Malpractice and Liability in Psychiatry

Peter Ash • Richard L. Frierson
Susan Hatters Friedman
Editors

Malpractice and Liability in Psychiatry

Springer

Editors
Peter Ash
Psychiatry and Law Service
Emory University
Atlanta, GA, USA

Richard L. Frierson
Neuropsychiatry and Behavioral Science
University of South Carolina School of Medicine
Columbia, SC, USA

Susan Hatters Friedman
Forensic Psychiatry
Case Western Reserve University
Cleveland, OH, USA

ISBN 978-3-030-91974-0 ISBN 978-3-030-91975-7 (eBook)
https://doi.org/10.1007/978-3-030-91975-7

This Springer imprint is published by the registered company Springer Nature Switzerland AG
The registered company address is: Gewerbestrasse 11, 6330 Cham, Switzerland

Preface

The goal of *Malpractice and Liability in Psychiatry* is to provide a comprehensive view of malpractice and liability issues in the practice of psychiatry. Psychiatrists are understandably concerned about being sued for malpractice. To help clinicians avoid claims, many chapters emphasize ways of preventing complaints from arising. When thinking of a title, we wondered if a suitable subtitle might be *A How Not-To Guide*. If prevention fails, and a suit is filed, the psychiatrist then enters into the unfamiliar world of legal process. Although defendant psychiatrists ultimately win most of the cases filed against them, the process can still be quite stressful, and this book details what the psychiatrist might reasonably expect. The practice of psychiatry may give rise to other complaints as well: ethics complaints, complaints to administrative agencies, medical boards, and complaints posted online. This book tries to provide useful guidance for managing those difficult situations as well.

The idea for this book grew out of prior work of the Group for the Advancement of Psychiatry (GAP). Several years ago, one of the editors (P.A.) was invited to guest edit an issue of *Focus: The Journal of Lifelong Learning in Psychiatry*. The Committee on Law and Psychiatry of GAP accepted his invitation to write articles for a journal issue on malpractice and risk management, and committee members authored the articles for the Fall 2019 issue of *Focus* titled *Forensic Psychiatry: Focus on Malpractice and Risk Management.* One journal issue could only cover a limited number of topics, which led to the idea of writing a more comprehensive work, an idea that was reinforced when we discovered there were no current comprehensive texts on this subject. Some of the conceptualization in chapters in this volume were previously presented in articles in the *Focus* issue (see acknowledgments in Chaps. 1, 12, 13, 14, 15, 21, and 33).

To provide a comprehensive discussion of malpractice and liability in psychiatric practice, different sections of this book approach these issues from different perspectives. The first section focuses on malpractice law – its principles and history. The second section discusses the process of litigation, from the time shortly after an adverse event through the course of a lawsuit, and discusses the perspectives and roles of the different players, from the defendant doctor to the plaintiff's attorney, defense attorney, and expert witnesses. The third section focuses on the most common allegations in malpractice litigation, with an eye to alerting the clinician to areas of risk, and with tips on preventive strategies and documentation without practicing overly defensive medicine. Although patient management receives considerable discussion, it should be emphasized that this book does *not* attempt to define the standard of care for any psychiatric condition and should not be construed as doing so. The section on practice areas also covers areas of risk and management, but does so from the perspective of different practice settings, such as inpatient and outpatient psychiatry, rather than focusing on types of allegations. While there is some overlap in content with the allegations section, the practice areas section highlights those issues that will be of particular interest to a clinician practicing in that specific arena. The section on special topics addresses variants of practice that cut across all practice areas: telepsychiatry, the Internet, and practicing under unusual conditions such as a pandemic or natural disaster. While most of the book has a focus on issues that give rise to malpractice litigation, the final section details special issues that arise from complaints against psychiatrists in other contexts.

While this book focuses on the practice of psychiatry, most of the chapters are also relevant to other practitioners (e.g., psychologists, social workers, licensed counsellors) who provide treatment for mental health conditions. Each of the chapter authors brings a wealth of knowledge and experience to their subject. We hope you find their writings useful.

Atlanta, GA, USA — Peter Ash
Columbia, SC, USA — Richard L. Frierson
Cleveland, OH, USA — Susan Hatters Friedman

Contents

Part VI Complaints

Contributors

Jacob M. Appel Department of Psychiatry, Icahn School of Medicine at Mount Sinai, New York, NY, USA

Peter Ash Psychiatry and Law Service, Department of Psychiatry and Behavioral Sciences, Emory University, Atlanta, GA, USA

Chinye Azuh-Showole Department of Psychiatry, Rutgers University-Robert Wood Johnson Medical School, Piscataway, NJ, USA

Richard Balon Departments of Psychiatry and Behavioral Neurosciences and Anesthesiology, Wayne State University, Detroit, MI, USA

Andrew J. Bond Eckert Seamans, Cherin & Mellott, Philadelphia, PA, USA

Charles D. Cash Professional Risk Management Services (PRMS), Arlington, VA, USA

Brian K. Cooke Department of Psychiatry and Behavioral Sciences, Emory University, Atlanta, GA, USA

Terri Day Barry University Dwayne O. Andreas School of Law, Orlando, FL, USA

Charles C. Dike Department of Psychiatry, Yale University, New Haven, CT, USA

Kevin F. Farrington Eckert Seamans, Cherin & Mellott, Philadelphia, PA, USA

Susan Hatters Friedman Division of Forensic Psychiatry, Case Western Reserve University, Cleveland, OH, USA

Departments of Psychiatry, Pediatrics, Reproductive Biology, and Law, Case Western Reserve University, Cleveland, OH, USA

Richard L. Frierson Department of Neuropsychiatry and Behavioral Science, University of South Carolina School of Medicine, Columbia, SC, USA

Michael H. Gendel Department of Psychiatry, University of Colorado School of Medicine, Denver, CO, USA

Colorado Physician Health Program, Denver, CO, USA

Doris C. Gundersen Department of Psychiatry, University of Colorado, Denver, CO, USA

Ryan C. W. Hall University of Central Florida, Orlando, FL, USA

University of South Florida, Tampa, FL, USA

Barry University Dwayne O. Andreas School of Law, Orlando, FL, USA

Peter J. Hoffman Eckert Seamans, Cherin & Mellott, Philadelphia, PA, USA

Trent C. Holmberg Department of Psychiatry, University of Utah School of Medicine, Salt Lake City, UT, USA

Brian Holoyda Martinez Detention Facility, Martinez, CA, USA

Abhishek Jain Department of Psychiatry, Columbia University Vagelos College of Physicians & Surgeons, New York, NY, USA

Kaustubh G. Joshi Department of Neuropsychiatry and Behavioral Science, University of South Carolina School of Medicine, Columbia, SC, USA

Anita S. Kablinger Department of Psychiatry and Behavioral Medicine, Carilion Clinic and Virginia Tech Carilion School of Medicine, Roanoke, VA, USA

Aimee Kaempf Department of Psychiatry, University of Arizona, Tucson, AZ, USA

Shabana Khan NYU Grossman School of Medicine, New York, NY, USA

Jacqueline Landess Department of Psychiatry, Medical College of Wisconsin, Milwaukee, WI, USA

Charles W. Luther Department of Psychiatry, Case Western Reserve University School of Medicine, Southwest General Health Center, Cleveland, OH, USA

Selena R. Magalotti Case Western Reserve University School of Medicine, Cleveland, OH, USA

Northcoast Behavioral Healthcare, Northfield, OH, USA

Richard Martinez University of Colorado at Anschutz Medical Center, Denver, CO, USA

Allison O. McKell Office of Organizational Integrity and Compliance, Carilion Clinic, Roanoke, VA, USA

Jeffrey L. Metzner Department of Psychiatry, University of Colorado School of Medicine, Denver, CO, USA

Alan W. Newman Department of Psychiatry, California Pacific Medical Center | Sutter Health, San Francisco, CA, USA

Stephen G. Noffsinger University Hospitals Cleveland Medical Center, Cleveland, OH, USA

Case Western Reserve University School of Medicine, Cleveland, OH, USA

Case Western Reserve University School of Law, Cleveland, OH, USA

University of Akron School of Law, Cleveland, OH, USA

Debra A. Pinals Program in Psychiatry, Law and Ethics, University of Michigan, Ann Arbor, MI, USA

Marilyn Price Assistant Professor of Psychiatry (PT), Law and Psychiatry Service, Massachusetts General Hospital, Harvard Medical School, Boston, MA, USA

Patricia R. Recupero Warren Alpert Medical School of Brown University, Providence, RI, USA

Phillip Resnick Department of Psychiatry, Case Western Reserve University School of Medicine, Cleveland, OH, USA

Alexandra Rogin Eckert Seamans, Cherin & Mellott, Philadelphia, PA, USA

Karen B. Rosenbaum Forensic Psychiatry Department, New York University Langone Medical Center, New York, NY, USA

Nina Ross Department of Psychiatry, University Hospitals/Case Western Reserve University, Cleveland, OH, USA

Adrienne Saxton Department of Psychiatry, Case Western Reserve University School of Medicine, Cleveland, OH, USA

Brooke Scicchitano Eckert Seamans, Cherin & Mellott, Philadelphia, PA, USA

Charles L. Scott Department of Psychiatry and Behavioral Sciences, University of California, Davis, Sacramento, CA, USA

Skip Simpson Law Offices of Skip Simpson, Frisco, TX, USA

Sherif Soliman Atrium Health, Charlotte, NC, USA

Department of Psychiatry, University of North Carolina, Chapel Hill, NC, USA

Renée Sorrentino Harvard Medical School, Boston, MA, USA

Joy Stankowski Northcoast Behavioral Healthcare, Northfield, OH, USA

Case Western Reserve University, Cleveland, OH, USA

Keri Ann Stevenson Department of Psychiatry and Neurobehavioral Sciences, University of Virginia, Charlottesville, VA, USA

Anthony Tamburello University Correctional Health Care, Piscataway, NJ, USA

Department of Psychiatry, Rutgers University-Robert Wood Johnson Medical School, Piscataway, NJ, USA

Robert L. Trestman Department of Psychiatry and Behavioral Medicine, Carilion Clinic and Virginia Tech Carilion School of Medicine, Roanoke, VA, USA

Donna Vanderpool Professional Risk Management Services (PRMS), Arlington, VA, USA

Ryan C. Wagoner Department of Psychiatry and Behavioral Neurosciences, University of South Florida, Tampa, FL, USA

Kenneth J. Weiss Department of Psychiatry, Perelman School of Medicine, University of Pennsylvania, Philadelphia, PA, USA

Sara G. West Department of Psychiatry, Case Western Reserve University School of Medicine, Cleveland, OH, USA

Part I

Malpractice Law

Principles of Malpractice Litigation in Psychiatry

1

Richard L. Frierson

Law and psychiatric medicine interact in a variety of ways, dealing with such important and profound issues as criminal responsibility (i.e., legal insanity), the right to die, civil commitment to a psychiatric facility, a psychiatrist's duty to protect third parties from violence by a patient, civil competencies (i.e., appointing a guardianship and conservatorship), informed consent, parental rights, confidentiality and privilege, etc. However, the most personal and painful nexus occurs when a physician is named in a malpractice lawsuit and must assume the role of defendant (Ryan, 2002). A majority of physicians (including a large minority of psychiatrists) will be involved in a medical malpractice case sometime in their career in some capacity: as a defendant, as a treating physician of a patient allegedly harmed by another physician, or as an expert witness for a plaintiff or defendant. For physician/defendants, being served a notice of a patient's intent to file a lawsuit, or being notified of a medical board complaint, is the first step in a complicated and nonintuitive legal process that the doctor must navigate. Additionally, physicians may be intimidated by the legal world of plaintiffs, discovery, evidence, expert witnesses, legal doctrines, state and federal law governing medical practice, and judicial application of the law (Ryan, 2002).

Malpractice litigation is frequently stressful because most physicians are not accustomed to being accused of wrongdoing, and the stress involved can lead to self-doubt, loneliness, guilt, embarrassment, and a sense of powerlessness (see Chap. 11). Psychiatrists may feel responsible for an undesired clinical outcome even when the care they provided to the patient was appropriate and did not fall below an acceptable standard. In order to reduce the associated stress of litigation and best navigate the litigation process, psychiatrists should become familiar with the underlying principles involved in malpractice litigation. In doing so, they may be better able to assist their defense attorneys and navigate the legal processes if they are sued, they may be better able to avoid lawsuits, and they may even be able to provide better care for their patients.

This chapter will review the theory of malpractice and its limitations, the frequency of lawsuits (and medical board investigations) against psychiatrists, and the four basic elements that must be proven in order for a plaintiff to win a malpractice claim. Additionally, this chapter will review the most common types of negligence allegations brought against psychiatrists and ways to reduce liability in psychiatric practice.

The Theory of Malpractice and Its Limitations

Medical malpractice litigation is designed to serve several important purposes. First and foremost, it exists to compensate patients for damages suffered due to the negligence of their treating physicians. Second, the possibility of being sued for a bad medical outcome also helps to deter physicians from engaging in unsafe practices. In this way, malpractice litigation serves to regulate medical practice by clarifying the nature of prevailing standards of practice (Halleck, 1983). Finally, malpractice litigation exacts corrective justice, i.e., the rectification of a wrong (Studdert et al., 2004). Providing corrective justice for injured persons produces psychological benefits. Corrective justice is also based on the notion that patients have a right to expect that the medical decisions made by their treating physician will be made in a professional, knowledgeable, and informed way that is commensurate with the medical practice of physicians practicing in the same specialty (Todd, 2011).

However, despite these benefits, medical malpractice litigation has numerous limitations and downsides. First of all, like other civil litigation matters, malpractice lawsuits are only decided after a lengthy legal process. The average amount of time required to close a litigated malpractice claim in the United States is now over 2 years (Jena et al.,

R. L. Frierson (✉)
Department of Neuropsychiatry and Behavioral Science, University of South Carolina School of Medicine, Columbia, SC, USA
e-mail: richard.frierson@uscmed.sc.edu

P. Ash et al. (eds.), *Malpractice and Liability in Psychiatry*, https://doi.org/10.1007/978-3-030-91975-7_1

2012), with a quarter of cases taking 3 to 5 years to resolve (Medscape, 2020). Additionally, medical malpractice litigation has been identified as one cause of the rising cost of healthcare in the United States through a variety of ways. The at-fault litigation-oriented system results not only in long delays but also large sums of money going to lawyers and litigation expenses rather than to the actual patients who were injured (Hoffer, 2019). The average contingency fee reported in the malpractice literature is fairly consistently in the range of 35–40% (Studdert et al., 2006).

Additionally, malpractice insurance is a substantial cost of operating a medical practice, and malpractice litigation also drives up the cost of this insurance for providers, a cost increase that is passed down to the patient and is factored into the overall cost of healthcare. The average cost for a malpractice insurance policy varies tremendously depending on the medical specialty; in 2019, the average malpractice insurance annual premium for psychiatrist was $5000, whereas an obstetrician/gynecologist paid around $46,000 (Medscape, 2019).

The adversarial malpractice litigation system may also discourage the reporting of adverse events, for fear that such reporting could lead to a lawsuit. While all physicians make mistakes, good physicians learn from their mistakes and share their learning with others. For example, the reporting of "near misses" can also benefit healthcare delivery systems, thereby reducing the likelihood of a bad outcome for future patients (Hoffer, 2019). For this reason, reporting of medical errors should be encouraged, not discouraged by the fear of litigation.

A final concern is the propensity for the fear of malpractice litigation to drive the expensive practice of defensive medicine. Practicing defensive medicine involves the ordering of expensive lab tests, procedures, or extra visits because of a primary concern about malpractice liability, not because of clinical indication. Several studies have estimated that the cost of defensive medicine in the United States is anywhere from $56 to $162 billion annually (Berlin, 2017). All combined, it is estimated that the total cost of the medical liability system accounts for 2.4% of all healthcare spending in the United States annually (Mello et al., 2010).

The Frequency of Psychiatric Malpractice Claims and Board Complaints

Fortunately, psychiatrists are less likely to be sued for negligence compared to physicians in other medical specialties. Across specialties, approximately 7.4% of all physicians face a malpractice claim annually, but the likelihood of being sued varies tremendously between specialties, with the rates much higher for specialties that are procedurally based. For example, the annual rate of physicians facing a malpractice suit is 19.1% for neurosurgeons, compared to 15.3% for general surgeons, 5.2% for family medicine practitioners, but only 2.6% for psychiatrists (Jena et al., 2011). According to data from the National Practitioner Data Bank (NPDB), while psychiatrists account for 4% of all active physicians, they only account for 1% of all paid medical malpractice claims in the United States (Studdert et al., 2016).

In a 2019 psychiatric malpractice survey, however, 41% of US psychiatrists reported that they had been sued for malpractice at least once in their career (Medscape, 2020). The vast majority (86%) believed the lawsuit was not warranted, and only a small percentage (2%) believed the lawsuit was justified, the lowest percentage of all physicians sued. The majority of those sued believed that the plaintiffs did not understand medical risks and blamed the doctor for bad outcomes, even if the care had been appropriate. Among the 35% of total malpractice cases that either settled or came to a verdict in favor of the plaintiff in 2019, almost half (48%) of monetary awards maxed out at $100,000, with 31% maxing out at $500,000, and 8% at $1,000,000 (Medscape, 2019; Medscape, 2020).

Although less likely than physician colleagues to be the defendant in a malpractice action, psychiatrists are overrepresented among complaints to medical boards and are much more likely to be the recipients of disciplinary actions from state medical boards (Reich & Schatzberg, 2014; Kohatsu et al., 2004). Perhaps due to the personal and private nature of the doctor-patient relationship in psychiatry, psychiatrists are also significantly more likely than nonpsychiatric physicians to be disciplined for boundary violations and having sexual relationships with patients (Dehlenhorf & Wolfe, 1998). For more information regarding types of medical board complaints and how to safely navigate these complaints, the reader is directed to Chap. 33.

The Elements of a Malpractice Action

A malpractice action is typically under the jurisdiction of state courts and is grounded in the concept of tort law. Medical malpractice laws vary depending on jurisdiction (i.e., the state where the action is brought), but in all jurisdictions, a "tort" can be defined as a civil wrong, for which a remedy may be obtained, usually in the form of damages (Black's Law Dictionary, 2004). Although there may be contractual aspects to the physician-patient relationship, a tort does not involve a breach of contract, but rather results from a negligent act that causes a claimant to suffer loss or harm, resulting in legal liability for the person who commits the tortious act. For example, one of the most common types of tort actions is a personal injury lawsuit arising from a car accident. In such a case, the injured party (i.e., the plaintiff) alleges that the tortfeasor (the defendant car driver) was negligent, through actions (e.g., speeding) or inactions (e.g., failure to stop at a red light), by failing to operate a motor vehicle with a reasonable degree of skill and caution. The actions of the defendant do not need to be purposeful or intentional. Likewise, in a medical malpractice action, the plaintiff (i.e., the patient or patient's estate) alleges that the defendant psychiatrist was negligent in the provision of medical care which resulted in damages to the patient (e.g., suicide, worsening of the condition, hospitalization, etc.).

In any tort or malpractice action, there are four separate elements that must be proven in order for the plaintiff to prevail. These elements have been commonly referred to as the "4 Ds": *duty* (to the patient), *dereliction* (i.e., negligence) in that duty, *damages*, and *direct causation* (Vanderpool, 2018). Furthermore, in most cases of medical negligence, the plaintiff must prove all four elements of his or her claim by a simple "preponderance of the evidence" standard. This means that the claims made by the plaintiff are more likely true than not (i.e., >50% likely true).

Duty

A doctor has a duty to a patient once a doctor-patient relationship has been established. Although there are jurisdictional variations in how this is defined, if is usually formed when a physician examines, diagnoses, treats, or agrees to treat a patient (Blake, 2012). While this may seem straightforward, there are many variations and subtleties as to what constitutes this duty. For example, can a psychiatrist incur liability for the care of a patient that he or she has never seen?

One example involves "curbside consults." These are usually informal opinions provided by one physician to another. The process typically involves a brief and informal discussion between colleagues, often about a very specific question. Given that such consults are usually sought for patients with complex conditions, the potential for error may be greater. Such consults can pose legal risks to the consultant including the provision of inappropriate advice, giving advice without adequate information about the patient, and having the consultant's name recorded in the record without the consultant's knowledge. Furthermore, in some jurisdictions, an implied treatment relationship may be found when a physician gives advice through another physician, thereby establishing a duty (Kreichelt et al., 2008).

Another more common example of being sued by a patient the psychiatrist has not necessarily examined is vicarious liability, a liability that a supervisory party bears for the actionable conduct of a subordinate or associate because of the relationship between the two parties (West, 2016) (See Chap. 3). In one type of vicarious liability, a psychiatrist may also have a duty to patients who are harmed through the actions of their employees (e.g., psychotherapists, counselors, supervisees, or trainees) under the legal doctrine of respondeat superior ("let the superior make answer"). In another type of vicarious liability, *agency liability*, a psychiatrist may be liable for the negligent actions of *non*employees who are perceived by the plaintiff to be the employer's agent or acting on the employer's behalf. For example, in academic settings, a voluntary supervising psychiatrist who has not employed a resident or medical student may nonetheless be liable for negligent supervision, such as not knowing what the resident or student is doing, and failing to teach, to regularly meet, or to provide proper oversight (Recupero & Rainey, 2007). Hospitals may also be held liable for actions of nonemployed physicians who practice in a hospital if the physician is perceived as an agent of the hospital.

While the concept of *duty* has traditionally applied to patients, there are a few areas where this duty has been expanded to non-patients. For example, psychiatrists are required by law to report known or suspected child abuse to the appropriate social service agencies in their state. In addition, many jurisdictions also have mandatory reporting laws for cases of elderly abuse or abuse of a vulnerable adult. Finally, in many jurisdictions, psychiatrists are required to protect third parties from harm when a patient has threatened violence against the third party (Tarasoff v. Regents of University of California, 1976; Johnson et al., 2014). Discharging this duty might involve warning the potential victim, notifying the police, or hospitalizing the patient.

Dereliction

Once a duty has been established, the plaintiff in a malpractice case must prove that the actions or inactions of the psychiatrist fell below an acceptable standard of care. A psychiatrist does not have to be exceptional in their care of the patient. They are simply held "to such reasonable care and skill as is exercised by the ordinary physician of good standing under like circumstances" (Clites v. Iowa, 1982, p. 919).

Jurisdictions vary in how the acceptable standard of care is determined, although there has been a long-standing trend away from reliance on a local standard (i.e., what most doctors do in the local community) toward the adoption of national standards of care (Halleck, 1983). In general, it is not necessary for a psychiatrist to use the treatment that would be used by a majority of practitioners. As long as the treatment provided is acceptable to a respectable minority of practitioners, the treatment should not be considered negligent (Hood v. Phillips, 1977). However, psychiatrists who fail to keep abreast of new developments in psychiatric practice – be it advances in pharmacotherapy or psychotherapeutic approaches – may find themselves at risk for being sued for poor clinical outcomes. For example, in the case of a patient with a treatment-resistant condition, if the treating psychiatrist knows an alternative treatment for a certain condition may be equally or more effective (e.g., ECT for depression compared to pharmacotherapy) and the psychiatrist does not practice or offer the alternative treatment, then the psychiatrist should consider referring to another practitioner who can provide the treatment. Failure to do so may also result in liability for the treating psychiatrist (Klerman, 1990).

Establishing the standard of care in a malpractice suit usually involves testimony provided by an expert witness – usually another psychiatrist – who has reviewed the medical record and can provide testimony through deposition and/or in court about the appropriate standard of care needed in a given clinical situation and whether the defendant psychiatrist met an acceptable standard of care. Expert witnesses who testify in malpractice cases are almost always required to engage in clinical practice (in addition to their forensic work and expert testimony) in order for their testimony to be admissible (see Chap. 9). In most cases, the expert, whether retained by the plaintiff's attorney or by the defense, will not directly interview or speak with the defendant psychiatrist. Experts generally rely on a review of the medical record and depositions taken in the discovery portion of the malpractice case (see Chap. 6). Therefore, if the defendant psychiatrist did not provide treatment or care that at least a significant minority of psychiatrists would have provided, or provided care that was unusual and deviated from the usual care for a particular condition, then the care should be reasonably justified in the medical record through the documentation of medical decision-making. This will assist the expert witness in assessing the appropriateness of the clinical decision-making.

There are a few situations in which an expert witness would not be needed in order to prove dereliction of duty. If the defendant psychiatrist engaged in negligent acts that were egregious (e.g., engaged in sexual activity with a patient, provided illicit drugs to a patient, assaulted a patient), then expert witness testimony would not be needed to prove negligence under the concept of res ipsa loquitur (i.e., "the thing speaks for itself") (Jerrold, 2004). In these types of cases, jurors can form a reasonable belief that the actions were negligent without needing to hear from an expert witness. (However, in these types of cases, expert witnesses may be still be used to assess and educate the jury about the extent of damages suffered by the patient.)

Damages

Regardless of the negligent actions or inactions of a defendant psychiatrist, a plaintiff must also establish that they were damaged in some way as a result of the care they received. For example, if a psychiatrist prescribes a medication to a patient who has a documented allergy to that medication and the patient suffers no adverse events, then he or she cannot claim damages, even though the act of prescribing the medication may have been negligent.

Between 2009 and 2014, the average medical malpractice payment amount in paid claims for psychiatrists was $ 269,870, and, unlike the vast majority of claims paid in malpractice cases involving other medical specialties, over 50% of claims paid in psychiatry involved a patient death (Schaffer et al., 2017). There are several types of damages that can be paid in a medical malpractice claim: actual damages, damages for wrongful death, and punitive (to punish) damages (Physician's Weekly, 2016).

Compensation for actual damages can be subdivided into two types: economic and noneconomic damages. Economic damages (sometimes called special damages) are designed to reimburse the victim for easily quantifiable financial costs related to the negligence. These would include financial coverage of medical expenses related to the treatment or therapy that was necessary to address the resulting injuries. Examples would include medical or psychiatric hospitalization expenses, medications, and future medical expenses. Economic damages can also cover lost income that resulted if the victim's injuries caused time loss from work. Economic damages are typically supported by documentation, such as medical bills and income tax earnings statements, but sometimes an expert will need to testify to support a request for future damages if the cost is speculative. In addition to economic damages, noneconomic damages (also known as general damages) may be recovered for pain and suffering that the victim experienced, for a reduction in the quality of life, and, in the case of a suicide, a loss of consortium on the part of a spouse. Many states place caps on noneconomic damages ranging from $250,000 to $500,000 (Hubbard, 2006). As of 2020, 23 states had passed limitations on noneconomic damages (Center for Justice Democracy, 2020).

In the event that a malpractice claim involves the death of a patient, the patient's estate and survivors may also be able to recover damages via a wrongful death claim. Damages in wrongful death claims are designed to compensate the family members of the victim for funeral expenses and the loss of future income based on the contributions that the victim would have made to their family. Depending on jurisdiction, some states also permit collection of damages for loss of companionship or guidance. Many clinicians fail to understand how they could be held responsible for the patient's actions in a case of suicide. However, because the doctor-patient contact creates a "special relationship," a psychiatrist is expected to have used his or her special knowledge and expertise to prevent the suicide by adequately assessing suicide risk and treating the underlying condition (Pinals, 2019).

The fact that a suicide occurred does not necessarily mean the psychiatrist was negligent as long as an appropriate risk assessment and treatment decisions were made and documented. Wrongful death claims are not only seen in cases of patient suicide. For example, in the case of the death of a third party who was killed by a psychiatric patient, the treating psychiatrist may incur liability if he or she was aware that the patient presented a serious danger of violence to another person and the physician did not act to protect that person (Tarasoff v. Regents of University of California, 1976; Felthous, 1999).

Punitive damages may be assessed against a defendant when the defendant's negligent conduct was overtly egregious, reckless, malicious, or intentional. Fortunately, punitive damages are rarely awarded in malpractice litigation, except in cases that involve allegations of sexual misconduct on behalf of the psychiatrist. Punitive damages are usually not assessed against defendants whose negligent conduct was merely unintentional. A victim typically needs to prove intent, recklessness, or another mental state that is greater than negligence in order to obtain punitive damages. Falsifying the medical record to hide negligence in a malpractice suit is also grounds for awarding punitive damages (Moskovitz v. Mt. Sinai Med. Ctr., 1994). In order to receive punitive damages, the defendant psychiatrist's behavior typically must border on being criminal. As the name implies, the purpose of punitive damages is to punish the medical professional for their conduct and send a message to similarly situated medical professionals not to engage in the same behavior. As a result of previous appellate case law, most malpractice insurance policies include the provision that the insurance carrier will not cover the payment of punitive damages because doing so would alleviate the insured of being personally and financially punished for intentional negligence (Aetna v. McCabe, 1983).

There are large differences in malpractice awards among state jurisdictions. For example, according to the National Practitioner Data Bank, in 2019 the average malpractice damages payout for each state (includes all medical specialties) ranged from as low as $3.93 per capita in Texas to $65.52 per capita in Alaska (Diederich Health Care, 2020). Larger awards are associated with death and permanent injuries.

All medical malpractice payments, whether settlements or verdicts, are reportable to the National Practitioner Data Bank (NPDB) which may provide future disclosures to hospitals, medical boards, professional societies, and various healthcare entities. The NPDB collects information on malpractice actions and other adverse actions taken against healthcare providers. It was established by Congress in 1986 for the purpose of preventing physicians and other practitioners from moving state to state to avoid the disclosure of previously negligent or poor medical practice (National Practitioner Data Bank, 2020). In addition to information about malpractice payments reported by insurers, the NPDB receives notices of adverse medical license actions taken by state medical boards, adverse hospital privilege actions taken by hospitals and other healthcare entities, adverse membership actions by provisional societies, adverse controlled substance registration actions by the Federal Drug Enforcement Agency (DEA), and finally, actions excluding participation in Medicare, Medicaid, or other federal health programs taken by the Office of Inspector General (OIG) (NPDB Guidebook, 2018).

Direct Causation

Poor results may occur in psychiatric practice even with the best possible care, and psychiatrists do not usually guarantee positive definitive results. Therefore, liability in psychiatric practice cannot be based on the fact that treatment was unsuccessful. Instead, the plaintiff must prove that the damages they suffered were the direct result of the psychiatrist's negligent actions.

The establishment of direct causation may be complicated by the existence of a preexisting condition. Malpractice defendants who have engaged in negligent practice have frequently attempted to attribute a plaintiff's alleged damages to a condition that was already present before the establishment of a doctor-patient relationship. Such plaintiffs in these cases have been colloquially referred to as "eggshell plaintiffs." For this reason, courts have frequently adopted a "relaxed causation" rule which prevents defendants from relying on preexisting conditions as a defense. Instead, a psychiatrist may be found negligent if their negligent practice increased the risk of illness or aggravated a preexisting mental illness (Stein, 2012). It is clear that a tortfeasor (i.e., negligent defendant) may be held responsible where the effect of his negligence is to aggravate a preexisting condition or disease (Hastie v. Handeland, 1969). A plaintiff is entitled to recover to the full extent that his condition has worsened as a result of defendant's tortuous act. Therefore, in malpractice cases, defendants take the patients that they injure as they find them (Rideau v. Los Angeles Transit Lines, 1954). If, by reason of some preexisting condition, the patient is more susceptible to injury, the psychiatrist is not thereby exonerated from liability.

Additionally, in determining direct causation, an expert must consider the proximity of the psychiatrist's negligence to the onset of damages. In determining legal fairness, the law holds that a negligent physician should not be liable for far-reaching and improbable consequences of his or her acts or omissions. Also, in determining proximate cause, experts must consider the possibility of both an intervening cause and a lack of foreseeability (Knoll & Gerbasi, 2006).

Causes of Action

There are numerous reasons that patients or their families sue psychiatrists. However, by far the two most common are suicide (or attempted suicide) and incorrect treatment (Frierson & Joshi, 2019). In general, in suicide cases, a psychiatrist may be accused of failing to identify and manage suicide risk factors, improper discharge from an inpatient psychiatric facility, failure to engage in means restriction (e.g., failure to inquire about access to firearms, failure to consider a gun violence restraining order [in jurisdictions where available], failure to inquire about social supports who can stay with patient, etc.), or other acts of omission. Acts of commission, such as prescribing a potentially lethal amount of medication at one time to a patient at chronic risk for suicidal behavior, may be also grounds for accusations of negligence. In regard to negligent treatment, allegations may involve failure to monitor potentially dangerous medications (e.g., lithium-associated nephropathy, neuroleptics, and tardive dyskinesia) (Clites v. Iowa, 1982; Rogers, 1981; Tancredi, 1988). Psychiatrists may also be held liable for failure to inform patients of alternative treatments when obtaining informed consent for treatment (Osheroff v. Chestnut Lodge, 1985). After suicide and incorrect treatment, other relatively common causes of action against psychiatrists include breach of confidentiality, failure to hospitalize or unnecessary hospitalization, and boundary violations (Resnick & Saxton, 2019; Hatters Friedman & Martinez, 2019). Finally, failure to properly terminate the doctor-patient relationship can lead to allegations of patient abandonment (Jung & McDowell, 2020; McMullen, 2007).

Liability Prevention

Receiving notice of a malpractice action is stressful for any psychiatrist. First and foremost, for psychiatrists who believe they are at risk of being sued for something that occurred during their medical practice or if they have received notice of a suit, they should contact their malpractice carrier (see Chap. 5). In some cases, if this is not done, it could be used as grounds for voiding the malpractice policy coverage. The vast majority of malpractice policies require that psychiatrists cooperate with the insurance provider when defending lawsuits. Psychiatrists should be honest with their attorneys, not withhold or misrepresent facts, and never make an attempt to alter the records (including attempts to recreate missing records). In the age of the electronic health record (EHR), alterations are easily discoverable, including who made the alteration as well as the time and date it was made.

There are many things psychiatrists can do to reduce their liability and the risk of being sued. First and foremost, thorough documentation of medical decision-making and clear treatment records are crucial. Typewritten notes are always preferable to handwritten notes, especially if the handwriting is illegible. Documenting a patient's symptoms and mental status, explaining the reasoning behind how diagnoses were reached and why certain treatment modalities were selected, and documenting medication dosages and amounts could potentially reduce the risk of erroneous assumptions being made by individuals reading these records in the future.

For patients at risk for suicidal or homicidal behavior, risk factors should usually be assessed and documented at each encounter. Because untoward events frequently happen at points of transition of care, ensuring appropriate follow-up for patients, especially when sending them to other providers or discharging them from a hospital, is crucial to reducing the risk of a bad outcome.

Psychiatrists should consider discussing challenging cases with colleagues. Conversely, when providing "curbside consults" for colleagues, it is best to do so using a hypothetical scenario and avoid using actual patient names. Open communication with a patient's other treating providers, establishing and maintaining open communication with patients, and practicing in a competent manner can provide a solid foundation to support a defense in the event of a lawsuit. Finally, psychiatrists should be involved in lifelong learning and stay abreast of evolving standards of treatment in the profession, new advances and techniques, and research findings that should guide clinical practice. Therefore, engaging in an active continuing medical education program is essential.

Key Points

- Malpractice litigation is designed to compensate injured patients for physician negligence, deter unsafe medical practices, and exact corrective justice.
- While much less likely than physicians of other specialties to face a malpractice lawsuit, a large minority of psychiatrists will be involved in a medical malpractice case sometime in their career.
- Psychiatrists are much more likely than nonpsychiatric physicians to be the subject of a medical board complaint and investigation.
- A successful malpractice action involves proving four elements: a duty on the part of the physician, dereliction of that duty, damages suffered by the patient, and that the negligence was the direct cause of the damages.
- The most common causes of malpractice actions against psychiatrists are patient suicide or attempted suicide and incorrect treatment.
- Thorough documentation of medical decision-making and clear treatment records are crucial in liability prevention.

Acknowledgments Some of the conceptualizations in this chapter were previously presented in Frierson, R. L. and Joshi, K. J. (2019). Malpractice law and psychiatry: An overview. *Focus 17*(4):332-336.

References

Aetna Life and Cas. Co. (Cas. & Sur. Div.) v. McCabe, 556 F.Supp. 1342 (1983).

Berlin, L. (2017). Medical errors, malpractice and defensive medicine: An ill-fated triad. *Diagnosis, 4*(3), 133–139.

Black's Law Dictionary, Eighth Edition. (2004), Edited by Bryan A. Garner. St. Paul, Minn, West Group, p.1526.

Blake, V. (2012). When is a patient-physician relationship established? *Virtual Mentor, 14*(5), 403–406.

Center for Justice and Democracy at New York Law School. (2020, August). *Caps on compensatory damages: A state law summary*. Available at: https://centerjd.org/content/fact-sheet-caps-compensatory-damages-state-law-summary. Accessed 8 Dec 2020.

Clites v. Iowa, 22 N.W.2d 917 (Iowa Ct. App. 1982).

Dehlenhorf, C. E., & Wolfe, S. M. (1998). Physicians disciplined for sex-related offenses. *Journal of the American Medical Association, 279*(23), 1883–1888.

Diederich Healthcare. (2020). *2020 Medical Malpractice Payout Analysis*. Available at: https://www.diederichhealthcare.com/the-standard/2020-medical-malpractice-payout-analysis/. Accessed 12 Dec 2020.

Felthous, A. R. (1999). The clinician's duty to protect third parties. *Psychiatric Clinics of North America, 22*(1), 49–60.

Frierson, R. L., & Joshi, K. G. (2019). Malpractice law and psychiatry: An overview. *Focus, 17*(4), 332–336.

Halleck, S. L. (1983). Malpractice in psychiatry. *Psychiatric Clinics of North America, 6*(4), 567–583.

Hastie v. Handeland 274 Cal.App.2d 599, 1969.

Hatters Friedman, S., & Martinez, R. P. (2019). Boundaries, professionalism, and malpractice in psychiatry. *Focus, 17*(4), 365–371.

Hoffer, E. P. (2019). America's health care system in broken: What went wrong and how can we fix it. Part 5: Malpractice, Fraud, Waste, and the EMR. *American Journal of Medicine, 132*(10), 1129–1132.

Hood v. Phillips, 554 S.W.160 (Texas 1977).

Hubbard, F. P. (2006). The nature and impact of the "tort reform" movement. *Hostra Law Review, 35*, 438–439.

Jena, A. B., Chandra, A., Lakdawalla, D., & Seabury, S. (2012). Outcomes of medical malpractice litigation against U.S. physicians. *Archives of Internal Medicine, 127*(11), 892–894.

Jena, A. B., Seabury, S., Lakdawalla, D., & Chandra, A. (2011). Malpractice risk according to medical specialty. *New England Journal of Medicine, 365*(7), 629–636.

Jerrold, L. (2004). Res ipsa loquitor: The thing speaks for itself. *American Journal of Orthodontics and Dentofacial Orthopedics, 26*(1), 131–132.

Johnson, R., Persad, G., & Siste, D. (2014). The *Tarasoff* rule: The implications of interstate variation and gaps in professional training. *Journal of the American Academy of Psychiatry and the Law, 42*(4), 469–477.

Jung, S., & McDowell, R. H.. (2020, Jan) Abandonment. (Updated 2020 Oct 11). In: StatPearls [Internet]. Treasure Island (FL): StatPearls Publishing. Available from: https://www.ncbi.nlm.nih.gov/books/NBK563285/. Accessed 12 Dec 2020.

Kohatsu, N., Gould, D., Ross, L. K., & Fox, P. J. (2004). Characteristics associated with physician discipline. *Archives of Internal Medicine, 164*(6), 653–658.

Klerman, G. L. (1990). The psychiatric patient's right to effective treatment: Implications of *Osheroff v.* Chestnut Lodge. *American Journal of Psychiatry, 147*(4), 409–418.

Knoll, J., & Gerbasi, J. (2006). Psychiatric malpractice case analysis: Striving for objectivity. *Journal of the American Academy of Psychiatry and the Law, 34*(2), 215–223.

Kreichelt, R., Hilbert, M. L., & Shinn, D. (2008). Minimizing the legal risk with 'curbside consultation'. *Journal of Health Care Risk Management, 28*(1), 27–29.

McMullen, L. (2007). Terminating the patient-physician relationship. Abandonment of the patient: What it means and how to avoid it. *Journal of the Mississippi State Medical Association, 48*(9), 289.

Medscape. (2019). *Malpractice premium report 2019*. Retrieved from https://www.medscape.com/slideshow/2019-malprac-prem-rep-6012332#7

Medscape. (2020). *Large percentage of psychiatrists sued for malpractice at least once*. Retrieved from https://www.medscape.com/viewarticle/924388?src=ppc_google_rlsa-traf_mscp_news-perspectives_t1-psych_us

Mello, M. M., Chandra, A., Gawande, A. A., & Studdert, D. M. (2010). National costs of the medical liability system. *Health Affairs, 29*(9), 1569–1577.

Moskovitz v. Mt. Sinai Med. Ctr. 69 Ohio St.3d 638, 1994 Ohio 324, 635 N.E.2d 331(1994).

National Practitioner Data Bank. (2020). *About us*. Available at: https://www.npdb.hrsa.gov/topNavigation/aboutUs.jsp. Accessed 12 Dec 2020.

NPDB. (2018). *Reporting medical malpractice payments*. Available at: https://www.npdb.hrsa.gov/resources/aboutGuidebooks.jsp Accessed 11 Dec 2020.

Osheroff v. Chestnut Lodge, 490 A. 2d. 720 (Md. App. 1985).

Physician's Weekly. (2016). *Understanding damages in a medical malpractice case*. Available at: https://www.physiciansweekly.com/understanding-damages-in-a-medical-malpractice-case/ Accessed 11 Dec 2020.

Pinals, D. (2019). Liability and patient suicide. *Focus, 17*(4), 349–354.

Recupero, P. R., & Rainey, S. E. (2007). Liability and risk management in outpatient psychotherapy supervision. *Journal of the American Academy of Psychiatry and the Law, 35*(2), 188–195.

Reich, J., & Schatzberg, A. (2014). An empirical data comparison of regulatory agency and malpractice legal problems for psychiatrists. *Annals of Clinical Psychiatry, 26*(2), 91–96.

Resnick, P. J., & Saxton, A. (2019). Malpractice liability due to patient violence. *Focus, 17*(4), 343–348.

Rideau v. *Los Angeles Transit Lines* 124 Cal.App.2d 466 (1954).

Rogers, G. A. (1981). Tardive-dyskinesia and lithium-associated neuropathy. *Journal of Clinical Psychiatry, 42*(9), 363–364.

Ryan, M. (2002). Medical malpractice: A review of issues for providers. *Hematology and Oncology Clinics of North America, 16*(6), 1331–1350.

Schaffer, A. C., Jena, A. B., Seabury, S. A., Singh, H., Chalasani, V., & Kachalia, A. (2017). Rates and characteristics of paid malpractice claims among U.S. physicians by specialty, 1992–2014. *Journal of the American Medical Association Internal Medicine, 177*(5), 710–718.

Stein, A. (2012). Toward a theory of medical malpractice. *Iowa Law Review, 97*, 1202.

Studdert, D. M., Biamark, M. M., Mello, M. M., Singh, H., & Spittal, M. J. (2016). Prevalence and characteristics of physicians prone to malpractice claims. *New England Journal of Medicine, 374*(4), 354–362.

Studdert, D. M., Mello, M. M., Gawande, A. A., Gandhi, T. K., Kachalia, A., Yoon, C., … Brennan, T. A. (2006). Claims, errors, and compensation payments in medical malpractice litigation. *New England Journal of Medicine, 354*(19), 2024–2033.

Studdert, D. M., Mello, M. M., & Brennan, T. (2004). Medical malpractice. *New England Journal of Medicine, 50*(3), 283–292.

Tancredi, L. R. (1988). Malpractice and tardive dyskinesia: A conceptual dilemma. *Journal of Clinical Psychopharmacology, 8*(4 Suppl), 71S–76S.

Tarasoff v. Regents of University of California, 17 Cal.3d 425, 551 P.2d 334,131 Cal. Rptr. 14 (1976).

Todd, N. V. (2011). Medical negligence: Legal theory and surgical practice. *Orthopaedics and Traumatology, 25*(1), 64–74.

Vanderpool, D. (2018). Professional liability in psychiatric practice. In L. H. Gold & R. L. Frierson (Eds.), *Textbook of forensic psychiatry* (3rd ed., pp. 169–183). American Psychiatric Association Publishing.

West, J. C. (2016). Vicarious liability: Is it an issue for your organization? *Journal of Healthcare Risk Management, 36*(1), 25–34.

2 History of Malpractice

Kenneth J. Weiss

Physicians, including psychiatrists, enjoy an elevated status in society, whether the culture regards them as communing with the supernatural or as highly trained technicians. In either case, their clientele—patients, those who suffer—place their health and life in their hands. In this dialectic, tension may arise between the healer's behavior and the patient's expectations. The regulation of physicians' conduct with patients originates in ethics: the duties owed to patients that foster balance, if not equality, in their interactions. When it can be proved that the physician breached the duty to the patient, allegations of negligence can lead to a determination of malpractice. This chapter will trace the evolution of the theory and adjudication of malpractice claims across millennia and geography, with emphases on the American system as it pertains to psychiatry and how that system differs from international models.

Early Cultural and Spiritual Formulations

Ancient societies regarded physicians as either godlike or especially skilled (American College of Physicians, 1984; Bal, 2009). In Egypt (ca. sixteenth century BCE) the priest-physician could be held accountable for trying a new therapy when the patient died; the penalty could include death (American College of Physicians, 1984). In the Mesopotamian model, the secular Code of Hammurabi (ca. 2000 BCE), medical practice was highly regulated and offenses punished (American College of Physicians, 1984); for example, "'If the doctor has treated a gentlemen with a lancet of bronze and has caused the gentleman to die, or has opened an abscess of the eye for a gentleman with a bronze lancet, and has caused the loss of the gentleman's eye, one shall cut off his hands'" (Bal, 2009).

In Greece (ca. 400 BCE), the secular Hippocrates emphasized doctor-patient communication and responsibility to the patient as a matter of oath while giving the appearance of "benign paternalism" (American College of Physicians, 1984). The Hindu, Islamic, and Chinese cultures also treated the medical profession as one with duty toward the patient. In Hebrew law, commentary on the Torah concerns obligations of citizens to one another and the specific duty of physicians to mitigate suffering (Ilani & Weinberger, 2020). Instead of the fatalistic view that, since all matters are in God's hands, no action need be taken, physicians have permission to heal and an obligation to do so. Those who stray from ethics or who disregard spiritual duties may suffer "heavenly" consequences, if not monetary damages (Dollin & Roth, 2018). Second-century *Tosefta* (supplemental oral Jewish law) indicates that iatrogenic injuries do not merit compensation, because physicians are too valuable to lose (Grossman et al., 2020). That model does not necessarily extend to medical errors involving excessive harm or loss of life (Dollin & Roth, 2018; Grossman et al., 2020).

In Roman civilization, the teachings of Galen, a Greek, successfully promoted the influence of Hippocrates. Under Justinian law, 533–534 CE, Roman physicians were held accountable for incompetence and liable for damages, a tradition that persisted through Europe's Dark Ages (Giesen, 1988). By about 1200 CE, Roman law recognized medical malpractice, and, over the ensuing centuries, the legal tradition spread to continental Europe and England. Medieval physicians were held to account for misfeasance, though the terms *negligence* and *malpractice* were not used in the fourteenth century (Silver, 1992). Gradually, the focus of malpractice law shifted from contract to tort considerations. It was not until the sixteenth century that expert testimony was first required by law to identify the standard of care (Bal, 2009). The reader is referred to Giesen (1988) for a detailed examination of malpractice law from ancient to modern times.

K. J. Weiss (✉)
Department of Psychiatry, Perelman School of Medicine, University of Pennsylvania, Philadelphia, PA, USA
e-mail: kenweiss@pennmedicine.upenn.edu

P. Ash et al. (eds.), *Malpractice and Liability in Psychiatry*, https://doi.org/10.1007/978-3-030-91975-7_2

Evolving Liability Law and the Problem of Quackery

During the fourteenth century, a patient collected damages for faulty medical practice under a standard comparing the practitioner to like individuals (Silver, 1992). Certification of physicians in England began with *An Acte conerning Phisicions* [spelling in original] in 1523, remaining until 1948 (Giesen, 1988). In this model, the medical profession policed its own for breaches of conduct, elevating itself to an exclusive position in society. Thus, a physician harming a patient was wrong per se (Silver, 1992). There was a subsequent but temporary shift in focus back to contract law, as Giesen (1988) observed in the comments of Blackstone regarding a 1694 case: "[I]t has been solemnly resolved that *mala praxis* is a great misdemeanor and offence at common law, whether it be for curiosity and experiment, or by neglect; because it breaks the trust which the party has placed in his physician, and tends to the patient's destruction" (Giesen, 1988, p 7). Since early nineteenth century, however, the theory of the tort of malpractice became standard, thereby necessitating expert testimony to define the standard of care.

Alongside the development of physician liability was preoccupation with medical fraud or quackery. During the prolonged plague in Europe (Black Death) in the fourteenth century, quackery emerged, with practitioners promising cures. This practice continued for centuries and was the predecessor of generations of charlatans (see Fig. 2.1). Many such frauds were perpetrated on the public by nonphysicians attempting to make money by selling ineffective treatments such as patent medicines, a matter not regulated by organized medicine in America (Holbrook, 1959; U.S. Senate, 1964). While the predatory practice of luring elderly patients to buy useless products was investigated by the US Senate in the mid-twentieth century (U.S. Senate, 1964), the same practice existed since 1682 (Holbrook, 1959). To the degree that licensed physicians took part in these schemes, they were possibly committing consumer fraud and misusing their high station, if not formally guilty of the tort of negligence.

Malpractice suits first appeared in the United States in 1794, when a Connecticut man charged a doctor with negligence after his wife died 3 hours after surgery (Sandor, 1957). The jury awarded the man £40 after his attorney argued in the English tradition of breach of contract. According to Sandor (1957), nineteenth-century American cases cited English decisions, sometimes reaching back centuries. The years 1835 to 1865 have been regarded as America's first malpractice "crisis," with the courts flooded with orthopedic cases (Spiegel & Kavaler, 1997).

Fig. 2.1 Plague doctor as quack. Johann Melchior Füssli (ca. 1721). The caption, translated, reads, "Sketch of a doctor of Marseilles clad in cordovan leather equipped with a nose-case packed with plague-repelling smoking material. With the wand he is to feel the pulse." (Credit: Plague doctor as a quack. Credit: Wellcome Collection. Attribution 4.0 International (CC BY 4.0). Downloaded October 29, 2020 from https://wellcomecollection.org/works/vsr5duqq)

Improvements in medical-surgical devices spawned riskier procedures and the possibility that lifesaving treatments could result in permanent disability. Thus, better clinicians might be bigger targets for disappointed patients (Spiegel & Kavaler, 1997).

The latter half of the nineteenth century witnessed a proliferation of American cases that relied on local precedents and procedures. There were 2500 physicians sued in 1936 individual cases in America between 1794 and 1955 (Sandor, 1957). Orthopedic cases were aided by the discovery of the X-ray in 1895, with use of a radiogram as "secondary evidence" by a plaintiff the next year (Weiss, 2011).

Psychiatric Malpractice Litigation in Nineteenth-Century America

Malpractice suits against psychiatrists were rare in early America, but challenges to authority, especially in matters of involuntary confinement, have been present since the dawn of psychiatry. Involuntarily admitted asylum patients had the ability, though rarely invoked, to request a *writ* of *habeas corpus* to argue their release. This section will review three examples of legal challenges by patients in the mid-nineteenth century: the confinement of Morgan Hinchman in Philadelphia, the malpractice suit against Dr. Isaac Ray by Isaac Hunt in Maine, and the exposé and activism by Elizabeth P.W. Packard regarding her confinement in Illinois. These former patients used varied arguments either to gain freedom or expose corrupt aspects of asylum conditions and commitment practices prior to the passage of the post-Civil War Fourteenth Amendment to the Constitution, which barred states from denying citizens life, liberty, and property without due process of law.

The Hinchman Case Morgan Hinchman, 30, was committed to Friends Asylum by family and friends in early January 1847 and remained there for 6 months. Afterward, he charged a number of people with conspiracy to steal his property, including the family physician, the physician issuing the insanity certificate, his sister and sister-in-law, the asylum manager and lay superintendent, two doctors at the asylum, and others. Since Mr. Hinchman had experienced "mania" since 1841 and breaches in social behavior over several years, it was plausible that his allegations of conspiracy were delusional (Cherry, 1978; D'Antonio, 2006). Mr. Hinchman's charges were unusual, since the facility, which opened in 1817, was operated on the Quaker principle of kindness (moral therapy) modeled at the York Retreat in England (D'Antonio, 2006). The highly publicized case angered supporters of the esteemed Quaker facility: "…that all this shocking violence was done to get possession of his property. The city has been shocked, and a cry of vengeance raised against the perpetrators of an outrage which shames the Spanish inquisition or the dungeons of the Bastile [sic]" (Anonymous, 1849).

This case was, by implication, about medical malpractice, but more squarely in the domain of misuse of commitment and false imprisonment. Mr. Hinchman was correct about the conspiracy to the degree that the friends and family had arranged to convince the doctors and hospital staff that he required confinement, but he was also significantly deranged. The jury, however, cleared the doctors and hospital administrator and found the family and friends liable, awarding Mr. Hinchman a whopping $10,000 in damages for the swindle.

The Hunt Case Following unsuccessful attempts at developing a private medical practice in Portland and Eastport Maine, Dr. Isaac Ray catapulted himself into the international spotlight by publishing *A Treatise on the Medical Jurisprudence of Insanity* (Ray, 1838). While the book was to be the linchpin of defense counsel's argument for acquittal by insanity in the famous 1843 London murder trial of Daniel M'Naghten, Ray's reputation helped to secure his first medical appointment, Superintendent of the Maine Insane Hospital in Augusta, in 1841. He remained there for several years before accepting a position as Superintendent of a new facility, Butler Hospital in Providence, Rhode Island. Shortly before he departed for Butler, in 1844, he treated Isaac Hunt. Unknown to Ray for several years, Mr. Hunt was gearing up for an exposé of what he considered Ray's nefarious practices in Augusta, publishing a pamphlet, *Astounding Disclosures!*, in 1852 (Hunt, 1852) (see Fig. 2.2) and attempting to file malpractice charges against Ray (Weiss, 2013). The campaign, which Mr. Hunt took to the Maine legislature, took place between 1848 and 1854 (Weiss, 2013).

The essence of Mr. Hunt's complaint was that he was held at the asylum against his will, that he was forced to take toxic medications, and that the conditions were inhumane. In his pamphlet, he previewed his intentions for the litigation, namely, "sending [Drs. Ray and Smith] to the State Penitentiary for the full term of twenty years for malpractice, and three years additional for conspiracy" (Hunt, 1852, p 5). He decried Dr. Ray's paternal and authoritarian manner and his "mal, barbarous and inhuman, and cruel treatment" in a letter to the legislature accompanying the civil complaint. The legislature rejected the claim in 1852 and his appeal in 1854. Mr. Hunt alluded to the practice of *habeas corpus* for committed patients and suggested that civil proceedings be decided by juries. Dr. Ray was never tried for malpractice. Throughout the remainder of his career, Dr. Ray defended physicians as the legitimate fact finders in commitment matters, rejecting the idea of trials and juries proposed by Mrs. E.P.W. Packard (see below).

The Packard Case Elizabeth P.W. Packard was trapped in a marriage to a Calvinist minister, Theophilus Packard. Mrs. Packard, an emerging feminist and abolitionist, vehemently opposed her husband's view of women's freedom. As a result, in 1860, while the Packards resided in Manteno, Kankakee County, Illinois, her husband arranged for a doctor to have her declared insane, resulting in forced confinement in the asylum at Jacksonville, Illinois, for 3 years. This was made possible by an 1851 law permitting her to be "legally kidnapped": "Married women and infants who, in the judgment of the Medical Superintendent [of the asylum] are evidently insane or distracted, may be entered or detained in the

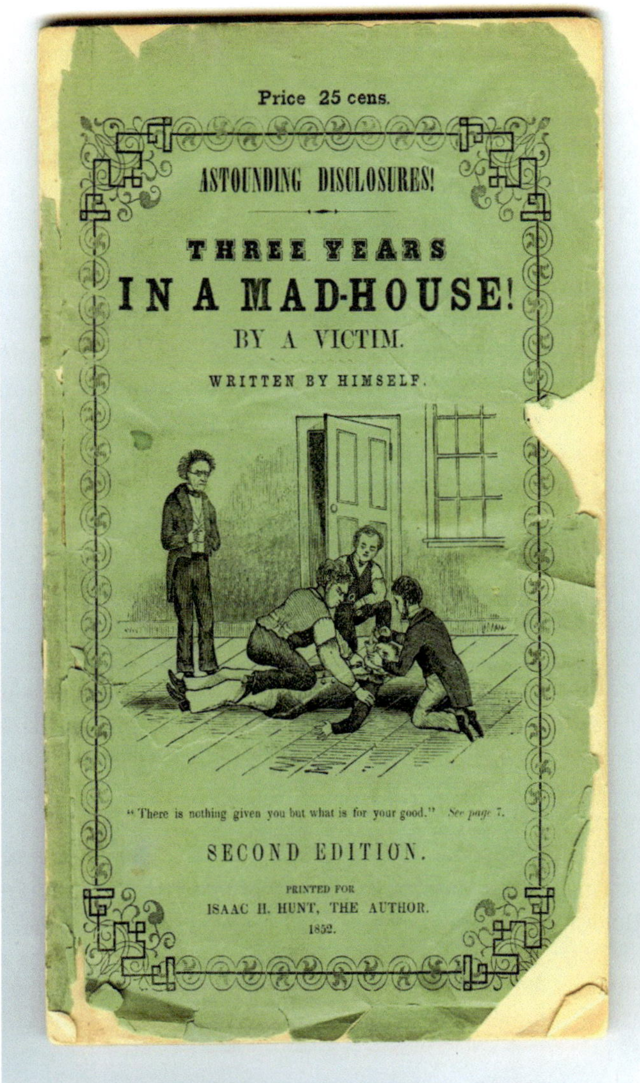

Fig. 2.2 Self-published book accusing Dr. Isaac Ray of medical malpractice, 1852, by Isaac H. Hunt. (Image obtained from the Disability History Museum (www.disabilitymuseum.org), accessed from https://www.disabilitymuseum.org/dhm/lib/catcard.html?id=2864 on October 20, 2020. Reprinted with permission of Pat Deegan. The illustration depicts the author, restrained by attendants, while Dr. Ray, observing, says, "There is nothing given you but what is for your good.")

hospital, on the request of the husband of the woman or the guardian of the infant, without the evidence of insanity required in other cases" (Packard, 1867, p 1). Mrs. Packard's doctor at Jacksonville, Dr. Andrew McFarland, whom she idolized (she wrote him love letters), was essentially a co-conspirator who, at the time of her discharge, declared her incurably insane (Sapinsley, 1991). When her husband barred her from returning home and threatened to commit her again, a sensational 5-day trial ensued in early 1864, resulting in her being declared sane (Sapinsley, 1991). While this was case about individual freedom, unlike Mr. Hunt's exposé, Mrs. Packard's was as much a direct accusation of Dr. McFarland as a statement of advocacy for humane care. As Sapinsley (1991) observed, however, when Mrs. Packard recovered from the transference love of her former psychiatrist, she sought to discredit him. Their battle was to take place in the Illinois legislature.

In the wake of her vindicating trial (*Packard v. Packard*) and unable to tolerate her oppressive husband, she moved to her home state of Massachusetts but later returned to Illinois, where her targets became broader, including a change in the commitment law and the unmasking of the physician-enablers of oppressive forces in her history. Now in post-Civil War America, she was empowered by her identification with other oppressed women, analogizing her former status to that of a slave (to her husband). Armed with letters attesting to her sanity, she found support from Governor Oglesby and some legislators. She delivered an impassioned address before the Illinois legislature (Packard, 1867). Mrs. Packard advocated for strict accountability of medical doctors for civil commitments. This included formal commitment trials and fines and imprisonment for doctors who deprived patients of due process. Dr. McFarland's objection to her view was that such procedures would traumatize the patients and have a chilling effect on families' obtaining care for their loved ones (Sapinsley, 1991). Ultimately, both legislative chambers and the governor signed the Personal Liberty Bill. The new law regarded deprivation of a sanity trial a "high misdemeanor" punishable by a fine of up to $1000 and possible imprisonment up to a year; some retroactivity applied. Accordingly, many of Dr. McFarland's patients at Jacksonville suddenly became cured (Sapinsley, 1991). Mrs. Packard had exposed him, achieving, in her mind, an outcome more valuable than a malpractice judgment. The ensuing sanity trials did not always end in release and the procedure received criticism in the press, which sometimes attributed Mrs. Packard's actions as a manifestation of insanity (Sapinsley, 1991). Undeterred, she wanted Dr. McFarland to repent, and was the star witness at a hearing on treatment of patients at Jacksonville. An independent investigation portrayed the doctor as cruel and abusive, while the hospital's own investigation acquitted him in 1868. The doctor stepped down and opened a private practice in 1872, in contrast to Mrs. Packard's assertion that she had "ruined" him (Packard, 1873). In 1891, he hanged himself.

Mrs. Packard's subsequent history, beyond the scope of this review, included a two-volume account of her struggles (Packard, 1873; Packard, 1874). Comparisons with Dorothea Dix, who exposed deplorable conditions and the housing of persons suffering from mental illness in jails and almshouses rather than hospitals, are inescapable, though it was a century until Mrs. Packard's contributions to the conversation on rights of persons with mental illness were recognized.

Late nineteenth-century treatises, for example, Dr. John Elwell's, which was in its fourth edition in 1881 (Elwell,

1881), devote much attention to the need for expert testimony in insanity cases but little to malpractice by psychiatrists. Elwell appeared to be especially concerned about quackery: "[T]he charlatan and pretender certainly should not be allowed to escape behind the ordinary skill and knowledge of honest practitioners, who actually are prepared to accomplish more than he, but promise and pretend less" (Elwell, 1881, p 24). Even in 1881, the state of psychiatry was such that, while Elwell regarded the testimony of physicians necessary to inform courts, such evidence could not be trusted: "Complexity, contradiction, difficulty, doubt and obscurity are the rules, if they may be so called, that guide him! These alone are certain, and present in every case" (Elwell, 1881, p 378). One can presume this would also apply to questions of standard of care.

Twentieth-Century Developments

Psychiatric malpractice cases were rare in the pre-pharmaceutical era (Bellamy, 1962; Dawidoff, 1966). Indeed, Dawidoff (1966) was hard pressed to identify suits against psychiatrists practicing psychotherapy and psychoanalysis. Sandor (1957) collected cases of medical liability from 1946 through 1956. Of 266 appellate decisions, 17 were coded "neuropsychiatric incidents." The incidents included allegations of falsely certifying patient as insane (11), alleged injury after electroshock treatment (3), allegations of inadequate restraints of psychiatric patients leading to suicide (2), and miscellaneous (1). Sandor (1957) also observed that there were many more suits against physicians under causes of action other than professional negligence, speculating that alternate pathways may have obviated the need for expert testimony on standard of care. They include: "breach of warranty by the physician,…technical assault and battery, fraud and deceit, false imprisonment and malicious prosecution, invasion of the right of privacy, interference with the family relationship, interference with contractual relations, defamation, and interference with property rights" (p 466, internal citations omitted).

International Comparisons

The adjudication of medical malpractice accusations in secular societies around the world has been addressed by Giesen (1988) and is beyond the scope of this chapter. Giesen noted that there is a split between nations that try malpractice claims via contract theory versus tort theory, whereas "the barriers between the two categories are breaking down" and could be merged (Giesen, 1988, p 9). Examples of contractually based systems include Austria, Belgium, France, Germany, Greece, Italy, and Switzerland, and tort-based include Japan and what were then Socialist countries of Eastern Europe. Practically speaking, Giesen (1988) stated that the outcomes should not differ, and there was no implication that psychiatric claims would differ from others, with the possible exception of liability of psychiatrists and psychologists for harm by patients to third parties.

A more recent publication regards comparative procedures in Canada, England and Wales, Germany, and India (Roudik, 2009). These countries have government-supported healthcare programs, whether single-payer or decentralized. The vast majority of cases are settled, with 8% litigated in Germany and 4% in England and Wales. Canadian cases are defended more vigorously compared to the types of dispute resolution seen in England and Wales. In all instances, patients may sue individual providers, and there is vicarious liability for the National Health Service (England and Wales) or hospitals (Canada). In cases involving death in India, there can be criminal proceedings, with the burden on the plaintiff to prove gross negligence. As of 2009, awards to plaintiffs were low in comparison to those in America. No punitive damages are permitted in Germany and India, and personal injury losses are borne by the social security systems of all nations studied. According to the report (Roudik, 2009), malpractice claims have little effect on healthcare delivery, and there was no indication that defensive medicine has driven up health costs.

Conclusions

With some variability in the details, medical malpractice has been established over time, culture, and geography, and applied to psychiatrists. As expected, adverse outcomes per se do not determine negligence. Instead, there have been numerous, nuanced versions of the principle that physicians have a contractual obligation to act with reasonable skill and care and that failure to do so may result in monetary and other sanctions. Aside from outright quackery and clear boundary violations, psychiatrists had not been the focus of malpractice claims prior to the advent of psychopharmacology, electroconvulsive therapy, and psychosurgery. Since the beginnings of American psychiatry in the nineteenth century, there has also been a focus on patients' rights, as demonstrated in the three vignettes. Tension between individual liberty of persons with mental disorders and the interests of the state and community have continued as salient issues alongside concerns about somatic therapies.

Key Points

- Allegations about medical malpractice have been adjudicated for centuries and across cultures.
- The theory on which malpractice allegations are adjudicated has migrated from contract law to analysis of standard of care.

- Expert testimony is required to define the standard of care on the negligence (tort) theory of malpractice.
- Historically, psychiatrists are among the physicians least likely to be sued for malpractice.
- The incidence of malpractice suits against psychiatrists has accelerated due to emphasis on somatic therapies.
- Some nations continue to use a contract theory of harm, whereby it is less likely to impose fault in cases of injury to third parties (tort claims).

References

American College of Physicians ad hoc committee on medical ethics. (1984). American College of Physicians Ethics Manual. Part I: History of medical ethics, the physician and the patient, the physician's relationship to other physicians, the physician and society. *Annals of Internal Medicine, 101*(1), 129–137.

Anonymous. (1849). Case of alleged conspiracy to confine a man in a lunatic asylum. *Boston Medical and Surgical Journal, 40*(21), 417.

Bal, B. S. (2009). An introduction to medical malpractice in the United States. *Clinical Orthopaedics and Related Research, 467*, 339–347.

Bellamy, W. A. (1962). Malpractice risks confronting the psychiatrist: A nationwide fifteen-year study of appellate court cases, 1946 to 1961. *American Journal of Psychiatry, 118*(9), 769–780.

Cherry, C. L. (1978). Friends Asylum, Morgan Hinchman, and moral insanity. *Quaker History, 67*(1), 20–34.

D'Antonio, P. (2006). *Founding friends. Families, staff, and patients at the friends asylum in early nineteenth-century Philadelphia*. Lehigh University Press.

Dawidoff, D. J. (1966). The malpractice of psychiatrists. *Duke Law Journal, 1966*, 696–716.

De Ville, K. A. (1990). *Medical malpractice in nineteenth-century America: Origins and legacy*. New York University Press.

Dollin, Y., & Roth, J. (2018). Psychiatric malpractice in Jewish law. *Journal of Jewish Ethics, 4*(1), 47–94.

Elwell, J. J. (1881). *Medico-legal treatise on malpractice, medical evidence, and insanity, comprising the elements of medical jurisprudence* (4th ed.). Baker, Voorhis.

Giesen, D. (1988). *International medical malpractice law: A comparative law study of civil liability arising from medical care*. M. Nijhoff.

Grossman, S. A., Gurley, K. L., & Wolfe, R. E. (2020). The ethics of error in medicine. *Rambam Maimonides Medical Journal, 11*(4), 1–6, e0033.

Holbrook, S. H. (1959). *The Golden age of quackery*. The Macmillan Co.

Hunt, I. H. (1852). *Astounding disclosures! Three years in a mad-house by a victim*. Self-published pamphlet available at Disability History Museum. www.disabilitymuseum.org

Ilani, Z., & Weinberger, Y. (2020). *The obligation to heal & medical malpractice*. Retrieved from https://www.jewishvirtuallibrary.org/jsource/Judaism/Malpractice.pdf. On November 2, 2020 (original posting date unknown).

Packard, E.P.W. (1867). *Mrs. Packard's address to the Illinois legislature, on the passage of the personal liberty bill*. Hartford: Case, Lockwood and Co.

Packard, E. P. W. (1873). *Modern persecution, or insane asylums unveiled*. Self-published in New York.

Packard, E. P. W. (1874). *Modern persecution, or married woman's liabilities* (Vol. II). Self-published in Hartford.

Ray, I. (1838). *A treatise on the medical jurisprudence of insanity*. Little and Brown.

Roudik, P. (2009). Comparative summary: Medical malpractice liability systems in selected countries. In *Medical liability: Canada, England and Wales, Germany, and India*. Law Library of Congress, Global Legal Research Center.

Sandor, A. A. (1957). The history of professional liability suits in the United States. *Journal of the American Medical Association, 163*, 459–466.

Sapinsley, B. (1991). *The private war of Mrs. Packard*. Paragon House.

Silver, T. (1992). One hundred years of harmful error: The historical jurisprudence of medical malpractice. *Wisconsin Law Review, 1992*, 1193–1241.

Spiegel, A. D., & Kavaler, F. (1997). America's first medical malpractice crisis, 1835–1865. *Journal of Community Health, 22*(4), 283–308.

U.S. Senate. (1964). *Special committee on aging, subcommittee on frauds and misrepresentations affecting the elderly. Part 3. Testimony on march 10, 1964*. U.S. Government Printing Office.

Weiss, K. J. (2011). Head, examined: Clarence Darrow's X-ray vision of criminal responsibility. *Journal of Psychiatry & Law, 39*, 627–661.

Weiss, K. J. (2013). Isaac Ray, malpractice defendant. *Journal of the American Academy of Psychiatry and the Law, 41*(3), 382–390.

Liability for the Acts of Others

3

Richard Balon and Sherif Soliman

There are numerous situations and settings in current day practice in which psychiatrists work and collaborate with other providers. The acts of those working with psychiatrists in various settings and relationships may present a significant risk of liability and malpractice lawsuits for practicing psychiatrists. Although there are exceptions, these situations and settings are usually not perfectly defined or regulated. Definitions and regulations may depend on the jurisdiction (i.e., state) that the psychiatrist is practicing in and the local standard of care. The risk of liability in these collaborative situations in psychiatry is not particularly high but may vary from state to state. As Vanderpool (2018) noted, professional negligence which could be subject of a malpractice action could occur only when the standard of care is not met. The standard of care is not always clear, frequently depending on local practice customs, and may require elucidation via expert witness testimony if the case reaches the court. Additionally, psychiatrists in supervisory, practice ownership, or even a collaborative relationship are exposed to more malpractice liability risk due to the "deep pocket" theory – malpractice lawyers prefer to sue the party with deep pockets, i.e., a person or organization with substantially more financial resources (assets, higher malpractice insurance), especially for the purpose of paying damages.

The literature on liability for the acts of others in psychiatry is sparse and does not include all situations and parties involved in current practice (e.g., NPs or PAs). Most publications focus on collaborative, consultative, or supervisory work with nonmedical therapists, where the psychiatrist is only providing medication management (also known as medication backup). This practice has become widespread in psychiatry during the last several decades. Appelbaum (1991) provided an analysis of this practice from a liability point of view and offered some guidelines for this practice. He made several important points regarding liability for the acts of others. He suggested that potential liability "is a function of the nature of the relationship among the psychiatrist, nonmedical therapist, and the patient. At a minimum, the prescribing psychiatrist will always risk liability for negligence associated with the evaluation of the patient, and the prescription and monitoring of the medication" [p. 281]. Nevertheless, he wrote that in regard to responsibility for the acts of others, two questions must be answered: (1) does the psychiatrist have supervisory responsibility for the nonmedical therapist and (2) what services has the psychiatrist agreed to provide? With regard to a supervisory relationship, Appelbaum (1991) stated that the supervisor is someone whose opinion the therapist (and for the purpose of this chapter, any supervised party) is obliged to follow, if reasonable supervision of patient care is provided. This, as Appelbaum wrote [2, p. 281], "does not mean that the psychiatrist will necessarily be held responsible for any negligence on the part of nonmedical therapist." If the supervisee acts unreasonably in a way the supervisor has not been able to foresee, no liability should accrue. Nevertheless, the psychiatrist has to monitor the supervisee according to accepted standard of care. However, as Appelbaum (1991, p. 281) pointed out, "If the therapist is the psychiatrist's employee, some jurisdictions will permit the psychiatrist to be held vicariously liable for all negligent and some intentional acts of the therapist regardless of the reasonableness of the psychiatrist's supervision." Regarding the extent of services agreed to, Appelbaum (1991, p. 281) warns that, at times, psychiatrists providing medication backup see patients less frequently, "relying on the nonmedical therapists to bring problems to their attention. This arrangement can be appropriate if the therapist is experienced and trustworthy."

R. Balon (✉)
Departments of Psychiatry and Behavioral Neurosciences and Anesthesiology, Wayne State University, Detroit, MI, USA
e-mail: rbalon@wayne.edu

S. Soliman
Atrium Health, Charlotte, NC, USA

Department of Psychiatry, University of North Carolina, Chapel Hill, NC, USA

P. Ash et al. (eds.), *Malpractice and Liability in Psychiatry*, https://doi.org/10.1007/978-3-030-91975-7_3

Definitions

In 1980, the American Psychiatric Association (1980) published guidelines for psychiatrists working in consultative, supervisory, or collaborative relationships with nonmedical therapists. While this document has never been properly updated and may not reflect all situations covered in this chapter (e.g., it speaks of psychologists [PhDs], social workers [MSWs], nurses [RNs], and mental health counselors [LPCs of LMHCs], but not nurse practitioners [NPs] and physician assistants [PAs]), it is useful to note the definitions of these relationships from this document as these are still applicable.

According to this document:

1. "*Consultative relationship between a psychiatrist and a therapist who is not a physician.* In this type of relationship, the psychiatrist does not assume responsibility for the patient's care. The psychiatrist evaluates the information provided by the therapist and offers a medical opinion which the therapist may or may not accept. In this instance, the therapist must have met professional and institutional standards for independent functioning (e.g., certification). Consultation is not a one-way process and psychiatrists do and should seek appropriate consultation from members of other disciplines in order to provide more comprehensive services to patients.
2. *Supervisory relationships between a psychiatrist and a nonmedical therapist.* In a supervisory relationship, the psychiatrist retains direct responsibility for patient care and gives professional direction and active guidance to the therapist. In this relationship, the nonmedical therapist may be an employee of an organized healthcare setting or of the psychiatrist. The psychiatrist is clinically responsible for the initial workup, diagnosis, and prescription of a treatment plan, as well as for assuring that adequate and timely attention is paid to the patient's physical status and that such information is integrated into the overall evaluation, diagnosis, and planning. The psychiatrist remains ethically and medically responsible for the patient's care as long as the treatment continues under his or her supervision. The patient should be fully informed of the existence and nature of, and any changes in, the supervisory relationship.
3. *Collaborative relationship between a psychiatrist and a therapist who is not a physician.* Implicit in this relationship is mutually shared responsibility for the patient's care in accordance with the qualifications and limitations of each therapist's discipline and abilities. The patient must be informed of respective responsibilities of each therapist; neither discipline's responsibilities diminish those of the other. Both the psychiatrist and nonmedical therapist are responsible for periodic evaluation of the patient's status to ascertain that the collaboration continues to be appropriate. The therapists must inform the patient, either jointly or separately, if they decide to terminate their collaborative relationship.
4. *Appropriateness of care.* It is unethical for the psychiatrist to continue an administrative supervisory, consultative, or collaborative relationship if it is ascertained that his or her role is being misinterpreted, or when he or she is convinced that the care being provided is inappropriate or inadequate. An exception may be made when the psychiatrist is specifically accepting a responsibility with the goal of raising the quality of care to an adequate level. Psychiatrists with ongoing administrative supervisory, consultative, or collaborative relationships should undertake such relationships with a therapist only if they are able to keep themselves appropriately informed of the nature of treatment and the progress of those patients for whom they are acting as supervisor, consultant, or collaborator, and can assure themselves that the treatment is being carried out competently and adequately."

The guidelines also address the legal responsibility, stating that "When psychiatrists extend their services to other professionals in meaningful collaboration (which includes supervision of cases or participation in interdisciplinary teamwork), they are obliged to know about and to be willing to assume the established legal responsibilities involved" (American Psychiatric Association, 1980, p. 1490). Mossman and Weston (2010) added to the permutations of types of split-care relationships, describing informal consultative relationships ("curbside") where "one practitioner describes clinical characteristics to another; patient's identity is unknown to consultant." This relationship does not routinely constitute a legal responsibility in the sense of liability for the acts of others.

Liability

The terms *vicarious liability* and *direct liability* are important in understanding a psychiatrist's liability for the acts of others in employment or supervisory relationships.

In an article on liability for failure to supervise adequately, Saccuzzo (1997) wrote that, in addition to *statutory liability* (responsibility for specific actions or omissions due to a related law or statute that is not open to interpretation), supervisors are liable under any negligence theory. These theories are divided into two main types of liability: "(1) *vicarious liability* in which the supervisor or employer is held liable for actions of the supervisee regardless of any fault on the part of the supervisor and (2) *direct liability* in which the supervisor is held directly liable for his or her own negligence, such as negligent supervision or hiring."

In the respondeat superior doctrine, an employer or supervisor is held principally responsible (i.e., vicariously liable) for the wrongful acts of an employee or agent such as supervisee or collaborator if such acts occur within the scope of the employment, agency, or relationship. Importantly, this liability applies whether or not the employer or supervisor breached a duty, providing that act "which injured the patient must be within the employee or supervisee's scope of employment" (Saccuzzo, p. 123). In simple language, this is "a doctrine in tort law that makes a master liable for the wrong of a servant" (Merriam-Webster Law, 2020). The literal translation from Latin is "let the master answer." The doctrine originated in the 1698 English case of *Jones v Hart*, which involved a pawnbroker who was held liable for an employee selling an item he should not have sold (*Jones v. Hart*, 1698; Lisk, 1991).

Two additional issues to consider in cases of vicarious liability are the *borrowed servant rule* (the employee or supervisee is directed or permitted by his primary employer or supervisor to work for or be supervised by another employer or supervisor) and *enterprise liability* (the supervisor earns money for supervision and thus should be willing to bear the risk of patient damages).

Parties and Situations Involved

Psychiatrists may work or collaborate with various other mental professionals, e.g., psychologists, social workers, NPs, PAs, therapists, other physicians, and trainees such as residents (of various specialties), medical students, and students in other disciplines, such as psychology interns or social work students. It is important to put in context whether the psychiatrist is (a) supervising or employing any of these parties (e.g., employing several other physicians or therapists in a clinic he or she owns or is a medical director of); (b) is supervised or employed by any of these parties (e.g., he or she works in a clinic or other entity run or owned by a psychologist or social worker); (c) is independently collaborating with any of these parties (e.g., seeing patients in private practice or a clinic who are also seeing another clinician in the community who is practicing independently); or (d) both parties, psychiatrist and nurse practitioner or physician assistant are employees of a hospital and each has his/her own chain of command although he/she collaborates in the care of patients..

In the first two situations (employing or supervising, being employed or supervised) and possibly even the third one, the previously mentioned doctrine of respondeat superior usually applies.

Psychiatrists should also be aware that the nature of working with several parties may increase the risk of malpractice just by the sheer increase of treated and supervised patient volume inherent to this type of practice (MacBeth, 1999), and less time with patients than he or she would spend when providing both psychopharmacology and psychotherapy. MacBeth (1999) lists a number of other situations and arrangements that may potentially increase the risk of liability in divided treatment, including lack of strong therapeutic alliance with the patient (and where relevant with his/her family), systemic information failure, lack of the psychiatrist's authority, system disorganization, and failure of a therapist to appreciate significance of information.

Supervising a resident or a fellow presents a special, not-well-explored situation. When a resident is being supervised, the supervising physician has a higher level of responsibility than he or she does in other collaborative relationships, because the resident's trainee status implies that he or she will not (generally) be individually held to the same standard as a fully trained psychiatrist. There is, as far as we know, no separate standard for a resident. As Recupero and Rainey (2007) point out, supervising physicians may be held vicariously liable (under the theory of respondeat superior) for resident's mistakes and negligence or may be directly liable for their own negligence in supervision and administration. As they expound, one of the premises of the training is that only qualified residents advance and residents, though not yet completely trained, are allowed to provide service with the expectation that their supervisor will remedy any deficiency. Under the theory of enterprise liability, a supervisor in private practice or a hospital may be held liable if they are compensated for the care provided by the resident (Recupero & Rainey, 2007). Many claims in psychotherapy and psychotherapy supervision also fall into categories of sexual misconduct and intentional torts. Resident supervisors could also be liable for mishandling of resident countertransference or for failing to respond appropriately to complaints of sexual misconduct. Recupero and Rainey (2007) recommend, among hosts of risk management strategies, that "Informed consent can be an ideal process for educating and involving the patient in the decision to receive treatment from a resident, as many states require informed consent from patients for treatment by supervision, at least in the context of psychology assistants" (p. 193). Finally, they suggest that tailored, consistent, and responsible supervision not only helps patients but improves education and lessens the risk for residents.

Case Laws and Clinical Examples

Medical malpractice, like other negligence claims, has traditionally relied on the presence of four elements: duty to the patient, deviation from the standard of care, causation, and damages (see Chap. 1). However, it is increasingly possible for physicians to be held vicariously liable for the care of patients whom they have never met nor examined. Consider the fictional case of Dr. Emily Blake, a psychiatrist in private practice who employs Allen Smith, a physician assistant (PA). PA Smith evaluates Mr. Jones, a 27-year-old man with major depression and passive suicidal ideation. PA Smith fails to inquire about past suicide attempts or whether Mr. Jones had access to firearms. Mr. Jones dies by suicide using a firearm shortly thereafter, and his estate sues PA Smith and Dr. Blake for negligence in assessing and managing his suicide risk. The relevant inquiries will vary by jurisdiction but will generally involve several questions. First, did PA Smith violate the standard of care and does PA Smith have a separate standard of care as a PA or is he subject to the same standard of care applicable to a psychiatrist? Second, is Dr. Blake liable for the acts of PA Smith? This question will largely depend on whether Dr. Blake had the ability to supervise or control PA Smith's conduct. The answers to these questions will largely depend on the law in the specific jurisdiction. A discussion of potential legal theories of liability and an examination of select cases will illustrate how the law views these issues. This discussion is not intended to constitute legal advice or a statement of the law in a particular jurisdiction. Rather, the cases are presented as an illustration of how legal decision-makers have approached issues of vicarious liability in medical malpractice.

A common theory of vicarious liability is the previously discussed doctrine of respondeat superior. This doctrine is partially rooted in public policy. The justification for the rule includes deterring negligent or risky conduct by large employers and ensuring that an injured party can be adequately compensated. For example, a nursing home corporation is aware that it may be liable for sexual abuse of its residents by an employee. This possibility provides additional motivation for the company to expend resources to train and monitor its employees and obtain background checks in order to reduce the likelihood of abuse. The critical inquiry under this doctrine is whether the physician has the authority to control how the other clinician performs their duties. As mentioned earlier, a related doctrine, the "borrowed servant" rule, extends respondeat superior liability to temporary employers. This may be relevant in medicine when a hospital employs a contract physician or when a medical resident, who is a hospital employee, performs surgery under the direction of an attending surgeon who is not employed by the hospital. The resident may be considered a "borrowed servant" of the surgeon if the surgeon has the authority to control how the resident performs the surgery.

In *Bazley v. Curry* (1999), the Supreme Court of Canada considered the case of the Children's Foundation, a nonprofit organization that operated residential care facilities for children. One of its employees, Mr. Curry, was convicted of 19 counts of sexual abuse, including two involving Mr. Bazley, who then filed suit against the Foundation. Mr. Curry was deceased at the time of the lawsuit. The lower court judge found that the Foundation could potentially face liability, even if it was not negligent in supervising or hiring Mr. Curry. The Supreme Court agreed and affirmed the decision. Applying prior Canadian precedent, the Court found that the sexual abuse was related to Curry's employment, even though it was obviously not a behavior that was sanctioned by his employer. In determining whether the behavior was sufficiently related to Curry's employment, the Court reasoned that the "…test for vicarious liability for an employee's sexual abuse of a client should focus on whether the employer's enterprise and empowerment of the employee materially increased the risk of the sexual assault and hence the harm" (*Bazley v. Curry*, 1999. p. 536).

In *Cox v. M.A. Primary and Urgent Care Clinic* et al. (2010), the Tennessee Supreme Court considered the case of Dr. Austin Adams, who was the supervising physician for PA Michael Maddox. PA Maddox saw Ms. Melissa Michelle Cox for fatigue and respiratory concerns. After a complicated course, she was eventually diagnosed at another facility with severe congestive heart failure. She filed suit against the clinic and Dr. Adams, alleging that the clinic had failed to properly diagnose her cardiomyopathy and that Dr. Adams owed her a duty of care. The trial court granted the defendants' motion to dismiss the case and ruled that the standard of care for a physician assistant was similar to that of the supervising physician. The Court of Appeals reversed the trial court on the issue of standard of care. The Tennessee Supreme Court ruled that physician assistants were held to a different standard of care than physicians, noting differences in training and scope of practice. The Court noted that different jurisdictions had resolved this issue differently, with some holding that physician assistants were held to the same standard of care as physicians. However, the Court found that plaintiffs had not presented any evidence that Maddox or Adams breached the applicable standards of care. In fact, the plaintiff's expert witness admitted that he was not familiar with the standard of care for physician assistants or their supervision. The Court specifically did not address the issue of negligent supervision, noting that it had not been raised at the lower court level and may not be raised for the first time on appeal.

In *Morvillo v. Shenandoah Memorial Hospital* (2008), the Virginia Supreme Court considered the case of Stephen Palmerton, a CRNA (certified registered nurse anesthetist), who was alleged to have injured the plaintiff's phrenic nerve while administering an interscalene block. The suit alleged in relevant part that Palmerton had performed the procedure negligently. The suit (in an amended complaint) also alleged that the supervising physician, Dr. O'Neal, was liable under the doctrine of respondeat superior. The Court, citing prior precedent, ruled that the test for whether a master-servant relationship existed included the power of selection of the

CRNA, payment of the employee, and the ability to dismiss and control the employee. The last element, power or control over the individual, was dispositive. The Court ruled that since it was undisputed that Dr. O'Neal supervised PA Palmerton, there was sufficient basis to have the jury decide whether Dr. O'Neal was vicariously liable.

The common theme that runs through these cases is an examination of the power the physician had or did not have to direct how the other practitioner practiced. Jurisdictions differ regarding the degree of control that is required for vicarious liability to apply and the factors that are relevant in making that determination. While different jurisdictions have different standards, the following questions may be helpful in determining the likelihood of vicarious liability:

1. What is the appropriate standard of care? For example, does the physician assistant, nurse practitioner, or therapist have their own applicable standard of care or are they governed by the physician's standard of care?
2. Was the standard of care breached?
3. Did the physician have the authority to control how the other practitioner practiced?
   (a) Does the law state that the practitioner may only practice under the supervision of the physician?
   (b) Does the law state explicitly that the practitioner is an agent of the physician?
   (c) Does the physician have the power to hire or fire the practitioner?
4. Was the physician negligent in hiring or supervising the practitioner?
5. Was the practitioner practicing within their scope of practice as defined by local laws and an agreement with the supervising physician?
6. Was the alleged act specifically forbidden, such as a crime or intentional tort?

How to Reduce the Risk of Liability from Others

There are several general ways to reduce the risk of liability for the acts of others: (a) knowing the rules and regulations of the relationship and practice; (b) practicing these rules and regulations; (c) knowing the parties involved and their skills and credentials, and understanding their scope of their practice; (d) performing a reasonable risk assessment in risk posing situations (e.g., suicidal threats, possible violence, discharge of the patient by supervisory or collaborative party); (e) determining, defining, and reviewing the nature of supervision; (f) possibly involving shared patients in discussing the roles of parties involved; and (g) properly documenting one's actions. In general, the risk is higher when psychiatrist is employing or supervising the other party(ies), and lower when he or she is collaborating with them or being employed or supervised by them.

Several authors have specifically addressed how to limit the risk of liability. Appelbaum (1991, pp. 281–282) wrote that "Liability prevention in the context of medication backup hinges on a clear definition of the psychiatrist's role. Unless otherwise specified, there will be a tendency for the courts, which traditionally have considered the physician to be the captain of the ship, to take expansive views of the psychiatrist's responsibilities." He added that there should be no "implied responsibilities," and all responsibilities should be "clearly specified, preferably in a written agreement among the patient, the psychiatrist, and the nonmedical therapist." However, it seems that the thinking about contracting has changed. Contracts are helpful, but a potential pitfall of written contracts in a divided treatment setting is that they tend to be overinclusive. Then, when there is a written agreement or policy, the failure to follow it creates liability, even if the policy was not necessary or applicable. Consequently, if for some reason something was not communicated that the policy says it should have been, the signers tend to become liable, even if the standard of care did not require it. There is no definite legal opinion on this issue available; however, the practice of written contracts seems controversial from the current point of view. Whether to write a contract or not may also depend on the character of the relationship (consultative, collaborative, supervisory). It may not be advisable to enter supervisory relationship without a (simple) contract unless both parties are employees of the same institution. The contract may be less useful in other types of relationships, such as consultative or collaborative. Thus, the pros and cons of using and writing a contract and its context should be carefully deliberated, and contracts, due to their over-inclusiveness, may not be advisable in many situations.

Mossman and Weston (2010) warned that essential aspects of clinical care should not be delegated to others no matter what the relationship is. They used a specific example of worsening of patient's suicidal thoughts – some patients may relate these thoughts to the therapist only, yet they should be instructed to relate them to the psychiatrist too. They also warned about working with uncredentialed or unlicensed therapists, as these may not be held to the same practice standards and may carry very little or no malpractice insurance, and thus the psychiatrist may be held accountable for not knowing their credentials and assuming most liability. Similar to others, Mossman and Weston (2010) urged the establishment of clear rules of collaboration, including division of responsibilities, outlining ways and circumstances of communication, types of problems that would prompt the patient to contact either party first, and coverage/availability during crises and vacations.

Sederer, Ellison, and Keyes (1998) noted that psychiatrists in working relationships with other providers should be monitoring the quality and safety of patient's care and well-being and when they believe "that the appropriateness of a diagnosis or the quality of treatment is questionable, he or she should take action commensurate with the level of concern to the patient's safety" (p. 1197). They emphasized the importance of documentation, recommending that all discussions, evaluations, and recommendations relevant to the patient's care should be included in medical records. They also suggested that the psychiatrist should inquire whether there are others clinically involved in the patient's care. They cited a case in which multiple therapists and multiple physicians were involved, but there was very little knowledge of involvement among those involved. Sederer, Ellison, and Keyes (1998) also thought that it is important to know why the psychiatrist was asked to assist or collaborate, as some reasons for collaboration may stem from unexpected or unrecognized wishes to deal with a difficult patient or the desire of the therapist to terminate or transfer the case. Further recommendations included addressing communication among all parties involved (ways of communications, i.e., phone, e-mail, letters; preference, in which situations); discussion of confidentiality and its limitations with all parties involved (disclosures to insurance companies; disclosure in situations involving risk of harm to patient and/or others); clarifying the responsibilities of parties involved (also to the patient); and awareness and discussion of transference and countertransference issues (difficult in triangular or even more complicated relationships). They also emphasized the need for open communication between treating parties that should happen with patient consent and warned that "continuing treatment with a patient who does not permit open communication of medically necessary information among treating clinicians may not be clinically responsible or feasible" (p. 1201). Sederer, Ellison, and Keyes (1998) further addressed consultation to a primary care physician and suggested that it may be useful for the psychiatrist to know the primary care physician's comfort with and knowledge of psychotropic medications.

MacBeth (1999) outlined several other risk mitigation measures, such as exercising continuing care and judgment in all practice circumstances, understanding operations and routines of every practice setting, weeding out problematic practice sites, understanding and using the system review and appeal procedures, deciding supervision and other discussion schedules based on patient's condition and need, and not indemnifying the system and other professionals for any damages connected to the patient's treatment.

Gutheil and Simon (2003) have addressed a special issue – the abandonment of patients in split treatment. Clinicians, as they noted, may choose to refuse to treat or cease treating patients except "The clinician may not cease treatment during a crisis or emergency and may not leave a patient in need of treatment completely without some recourse, such as referral or alternative care. To do either of these actions constitutes legal abandonment" (p. 175). Additionally, refusal to accept some patients as required by regional rules (e.g., catchment areas) can also constitute abandonment. All three situations might constitute "the legal cause of action of abandonment as an element of tort of medical malpractice" (p. 175).

There are specific situations related to the issue of abandonment in split or collaborative treatment. Failure to properly monitor or attend to a patient in this setting may constitute an abandonment. Unilateral ceasing of patient care without proper referral, but relying on the therapist continuing therapy, is a more complex issue. However, the therapist cannot prescribe medications, and therefore a lack of further arrangements by the psychiatrist could be considered abandonment (unless it is clear that need for medication ceased and it was properly documented). Gutheil (1994) described the "eight Cs" of the role of prescribing physician working with a nonmedical collaborator: Clarity (about roles), Contract (preferably written), Communication (ongoing, active), Consent (by all parties), Contact (regular, between treaters), Comprehensive view, Credentialing, and Consultation (if there is disagreement between clinicians).

Finally, in his article on organizational liability, Reid (2004) warned that clinicians working for healthcare organization may be assigned duties that go beyond the simple concept of respondeat superior. At times, clinicians may believe that they are fully indemnified by their employment status and thus protected from malpractice claims. However, if they oversee clinical work as part of their employment, that part of their work could be considered "discretionary." That means that in addition to their administrative duties, they may be considered to be practicing clinical care or be involved in working with others outside of their administrative work. This part of their work may be considered separately from their administrative role, and they may me sued personally if any negative outcome of this part of their work occurs.

Conclusion

Divided treatment with its numerous possible combinations of relationships among parties, various situations, and dynamics constitutes a fertile ground for the liability for actions of others. This chapter has not covered all possible liabilities and how to reduce their risk. Nevertheless, it seems clear that the psychiatrist has to understand the risks of divided treatment; practice according to standard of care; be familiar with professionals he or she works with and know their credentials, abilities, and competency; monitor the work of other clinicians involved; document issues related to divided treatment carefully; and be clear about responsibilities and the comprehension of all parties involved, including patients.

Key Points

- Divided treatment arrangements (collaborative, consultative, supervisory) may expose psychiatrist to liability for the acts of others.
- The character of the relationship between psychiatrist and other parties such as other physicians, residents and fellows, NPs, PAs, and social workers should be discussed and clarified.
- It is unclear whether written contracts between psychiatrists and other parties are decreasing the chance of liability, and therefore such contracts are probably not advisable.
- Various strategies to decrease liability for the acts of others include, for instance, monitoring quality and safety of care; open, frequent two-way exchange of information; careful documentation; and timely addressing of patient's complaints and countertransference issues.

References

American Psychiatric Association. (1980). Guidelines for psychiatrists in consultative, supervisory, or collaborative relationships with nonmedical therapists. *American Journal of Psychiatry, 137*(11), 1489–1491.

Appelbaum, P. S. (1991). General guidelines for psychiatrists who prescribe medications for patients treated by nonmedical psychotherapists. *Hospital and Community Psychiatry, 42*(3), 281–282.

Bazley v Curry, 2 SCR 534 (1999).

Cox v. MA Primary and Urgent Care Clinic, 313 S.W.3d 240 (2010).

Gutheil, T. G. (1994). Risk management at the margins: Less-familiar topics in psychiatric malpractice. *Harvard Review of Psychiatry, 2*(4), 214–221.

Gutheil, T. G., & Simon, R. I. (2003). Abandonment of patients in split treatment. *Harvard Review of Psychiatry, 11*(4), 175–179.

Jones v. Hart, 90 Eng. Rep. 1255 (1698).

Lisk, L. D. (1991). A physician's respondeat superior liability for negligent acts of other medical professionals-when the captain goes down without the ship. *University of Arkansas Little Rock Law Review, 13*(2), 183–207.

MacBeth, J. E. (1999). Divided treatment: Legal implications and risks. In I. M. B. Riba & R. Balon R. (Eds.), *Psychopharmacology and psychotherapy. A collaborative approach* (pp. 111–158). American Psychiatric Press, Inc.

Merriam-Webster Law. https://www.merriam-webster.com/legal/respondeat%20superior. Accessed 27 Dec 2020.

Morvillo v. Shenandoah Memorial Hosp., 547 F. Supp. 2d 528 (W.D. Va.) (2008).

Mossman, D., & Weston, C. G. (2010). Splitting treatment: How to limit liability risk when you share a patients' care. *Current Psychiatry, 9*(3), 43–46.

Recupero, P. R., & Rainey, S. E. (2007). Liability and risk management in outpatient psychotherapy supervision. *Journal of the American Academy of Psychiatry and the Law, 35*(2), 188–195.

Reid, W. H. (2004). Organizational liability: Beyond Respondeat superior. *Journal of Psychiatric Practice, 10*(4), 258–262.

Saccuzzo, D. P. (1997). Liability for failure to supervise adequately mental health assistants, unlicensed practitioners and students. *California Western Law Review, 34*(1)., article 10,, 115–152.

Sederer, L. I., Ellison, J., & Keyes, C. (1998). Guidelines for prescribing psychiatrists in consultative, collaborative, and supervisory relationships. *Psychiatric Services, 49*(9), 1197–1202.

Vanderpool, D. (2018). Professional liability in psychiatric practice. In L. H. Gold & R. C. Frierson (Eds.), *The American Psychiatric Association Publishing Textbook of Forensic Psychiatry* (3rd ed., pp. 169–183). American Psychiatric Association Publishing.

4 Professional Liability Insurance

Donna Vanderpool

When practicing any type of medicine, including psychiatry, there is the risk of a professional liability action being brought against the physician. As can be seen in Fig. 4.1, there are many different types of professional liability actions that can potentially be brought against psychiatrists. Civil litigation involves one citizen versus another citizen, such as a patient, or the patient's estate, versus the psychiatrist. Medical malpractice is the most common action, but there could be other causes of action, such as wrongful death. There are also government actions against psychiatrists. These actions could be civil, such as a state attorney general bringing a civil action based on breach of confidentiality, such as related to cybersecurity, or based on billing. Or, the government could bring criminal actions, such as those alleging fraudulent billing or homicide for excessive opioid prescribing that resulted in death.

Administrative actions by the government are also possible. Psychiatrists have many government agencies as regulators, all of which can investigate and impose penalties. Data from Professional Risk Management Services (PRMS, 2021) shows that psychiatrists are more likely to have an administrative action brought against them than a malpractice lawsuit. While the term "claim" is used in the malpractice realm to include any action brought against a physician, a claim is technically a demand for money outside of litigation. In 2020, 68% of incoming actions were administrative actions and 32% were claims and lawsuits. The vast majority of those administrative actions were licensing board investigations, triggered by any number of things such as patient complaints or news headlines.

Other regulatory agencies can also initiate investigations. At the federal level, examples include the Drug Enforcement Agency for improper prescribing of controlled substances, or the Department of Health and Human Services for a violation of the Health Insurance Portability and Accountability Act (HIPAA). There are additional entities that can investigate psychiatrists: hospitals related to poor patient care, health plans related to billing irregularities and adverse events, and professional organizations, such as the American Psychiatric Association for alleged ethical violations. These actions are not mutually exclusive, and professional liability insurance policies may not cover all of these actions, such as criminal investigations. However, psychiatrists should notify their insurer upon notice of any action or investigation being brought against them (see Chap. 5).

How to Manage Professional Liability Risk

There are two strategies to manage professional liability risk. The first strategy is to avoid an action all together, by practicing good medicine and minimizing the clinical risks of patient harm. However, even with the best clinical care, psychiatrists can still have professional liability actions brought against them. The second strategy, in case there is an action, is to transfer the risk, specifically the cost of paying for the liability action, to an insurance company, or other insurer. By purchasing professional liability insurance, the financial risk is transferred to the insurer.

What Professional Liability Insurance Is and Is Not

Insurance is a highly regulated industry and each state has its own legal requirements. While not all types of policies are offered in each state, there are basic elements of all professional liability insurance policies. Medical professional liability insurance is a contract between the insured psychiatrist and the insurer, where in exchange for the insured's paid premium, the insurer provides coverage for professional liability claims brought against the insured based on acts and omissions incurred in the rendering of professional services, the practice of psychiatry. Coverage lasts for the policy

D. Vanderpool (✉)
Professional Risk Management Services (PRMS), Arlington, VA, USA
e-mail: vanderpool@prms.com

P. Ash et al. (eds.), *Malpractice and Liability in Psychiatry*, https://doi.org/10.1007/978-3-030-91975-7_4

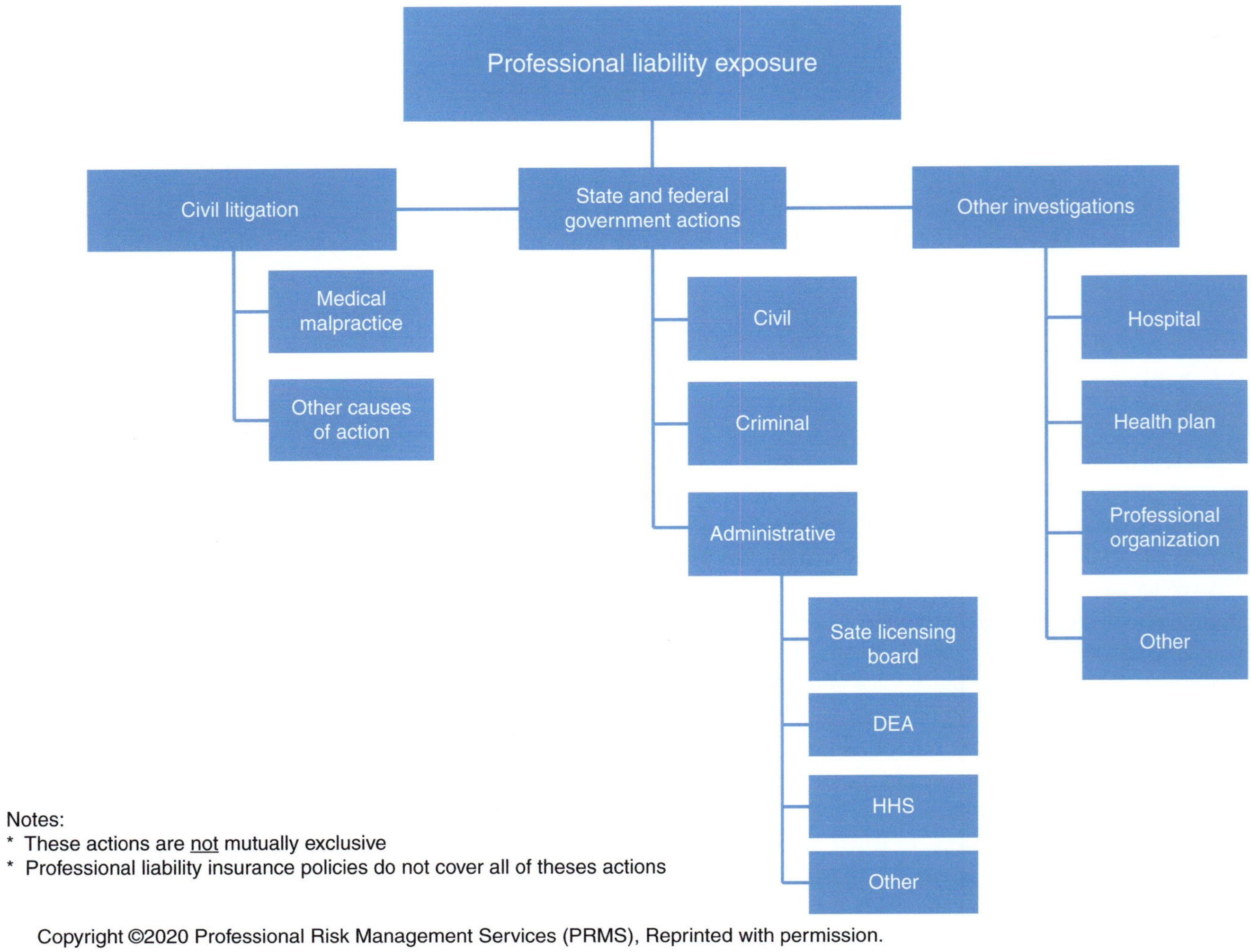

Fig. 4.1 Physicians professional liability exposure

period, discussed further below. In the event of coverage issues, courts have made it clear that limitations of coverage must be clearly expressed in the policy, and any ambiguities are construed against the insurer and in favor of the insured (*Mazza v. Medical Mutual Insurance Co. of North Carolina*, 1984).

Policies generally cover two types of costs:

- "Indemnity" is money paid to resolve the claim (whether pursuant to a court judgment or a settlement) as compensation to a plaintiff for the physician's act or omission. Indemnity includes economic (such as medical bills) and noneconomic (such as pain and suffering) damages. States may, or may not, allow insurance coverage for punitive damages (for outrageous behavior, imposed to deter such behavior). In those states that allow such coverage for punitive damages, insurers may have to pay punitive damages unless they are explicitly excluded under the policy (*Mazza v. Medical Mutual Insurance Co. of North Carolina*, 1984).
- "Defense" or "expense" is money paid to defend the action, such as attorneys' fees, court fees, and expert witness fees.

Medical professional liability insurance policies only cover professional services and are not general liability policies. Accordingly, they typically will not cover the theft of office equipment. Other types of insurance policies that may be needed include general liability, business owners, workers' compensation, etc.

Professional Liability Insurance Policies

Occurrence Versus Claims-Made Insurance Policies

There are two main types of professional liability policies: claims-made and occurrence. With an occurrence policy, coverage is given for an incident giving rise to a claim that occurs while the policy is in place, regardless of when it is reported to the insurer, even if that reporting occurs after the policy has expired. Each year that an occurrence policy is renewed, the insured is given a new set of policy limits, and previous years' limits remain available to defend claims that may arise from incidents occurring in those previous years. By contrast, a claims-made policy only covers those claims reported while the policy is in effect. Under a claims-made policy, even if a physician had insurance at the time the incident giving rise to the claim occurred, if it is reported after the policy has expired, there will be no coverage for that claim, unless extended reporting coverage ("tail" coverage) has been purchased or was provided by the insurer. When a claims-made policy is renewed, the insured is given a new set of policy limits, but the prior years' limits are not retained.

To illustrate the differences between the two types of policies, consider this example: there is an event – a patient death allegedly due to suicide – on February 1, 2018. The claim was filed on January 15, 2019. If the psychiatrist had an occurrence policy covering January 1, 2018, through December 31, 2018, but did not renew in 2019 because she took a job with the Department of Veterans Affairs (VA) and did not need insurance, the policy would still cover the claim even though there was no policy in effect at the time the claim was filed. An occurrence policy covers an event that took place during the policy period, regardless of when the claim is filed. In contrast, if the psychiatrist had a claims-made policy covering the same period (January 1, 2018, through December 31, 2018) but did not renew in 2019, again because she took a job at the VA and did not need insurance, the policy would not cover the claim because even though the event occurred during the covered period, the claim was filed when there was no coverage, unless the psychiatrist bought "tail" coverage to extend the reporting period.

As long as the claims-made policy is renewed yearly, there is coverage. Once the policy is terminated, purchasing tail coverage will extend the reporting period. Tail coverage will not cover events that happened after the termination date of the original policy. Tail coverage can be very expensive to purchase, but there may be circumstances where tail coverage may be offered at no charge by the insurer, such as after 10 years of continuous liability coverage. An occurrence policy is more expensive initially, as the equivalent of tail coverage is included in the premium. Claims-made policies are cheaper initially because if the policy is terminated, tail coverage will need to be purchased. But tail coverage can be very expensive, and it is due all at once (see more below). While claims-made is cheaper initially, the premium increases each year because of the increased chance of a claim being reported in the prior years. The more years into a policy, the more chances of a claim being filed, so the price increases each year. Eventually the price stabilizes and becomes equal to an occurrence premium policy after approximately 4–7 years.

The choice of a type of policy comes down to how the psychiatrist wants to finance the necessary extended reporting provision. The premium for claims-made will start out lower, and then after a number of years of increasing, it will stabilize. Tail coverage will still be needed if the policy is discontinued.

Limits of Liability

Medical malpractice insurance policies come with two limits of liability – per incident limit and aggregate limit for a "policy period." Typical policy limits are $1 million/$3 million, meaning per claim, the maximum available to pay out is $1 million, and per policy period, the maximum available to pay out all claims is $3 million. If there is only one claim in policy period, and it settles for $1.1 million, the policy pays $1 million, and the insured psychiatrist is responsible for $100,000. If there are four claims in the policy period, and each has $500,000 payout, the policy pays the entire $2 million.

Policy Period

The "policy period" is different for claims-made and occurrence policies. For an occurrence policy, the policy period is each year the policy is renewed. The number of policy periods is equal to the number of years that the premium is paid. So for a policy in place for 10 years, there are ten policy periods. Each policy period has the liability limits, such as $1 million/$3 million. For a claims-made policy, the policy period is always one period, from start date of policy (retroactive date) through current term or termination date. The number of policy periods is always one, even if the psychiatrist has renewed the policy for 10 years.

This can be thought of like wine in a wine cellar. For an occurrence policy, each year the policy is renewed, the insured gets a bottle of wine for that period. As the years go by, the insured has a cellar full of bottles because each bottle is a year's coverage. But with a claims-made policy, each year it is renewed, the same bottle is topped off. As the years go by, there continues to be only one bottle, filled each year the policy is renewed, in the cellar.

In terms of the significance of the policy period, consider if the psychiatrist has ten claims come in this year, each with a payout of $500,000. Four are from events in year 1 of policy, three are from events in year 2, and three are from events in year 3. With an occurrence policy with limits of

$1,000,000/$3,000,000, each year is a separate policy period with separate limits, and all claims will be covered as follows:

- For the year 1 policy, each claim is $500,000, and that is within the per incident limit of $1 million. There is $2 million total in claims for the policy period, and that is within the limit of $3 million per policy period.
- For the year 2 policy, each claim is $500,000, and that is within the per incident limit of $1 million. There is $1 million total for claims in the policy period, and that is within the limit of $3 million per policy period.
- For the year 3 policy, each claim is $500,000, and that is within the per incident limit of $1 million. There is $1 million total for claims in the policy period, and that is within the limit of $3 million per policy period.

With claims-made, there is only one policy period, starting from the retroactive date (when policy first started) through current policy year. In the example, not all ten claims this year with payouts of $500K will be covered. Each claim is within per incident limit of $1 million, but the aggregate incurred for policy period is $5 million, which is $2 million over the aggregate limit of $3 million. In this event, the insured would be personally responsible for the extra $2 million. Note that while this example is useful to illustrate the significance of policy periods, it is an extreme example. While not unheard of, it is extremely rare for ten claims to be filed in the same year against a psychiatrist.

Extended Reporting (Tail) Coverage

As discussed above, an occurrence policy covers claims reported even after the policy ends, but this is not the case with claims-made policies. For psychiatrists with a claims-made policy, to protect themselves from personal exposure, it may be necessary to obtain tail coverage. Tail coverage does not extend the policy period, but rather the period of time during which claims may be reported. In other words, if after the policy is canceled, a claim is filed based on an incident that occurred while the policy was active, a tail policy would provide coverage for that claim. If on the other hand, after the policy was canceled, the psychiatrist rendered care which resulted in a claim being filed, that would not be covered.

Purchasing tail coverage is very expensive, often double the annual premium amount. Moreover, payment for tail coverage is typically due in full within a very short time frame. If an employer is providing professional liability insurance, an employer's agreement to pay for tail coverage should be documented in the employment agreement. In one case (*Patel v. Assoc. in Obstetrical Gyn.*, 2010), an obstetrician signed an employment agreement with a group practice. The agreement provided that the employer would "provide and pay the premium for malpractice insurance coverage covering employee." When she decided to terminate her employment with the group, she was covered by a claims-made policy. Since she was practicing in one of the highest risk specialties, the bill for her tail coverage was $146,000. The employer refused to pay, so the physician paid it and then sued the group for breach of contract. The court ruled against her, finding the obligation of the group to pay for tail was not in the agreement. This was likely due to the fact that when she joined the group, they had an occurrence policy. However, they subsequently changed to a claims-made policy.

The importance of having the tail coverage is to avoid a gap in coverage. In the event of a gap, the psychiatrist would be personally responsible for all expenses related to any claims filed after her termination date. Also, insurance companies are reluctant to cover physicians following a gap in coverage. They do not want to risk the chance of being brought into a claim when there was no coverage. Rather than tail coverage from the prior insurer, another possible way to avoid gaps in coverage is to obtain coverage for prior acts, also known as "nose coverage" from the new insurer. This coverage, if available, covers claims arising from acts or omissions that occurred when the insured was covered under a prior claims-made policy.

The Insurance Contract

There are five basic parts to the insurance policy: (1) the declarations page, (2) the insuring agreement, (3) conditions, (4) exclusions, and (5) endorsements.

The Declarations Page

The declarations page is the summary of coverage. It is critical to read this to ensure all information is correct, such as name of insured, practice locations, policy effective and termination dates, policy type, and coverage limits.

The Insuring Agreement

The insuring agreement spells out the insurance company's grant of coverage.

Conditions

Conditions are what the insured must do. Coverage is contingent on conditions (spelled out in the insurance policy) being met. For example, the insured must pay the premium.

Another condition is that the insured must cooperate in the defense of a claim. The record will be needed for the psychiatrist's defense; if he chooses not to provide it, he has not met this condition and may not have coverage.

The insured must also give the insurance company notice of potential claims and anything that could possibly lead to a claim. With a claims-made policy, it is important to document the report date. Also, the insurance company should assist in mitigating additional exposure after an event, such as a patient suicide or suicide attempt. Insured psychiatrists must also update the insurance company on practice changes. If the declarations page is missing a practice location, there is no coverage for claims arising from that location.

Exclusions

Exclusions spell out what is not covered. Exclusions, if proven, mean there is no coverage. Insurers contract with physicians to provide coverage, and they are obligated to cover as they wrote in the policy. But there are activities that may be excluded from coverage, such as the unauthorized practice of medicine. There may, however, be a defense provided under a "reservation of rights." To exclude coverage for a claim, the insurer must notify the insured of the exclusion from coverage in the policy. This is typically done in a "Reservation of Rights" letter, advising that the insurer will provide a defense for the action, but the insurer "reserves the right" not to pay for certain expenses, such as those related to sexual misconduct (discussed further below). Examples of exclusions include:

- Criminal acts: If a psychiatrist intentionally alters the clinical record, there could be a coverage issue since altering records is a crime under many states' laws. If a psychiatrist believes something needs to be changed in the record after an adverse event, he or she should seek advice from the insurer prior to making changes or corrections.
- Statutory or regulatory violations: If a psychiatrist is found to be violating a statute or regulation, such as the unauthorized practice of medicine, the claim is excluded from coverage. Insurance policies cannot cover such bad acts, but until those allegations are proven, the insurance may provide a defense.
- If practicing within a correctional system, psychiatrists need to ensure the insurance policy will cover a specific statutory violation, known as a "Section 1983 claim." Section 1983 refers to 42 USC §1983, which is a federal civil rights statute from 1871 that imposes liability on government employees, or those linked to the government (such as private contractors) for deprivation or violation of constitutional rights. Inmates are the only people in America with a constitutional right to medical care, specifically the following three rights: the right to access care, the right to a professional judgment, and the right to receive care ordered. Inmates often assert deprivation of their rights by filing Section 1983 claims against correctional psychiatrists alleging their constitutional rights were violated due to the delay or denial of medical treatment. A Section 1983 claim is actionable regardless of whether the deliberate indifference to the serious needs of inmates is by correctional healthcare providers, or by correctional staff in intentionally delaying or denying access to medical care, or intentionally interfering with treatment that has been ordered.
- Sexual misconduct: In states that consider sex with a patient to be a criminal act, coverage for a malpractice action will be excluded. Insurers may also explicitly exclude coverage for sexual misconduct. Or, insurers could cap their exposure by limiting coverage to defense only, and for a limited amount, such as $25,000.
- Penalties: Since penalties are meant to punish, insurance companies are typically prohibited from covering them by state insurance departments. But, there could be exceptions, such as coverage for penalties imposed by the Office of Civil Rights for a HIPAA violation. If covered, it may be subject to a sublimit, which is less than the full policy amount. For example, a $1 million/$3 million policy may have a sublimit maximum of $100K for HIPAA penalties.

Endorsements

Endorsements amend or change the coverage under the insuring agreement by restricting or expanding coverage. For example, some policies add defense coverage for administrative actions, such as licensing board actions, by an endorsement. They can also restrict coverage. For example, some policies will not cover services provided in correctional facilities.

Things to Look for in a Professional Liability Insurance Policy

About the Policy

When shopping for an insurance policy, important things to look for include:

- Coverage: If a policy only covers "psychiatric services," this would typically include such things as evaluating, diagnosing, and treating patients for psychiatric conditions. It is important to note that just because an activity such as telepsychiatry or forensic practice is a well-established aspect of psychiatric practice, it does not mean that a particular insurer will cover that activity.

- Definitions: Definitions will spell out exactly what is covered. A policy covering "psychiatric services" may or may not include medical director services. As another example, many policies exclude coverage for forensic services because there is no treatment. And another example is coverage for supervision, such as for nurse practitioners.
- Territory: Will the policy cover the insured if an action is brought in a different state? Psychiatrists practicing telepsychiatry with patients out of state will typically be sued in the patient's state, not in the state where the psychiatrist is located. Insurance companies can only operate in states where they are licensed, so coverage for out-of-state services needs to be confirmed with the insurer. Additionally, a psychiatrist should ensure licensure requirements are met in the state where the patient is located (see Chap. 30).
- Consent to settle: An insured's ability to consent to settlement of a case varies, depending on the type of consent provision in a policy. While a physician may not have any monetary exposure in the event of a claim, there is still a personal cost that comes whenever a claim is settled. Any time an insurer makes an indemnity payment on behalf of a physician, in addition to other reporting requirements that may exist (such as to the state), the insurer must report that settlement to the National Practitioner Data Bank (NPDB). NPDB records are available to state licensing boards, hospitals and other healthcare entities, professional societies, and others. Additionally, this information would be made available to health insurers, professional liability insurance carriers, and other entities based on an authorization from the psychiatrist to obtain a claim summary. Because a negative claims history can impact the psychiatrist professionally, it is important that the psychiatrist have a say in the decision to settle versus defend.
- There are four basic types of consent language possible in a professional liability insurance policy; see Table 4.1.
- Defense costs: Money paid to defend the insured can be "inside" or "outside" policy limits. If inside policy limits, defense costs are deducted from the policy limit available to pay a settlement or judgment. For example, if there are $500,000 in defense costs, and a $1 million/$3 million policy, there is only $500,000 left available if needed to pay a settlement or judgment. On the other hand, if defense costs are outside policy limits, the $1 million limit would all be available for settlements or judgments, regardless of how much is spent on defending the case.

Table 4.1 Types of consent to settle provisions

Type of consent	Who ultimately decides whether to settle	Notes
Unlimited consent: Insured controls	Only the insured	Most expensive consent provision – insured controls settlement decision
Limited consent with arbitration: When the insured and insurer disagree, it goes to an arbitrator	Arbitrator, in the event the insured and insurer disagree	Most common consent provision
Hammer clause: If the insurer wants to settle a case and the insured refuses, the insurer only has to pay up to the amount the insurer wanted to settle for, regardless of what the actual settlement or judgment is The insured is personally responsible for any excess amounts.	Insured, but may be personally responsible for settlement or judgment amount that exceeds the insurer's initial settlement amount	Insurer's settlement amount can be capped; may be risky for the insured
No consent: Insurer controls	Only the insurer	Least expensive consent provision – insurer solely controls settlement decision

- Loss of earnings: If there is a case that goes to trial, and the psychiatrist is not working on the days he or she is attending the trial, some policies will reimburse for loss of earnings.

About the Insurer

In addition to the policy, it is important to look at the insurer from a variety of perspectives. First, financial viability is important. Potential insured psychiatrists should review AM Best and other ratings to ensure that the company is viable. It may also be worthwhile to check the state insurance department's website to see whether any complaints have been made against the company. Second, consider what the insurer offers in addition to the policy. Many companies provide risk management consultation and education. Finally, the insurer's claims philosophy is worth seeking. Does the company try to simply resolve cases as quickly and as inexpensively as possible, or do they aggressively defend every case? An insurer that takes the middle position is ideal – aggressively defending non-meritorious claims and promptly resolving those that do have merit.

Professional Liability Insurance Policy Pricing

There are many factors that will determine the cost of a professional liability insurance policy, including:

- Specialty coverage. The frequency of claims varies by medical specialty. The cost of a psychiatric liability insurance policy will reflect the fact that psychiatry is one of the least often sued medical specialties (AMA, 2017).
- Consent to settle. As discussed above, a policy where the insurer has the sole decision-making authority regarding settlement will be less expensive than the policy under which the insured solely has that authority.
- Geographic territory. Claims experience and payouts vary by region.
- Type of coverage. As described above, claims-made policies are initially less expensive than occurrence policies, but the premium increases yearly until it reaches the "mature" rate, typically after 5 years.
- Coverage for administrative actions. This additional coverage could increase the premium.
- Policy limits. The higher the limits, the higher the premium.
- Discounts. Insurers may offer premium discounts, such as for part-time work, and completion of risk management continuing medical education.

When the Policy Is Received

Once the policy has been received, there are additional actions that should be taken by the insured. First, it is important to review the policy once received to confirm accuracy. Also, copies of all insurance policies should be retained. And, insureds are obligated to notify the insurer of practice changes, as well as incidents that could possibly lead to a claim. If there is an adverse event that needs to be disclosed, possibly with an apology, prior guidance from the insurer should be sought (see Chap. 5). As discussed above, one condition of coverage is that the insured not impair the insurer's ability to defend the claim, such as by admitting liability when there was no liability. And lastly, the insured should notify the insurer immediately upon notice of any claim, lawsuit, or administrative action being initiated against the insured.

Key Points

- Professional liability insurance allows a psychiatrist to transfer the financial risk of having to defend a professional liability action to a liability insurer.
- Professional liability insurance policies typically cover two types of costs: (1) indemnity, paid to plaintiff pursuant to a settlement or court judgment, and (2) expense, paid to defense counsel, expert witnesses, etc. to defend the action.
- Professional liability insurance policies cover only professional services, and are not general liability policies.
- There are two main types of professional liability insurance policies: (1) claims-made and (2) occurrence.
- With an occurrence policy, coverage is given for an incident giving rise to a claim that occurs while the policy is in place, regardless of when it is reported to the insurer.
- Under a claims-made policy, only those claims that occur and are reported while the policy is in effect are covered, unless extending reporting coverage ("tail coverage") has been purchased or provided by the insurer.
- Professional liability insurance policies have two limits of liability: (1) per incident limit and (2) aggregate limit for a policy period.
- There are five basic parts to a professional liability insurance contract: (1) the declarations page, (2) the insuring agreement, (3) conditions (what the insured must do), (4) exclusions (what is not covered), and (5) endorsements (can restrict or expand coverage).
- When shopping for a professional liability insurance policy, things about the policy to look for include (1) type of coverage, (2) definitions, (3) territory covered, (4) consent to settle provision, (5) defense costs (inside or outside of policy limits), and (6) reimbursement for loss of earnings. Things about the insurer to look for include (1) financial stability; (2) services offered under the policy, such as risk management education; and (3) the insurer's claim philosophy.
- Factors that determine the price of a professional liability insurance policy include (1) specialty, (2) geographic coverage, (3) type of coverage, (4) consent to settle provision, (5) coverage for administrative actions, (6) policy limits, and (7) discounts.

References

AMA. (2017). *Medical liability claim frequency among U.S. physicians*. Available at: www.ama-assn.org/media/21976/download. Accessed December 29, 2020.

Mazza v. Medical Mutual Insurance Co. of North Carolina, 319 S.E.2d 217 (1984).

Patel v. Assoc. in Obstetrical Gyn, 2010 WL 2347015 (2010).

PRMS. (2021). *2020 year in review*. Available at: https://www.prms.com/media/2554/prms-2020-year-in-review.pdf. Accessed February 20, 2021.

Part II

Litigation

Do's and Don'ts After an Adverse Event

5

Charles D. Cash

Broadly, an adverse event is any unwanted outcome related to a patient's treatment. Adverse events fall on a broad continuum from a known risk of treatment that materializes to an outright error by the psychiatrist that results in harm to the patient. Various organizations have defined the concept differently to suit their particular missions (Patient Safety Network, 2019; The Joint Commission, 1996; United States Department of Health and Human Services, 2020; United States Food and Drug Administration, 2020).

The appearance that one's actions – or inactions – may have actually brought harm to a patient cuts to the core for most psychiatrists. However, adverse events can occur even in the absence of negligence (i.e., failure to meet the standard of care). As negligence is one of the elements that must be proven in order for a plaintiff to prevail in a medical malpractice lawsuit, the fact that there can be an adverse event without negligence should be kept in mind when contemplating the situation as well as when discussing the adverse event with the patient.

Even when the care and treatment rendered were flawless, though, an adverse event can result in a claim, lawsuit, and/or administrative complaint. It may seem that the psychiatrist has been placed in a situation where he or she is powerless to affect the course of events, but this is not true. By implementing a few risk management strategies, the psychiatrist can mitigate harm to the patient, reduce his or her own anxiety, and provide tremendous assistance to his or her defense should a complaint materialize.

Risk Management After an Adverse Event

While the primary goal of risk management activities is to prevent the occurrence of adverse events, it is not possible to prevent all adverse events. After an adverse event materializes, risk management activities focus on halting or lessening the severity of the adverse event.

Immediate Clinical Interventions

When confronted with an adverse event, a psychiatrist should, first and foremost, take care of the patient. The patient's immediate clinical needs should be met. This seemingly obvious first step of intervening clinically to halt or mitigate a potential patient harm can be overlooked as anxiety levels about the adverse event and the potential outcomes increase. The psychiatrist should consider actions that will impact the patient's immediate safety and intervene. The patient's medication may need to be discontinued, the patient may need admission to a psychiatric facility, or the patient may need to be evaluated in an emergency department.

Report the Adverse Event to Your Professional Liability Insurance Carrier

Psychiatrists should report the adverse events to their professional liability carrier. This step is important for two reasons. First, most professional liability insurance policies require insured psychiatrists to report events that might lead to a claim. This reporting is mandatory and a condition of coverage. Second, the insurance carrier can assist a psychiatrist with risk mitigation.

This reporting is an ongoing task. New information that comes to light, such as progress in mitigating the adverse event, medical examiner determinations, and so forth, should also be reported. A request for a copy of the medical record from a patient's personal injury attorney can be the first sign that the patient is contemplating legal action. This request should also be reported to the professional liability carrier. For assistance with taking the steps below, consider requesting an attorney be assigned to the matter or request assistance from a risk management professional.

C. D. Cash (✉)
Professional Risk Management Services (PRMS),
Arlington, VA, USA
e-mail: cash@prms.com

P. Ash et al. (eds.), *Malpractice and Liability in Psychiatry*, https://doi.org/10.1007/978-3-030-91975-7_5

Discussing the Adverse Event with the Patient

An adverse event should be discussed with the patient as soon as possible after it is discovered. This discussion is clinically required so that the patient can make informed decisions about future care and treatment. Additionally, if the patient is not dealt with honestly, he or she may pursue legal action. When patients and their families feel as if they are not receiving adequate or truthful information, they become angry and frustrated and may end up taking their case to an attorney. Communication with the patient and/or the patient's family can diffuse that anger.

It is important that the psychiatrist not jump to conclusions about causation and assume that the adverse event was caused by something that the psychiatrist either did or should have done. Patients and family members are often eager to know why an adverse event occurred and may press the psychiatrist for answers. Before making any statements about causation, it is important to gather whatever information is needed to make a reasonable determination about what actually happened.

It is important, also, to avoid making any statements that might be viewed as an admission of liability. There have been cases where a physician's untimely admission of fault resulted in a jury verdict. In one instance, a surgeon apologized to the patient for an infection the surgeon assumed was acquired during surgery. The investigation actually revealed that the patient had the infection upon admission, but the jury, in finding the surgeon liable, focused on the initial apology and discounted the surgeon's expert's testimony (Szostak, 2011).

Some states have adopted "benevolent gesture" laws that purportedly allow physicians to apologize for mistakes without that apology later being used against the physician in court (Cal. Evidence Code § 1160, 2000; Fla. Evidence Code § 90.4026, 2011). However, there are several limitations related to these benevolent gesture laws. Additionally, not all states have such laws, and even in states that do, the laws vary greatly among the states in terms of:

- Who may apologize
- To whom the apology may be made
- What exactly can and cannot be used against the physician in litigation:
  - Most states with these laws do not allow the apology to be used in court.
  - Only a few states keep an expression of fault from coming out in litigation – most states will keep the apology out of court but allow the expression of fault to come into evidence at trial as an admission of liability.

For one example, consider the California Evidence Code:

> The portion of statements, writings, or benevolent gestures expressing sympathy or a general sense of benevolence relating to the pain, suffering, or death of a person involved in an accident and made to that person or to the family of that person shall be inadmissible as evidence of an admission of liability in a civil action. *A statement of fault, however, which is part of, or in addition to, any of the above shall not be inadmissible pursuant to this section* [emphasis added] (Cal. Evidence Code § 1160, 2000).

Upon a psychiatrist's statement, "I'm sorry I failed to check your lithium level," the "I'm sorry" would be inadmissible. Presumably, "I failed to check your lithium level" would be admissible as an admission against the psychiatrist's interests.

Rather than parsing benevolent gesture laws, it is preferable to convey empathy through one's actions in addressing the patient's immediate clinical needs and one's honest and open discussions with the patient. In this way, if the psychiatrist were not at fault, or causation has not yet been determined, the psychiatrist can express care and concern without placing blame or risking admitting liability. This is particularly true if there is a prior positive communication history with the patient. If issuing an apology is appropriate, it should be done with the advice and assistance of an attorney assigned to the matter or a risk manager.

Consideration of whether treatment can continue after the adverse event will be appropriate. If negligence on the part of the psychiatrist is clear, it may be impossible to remain in the treatment relationship. In that case, the discussion should include the need to transfer the patient's care. The patient should be reassured that his or her clinical needs will be met in the meantime. Even in the absence of negligence, the patient still may blame the psychiatrist for the adverse event, creating a significant barrier to successful treatment.

Ultimately, the discussion of the adverse event with the patient should not revolve around efforts to avert litigation, but rather around the shared goal of providing the patient with the information that he or she needs to make informed decisions about future healthcare issues. Focusing on good patient care is the best risk management.

Do's and Don'ts if Sued

Despite concerted risk management efforts to mitigate the effects of an adverse event, a psychiatrist may still face a claim, lawsuit, and/or administrative action. If a patient makes a claim, a written demand for money without filing a lawsuit, the psychiatrist will likely receive a letter from the patient's attorney stating such, and asking the psychiatrist to have their professional liability carrier contact the attorney.

Similarly, for an administrative action, the psychiatrist likely will receive a letter from the administrative body (usually the relevant medical or osteopathic licensing board) stating that a complaint has been filed and asking for a response. This correspondence should be submitted to the professional liability carrier immediately.

In most jurisdictions, when a psychiatrist is sued, a process server will personally deliver a summons and complaint to the psychiatrist. The summons is the court's notice to the psychiatrist that it is asserting jurisdiction over the matter. A psychiatrist should not attempt to evade the process server as there rarely exists a reason to do this. The legal system is procedure oriented. Accordingly, each step starts the clock ticking for the next step. Therefore, it is best to get served with the summons and complaint as quickly as possible so the professional liability carrier can start working on it right away.

Clinicians should not ignore any lawsuit, claim, or administrative action, even those that they know are meritless. These types of legal matters will not go away on their own. An ignored claim that might have been easily dealt with can morph into a lawsuit. Likewise, a licensing board may suspend a psychiatrist's medical license if correspondence about a complaint is ignored.

Court rules allow for default judgment when a complaint goes unanswered within a certain amount of time, usually 20–30 days. Although the specific rules vary by jurisdiction, generally speaking, when a defendant ignores a complaint and fails to file an answer within the allotted time, a plaintiff may have the court enter a default judgment against the psychiatrist, meaning that the case has been resolved in favor of the plaintiff. By failing to respond to the complaint in a timely manner, a default defendant effectively admits to the allegations in the complaint, admits liability for them, and agrees to the amount of damages sought.

Generally, after such a judgment is entered, the defaulting defendant will receive a notice that judgment has been entered. Sometimes there will be one last chance to respond, but not always. Additionally, by failing to notify the insurer when the complaint was received, the psychiatrist may have jeopardized his or her insurance coverage altogether. Most professional liability policies require that the insured psychiatrist, as a condition of coverage, cooperate with the insurer in the defense of the suit. In that vein, the insured psychiatrist is prohibited from admitting liability, which he or she would be doing (by their silence) if a default judgment were entered.

The insurance carrier has the right and duty to defend the insured psychiatrist in a lawsuit, even one that is groundless. If the psychiatrist fails to notify the carrier of the suit and goes into default as a result, the psychiatrist has interfered with the insurer's right to defend, and that interference may be considered a breach of the insurance contract. One of the rights the insurance company may have in such a situation is to refuse to pay any monetary judgment against the psychiatrist or help the psychiatrist to challenge the default judgment (see Chap. 4). The fallout from a default judgment can be calamitous. The plaintiff may file a lien on the psychiatrist's property, or seize his or her bank accounts, or report the judgment to credit agencies.

Reporting the suit to the professional liability carrier quickly and forwarding a copy of the complaint to the claims examiner will allow the claims examiner the opportunity to obtain specific information about the patient and review the complaint. Once coverage is confirmed, the examiner will assign an attorney to defend the psychiatrist at the insurer's expense.

When the assigned attorney attempts contact, a psychiatrist should make him or herself available to talk with the attorney privately, without interruptions or distractions. Remember, not only is the conversation with the attorney confidential and privileged, but the psychiatrist will be talking about the confidential relationship between him or her and the patient. The psychiatrist should protect attorney-client communications from eavesdroppers while fulfilling the obligation to protect the patient's privacy by discussing the clinical care where it cannot be overheard. If the attorney calls while the psychiatrist is out in public, the psychiatrist should schedule a time to call back when he or she will have more privacy. The psychiatrist should be ready to discuss the patient's care and the incident that is the subject of the suit. If the psychiatrist is the custodian of the patient's records, the chart should be copied and sent to the attorney. If the psychiatrist is a covered entity under HIPAA, he or she should ask the attorney for a business associate agreement.

A psychiatrist served with a lawsuit should not call or write to the court or plaintiff in an attempt to convince them to dismiss the case. This is highly unlikely to result from such extremely risky conduct. While it is understandable to think that a commonsense explanation from the psychiatrist will resolve a misunderstanding, the realities of the justice system frequently run counter to common sense. Moreover, if the psychiatrist acts without notifying the insurer, he or she may jeopardize coverage altogether. Remember, most professional liability insurance policies prohibit the insured from admitting liability or compromising the insurance company's right to defend the case. An innocent comment in a conversation between the insured psychiatrist and the plaintiff's attorney or court may have this effect.

Most plaintiff's attorneys will usually refuse to speak at all with an opposing party who is represented by counsel, but a crafty plaintiff's attorney may manipulate a conversation in such a way that the psychiatrist divulges information that shouldn't be divulged, or unwittingly makes admissions that may adversely affect the defense and compromise insurance coverage. As a party to a lawsuit, everything a clinician says can be used against him or her. Without realizing it, the psychiatrist may identify potential adverse witnesses or suggest additional defendants. Of all potential results, the one outcome of a conversation with plaintiff's counsel that is highly unlikely is a spontaneous, voluntary dismissal of the lawsuit.

It is equally unwise to contact the court. Although common sense may suggest that a simple phone call to the court with an explanation may cause a judge to dismiss the complaint, there is no mechanism in court procedure for such a dismissal. Instead, frustration will be the likely result. Just as a psychiatrist's office staff screens calls, so does the court staff screen calls to judges. Calls to the court are unlikely to get any further than the judge's law clerk, who may sympathize, but is not permitted to give legal advice. The clerk likely will advise contacting an attorney and filing a written response.

A psychiatrist should never attempt to answer the suit to avoid unnecessary legal fees or malpractice insurance premium increases. Again, this is highly unlikely to be successful and extremely risky. Defending a lawsuit is a highly technical pursuit. The allegations of a complaint must be analyzed and responded to in a specific manner. Attempting to file an answer to the complaint without the benefit of legal counsel risks prejudicing the defense of the lawsuit. For example, trying to answer the complaint without properly addressing all the allegations in the complaint may lead the court to assume that the allegations not properly addressed are admitted to. Moreover, there are important affirmative defenses that must be raised in the answer or else they will be considered waived. If an attempt to respond to the complaint contains admissions or fails to raise significant defenses, defense of the lawsuit will be prejudiced.

Professional liability insurance policies prohibit insureds from admitting liability or doing anything to prejudice the defense of a lawsuit. Undermining the insurer's right to defend may void coverage altogether. It is certainly understandable to worry about malpractice insurance premiums, but simply being named in a lawsuit is a far cry from premium increases. Remember that defense and indemnification are the reasons psychiatrists have insurance.

Psychiatrists should make themselves available during the pendency of the lawsuit. Unfortunately, being a defendant in a lawsuit is time-consuming, and it will be very difficult to get through the entire process without having to give up time during work hours. This is an inconvenience, to be sure, and it certainly adds insult to injury when the case against the psychiatrist has no merit. As tempting as it may be to try, it is inappropriate to bill the plaintiff or his or her attorney for the psychiatrist's time.

The psychiatrist will be asked to meet with the defense attorney multiple times and will probably need to reschedule some patients to facilitate those meetings. There will be an initial meeting when the psychiatrist and the defense attorney will discuss the psychiatrist's background, the patient's care, and the incident that is the subject of the complaint. The psychiatrist should remain available to the defense attorney to educate him or her on the medical and psychiatric issues in the case. The psychiatrist may be asked to find medical literature relevant to the lawsuit and forward it to the defense attorney.

Later, the attorney will need the psychiatrist to help respond to interrogatories, which are written questions answered under oath. The psychiatrist's deposition testimony will require preparation with the attorney, perhaps in multiple sessions, as well as on the day or days of the deposition itself. The psychiatrist may be required to attend mediation or court-mandated settlement conferences. Unhappily, these meetings can take all day, and the psychiatrist should be prepared for long periods during which he or she and the attorney sit in a room or hallway and wait.

Finally, should the lawsuit proceed to a trial, the psychiatrist should be present for jury selection and for each day of the court proceeding. Having an empty chair at the defense table is not as effective as having the psychiatrist actively participate in the trial.

More often than not, all parties involved in a legal proceeding are sensitive to the fact that every moment the psychiatrist devotes to the defense of the lawsuit is one that could have been spent caring for patients. They are also aware that the psychiatrist did not ask to be sued and to have to give up so much time. The attorneys usually will make an effort to accommodate the psychiatrist's schedule, but the reality is that much of what needs to be done has to happen during business hours. Some malpractice insurance policies include a provision for reimbursement of a portion of the earnings lost due to time spent defending a case. The claims examiner can provide details about this provision if it is available.

A treatment record should never be altered once a psychiatrist has received notice of a lawsuit. This admonition even includes:

- Properly entering corrections according to accepted procedures
- Attempting to recreate missing records
- Clarifying medications and doses that don't correlate with prescription records
- Creating late entries after an adverse event
- Expanding on scant notes
- Correcting nonstandard or confusing abbreviations
- Rewriting illegible entries

Regardless of the intent or rationale, changing, editing, rewriting, or otherwise altering the original record is very dangerous. Doing so negatively impacts the defense of the lawsuit. It is also a crime in many states, punishable by a stiff fine and/or potential jail time, especially when the alteration is done with nefarious intent. If this is not discouragement enough, alteration of medical records may also void professional liability insurance coverage. Professional liability insurance policies typically contain the following or similar language:

> Any alteration of medical records or intentional misrepresentation or concealment of material facts by any insured will constitute a violation of this condition as respects such insured (Fair American Insurance and Reinsurance Company, 2012).

There is no such thing as a perfect medical record. When viewing care through a plaintiff's eyes, it is very easy to find flaws in the treatment record documentation. However, defense attorneys understand that there is no such thing as a perfect record and are prepared to defend a psychiatrist's care even when faced with less-than-ideal documentation. What they cannot defend is an altered treatment record. Any indication that the treatment record has in any way been altered will call into question every statement that the psychiatrist has made and will irreparably damage the psychiatrist's credibility.

Treatment record documentation typically is key to the psychiatrist's defense in a lawsuit. Treatment records are easily admitted into evidence because they are typically created contemporaneously to patient encounters, before any adverse event has occurred. This causes the documentation to be viewed as honest, truthful, and reliable. Treatment record documentation created after an adverse event or after a lawsuit is filed will be viewed as documentation created in anticipation of litigation, which is self-serving and not honest, truthful, or reliable.

For example, after producing a set of illegible handwritten notes, the attorney may ask the psychiatrist to dictate the notes as written so that the dictation may be transcribed. If, however, the psychiatrist discovered the problem with the original and dictated a replacement on his or her own, and then produced the transcription, the psychiatrist would risk being accused of making self-serving changes to the record. No matter how innocent or helpful the motivation, an altered treatment record can render an otherwise defensible case virtually indefensible because it has such a negative impact on the psychiatrist's credibility.

A psychiatrist should advise the defense attorney of any concerns he or she has regarding the treatment record documentation and follow the advice of the attorney. If changes to the record need to be made, the attorney can assist in making them in such a way that neither the entire record nor the psychiatrist's credibility are thrown into doubt. If the record cannot be amended, the attorney may be able to otherwise get the information into evidence.

Beyond the confines of the lawsuit, altering a chart can be a career devastating action. Many licensing boards treat the alteration or destruction of medical records by a healthcare provider as a basis for revocation of a medical license.

A lawsuit should not be discussed with anyone other than the assigned attorney and claims examiner, except in relationships where communications are privileged as described below. The psychiatrist in the lawsuit can expect to be asked more than once for the names, addresses, and phone numbers of anyone with whom the psychiatrist discussed the case or the underlying treatment. Unless the discussions were protected by a legal privilege, such as the attorney-client privilege, the psychiatrist will be asked to describe what was said, and the person talked to will certainly be interviewed.

It is understandable to want to discuss the treatment rendered in the underlying case with colleagues. However, those discussions are unlikely to be protected by any legal privilege and likely would be discoverable. Participants in the conversation may become witnesses against the psychiatrist and have to repeat in court any concerns raised in discussions by the psychiatrist about care and treatment of the patient. This admonition includes not participating in treatment reviews (such as Morbidity and Mortality conferences, etc.).

Should the psychiatrist have a patient who is a physician, discussing the case with the patient is fraught with peril. First, the physician-patient privilege belongs to the patient, not the psychiatrist. While the patient's statements, treatment, and information are confidential and subject to a legal privilege, the psychiatrist's statements about the lawsuit are not and could be discoverable. (Moreover, a conversation with a patient about events in the psychiatrist's life may be seen as a failure to maintain appropriate boundaries in the treatment relationship.)

This admonition also applies to any expert witnesses retained by the defense. Should the defense attorney not provide much detail when retaining the expert witness or when the psychiatrist disagrees with the expert witness's findings, resist the temptation to talk to the expert witness personally. The temptation is understandable given the expert witness's critical role in the defense of the lawsuit. The attorney may have made a conscious decision not to communicate much detail to the expert in writing. While the psychiatrist's discussions with his or her attorney are protected by a legal privilege, the attorney's communications with the expert – particularly if the expert is not ultimately retained – may be discoverable. As a litigant, the psychiatrist's statements to the expert witness are usually subject to discovery. Any concerns about the expert witness's findings should be raised with the defense attorney.

If the psychiatrist must talk to another party outside of the attorney-client relationship, the conversation should be within the confines of another legal privilege, such as therapist-patient or clergy-penitent privilege, or marital privilege. Legal privileges vary by jurisdiction. The psychiatrist should discuss the need to speak with another with the defense attorney and seek guidance before conversing with another about the lawsuit or the treatment underlying the lawsuit.

A psychiatrist may self-query the National Practitioner Data Bank. Insurance carriers are required to report any medical malpractice insurance payments to the National Practitioner Data Bank, regardless of the amount. After a report is submitted, the defendant psychiatrist will receive a copy and be able to comment on it. While Data Bank information is not available to the public, psychiatrists can see reports about themselves. A self-query can be submitted online for a small fee.

Being named in a lawsuit is stressful (see Chap. 11). The defendant psychiatrist should take care of him or herself throughout the process. Whatever stress-reduction activities the psychiatrist participates in, they should continue them during the pendency of the lawsuit. The defense attorney can offer guidance on talking to a provider within the shelter of a legal privilege. There are some fortunate truths that may be helpful:

- Being sued is ≠ being found liable.
- It is actually difficult for a plaintiff to successfully sue a psychiatrist.
- The defendant psychiatrist can – and should – be very involved in his or her defense
- In the vast majority of cases that go to trial, the defendant psychiatrist prevails.

Key Points

- After an adverse event, the patient's immediate clinical needs should be addressed.
- The psychiatrist should report the adverse event to their professional liability carrier.
- Without jumping to conclusions about causation, the psychiatrist should discuss the adverse event with the patient.
- Should a lawsuit, claim, or administrative action materialize, the psychiatrist should notify their professional liability carrier immediately.
- Treatment record documentation should never be altered once notified of a lawsuit, claim, or administrative action.
- The pending action should not be discussed with anyone other than the attorney assigned to the matter and the liability carrier's claims examiner.
- Being named in a lawsuit, claim, or administrative action is stressful. The psychiatrist should practice self-care while the action proceeds.

Disclaimer This chapter is expressly intended for informational purposes only and is not intended for any particular purpose. The views expressed herein do not represent the views of Fair American Insurance and Reinsurance Company and its affiliates, subsidiaries, management, and/or shareholders. The author shall not be held responsible in any way for use of any of the information contained in or referenced in this chapter. The information contained in this chapter is not intended to constitute and should not be considered legal advice, nor shall it serve as a substitute for obtaining legal advice specific to any particular needs that may be presented.

References

Cal. Evidence Code § 1160. (2000). Retrieved from: http://leginfo.legislature.ca.gov/faces/codes_displaySection.xhtml?lawCode=EVID&sectionNum=1160

Fair American Insurance and Reinsurance Company. (2012). *Occurrence-based psychiatrists' professional and business liability policy*. Author.

Fla. Evidence Code § 90.4026. (2011). Retrieved from: https://www.flsenate.gov/Laws/Statutes/2011/90.4026

Patient Safety Network. (2019). *Adverse events, near misses, and errors*. Retrieved from: https://psnet.ahrq.gov/primer/adverse-events-near-misses-and-errors

Szostak, D. C. (2011). Apology not accepted: Disclosure of medical errors and legal liability. *DePaul Journal of Health Care Law, 13*, 367. Retrieved from: https://via.library.depaul.edu/jhcl/vol13/iss3/4/

The Joint Commission. (1996). *Sentinel event policy and procedures*. Retrieved from: www.jointcommission.org/resources/patient-safety-topics/sentinel-event/sentinel-event-policy-and-procedures/

United States Department of Health and Human Services – Office of Inspector General. (2020). *Spotlight on...adverse events*. Retrieved from: https://oig.hhs.gov/newsroom/spotlight/2012/adverse.asp

United States Food and Drug Administration. (2020). *Code of federal regulations title 21 (21CFR312.32)*. Retrieved from: www.accessdata.fda.gov/scripts/cdrh/cfdocs/cfcfr/cfrsearch.cfm?fr=312.32

The Litigation Process

6

Richard L. Frierson

All psychiatrists are taught the basic elements when conducting an initial psychiatric evaluation: a chief complaint, the history of the present illness, the psychiatric history, an alcohol and drug use history, a medical history, a family history, a social history (including birth and development, educational history, occupational history, marriage and relationship history, legal history), and a formal mental status examination. While it may seem complicated to an outsider, this process becomes routine and the elements embedded in our consciousness as second nature over time, requiring little concentrated effort to remember them on the part of the psychiatrist. Similarly, for attorneys the process and different stages of a civil lawsuit become second nature, and many attorneys routinely handle several cases, all of which may be in different phases of the litigation process. This chapter will review the litigation process and different stages that typically occur in a malpractice lawsuit, from the serving of notice of intent to sue and the initial complaint to the negotiated settlement or jury verdict. Additionally, the different approaches to malpractice tort reform and their effect on the litigation process will be reviewed.

Basic Legal Terms in Malpractice Litigation

Jurisdiction

Jurisdiction involves a government's power to exercise authority over all persons and things within its territory. This term also refers to a court's power to decide a case or issue a decree (Garner, 2004). Malpractice actions are governed by the rules of civil procedure, and malpractice cases are typically heard under the jurisdiction of state courts. Therefore, every state has its own rules of civil procedure which govern the litigation process, and there can be significant jurisdictional differences, from the length of the statute of limitations to the amounts of money that can be awarded for damages. Additionally, state law governs which courts within a state are charged to adjudicate different legal matters. Coverage of these rules in every US jurisdiction is beyond the scope of this chapter. However, some generalizations can be made. For the purpose of malpractice litigation, most states allow for the adjudication in a superior court, rather than a magistrate or lower level court.

However, if a negligent health-care provider commits malpractice at a VA hospital or on property owned by the US government (e.g., post office or federal building, armed forces base, etc.), the case may be brought in federal court as permitted by the Federal Tort Claims Act (FTCA) instead of in state court. The FTCA is a federal law passed by the US congress that allows plaintiffs injured by the negligent acts of federal employees (e.g., a Veteran's Administration-employed psychiatrist) to file claims against the United States for damages (Federal Tort Claims Act, 1946). Under this act, an injured party must prove that (1) he or she was injured or his or her property was damaged by a federal government employee; (2) the employee was acting within the scope of his or her official duties; (3) the employee was acting negligently or wrongfully; and (4) the negligent or wrongful act proximately caused the injury or damage (U.S. House of Representatives, 2020). Although these cases are heard in federal court, the state's medical malpractice litigation rules may still apply, such as the statute of limitations (see below) and limitations on damage awards.

Burden of Proof and Standard of Proof

The term *burden of proof* is used to identify which of the parties in the litigation is obligated to prove an assertion. In a medical malpractice action, the burden of proof lies with the plaintiff (i.e., the patient or deceased patient's survivors) to prove negligence on the part of the psychiatrist. The

R. L. Frierson (✉)
Department of Neuropsychiatry and Behavioral Science, University of South Carolina School of Medicine, Columbia, SC, USA
e-mail: richard.frierson@uscmed.sc.edu

P. Ash et al. (eds.), *Malpractice and Liability in Psychiatry*, https://doi.org/10.1007/978-3-030-91975-7_6

psychiatrist is not obligated to prove anything. The burden of proof also includes two elements: the burden of production and the burden of persuasion. The burden of production requires the plaintiff to introduce enough evidence on an issue to have it decided by the jury. The burden of persuasion is the duty of the plaintiff to convince the jury to view the facts in their favor (Garner, 2004).

The term *standard of proof* refers to the degree or level of proof demanded in a specific case (Garner, 2004). For example, in criminal proceedings, because defendants' liberty interests are at stake and they may be incarcerated, the highest possible standard of proof (i.e., *beyond a reasonable doubt*) is required for conviction. For most civil cases where the interest is monetary rather than liberty, a lower standard of proof is required. In most US jurisdictions, this standard is a *preponderance of the evidence* standard, which generally means "more likely than not" (i.e., >50% likely). In some jurisdictions, tort reform measures have led to legislation that increased the standard of proof in medical malpractice cases to *clear and convincing evidence*, the highest standard used in civil cases (Latner, 2010; Law Firm Newswire, 2013). Under this standard, the evidence is *highly* and *substantially* more likely to be true than untrue (*Colorado v. New Mexico*, 1984).

Statute of Limitations

Every state has different rules and procedures for bringing medical malpractice claims, but in general, they must be brought quickly. The *statute of limitations* is a law that bars claims after a certain period (Garner, 2004). It establishes a time limit for suing in a civil case based on the date the injury occurred or the date that the injury was first discovered. This law requires diligent prosecution of known claims at a time where evidence is reasonably available and fresh. It also offers some degree of predictability and finality in legal affairs. In medical malpractice cases, the statute of limitation varies by jurisdiction. In the majority of states, the statute of limitations is 2 years; however, jurisdictions vary from 2 years to up to 7 years (National Conference of State Legislatures, 2014a, 2014b), and for minors, in most jurisdictions, the statute of limitations clock begins after the minor turns 18.

Stages of Litigation

The amount of time from the beginning to the end of a malpractice case can vary depending on the number of litigants and attorneys involved (e.g., multiple defendants), the amount of records that must be reviewed, the complexity of both the medical treatment that was rendered and the allegations of negligence, and the number of witnesses and medical experts that must be deposed. Three out of four psychiatric malpractice cases have more than one defendant (Medscape, 2020). Also, on average, most psychiatrists spent more than 40 hours over the course of a lawsuit assisting their lawyer in preparing their defense (Medscape, 2020). The litigation process itself may be quite lengthy. According to a 2019 survey specific to psychiatrist malpractice defendants, 46% of the cases were resolved in 2 years, 23% took 3–5 years, and 12% took more than 5 years to be resolved; only 16% went to trial with about 34% settling prior to trial and 37% being dismissed prior to settlement (Medscape, 2020).

The stages of litigation are fairly consistent across jurisdictions and are listed in Table 6.1 (Vanderpool, 2018). A malpractice case typically begins with a potential plaintiff consulting with a lawyer about the possibility of filing a malpractice action. The lawyer then interviews the plaintiff and decides whether the facts as presented are deserving of investigation. In many large law firms, there are in-house employees who are either nurses or physicians who are typically used to screen cases. If not, there are companies who exist to provide attorneys with experts who can perform the initial review of records. Attorneys usually turn down many more cases than they accept (see Chap. 7). This may happen not only because of an apparent lack of evidence of negligence or causation but also because most malpractice attorneys are compensated through a contingency agreement, and therefore a case may be declined if the potential monetary damages do not warrant the time and expense involved with the litigation. However, the opposite is also true: attorneys may pursue a case with scant evidence of negligence on the part of the physician if the potential monetary awards are

Table 6.1 The stages of litigation in a malpractice suit

Pre-filing activities	Communication and Resolution (C&R) programs; securing affidavit or certificate of merit from expert; notice of intent to sue; medical malpractice tribunals
Summons and complaint	Establishes jurisdiction; establishes parties involved; establishes allegations against psychiatrist and/or facility
Answer	Point by point acknowledgment, rejection, or failure to confirm or deny each element contained in the complaint
Discovery	Subpoena of medical records and other documents, filing of interrogatories and answers to interrogatories, depositions of fact witness and expert witnesses
Mediation	May have arbitration that is binding or non-binding
Pretrial Motions	Admissibility of evidence, witnesses, etc.
Trial	Jury selection, opening arguments, plaintiff's case (including expert testimony), defense case, closing arguments, jury deliberations, verdict, judgment
Prejudgment motions	Judgment notwithstanding the verdict

large (Bookman & Zane, 2020). Once a plaintiff's attorney decides a case is meritorious, they may state a claim and notify the defendant prior to initiating a lawsuit. The hospital or psychiatrist may decide to investigate the claim and decide whether to defend the claim or negotiate a settlement.

Pre-filing Requirements

In some jurisdictions, there are certain requirements a potential plaintiff/litigant must meet before they can file the notice of a lawsuit. Many of these requirements were the result of tort reform measures aiming at reducing the cost of malpractice litigation as it contributes to total health-care costs.

Some states (including Massachusetts in 2012, Oregon in 2014, and Iowa in 2015) have enacted Communication and Resolution (C&R) programs, also known as Early Discussion and Resolution (EDR) programs that create requirements for early disclosure and communication about unanticipated adverse outcomes and medical errors when they occur prior to potential litigation. When appropriate, insurers offer fair financial compensation for avoidable medical harm without the patient or family having to file a lawsuit (American Medical Association, 2017a). If an agreement is not reached, certain evidence discussed in the negotiations will be confidential and cannot be used by plaintiffs in a lawsuit without going through the usual process of discovery. These programs also encourage health-care facilities or health-care providers to communicate with the patient (and/or family) the steps that the health-care facility or health-care provider will take to prevent future occurrences of the adverse health-care incident. Finally, if the hospital or medical provider believes that the care leading up to the injury was reasonable, the patient and/or family are given a reasonable explanation and chance to ask questions about what actually occurred. The health-care entity may also indicate that they will stand behind the providers and defend the care that was rendered if the patient or family were to bring legal proceedings.

In most jurisdictions, there is a mandatory requirement that notice be provided to the medical provider prior to the initiation of the lawsuit. This is known as "the notice of intent to sue" and must be served upon the potential defendant. Each state's rules of civil procedure outline the amount of notice a defendant must be given (usually between 90 and 180 days). This requirement serves two purposes: (1) to allow the potential defendant(s) the opportunity to evaluate and potentially resolve any claim in advance of the commencement of litigation and (2) to avoid the element of surprise to the health-care provider, as well as provide a reasonable opportunity to prepare a defense. The notice of intent to sue must usually be received by certified mail before the expiration of the statute of limitations. The notice of intent generally contains a short and plain statement of the facts showing that the plaintiff is entitled to some sort of relief. In some jurisdictions, the notice of intent must be accompanied by an expert witness affidavit.

A majority of states (29 as of 2017) require that a plaintiff produce an affidavit or certificate of merit from a medical expert who has already reviewed the medical record before or within a few weeks of the filing of the actual complaint (American Medical Association, 2017b). The requirements of the contents of the affidavit vary by jurisdiction but could include the expert's familiarity with the standard of care, the expert's qualifications, the expert's opinion regarding whether there was a breach in the standard of care, and the expert's opinion as to how the breach resulted in injury or death of the patient. Therefore, a plaintiff attorney's work in having an expert review medical records and offer an opinion in a malpractice suit actually begins prior to the suit being filed in these jurisdictions. Finally, the expert who writes the affidavit or certificate of merit will not necessarily be the same expert who testifies for the plaintiff at deposition or trial.

Finally, state jurisdictions may enact other requirements prior to the filing of a malpractice lawsuit. Massachusetts, for example, has enacted a medical tribunal consisting of a superior court judge, a physician in the same specialty but from a different county jurisdiction, and a lawyer. At the tribunal, the plaintiff presents an offer of proof, and the tribunal determines if the evidence presented, if properly substantiated, is sufficient to raise a "legitimate question of liability appropriate for judicial inquiry or whether the plaintiff's case is merely an unfortunate medical result" (Mass, 2007). However, even if the tribunal denies the suit, the plaintiff may override the refusal by posting a $6000 bond which will be returned if the plaintiff wins the suit (Bookman & Zane, 2020).

Summons and Complaint

The actual initial filing in a medical malpractice suit is called the summons and complaint. This document is filed in the court of jurisdiction and also delivered to the defendant(s) by the plaintiff. The document establishes that the court where it is filed is the proper jurisdiction (i.e., the alleged negligent act took place in that county). The complaint also lists all the parties that are involved, the party locations, and the initial allegations against the defendant. The complaint usually contains a series of numbered paragraphs or sentences. Each paragraph or sentence contains a statement of facts that are pertinent to establish the allegations against the psychiatrist. The complaint also contains all of the causes of action that are being pursued (e.g., medical malpractice negligence, wrongful death, loss of consortium, etc.). Sometimes, the complaint also contains the types of damages being sought (compensatory, punitive, etc.), and on occasion, the amount of damages being sought. The filing of the summons and complaint requires the payment of a filing fee and begins the official legal process of a malpractice suit.

Answer

The answer is a document prepared by the defense and filed with the court after the summons and complaint has been received. It is designed to respond to all the facts or allegations contained in the complaint. Because the complaint usually contains a series of numbered paragraphs or sentences, the answer typically corresponds number by number to each of the stated facts and allegations. The typical responses in the formal answer include that the defendant confirms an item in the complaint, denies an item in the complaint, or neither confirms nor denies an item in the complaint. The facts or allegations that are denied by the defendant must be proven in court by the plaintiff. The process of discovery is designed to clarify those items in the complaint that can neither be confirmed nor denied by the defendant.

Discovery

The discovery period of a malpractice case typically last months to years and consists of a time where both the plaintiff and defense obtain facts relevant to the case. In general, the discovery process begins with a subpoena of documents including medical records of the plaintiff, hospital (or office practice) policies and procedures, and, in the case of an inpatient setting, rosters of employees working at the time of the event (to identify any relevant fact witnesses). However, subpoenas can also extend to financial records of the plaintiff (e.g., if there are alleged financial losses due to a loss of income), medical board complaints concerning the defendant psychiatrist, etc. In cases where a party does not want to relinquish the information requested, the party can file a motion to suppress the subpoena and have the matter heard by the judge in the case.

Many state jurisdictions allow the use of interrogatories. Interrogatories are specific written questions that either side in the suit may pose to the opposing party. They are usually sent via certified mail and, in some jurisdictions, may be filed into the official court records. Like the initial complaint, interrogatory questions are typically numbered and require written answers within an allotted time frame that is determined by the rules of civil procedure. The answers are typically prepared by the attorneys with input from the defendant or plaintiff, depending on which side is answering. Information contained in interrogatories is considered to be sworn testimony, and therefore can be used in cross-examination if contradicted later in the ligation process.

In addition to subpoenas and interrogatories, depositions are generally taken during discovery. A deposition is an oral examination under oath that creates a written record produced by a stenographer (commonly known as a reporter). Depositions are generally taken from the plaintiff and/or plaintiff's survivors (in the case of suicide), the defendant psychiatrist, any factual witnesses, and the expert witnesses who have been retained by either party. The expert witnesses will have reviewed the medical records and subpoenaed policies, but may or may not have reviewed depositions of the parties and opposing experts. An expert witness is typically deposed by the opposing attorney and experts must be disclosed by both sides. Attorneys are not required to disclose experts who were retained to review the case but whose opinions were not favorable to their side of the case. In a few jurisdictions, depositions of expert witnesses are not routinely conducted as part of the discovery process. For example, the Pennsylvania rules of discovery require that the dissemination of expert opinions prior to trial be done through interrogatories or an expert witness report, and depositions are not done unless either special permission is obtained from the judge or both parties agree to a deposition (Pa.R.Civ.P. §4003.5., 2021).

Mediation/Arbitration

In many cases, after the discovery process is nearing completion, the opposing parties may meet to discuss a possible settlement and avoid a trial. The malpractice insurer may become a major broker in this decision. Some malpractice policies will allow the company to settle a case without the defendant psychiatrist's consent, whereas other policies require consent to settle (Frierson & Joshi, 2019). The most common medical malpractice insurance policies allow for a limited consent to settle with arbitration. Under this provision – defendant psychiatrist wants to settle but the insurer does not – the issue of settling may also be arbitrated (see Chap. 4).

Arbitration is a form of alternative dispute resolution (ADR) and a way of resolving disputes outside of a court of law. With arbitration, the parties agree to have the case decided by a neutral third party, known as an arbitrator. Arbitration may be binding or non-binding. In most cases, they are non-binding, allowing the case to proceed to trial if both parties do not accept the arbitration recommendations. In binding arbitration, there is usually more than one arbiter (e.g., a three person panel), and decisions about deviation in the standard of care, causation, and damages are final (Bookman & Zane, 2020).

Trial

After resolution of any pre-trial motions, a trial begins with jury selection. A process known as *voir dire* (literally, "to see, to say" in French) is used to select jurors. In this process, each opposing attorney is allowed to ask potential jurors questions to determine if they believe the juror will be unbiased and fair (i.e., to see what each potential juror has to say). Special experts may be hired by the attorneys to advise them on jury selection. Each side will have a number of preemptory challenges, meaning that a potential juror may be excused without the reason being specified.

After jury qualification, opening arguments proceed, with the plaintiff going first. Each side will set the agenda for the trial during opening arguments and there are very few rules governing them. However, opening arguments are not evidence. After opening arguments, the plaintiff's attorney will present the case, call fact witnesses, and call an expert witness or witnesses (who must first be qualified as an expert by the judge before they can offer testimony). Expert qualification involves the court reviewing the proposed expert's education, background, and experience. The plaintiff's attorney will ask open-ended questions (e.g., who, what, where, when, why), which is known as direct examination of the witness. Following direct examination, the defense attorney can cross-examine the witness. Cross-examination questions can be much more pointed and leading, and sometimes require a "yes" or "no" answer (e.g., "You testify as an expert much more often for plaintiffs in malpractice cases than for the defense, correct?").

After the plaintiff's case is presented, the defense attorney may ask for summary judgment from the judge if he or she believes the plaintiff has not proved one of the necessary elements of liability (see Chap. 1). If summary judgment is denied, the defense will then present their case, with a similarly qualified expert testifying that the defendant psychiatrist met the standard of care and did not contribute to any alleged plaintiff injury or damages. The defendant psychiatrist may or may not testify, depending on the particular facts of the case.

Following the defense case, both attorneys will make closing arguments and the judge will instruct the jury on the laws of negligence in the particular jurisdiction. The jury will then deliberate with a certain majority of jurors (or all, depending on jurisdiction) needed to reach a verdict by a preponderance of the evidence. If the jury finds negligence and liability on the part of the psychiatrist, the jury will then decide damages (see Chap. 1 for types of damages). After the jury verdict, the judge will enter a judgment. After the verdict, either party may make a motion asking the court to enter a judgment notwithstanding the verdict (JNOV). This motion argues that no reasonable jury could have reached the verdict that the jury did in this case. In other words, it claims that the jury did not follow proper instructions and ruled for the opposing party based on legally insufficient evidence. JNOVs are rarely granted. More commonly, a defense attorney may request a reduction in the damage amounts rewarded by the jury prior to the judgment being entered, if the awarded amount seems excessive.

In medical malpractice actions, whenever money is paid to a plaintiff, either through settlement or through an award of damages by a jury, the payment must be reported to the National Practitioner Data Bank (National Practitioner Data Bank, 2018). The National Practitioner Data Bank is required to provide future disclosures of these payments to hospitals (during credentialing), medical boards, professional societies, and various health-care entities in response to inquiries from these entities.

Tort Reform

The frequency of malpractice claims increased during the last half of the twentieth century. Many states have enacted medical malpractice litigation reforms over the past 30 years with the goal of reducing malpractice insurance premiums for physicians, increasing the supply of physicians, reducing the cost of health care, and increasing efficiency (i.e., decreasing the practice of defensive medicine and the expenses involved with ordering excessive tests to prevent liability) (Agarwal et al., 2019). The largest effort, with around 30 states participating, involves placing caps on the amount of economic damages that can be awarded (American Medical Association, 2017c). However, several state supreme courts have found that limiting damage awards is a violation of the state's constitution. Additional tort reform measures include increasing the required standard of proof in medical malpractice trials to a standard of clear and convincing evidence, placing caps on plaintiff attorney contingency fees, creating governmental patient compensation funds to augment malpractice liability insurance, and allowing insurers to administer malpractice awards as payments over time rather than as a lump sum.

Many tort reform measures have targeted the "hired gun" expert witness – one that typically offers the opinion the retaining attorney is looking for regardless of the facts in the case. Because many expert witnesses in malpractice cases come from a different state than the trial, one approach has been for the state medical board to declare the provision of expert testimony to be considered the practice of medicine. By doing so, the expert is subject to the review of the state medical board, and the provision of expert testimony may require a medical license or special permit in the state where testimony is given. For example, if a physician wishes to provide medical expert testimony in Florida and does not have a

Florida medical license, he or she must first apply for and receive an expert witness certificate from the Florida Board of Medicine (Fla. Stat. § 458.3175, 2021).

The total impact of tort reform measures is not known, in part because the varied approaches to tort reform across jurisdictions have been hard to study. However, early research suggests that tort reform efforts may decrease the practice of defensive medicine, increase the physician supply, decrease health-care spending, and have no effect on the quality of health care (Agarwal et al., 2019).

Key Points

- Malpractice actions are governed by the rules of civil procedure, and malpractice cases are typically heard under the jurisdiction of state courts; however, the case may be brought in federal court and as permitted by the Federal Tort Claims Act (FTCA) if the negligent act occurred on federal property.
- In most US jurisdictions, this standard or proof in a malpractice case is a preponderance of the evidence standard, which generally means "more likely than not."
- The statute of limitations establishes a time limit for suing in a civil case based on the date the injury occurred or the date that the injury was first discovered.
- Pre-filing requirements include Communication and Resolution (C&R) programs, a notice of the intent to sue, an affidavit or certificate of merit from a medical expert, and, in some jurisdictions, appearance before a medical tribunal.
- The stages of a malpractice suit include the following: summons and complaint, answer, discovery (subpoenas for records, interrogatories, depositions), arbitration (binding or non-binding), and trial.
- Tort reform measures have included caps on damages, raising the standard of proof, limiting plaintiff attorney contingency fees, allowing malpractice award payments to be made over time, and placing restrictions on expert witnesses.

References

Agarwal, R., Gupta, A., & Gupta, S. (2019). The impact of tort reform on defensive medicine, quality of care, and physician supply: A systemic review. *Health Services Research, 54*(4), 851–859.

American Medical Association Advocacy Resource Center. (2017a). *Communication and resolution programs*. Available at: https://www.ama-assn.org/sites/ama-assn.org/files/corp/media-browser/specialty%20group/arc/early-disclosure-compensation-programs.pdf. Accessed December 28, 2020.

American Medical Association Advocacy Resource Center. (2017b). *State laws chart II*. Available at: https://www.ama-assn.org/sites/ama-assn.org/files/corp/media-browser/premium/arc/state-laws-chart-2_0.pdf. Accessed December 29, 2020.

American Medical Association Advocacy Resource Center. (2017c). *Caps on damages*. Available at: https://www.ama-assn.org/sites/ama-assn.org/files/corp/media-browser/premium/arc/caps-on-damages_0.pdf. Accessed January 2, 2021.

Bookman, K., & Zane, R. D. (2020). Surviving a medical malpractice lawsuit. *Emergency Medicine Clinics of North America, 38*(2), 539–548.

Colorado v. New Mexico, 467 U.S. 310 (1984).

Federal Tort Claims Act, 28 U.S. Code § 1346 (1946).

Fla. Stat. § 458.3175. (2021). Available at: http://www.leg.state.fl.us/statutes/index.cfm?App_mode=Display_Statute&Search_String=&URL=0400-0499/0458/Sections/0458.3175.html. Accessed January 2, 2021.

Frierson, R. L., & Joshi, K. G. (2019). Malpractice law and psychiatry: An overview. *Focus, 17*(4), 332–336.

Garner, B. A. (Ed.). (2004). *Black's law dictionary* (8th ed.). West Group.

Latner, A. W. (January 22, 2010). *Arizona toughens burden of proof in malpractice cases. Renal & Urology News*. https://advance.lexis.com/api/document?collection=news&id=urn:contentItem:7XPB-VP11-2SM0-Y0GN-00000-00&context=1516831. Accessed December 28, 2020.

Law Firm Newswire. (April 1, 2013 Monday). *Does a higher standard of proof for medical malpractice help or hinder victims?* https://advance.lexis.com/api/document?collection=news&id=urn:contentItem:583D-SKP1-F03R-N1WF-00000-00&context=1516831. Accessed December 28, 2020.

Mass, Gen. Laws Ann, ch. 231, § 60B (2007).

Medscape. (2020). *Psychiatrist malpractice report 2019*. Available at: https://www.medscape.com/slideshow/2019-malpractice-report-psych-6012450#1. Accessed December 28, 2020.

National Conference of State Legislatures. (2014a). *Medical liability/malpractice statutes of limitation*. Available at: https://www.ncsl.org/research/financial-services-and-commerce/medical-liability-malpractice-statutes-of-limitation.aspx. Accessed December 28, 2020.

National Conference of State Legislatures. (2014b). *Medical malpractice reform – health cost containment*. Available at: https://www.ncsl.org/research/health/medical-malpractice-reform-health-cost-brief.aspx. Accessed December 28, 2020.

National Practitioner Data Bank (NPDB). (2018). *Reporting medical malpractice payments*. Available at: https://www.npdb.hrsa.gov/guidebook/EMMPR.jsp

Pa.R.Civ.P. §4003.5. (2021). Available at: https://casetext.com/regulation/pennsylvania-code-rules-and-regulations/title-231-rules-of-civil-procedure/part-i-general/chapter-4000-depositions-and-discovery/rule-40035-discovery-of-expert-testimony-trial-preparation-material. Accessed January 2, 2021.

United States House of Representatives. (2020). *Federal tort claims act*. Available at: https://www.house.gov/doing-business-with-the-house/leases/federal-tort-claims-act. Accessed December 28, 2020.

Vanderpool, D. (2018). Professional liability in psychiatric practice. In L. H. Gold & R. L. Frierson (Eds.), *Textbook of forensic psychiatry* (3rd ed., pp. 169–184). American Psychiatric Association Publishing.

The Plaintiff Attorney's Perspective: Avoiding the Malpractice Snare

7

Skip Simpson

He who fears he shall suffer, already suffers what he fears.
Michel de Montaigne, 1570–1592, The Complete Essays

The best way for a psychiatrist to avoid a malpractice action is simply to be competent, do the hard work of treatment, and document thoughtfully. The psychiatrist's focus cannot be on the patient if there is a fear of lawsuits. A focus on the potential for lawsuits constitutes a focus on the psychiatrist and not the patient; it is a focus destined for failure in any area of medicine. This chapter will examine the following: (1) taking the fear out of practicing psychiatry; (2) how a plaintiff's attorney may decide to select medical malpractice cases for prosecution (and how a psychiatrist can avoid being selected); (3) a vignette about a psychiatrist as a leader; (4) the physician's promise to protect the patient; and (5) cross-examination areas for a defendant psychiatrist in a medical malpractice lawsuit.

Causes of action for misdiagnosis, negligent treatment, sexual exploitation, and the implanting of false memories are all examples of potential malpractice suits against mental health clinicians. Suicide, however, is the most common reason for a medical malpractice case against a psychiatrist. Therefore, this chapter will focus on psychiatric malpractice involving a death by suicide.

Note: Mr. Simpson is a plaintiff's counsel who focuses primarily on suicide and false memory cases for the past 34 of his 45 years of practice of law. Each year he reviews about 80 cases for potential litigation against psychiatrists and accepts about 6 for prosecution. Before his malpractice career, he was an Air Force judge advocate serving mostly as a prosecutor, but also as a criminal defense lawyer and military judge. Later he served as an assistant district attorney for Dallas County, Texas. He was called back to duty by the Department of Defense and the Department of Justice (DOJ) to prosecute public corruption cases for DOJ and later prosecuted Organized Crime, Narcotics for DOJ.

S. Simpson (✉)
Law Offices of Skip Simpson, Frisco, TX, USA
e-mail: ssimpson@skipsimpson.com

Many clinicians and the general public do not understand why psychiatrists are sued in suicide cases, what the violations of patient safety rules are, and how a psychiatrist can be held responsible for a death from suicide. However, when examining an uncomplicated fact pattern about an inpatient suicide, it becomes clear. Patients so overwhelmed that they consider suicide are frequently hospitalized to prevent self-harm. Additionally, the most common method of suicide in a psychiatric hospital is hanging (Frierson, 2020). Individuals at risk of suicide who are being monitored in psychiatric hospital facilities need to be under constant direct visual surveillance to prevent strangulation. A significant deficiency in brain oxygenation can be rapidly induced when a patient hangs himself or otherwise stops breathing.

In about 30–180 seconds, a patient may lose consciousness. If that happens, any change of heart to end life is too late. At 2 minutes, neurons suffer extensive damage and lasting brain damage becomes likely. At 5 minutes, death becomes imminent. At 10 minutes, even if the brain remains alive, a coma and lasting brain damage and death are almost inevitable. Yet, most suicide observation levels are every 15 minutes. Therefore, significant damage can be done if a patient is left alone in a room with the means to die by suicide (Gilbert et al., 2008).

Removing the Fear of Lawsuits: Make the Main Support Person a Part of the Treatment Team

The traditional, legalistic approach to risk management is to avoid or minimize family contact after a patient suicide to reduce the threat of litigation. However, compassion over

P. Ash et al. (eds.), *Malpractice and Liability in Psychiatry*, https://doi.org/10.1007/978-3-030-91975-7_7

caution is likely a better approach. Avoidance of family contact increases distrust, animosity, and litigation, whereas compassionate contact reduces the likelihood of litigation. When a psychiatrist is sued, it is prudent to consult with a lawyer and the doctor's malpractice carrier immediately. The psychiatrist needs to know from the carrier if contacting family members after being sued will cause the carrier to deny coverage.

Most lawsuits could be avoided by the psychiatrist if the second rule of medicine was to be a nice human. So first, do no harm, and second, be nice. When a suicide occurs while a loved one is under the care of a psychiatrist, family members may not understand how a suicide could occur when a psychiatrist is in charge of the patient's safety; they want to make sense of the suicide. After a suicide, family members often call the psychiatrist to inform him or her of the death. The first exchange the psychiatrist has with the family member may determine if the family member decides to call a lawyer.

Properly preparing for such a call can be likened to an athlete's training for the marathon. A marathon may seem like an intimidating and exhausting endeavor, but with the proper planning and preparation, the athlete can make it through the 26.2 miles successfully. Likewise, with solid planning, a psychiatrist can make it through a suicide of a patient without being sued. Additionally, receiving a call from a family member that a patient has died from suicide can provoke unfortunate legal consequences if this is the psychiatrist's first interaction with the caller. However, being empathetic is both good medicine and good risk management. If the family member hears a kind, familiar, and compassionate psychiatrist forthcoming with answers, a lawyer will likely not be called. The ground work for a good conversation with the family is paved by making the family member a part of the treatment team, if possible. The patient should be encouraged to involve family or significant others in the treatment. The psychiatrist should obtain documented permission to speak with collateral sources when necessary to help obtain the best outcome for the patient. Frequently, what is good for the patient is good for the family; likewise, what is good for the family is good for the patient.

If family members are involved in the patient's care, the psychiatrist can inform them of the importance of suicide means restriction, the importance of therapy, and the necessity to keep the psychiatrist informed if the patient is not adherent to treatment or if a significant event is occurring and causing the patient to be overwhelmed. The family can anticipate problems on the horizon for the patient and warn the psychiatrist of stormy seas. Although the clinical reasons for being involved with collaterals and assisting the psychiatrist with means restriction is part of the psychiatric knowledge base in managing suicidal patients, the prior involvement with collaterals will also be powerful and consequential when that call to the psychiatrist to report a death occurs. Therefore, establishing a good relationship with collaterals is a prudent risk management technique. It may be a mistake to rely solely on an at-risk suicidal patient, whose judgment and insight are likely flawed and whose motivations are often unclear, when other reliable sources of information are available (Reid, 2007).

Case Selection: Method (and How to Avoid Being Selected)

In accepting or declining a case, a plaintiff's attorney begins by listening to the potential new client. As the lawyer listens to the story, there are other matters of interest besides determining if there is a violation of the standard of care. The lawyer also wants to know – if there indeed was a breach of a patient safety rule – what other potential victims could have been affected by the breach. Would the community care about the violation? Finally, was there a system failure involved?

If the information gathered warrants more investigation, the first step is to obtain the medical records from the psychiatrist. When a lawyer initially reviews a potential case, all he or she typically has are the medical records. Nothing will stop a malpractice plaintiff's lawyer dead in his or her tracks quicker than a well-documented chart reflecting compassionate care and careful and thoughtful suicide assessments.

Documentation is a basic tool to the defense of a suicide case. To be clear, it is axiomatic there is no substitute for good ethical care. However, good care combined with good documentation is the surest way to avoid being a defendant in a malpractice action. From the perspective of an attorney who reviews medical malpractice matters for prospective plaintiffs daily, authentic quality documentation will determine whether a malpractice attorney accepts or declines a psychiatric malpractice case. The attorney also knows the importance juries attach to the written record. A well-documented case reflecting good compassionate care means a plaintiff's lawyer is likely to lose the case, even if the lawyer is so unprincipled that such a case would be pursued.

If being unconscionable is not enough to deter a lawyer from filing a frivolous lawsuit, economics will: losing a malpractice case means the lawyer will lose hundreds of hours of attorney time preparing the case (for no fee), along with approximately $30,000 to $140,000 in expenses the lawyer has advanced for the cost of litigation (Simpson, 2004).

In determining whether a malpractice case should be filed, a lawyer looks closely at the defendant's conduct in managing the patient's care. A good plaintiff's attorney might spend 30 minutes reading one page of a doctor's note. The attorney is not just reading the written words, but imagining the scene, preparing opening arguments, thinking about who he or she wants on a jury, and preparing cross-examination of the author of the note.

Hours are spent combing through the medical charts of potential cases and paying attention to details: does the word *suicide* appear anywhere in the record? Were the services medically or therapeutically focused? Were symptoms properly documented? Was psychosis assessed? Is there sufficient information to warrant the diagnosis? Are chart entries dated and timed? Medical records that only document existing symptoms may be a tip that the psychiatrist may not have been careful. It is analogous to saying a tire is low on air without saying if the car can be driven. The severity of the problem depends on how low on air the tire is. When did the problem start? What was done to address the problem?

Careless documentation may not be the proximate cause of an injury, but it may encourage the lawyer to keep digging because now the psychiatrist's competence is in question (Wiger, 2011).

In all medical specialties, core competencies represent what physician specialists should be able to do to be considered minimally competent in their field. Core competencies are nonnegotiable. A core competency for a psychiatrist is comprehensively assessing and documenting a patient's potential for suicide and homicide (American Board of Psychiatry and Neurology, 2003). The lawyer will therefore look for a systematic suicide and homicide assessment in the physician's records. Cross-examination questions about the assessment can be devastating to the psychiatrist in front of a jury. If a psychiatrist does not know the answers to certain questions about the assessment, the jury will conclude no real assessment was done.

When done properly, the suicide and homicide risk assessment is recorded in the chart contemporaneously (i.e., recorded when done, not as an afterthought once notice of a lawsuit is filed). A timely dictated note is more reliable and credible to a jury than a later one, since it is recorded before the doctor can be alleged to have motive to fabricate an assessment. Conversely, post-suicide entries in a medical chart are looked upon with great suspicion by both lawyers and jurors (Simpson, 2004).

Failure to carefully assess for suicide and homicide is a major infraction of patient safety rules. Who else could have been or was injured or died because of the psychiatrist's decision not to properly assess the patient for suicidal and homicidal thinking? If the malpractice occurred on a hospital unit, mental health techs, social workers, nurses and doctors, other patients and visitors, janitorial crew, and maintenance workers could conceivably be harmed.

The focus on these "random" victims impacts the role of foreseeability in the law and the basic premises underlying tort law. For example, if an outpatient psychiatrist fails to properly access a patient for suicide or homicide, harms that could arise from tortious behavior will vary (MacDougall, 2018). Forensic psychiatrists may explain the damages to random victims during their discussion of the purpose of the safety rules (i.e., the standard of care). For example, the testimony would be: "[Expert], let's discuss the standard in assessing a young mother at risk for suicide and filicide, who is the standard intended to protect?" The expert then says obviously the mother and her children and then details other foreseeable "random" victims: first responders and bystanders in the line of fire.

A lawyer – in accepting or declining a potential case – considers why the community should care about this case. How would members of the community (represented by the jury) want their family member treated if he or she were under the care of a psychiatrist?

What is the importance of keeping dangerous items away from teenagers in the community if they are at risk for suicide? Does the community believe it is prudent for psychiatrist to protect teens from suicide? If so, how? If a safety rule is to have future application, then one can't choose when the rule is enforced; it must be enforced constantly. Safety rules become stronger the more they are enforced. Therefore, the rule of keeping dangerous instruments away from those at risk for suicide needs to continue at all times and in every place. In the view of the plaintiff's attorney, conduct forgiven is conduct repeated. The juror's amygdala, our neurological burglar alarm, is blaring when it knows how important preventing suicide is to the survival of a juror, his or her children, and the community. For example, the horror of murder-suicides looms large in the public's consciousness. Of the approximately 47,173 recorded suicides in the USA annually, about 2% (943) are murder-suicides. In these cases, suicide prevention can also prevent homicides (Joiner, 2014).

Vignette: Inpatient Suicide

A patient is admitted to a psychiatric unit by an admitting psychiatrist after receiving a call from a hospital social worker in the hospital admissions department. The social worker had earlier been called by an emergency department (ED) crisis assessor from a nearby hospital. The ED crisis assessor told the social worker that the patient was brought to the ED by the police after causing a disturbance at his workplace. When the officer arrived at the office, the workplace employees told the officer a fellow employee had "snapped" and was having a complete breakdown. The officer met with the employee in his office and observed him to be very emotional, crying, and not making much sense. He was quickly pacing around the office and wouldn't answer the officer's questions directly. The officer attempted to ask the employee questions about suicide and homicide, but the employee would not answer the officer's questions. The distressed employee seemed panic-stricken and inconsolable and made statements such as "I have to make sure my wife knows how to get access to the money," "I need to make sure she has all the account numbers first," and "I need to make sure my kids are going to be taken care of." The officer considered these statements evidence of a possible suicide or suicide behavior. The officer also did not think that the employee was able to properly care for himself or prevent himself or another person from harm in his current condition.

The officer took the employee to the ED. Upon arrival the patient appeared catatonic and would not answer questions. After about an hour in the ED, the patient began pacing and rambling with pressured speech, racing thoughts, and agitation. The patient made statements about not wanting to live and wanting to "leave this earth." The patient stated he wanted to be left in a room to die. The ED crisis counselor determined the patient was at high risk for suicide. The hospital admissions social worker never personally assessed the patient. The social worker charted after admission: "Although the patient has not stated that he is directly suicidal, he has said multiple things that indicate that he has a plan and intent to harm himself."

The admitting psychiatrist, without personally assessing the patient, placed the patient on every 15-minute suicide observations. No psychotropic medication was administered by the admitting or attending psychiatrist. During a safety assessment within hours of his admission, the patient stated he was having thoughts of killing himself. No one determined the content of the thoughts. The attending psychiatrist evaluated the patient. The chief complaint was listed as "psychosis." The patient admitted to suicide ideation and hopelessness. The attending psychiatrist continued the patient on an "every 15 minute" suicide observation level. Seventeen hours after being admitted to the unit, the patient choked himself to death with food brought to his room by hospital staff. In a deposition, the attending psychiatrist believed his care was good and would do nothing different if a similar patient was under his care again. The attending psychiatrist previously had a patient die from suicide while on an every 15-minute observation level.

In considering this vignette, several questions arise: Was the care adequate? What, if anything, might have prevented this tragic event? What is the legal risk to the admitting psychiatrist and/or attending psychiatrist? Does the medical director (also a psychiatrist) or hospital administrator bear any responsibility? How could this event impact random victims? What system failures contributed to the outcome? Was this event preventable?

The Joint Commission in 2006 published *The Physician's Promise: Protecting Patients from Harm,*" *second Edition* (The Joint Commission, 2006). On the title page of *Reducing Suicide: A National Imperative*, a publication of the Institute of Medicine, there is a quote by Johann Wolfgang von Goethe (The Institute of Health, 2002): "Knowing is not enough; we must apply. Willing is not enough; we must do." In litigated cases, many psychiatrists do not know appropriate safety practices, let alone apply them. If they do know safe practices but don't apply them, there must be proper justification documented in the chart.

The *Physician's Promise* impacts some answers to the questions following the vignette.

- "With an ability to serve as a bridge between patients and staff as well as staff and management, physicians play a unique leadership role in fostering improvements in care." (Joint Commission Resources, 2006, p.12)
- "Strong and sustained physician leaders can help eliminate adverse events and dramatically reduce medical errors. As physician leaders continue to encourage an open discussion of organizational fallibility, innovations is enabled, provoking a collective effort of all to enhance the health care system" (Joint Commission Resources, 2006, p.11).
- "Approximately 2%–6% of suicides are by individuals receiving treatment from health care professionals in hospital settings" (Joint Commission Resources, 2006, pp. 71–72).
- The purpose of suicide assessment is to identify individuals at increased risk for suicide and to obtain clinical information relevant to their treatment planning" (Joint Commission Resources, 2006, p.72).
- "Psychiatrists are normally assumed to be the type of physician most likely to evaluate suicide patients" (Joint Commission Resources, 2006, p.72).
- "The purpose of assessment is to obtain appropriate and necessary information about each patient at the time of entry into or transition within a health care setting or experience. The information gleaned from an initial assessment is used to match an individual's need with the appropriate setting, care level, and interventions" (Joint Commission Resources, 2006, p.72).
- "Findings from an initial admission assessment should be thoroughly documented, signed and validated by a physician, and properly communicated to all clinical staff within the required time frame" (Joint Commission Resources, 2006, p. 76).
- "...if assessment findings indicate that an individual is at high risk for suicide, staff must be informed immediately to implement line-of-sight or even arm's length, one-to-one observation procedures" (Joint Commission Resources, 2006, p. 76).

- "To ensure and maintain a successful risk assessment process, organization leaders must ensure that all staff members with direct contact with patients are educated about the prevalence of suicide in health care settings, the physiology of suicides, the risk factors of suicide, and about specific patients at risk for suicide" (Joint Commission Resources, 2006, p. 77).
- "Physicians, along with nursing staff, must also be aware of areas and elements of the environment that represent opportunities for an individual's intent to [die by suicide]" (Joint Commission Resources, 2006, p. 75).
- "Physicians must be familiar with the environment in which their patients receive care and must work with organization leaders to ensure a safe environment of care" (Joint Commission Resources, 2006, p. 75).
- "Making certain that the patient's clinical record contains sufficient information to support clinical decisions, and that the transmission of data and information is timely, accurate, and complete among all heath care professions, are crucial measures in providing care that revolves around safety" (Joint Commission Resources, 2006, p. 76).

In the vignette, an anticipation of the possibility of a sudden surge of suicidal ideation with lethal suicide intent, and the implications thereof for line of sight monitoring for an unmedicated anxious and psychotic patient, might have saved this patient.

In summary, to avoid the malpractice snare, be competent, document formulations of risk, and have significant others be a part of the treatment team. Under these tenets, hopefully the psychiatrist will not be sued. However, if a good lawyer has sued a psychiatrist, it is not a pleasant experience and if the case is not settled, a trial will occur.

Cross-Examination of the Defendant Psychiatrist

When a psychiatrist has violated the safety rules (standard of care), thereby causing harm or death, it is now time to enforce those rules by prosecution. Breaking rules with no consequences is not a way to keep patients safe. Giving a psychiatrist a pass for not following patient safety rules condones unsafe behavior. This portion of the chapter explores one part of a malpractice trial: cross-examination. Before cross-examination there is *voir dire*, opening statements, and direct examinations. Following the examination of witnesses, closing arguments are given by the opposing lawyers, followed by jury instructions from the judge.

Cross-examination, unlike the other stages of trial, is one of the only unscripted person-to-person interactions in the trial; it is analogous to hand-to-hand combat. Sometimes a jury will see interactions between counsel and the judge; but cross-examination is the only time to show the jury who the witnesses are and if they can be believed. Cross-examination of a witness before a jury is said to be the greatest engine ever invented for the discovery of truth. Dragging *the* truth out of witnesses who are supporting a defendant psychiatrist in a jury trial is the goal in cross-examination. A defendant psychiatrist, and those aligned with the psychiatrist, either did something or omitted doing something, which caused the plaintiff to lose a family member. In the plaintiff attorney's mind, the psychiatrist started the war.

The mindset of the plaintiff's attorney in cross-examining a witness is that any witness taking the stand to support the defendant in a medical malpractice case is the enemy of patient safety. The defense lawyer puts his or her witnesses on the stand to harm the plaintiff's case; the plaintiff's attorney cannot let that happen. The plaintiff attorney carefully selects points to highlight and aims to be concise in their attack.

The objective of cross-examination is to cause an appearance of the witness that makes a negative impression on the jury. In a psychiatric malpractice case, the jury needs to know the good guys from the bad guys. The good guys are those fighting for patient safety; the bad guys are in trial to escape responsibility for not protecting a patient. In the hand-to-hand combat with the witness, if the witness wins, it may mean, and likely does mean, the plaintiff attorney will lose the fight for patient safety. Louis Nizer, a famous New York lawyer, stated: "In cross-examination, as in fishing, nothing is more ungainly than a fisherman pulled into the water by his catch."

The malpractice trial of the psychiatrist occurs when the plaintiff and the defendants cannot resolve the case, usually in mediation. Often the psychiatrist is being tried along with other defendants (e.g., the psychiatric hospital and the management company of the hospital). Because the suicide of the patient resulted from systemic negligence, there are often multiple defendants.

In the above vignette, multiple parties were involved in the failure to prevent the suicide. If any one person had done their job to protect the patient, a death would likely not have occurred. The key point is that the checks and balances in the system failed. The Joint Commission has written and talked about highly effective organizations for years. Highly effective organizations rarely have a catastrophic incident.

The death in the vignette occurred, in part, due to normalization of deviance. Normalization of deviance occurs for many reasons, such as when people within a group become so insensitive to a deviant practice it no longer feels wrong; when continuing a deviant practice repeatedly fails to create bad consequences; or when safer practices are inconvenient or expensive and people in authority eventually say they are unnecessary (Price, 2018).

One goal of cross-examination of all parties, including the psychiatrist and the psychiatrist's expert, will be to show how normalization of deviance has occurred. Cross-examination will be directed at proving that the goal of the expert hired by the defendant psychiatrist is to condone bad and dangerous care in order to trick the jurors into believing that what is bad care is actually good care (Simpson, 2019). Whenever a psychiatrist takes the witness stand, the overriding issue is the credibility and the believability of the psychiatrist. The impression that each witness makes can be very important in the end result.

Some jurors may think that since the case is about an individual suicide and lack of monitoring, they have no interest in the trial; they may be upset they have to miss work to oversee a dispute between a psychiatrist and a family member who is blaming a suicide on a physician. In illustrating that the case is not only about suicide but about protecting (monitoring) patients, the following cross can occur:

Q. Isn't it true every department of the hospital must adhere to the rule of adequate monitoring? [This question wakes up the juror – "maybe my own safety or that of my family is on the line."]

Q. Isn't it true all departments of the hospital have a monitoring aspect?

Q. The obstetrics floor is an example, right? The cardiology floor? The pulmonology floor? The oncology floor?

Q. Isn't it true every aspect of the hospital has as a key ingredient in the absolute necessity of safe monitoring?

Q. Monitoring involves concepts like electronic fetal monitoring, reporting of vital signs, monitoring the heart by EKG, and the monitoring taking place in an ICU, right?

Q. Failure to monitor a patient in an ICU compares to failing to monitor on an acute psychiatric unit, right?

Jurors may now understand the risk of not supervising a patient at risk for death, suicide just an example of what can go quickly wrong if a doctor is not ordering safe observation levels.

The witness has a choice in answering these cross-exam questions: answer yes or no to each question, or quibble with the question. Any answer but "yes" calls the psychiatrist's or expert's credibility into question; impressions about truth-telling matter.

Jurors may believe myths about suicide that patients who die from suicide are bad, selfish, and sinful. If the defendant psychiatrist answers questions which dispel these myths, it helps jurors to decide the case without bias and prejudice against the mentally ill.

Q. Do you agree that mental disorders are not character flaws?

Q. Do you agree that mental disorders are legitimate illnesses that respond to specific treatments, just as other health conditions respond to medical assistance?

Q. Do you agree it is a myth that asking a patient about suicide will somehow give the patient the idea to kill themselves?

Q. Do you agree most suicidal people are ambivalent about suicide? What does that mean? [Questions are asked on cross-examination when the lawyer does not care what the answer is. Any answer will work as a springboard to more questions designed to show a lack of credibility.]

Q. Do you agree suicide results from a disease which, like all diseases, is involuntary?

Q. Do you agree that psychiatrists can fall below the standard of care?

Q. Do you agree that when a psychiatrist does not provide safe care, a patient can die as a result?

The psychiatrist can expect cross-exam questions relating to patient safety rules and how he or she applied them in case being tried. As the psychiatrist answers questions, the jury is again assessing credibility: Are the answers disingenuous? Dishonest? Self-serving? Prideful supplanting of testimonial responsibility to tell the truth and encourage safe patient care? Is the testimony encouraging normalization of deviance? Is the witness arrogant? Is testimony moving the profession toward unsafe patient care? Are the answers misleading? Are the questions asked being answered?

There are other areas of cross-examination which may be explored (see Table 7.1).

Witness believability is tested in the courtroom by putting the psychiatrist in a wind tunnel to see where and when the cracks occur. The lawyer knows the psychiatrist cannot be telling the truth, the whole truth, and nothing but the truth. If the psychiatrist was telling the truth, there would likely be no lawsuit. Remember, the lawyer has spent at least 100 hours and thousands of dollars on this case. It is unethical for a lawyer to attack the credibility of any witness unless the lawyer has a good faith belief that the witness is not being truthful.

Q. Please repeat the oath you just took. What does it mean to you?

Q. Not just the truth, but the whole truth? What does that mean to you?

The psychiatrist, like any other witness, must have *perceived* something relevant to the subject of the trial.

Table 7.1 Sample additional cross-examination questions

Q. Isn't it true there are several reasons a patient may deny being suicidal, when he or she is suicidal?
Q. Isn't it true if a person has a large number of risk factors for suicide, yet denies any thoughts about suicide, could such an inconsistency signal that the client is hiding information?
Q. Do you agree that a total lack of suicidal ideation in clients riddled with risk factors is not the norm?
Q. Do you agree that a psychiatrist should not rely solely on a patient's denial of suicidal thinking?
Q. Isn't it true that even patients who respond honestly they are not suicidal often misunderstand their own symptoms, condition, and risk?
Q. Isn't it true that those patients who think they are being honest can't predict their future condition, impulses, and behaviors?
Q. Isn't it true in this case that you charted Ms. Smith's judgment and depth of insight as poor?
Q. Didn't you chart Ms. Smith having poor impulse control?
Q. Isn't it true that information from patients with conditions such as severe depression, serious suicide potential, borderline personality traits, or psychosis is often unreliable?
Q. Do you agree that these factors impede risk assessment and increase the need for caution and collateral information?
Q. Do you agree that Ms. Smith was suicidal but could be safely watched by her family?
Q. Have you read any literature suggesting having a suicidal patient watched by family is a bad idea?
Q. What is means restriction? What did you ask Ms. Smith's family about guns?
Q. Do you agree that "professional judgment" can sometimes fall below the standard of care?
Q. Do you agree when exercising judgment, a psychiatrist must act as a reasonably careful psychiatrist under similar circumstances?
Q. Do you agree that doctors who make treatment decisions which are not the product of a careful evaluation can fall below the standard of care?
Q. Do you agree that hospital policies regarding suicide must be followed if the patient is at risk for suicide?
Q. Is documentation important for continuity of care? Is accurate documentation required by any rule or policy? Is documentation important for tracking whether treatment is working?
Q. Do you agree that the least-restrictive-placement policy is relevant to the standard of care? How?
Q. For the concept of the least-restrictive-placement policy to be within the standard of care, must the particular placement must be suited to a particular patient's safety needs?
Q. Isn't it true that whether a psychiatrist's choice of a patient's placement met the psychiatrist's duty of care to the patient depends on whether the placement was safe?

Q. You say everyone does it that way; tell me the last person you spoke to who told you it is proper to take the patient's word for it when the patient says "I am not suicidal?"

Q. You say the nurse asked all the right questions at discharge, but were you present when he asked those questions?

Q. You say that suicide cannot be foreseen. Who told you that? When? Where? Why was that a subject for discussion?

Q. Can a suicide be anticipated? What is the difference between foreseeability and anticipation? What is prediction?

Once the witness has perceived something, the psychiatrist needs to *remember* what she perceived. The memory of the event the psychiatrist is testifying about is worthless unless it can be *communicated* to the fact finder. Additionally, how the witness communicates to the jury can be questioned. At times the testimony is so rehearsed that a simple question can uncover this fact.

Q. Sir you just testified to a set a facts, will you repeat your answer?

Lawyers are permitted to ask any witness, including defendants, questions to expose bias, prejudice, interest, corruption, bribery, or a motive to misrepresent. Any psychiatrist knows his or her own vulnerabilities when taking the witness stand. The psychiatrist should also know the vulnerabilities of all witnesses testifying on his or her behalf.

Q. You say sertraline is the drug of choice for all your patients; don't you have a close relationship with the drug representative from Pfizer?

Q. You are testifying on behalf the hospital; don't you have an interest in the outcome of this case?

Q. You are an expert for Dr. Smith; didn't you make $700,000 last year only testifying for defendant psychiatrists?

Q. You testified Dr. Smith abided by the standard of care in all respects; why haven't you told the jury Dr. Smith is a business partner of yours?

Lawyers are permitted to impeach witnesses convicted of a felony or any offense involving a dishonest act or false statement.

The rules of evidence specifically permit questioning on a witness's character for truthfulness or untruthfulness to assess the witness's honesty and credibility. The rules are an explicit acknowledgment that every witness who testifies places their character for truthfulness or untruthfulness at issue. Even one instance of dishonesty or deceit can be enough to call into question a witness's credibility on the stand. The following questions relate to specific instances of conduct probative of untruthfulness because they involve dishonesty or false statements, i.e., some element of deceit, untruthfulness, or falsification – some element of active misrepresentation.

Q. Dr. Smith, isn't it true you submitted to your last employer a false CV?

Q. Dr. Smith, isn't it true you lied to a bankruptcy court regarding your assets?

Q. Dr. Smith, isn't it true you hid assets in a divorce proceeding?
Q. Dr. Smith, isn't it true you falsified data in a drug trial?

A psychiatrist can be impeached by prior inconsistent statements. Usually this comes about when the psychiatrist has given a deposition or has authored articles or books where he said something different at trial from what he previously wrote. A statement's inconsistency may be determined from the circumstances and is not limited to cases in which diametrically opposite assertions have been made. Thus, inconsistencies may be found in changes of position, they may be implied through silence, and they may also be found in denial of recollection.

When a decision to sue a psychiatrist has been made, the ethical plaintiff's attorney spends hundreds of hours reading professional literature, consulting with the top forensic psychiatric experts, and having the experts specifically review the records and facts of the case before it is filed. When filing a malpractice case, there is no room for errors or bad decisions. The lawsuit, like an indictment for criminal negligence, is stating that the physician is responsible for another human's death or serious injury. The lawyer also knows there will be an impact on the physician and his or her family because it strikes at their livelihood. However, the fight is for patient safety. Patients have entrusted their mental health and lives to those with a duty to first do no harm.

There is no legal substitute for cross-examination to get to the truth in a medical malpractice trial. Traps are set for the psychiatrist to trip in front of the jury. When a psychiatrist is cross-examined, there are no honest disagreements between the witness and plaintiff attorney. The plaintiff attorney never "understands" anything the psychiatrist says except that his or her testimony is misleading or false. To the attorney, the psychiatrist in a medical malpractice case does not have "opinions," or "beliefs"; they have stories, excuses, rationalizations, and justifications.

Key Points

- Malpractice suits serve a dual purpose: to make an injured party whole and to protect patient safety through enforcing the standard of care.
- The best way for the psychiatrist to avoid a malpractice action is to simply be competent, do the hard work of treatment, and document thoughtfully.
- Following a patient death from suicide, being empathetic toward family members is both good medicine and good risk management.
- In determining whether a malpractice case should be filed, a lawyer looks closely at the defendant's conduct in managing the patient's care.
- Timely contemporaneous documentation of suicide or violence risk assessment is prudent, and notes entered into a record after a bad outcome will be viewed with suspicion.
- The mindset of the plaintiff's attorney in cross-examining a witness is that any witness taking the stand to support the defendant in a medical malpractice case is the enemy of patient safety.

References

American Board of Psychiatry and Neurology. (2003). *Core competencies for psychiatric practice: What Clincians need to know*. American Psychiatric Publishing.

Frierson, R. L. (2020). Inpatient treatment. In L. H. Gold & R. L. Frierson (Eds.), *Textbook of suicide risk assessment and management* (3rd ed., pp. 201–212). American Psychiatric Association Publishing.

Gilbert, J. D., Jensen, L., & Byard, R. W. (2008). Further observations on the speed of death in hanging. *Journal of Forensic Sciences, 53*(5), 1204–1205.

Joiner, T. (2014). *The perversion of virtue: Understanding murder-suicide*. Oxford University Press.

Joint Commission Resources. (2006). *The Physician's promise: Protecting patients from harm* (2nd ed.). The Joint Commission.

MacDougall, V. L. (2018). *Negligence purpose, elements, and evidence the role of foreseeability in the law of each state*. Balloon Press.

NR Price, T. W. (2018). When doing wrong feels so right: Normalization of deviance. *Journal of Patient Safety, 14*(1), 1–2.

Reid, W. (2007). Practice well: Risk and suicide prevention. *Journal of Psychiatric Practice, 13*(6), 403–404.

Simpson, S. (2004). Avoiding the malpractice snare: Documention suicide risk assessment. *Journal of Psychiatric Practice, 10*(3), 185–189.

Simpson, S. R. (2019). Clinician testimony in suicide litigation: A case to be uneasy. *Behavioral Sciences & the Law, 37*(3), 313–328.

The Institute of Health. (2002). *Reducing Suicide: A National Imperative*.

The Joint Commission. (2006). *The Physician's promise: Protecting patients from harm* (2nd ed.).

Wiger, D. (2011). *The psychotherapy documentation primer*. Wiley.

8 The Defense Attorney's Perspective

Peter J. Hoffman, Alexandra Rogin, Kevin F. Farrington, Andrew J. Bond, and Brooke Scicchitano

An unfortunate fact for many US psychiatrists is that they will contend with malpractice suits at some point in their careers. Forty-one percent of psychiatrists in the United States have been sued for malpractice at least once (Martin, 2019).

The process will be an unpleasant experience. This chapter outlines opportunities to decrease the chances of being sued along with steps for a psychiatrist to assist in his or her defense if they have been sued. All of the following suggestions are based on our experience as defense attorneys who practice in the arena of professional malpractice.

Basis of Liability

Patients can allege or establish malpractice liability against a psychiatrist based on a number of claims.

Duty

A claim for medical malpractice is not cognizable unless the healthcare provider owes a duty to the patient or a third party. A duty usually attaches when the provider undertakes to care for the patient. Typical claims alleging a failed duty include wrongful death, failure to treat, suicide, errors in medication administration, complications from treatment, and failure to diagnose. Many times, whether such a duty exists is a question of law.

Once duty is generally established, the specific duty owed must be established. A provider owes a duty of care to his or her patients to conform to a certain standards of reasonable medical care. Generally, a provider's standard of care is measured by the degree of care and skill possessed by other physicians within the same specialty under similar circumstances. Most arguments during litigation surround the proper standard of care and whether the standard was breached.

P. J. Hoffman (✉) · A. Rogin · K. F. Farrington · A. J. Bond · B. Scicchitano
Eckert Seamans, Cherin & Mellott, Philadelphia, PA, USA
e-mail: phoffman@eckertseamans.com; abond@eckertseamans.com

Third-Party Duty

Most states have implemented the general rule that a provider does not owe a professional duty to a third party. Some states have limited this "no duty" rule by recognizing a duty to non-patient bystanders when the patient poses a danger of harm to an identifiable third party.

A growing number of jurisdictions have moved away from a strict privity rule in claims by non-patients against physicians and instead look to public policy concerns such as (1) the relationship between the parties, (2) the social utility of the actor's conduct, (3) the nature of the risk imposed and foreseeability of the harm incurred, (4) the consequences of imposing a duty upon the actor, and (5) the overall public interest (*Althaus v. Cohen*, 2000).

Since the landmark case of *Tarasoff v. Regents of University of California* (1976), a majority of states have imposed some form of the *Tarasoff* duty to protect an identifiable victim either by statute or case law, thereby creating an exception to the confidentiality of the physician-patient relationship (see Chap. 13).

Negligence

One of the most common theories that a medical provider may be sued under is negligence. To state a negligence claim against a medical provider, a plaintiff must show that the provider owed the patient a duty recognized by law, that the provider breached that duty – the standard of care – that the alleged breach resulted in injury to the patient, and that the patient sustained legally recognized damages as a result.

P. Ash et al. (eds.), *Malpractice and Liability in Psychiatry*, https://doi.org/10.1007/978-3-030-91975-7_8

Many states have a Mental Health Procedures Act, which gives the defendant physician "qualified immunity." In such jurisdictions, the plaintiff would be required to prove gross negligence.

Informed Consent

Another theory under which a provider might be sued is lack of informed consent. A patient's lack of consent claim is premised on the allegation that the provider failed to reveal a significant risk, which caused harm to the plaintiff, and that, had the potential risk been disclosed, a reasonable person would not have consented to the treatment or procedure. Informed consent requires more from a physician than simply having the patient sign a form. The provider must ensure that the patient is aware of and understands the benefits of the proposed treatment, the material risks of the treatment, alternative options to the proposed treatment, and possible consequences of declining the treatment. In some jurisdictions, it may be expanded to include the use of certain therapies including medication interventions or the use of certain psychotropic medications. This is most applicable to the psychiatrist.

Relations with Patient

Psychiatrists must maintain strictly professional relationships with their patients. Sexual relations between doctor and patient are unethical and are held as unethical by a number of professional associations, including the American Psychiatric Association. This ban extends beyond the termination of the individual therapy. Additionally, it applies not only to the patient but also to people related to the patient, such as the patient's spouse (see Chap. 34).

Common Situations in Psychiatric Settings

There are a number of situations in which psychiatrists are typically sued. Common situations include, but are not limited to, failing to document monitoring and evaluation of suicide risk, neglecting to document a change in the level of patient supervision, failing to evaluate the safety of the environment for a patient with suicidal behaviors, prescribing psychotropic medications without going through the informed consent process, prescribing off-label use of medication, and failing to document what medications have been ordered.

Damages

In any malpractice action, the plaintiff must establish its damages were a direct result of the clinician's failure to exercise reasonable standard of care. Typically, the plaintiff is eligible for two types of damages – economic and noneconomic (see Chap. 1). Economic damages are awarded to compensate the injured patient for financial expenses and losses resulting from the defendant's negligence. Noneconomic damages, on the other hand, compensate the patient for losses that do not carry an inherent financial value, such as loss of life's enjoyment. Recoverable damages vary from state to state, and some states have a monetary cap on recoverable damages.

How to Minimize the Chance of Being Sued, and What to Do Before Being Sued

Opportunities exist to decrease the chances of being sued, and to protect oneself before being sued.

Keeping Up to Date

All medical providers must keep up to date on the state of medicine. Psychiatrists should be particularly aware of the developments involving psychotropic medications, including their discussion in literature, clinical practice, and manufacturer warnings. Psychiatrists must also stay up to date on the laws and regulations affecting their practice. This includes issues such as consent to speak with family members of patients who are in crisis. Psychiatrists should maintain all licensure requirements and complete all renewal requirements with their state board of medicine in a timely manner. Psychiatrists should also obtain their continuing medical education requirements yearly. Finally, malpractice insurers can provide resources regarding important developments impacting psychiatric practice in certain geographic locations and jurisdictions.

Communication and Continuation of the Patient Relationship

A good patient-psychiatrist relationship can mean the difference between a patient (or family) bringing a lawsuit, or not. Communication, within professional boundaries, is key to fostering this relationship. Patients should feel like they are being heard, and that their concerns are not being summarily dismissed. Time and care should always be devoted to making sure the patient understands his or her care plan, and why certain recommendations have been offered. Psychiatrists should also make it a top priority to have a system in place to return patient calls and refill necessary medications. Furthermore, it goes without saying, but the psychiatrist should be sure to review the patient's chart and history before engaging in any contact with the patient. Remembering the small details is important and can help the patient feel that their psychiatrist is an advocate for his or her health and well-being.

Once a relationship is established with the patient, treatment may not be withdrawn without providing adequate notice to the patient in time to obtain alternative care. Terminating the relationship without safeguards in place is called abandonment, and can result in professional discipline, in addition to civil liability. The American Psychiatric Association (APA) advises that it is ethical to terminate a relationship in certain situations, for example, where the patient no longer needs services, where the patient is not likely to benefit from the services provided, where the patient would be harmed by continuation of the relationship, or when the psychiatrist does not feel that he or she can safely care for the patient. However, in terminating the relationship, the psychiatrist must consider the needs of the patient, document that he or she has provided notice of intent to terminate the relationship (and the basis therefore), and provide recommendations for alternative treatment options and/or providers. The APA recommends that a psychiatrist terminating a patient relationship should ensure there is written evidence of patient receipt and acknowledgment of such notice, for example, by certified mail or email (American Psychiatric Association, 2014). The APA routinely publishes its recent ethics opinions, and providers should access these resources for further guidance into specific situations (American Psychiatric Association, 2020).

Documentation

The importance of documentation cannot be emphasized enough, as the patient's records will serve as the basis of litigation. Psychiatrists and all office staff should ensure notations are legible so that lawyers, jurors, and others participating in the patient's care do not misunderstand the records. Records should also be comprehensive, including the identity of all individuals involved in the care (i.e., nurses, patient, and family members). A psychiatrist must be sure to document all factors that contribute to, and form the basis of, clinical judgment or decision-making.

Documentation should be kept contemporaneously with treatment to maintain accuracy and avoid the appearance of impropriety. Notes should be timed, as this will help create a timeline of events at trial. Subsequent entries must be clearly identified and dated. Medical records should never be changed after a patient commences a suit against a clinician. Everything that is written in the medical record can come out in discovery and may also be shown to a jury at trial.

Phone records are also an important part of the patient's record. Many office practices do not consistently document when they have received a call from a patient, whether that call was returned, and the contents of any phone discussions. Keeping detailed phone records can prevent entering a he-said she-said situation at trial. Detailed records are key, as often times, they are the only hard evidence of what transpired between a patient and psychiatrist.

What to Do After Being Sued

Various steps exist to simplify the legal process, and for psychiatrists to protect themselves while in a lawsuit. (More details can also be found in Chap. 5.)

Notify the Malpractice Insurer Immediately

When an adverse treatment event occurs, or upon receiving a records request or letter from an attorney, and certainly upon service of a lawsuit, the clinician should report the event or complaint to his or her malpractice insurer immediately. Actual physical or emotional harm to the patient is not a condition precedent to the clinician reporting an event. Early reporting allows for a comprehensive investigation and may result in intervention. In fact, many professional liability insurance policies have reporting requirements as certain information must be reported in order for the event to be covered under the policy. These include:

- When and how the psychiatrist first became aware of the event(s)
- The reasons for anticipating the claim, including the nature and dates of the alleged event(s)
- Any alleged injuries or damages sustained from the event(s)
- The names of potential claimants, if available

After notifying the insurer, the insurer then determines how it would like to proceed in the matter and may assign counsel.

The Attorney-Client Privilege and Communications with Third Parties

Importantly, psychiatrists who are sued should not discuss their case with anyone other than the counsel assigned to their case. Federal and state laws have codified the attorney-client privilege which protects the disclosure of communications between the attorney and the client (i.e., clinician). It is an essential component of the legal system and promotes full and candid communication between an attorney and the client. The privilege belongs to the client and the attorney is responsible for keeping client communications in the strictest of confidence. Therefore, it is recommended that the defense attorney participate directly in all discussions involving the lawsuit and allegations in the complaint. It is also best to avoid discussions with the attorney while in public. The privilege is not absolute, and inadvertent disclosure may lead to waiver. If an inadvertent disclosure occurs, the psychiatrist should take immediate action by consulting his or her attorney, advising the recipient that disclosure was unintentional, requesting return of the materials, and confirming in writing that the aforementioned steps have been taken.

Questions about the lawsuit should be directed to the defense attorney only. The attorney is the best person to answer questions and the person with whom these communications are likely confidential.

Altered Medical Records

Once a potential claim or lawsuit is known, the medical or treatment record should not be accessed, other than to organize for the attorneys' review, and the medical or treatment record should never be altered. If a psychiatrist makes a notation in the records and later, before knowledge of a claim or litigation, discovers a mistake in the records, the psychiatrist should correct the mistake and then initial and date it. The original notation should not be deleted or altered. Plaintiff's attorneys have many ways to discover, interrogate, and prove changes in the records. If proven, the clinician will essentially lose all credibility, and his or her chances of avoiding liability are significantly reduced.

Assessing the Strengths and Weaknesses of a Malpractice Case

Many factors go into an attorney's assessment of a lawsuit. The assessment will direct whether a case should be settled in mediation or whether the case should be decided at trial.

First Impressions

First impressions are always important and they color the attorney's assessment. However, the assessment of the case is a dynamic process and the analysis may change over time.

Optics

Optics are very important. Such things as "bad" or "hot facts" may become issues in and of themselves. These facts may include the number of previous lawsuits against the doctor, allegations of sexual contact with the plaintiff, "grisly" facts, suicide, violence toward third parties by the patient, and media coverage. It must then be determined if any of these facts are admissible at trial or have already been judged by the public through media coverage.

Assessing the Physician as to Appearance and Attitude

It is sad to say, but appearance matters. The physician's appearance will matter for both a deposition and trial. The physician's appearance will be evaluated during their deposition. The jury will evaluate the physician's appearance during trial. If a physician has an uncaring or patronizing attitude, that also has to be considered.

Medical Records Review

A careful review of the medical records must be undertaken immediately after a lawsuit is filed. If there are notations in the documentation which are harmful, they must be considered and explanations should be given. If the records have been in any way altered, it creates a critically bad optic, but more importantly, becomes an issue itself, and negatively affects credibility.

Analysis of Plaintiff and Plaintiff's Family, and the Defendant Physician

An analysis of the plaintiff and the plaintiff's family, including social media searches, or other searches to determine who the parties really are is important. Care must also be taken to investigate the defendant physician, including prior reports to the National Practitioner Data Bank, licensure issues, and prior litigation.

The Key Next Step

The next step is the analysis of the complaint, all of the records, emails, and text messages. Initially, the defendant physician and the staff must be advised to "hold" and maintain all records, emails, and text messages. In addition to examining the records, it is important to perform an audit trail. Audit trails are a common form of discovery in these cases given the current malpractice climate. If the doctor has been in and out of the records many times, it can be a potential red flag and must be explored.

The office or hospital setting is critical. A view of the location, if it is an office case, should take place. The doctor's office and the staff should be considered. Is it a calm place or is it chaotic, and how does the staff seem? All of this may be problematic, or helpful. If it is a hospital case, then the unit should be observed, particularly if it is a suicide case. Moreover, the documentation of all of the observations should also be reviewed very carefully. All negative factors must be carefully analyzed and considered.

The review of the chart, and all other documentation, including emails and text messages, must be undertaken with care and diligence. At this time, an initial review of pertinent literature is usually done before meeting the physician. The literature should be analyzed with comparison to the complaint and the records.

Meeting with the Doctor

The initial meeting with the defendant psychiatrist is the most important step, and experienced counsel should conduct the meeting. Most lawyers prefer to have the meeting in their office. As noted above, it may be more important (although more inconvenient) for the lawyer to consider meeting at the psychiatrist's office or the hospital location. The initial meeting must be done in a quiet place, if possible, and be uninterrupted. The psychiatrist should be prepared to block out at least 2 hours for the meeting. The lawyer should have an agenda including review of the doctor's CV, the medical record, the complaint, and medical principles. At this point, it is important to assess the doctor as a potential witness. The doctor's background must be vetted and explored, including prior lawsuits, any disciplinary actions, etc.

The attorney should be aware as to whether the doctor has psychological or emotional issues with the case. It is difficult to do so if the doctor is overly defensive or aggressive. The assessment of the defendant doctor cannot be overstated. The doctor will be viewed by the fact finder as a witness. The key fact will be whether "the fact finder would want the defendant physician to be their 'doctor'." If not, that is another red flag. The discussion with the doctor must be candid and the doctor should understand attorney-client privilege. It is advisable that the meeting be with the doctor, and that his staff or family not be present. The attorney may be accompanied by an assistant, paralegal, or someone else to aid in the meeting and to take careful notes. Third parties should not be at this meeting, including insurance representatives, risk managers, office managers, etc. The reason is twofold: the first is the potential waiver of the privilege and the second is whether the conversation will be less than candid.

Initial Assessment

With all the above in mind, the lawyer will reach tentative conclusions about defending the case. A dynamic defense trial outline will be undertaken, containing all of the key allegations against the physician, and an analysis of the complaint, and what the evidence is favoring each side. The lawyer should know which of the allegations of the complaint are factually correct, which are medically tenable, and which are legally tenable. To best serve the psychiatrist and the litigation as a whole, this must be done in a straightforward and neutral fashion.

Selection of Expert Witnesses

Counsel should reach out to a qualified expert to get a preliminary review. Counsel may use multiple sources to obtain qualified experts such as relationships from prior cases, word of mouth, or recommendations from colleagues. A qualified expert can further help in preparing the defense, challenging the plaintiff's assertions, and preparing the doctor for deposition. Counsel may inquire of the defendant physician as to his choices of potential experts. If there is a close relationship between the defendant physician and the proposed expert, the expert should not be retained. The defendant physician must be counseled as to consulting with any potential experts, or discussing the case with anybody other than counsel. The importance of counseling the doctor to refrain from discussing the case with a potential expert, or anyone else, is vitally important for the success of the defense.

Discovery

Written discovery should be taking place, and extreme care should be taken in responding to document requests and answering interrogatories. Written discovery to the plaintiff should be received and analyzed to determine whether there are potential problems, i.e., "new facts," and key witnesses. Obviously, all potential witnesses should either be interviewed or deposed. Again, this is part of the dynamic process of assessment.

The Deposition of the Defendant

The plaintiff's deposition may or may not be important, but any key witnesses and the plaintiff himself should take place and an analysis be made of the witnesses as potential trial witnesses.

The deposition of the defendant psychiatrist is probably the single most important factor in preparation of the case. The defendant psychiatrist must be thoroughly and adequately prepared. Ideally, there should be no area of inquiry into which the defendant psychiatrist has not been well prepared.

Plaintiff's attorney will strive to obtain concessions that establish the standard of care, breach of the standard, causation, and damages. It is important that the defendant physician be aware that everything said at the deposition is for the benefit of the plaintiff. It is not the time to offer information that the doctor thinks may be helpful in his defense. Rather, it is the time to answer specific proper questions posed by counsel without volunteering additional information. The deposition is not the opportunity to explain the defense side of the story. As a general proposition, less is more.

Further, more often than not, physicians are videotaped. How the defendant appears as a witness is critically important to the evaluation of the case. In some cases, depositions are done remotely. While this is clumsy and cumbersome, the physician should be made aware of it, but it is not a major problem. This video, whether in person or remote, will provide a good indication of how well the physician will do as a witness and how he or she will be perceived by the jury. The trial will likely build on what occurs during the deposition of the defendant psychiatrist.

The plaintiff attorney will evaluate the defendant physician as a potential witness, but so should the defense lawyer. An analysis of the videotape after the deposition has been taken is another important step. How the defendant appears as a witness is critically important to the evaluation of the case.

In all likelihood, the plaintiff's counsel will schedule the doctor's deposition. The deposition will give all of the parties the opportunity to evaluate the strengths and weaknesses of the other side's case before trial as well as help to predict the outcome of the case and facilitate settlement before trial occurs.

The key to the deposition is witness preparation. Years ago lawyers would meet with the client an hour or two before the deposition and that would suffice as the preparation. Today, that is nothing other than a roadmap for failure. Preparation cannot take place in a single session a few hours before the deposition. Rather, preparation begins with the first meeting with counsel. Thereafter, a number of sessions should take place. Very often defense attorneys may videotape their client prior to the deposition so that they can see how their client performs when certain questions are asked, and learn from the experience. The first step in preparation is making sure the psychiatrist knows a few basic rules:

- Do not volunteer information.
- Do not guess or speculate.
- If the psychiatrist does not know the answer, the best answer is "I don't know."
- If the psychiatrist does not remember, the best answer is "I don't remember," as guessing will only cause problems.
- The psychiatrist should strive to show confidence without being patronizing, condescending, or overbearing.

The key step in preparation is knowing the records. That doesn't just mean being familiar with them, but knowing them – cold. Counsel should go over key and important medical principles with the defendant doctor prior to the deposition. At some point in the preparation process, the attorney should interrogate the doctor as if he were the opposing counsel. Often another attorney is used to play that role.

It is likely the physician will be anxious prior to the deposition, which is a natural reaction. A deposition can be a rather unpleasant process, and it has been compared to having a kidney stone. The best way to deal with anxiety is to be prepared and have frank discussions with counsel. Opposing counsel may be aggressive and attempt to aggravate the witness into giving "bad answers." However, it is important to maintain composure and not show anger.

Other attorneys may take a "more gentle approach" and ask easy questions in order to establish a pattern of getting concessions. It is important to be aware of that tactic. Again, it is important that the witness only answer a question posed and not volunteer additional information. It is also important that the physician does not attempt to "teach" the opposing lawyer.

A good plaintiff's attorney will be prepared as to the records, as well as to the literature, and it is likely that the witness will be asked questions about literature. Many attorneys will ask the physician if they have read certain medical articles or texts, and be asked to comment on them. They will likely be asked whether they consider the author, the text, the journal, etc. to be "authoritative" or "reliable." It is important that the witness be prepared to answer the question. Stating that a medical article is "authoritative" can result in its use at trial by the plaintiff's attorney in cross-examination.

Experts

In the course of discovery, plaintiffs and defendants will submit expert reports or name experts who may be a witness at trial so that they may be deposed prior to trial. Attorneys use a detailed analysis and process to learn as much as possible about every opposing expert, including accuracy of the CV, background, detailed Internet and social media searches, and all prior deposition transcripts and reports. This step is time consuming and expensive, but its importance cannot be underestimated. Counsel will work with the defense expert to make sure that all of the issues that are important will be covered in the report or deposition, and if there is going to be a dispute, it is important to determine how it is likely to play out. A careful literature search should be made in order to assess the case and determine whether the plaintiff's theories as well as the defense theories are well grounded in the literature. In some jurisdictions, experts do not write reports and are only deposed. Moreover, under the Federal Rules of

Civil Procedure, experts are permitted to be deposed. In other jurisdictions (e.g., Pennsylvania), experts are not routinely deposed in state courts.

Final Pretrial Analysis

Once all of this information is gathered, digested, and understood, the lawyer should be in a position to evaluate the case. Is it a strong case for the plaintiff, or is it a strong case for the defendant? Are there strengths and weaknesses on the defense side, and if there are weaknesses, are they insurmountable?

Some of the factors which may be considered in the final analysis include:

- Optics
- Media coverage
- Grisly facts
- The defendant physician
  - Caring
  - Patronizing
  - Quality as a witness
  - How the deposition went
- Documentation, including review of audit trail and whether there are any alterations
- Assessment of the plaintiff and the plaintiff witnesses
- Strengths and weaknesses of each expert
- Is the case defensible? Is it "winnable"?

As noted above, this is a dynamic process and is subjective, or, put another way, it is really more art than science, but the lawyer should then be in a position to honestly and professionally assess the case. While the defendant physician, and insurance companies, wants to know the percentage of the chance of a defense verdict, lawyers typically refrain from this exercise.

The Trial

Much is written about how cases are tried, but the truth is that far less than 5% of the cases that are actually put into a lawsuit will end up with a trial that goes to a verdict (Hadfield, 2004). Nevertheless, the defendant physician should be aware of basic principles about a trial.

A trial can last anywhere from a few days (very unlikely with a jury trial) to 3 or 4 weeks. It is essential that the defendant physician be at trial in all phases, including jury selection. Consequently, this will be a drain on the physician's practice and scheduling of patients will require large sacrifices. The physician's behavior at trial is also important. Jurors do not miss a thing. The collective jurors will see everything about the defendant physician; they will be keyed in to everything he or she says and does, his or her mannerisms, dress, demeanor, and jewelry. Consequently, the physician should listen to counsel and maintain a rather cool exterior during the trial. It is certainly advisable for the physician to have a tablet or pad and to make notes.

In terms of trial preparation, the physician should thoroughly review the documents in the case, key medical literature, and the deposition. It is also likely that the defendant physician will be called as an adverse witness, very often as the first witness in trial. If the physician is unprepared, and is not familiar with the deposition and the records, the outcome could be a disaster. If the physician's testimony at trial differs from the deposition testimony, the jury may infer that the physician is being less than honest. The jurors will have the juxtaposition of the doctor on the stand at trial and the video of the doctor at deposition, making two inconsistent statements.

Settlement and Negotiations

In most jurisdictions, the court will hold one or more settlement conferences, either with the trial judge, a settlement master, or a magistrate. Settlement conferences done too early in the process are usually ineffective. Settlement conferences done late in the process have the benefit of the development of more information, but are very often on the eve of trial when most of the money for defense has been spent. Additionally, many courts require mediation, and often the parties or their attorneys strive to have the case mediated before an experienced mediator. This is very often more beneficial than having a trial judge who only has limited time for the conference. Counsel may choose to negotiate the case in person or on the telephone.

There are different styles for negotiation either informally, before the court, or in front of a mediator. In our experience, plaintiffs often have a "demand" which may or may not be tied to reality. The "demand" number may be a multiple of what the case's real value is, or what the plaintiff will take. The response by the defense can take various forms, including the "low-ball offer," or an offer, based on an analysis of the case, and strengths and weaknesses, etc. While the latter course may make more logical sense, the problem is that plaintiff's lawyers, judges, and mediators look for the "midpoint." If the offer is a realistic offer, then, that becomes the floor against the astronomical demand, and the midpoint becomes unattainable.

There are no black and white rules as to how to negotiate the case. The attorney should be aware of who the settlement conference judge, mediator, or magistrate is and how they want to conduct negotiations. The assessment of the plaintiff's demand should also be considered, as well as an understanding of how the plaintiff's attorney behaves in other cases. Most plaintiff's attorneys have learned two basic principles: (1) "I'm not going to bid against myself" (even if the initial demand is ridiculous) and (2) searching for the midpoint. Sophistication by the defense lawyer is important. The defense counsel often comes up with what is believed to be a realistic opening offer, based on the value of the case, and advise plaintiff's counsel and the court or mediator that there is no interest in auction bidding or finding a midpoint. In these situations, the defense counsel may be prepared to negotiate, but the ultimate number must be closer to the defense assessment than the plaintiff's assessment. If the insurance carrier, risk retention group, hospital, or whoever is paying to defend and settle the case is involved, it may extremely hamper the lawyer's ability to negotiate the case as he or she sees fit. Very often the large excess carriers will send their "negotiation experts" to settlement conferences or mediations, and that has not been an extremely beneficial process. In our experience, a realistic discussion between the defense lawyer and the plaintiff's lawyer should take place with a sounding out of the values in an attempt to look for a range for settlement of the case. This requires that there be some respect between the lawyers.

Recommending Settlement

In making a settlement recommendation, counsel must first determine whether the case has a chance of a defense verdict. Settlement should be recommended if the case is not defensible. If there are allegations and claims which may not be covered by insurance, the lawyer would do well to try to attempt to settle the case within the policy coverage in order to avoid extra-contractual damages such as punitive damages on the part of the defendant. If the potential damages in the case far exceed the insurance coverage, thought should be given to try to achieve a settlement within the insurance coverage. When the case is defensible, but there is a large potential damage exposure, the analysis becomes difficult as to whether to recommend settlement.

Where there is an insurance policy at issue, the physician should determine if there is a "consent to settle" clause (See Chap. 4). A "consent to settle" clause requires the physician to consent to any settlement terms. If there is no "consent to settle" clause, then the case can be settled without the doctor's consent. This presents ethical problems to the attorney. An attorney owes a fiduciary duty to their client. The client in these cases is usually not the insurance company but the defendant physician. There have been lawsuits by physicians against attorneys and insurance companies where a case was settled without the doctor's consent, even in a policy which does not have a "consent to settle" clause. Any discussion of settlement should take place in a realistic and straightforward and candid way with the defendant physician.

Key Points

- There are things psychiatrists can do both before and after being sued to minimize litigation and its impact; psychiatrists should stay current with medical advances, take the time to create a relationship with patients involving quality communication, and thoroughly and legibly document all aspects of care provided.
- After a suit is filed, a psychiatrist should notify their malpractice carrier immediately.
- Medical records should never be altered and the psychiatrist should not discuss the case with anyone other than their lawyer.
- Defendant psychiatrists should strive to create a productive and honest relationship with their lawyer as this relationship will be invaluable during the difficult and time-consuming work of preparing for deposition and trial; it can help endure and successfully navigate the litigation process.

References

Althaus v. Cohen, 756 A.2d 1166, 1168 (Pa. 2000).

American Psychiatric Association. (2014). *Online practice handbook*. Available at: https://www.psychiatry.org/psychiatrists/practice/practice-management/starting-a-practice/online-practice-handbook. Accessed December 8, 2020.

American Psychiatric Association. (2020). *Ethics*. Available at https://www.psychiatry.org/psychiatrists/practice/ethics. Accessed December 8, 2020.

Hadfield, G. K. (2004). Where have all the trials gone? Settlements, nontrial adjudications, and statistical artifacts in the changing disposition of federal civil cases. *Journal of Empirical Legal Studies, 1*(3), 705–734.

Martin, K. L. (2019). *Medscape psychiatrist malpractice report 2019*. https://www.medscape.com/slideshow/2019-malpractice-report-psych-6012450#4. Accessed November 18, 2020.

Tarasoff v. Regents of University of California, 17 Cal. 3d 425 (Cal. 1976).

Expert Witnesses

9

Charles L. Scott

Approximately 41% of psychiatrists in the United States have been sued at least once for medical malpractice (Martin, 2020). Being sued for medical malpractice is an extremely stressful experience, and the defendant doctor may reasonably wonder, "Who determines if my care was negligent?" Although the ultimate answer to this question may come from a jury, in most claims of psychiatric malpractice, the treating psychiatrist's care is reviewed by independent psychiatrists who serve as "expert witnesses." Psychiatric expert witnesses have a very different role than treating psychiatrists. This chapter highlights key differences between a treating psychiatrist and an expert witness psychiatrist and outlines common tasks of an expert witness retained to evaluate potential malpractice claims.

Fact Witness Versus Expert Witness

Psychiatrists should have a clear understanding of the difference between a fact witness and an expert witness in medical malpractice cases. Fact witnesses have firsthand knowledge about a case they obtained through their sight, sound, smell, taste, or touch. Fact witnesses can testify about their observations and experience but are generally not permitted to provide personal expert opinions on case-related issues. In contrast, expert witnesses have "special knowledge" deemed relevant to assist the judge or jury in understanding the facts of a case (Resnick & Piel, 2017). The Federal Rule of Evidence (FRE) 702 outlines conditions that qualify a witness as a court expert as follows (Rule 702, 2011):

A witness who is qualified as an expert by knowledge, skill, experience, training, or education may testify in the form of an opinion or otherwise if:

(a) The expert's scientific, technical, or other specialized knowledge will help the trier of fact to understand the evidence or to determine a fact in issue
(b) The testimony is based on sufficient facts or data
(c) The testimony is the product of reliable principles and methods
(d) The expert has reliably applied the principles and methods to the facts of the case

A psychiatrist who is sued for medical malpractice is a defendant in civil litigation, and serves as a fact witness if testimony is provided in a deposition or trial. As such, defendant doctors can provide testimony about the facts they recorded in their record, their diagnoses, specific treatments they provided, and their knowledge of relevant governing policies and procedures. The deposition exchange below illustrates common fact witness questions for a named defendant. Pay attention to the precise way the treating doctor answers only the question being asked and does not volunteer information not asked of him.

Attorney: Doctor, how many appointments did you have with Ms. Jones?
Doctor: Five.
Attorney: What was your diagnosis in the chart?
Doctor: Major depressive disorder.
Attorney: Did you ever ask her if she was having suicidal thoughts?
Doctor: Yes.

A sued psychiatrist would not typically provide expert witness testimony about the standard of psychiatric care, even though he or she would likely possess such knowledge. The interchange below illustrates how the attorney is attempting to shift the defendant doctor away from their role as a fact witness to that of an expert witness. The defendant psychiatrist recognizes that she is inappropriately being asked to provide expert witness testimony that could potentially be used to impeach her own care and she adheres to her fact witness role.

C. L. Scott (✉)
Department of Psychiatry and Behavioral Sciences, University of California, Davis, Sacramento, CA, USA
e-mail: clscott@ucdavis.edu

P. Ash et al. (eds.), *Malpractice and Liability in Psychiatry*, https://doi.org/10.1007/978-3-030-91975-7_9

Attorney: Doctor, isn't it true that your patient was suicidal on five occasions during your treatment?
Doctor: No.
Attorney: How many times did your patient tell you that he was suicidal?
Doctor: Four.
Attorney: Did you conduct a suicide risk assessment?
Doctor: Yes.
Attorney: And doctor, what book or article do you consider authoritative in how to conduct a suicide risk assessment?
Doctor: That requires an expert witness opinion. I am here today as a named defendant providing fact witness testimony only.

In contrast, an expert witness psychiatrist can provide opinions on a wide range of relevant topics related to a malpractice case, including whether or not the standard of care was met, if any breach in care resulted in damages, the degree of resulting damages, future treatment requirements and estimated costs, and long-term prognosis. A psychiatric expert witness often states in writing or testimony that their opinion is provided with a "reasonable degree of medical certainty." The precise meaning of the phrase "reasonable medical certainty" is subject to interpretation, and no universally accepted definition exists. Although this phrase suggests some level of confidence in a rendered opinion, the definition of "reasonable medical certainty" may vary according to jurisdiction and to the questions presented to the expert (Rappeport, 1985).

Expert Witness Tasks in Psychiatric Malpractice Cases

Screening the Referral

An expert witness typically receives a referral to review a medical malpractice claim from a plaintiff or defense attorney. The expert witness should seek answers to the following three questions during their first referral contact:

1. Who is requesting my expert witness review (i.e., plaintiff or defense)?
2. What am I being asked to do?
3. What are the specific allegations?

In many cases, a plaintiff's written complaint outlines the allegations known at the time of the referral and is a useful document to understand the plaintiff's version of the facts, alleged derelictions of duty, how these alleged derelictions resulted in harm, and the specific alleged harms. In situations where a formal complaint has not yet been generated, the attorney may provide an affidavit that describes a written notice to sue, or the attorney may provide his or her version of the case facts and claims.

After considering information provided by the contacting attorney, the psychiatrist (potential expert witness) should determine if they have the expertise appropriate to evaluate the case. Consider a lawsuit claiming that the treating provider negligently prescribed a medication to treat attention deficit/hyperactivity disorder in a 5-year-old boy and the boy was harmed as a result. The potential expert should carefully consider if they have the appropriate training and experience to render an informed opinion on this standard of care issue in such a young child, particularly if they are not trained in child and adolescent psychiatry.

If the psychiatrist decides that they have the appropriate background to accept the case referral, then he or she should consider other factors that may determine if they want to accept the referral. First, are there any ethical conflicts that would deter case acceptance? Ethical conflicts include accepting fees for services contingent on the outcome of the case, agreeing to give an opinion regardless of the case facts, having treated the plaintiff, or having already been retained by opposing counsel. Second, is there a request to evaluate the plaintiff? In some circumstances, family members sue for emotional damages, and the possibility of family member evaluations should be clarified up front. When a plaintiff and/or a family member is being evaluated, the psychiatrist should also inquire if an additional assessment by a forensic psychologist to help evaluate the claim will be allowed.

Third, what is the jurisdiction where the case is being heard? Most medical malpractice cases are heard in state courts; however, there are circumstances where standard of care issues are heard in federal court. Experts need to carefully vet any special licensure and/or current practice requirements for expert witness evaluations or opinion testimony in states where they are not currently licensed. Fourth, are there any agreed upon limitations on the expert witness review and evaluation? Possible limitations that both plaintiff and defense counsel may have agreed to include limiting the extent of records available for review, restricting the time allowed for evaluation of the plaintiff, and prohibiting certain inquiries into the background of the plaintiff's life during the psychiatric evaluation. The expert witness will need to evaluate if court-imposed restrictions impair their ability to perform an appropriate evaluation, and therefore impact their willingness to accept the case. Consider the scenario where a young woman is suing a doctor alleging that a prescribed medication made her suicidal, but a court order dictates that the expert witness psychiatrist is not allowed to inquire about a prior history of suicidal thinking or behavior. In this situation, an expert may determine that they are unable to provide a fair analysis of an alleged treatment causing suicidality and decline to accept the case.

Fifth, what are the proposed time frames for the record review, evaluation of the plaintiff or other parties, and submission of a written report if one is required? In determining if the evaluation can be done in the required time frame, the expert will need to gather information about the proposed scope of work, such as the volume of medical records, depositions, policies and procedures, or other documents to be reviewed. When an expert is contacted on very short notice, they may be unable to accept the case due to time limitations. Finally, how is the expert being paid for his or her time? As noted above, experts should not accept payment on a contingency basis as this could result in the expert consciously or unconsciously shaping their opinions to ensure their side wins the case as opposed to reaching opinions in an objective manner based on the available evidence. The expert should also inquire as to who is responsible for paying their fees, when fees are typically paid, and if there are any caps on their payment.

Initial Steps in Malpractice Case Review Organization

If the expert decides to accept the case, the attorney will typically request a copy of the expert's fee agreement and curriculum vitae. Attorneys may contact more than one potential expert before choosing which expert they determine is best suited for their case. An attorney's selection of an expert is based on a wide array of factors including the specific expertise relevant to the case, the ability of the expert to clearly communicate their findings, and the expert's background and training. The expert's curriculum vitae can assist the requesting attorney by including their educational background and training, their specific board certifications, as well as their publications, presentations, awards, organizational involvement, and research.

An expert witness fee agreement outlines the expert's fee for their time. Some experts charge an hourly rate for any time spent on the case, whereas other experts have different rates depending on the specific activity, such as record review, evaluation of the plaintiff, or deposition/court testimony. Experts commonly include a retainer agreement in their fee agreement, which helps ensure that the attorney is retaining them for their services as opposed to "hiring" them so they cannot be retained by the opposing counsel. When billing for their time, experts should outline each date that they worked on the case, what specific work they did on that date, and how much time they spent on that activity.

Once the attorney notifies the psychiatrist that they are the selected expert, the psychiatrist should request the language from statute or case law defining the relevant malpractice standard and delineate records needed for the malpractice review. Records often requested before beginning the case review are listed in Table 9.1.

Table 9.1 Potentially relevant records for malpractice review

Jurisdictional definition of medical malpractice
Plaintiff complaint or notice to sue
Interrogatories and response to interrogatories
Mental health treatment records
Medical treatment records
Educational records
Occupational records
Governing policies and procedures
Organizational investigations on standard of care
Deposition of fact witnesses
Deposition of defendant psychiatrist
Written report and notes of opposing expert
Deposition of opposing expert
Psychological testing to evaluate plaintiff
Written letters/notes/diaries by plaintiff addressing alleged harms

Many attorneys provide the requested records in an electronic version rather than printing them out. If received in an electronic format, the expert should attempt to open all documents when initially received to ensure that they can access all the documents. In legal cases, records typically have a number on the left-hand bottom of the page referred to as a "Bates stamp" or "Bates numbering." This system places a number on each page allowing all parties to readily identify a single referenced page. When experts are reviewing a case and identifying key facts on a page, they often will cite the specific related Bates stamp number so that all parties can track the specific source of information. Experts should be aware that any markings they make on documents or notes that they take while reviewing records are potentially discoverable during litigation and are subject to cross-examination.

Communications with Retaining Counsel

After being retained by an attorney, the expert typically reviews the available records which may be sent in hard copy or electronically. Experts should be fully aware that written communications with the retaining attorney are generally subject to subpoena. Such communications typically include written letters, faxes, fee agreements, billing statements, and emails between the expert and/or his representatives and the attorney. Experts should anticipate that they may be cross-examined on such correspondence and therefore use caution in prematurely expressing any case opinions or writing any comments that may be viewed as unprofessional. Consider the contrasting two emails below from different experts to the retaining attorney and how each might be perceived by a judge or jury.

Email 1

- Hey Jasper,
- You are going to really like my attached report. The treating psychiatrist was a real quack and I nailed him! I emphasized the points you brought up during our conversations and came around to your viewpoint. Let me know if there is anything else you want me to say or to change.
- Carl

Email 2

- Dear Mr. Jones:
- My report is attached.
- Dr. Smith

Email 1 is unprofessional and likely unethical. The retained expert appears to be providing an opinion that is bought by the retaining attorney, who is unnecessarily disparaging the treating provider, and who is morphing his opinions to please the attorney. The American Academy of Psychiatry and the Law (AAPL) provides ethics guidelines for the practice of forensic psychiatry to help avoid this "hired gun" appearance. The section titled "Honesty and Objectivity" notes:

> When psychiatrists function as experts within the legal process, they should adhere to the principle of honesty and should strive for objectivity. Although they may be retained by one party to a civil or criminal matter, psychiatrists should adhere to these principles when conducting evaluations, applying clinical data to legal criteria, and expressing opinions (American Academy of Psychiatry and the Law, 2021).

Although this email may be a rather extreme example of what not to do, the lesson here is clear: keep all correspondence with attorneys to a minimum with the expectation that every word written will be closely scrutinized. Many experts prefer to have communications with an attorney via a phone call. Although there may be no written record of these calls, the opposing attorney can ask the expert what was discussed during each telephone conversation. Experts typically discuss with attorneys their impressions of reviewed records, any additional documents that may assist in understanding the case, as well as potential questions that the attorney may ask a fact or opposing expert witnesses in subsequent depositions.

Defendant doctors are typically deposed during malpractice litigation, and the plaintiff's attorney can ask the sued doctor specific questions about the care they provided. Although plaintiff psychiatric experts are not usually allowed to speak directly with the sued doctor, the expert can nevertheless gather significant information that may be relevant to their malpractice opinion through the answers provided by the defendant doctor in a deposition. As a result, plaintiff experts often suggest relevant questions to the plaintiff attorney for this purpose.

Whether or not draft reports submitted by an expert to an attorney for review are discoverable depends on the jurisdiction where the case is heard. In federal court, experts may submit draft reports to an attorney and these draft reports are not subject to discovery. In contrast, state courts do not typically offer this level of protection. Therefore, the expert should review with the attorney any discovery issues relevant to their documents, correspondence, and draft reports.

Scheduling a Plaintiff's Evaluation

The logistics for an expert scheduling an evaluation of a plaintiff depend largely on who retained the expert. If hired by the plaintiff, the expert can generally determine the length of the evaluation, questions asked, who is present or not present, whether or not the evaluation is audio or video recorded, relevant collateral interviews, if a psychologist will conduct testing, and what specific assessment tools will be utilized. In contrast, a defense expert is often required to submit a declaration to plaintiff's counsel outlining detailed specifics of their scope of work for the proposed evaluation. Plaintiff counsel may object to multiple aspects of the proposed evaluation. In this situation, a court hearing may be necessary for the judge to issue an order regarding what the defense expert may or may not do. Defense experts are not allowed to conduct third-party interviews without expressed permission by the plaintiff's attorney. To avoid any conflict or confusion about the examination, defense experts should carefully consider having both parties sign a consent form in advance of the evaluation. A consent form in this context typically delineates who has retained the defense expert, limits on confidentiality, a clear statement that the evaluator is not the treating doctor, who receives the evaluation information, any legal duties to report information to a third party (e.g., child abuse, elder abuse, or threat to harm others), and an agreement to audio or video record when approved. Even when consent forms are signed in advance, questions may nevertheless arise on the evaluation day. For this reason, experts should have a method to contact the retaining attorney should any misunderstandings develop that need clarification before proceeding.

Assessing the Plaintiff

The course of litigation and psychiatric evaluations can be stressful for plaintiffs who are being examined to determine the nature and extent of their claims. When examined by the defense expert, the plaintiff may experience heightened apprehension and mistrust about the evaluation process. Defense experts can help ameliorate such concerns by asking the plaintiff how they are feeling and if they have any ques-

Table 9.2 Key areas in evaluating plaintiff's medical malpractice claim

Collateral records outlined in Table 9.1
Biopsychosocial history
Claimed harms and current status of harms
Life event traumas and stressors (outside of malpractice claim)
Impact of alleged harms on activities of daily living
Relevant favorable and unfavorable prognostic indicators
Inconsistencies between reviewed records and plaintiff's report
Inconsistencies between plaintiff's presentation during the evaluation
Psychological testing as appropriate

tions at the onset of the assessment. Experts for both sides should review the consent form and remind the plaintiff that the evaluator is not the treating doctor and that the evaluation is not confidential.

A significant aspect of the evaluation will focus on the plaintiff's claimed harms resulting from alleged improper care. To determine the relationship, if any, of a plaintiff's alleged emotional distress and/or mental disorder to their mental health care, the expert generally reviews the key areas outlined in Table 9.2 during the assessment.

Finalizing the Expert Opinion on Alleged Malpractice

After reviewing the records and completing the evaluation of the plaintiff to assess damages, the expert synthesizes that data to reach on opinion on whether or not the defendant doctor was negligent in the care provided. In reaching their opinion on whether medical negligence occurred in the case reviewed, the expert should answer the following four questions, commonly known as the 4 "Ds" necessary to substantiate a negligence claim (Scott & Resnick, 2006):

1. Did the defendant doctor have a *duty* to the plaintiff?
2. Did the defendant doctor have any *derelictions* in the care provided? If so, how?
3. Were the identified derelictions *directly* related to alleged harms?
4. What are the specific *damages* resulting from the care provided?

Even if an expert identifies specific areas where the standard of care was breached, these derelictions of duty do not automatically determine that the patient was harmed as a result. For example, consider the situation where a defendant doctor mistakenly prescribes a potentially toxic medication at a dose 1000 times greater than the maximum recommended dosage. Fortunately, the pharmacist identifies the medication prescription error and the medication is never given to the patient. As a result, there is no resulting harm from the improper order and therefore no financial recovery for damages. The expert must also consider the degree to which the alleged harms are causally related to standard of care violations. When considering the relationship, if any, of claimed harms to standard of care violations, the expert psychiatrist can consider four possible conclusions:

1. All damages are causally related to the mental health care at issue.
2. All damages are causally related to factors unrelated to the mental health care at issue.
3. Some damages are related to the mental health care at issue and some damages are due to unrelated factors.
4. The plaintiff has no damages from any source.

Table 9.3 Medical malpractice report components

Statement identifying who retained expert and referral questions
Circumstances of the evaluation (e.g., location, duration of evaluation, whether recorded, presence of third parties)
Sources of information reviewed
Statement of non-confidentiality
Psychiatric interview and mental status examination
Psychological testing results
Summary of records
Current diagnoses
Consideration of malingering
Opinion as to whether the defendant doctor was negligent with supportive reasoning
Prognosis (when requested)
Treatment recommendations (when requested)
Estimated cost of treatment (when requested)

Experts who render an opinion that is not favorable to the side who retained them are unlikely to be used as an expert witness in the case. However, the attorney may ask for a written summary of the expert's opinions for the attorney's file. In situations where the expert's opinion supports the position of the retaining party, the attorney may request a report, depending on the jurisdiction and litigation stage (see Chap. 6). General components of a medical malpractice report and opinion are outlined in Table 9.3.

Some medical malpractice cases are heard in federal court which has specific report submission guidelines outlined by Rule 26 of the Federal Rules of Civil Procedure. Under this rule, experts are required to submit a signed written report that includes the following (Rule 26, 1993):

- A complete statement of all opinions to be expressed and the basis and reasons for their opinions
- The data or other information considered in reaching their opinions
- Any exhibits to be used as a summary of or support for the opinions

- Qualifications of the expert, including a list of all publications authored by the expert within the preceding 10 years
- The compensation to be paid for the forensic review and testimony
- A listing of any other cases in which the witness has testified as an expert at trial or by deposition within the preceding 4 years

Providing Expert Witness Testimony

Expert witness testimony is not required in all cases. Many cases settle after expert witness reports or verbal opinions are received and the attorneys have assessed the strengths and weaknesses of their case. If the case does not settle, the expert witness usually receives a subpoena by opposing counsel that outlines documents that must be provided. Such requests can be extremely broad and may include written notes related to the expert's review of records and evaluation of the plaintiff, testing data or administered questionnaires, written communications with retaining attorney, a curriculum vitae, authored publications, copies of all records reviewed, billing statements, list of all prior testimony history, and any publications relied upon in rendering opinions. Experts can work with the attorney who retained them on how to best address overly broad demands. For example, a subpoena requesting every single psychiatric article or book ever read by an expert during their education and career would be impossible to provide, and it is unlikely the court would require this from the expert.

Subpoenas specify a date and time where the expert must appear for their sworn testimony. The requesting attorney has multiple goals when taking the deposition of an expert witness. These goals include learning what the expert knows, committing the expert to sworn statements, obtaining concessions to help their case, gaining information to discover more facts, and determining the expert's weak points in knowledge and presentation style. The attorney typically asks specific questions about how the expert became involved in the case, the background of the expert witness, their opinions, the database used to reach their opinions, the evidence to support their opinions, and any critiques the expert witness may have of the opposing expert witness or defendant doctor. When answering questions about a provider or opposing witness, an expert is best served by sticking with the evidence used to support their own opinions rather than personally disparaging another party. After the deposition is completed, the expert witness is provided the option to review their deposition to correct any possible transcription errors made by the court reporter.

Many malpractice cases settle after expert witness depositions have been taken. If the case does not settle, the expert witness may be asked to provide testimony at a trial. At this hearing, a judge or jury will hear evidence from both the plaintiff and defense to reach a verdict as to whether the treating doctor committed medical malpractice. If the expert witness testifies, he or she should carefully review their deposition testimony in advance because inconsistencies between deposition and trial testimony can be used to impeach the credibility of the expert witness. Key principles for expert witness testimony in any setting include telling the truth, acknowledging when you don't know the answer to a question, having a solid understanding of the case facts and basis of all opinions, presenting in a professional manner, carefully listening to the specific question asked and answering that question, and communicating to the judge or juror in a logical and relatable manner.

Summary

The role of a psychiatrist who serves as an expert witness in a medical malpractice case is significantly different than the role of a treating psychiatrist. If a treating psychiatrist is sued, understanding how expert witness opinions should be formulated may assist the defendant doctor in responding to the heightened legal and professional scrutiny of their care. Although the treating psychiatrist is not allowed to serve as their own expert witness, he or she can assist their attorney in the review of records, understanding their perspective of the case, and formulating cross-examination questions of the plaintiff's expert. Psychiatric experts on both sides should aim for objective reviews in rendering their opinions as the potential consequences for both the treating doctor and the allegedly harmed patient are substantial.

Key Points

- A treating psychiatrist who is sued for medical malpractice may be asked to serve as a *fact witness* and provide testimony about the facts of the care he or she provided.
- A forensic psychiatrist retained to review a medical malpractice case provides *expert witness* opinions about the standard of care provided and any causally related damages.
- Expert witnesses should carefully screen case referrals to evaluate if they have the appropriate expertise and if there are any ethical conflicts in accepting the case.
- Expert witnesses should evaluate the relationship, if any, of claimed damages to alleged derelictions of duty.
- Expert witnesses should consider the possibility of malingering in evaluating alleged damages.

References

American Academy of Psychiatry and the Law. (2021). *Ethics guidelines for the practice of forensic psychiatry*. Available at: https://aapl.org/ethics.htm. Accessed on 4 Mar 2021.

Martin, K. L. *Medscape psychiatric malpractice report 2019*. Available at: https://www.medscape.com/slideshow/2019-malpractice-report-psych-6012450. Accessed on 4 Jan 2020.

Rappeport, J. R. (1985). Reasonable medical certainty. *Bulletin of the American Academy of Psychiatry and the Law., 13*(1), 5–15.

Resnick, P. J., & Piel, J. L. (2017). Guidelines for courtroom testimony. In R. Rosner & C. Scott (Eds.), *Principles and practice of forensic psychiatry* (3rd ed., p. 43). CRC Press.

Rule 26. Duty to Disclose; General Provisions Governing Discovery. Fed. R. Civ. P. 26(a)(2), 1993.

Rule 702. Testimony by Expert Witnesses. Pub. L. 93–595, §1, Jan. 2, 1975, 88 Stat. 1937; Apr. 17, 2000, eff. Dec. 1, 2000; Apr. 26, 2011, eff. Dec. 1, 2011.

Scott, C. L., & Resnick, P. J. (2006). Patient suicide and litigation. In R. I. Simon & R. E. Hales (Eds.), *The American Psychiatric Publishing textbook of suicide assessment and management* (pp. 527–544). American Psychiatric Publishing, Inc.

The Defendant Psychiatrist as Witness

10

Ryan C. W. Hall and Terri Day

Defendant psychiatrists can potentially testify in three different ways during the course of a malpractice suit: via interrogatories, in depositions, and at trial. Although psychiatrists as a group may have some experience testifying in civil commitment proceedings, for many this will be the first time when their actions, not their patient's, are being directly scrutinized. When a psychiatrist discovers that he or she has been named in a malpractice lawsuit, he or she may experience various emotional reactions (e.g., anger, fear, guilt) or ego defense formations (e.g., narcissism, denial, avoidance) which, if not understood or addressed, can hinder the ability to respond appropriately (Knoll & Resnick, 2008; Gutheil, 2012; Brodsky et al., 2017). Chapter 11 addresses the psychological responses to being named in a malpractice suit and various coping mechanisms. Additionally, remembering the ABCs of testifying as a malpractice defendant can be most helpful: A, *A*nswer Honestly; B, Be *B*rief (especially during a deposition); and C, Remain in *C*ontrol, *C*lassy, and *C*lear.

Interrogatories

The first time a defendant testifies in a malpractice action is often in written responses to interrogatories. Interrogatories are questions proposed by the plaintiff's counsel (Zane, 2009) (see Chap. 6). Although interrogatories require a defendant's answers to the plaintiff's questions, the defense attorney usually drafts the responses (Whitmore, 2005; Feld & Moses, 2009). It is important for defendants to review and be aware of their answers since interrogatories may be referenced during later depositions.

Depositions

The most important testimony a defendant psychiatrist will give in a malpractice suit is usually the deposition (see Chap. 8 and Hoffman et al., 2005; Prevatt et al., 2007; Gutheil, 2012; Lundy & Teuscher, 2013; Shah et al., 2016). Most malpractice cases settle before trial, negating the necessity of in-court testimony (Whitmore, 2005; Knoll & Resnick, 2008). However, depositions often occur relatively early in the life of the lawsuit. Reasonable expectations of what a deposition can accomplish are important. Well-prepared defendants may be able to improve their case by significantly limiting damages or encouraging a plaintiff to consider a reasonable settlement (Whitmore, 2005; Williams, 2008; Knoll & Resnick, 2008; Gutheil, 2012). However, defendants should be cautioned against the fantasy that if they do well in their deposition the case will just be dismissed or they will "win" (Whitmore, 2005; Reid, 2006; Williams, 2008). By the time depositions are taken, the plaintiff's attorney has reviewed enough information to conclude that the case has some value in either a jury verdict or a settlement (Feld & Moses, 2009).

The most common advice attorneys give regarding deposition testimony is to give brief, clear, and truthful answers, and avoid volunteering information (Hoffman et al., 2005; Knoll & Resnick, 2008; Williams, 2008; Feld & Moses 2009; Gutheil, 2012; Brodsky et al., 2017). The purpose of the defendant's deposition is for the plaintiffs to gain information, lock in the defendant's testimony, and determine how well the physician will do on the witness stand if there is a trial (Hoffman et al., 2005; Knoll & Resnick, 2008; Williams, 2008; Gutheil, 2012). Overly detailed answers may provide too much information, reveal more of the defense strategy than the defendant intended, highlight concerns which the defendant has but that the plaintiff's side

R. C. W. Hall
University of Central Florida, Orlando, FL, USA

University of South Florida, Tampa, FL, USA

Barry University Dwayne O. Andreas School of Law, Orlando, FL, USA

T. Day (✉)
Barry University Dwayne O. Andreas School of Law, Orlando, FL, USA
e-mail: tday@barry.edu

P. Ash et al. (eds.), *Malpractice and Liability in Psychiatry*, https://doi.org/10.1007/978-3-030-91975-7_10

may not have considered, or lead to follow-up questions that provide more information than would have originally been discovered (Hoffman et al., 2005; Knoll & Resnick, 2008; Feld & Moses, 2009; Shah et al., 2016). Therefore, it is important to try to avoid "gamesmanship" or try to outdo the opposing council in a deposition (Reid, 2006). Although the defendant psychiatrist is an educated doctor, the lawyer is much more knowledgeable and comfortable in the legal setting. In addition, the defendant doctor should not take the questions or the tone personally (Reid, 2006). Often, being overly emotional or needing to "win" results in testimony of poorer quality (Lundy & Teuscher, 2013).

Once deposition testimony is given, it cannot be altered at trial. If a defendant gives conflicting testimony between deposition and trial statements, the plaintiff is allowed to use the deposition transcript to "impeach" the witness at trial (Knoll & Resnick, 2008; Gutheil, 2012). However, further explanation or a more in-depth response to a deposition answer is possible at trial, as long as the trial testimony does not contradict the original statements made during a deposition. Therefore, brief answers during deposition are usually more helpful than harmful if a case does go to trial.

There is a general structure and progression of the questions in depositions (background of the defendant, linear questions related to treatment, follow-up or clarification); however, attorneys are not required to follow this pattern (Gutheil, 2012). Some attorneys intentionally change the format in order to confuse the defendant (Knoll & Resnick, 2008; Gutheil, 2012). For example, attorneys may ask three or four questions related to one topic, then switch to another, and then switch back to the original topic. Although this can happen in depositions, it is less likely during a trial where the attorney must be careful not to lose the jury.

A defendant psychiatrist is most likely a *fact* witness. Therefore, the psychiatrist should not serve as their own expert witness since that would allow the plaintiff's attorney more latitude in asking questions (Rich, 2006). As a fact witness, a psychiatrist should limit testimony to only what he or she knows personally and recollects from medical charts or what standard practices are commonly used with their patients (Hoffman et al., 2005; Williams, 2008). When asked questions, the psychiatrist should listen carefully to the entire question and answer only the question asked (Hoffman et al., 2005; Rich, 2006; Williams, 2008). The witness should not answer anticipated "future" questions until they are asked (Hoffman et al., 2005).

Depositions are often very stressful, can last for hours, and can be physically and emotionally draining (Hoffman et al., 2005; Knoll & Resnick, 2008; Gutheil, 2012). Plaintiffs' attorneys are aware of this and sometimes try to use this to their advantage. Skilled attorneys may be able to complete a deposition within 2 to 3 hours (Knoll and Resnick 2008). However, some attorneys may draw out depositions, believing that the longer they go and the more fatigued a defendant becomes, the higher the likelihood that the defendant will reveal new information or agree to inaccurate statements. Deponents should ask for breaks when needed, but a break may not be taken when a question is pending (Hoffman et al., 2005; Knoll & Resnick, 2008; Gutheil, 2012).

It is often best to schedule the deposition in the morning with the assumption that it will take all day (Knoll & Resnick, 2008). If the deposition is at the end of the clinical workday, the deponent will likely be more fatigued. Additionally, patients should not be scheduled after a deposition as this may add additional stress or a sense of urgency to the proceedings if the deposition runs long or starts late.

At the end of a deposition, the psychiatrist will be asked whether he or she wants to read the transcript or waive that opportunity. It is generally recommended that the transcript be read (Solle, 2001; Knoll & Resnick, 2008; Gutheil, 2012). This way, minor typographical errors can be corrected. Although major errors also can be addressed, attempting to correct them post-deposition can lead to a request for additional depositions or be heavily scrutinized at trial (Solle, 2001; Knoll & Resnick, 2008). Also, before trial testimony, it is important to review the deposition transcript, since it may be months to years between deposition and court testimony (Zane, 2009).

Preparing for a Deposition

Prior to giving a deposition, the defendants should consult with their lawyer and prepare what to bring to the deposition (Soller, 2001; Knoll & Resnick, 2008; Vandercar & Resnick, 2020). Conversations or information shared between defendant psychiatrists and their representing attorney may be protected by attorney-client privilege, thereby prohibited from compelled disclosure (Hoffman et al., 2005). In a deposition, if questions are likely to violate this privilege, the attorney will often object by asserting such privilege. The psychiatrist may also want to ask the attorney if outside medical literature should be reviewed in preparation for the deposition. If medical literature is reviewed, the deponent could be questioned about it. However, if a literature review was completed to better prepare the attorney for the case, such a review could be covered under attorney-client privilege (Hoffman et al., 2005; Feld & Moses, 2009; Williams, 2008). Counsel can best advise on how best to answer that question if it comes up during a deposition.

Attorneys will likely meet with defendant psychiatrists multiple times prior to a deposition (Hoffman et al., 2005). At these meetings, the attorney will review key issues, rules of the deposition, and what to expect from plaintiff's counsel. Mock questioning may be used to ensure the deponent understands what to expect (Knoll & Resnick, 2008;

Williams, 2008). The type of questions and style of the plaintiff's counsel during a deposition may differ from how they will behave at trial (see Table 10.1). Once the deposition starts, the defense attorney will have little opportunity to guide the deponent on how to answer a question (Williams, 2008). However, actively listening to the objections raised by the defense attorney may reveal a concern over what is being asked (Hoffman et al., 2005).

Defense attorneys are not supposed to argue their objections (on or off the record) at a deposition. This is often referred to as "speaking objections," a legal term for an objection that contains more information than needed. Whether an objection is a speaking objection or utilizes a standard term to identify a type of objection (e.g., "Objection. Speculation"), the deponent should always pay close attention to the question asked when an objection is made (Table 10.2) (Hoffman et al., 2005; Gutheil, 2012). Of note, some attorneys object more than others and the number of objections depends on the situation; hence, the deponent should not read anything into their performance based on the number of objections made.

During meetings with the attorney, he or she will advise about issues that may be important for the case, and how certain words may be more relevant (Knoll & Resnick, 2008). For example, it is not uncommon in everyday situations for people to say they are "sorry" (e.g., "sorry to hear that"). However, in a legal context, the use of the word "sorry" may be construed as admitting guilt or responsibility for an outcome (Feld & Moses, 2009; Shah et al., 2016). One may "regret" a negative outcome and express empathy/sympathy for the plaintiff's situation even though he does not feel responsible for the outcome (Feld & Moses, 2009).

Before a deposition, it is important for the psychiatrist to review the medical chart thoroughly (Reid, 2006). Although depositions are not a memory test, detailed knowledge can be very helpful (e.g., treatment plan, medications prescribed, differential diagnosis, important lab values) (Reid, 2006; Knoll & Resnick, 2008; Lundy & Teuscher, 2013). This helps to prevent simple errors, reduce the chance of becoming flustered during questioning, and also make the defendant look like somebody who would be prepared if he had to testify in front of a jury (Hoffman et al., 2005). Even with good preparation, mistakes can occur, such as giving the wrong date or remembering an event out of order. Factual errors of this nature in a deposition rarely benefit any party. Your counsel may try to clarify or even the plaintiff's counsel may make an attempt to let you know of a legitimate error (e.g., "Doctor I propose to you the date might have been…").

Table 10.1 Potential plaintiff attorney styles (Solle, 2001; Hoffman et al., 2005; Knoll & Resnick, 2008; Gutheil, 2012)

Style	What to expect	Risks
"Joe Friday" after the old television show *Dragnet*	Professional, but wants "just the facts"; usually efficient deposition without a lot of emotion	Is anticlimactic and can result in rushed answers without taking time to weigh responses appropriately
Bully	Very angry and accusatory leading to an emotional and dysphoric experience; may focus on minor issues or editorialize to intimidate or distract from weakness in own case	Due to feeling attacked, may come across as overly defensive; may become aggressive or angry in return
Monotone	Low energy attorney who goes slow and leaves a lot of time between a response and the next question	Risk of defendant losing attention to what is being asked, or talking too much in an effort to fill space or speed things along
Friendly	Appears very civil and almost understanding of defendant; is generally polite and may engage in conversation outside the formal deposition	May result in testimony that is too casual, resulting in answers that provide more information than needed; nothing is truly off the record
Collegial or professorial	General low pressure but comes across as knowing more than the defendant	Defendant provides lengthy answers to try to show he is the professorial equal to the learned attorney and may provide too much information
Clueless or disorganized	Does not seem well prepared and asks questions that seem unfocused; this may be a ploy or the attorney may really be this disorganized	Defendant talks too much to try to educate the opposing counselor or identifies key points for the counselor to move the deposition along
Controlling but not an outward bully	Tries to be the alpha in the room by controlling everyone else (e.g., where people sit, when breaks are taken, control of exhibits and records, educating your attorney about the law and procedural rules)	If defendant sees the attorney as an authority in control, the defendant may start to question his own attorney's abilities, be less likely to defend him or herself against some of the attorney's more pointed questions, or may be provoked into confrontation that makes the defendant look out of control compared to the calm, confident, and controlled demeanor of the attorney
Mixed	May begin with style like "Joe Friday," becomes a "bully," then reverts to "Joe Friday" or controlling	Keeps the defendant off guard and can result in overly defensive testimony and points of hostility; often results in defendant having testimony set in stone, in the worst ways if done effectively

Table 10.2 Examples of common types of objections, what they mean, and what to remember to testify effectively (Hoffman et al., 2005)

Objections	What to keep in mind
Attorney-client privilege: relies on information or discussions you had with your attorney	Wait for your attorney to instruct whether to answer; one of the few times where a deponent may not answer after an objection is made in a deposition
Leading: suggest an answer not allowed in direct exam that may be allowed in cross-examinations	Make sure not to endorse something that is not factual or accurate
Compound: multiple questions linked by "and" or "or"	Answer each question separately; avoid giving a blanket "yes" or "no" for both questions
Argumentative: question is overly aggressive, directly arguing with the witness, or badgering	This is often the defense attorney trying to make sure the situation does not get out of control; deponent should refocus, take a deep breath, and stay in control
Asked and answered: same question asked again and again	Be aware that the opposing attorney is trying to get a different response by repeating the same question multiple times; deponent should stay consistent, even if different verbiage is used
Vague: question asked does not have enough specifics for witness to understand what is being asked (e.g., which admission to a hospital since there are several)	Pay attention to what exact event or time period is being asked about; avoid an overly broad response; ask for clarification about what specifically is being asked
Nonresponsive answer: question asked is not what the witness is discussing	At times deponent may misunderstand a question or answer the question he or she wished were asked; pay close attention to the question and, if needed, explain how answer is related to the question asked
Form: plaintiff's attorney may ask defense to only object to "form of the question" to reduce the potential for coaching the witness. Form implies the attorney believes there is some "form" of error in the question	Listen closely to the question, make sure the statements in it are correct, that it is not calling for speculation, and not bringing in facts that are not part of the cases
Relevance: irrelevant information is being brought up or asked about	Plaintiff's attorney may be looking for information to bring others into the suit, use testimony against others, or trying to bring facts into the case to potentially impugn character or make defendant look bad later in front of a jury
Lacks foundation: rules of a deposition require that certain facts must be established first before a later question is asked (e.g., need to know someone was in a room before asking what happened in the room)	Usually a technical issue just to make sure that the deponent has knowledge about the question being asked and how that knowledge was obtained
Speculation: lacks personal knowledge	Refocus on the exact question asked and avoid guessing

If you did make a mistake earlier in your deposition which you later recognize, it is often best to correct it during the deposition if possible.

Etiquette and Demeanor During a Deposition

A deposition is not a normal social interaction (Soller, 2001, Gutheil, 2012). Although it is important to be professional, one does not have to engage in certain courtesies that normally would be expected in a typical social environment. For example, it is acceptable and appropriate if done in a truthful manner to disagree (e.g., "Would you agree doctor?… No, I would not."), to reject compromise or middle ground ("Do you think that view is extreme or too one sided?… No, I do not."), and to state the information as you believe it to be (Solle, 2001; Knoll & Resnick, 2008). This is not a sign of being rude, but an integral part of the formal fact-finding process. What is most important is that deponents are clear in conveying their statements (Gutheil, 2012). The use of humor during a deposition may be misconstrued or potentially used against the defendant (e.g., "Doctor, this is a serious matter, and you are making jokes.") (Knoll & Resnick, 2008). Additionally, when testifying, a defendant should not editorialize on how unfair the lawsuit is or how ungrateful the plaintiff is (Brodsky et al., 2017). It is also important not to overstate one's virtues or to get argumentative with the plaintiff's attorney (Knoll & Resnick, 2008; Vandercar & Resnick 2020).

A general rule for depositions and trial testimony is that only one person should talk at a time (Gutheil, 2012). A defendant should wait for the plaintiff's attorney to finish his question completely before answering (Knoll & Resnick, 2008; Gutheil, 2012). Also, the defendant may reflect after the question is finished before speaking. The slow speed and breaks make it easier for the court reporter to obtain a clean record (Gutheil, 2012), and the brief pause before answering allows the defendant time to compose thoughts and allows time for the defense attorney to object (Knoll & Resnick, 2008; Shah et al., 2016). The slow answering also allows the defendant some control over the pacing of the questions and reduces the risk of accidently agreeing to something untrue (e.g., answering too quickly to rapid-fire questioning, continuing to answering yes after a string of methodical yes answers) (Knoll and Resnick, 2008; Brodsky et al., 2017). In general, haste makes waste, and although many defendants want to get a deposition over as quickly as possible, it is best to take one's time.

Normally in a deposition, the deponent should make eye contact with the attorney who is deposing. However, if the deposition is videotaped, it is recommended that the deponent look directly into the camera and treat deposition testimony as if it were courtroom testimony (Knoll & Resnick, 2008). Speaking directly to the jury is always preferred, and in video depositions, the camera is the jury's surrogate (Prevatt et al., 2007; Knoll & Resnick, 2008; Gutheil, 2012). Along those lines, it is important to dress professionally for a deposition whether being video recorded or not. It is not uncommon for physicians to wear court attire during a deposition, even though the attorney may be dressed more casually (Prevatt et al., 2007).

If the attorneys engage in a legal discussion, it is best for the defendant to sit quietly and let the lawyers resolve the issue on their own (Hoffman et al., 2005; Gutheil, 2012). During a deposition, if a question is answered, it is assumed that it was understood. If a question is not understood, the deponent can request the question be repeated, clarified, or restated (Soller, 2001; Hoffman et al., 2005; Williams, 2008). If an objection is raised, unless instructed by the defense attorney not to answer a question, the defendant should answer the question. Finally, only the attorneys may object to the questions asked; the psychiatrist may not object.

In depositions, it is generally good advice to avoid protestations of honesty (e.g., "to tell the truth…", "honestly…") (Gutheil, 2012). In addition, answering questions with absolute words like "always" or "never" should generally be avoided (Knoll & Resnick, 2008). There are very few, if any, "always" or "never" situations in medicine; however, there may be a lot of "my standard practice is…."

If the plaintiff attends the deposition, the deponent should be polite but not engage the plaintiff in conversation (Lundy & Teuscher, 2013). When answering questions, the deponent should either address the plaintiff's counsel or the video camera but not the plaintiff. The deposition begins the moment a deponent walks into the room and ends when he or she leaves the building. There may be times where the psychiatrist is off the record, but always being observed by the plaintiff's attorney (Knoll & Resnick, 2008). The impression a deponent makes may be as important as his or her answers in determining if the case does go to trial (Knoll & Resnick, 2008).

Potential Types of Questions and How to Answer

In a defendant's deposition, the plaintiff's attorney often starts with the defendant's educational background and employment history. Counsel may ask questions such as "have you ever lost hospital privileges or failed a board exam?" (see Table 10.3). The deponent should answer these

Table 10.3 Potential deposition questions (Hoffman et al., 2005; Knoll & Resnick 2008, Gutheil, 2012)

Basic questions about your background
Q. What did you do to prepare for this deposition?
Q. Have you discussed this case with anyone else besides your attorney?
Q. Ever lost privileges at a hospital or had a disciplinary action?
Q. Ever had a complaint filed with a state board of medicine?
Q. Ever arrested or convicted of a felony?
Q. Ever been named in a malpractice suit before?
Q. What is your educational background?
Q. Have you ever failed a board certification exam?
Q. Name places you have worked or titles you have held?
Q. Have you had any [other] patients commit suicide (suicide frequent basis of suit)?
Basic questions for an event-based suit
Q. Do you have an independent memory of this patient and/or event? (Deposition may be years after the event and deponent may or may not remember the patient except for what is in notes.)
Q. When did you first meet the plaintiff?
Q. How did you come to be taking care of the plaintiff (covering for another physician, consulted, outpatient treatment relationship)?
Q. What was the diagnosis?
Q. What are the diagnostic criteria for that condition?
Q. What was the treatment (e.g., depending on records and degree of documentation, question may go more or less in-depth regarding treatment)?
Q. Anyone you consulted with or discussed care with?
Q. I don't see that in your notes. Where are you getting that from?
Examples of "gotcha"/stress questions
Q. Have you ever told a lie, doctor? A. I think we all have told a lie at some point (Answering "no" sets you up to be questioned on virtue; after all, questions like this are used in standardized testing to measure validity.)
Q. Are you ever wrong doctor? A. Yes (If you answer "no," often lawyer will point out that no one is infallible and that you have unrealistic expectations of your abilities.) Q. Could you be wrong here Doctor? A. No, because of X, Y, and Z
Q. What professional associations do you belong to doctor? (Is a way to bring up guidelines to try and show deviation from standard of care from an organization you belong to. Although it is good to belong to organized medical groups, no association's views are 100% accepted by all physicians, and guidelines are just that guidelines, not standard of care treatises.)
Q. Do you know or follow the ethical codes of these professional organizations? (No one has these memorized, so be careful on what you agree to because lawyers may read parts of the codes out of context or omit words.)
Q. What journals do you read or what texts do you identify as authoritative? (No journal or text is authoritative since new information is constantly coming out.)
Q. Would you not agree doctor that…? Or: The truth is Doctor…? (These question prompts are often designed to lock a doctor's testimony in or to put them on the defensive. Remember it is *ok* to say "no.")
Q. Looking back would you have done things differently? (Question often helps to identify the weaknesses you see in your own case.)

(continued)

Table 10.3 (continued)

Q. Is there anything else you "should have" done? ("Should-have" statements often speak directly to the issue of the suit so always answer those questions carefully.)
Q. So are you saying it is impossible…? (Often it is best to say "something was not probable" rather than impossible.)
Q. Is there anything else relevant to this case or that you remember that we have not discussed? (Although this may be a fair standard question, it is also somewhat of a "gotcha" question since it may lead you to reveal more than needed. You want to talk with your attorney during deposition preparation on how best to respond. Remember, it is not your job to do the other counsel's work and a reasonable response is "That is all that I can recall at this time.")
Q. Doctor what is your opinion regarding… future treatment needed? A codefendant? Or some other question… (You are likely a fact witness so you should not be giving opinions. Your lawyer will likely object. If you need to give an answer, it is again acceptable to state: "I do not have an opinion." It may be a question you have not considered; therefore, you have not formed an opinion, or you do not have enough current information to form an opinion in good faith.)
Q. Hypothetically Doctor… (Again, you are a fact witness; it is not your realm to enter into hypothetical questions. Your lawyer will likely object. If you do have to answer a hypothetical question, qualify that it does not necessarily fit with the fact pattern of the case if that is true.)
Q. With all your training and knowledge, you don't know or have an answer Doctor? (This type of question begins to border on badgering the witness; so, wait to see if your attorney objects. In addition, this question is designed to elicit an emotional response such as anger or shame. Do not take the bait.)

questions with a "yes" or "no" response and keep follow-up answers brief. The scope of questioning in a deposition is usually broader than at trial, meaning attorneys may ask deponents for information that would be inadmissible at trial. It is not uncommon for attorneys to ask questions, such as "Have you ever been convicted of a crime or been sanctioned for dishonest behavior?" A deponent should not take these questions personally. Some of these questions, even the ones that may seem attacking or inflammatory, are actually common questions. These types of questions are akin to questions psychiatrists frequently ask during an evaluation such as "Do you use recreational drugs?" In addition, another basic question often asked is who else the defendant has had conversations with regarding the case. Realize that any names provided may result in those individuals being deposed and could jeopardize aspects of attorney-client privilege (Feld & Moses, 2009).

If there is a question that the deponent does not know the answer to, the deponent should not speculate, make assumptions, or guess (Solle, 2001; Gutheil, 2012). "I don't know" or "I don't recall" is not a bad answer and is preferable over speculating or saying something incorrect (Hoffman et al., 2005; Williams, 2008; Gutheil, 2012; Brodsky et al., 2017). Speculative answers may be interpreted in ways not intended and can lead to questioning that the defendant is not prepared to answer. However, it is acceptable to acknowledge that certain statements are "within my best recollection" or "not as I recall" (Knoll & Resnick, 2008). In addition, the deponent should acknowledge obvious points (Knoll & Resnick, 2008; Gutheil, 2012). Although admitting a fact that is not necessarily supportive of the defense's case seems to be going against one's own self-interest, trying too hard to deflect or obfuscate may make the questioning worse and create an impression of being overly defensive or dishonest (Brodsky et al., 2017).

When answering questions, deponents should give clear audible answers such as "yes" or "no" and avoid saying "uh-huh" or "unh-uh" or nodding their head (Gutheil, 2012). Although these are common expressions in regular speech, it is hard to understand their meaning in a written deposition transcript. It is also difficult for court reporters to accurately record gestures, movements, or distance descriptions (e.g., "yay big" [holding up hands] or "It was from here to the door") (Hoffman et al., 2005).

Attorneys may ask doctors to limit responses to just "yes" or "no" answers. Whether this is permissible may depend on the jurisdiction, as well as the defense attorney's desire to be confrontational (Knoll & Resnick, 2008; Williams, 2008). These questions may not necessarily fully encapsulate all aspects of the case. In this situation, the deponent should not be defensive and just answer the question "yes" or "no," or "I can't answer that 'yes' or 'no'" or add the qualifier "with qualification" or "with explanation" (Knoll & Resnick, 2008; Williams, 2008). This allows further explanation or at least alerts the defense attorney that there is additional information or a different full answer to the question.

When asked to comment on a note or document, the deponent should ask to read the document to refresh his or her memory (Solle, 2001; Knoll & Resnick, 2008; Gutheil, 2012). Also, note that plaintiff's attorney can ask the deponent to read a sentence into the record. It may be worthwhile to go back at least two or three prior sentences, if not the entire page, just to make sure you have the full context of the sentence within the document (Knoll & Resnick, 2008). Putting the entire sentence into context may prevent a single sentence from being used to potentially impeach the defendant at trial. Finally, a deponent should take time to look up information in the chart or reread a section in order to best answer a question (Knoll & Resnick, 2008).

There is an adage in lawsuits that if it is not written down, it did not happen. Even the best documentation at times may miss a point. Although it may not be written down, one can always comment on one's usual practice or on information for which the deponent has independent memory. The defendant just needs to be ready for questions to clarify how he or she remembers that one point or if standard practice explains why the information is not in the notes. In general, clinical notes are a tool to help document the treatment of a patient and inform the treatment staff of information of significance or events that have occurred. As such they are not a transcript of every action said or done.

As a general concept, in testimony, if the deponent identifies "definitive" texts, these texts can be used in cross-examination. Although there may be prestigious textbooks that are recognized as informative, in general medical textbooks are not considered definitive or authoritative because their information often lags 2–3 years behind current journal publications. No article or journal is definitive in the sense that research is ongoing, conflicting studies exist, and even well-respected journals can publish a bad article. For example, *The Lancet* had to retract an article written by Dr. Benjamin Wakefield 12 years after it was published that concluded vaccines caused autism (Lancet, 2010).

A psychiatrist under oath in a deposition is expected to answer questions honestly. The attorney asking the questions, however, is not. Although most attorneys refrain from dishonest or "massive distortions" as part of their questioning styles during a deposition, some will not (Gutheil, 2012). With adequate preparation and confidence, even this worst-case scenario can be dealt with in a controlled and effective manner.

Trial Testimony

When preparing for trial testimony, the deponent should be well rested. A psychiatrist/witness may not be able to give effective testimony if he or she is run down or sleep-deprived (Reid, 2006). When it comes to trial preparation, the defendant will not likely meet with the defense expert ahead of time. Most experts do not want to meet or directly communicate with the defendant because they do not want to give the impression that they are biased or influenced by a personal relationship (Hoffman et al., 2005). Defendants should understand that they have already communicated with their experts through their chart, through their deposition statements, and through their interactions with their attorneys. If there are specific points or questions that a defendant wants to ask the expert, often the defense attorney is the best conduit (Hoffman et al., 2005).

Once again, defendants need to review in detail the chart and their deposition transcript in preparation for trial (Hoffman et al., 2005). Like the deposition, there should be meetings with the attorney before the trial (Lundy & Teuscher, 2013). The defense attorney will likely review the questions that will be asked during his direct examination (Williams, 2008). Additionally, the defense attorney should also go over the questions opposing counsel is likely to ask during cross-examination. If there has been extensive pre-trial discovery, the defense attorney should have a good sense of the strengths and weaknesses of plaintiff's case and be able to anticipate the line of questioning on cross-examination. Once the trial is underway, the defense attorney will be managing multiple issues (e.g., experts, preparing for direct and cross-examinations, filing motions, etc.) and may not be as available as he or she was pre-trial. Therefore, it is advantageous to ask questions and prepare during pre-trial meetings (Williams, 2008).

The defendant should be present for the full length of the trial (Prevatt et al., 2007; Williams, 2008; Feld & Moses, 2009). Even though the defendant may only testify for a few hours, the jury will be able to observe the defendant throughout the duration of the trial (Lundy & Teuscher, 2013). Therefore, it is important for the defendant to maintain professional dress and positive demeanor and not appear angry. In general, most individuals perceive doctors as healers who have undergone significant training and intend to help their patients (Williams, 2008). However, a hostile-appearing defendant may undermine the generally neutral-to-positive view the jurors hold for the profession.

A trial has a usual pattern with the plaintiff going first and then the defense (Vandercar & Resnick, 2020). There is no constitutional right for the defendant to remain silent or refuse to be cross-examined in a civil proceeding. The plaintiff's attorney can ask the defendant all questions that are deemed relevant and not overly prejudicial to the case (Williams, 2008). The judge decides what is relevant based on the rules of evidence (Bookman & Zane, 2020). Both attorneys may make objections to questions they believe violate the evidentiary rules. However, unlike in the deposition, the defendant should not answer a question until the judge has made a decision to sustain (agreed with the objection) or to overrule (disagree with the objection) an objection. If a witness is not sure if he or she should answer, the judge may be respectfully asked for clarification.

The style of testimony at trial may be somewhat different from the deposition (Gutheil, 2012). In court, the defendant will want to come across as relatable. There should be eye contact with the jury when answering questions, and explanations should not contain jargon or complicated medical terminology that is not easily understood (Shah et al., 2016; Brodsky et al., 2017). Much like the deposition, a witness should take time, listen closely to the questions, pay attention to objections, and try to be consistent with the answers given during deposition. If there are huge variations, the plaintiff's attorney may refer to parts of the deposition to challenge the defendant or to make it look like the defendant changed his or her testimony (Hoffman et al., 2005; Gutheil, 2012). It is important to have faith in the defense attorney and trust that he or she can rehabilitate and redirect if a mistake was made during the cross-examination (Brodsky et al., 2017; Vandercar & Resnick, 2020).

Occasionally, if there is a disagreement between the attorneys, a sidebar may occur – where the attorneys go up and speak to the judge. A white noise machine is often used, which prevents the jury or the witness from hearing what is being discussed. If such an event occurs, remain calm and professional, remember the jury is observing you, and try to have a positive, relaxed demeanor.

Conclusion

In conclusion, there are three forms of testimony. One is the written responses to interrogatories where your attorney will often assist you. The second, and perhaps most important, is the deposition where a deponent should stay brief in responding and know the medical record well. Although most cases resolve after the deposition, in rare incidences cases do go to a full trial. While there are slight variations in style between deposition testimony and trial testimony, overall content needs to remain consistent. It is the defense psychiatrist who is in the best position to give a factual account of what occurred.

Key Points

- There are three types of testimony in a malpractice action: interrogatories, depositions, and trial testimony.
- The most common advice attorneys give regarding deposition testimony is to give brief, clear, and truthful answers, and avoid volunteering information.
- Deponents should review all records carefully and meet with the defense attorney prior to a deposition.
- The ABCs of testifying are A, Answer Honestly; B, Be Brief (especially during a deposition); and C, Remain in Control, Classy, and Clear.
- During depositions and trial testimony, it is important that only one person talk at a time.
- If a defendant gives conflicting testimony between his deposition and trial statements, the plaintiff is allowed to use the deposition transcript to "impeach" the witness at trial.
- During trial, it is important for the defendant to maintain professional dress and positive demeanor and not appear angry.

References

Bookman, K., & Zane, R. D. (2020). Surviving a medical malpractice lawsuit. *Emergency Medicine Clinics of North America, 38*(2), 539–548.

Brodsky, S. L., Dvoskin, J. A., & Neal, T. (2017). Temptations for the expert witness. *The Journal of the American Academy of Psychiatry and the Law, 45*(4), 460–463.

Feld, A. D., & Moses, R. E. (2009). Most doctors win: What to do if sued for medical malpractice. *The American Journal of Gastroenterology, 104*(6), 1346–1351.

Gutheil, T. G. (2012). Deposition dos and don'ts: Strategies for the expert witness. *The Psychiatric Clinics of North America, 35*(4), 947–956.

Hoffman, P. J., Plump, J. D., & Courtney, M. A. (2005). The defense counsel's perspective. *Clinical Orthopaedics and Related Research, 433*, 15–25.

Knoll, J., & Resnick, P. (2008). Deposition dos and don'ts: How to answer 8 tricky questions. You must tell the truth, but you can answer honestly without hurting your case. *Curr Psychiatry, 7*(3), 25–28, 36, 39–40.

Lundy, D. W., & Teuscher, D. D. (2013). Surviving and winning a professional negligence lawsuit. *Instructional Course Lectures, 62*, 595–601.

Prevatt, H. A., Sturgill, T. C., Jr., Austin, J. B., Seif, E. R., & Schwartz, R. W. (2007). Anatomy of a malpractice lawsuit. *Surgical Innovation, 14*(1), 62–64.

Reid, W. H. (2006). When clinicians must testify in court. *Journal of Psychiatric Practice, 12*(3), 176–179.

(2010). Retraction--Ileal-lymphoid-nodular hyperplasia, non-specific colitis, and pervasive developmental disorder in children. *Lancet (London, England), 375*(9713), 445.

Rich, B. A. (2006). The treating physician as expert witness: Ethical and pragmatic considerations. *Pain Medicine (Malden, Mass.), 7*(5), 460–463.

Shah, V. V., Kapp, M. B., & Wolverton, S. E. (2016). Medical malpractice in dermatology-part II: What to do once you have been served with a lawsuit. *American Journal of Clinical Dermatology, 17*(6), 601–607.

Soller, I. (2001). Legal testimony: The dos and don'ts. *Biomedical Instrumentation & Technology, 35*(1), 61–63.

Vandercar, A., & Resnick, P. (2020). Tips for testifying in court. *Psychiatric Times.* https://www.psychiatrictimes.com/view/tips-for-testifying-in-court?utm_source=sfmc&utm_medium=email&utm_campaign=10062020_PT_CAL-20-PSD0035_WRS-19-CBD0062__Reg%20Sched_CA%20Correctional%20Health_WRS&eKey=c3R6dWNob0BnbWFpbC5jb20=. Accessed 7 Oct 2020.

Whitmore, M. R. (2005). Help! I've been sued: A guide to surviving a physician's nightmare. *Minnesota Medicine, 88*(6), 40–41.

Williams, E. J. (2008). Managing a lawsuit if all else fails. *Clinical Obstetrics and Gynecology, 51*(4), 731–739.

Zane, R. D. (2009). The legal process. *Emergency Medicine Clinics of North America, 27*(4), 583–592.

The Stress of Being Sued

11

Jeffrey L. Metzner and Michael H. Gendel

Psychiatrists are the least likely of medical specialists to get sued and statistically are likely to prevail at trial (Jena et al., 2011). However, the stress associated with being a defendant in a malpractice suit is significant. Malpractice stress is one of two well-described work stress syndromes, the other being burnout; they are not mutually exclusive. Being sued can be one of the most devastating experiences for physicians in their career (Gendel, 2015). There are specific characteristics of malpractice stress, ways to conceptualize it, and approaches to managing it.

Charles et al. (1988) reported that 97% of 64 responding physicians, none of whom were psychiatrists, experienced physical and/or emotional reactions in response to being sued for malpractice. Charles et al. (1984) surveyed 450 physicians sued for malpractice and identified three symptom clusters that developed among these physicians in response to the litigation. Their findings suggested several response patters to litigation: (1) a possible major depressive disorder; (2) an adjustment disorder with symptoms of pervasive anger associated with affective symptoms, frustration, fatigue, insomnia, GI symptoms, and/or headache; and (3) onset or an exacerbation of physical illness. Additional findings included alteration of certain aspects of their medical practice in response to the litigation, such as practicing defensively or choosing not to see or treat patients who may represent a higher risk of a poor outcome, or who seem "litigious." Many respondents also reported feelings of loneliness during the litigation process. This was likely related to shame or embarrassment about having been sued, resulting in a degree of social withdrawal, and to being told by their attorney that they should avoid discussing details with anyone. It should be noted that the above referenced studies were conducted before there was much understanding of the nature and significant emotional effects of occupation stress itself, even absent a clear psychiatric diagnosis.

Litigation-related stress has been referred to as medical malpractice stress syndrome (MMSS). The primary manifestations of MSSS are psychological symptoms (e.g., anxiety and depression) and physical symptoms related to stress (Sanbar & Firestone, 2007). Psychological symptoms may include excessive worrying, fatigue, concentration impairment, insomnia, and irritability. Rumination about the case may be very disruptive. Anxiety may be triggered by nothing more than seeing a letter with the opposing attorney's letterhead. Guilt and decreased self-esteem, even in the absence of medical wrongdoing, are common. Some physicians feel that when they visit their lawyer's office that the attorney's staff "know" that they are a bad doctor. Anger may be demonstrated by anger outbursts, feelings of bitterness, and/or frustration. Feelings of isolation are also commonly reported (Andrew & Pfifferling, 2015). However, not every physician who is sued for malpractice experiences severe stress.

Multiple factors contribute to MMSS, including the personality characteristics of physicians and the nature of tort law. Doubt, guilt feelings, and an exaggerated sense of responsibility form a compulsive triad in the personality of the physician (Gabbard, 1985), which creates a vulnerability to developing MSSS. The litigation process, which is based on the plaintiff attempting to establish that the doctor was at fault, and failing to meet the standard of care and causing damage, can cause self-doubt, guilt, and feeling responsible even when there was no substandard care. Other factors contributing to the physician's reactive stress include the nature of the relationship between the physician and patient, the nature of the patient's alleged injury, and the potential or actual publicity generated by the allegations (Charles, 2001).

Being competent and helpful to patients is key to a physician's identity. A malpractice suit attacks one's professional integrity and self-perception of being a competent and well-

J. L. Metzner (✉)
Department of Psychiatry, University of Colorado School of Medicine, Denver, CO, USA
e-mail: jeffrey.metzner@cuanschutz.edu

M. H. Gendel
Department of Psychiatry, University of Colorado School of Medicine, Denver, CO, USA

Colorado Physician Health Program, Denver, CO, USA

P. Ash et al. (eds.), *Malpractice and Liability in Psychiatry*, https://doi.org/10.1007/978-3-030-91975-7_11

respected physician, which can cause profound injury to identity. Despite being told by others that such litigation is an expected part of most medical practices and not to be taken personally, it is understandably perceived by the sued physician to be a very personal attack.

Another way to conceptualize why doctors are so vulnerable to litigation stress is to understand the nature of occupational stress generally. The foundation of occupational stress is twofold: high mental workload and diminished decision latitude (or autonomy). When sued, the defendant physician's mental workload escalates dramatically, reviewing every memory of the patient, every aspect of the case, and every note in the chart; considering all possibilities of what they might have done wrong; imagining what colleagues might think; and worrying what an expert or a jury might conclude. The sense of dread may be pervasive, taking much mental energy. Adding to this, decision latitude is minimal as the lawsuit is not a medical action and no amount of authority or power in the medical workplace will provide much control at all over the process because it is a legal action. Other dimensions contributing to occupational stress include biological vulnerability to stress reactions, preexisting physical or mental illness, the social setting of the matter (e.g., small town where many people know each other, prominence of the plaintiff or defendant) (Gendel, 1999), and the nature of the alleged patient injury (loss of life versus delayed recovery).

Common reasons for litigation against a psychiatrist are the suicide of a patient, an adverse medication reaction, and medical board complaints. While medication reactions can be serious, loss of life and potential loss of one's medical license are very serious matters. This means that the most common legal issues are by their nature those most like to cause maximum stress for psychiatrists.

Unlike in malpractice litigation, doctors are generally not advised to refrain from talking with others about medical board matters. Talking with colleagues allows the doctor to understand that these issues are common and usually leads to expressions of support for the competence and well-being of the doctor. This may prove difficult to do because shame and embarrassment may also accompany these matters. Support may not be forthcoming if the medical board matter is an emotional trigger, such as a sexual boundary allegation. In these cases, talking with one's own family may be helpful. Some physicians avoid this by telling themselves that they are protecting their spouse or other family members from worry about being able to make a living. This is almost always a rationalization borne of shame and embarrassment.

Medical board matters have complexities that require having an attorney with specific experience in that area. Referrals to such skilled attorneys can be obtained from one's malpractice carrier, colleagues, and the state's physician health program.

Part I: Understanding the Process of a Lawsuit and Vulnerabilities to Stress in Each Phase

The stress experienced by defendant physicians, especially if they have not previously been sued, is often exacerbated by unfamiliarity with the litigation process, having minimal control relevant to the timing of the process (e.g., discovery and trial dates being changed), and the nature of the adversarial process.

Becoming knowledgeable about the litigation process, which may last 1–5 years, is a key element of effectively managing the associated stress as is developing a support system throughout the process (see Chap. 6 for additional detail). The legal process can be characterized as involving the following four stages:

1. Receiving the complaint, which may have been preceded by a demand letter from the plaintiff's attorney
2. The discovery process
3. The trial
4. The appeals process

The Complaint

The complaint is a legal document filed with the court of appropriate jurisdiction that details the allegations of the physicians' negligence that led to the alleged damages to the patient. It may contain inaccurate information due to many reasons, which subsequently may be clarified during the discovery process that can lead to an amended complaint being filed. Receiving the complaint is often unexpected and a shock to the physician. Physicians often feel guilty and shameful after reading the complaint and thinking, retrospectively, that they had not met the standard of care with that particular patient. However, such thoughts should not be shared with others until meeting with their malpractice attorney because conversations with others about the allegations in the complaint may be discoverable by the plaintiff's attorney.

Physicians should immediately contact their malpractice carrier, which will then assign them an attorney who specializes in medical malpractice. Prior to being assigned an attorney, the physician may find it very helpful to consult with colleagues to suggest an attorney who specializes in malpractice cases and is known to them. The selection of an attorney is one of the four key factors in prevailing in a malpractice suit. In our opinion, in order to prevail, the following four factors are key in order of importance:

1. The members of the jury (i.e., jury selection)
2. The physician's attorney

3. The judge
4. The facts of the case

The physician should meet with the assigned attorney as soon as possible for many reasons, including becoming more informed of the subsequent process. One of the first actions of the attorney will be to take possession of the original patient's chart and provide the physician a copy. Most physicians will have reviewed the chart upon receipt of the complaint, often multiple times. The physician should not alter or post-date new entries in the patient's medical record because such entries will be eventually discovered by the plaintiff's counsel and will almost always be detrimental to their defense.

During the initial meeting with the attorney, physicians will learn more about their malpractice insurance, such as whether they have a choice to settle, which may impact whether an attorney hired by and paid for by the physician (in contrast to the attorney retained by the malpractice insurer) may also be needed. Initial discussion with the attorney regarding possible defense experts will occur. Consultation with colleagues may be helpful in choosing the defense experts. During this initial meeting, the physician should summarize the patient's course of treatment with a focus on the physician's response to the allegations included in the complaint, which will assist the attorney in the selection of the defense experts.

The attorney will clarify issues around discoverability of statements made to others regarding the litigation, which will help frame the structure for development of the physician's support system during the litigation process. The main support system for the physician will likely be their attorney, in addition to their spouse, related, in part, to such shared information not being discoverable. It is important to alert one's spouse and older children to the occurrence of the suit so that they can understand when the doctor appears stressed at times and can offer their support. Children may need reassurance that there is no danger of the doctor going to jail as a result of the lawsuit.

The Discovery Process

The discovery process is the longest stage of the litigation process. This pretrial procedure involves each party, through the law of civil procedure, obtaining evidence from the other party or parties by means of discovery mechanisms such as interrogatories, requests for production of documents, and requests for admissions and depositions. Interrogatories are written questions by each litigant to the other litigant(s) regarding relevant facts that result in written responses by the adversary. The answers may be used later at deposition or trial. Questions are frequently based on information documented in the medical records, but some questions inquire about the physician's background, finances, family matters, and professional associations. Depositions involve questions asked directly to the deponent by the other side's attorney, which is taken under oath and recorded by a court stenographer. Depositions may also be videotaped.

Expert witnesses provide deposition testimony related to the facts of the case and the relevant standard of care. The court, with input from the parties, will establish a scheduling order that addresses the length of the discovery process as well as the trial date. The activity during the discovery process waxes and wanes, which often results in the physician not feeling in control. Discovery deadlines often change as do scheduled trial dates.

The physician and the physician's expert witness(es) will assist the attorney in both formulating interrogatory questions and answers and helping the attorney formulate deposition questions. This process, based on experience, may help the physician gain some measure of control in the litigation process, which may decrease some MMSS symptoms (Halleck, 1983). However, the deposition process often exacerbates such symptoms due to the answers being provided by various deponents that are not consistent with the physician's memory, perceptions, and/or opinions. Depositions that are key include the deposition of the plaintiff patient (or in the case of suicide, the patient's family), the experts on both sides, and the defendant physician. The depositions of the plaintiff's expert and the patient are frequently distressing to the physician because they will result in information and/or opinions that are unfavorable to the defense.

Discussion with the physician's attorney should determine whether any deposition should be attended by the physician. It is not uncommon for the physician to painfully learn that various deponents (e.g., consultants used during the treatment of the patient) are not helpful, and at times are harmful, to their defense. The dynamics involved often include the consultants being concerned that they will become named defendants. Even when the plaintiff's expert has a good reputation based on publications and professional organization involvement, it is not uncommon to discover that their reputation is not consistent with their role as an objective expert witness. Based on experience, such a discovery often contributes to the development and/or exacerbation of MMSS.

The defendant physician's deposition is a crucial and very stressful event that requires extensive preparation by his or her attorney. The physician needs to be extremely familiar with the relevant patient's medical record and history with a laser focus on all notes written by the physician. Many physicians have little, if any, experience with the deposition process which may be very distressing to them as the attorneys voice objections on the record during the deposition and demonstrate hostile verbal interactions during the deposition that would not be tolerated in a courtroom setting with a judge present. The physician needs to be ready to address the allegations described in the complaint. It is common for the plaintiff patient to be present during the deposition, which often results in a very uncomfortable situation, especially when they react to the physician's answers to deposition questions.

The Trial

Prior to trial, the parties will engage in settlement discussions in an attempt to resolve the case either by a financial agreement or some other agreement. The physician may choose to settle the case to limit emotional distress or avoid a feared trial outcome. A trial is very stressful but time-limited. However, the ramifications of the trial's outcome may not be so time-limited, especially if it is a negative outcome for the physician, as malpractice payments are reported to the National Practitioner Data Bank and may follow the physician for years (National Practitioner Data Bank, 2020).

During the jury selection process, the physician learns that neither side wants an impartial jury but, instead, jurors partial to their side. During the trial, the physician will learn about the rules of evidence, which determine what evidence may be admitted during the trial. The crucial role of the judge will become more apparent as the judge interprets and applies the rules of evidence. It will become overtly obvious that the plaintiff's attorneys and experts are prepared and planning to attack the physician's credibility and medical competence in the context of the treatment provided to the plaintiff patient.

The trial process involves the following:

1. Pretrial motions
2. Jury selection
3. Opening statements
4. Plaintiff's presentation of their case via witnesses
5. Defendant's presentation of their case via witnesses
6. Closing arguments
7. Jury instructions
8. Jury deliberations
9. Verdict
10. Appeals process

The pretrial motions generally involve issues of admissibility of evidence that one side is disputing which is either relevant or not admissible for other reasons.

During jury selection, each side has the ability to exclude a set number of potential jurors without cause, although such exclusion is almost always based on a perception that the potential juror would not be favorable to the side excluding him or her. The physician will often feel distressed when the plaintiff's attorney excludes a juror who had been perceived to be favorable to the defendant physician.

Opening arguments are designed to allow each side, via statements by the attorneys, to familiarize the jury with the case and to provide a framework for what they will learn from the testifying witnesses. Opening arguments by the plaintiff's attorney may include statements that are either untrue or misleading, which provide another source of distress for the physician, especially when such statements are about the physician.

The plaintiff's attorney will then call witnesses in order to present the plaintiff's case. Cross-examination of the plaintiff's witnesses will demonstrate to the defendant physicians the critical role of their attorney. Related to decisions by the judge specific to admissibility of various statements by the witnesses and the changing and/or new testimony by various witnesses (when compared to their deposition testimony), it will become apparent the benefit of having an attorney who can "think on his or her feet" and rapidly adapt to changing circumstances.

Following completion of the plaintiff's case, the defendant's attorney will almost always make a motion for a directed verdict by the judge (in favor of the defense), which is rarely granted.

Physicians will begin to feel less distressed during the presentation of the defense's case although their testimony will be stressful, especially during the cross-examination phase. During this phase, the defense will present evidence via fact witnesses, expert witnesses, and the defendant physician. Even more important than the preparation for deposition will be the physician's preparation for both direct and cross-examination at trial. It is essential that the physician be completely familiar with the plaintiff's medical record, especially (but not exclusively) with the physician's progress notes.

Following completion of the defense case, the opposing attorneys will speak to the jury via closing arguments that attempts to summarize witness statements that were favorable to their side. The judge will then provide jury instructions that guide the jurors in their deliberations by helping them understand the specific legal issues and laws specific to the case in question, which will include the applicable proper burden of proof.

Specific Strategies for Reducing the Stress of the Legal Process and Increasing Resilience and Enhancing Self-Care

Reducing Stress of the Legal Process

Sued physicians should be as realistic as possible about the case rather than allowing themselves to be overrun by inaccurate cognitions based on self-doubt, guilt, and an exaggerated sense of responsibility so common among physicians (Gabbard, 1985; Gendel & Cooper, 2017). It is useful to conceptualize being sued and the effort to defend the case as being among the normal duties of the job. Reminding themselves of this, which may be necessary to do frequently, makes it a little easier to tolerate the pressure and less aggravating to spend the considerable time and energy required in helping with the defense. Talking openly with defense counsel about their doubts and fears will give the lawyer the ability to specifically address what is normal, what is likely, and what is extremely unlikely and simply a product of the doctor's fearful state of mind and inexperience of being sued (i.e., a cognitive distortion). The defense counsel is often the doctor's most important and effective social support system. It can be very helpful to ask their attorney what is worth worrying about, what it is best for the attorney to worry about, and what is not worth any worry at all. This potentially reduces mental workload. The corollary of this step is to ask one's attorney what one can do to help defend the case. In accepting such an assignment, the defendant doctor can reduce the sense of having no control or autonomy in the legal process, which also reduces stress.

If the defendant physician suffers from preexisting psychiatric illness or develops a diagnosable disorder (e.g., major depression, panic disorder) in the context of having been sued, it is essential that treatment for these conditions be as effective as possible. Alerting those treating the physician to the lawsuit and talking about any distress produced can go a long way to keeping the condition stable and reducing added stress. Ideally, those involved in the care of the doctor have experience in helping physicians through malpractice litigation. If looking for a referral of a clinician knowledgeable in this regard, obtaining a name from the defense attorney or from the state's Physician Health Program (PHP) can be helpful. Many PHPs provide direct help for those suffering from litigation stress and from psychiatric illness; therefore consulting with those organizations can provide major benefits (Gendel & Cooper, 2017). Similarly, many other kinds of medical conditions are subject to worsening due to stress. Those who suffer from these conditions should consult with their physicians about how to manage those conditions during the lawsuit.

Malpractice insurance companies have an interest in helping physicians with litigation stress because they recognize that such stress can negatively affect the sued physician's practice. They are concerned that under the pressures of a lawsuit doctors may be less nimble in their clinical reasoning, preoccupied by their worries, and less able to concentrate on current patients. Thus, they may be at risk for further malpractice litigation. As a result, many malpractice insurers offer support groups and other services that can help mitigate litigation stress. Some policies provide minimal wage replacements for the physician during the trial process. Physicians should learn about and take advantage of these options.

When a lawsuit is settled or adjudicated in court, or a medical board issue is resolved, sued physicians expect that if they prevail (or their settlement reflects a positive outcome) their stress level will be immediately reduced. This is almost never the case. Lawsuits often last years, even if the physician ultimately prevails. The stress of the litigation tends to become embedded in the everyday life of the sued doctor and does not simply dissipate with a favorable verdict. It often takes months or longer for physicians to return to a pre-lawsuit stress level, as they slowly begin to live life without constantly associating to their feeling of vulnerability. When the case is finally adjudicated, it is a time to speak to loved ones and colleagues about what they have been through and what residual stress the sued doctor continues to experience.

Increasing Resilience and Enhancing Self-Care

Activities that are not specific to managing litigation stress are also useful when coping with the stress of a lawsuit. The range of activities often captured by the phrase "self-care," always important to the well-being of doctors, becomes essential when under litigation stress. These include eating and sleeping well, exercising regularly, staying in close touch with friends and loved ones, sharing one's feelings and listening to others, taking time alone away from work, finding spiritual refreshment and renewal (spending time in nature, listening to music, meditating, praying and/or attending religious services, etc.), and avoiding excessive use of substances. Because of the danger of worry and rumination, learning and practicing a relaxation technique can be especially beneficial. Mindfulness and mindfulness meditation are easy to learn, help one focus on the present and clear one's mind, and can be practiced anywhere and almost any time. Other forms of meditation, progressive muscle relaxation, and a variety of "time-out" practices (moments of deep breathing, taking a minute of time out between activities, attending to muscle stiffness) are also helpful. There is much individual variation in what doctors may find relaxing or nourishing.

Conclusion

Malpractice litigation is often a very stressful and prolonged experience for the defendant physician, even when the ultimate legal outcome is favorable for the physician. Minimizing and managing litigation stress is facilitated by becoming knowledgeable about the litigation process and well prepared for the various phases of litigation. Developing a support system specific to the litigation and enhancing self-care will foster the physician's resilience during this difficult time.

Key Points

- A vast majority of physicians experience physical and/or emotional reactions in response to being sued for malpractice.
- Sued physicians are usually advised not to discuss the litigation with others, which may exacerbate a sense of litigation related loneliness and isolation and can lead to development of clinically significant anxiety and/or depression, as well as physical reactions.
- Becoming knowledgeable about the litigation process, which may last 1–5 years, is a key element of effectively managing the associated stress.
- The defense counsel is often the doctor's most important and effective social support system.
- The range of activities often captured by the phrase "self-care," always important to the well-being of doctors, becomes essential when under litigation stress.

References

Andrew, L., & Pfifferling, J-H. (2015). Managing medical malpractice stress. https://www.themphp.org/Archive/Articles/tabid/98/ArticleID/114/Managing-Medical-Malpractice-Stress-by-Louise-Andrew-MD-JD-and-John-Henry-Pfifferling-PhD.aspx. Accessed 25 Oct 2020.

Charles, S. C. (2001). Coping with a medical malpractice stress. *Western Journal of Medicine, 174*(1), 55–58.

Charles, S. C., Pyskoty, C. E., & Nelson, A. (1988). Physicians on trial-self-reported reactions to malpractice trials. *Western Journal of Medicine, 148*(3), 358–360.

Charles, S. C., Wilbert, M. A., & Kennedy, E. C. (1984). Physicians' self-report of reactions to malpractice litigation. *American Journal of Psychiatry, 141*(4), 563–565.

Gabbard, G. O. (1985). The role of compulsiveness in the normal physician. *Journal of the American Medical Association, 254*(20), 2926–2929.

Gendel, M. (2015). Malpractice stress. https://www.themphp.org/Arc,hive/Articles/tabid/98/ArticleID/220/Malpractice-Stress-by-Michael-H-Gendel-MD-Colorado-Physicians-Health-Program-Medical-Director-Emeritus.aspx. Accessed 25 Oct 2020.

Gendel, M. (1999). Assessment and Management of Physician Work Stress. *Directions in Psychiatry, 19*, 281–291.

Gendel, M., & Cooper, P. D. (2017). The law and the ill physician: Ill physicians. In R. Rosner & C. L. Scott (Eds.), *Principles and practice of forensic psychiatry* (3rd ed., pp. 203–211). CRC Press, Taylor and Francis Group.

Halleck, S. L. (1983). Malpractice in psychiatry. *Psychiatric Clinics of North America, 6*(4), 567–583.

Jena, A. B., Seabury, S., Lakdawakka, D., & Chandra, A. (2011). Malpractice risk according to physician specialty. *New England Journal of Medicine, 365*(7), 629–636.

National Practitioner Data Bank. (2020). *What is the NPDB?*. https://www.npdb.hrsa.gov/resources/whatIsTheNPDB.jsp. Accessed 4 Nov 2020.

Sanbar, S. S., & Firestone, M. H. (2007). Medical malpractice stress syndrome. In S. Sanbar (Ed.), *The medical malpractice survival handbook* (pp. 9–15). Mosby Elsevier.

Part III

Malpractice Allegations

Suicide

12

Debra A. Pinals and Peter Ash

National, comprehensive data on causes of action in malpractice cases are not available, but several recent studies suggest that suicide is the most common reason for a malpractice case against a psychiatrist, accounting for about a quarter of all claims (Frierson & Joshi, 2019; Medscape, 2020). There is no published data on how many claims also arise from serious suicide attempts leading to damages (e.g., paralysis, brain injury from anoxia) but not actual death. Appropriately assessing risk for suicide, taking steps to ameliorate the risk, and monitoring ongoing care are critical issues in managing the risk of being sued in the event of a patient's suicide attempt or actual suicide.

Legal Framework

The law considers the relationship between a doctor and a patient to be a special relationship. By engaging in this special relationship, the psychiatrist assumes a duty to meet the standard of care for preventing suicide. Since Pokorny's landmark study (1983), it has been generally recognized that prediction models based on risk factors are not sufficiently strong to be able to make an accurate prediction that a given patient will die by suicide (Belsher et al., 2019). Even in more recent studies that consider the use of artificial intelligence and machine learning to predict who might be at greater risk of suicide, there will still be a treating physician's individual assessment and management in a particular case (Bernert et al., 2020). Specifically, in a malpractice case involving a patient's suicide, the question turns on whether the particular suicide attempt or actual suicide was reasonably foreseeable and, if so, what steps the psychiatrist took to reduce the risk. There is no clear standard of care applicable to all cases: the standard varies depending on the legal jurisdiction and the details of the particular case (Obegi, 2017). Judgments as to whether the psychiatrist met the standard of care typically focus on three main steps: the assessment of risk, the treatment plan and safety plan implemented to ameliorate the risk, and the continuing monitoring of both risk and treatment efficacy.

Since suicide is, by definition, an intentional act, the patient had an active role in suicide, and therefore the question may arise as to how a psychiatrist can be held legally liable for a patient who took his or her own life. The psychiatrist, after all, is not the one who forces the overdose or shoots a gun at a patient. Some states have contributory negligence statutes or court precedents that take into account whether the patient was capable of following the doctor's instructions and, if so, the extent to which the patient's actions contributed to the bad outcome (Appelbaum, 2000). Other states do not have such statutes and assume that the special relationship confers the duty on the psychiatrist to prevent the action that leads to the damages, assuming the action (i.e., the suicide action) results from the illness the doctor is there to treat.

Epidemiology and Phenomenology of Suicide

Definitions of suicide and surrounding terms are important to distinguish. According to the National Institute of Mental Health (2021), suicide is "death caused by self-directed injurious behavior with any intent to die…," whereas a suicide attempt is "a non-fatal, self-directed, potentially injurious behavior with intent to die as a result of the behavior," and suicidal ideation refers to "thinking about, considering, or

D. A. Pinals
Program in Psychiatry, Law and Ethics, University of Michigan, Ann Arbor, MI, USA
e-mail: dpinals@med.umich.edu

P. Ash (✉)
Psychiatry and Law Service, Department of Psychiatry and Behavioral Sciences, Emory University, Atlanta, GA, USA
e-mail: peter.ash@emory.edu

P. Ash et al. (eds.), *Malpractice and Liability in Psychiatry*, https://doi.org/10.1007/978-3-030-91975-7_12

planning suicide." Given those definitions, although some people die by their own hand, not all self-inflicted deaths are suicides (Abiragi et al., 2020; Sorenson et al., 1997), and it is important in considering malpractice actions to ensure the establishment that the manner of death has been sufficiently determined. This is a complicated area of practice for medical examiners and may benefit from a psychological autopsy, but it may become a point of contention in responding to a malpractice complaint. In some malpractice cases, a manner of death listed to be "undetermined" may be treated as a suicide for the civil litigation and in these authors' experience may be accepted by both parties – or may be contested – as a suicide or a self-injurious action for the purpose of the plaintiff's complaints and the defendant's response.

According to the American Foundation for Suicide Prevention (2021), in 2019, 47,511 individuals in America died from suicide, and there were 1.38 million suicide attempts. Data from the Centers for Disease Control and Prevention (CDC) from 2019 show that suicide was the second leading cause of death after accidents for individuals age 10 to 34 and the fourth leading cause of death for individuals age 35 to 54 (Centers for Disease Control and Prevention, 2021c). The CDC (2021b) makes available on the web data analytic tools that allow for easy analysis of fatal injuries. Analyses of that dataset show that in the 20 years prior to 2019, suicide rates increased over 25% for those over age 14, with men dying from suicide at over four times the rate of women (28/100,000 for men, 6.3/100,000 for women). Firearms were used in over half of these deaths.

Data collected in the National Survey on Drug Use and Health (NSDUH) from 2019 showed that 4.8% of the adult population over age 18 had serious thoughts about suicide and .6% made a suicide attempt (National Institute of Mental Health, 2021). Younger age was associated with more suicidal thinking (see Chap. 21 for discussion of even higher rates among adolescents). The impact, if any, of the COVID-19 pandemic on suicide rates is still not fully known.

Self-Injury Labeled as "Non-suicidal" and Self-Injury Unrelated to Suicide

The act of harming oneself is complex. Some self-harm is accidental or an incidental by-product of risky behavior where there was no original intent to harm oneself (e.g., a patient who dies in a single car motor vehicle accident while intoxicated), which can occur even if the patient had some suicidal thoughts. Some self-harm may be intentional, but the death that ensues was not intentional (e.g., a patient who cut herself to relieve distress, or a patient who derived sexual gratification from auto-asphyxiation). And, of course, self-harm that was intended as suicide may not result in death (e.g., a patient who overdosed, survived, but had residual liver damage) and may be classified as a non-lethal suicide attempt. Thus, suicidal ideation and attempts require an understanding of the interplay between the intentions of the individual, the actions they take, and the resultant harm. This will all be analyzed with regard to the elements of malpractice to understand whether the self-harm was foreseeable and what damages were related to the self-injury. There are specific diagnoses in which non-suicidal self-injury (NSSI) may be more common, such as personality disorders (Hauber et al., 2019), but NSSI is also seen in other populations without this condition (Turner et al., 2015). When an individual engages in repetitive NSSI, it is incumbent upon the psychiatrist to assess the behavior and develop a treatment plan that is aimed at reducing it, often in the context of enhancing the patient's ability to self-regulate around emotional distress.

Types of Allegations

Allegations about failures to meet the standard of care generally allege that the psychiatrist failed in one or more of the following areas: assessing the patient's risk for suicide, developing an appropriate treatment plan and safety plan to ameliorate the risk, or continuing to monitor both risk and treatment efficacy. Most commonly, in the case of an outpatient suicide, the decision not to hospitalize the patient will be carefully scrutinized; in the case of an inpatient suicide, the level of monitoring by unit staff will be assessed; and for a patient recently discharged from an inpatient unit, the discharge decision and follow-up treatment plan will be examined.

Screening and Assessment of Suicide Risk

Because of its clinical importance, suicide risk assessment has an extensive literature (Gold & Frierson, 2020; Jacobs et al., 2003). Borne out of research looking at specific suicide risk factors (discussed further below), screening and assessment tools have gained attention. The Columbia Suicide Severity Rating Scale (CSSRS) (Interian et al., 2018) and the PHQ-9 (Simon et al., 2013) are two of the tools that are commonly referred to in the suicide risk identification discourse. The idea behind these tools is to develop a method of screening for basic suicide risk and then identifying who should have a more in-depth assessment. As noted above, the field of artificial intelligence and machine learning is also advancing to comb through medical records, for example, to cull out who might be more likely to make a suicide attempt in the near future. These advanced methods are yet to be incorporated into mainstream clinical care or become part of care standards, but it will be important from a malpractice standpoint to pay attention to their evolution. In the meantime, the elusive screening tool is promoted often as a best practice. At the same time, the desire for a briefer way of detecting suicide risk has yet to be identified. As a case in point, the PHQ-2 is a two-question version of the PHQ-9, and although it has been shown as a good abbreviated screening tool for depression, it has not shown as much promise as a screening tool for suicide risk (Dueweke et al., 2018). Furthermore, although the screening tools like the CSSRS are increasingly utilized and recommended, there is no definitive rule that a psychiatrist would have breached the standard of care if they had not been used, if all other data demonstrated a robust suicide risk assessment.

Different institutions have published basic clinical resources to aid in suicide risk assessment, such as the American Psychiatric Association's guideline on psychiatric evaluation of adults (APA Work Group on Psychiatric Evaluation, 2016). Another example comes from the Veterans Administration, where suicide risk has become a main focus, related to the unfortunate high suicide rates seen among veterans (Department of Veterans Affairs, 2019). These guidelines attempt to parse out the various static and dynamic factors associated with suicide risk. Static risk factors are those factors that cannot be changed (e.g., age, race, history of prior suicide attempts), and dynamic factors are those that can be addressed in treatment (e.g., depression, unemployment, access to firearms, etc.). They also attempt to guide practice, cite literature where it is known, or bring forth the views of the guidelines in an "expert consensus"-type format.

As an example of an attempt to cull out specific guidance in suicide risk assessment, the American Psychiatric Association has put forth key variables in the effort to "stop a suicide," suggesting that psychiatrists inquire about suicide intent and also access to lethal means, motivations for suicide (including attention, revenge, shame, guilt, psychotic beliefs) as well as about a patient's purpose to go on living, the quality of the relationship with the psychiatrist, and family history of suicide (APA Work Group on Psychiatric Evaluation, 2016).

Overall, expert witnesses may use clinical practice guidelines as a means of considering the details of the case before them, yet these guidelines may or may not be accepted by courts in malpractice cases as a learned treatise that helps the court understand a standard of care. In court cases, it will be up to experts on either side to explain how the clinical practice guideline demonstrates or fails to demonstrate that the physician operated within the standard of care (Moffett & Moore, 2011; Recupero, 2008). Ultimately, it is important for psychiatrists to recognize that although helpful, these guidelines generally cannot inform specifics of every individual case, thus leaving to clinical judgment any ultimate assessment and management decisions.

With the above in mind, psychiatrists must assess patients carefully and formulate treatment plans surrounding those assessments. Such assessments typically should include a review of the patient's biopsychosocial history and a current mental status examination. A focused evaluation of suicide risk includes understanding the patient's history of suicide and suicide attempts, the severity of prior attempts, and the current thoughts about suicide, typically framed as suicide ideation, intent, and plans. There is also the need to assess the patient's access to suicidal means (e.g., a firearm or large quantities of pills). In assessing these factors, it is also important to evaluate the sense of helplessness, hopelessness, and worthlessness a patient may feel, and any factors that they see as protective (e.g., family, religion).

Clinical assessments must thus be individualized, and different theoretical orientations suggest different approaches. For example, the interpersonal-psychological theory of suicide (Van Orden et al., 2010) emphasizes assessing depressed patients' perceived burdensomeness and an unmet need to belong. Individual characteristics might be associated with higher risk of suicide, such as for transgender individuals (Peterson et al., 2017), veterans (Nelson et al., 2017), and older adults (see Chap. 26 and Morgan et al., 2018). The setting in which the clinical assessment is conducted may also require more specific analyses for that setting, such as in emergency departments, correctional environments, inpatient psychiatric units, or outpatient settings (see Chaps. 19–27).

Challenging aspects of suicide risk assessment and mitigation include the analysis and formulation, which requires the clinical judgment to weigh the risk and protective factors to formulate the overall assessment and plan. Such judgment does not seek to have the physician predict the suicide but to assess the risk and navigate it safely. In this way, a successful malpractice claim is less likely if the psychiatrist foresaw that there was a high risk, and took appropriate steps to mitigate it, even if in the end the patient ultimately died from suicide. The SAFE-T guide (Suicide Assessment and Five-Step Evaluation and Triage) is a framework promoted by the federal Substance Abuse and Mental Health Services Administration (2009) that outlines several steps in the suicide prevention process (see Table 12.1).

Another tool that has gained traction and attention stems from the Zero Suicide model (Zero Suicide Institute, 2020). This model stemmed from work done that provides resources to create systemic approaches to quality improve-

Table 12.1 SAFE-T framework

1. Identify risk factors
2. Identify protective factors
3. Conduct the suicide inquiry
4. Determine risk level/intervention
5. Documentation

Substance Abuse and Mental Health Services Administration (2009)

ment in suicide prevention (Labouliere et al., 2018). The AIM framework embedded in the model stands for aim, intervene, and monitor (Stanley et al., 2021). The idea of healthcare systems setting up screening and assessment align with the National Patient Safety Goals of suicide prevention articulated by the Joint Commission (The Joint Commission, 2019). With all this focused effort on systemic identification and drive toward suicide prevention, there is arguably more weight on psychiatrists both within large hospital systems and in outpatient practice to identify risk and effectively manage it.

Suicide Risk and Protective Factors

Even in the best of systems, as noted above, malpractice cases will turn on what happened in an individual circumstance. Plaintiffs may argue that systemic failures contributed to the individual's death, but it is nonetheless critical for psychiatrists to understand suicide risk factors and how to balance protective factors. Table 12.2 lists risk factors commonly associated with suicide, and Table 12.3 lists commonly noted protective factors.

The analysis of the risk and protective factors implies that there is not a simple checklist in which one risk factor balances with one protective factor. Similarly, ten risk factors can be mitigated by one protective factor. For example, an individual who has a spinal cord injury and is quadriplegic can have a host of risk factors but may not be able to execute a suicide plan due to his or her physical limitations. This example can help triers of fact understand why the analysis of risk and protective factors does not boil down to simple math equations but rather requires clinical judgment and an understanding of the totality of the circumstances.

Table 12.2 Risk factors commonly associated with suicide

Family history of suicide
Family history of child maltreatment
Previous suicide attempt(s)
History of mental disorders, particularly clinical depression
History of alcohol and substance abuse
Feelings of hopelessness
Impulsive or aggressive tendencies
Cultural and religious beliefs (e.g., belief that suicide is noble resolution of a personal dilemma)
Local epidemics of suicide
Isolation, a feeling of being cut off from other people
Barriers to accessing mental health treatment
Loss (relational, social, work, or financial)
Physical illness
Easy access to lethal methods
Unwillingness to seek help because of the stigma attached to mental health, substance abuse disorders, and suicidal thoughts

Adapted from Centers for Disease Control and Prevention (2021a); US Public Health Service (1999)

Table 12.3 Protective factors

Effective clinical care for mental, physical, and substance abuse disorders
Easy access to a variety of clinical interventions and support for help-seeking
Family and community support (connectedness)
Support from ongoing medical and mental healthcare relationships
Skills in problem solving, conflict resolution, and nonviolent ways of handling disputes
Cultural and religious beliefs that discourage suicide and support instincts for self-preservation

Adapted from Centers for Disease Control and Prevention (2021a); US Public Health Service (1999)

Assessment of Foreseeability

Foreseeability is not the same as predictability, yet there is an element of prediction in foreseeing a future harm. Furthermore, suicides can be impulsive (Smith et al., 2008). In tort claims (the type of case that covers civil liability for malpractice actions), the courts will examine whether the psychiatrist had sufficient information or should have accessed such information, so as to make a reasonable judgment. In that sense, foreseeability is not absolute, but courts will often look at what was considered "reasonably foreseeable." Some authors have cautioned against the magical thinking associated with hindsight bias – in which foreseeability is exaggerated by knowing what harm ensued (LeBourgeois et al., 2007). Other types of bias, such as confirmatory bias, can be a risk in reviewing a suicide retrospectively when one is simply or unconsciously confirming the plaintiff's or defendant's hypotheses a priori. According to Bursztajn et al. (1988), in suicide malpractice cases, the legal analysis and the expert's work should examine factors beyond how the patient committed suicide and instead fold into the analysis a reconstruction of the conditions under which the psychiatrist exercised foresight, which includes considering the uncertainty of clinical judgments, the multicausal explanations for suicide, the role of the physician as an active agent in the resultant decisions that led to the suicide, the role of the patient as a passive victim or active competent participant, and the overemphasis on the means of death as relevant to whether the suicide could have been foreseen or prevented. In a malpractice analysis, there is also the question of examining whether the standard of care was met, which typically incorporates considerations of how other psychiatrists who were similarly situated would have acted. It does not call for the assessment of idealized practice but standard practice. This issue can get even more complex with geographic variations (e.g., some jurisdictions have limited access to electroconvulsive therapy or day programming that might mitigate risk of a patient's suicide).

Suicide and Firearms

Firearms are the method utilized in over half of suicides in the United States (Centers for Disease Control and Prevention, 2021b). Clinical risk assessments that generally assess substance use and impulsivity help shape contours around suicide risk with firearms. Wintemute (2015) highlights the correlation between firearm ownership, risky behaviors, and alcohol misuse. Suicide risk assessment with regard to firearms can be broken down for the psychiatrist into two levels, with the first level incorporating general inquiry about firearm access, storage, ammunition access, and whether there are ways to remove the firearm if the person is at risk, with the more in-depth second level in inquiry covering, for example, how the patient is thinking about the use of a firearm itself for a possible suicide and the relationship the patient has toward guns (Pinals & Anacker, 2016). The first level of inquiry has gained acceptance as a standard approach at least to individuals expressing suicidal ideation. Given the higher risk of suicide in adolescents in homes where there is firearm access, psychiatrists should especially deliberate their inquiry in these populations (Knopov et al., 2019).

After a careful suicide risk assessment, the next step is to manage foreseeable risks. A multidisciplinary approach has been suggested for inpatients whose suicidal ideation surrounded the use of firearms (Sherman et al., 2001). Restriction of access to firearms and associated counseling may be helpful in certain veterans (Smith et al., 2015). So-called "red flag" or "extreme risk protection orders" (ERPO) laws have been promoted in many states that allow for the removal of firearms from individuals for whom there appears to be a firearm-associated risk of harm to self or others. These laws generally do not require the individual to have a defined mental illness to permit the removal. Rather they focus on a layperson's ability to petition for firearm removal for anyone posing a risk related to the firearm. This also means that psychiatrists may not be included in the ability to breach confidentiality and seek the removal of the firearm directly but may need to consider these laws in balancing with other legal obligations and still work to mitigate risk and potentially effectuate separation of the suicidal patient from the firearm (such as through hospitalization or advocacy with family members). More details about these approaches are articulated in a recent resource document developed by the American Psychiatric Association (Kapoor et al., 2019).

Risk Mitigation Strategies

Once the psychiatrist concludes that a patient poses a significant risk of suicide, it is incumbent on the psychiatrist to establish treatment approaches to minimize the risk. Courts in liability claims will examine these mitigation responses as part of determining whether the psychiatrist acted negligently. As such, basic approaches to treating any associated symptoms of mental illness and accessing substance use treatment services and other needed services are important. The American Psychiatric Association's practice guideline about suicide assessment (Jacobs et al., 2003) addresses the importance of accessing the proper level of care that matches the patient's need. This might include accessing inpatient treatment or crisis services. There is a major effort to advance crisis services across the United States, beginning with the promulgation of the phone number 988 as the future number for the national suicide prevention lifeline and the build out of an array of crisis services (Pinals, 2020). It will thus be important for psychiatrists to be aware of the availability of these services in order to direct patients to them when needed.

The use of legal mechanisms to involuntarily hold and then potentially hospitalize individuals is a mechanism that is available when an individual's suicide risk is high and the patient is unwilling to engage in voluntary care (Hedman et al., 2016; Pinals & Anacker, 2020). Suicide across all levels of care is still possible, and thus the management of suicide risk cannot be ignored when an individual is sent for more intensive treatment, whether voluntarily or involuntarily (for the particular issues related to managing suicide risk on inpatient units, see Chap. 19).

Beyond determining the most clinically appropriate venue for proper care and risk mitigation, the means of care is also critical. Here, a biopsychosocial approach is relevant. For example, psychopharmacological strategies will be necessary for patients with active symptoms of mental illness such as depression or psychosis. Clozapine and lithium may have unique properties that reduce suicide risk, though they need to be prescribed for the patients whose symptom pattern and severity justify these medications (Bastiampillai et al., 2017). On the flip side, some medications, such as selective serotonin reuptake inhibitors (SSRIs), have black box warnings that suggest their use is correlated with elevated suicide risk, especially in specific populations such as youth and older adults (see Chaps. 21 and 26). Thus the prescriber must be cognizant of risks and benefits of medications with regard to the symptoms being addressed, specific population, and suicidal risk. Psychotherapeutic approaches are also important in the suicide risk mitigation armamentarium. Cognitive behavioral therapy and dialectical behavioral therapy, for example, have been shown to reduce the likelihood of suicide and non-suicidal self injury (NSSI) in specific patients (Zalsman et al., 2016).

Because of the very high correlation between substance use and suicide risk, substance use-specific treatment is also an important component of risk mitigation, whether the patient's pattern consists of binge use or more persistent regular use. Data surrounding this is extremely compelling, such as that showing the strong relationship between the misuse of alcohol (Brady, 2006), opioids (Braden et al., 2017), and suicide. In the substance use disorder and suicide risk mitigation formulation, therapy and other evidence-based practices, along with medications to address the substance use directly (i.e., "medications for addiction treatments" or "medication-assisted treatments"), should both be considered (Braden et al., 2017), though not all substances of misuse can be treated with medication. Other social supports, including peer support or Alcoholics Anonymous-type interventions, may also be useful. Encouraging patients who continue to use to have someone nearby to mitigate risk has been another strategy (e.g., encouraging rescue with naloxone in the case of opioid overdose), and this can also extend to persons who binge drink (such as college students or others) to ensure proper safety net approaches. Engaging patients in the discussion about how substance use fits into their lives and its relation to potential suicide risk can be critical. In other words, risk mitigation strategies can involve a number of actions that help lessen the patient's risk and protect the psychiatrist who will be scrutinized for how they addressed and managed risk as well as monitored the patient over time.

In the AIM (aim, intervene, and monitor) model, the monitoring of patients is incorporated as the means to continue to mitigate risk. Because patient presentations range from those with chronic suicidal ideation and histories of multiple suicide attempts to those with new onset suicidal ideation and no prior mental health history, the monitoring will differ from patient to patient. Also, some significant proportions of suicides are impulsive or associated with substance use, and their foreseeability will be limited. In those situations where a sufficient risk assessment has been conducted and risk has been identified, a supportive plan that involves a safety net of collateral supports and proper follow-up and monitoring can be critical. Typically, collateral supports include outreach to family and friends to help weave them into the planning for risk mitigation. This can be fraught with challenges if patients decline to allow the psychiatrist to communicate with others. In those instances, the psychiatrist should work with the patient to educate them as to why such communication is desired to help build a safety net and mitigate risk. If the patient continues to decline authorization to communicate, the psychiatrist should document the refusal, and may consider a higher level of care, including involuntary hospitalization, or determine whether the urgency of the suicide risk rises to the level that warrants an emergency exception to confidentiality.

The psychiatrist may also educate the potential supports about suicide and risk reduction and discuss a proposed safety plan and its feasibility. The psychiatrist could be found negligent in simply leaving the safety planning to family, for example, rather than serving as the "learned intermediary" to help navigate risk mitigation. For example, it may be critical to assist family members by educating them about the risk of leaving patients, especially during high-risk periods or when there is access to lethal means or substances that might create increased risk of self-harm.

From a liability perspective, there are other advantages to safety planning, as engagement with family can ensure that there is awareness that an individual had access to treatment and that the family had information about whom to contact should a situation worsen. In this way, there may be a chance that the bad feelings toward the psychiatrist that sometimes catalyze litigious actions can be mitigated by involvement and engagement in the difficult task of risk mitigation. Yager and Feinstein (2017) provide an example of how family and mental health professionals can work together to continually attend to known warning signs of increasing risk and re-review safety plans for persons with chronic suicidal ideation.

It is important for psychiatrists to realize that the mitigation responsibility, from a tort claim perspective, will fall to them, such that if the safety plan is inadequate in the community, the negligence may stem from a question of whether the patient should have been moved to a higher level of care. And, as noted above, safety planning requires a balance between patient privacy and enlisting others in the plans. One other important element is the idea that a psychiatrist and patient may have varying levels of therapeutic alliance. For example, this will differ for new patients seen in emergency rooms compared to patients with whom a psychiatrist has worked for years to mitigate against chronic suicide risk. The idea of "contracting for safety" as insurance from liability has been debunked (Garvey et al., 2009). However, a treatment agreement with a competent patient who has engaged in long-standing care may incorporate the idea that the patient will alert the psychiatrist if they are having increased suicidal thoughts. In the overarching approach to risk mitigation, means restriction counseling has been considered a valuable addition (Sale et al., 2018), and not just with firearms as noted above. Working with patients to remove risks related to their suicidal thoughts, such as removing pills from medicine cabinets, prescribing fewer pills at any given time, asking for pill counts, and other similar actions, can be developed on an individual basis. At a population level, there are many strategies including putting fencing up on parking structures or statutorily requiring waiting times for firearms purchases. The goal of these strategies is to create space between the suicidal thought and the access to the means to carry it out, especially given the high potential for suicide to be impulsively executed. In this chapter we focus on individual liability, but systems failures to reduce liability may also be examined in cases, such as in correctional settings, within the Veterans Administration, and on college campuses. Malpractice claims toward an individual psychiatrist may be linked to systemic challenges. Psychiatrists should thus be aware of the general community efforts at risk mitigation through means restriction.

Documentation

As with other types of malpractice cases, in the event of an adverse outcome and scrutiny of the chart by a plaintiff attorney, good documentation is key to defending a case. Although not every word or act needs to be documented, the suicide risk assessment should be documented, and, if there is significant risk, the safety plan and ongoing monitoring should be clearly documented as well. In cases of significant risk, Gutheil (1980) recommends writing as though a plaintiff attorney is looking over your shoulder, but writing only the information necessary to convey the clinical thinking that led to the particular decision. In addition to documenting what was done, if the psychiatrist is not taking the most conservative course (e.g., they are not hospitalizing a patient who demonstrates some risk), it is very useful to document the reasoning process – how the risk and protective factors and the pros and cons of a particular action were weighed. The psychiatrist does not have to be right – the psychiatrist just has to be reasonable, based on what were reasonably foreseeable risks. Documenting the reasoning process can go a long way in combatting the hindsight bias of a plaintiff expert opining well after the fact. As noted above, hindsight bias is a particular problem in suicide cases (Knoll & Gerbasi, 2006; LeBourgeois et al., 2007). Another useful strategy in high-risk situations is to follow Jonas Rappeport's (1984) advice: "When in doubt, Shout!" Get a second opinion and have it documented. This can be particularly helpful in an emergency department when the decision is not to hospitalize a patient who demonstrates some risk but on balance is judged appropriate for an outpatient safety plan. The contemporaneous second opinion by another reasonable psychiatrist can go a long way in combatting the opinion of a plaintiff expert looking back through the "retrospectoscope," when hindsight and confirmatory biases, as described above, may be more likely.

Conclusion

Suicide is on the rise in the United States. When psychiatrists are involved in an individual's care, suicide can be a major cause of liability. The work of treating patients is rewarding, but the fear of liability can greatly hamper psychiatrists' willingness to work with patients at risk of suicide. In civil tort liability that involves plaintiff's allegations toward a psychiatrist, the plaintiff will be pursuing damages and need to prove that there was a dereliction of duty by the physician that directly led to the damages. The foreseeability of the patient's suicidal behavior will be scrutinized. The best strategy therefore to mitigate against successful liability is to provide and document sound clinical care. This should at a minimum include an appropriate assessment of risk based on what is known and what should be known by the psychiatrist, developing a treatment plan with the patient (and possibly others such as family) that mitigates that risk and then monitoring the patient for evolving circumstances.

Key Points

- Prediction models based on risk factors are not sufficiently strong to be able to make an accurate prediction that a given patient will die by suicide.
- Malpractice cases involving a patient's suicide turn on whether a suicide was reasonably foreseeable and, if so, the steps the psychiatrist took to reduce the risk.
- Judgments as to whether the psychiatrist met the standard of care typically focus on three main steps: the assessment of risk, the treatment plan and safety plan implemented to ameliorate the risk, and the continuing monitoring of both risk and treatment efficacy.
- Over half of American suicides are completed with the use of a firearm.
- Good documentation, including documentation of the reasoning involved in weighing risk and protective factors, is a key factor in protecting the psychiatrist in the event of an adverse outcome.

Acknowledgment Some of the conceptualizations in this chapter were previously presented in Pinals DA (2019). Liability and patient suicide. *Focus, 17*(4), 349–354.

References

Abiragi, M., Bauler, L. D., & Brown, T. (2020). Importance and approach to manner of death opinions in opioid-related deaths. *Journal of Forensic Sciences, 65*(3), 1009–1011. https://doi.org/10.1111/1556-4029.14266

American Foundation for Suicide Prevention. (2021). *Suicide statistics*. https://afsp.org/suicide-statistics. Accessed 9 July 2021.

APA Work Group on Psychiatric Evaluation. (2016). *The American Psychiatric Association practice guidelines for the psychiatric evaluation of adults*. American Psychiatric Association. https://psychiatryonline.org/doi/pdf/10.1176/appi.books.9780890426760

Appelbaum, P. S. (2000). Patients' responsibility for their suicidal behavior. *Psychiatric Services, 51*(1), 15–16.

Bastiampillai, T., Sharfstein, S. S., & Allison, S. (2017). Increasing the use of lithium and clozapine in US suicide prevention. *JAMA Psychiatry, 74*(4), 423. https://doi.org/10.1001/jamapsychiatry.2016.3866

Belsher, B. E., Smolenski, D. J., Pruitt, L. D., Bush, N. E., Beech, E. H., Workman, D. E., Morgan, R. L., Evatt, D. P., Tucker, J., & Skopp, N. A. (2019). Prediction models for suicide attempts and deaths: A systematic review and simulation. *JAMA Psychiatry, 76*(6), 642–651. https://doi.org/10.1001/jamapsychiatry.2019.0174

Bernert, R. A., Hilberg, A. M., Melia, R., Kim, J. P., Shah, N. H., & Abnousi, F. (2020). Artificial intelligence and suicide prevention: A systematic review of machine learning investigations. *International Journal of Environmental Research & Public Health, 17*(16), 15. https://doi.org/10.3390/ijerph17165929

Braden, J. B., Edlund, M. J., & Sullivan, M. D. (2017). Suicide deaths with opioid poisoning in the United States: 1999-2014. *American Journal of Public Health, 107*(3), 421–426. https://doi.org/10.2105/AJPH.2016.303591

Brady, J. (2006). The association between alcohol misuse and suicidal behaviour. *Alcohol and Alcoholism, 41*(5), 473–478. https://doi.org/10.1093/alcalc/agl060

Bursztajn, H., Gutheil, T. G., Brodsky, A., & Swagerty, E. L. (1988). "Magical thinking," suicide, and malpractice litigation. *Bulletin of the American Academy of Psychiatry and the Law, 16*(4), 369–377.

Centers for Disease Control and Prevention. (2021a). *Risk and protective factors*. Centers for Disease Control and Prevention. https://www.cdc.gov/suicide/factors/index.html?CDC_AA_refVal=https%3A%2F%2Fwww.cdc.gov%2Fviolenceprevention%2Fsuicide%2Friskprotectivefactors.html. Accessed 13 Feb 2021.

Centers for Disease Control and Prevention. (2021b). *WISQARS fatal injury and violence data*. Centers for Disease Control and Prevention. https://www.cdc.gov/injury/wisqars/fatal.html. Accessed 21 Jan 2021.

Centers for Disease Control and Prevention. (2021c). *WISQARS leading causes of death reports, 1981–2019*. Centers for Disease Control and Prevention. https://webappa.cdc.gov/sasweb/ncipc/leadcause.html. Accessed 13 Feb 2021.

Department of Veterans Affairs. (2019). *VA/DoD clinical practice guideline for assessment and management of patients at risk for suicide, Ver. 2*. https://www.healthquality.va.gov/guidelines/MH/srb/VADoDSuicideRiskFullCPGFinal5088212019.pdf. Accessed 21 Feb 2021.

Dueweke, A. R., Marin, M. S., Sparkman, D. J., & Bridges, A. J. (2018). Inadequacy of the PHQ-2 depression screener for identifying suicidal primary care patients. *Families, Systems & Health, 36*(3), 281–288. https://doi.org/10.1037/fsh0000350

Frierson, R. L., & Joshi, K. G. (2019). Malpractice law and psychiatry: An overview. *Focus, 17*(4), 332–336. https://doi.org/10.1176/appi.focus.20190017

Garvey, K. A., Penn, J. V., Campbell, A. L., Esposito-Smythers, C., & Spirito, A. (2009). Contracting for safety with patients: Clinical practice and forensic implications. *Journal of the American Academy of Psychiatry & the Law, 37*(3), 363–370.

Gold, L. H., & Frierson, R. L. (2020). In L. H. Gold & R. L. Frierson (Eds.), *The American Psychiatric Association Publishing textbook of suicide risk assessment and management* (3rd ed.). American Psychiatric Association Publishing.

Gutheil, T. G. (1980). Paranoia and progress notes: A guide to forensically informed psychiatric recordkeeping. *Hospital and Community Psychiatry, 31*(7), 479–482.

Hauber, K., Boon, A., & Vermeiren, R. (2019). Non-suicidal self-injury in clinical practice. *Frontiers in Psychology, 10*, 502. https://doi.org/10.3389/fpsyg.2019.00502

Hedman, L. C., Petrila, J., Fisher, W. H., Swanson, J. W., Dingman, D. A., & Burris, S. (2016). State Laws on emergency holds for mental health stabilization. *Psychiatric Services, 67*(5), 529–535.

Interian, A., Chesin, M., Kline, A., Miller, R., St Hill, L., Latorre, M., Shcherbakov, A., King, A., & Stanley, B. (2018). Use of the Columbia-Suicide Severity Rating Scale (C-SSRS) to classify suicidal behaviors. *Archives of Suicide Research, 22*(2), 278–294. https://doi.org/10.1080/13811118.2017.1334610

Jacobs, D. G., Baldessarini, R. J., Conwell, Y., Fawcett, J. A., Horton, L., Meltzer, H., Pfeffer, C. R., & Simon, R. I. (2003). Practice guideline for the assessment and treatment of patients with suicidal behaviors. *American Journal of Psychiatry, 160*(11 Suppl), 1–60.

Kapoor, R., Benedek, E., Bonnie, R. J., Gandhi, T., Gold, L., Judd, S., & Pinals, D. A. (2019). Resource document on risk-based gun removal laws. *Focus, 17*(4), 443–451. https://doi.org/10.1176/appi.focus.17403

Knoll, J., & Gerbasi, J. (2006). Psychiatric malpractice case analysis: Striving for objectivity. *Journal of the American Academy of Psychiatry & the Law, 34*(2), 215–223.

Knopov, A., Sherman, R. J., Raifman, J. R., Larson, E., & Siegel, M. B. (2019). Household gun ownership and youth suicide rates at the state level, 2005-2015. *American Journal of Preventive Medicine, 56*(3), 335–342. https://doi.org/10.1016/j.amepre.2018.10.027

Labouliere, C. D., Vasan, P., Kramer, A., Brown, G., Green, K., Rahman, M., Kammer, J., Finnerty, M., & Stanley, B. (2018). "Zero Suicide" - a model for reducing suicide in United States behavioral healthcare. *Suicidologi, 23*(1), 22–30.

LeBourgeois, H. W., 3rd, Pinals, D. A., Williams, V., & Appelbaum, P. S. (2007). Hindsight bias among psychiatrists. *Journal of the American Academy of Psychiatry and the Law, 35*(1), 67–73.

Medscape. (2020). *Medscape psychiatrist malpractice report 2019*. https://www.medscape.com/slideshow/2019-malpractice-report-psych-6012450#1. Accessed 8 Feb.

Moffett, P., & Moore, G. (2011). The standard of care: Legal history and definitions: The bad and good news. *The Western Journal of Emergency Medicine, 12*(1), 109–112.

Morgan, C., Webb, R. T., Carr, M. J., Kontopantelis, E., Chew-Graham, C. A., Kapur, N., & Ashcroft, D. M. (2018). Self-harm in a primary care cohort of older people: Incidence, clinical management, and risk of suicide and other causes of death. *Lancet Psychiatry, 5*(11), 905–912. https://doi.org/10.1016/s2215-0366(18)30348-1

National Institute of Mental Health. (2021). *Suicide*. Centers for Disease Control and Prevention. https://www.nimh.nih.gov/health/statistics/suicide.shtml. Accessed 13 Feb 2021.

Nelson, H. D., Denneson, L. M., Low, A. R., Bauer, B. W., O'Neil, M., Kansagara, D., & Teo, A. R. (2017). Suicide risk assessment and prevention: A systematic review focusing on veterans. *Psychiatric Services, 68*(10), 1003–1015. https://doi.org/10.1176/appi.ps.201600384

Obegi, J. H. (2017). Probable standards of care for suicide risk assessment. *Journal of the American Academy of Psychiatry and the Law Online, 45*(4), 452. http://jaapl.org/content/45/4/452.abstract

Peterson, C. M., Matthews, A., Copps-Smith, E., & Conard, L. A. (2017). Suicidality, self-harm, and body dissatisfaction in transgender adolescents and emerging adults with gender dysphoria. *Suicide and Life-threatening Behavior, 47*(4), 475–482. https://doi.org/10.1111/sltb.12289

Pinals, D. A. (2020). *Crisis services: Meeting needs, saving lives*. National Association of State Mental Health Program Directors. Also available at https://nasmhpd.org/content/crisis-services-meeting-needs-saving-lives

Pinals, D. A., & Anacker, L. (2016). Mental illness and firearms: Legal context and clinical approaches. *Psychiatric Clinics of North America, 39*(4), 611–621. https://doi.org/10.1016/j.psc.2016.07.013

Pinals, D. A., & Anacker, L. (2020). *Legal issues in crisis services*. National Association of State Mental Health Program Directors. Also available at https://www.nasmhpd.org/sites/default/files/2020paper5.pdf

Pokorny, A. D. (1983). Prediction of suicide in psychiatric patients. Report of a prospective study. *Archives of General Psychiatry, 40*(3), 249–257. https://doi.org/10.1001/archpsyc.1983.01790030019002

Rappeport, J. R. (1984). *Malpractice prevention*. Spring Grove State Hospital Center.

Recupero, P. R. (2008). Clinical practice guidelines as learned treatises: Understanding their use as evidence in the courtroom. *Journal of the American Academy of Psychiatry and the Law, 36*(3), 290–301.

Sale, E., Hendricks, M., Weil, V., Miller, C., Perkins, S., & McCudden, S. (2018). Counseling on Access to Lethal Means (CALM): An evaluation of a suicide prevention means restriction training program for mental health providers. *Community Mental Health Journal, 54*(3), 293–301. https://doi.org/10.1007/s10597-017-0190-z

Sherman, M. E., Burns, K., Ignelzi, J., Raia, J., Lofton, V., Toland, D., Stinson, B., Tilley, J. L., & Coon, T. (2001). Firearms risk management in psychiatric care. *Psychiatric Services, 52*(8), 1057–1061. https://doi.org/10.1176/appi.ps.52.8.1057

Simon, G. E., Rutter, C. M., Peterson, D., Oliver, M., Whiteside, U., Operskalski, B., & Ludman, E. J. (2013). Does response on the PHQ-9 depression questionnaire predict subsequent suicide attempt or suicide death? *Psychiatric Services, 64*(12), 1195–1202. https://doi.org/10.1176/appi.ps.201200587

Smith, A. R., Witte, T. K., Teale, N. E., King, S. L., Bender, T. W., & Joiner, T. E. (2008). Revisiting impulsivity in suicide: Implications for civil liability of third parties. *Behavioral Sciences & the Law, 26*(6), 779–797. https://doi.org/10.1002/bsl.848

Smith, P. N., Currier, J., & Drescher, K. (2015). Firearm ownership in veterans entering residential PTSD treatment: Associations with suicide ideation, attempts, and combat exposure. *Psychiatry Research, 229*(1–2), 220–224. https://doi.org/10.1016/j.psychres.2015.07.031

Sorenson, S. B., Shen, H., & Kraus, J. F. (1997). Undetermined manner of death. A comparison with unintentional injury, suicide, and homicide death. *Evaluation Review, 21*(1), 43–57.

Stanley, B., Labouliere, C. D., Brown, G. K., Green, K. L., Galfalvy, H. C., Finnerty, M. T., Vasan, P., Cummings, A. K., Wainberg, M., Carruthers, J. W., & Dixon, L. B. (2021). Zero suicide implementation-effectiveness trial study protocol in outpatient behavioral health using the A-I-M suicide prevention model. *Contemporary Clinical Trials, 100*, 106224. https://doi.org/10.1016/j.cct.2020.106224

Substance Abuse and Mental Health Services Administration. (2009). *SAFE-T pocket card: Suicide assessment five-step evaluation and triage for clinicians*. Substance Abuse and Mental Health Services Administration. https://store.samhsa.gov/product/SAFE-T-Pocket-Card-Suicide-Assessment-Five-Step-Evaluation-and-Triage-for-Clinicians/sma09-4432. Accessed 13 Feb 2021.

The Joint Commission. (2019). *National Patient Safety Goal for suicide prevention*. https://www.jointcommission.org/-/media/tjc/documents/standards/r3-reports/r3_18_suicide_prevention_hap_bhc_cah_11_4_19_final1.pdf. Accessed 21 Feb 2021.

Turner, B. J., Dixon-Gordon, K. L., Austin, S. B., Rodriguez, M. A., Zachary Rosenthal, M., & Chapman, A. L. (2015). Non-suicidal self-injury with and without borderline personality disorder: Differences in self-injury and diagnostic comorbidity. *Psychiatry Research, 230*(1), 28–35. https://doi.org/10.1016/j.psychres.2015.07.058

U. S. Public Health Service. (1999). The surgeon General's call to action to prevent suicide. .

Van Orden, K. A., Witte, T. K., Cukrowicz, K. C., Braithwaite, S. R., Selby, E. A., & Joiner, T. E., Jr. (2010). The interpersonal theory of suicide. *Psychological Review, 117*(2), 575–600. https://doi.org/10.1037/a0018697

Wintemute, G. J. (2015). Alcohol misuse, firearm violence perpetration, and public policy in the United States. *Preventive Medicine, 79*, 15–21. https://doi.org/10.1016/j.ypmed.2015.04.015

Yager, J., & Feinstein, R. E. (2017). General psychiatric management for suicidal patients, with remarks on chronicity: Contending with the angel of death. *Journal of Nervous and Mental Disease, 205*(6), 419–426. https://doi.org/10.1097/NMD.0000000000000701

Zalsman, G., Hawton, K., Wasserman, D., van Heeringen, K., Arensman, E., Sarchiapone, M., Carli, V., Hoschl, C., Barzilay, R., Balazs, J., Purebl, G., Kahn, J. P., Saiz, P. A., Lipsicas, C. B., Bobes, J., Cozman, D., Hegerl, U., & Zohar, J. (2016). Suicide prevention strategies revisited: 10-year systematic review. *Lancet Psychiatry, 3*(7), 646–659. https://doi.org/10.1016/S2215-0366(16)30030-X

Zero Suicide Institute. (2020). *Zero suicide*. https://zerosuicide.edc.org/. Accessed 13 Feb 2021.

13 Patient Violence

Adrienne Saxton and Phillip Resnick

Assessment of violence risk is a core competency for psychiatrists. A patient's risk of violence is considered in everyday clinical decisions ranging from whether to admit a patient to the hospital, readiness for discharge, the need for civil commitment, and whether medication changes may be necessary. In addition to routine clinical scenarios, violence risk assessment is essential when faced with a patient making a threat toward another individual.

Due to significant variability of *Tarasoff*-limiting statutes and case law from state to state, psychiatrists may be unsure of how to proceed when they determine that their patient presents a serious risk of harm to another. Is an explicit threat required to breach confidentiality to warn a potential victim? Is there legal justification to breach confidentiality in the absence of an explicit threat? What about a moral justification? Can a psychiatrist be found liable for patient violence in the absence of an explicit threat?

This chapter provides an overview of the legal framework underlying malpractice liability for patient violence, reviews principles of violence risk assessment, and offers practical risk management strategies to reduce psychiatrists' risk of liability for patient violence.

Legal Framework

Tarasoff v. Regents of the University of California (1976) is considered the most influential case related to a mental health professional's liability for patient violence. In 1969, a graduate student who had been receiving psychotherapy at a university clinic stabbed and killed Tatiana Tarasoff. In one therapy session leading up to the killing, the student threatened to buy a gun and kill Ms. Tarasoff. Although the therapist contacted police about this threat, he did not warn Ms. Tarasoff or her family. Ms. Tarasoff's parents sued the university and the therapist for failing to warn them that their daughter was in danger.

The trial court dismissed the case, concluding that there was no cause of action since the therapist had a duty only to his patient, not to a third party. The appellate court affirmed this dismissal. However, the California Supreme Court in 1974 reversed the appellate court decision and created a "duty to warn." In this decision, known as *Tarasoff I*, the court held that when a doctor or therapist "…determines, or should determine, that a warning is essential to avert danger arising from the medical or psychological condition of his patient, he incurs a legal obligation to give that warning" (*Tarasoff v. Regents of the University of California*, 1974, p. 555).

Due to outcry from psychiatrists and police about the inaccuracy of violence prediction and the potential for patients to stop seeking care due to lack of confidentiality, the California Supreme Court took the unusual step of hearing the case again. In their 1976 ruling, known as *Tarasoff II*, the court held that "when a therapist determines, or pursuant to the standards of his profession should determine, that his patient presents a serious danger of violence to another, he incurs an obligation to use reasonable care to protect the intended victim from danger…it may call for him to warn the intended victim or others likely to apprise the victim of the danger, to notify the police, or to take whatever other steps are reasonably necessary" (*Tarasoff v. Regents of the University of California*, 1976, p. 431). This holding created a "duty to protect."

The defendants in the *Tarasoff* case argued that creating a duty to exercise reasonable care to protect third persons was unworkable because therapists were not able to accurately predict a patient's violent behaviors. *Amicus curiae* briefs submitted by the American Psychiatric Association and several other professional organizations cited research showing that therapists consistently over-predict violence and were more often wrong than right.

The California Supreme Court majority in *Tarasoff II* responded that they do not require a therapist to achieve

A. Saxton (✉) · P. Resnick
Department of Psychiatry, Case Western Reserve University School of Medicine, Cleveland, OH, USA

P. Ash et al. (eds.), *Malpractice and Liability in Psychiatry*, https://doi.org/10.1007/978-3-030-91975-7_13

perfect performance in predicting violence. Instead, a therapist need only exercise "that reasonable degree of skill, knowledge and care ordinarily possessed and exercised by members of [that professional specialty] under similar circumstances" (*Bardessono v. Michels*, 1970, p. 788) (*Tarasoff v. Regents of the University of California*, 1976, p. 438), adding that "proof aided by hindsight" was not sufficient to establish negligence. Furthermore, in the Tarasoff case, the therapist's concerns about the student's potential for violence proved warranted. The majority opined that the risk of unnecessary warnings was a reasonable price to pay for the lives of possible victims who might be saved and that the public's interest in safety from violent acts outweighed concerns about protecting patients' privacy.

The *Tarasoff* case was unique in its creation of a legal duty to third parties and added a new exception to therapist-patient confidentiality. Prior to *Tarasoff*, lawsuits related to harm to third parties were rarely successful due to the common law principle that people do not generally have duties to "third parties" unless they have a special relationship with them. For example, if a person sees a stranger drowning in a public pool and a life preserver is readily available, that person generally has no legal duty to assist the drowning person and thus cannot be held liable for their injuries or death. In contrast, a lifeguard on duty, who does have a "special relationship" with the drowning person due to his occupation, would have a legal duty to try to save the stranger.

In *Tarasoff*, the court cited some other case law exceptions to this general principle. For example, they noted that doctors had been held liable for negligent failure to diagnose a contagious disease and for failing to warn family members of their patient's diagnosed contagious illness (*Tarasoff v. Regents of the University of California*, 1974). Perhaps even more relevant, in *Merchants Nat. Bank & Trust Co. of Fargo v. United States*, the Veterans Administration was held liable for arranging for a patient to work on a farm but failing to warn the farmer of the man's dangerous background. The patient, being allowed to come and go freely, rented a car, drove to his wife's home, and killed her (*Merchants Nat. Bank & Trust Co. of Fargo v. United States*, 1967). The *Tarasoff* court concluded that patients with severe mental illness and "dangerous proclivities" may present a danger that is both serious and foreseeable, akin to a person with a contagious disease or a driver with a medical condition that affects his ability to drive safely (*Tarasoff v. Regents of the University of California*, 1974).

Expansions of the *Tarasoff* Doctrine

The *Tarasoff* case has had far-reaching implications. Although the decision applied only to California, new case law developed in states across the country citing the *Tarasoff* precedent. Subsequent court decisions in other states found psychiatrists liable for failing to prevent violent acts by patients (Soulier et al., 2010). Some of these decisions broadened the *Tarasoff* holding, finding liability for violence toward unidentified victims in the general public (*Lipari v. Sears, Roebuck & Co.*, 1980), for discharging psychiatric inpatients who were at foreseeable risk of reckless driving (*Naidu v. Laird*, 1988; *Petersen v. Washington*, 1983), and for violent acts against property (*Peck v. Counseling Service of Addison County*, 1985).

In *Lipari v. Sears, Roebuck and Co.*, 1 month after leaving a VA day treatment program, a man fired a shotgun into an Omaha nightclub, killing Mr. Lipari. Mrs. Lipari filed suit against the VA arguing that the staff should have known that the man was dangerous and should have taken appropriate steps to manage him. A federal district court in Nebraska denied the defendant's motion to dismiss (for no cause of action), reasoning that a therapist has a duty to "initiate whatever precautions are reasonably necessary to protect potential victims of his patient" (*Lipari v. Sears, Roebuck & Co.*, 1980, p. 193). This case created a duty to any class of individuals who are at a reasonably foreseeable risk of harm (in contrast to *Tarasoff* which was limited to identifiable victims).

In *Naidu v. Laird*, the Delaware Supreme Court upheld a trial court ruling in which a psychiatrist employed by Delaware State Hospital was found liable. His patient had caused a deadly auto accident more than 5 months after hospital discharge and hundreds of miles away from the hospital (*Naidu v. Laird*, 1988). These decisions, not surprisingly, fueled fear of liability among psychiatrists who were increasingly being expected by courts to predict violence at distant locations and dates and toward unidentified individuals (Soulier et al., 2010).

Limitations of the *Tarasoff* Doctrine

In response to court decisions that were trending toward seemingly endless mental health professional liability for patients' violent acts, mental health professionals lobbied state legislatures to provide specific guidelines for their duty to protect third parties. Over 20 states have now enacted "*Tarasoff*-limiting statutes" that are intended to specify the situations that trigger a duty to protect third parties, and exactly what should be done to discharge that duty. In most states, these statutes attempt to shield mental health professionals from liability for patient violence in situations that do not meet a specific threshold for a duty to protect (Soulier et al., 2010).

California, where the original *Tarasoff* case took place, passed the first *Tarasoff*-limiting statute. Compared to the relatively broad *Tarasoff* holding that required a duty to protect when a patient "presents a serious danger of violence to another," the California statute (updated in 2013) limits liability to situations in which the patient communicated a serious threat. Specifically: "There shall be no monetary liability…. and no cause of action shall arise against, any … psychotherapist … in failing to predict and protect from a patient's violent behavior except if the patient has communicated to the psychotherapist a serious threat of physical violence against a reasonably identifiable victim or victims" (California Civil Code § 43.92 [2013]). This statute protects therapists in situations where patient violence occurs in the absence of an explicit threat, even if the patient had many violence risk factors. In addition to limitations on psychiatrist liability for patient violence offered by some states, *Tarasoff*-limiting statutes almost uniformly offer immunity for a breach of confidentiality made in good faith in a duty to warn or protect scenario.

Tarasoff-limiting statutes have been helpful in reducing clinician liability for patients' violent acts. Soulier et al. analyzed 70 Tarasoff-related appellate cases from 1985 to 2006 and found that overall, defendants were rarely found to be negligent on the grounds of failure to warn or protect (Soulier et al., 2010). Soulier and colleagues noted, "In the early days after *Tarasoff*, courts found negligence in cases with fact patterns similar to those that are now being decided for defendants" (Soulier et al., 2010, p. 469). In Soulier and colleagues' analysis, appellate courts "almost always found that defendants owed no duty to the public at large" (Soulier et al., 2010, p. 470). Further, courts in several cases found that the duty did not extend to victims who were already aware of the danger from a patient and that clinicians could not be held liable for violence that occurred long after termination of treatment. In states that mandate or permit a clinician warning, courts consistently found no duty when the patient had not communicated a threat to the therapist (Soulier et al., 2010).

Despite these promising findings, it is important to note that the protection (if any) offered to mental health professionals in the event of violent acts by patients varies by state and is still subject to interpretation by courts. Soulier and colleagues described six plaintiff verdicts that demonstrated "*Tarasoff*'s inability to protect clinicians from clinical assessments that the courts found to be seriously lacking or missing all together" (Soulier et al., 2010, p. 470). Michaelsen commented regarding this finding, "The protection of *Tarasoff*-limiting laws did not extend to negligent care and poor clinical judgment—that is, when a clinician's care failed to meet the standards that could be reasonably expected for clinicians in a similar position—such as failing to assess a patient's risk of violence when there are clearly reasons for concern (e.g., agitation with a history of violence)" (Michaelsen, 2017, p. 39). Soulier and colleagues' analysis was limited to appellate level cases, so the details of *Tarasoff*-related cases settled in favor of the plaintiff or dismissed at the trial court level without appeal are unknown.

Some state supreme courts (e.g., Michigan) have narrowly interpreted their state's *Tarasoff*-limiting statute in such a way that liability for violent acts by patients in the absence of an explicit threat is still possible under a common law suit (Hartwig et al., 2011). In *Volk v. DeMeerleer*, the Washington Supreme Court similarly found that psychiatrists need to exercise "reasonable care to act consistent with the standards of the mental health profession, in order to protect the foreseeable victims of his or her patient" even in the absence of an explicit threat toward an identifiable victim (*Volk v. DeMeerleer*, 2016, p. 266).

Tarasoff Duties by State

Tarasoff duties across the states can be classified into four general categories:

1. States with a mandatory duty to warn or protect codified in legislative **statute** (23 states)
2. States with **common law** precedent that describes a duty to warn or protect (10 states)
3. States that **permit** a breach of confidentiality if there is a threat but do not have a statute or case law mandating it (11 states)
4. States without case law or statutes providing guidance (6 states) (Johnson et al., 2014)

Some authors group the first two categories into one, referring to these as "mandatory duty" states. The states that permit a breach of confidentiality but do not require it are considered "permissive" states.

In addition to variability among states on the issue of mandatory versus permissive warnings, states vary with respect to whether the threat must be imminent or serious, whether the victim must be an identifiable person (usually) versus "reasonably foreseeable," and whether threats toward property qualify (Johnson et al., 2014; Michaelsen, 2017). The necessary interventions may also vary from warning the victim and/or police, to hospitalization of the person making the threat, to developing a treatment plan designed to eliminate the risk. Psychiatrists should familiarize themselves with the specific *Tarasoff*-limiting statute or case law in the state where they practice.

Tarasoff-Limiting Statute Protections

Although *Tarasoff*-limiting statutes are usually protective for clinicians, it is not safe to assume that a psychiatrist will be free from liability in all cases where the patient does not make an explicit threat. Soulier and colleagues' study found that the protections did not completely insulate clinicians who "failed to exercise sound clinical judgment" nor did they prevent liability in cases where clinical assessments were "seriously lacking" (Soulier et al., 2010). The 2016 *Volk v. DeMeerleer* case in Washington raised concerns among psychiatrists that the pendulum may be swinging back toward increased liability for violent acts of patients (*Volk v. DeMeerleer*, 2016). In *Volk*, the Washington Supreme Court ruled that clinicians must exercise "reasonable care to act consistent with the standards of the mental health profession, in order to protect the foreseeable victims of his or her patient" (*Volk v. DeMeerleer*, 2016, p. 266). In *Volk*, Mr. DeMeerleer, a man with a history of bipolar disorder, shot and killed his ex-fiancé and her 9-year-old son. Mr. DeMeerleer was treated by a psychiatrist in the outpatient setting. During his last appointment, Mr. DeMeerleer expressed no homicidal ideas. He reported some suicidal thinking when depressed, but he denied suicide intent. He was continued on his medications. The killings took place 3 months after that appointment. The malpractice case was allowed to proceed against the defendant doctor, even though the patient made no threats toward the victims. The case subsequently settled out of court.

Although psychiatrists and other mental health professionals are not expected to accurately *predict* violence, reasonable care generally requires conducting an adequate violence risk assessment. The risk of being found liable for patients' violent acts is reduced if an adequate violence risk assessment is documented and interventions were made that were appropriate for the risk level. This is particularly important if the patient has engaged in threatening behavior or demonstrates other signs indicating an elevated risk of violence (Michaelsen, 2017).

Failure to warn or protect is relatively rarely the cause of a malpractice verdict against psychiatrists. According to Professional Risk Management Services (PRMS) (a malpractice insurance provider) Cause of Loss data from 1986 to 2019, less than 1% of claims were related to duty to warn or protect (PRMS, 2020). This is not surprising since most psychiatrists are familiar with their *Tarasoff* duty and have a sense of what to do when faced with a patient making an explicit threat. Many state *Tarasoff*-limiting statutes offer fairly specific guidance. However, as we have seen in case law and Soulier and colleagues' analysis, liability can occasionally be attached to patient violence without an explicit threat. A patient with many violence risk factors who makes no overt threat presents a greater clinical challenge and requires a more nuanced approach.

Examples of Malpractice Allegations Related to Patient Violence

Psychiatrists may face potential liability in the following scenarios:

1. Failure to hospitalize a patient with both mental illness and a high violence risk (even in the absence of threats). For example, failing to hospitalize a patient with acute paranoia who has a recent history of violence while psychotic
2. Premature discharge of a patient from a psychiatric hospital who remains at a substantial risk of violence and in need of further treatment. For example, discharging a patient who continues to show signs of mania and has been recently assaultive toward other patients
3. Failure to schedule an outpatient follow-up appointment at an appropriate interval to monitor a patient with schizophrenia and a history of recent serious violence
4. Failure to reach out to a high-risk patient who has missed three consecutive appointments and has no refill of antipsychotic medication available
5. Discontinuing or markedly reducing psychotropic medications without reviewing past records detailing a patient's pattern of prior symptoms and violence
6. Failure to conduct a violence risk assessment of an individual with homicidal fantasies even though the patient denies any intent to act on the fantasies
7. Offering an opinion that a patient who made a serious threat can safely return to work without a doing an appropriate violence risk assessment
8. Failure to gather collateral information relevant to violence risk in a patient with a substantial number of risk factors (list of examples adapted from Resnick & Saxton, 2019)

Whether or not these allegations will lead to the defendant psychiatrist being found liable depends on a number of factors including:

1. Whether or not the state has a *Tarasoff*-limiting statute that prohibits liability if a patient made no explicit threat
2. How the court interprets and applies a *Tarasoff*-limiting statute
3. Expert opinions regarding whether the psychiatrist's actions met the standard of care for assessing violence risk
4. Whether the jury believes that the doctor met the standard of care

Malpractice insurers and healthcare institutions may be motivated to settle a case in which a patient's violent act led to considerable damages. Malpractice insurers may be concerned that a jury will sympathize with the victims of severe violence or be influenced by hindsight bias. However, a well-documented violence risk assessment and rationale for the clinical decisions made prior to the violent act will strongly support the conclusion that the psychiatrist's care met the standard of care. Such documentation will increase the willingness of insurers to fight an allegation in a trial rather than settle the case.

A Systematic Approach to Violence Risk Assessment Reduces Liability Risk

The following recommendations are aspirational and are not meant to suggest a standard of care for violence risk assessments.

The key themes in violence risk management are (1) identifying the level of risk and (2) addressing the risk appropriately. A psychiatrist should perform an adequate violence risk assessment if a patient has recently made threats or recently exhibited violent behavior. Violence risk should also be assessed in manic and psychotic patients. Psychiatrists should collect data regarding static (not subject to change by intervention) and dynamic (subject to change by intervention) risk factors for violence in a systematized fashion. Consider the use of a structured violence risk assessment instrument which can help guide data collection to ensure that relevant information is not missed. Important risk factors are listed in Table 13.1.

A recent review of meta-analyses by Fazel and colleagues found that among neuropsychiatric risk factors for violence, substance use disorders convey the largest effect at the population level. Among historical risk factors for violence, witnessing or being the victim of childhood violence had the greatest effect. They found that the top five risk factors for interpersonal violence ranked by quality of the evidence are antisocial personality disorder, bipolar disorder, schizophrenia, non-schizophrenia psychoses, and victimization by bullying (Fazel et al., 2018).

In contrast to *static* risk factors which are not generally subject to intervention, *dynamic* risk factors present opportunities for intervention. Major *dynamic* risk factors for violence are substance use and active psychiatric symptoms. It is well established that although certain symptoms of mental illness raise the risk of violence, the vast majority of violence in society is not due to mental illness (Skeem et al., 2016). Nonetheless, as psychiatrists, it is crucial that we assess the contribution of psychiatric symptomatology to violence risk. Psychosis is a key symptom associated with increased violence risk. Paranoid patients are at risk of killing someone in misperceived self-defense. Command hallucinations, especially if related to a delusion, elevate the risk of violence (Scott & Resnick, 2017). Patients with poor insight into their illness are likely to discontinue their medication and are also at higher risk of violence. Traumatic brain injury and poor executive functioning have also been linked to violence (Fazel et al., 2018).

Table 13.1 Risk factors for violence

Risk factor	Example
Violence	Past episodes of assault
Antisocial behavior	History of repeated arrests
Relationship problems	Lack of long-term relationships, frequent infidelity
Employment problems	Frequent unemployment
Substance abuse	Alcohol abuse
Major mental disorder	Paranoid psychosis
Personality disorder	Antisocial personality disorder
Traumatic experiences	Victim of child abuse
Violent attitudes	Views violence as an acceptable way to solve problems
Problems with treatment or supervision response	Failure to successfully complete probation

Adapted from Douglas et al. (2013)

The well-established link between substance abuse and interpersonal violence is likely multifactorial. The direct psychopharmacological effects of substances, economic issues (e.g., commission of crime and/or violence to fund drug use), and systemic factors (e.g., violence as an inherent part of the illicit drug market) may all play a role (Atkinson et al., 2009). According to a 2009 publication by the World Health Organization, 35% of methamphetamine users between the ages of 18 and 25 in Los Angeles, CA, committed violence while under the influence (Atkinson et al., 2009). According to a study in Memphis, TN, victims and family members of the victims and/or perpetrators of domestic violence believed that 92% of the perpetrators had used drugs or alcohol on the day of the assault (Atkinson et al., 2009). In a 2004 survey of state and federal prisoners, 17% and 18% of inmates reported committing their violent offense to obtain money for drugs (Mumola & Karberg, 2006). Because the majority of violence risk factors are historical and not subject to change by intervention, psychiatrists should pay special attention to the factors that are potentially modifiable, such as active substance use.

It is useful to inquire about any preparation the patient has made for violent acts (e.g., journaling plans, purchasing a weapon, or surveilling a target for an attack). Contextual factors that may lead to violence should be explored (e.g., stress, financial problems, narcissistic injury, romantic problems). The risk level is elevated in contexts with similar situational factors that precipitated prior violent acts. It is essential to ask about access to weapons, particularly firearms. Patients may not always be forthcoming with information related to their risk of violence, particularly if they wish to avoid hospitalization. In a situation with a high level of concern, collateral sources become especially important.

Once the risk assessment data are collected, the next step is formulating a treatment plan that is designed to reduce the patient's level of risk. Ideally, the treatment plan should address each modifiable risk factor for violence. For example, in a psychotic patient with poor insight and a history of medication non-compliance, initiating a long-acting injectable antipsychotic medication can reduce risk. Other steps to improve compliance could include pursuing an outpatient commitment order or guardianship. For patients with substance use disorders, consider the use of a medication to assist with sobriety (e.g., buprenorphine, naloxone, naltrexone) and referral to a substance use treatment program (Resnick & Saxton, 2019).

Even if the best treatment is made available during an inpatient stay, many individuals will still carry some elevated risk of violence at the time of discharge due to the burden of historical non-modifiable factors. Additionally, some dynamic risk factors are unlikely to change completely during the inpatient stay and will require further treatment in the outpatient setting (e.g., substance use disorders, poor coping skills, impulsivity). However, the most critical modifiable risk factors should be addressed during the inpatient stay.

For example, consider a mother with postpartum psychotic depression who believes that her baby is possessed by the devil. Postpartum psychosis is considered a psychiatric emergency that requires hospitalization in almost all cases. This aforementioned delusion about her infant is a major risk factor that should be treated and resolved prior to discharge. The depression should also be treated in the hospital, though it may not fully resolve prior to discharge. A pre-discharge meeting with family to provide education, including emphasizing the importance of support in the home to allow patient to get adequate sleep, the need for regular outpatient follow-up, and warning signs of potential decompensation to look out for, is also recommended to mitigate risk. Further, a child protective services referral may be warranted given the potential risk to the baby (Friedman et al., 2019). If the patient also has a history of chronic poor coping skills, a plan to continue to address these issues in outpatient therapy is reasonable (Resnick & Saxton, 2019). The discharge plan should mention unresolved dynamic risk factors that should be addressed as an outpatient.

After collecting the relevant information about violence risk and formulating a strategy to address risk factors, the final step is documentation. The documentation should include an overall estimation of risk and how the treatment plan addresses the modifiable risk factors. Be sure to add the clinical rationale for decisions, including why the proposed treatment plan is the least restrictive setting that is appropriate for a patient's level of violence risk (Saxton et al., 2018). This is particularly important when a potentially violent patient is stepped down from a higher level of care. "You can do a good job and write a bad note, but it is hard to write a good note if you have done a bad job" (Kontos et al., 2018). Thorough documentation can strongly reduce risk of liability in the event of a negative outcome (Resnick & Saxton, 2019).

After discharge from the hospital, a patient with elevated risk of violence is likely to require frequent follow-up appointments to monitor their condition. Psychiatrists should avoid major medication changes in patients with a history of psychosis or severe mood disorders when there is a lack of knowledge of their violence history. A psychiatrist could be found liable in the case of a careless medication reduction that leads to psychotic decompensation and violence. This would be more likely if the past medical records documented agitation, paranoia, or violence at lower dosages. If patients with serious risk factors fail to attend their follow-up appointments, reasonable efforts to reach out to them should be made; home visits by case managers and efforts to contact family members should be documented.

Additional Suggestions to Reduce Potential Liability for Violence by Patients

The following suggestions are adapted from Resnick and Saxton (2019):

Obtain Collateral Information

Violence risk assessments should not rely solely on a patient's denial of violent plans or intent if there is other information that points to an elevated risk level. Potential sources of collateral information include friends, family, co-workers, online court dockets, controlled substance databases, and police reports. As the severity of the potential risk rises, the amount of collateral data collected should rise proportionately.

Inquire About Access to Weapons

When firearms are used in violent acts, the risk of severe injury or death increases. Individuals who are planning an attack may be reluctant to disclose their weapons access. For example, James Holmes, the 2012 Aurora Colorado movie theatre shooter, disclosed homicidal fantasies to his treating psychiatrist but denied plans to act on these thoughts. He went on to secretly purchase weapons and thousands of rounds of ammunition on the internet in the weeks before the shooting (Patterson, 2012). Seeking collateral information about weapons access may reveal important data regarding risk.

In acutely high-risk situations, efforts should be made to avoid discharging a patient from the hospital if they will have access to firearms. A friend or family member should remove the firearms from the home and confirm with the treatment team that this task has been done. Patients should not be trusted to remove their own firearms from the home.

Involuntary commitment may be a way of preventing a patient from legally purchasing firearms from a licensed dealer in the future since the federal government and many states have laws banning gun ownership by individuals who have been involuntarily committed (Gold & Vanderpool, 2018).

A growing number of states now have some form of "red flag law," also known as extreme risk protection orders (ERPO), or gun violence restraining orders (GVRO), depending on the state. These types of laws do not require that the individual be involuntarily committed to restrict firearms access. As of 2019, at least 17 states have approved some variation of a red flag law (Williams, 2019). In contrast, prior to the 2018 mass shooting at Marjory Stoneman Douglas High School in Parkland, Florida, only five states had such laws (Williams, 2019). These laws allow law enforcement, and sometimes mental health professionals or family members, to petition state courts to restrict firearms access for people who are deemed a threat to themselves or others (Arnold et al., 2018). California is an example of a state that allows families to apply for a GVRO (Ask for a Gun Violence Restraining Order, 2021). Psychiatrists should familiarize themselves with their state's red flag law, if present, since this can be a useful tool to mitigate violence risk.

Issue a Warning

If a patient threatens harm toward an identifiable third party, appropriate steps should be taken in compliance with state *Tarasoff* regulations. This could include warning the victim and law enforcement, or admitting the patient to the hospital. In states without a mandatory or permissive duty to warn or protect, a conflict may arise between the psychiatrist's legal duty to protect confidentiality and their moral obligation to prevent harm. A similar dilemma may occur when a patient does not make an explicit threat yet implies a serious threat. In these scenarios, one should consider consulting risk management personnel (if available) or consulting one's malpractice insurer. Seeking a second opinion from a colleague may also be useful. It is easier to defend a malpractice suit for a breach of confidentiality done in good faith than a suit for a wrongful death.

When the violence risk appears to be primarily due to antisocial personality traits, psychiatrists should still complete a violence risk assessment, address modifiable risk factors, and carry out appropriate *Tarasoff* duties. Short-term voluntary hospitalization may be indicated in a crisis; however, involuntary hospitalization may not be legally permissible if the dangerousness does not flow from mental illness. Some states specifically define mental illness (e.g., Ohio), and antisocial personality disorder usually does not meet the definition or is specifically excluded (hospitalization of mentally ill definitions, 2004). Other states are less specific about what constitutes a mental illness, in which case antisocial personality disorder might qualify since it is found in the *Diagnostic and Statistical Manual of Mental Disorders*. Nonetheless, prolonged hospitalizations for patients who are dangerous due to antisocial personality alone is generally not helpful nor clinically indicated. Instead, clinicians should address dynamic risk factors, including access to guns; carry out a duty to protect, if applicable, document thoughtfully; and discharge when there is no further clinical indication for hospitalization (Saxton et al., 2018).

Risk Mitigation Strategies

Court-ordered probation after a violent offense can sometimes help to reduce violence risk due to mandated abstinence from substances (monitored by drug and alcohol screens). Probation may also reduce risk by requiring compliance with mental health appointments and psychiatric medication. If a patient is on probation, consider seeking a release of information to coordinate care with their probation officer. In a patient whose mental condition raises reasonable concerns about their ability to safely parent their child (e.g., abuse, neglect, or a significant risk of violence), Child Protective Services (CPS) must be notified. CPS may be able to offer some services and monitoring to reduce risk.

Documentation

As indicated previously, proper documentation is crucial and can be highly protective against liability if a bad outcome occurs. Good documentation includes information about violence risk factors, an overall estimation of risk, and a plan that addresses the modifiable risk factors for violence. Further, the clinical rationale for the proposed treatment plan should be noted.

Seek a Second Opinion in Difficult Cases

Medical malpractice claims frequently allege that a psychiatrist did not provide reasonably prudent care and was thus negligent in their assessment or management of the patient's condition. Seeking a second opinion can be helpful, not only to offer new ideas and risk mitigation strategies but also to show that the psychiatrist took the case seriously and pursued additional advice to lower the risk.

Conclusion

Despite the fact that violent acts are extremely difficult to accurately predict, psychiatrists are expected to make reasonable efforts to assess and reduce the risk when faced with a potentially violent patient. While some states have enacted statutes to reduce mental health clinicians' liability for the violent acts of their patients, courts have varied in their interpretation of these statutes. In order to reduce the risk of liability, an adequate violence risk assessment should be completed and documented. Documenting only disavowal of homicidal intent may be insufficient in some cases, particularly if other information points to a high-risk level. It is much more difficult for a plaintiff to prove negligence when a psychiatrist collects sufficient information (including collateral), asks about access to weapons, and documents the reasoning for their clinical decisions.

Key Points

- Learn the state-specific *Tarasoff*-type duty.
- *Tarasoff*-limiting statutes offer some liability protection but may not protect against inadequate assessment or frankly unsound clinical judgment.
- Collect data about violence risk in a systematized fashion and always ask about weapons.
- When there is a clinical concern for acutely elevated risk of violence, seek collateral information regarding prior threats of violence, violent acts, and substance use, rather than relying only on the patient's word.
- Initiate efforts to mitigate dynamic risk factors.
- Document the overall risk level, how dynamic risk factors are being addressed, and why the treatment plan is appropriate for the patient's risk level.
- When in doubt, consult a colleague, risk management services, and/or malpractice insurer.

References

Arnold, S., Deai, A., & DeMatteo, D. (2018). Keeping guns away from potentially dangerous people. *Monitor on Psychology, 49*(8). Retrieved from http://www.apa.org/monitor/2018/09/jn

Ask for a Gun Violence Restraining Order. (2021). Retrieved from https://www.courts.ca.gov/33679.htm

Atkinson, A., Anderson, Z., Hughes, K., Bellis, M., Sumnall, H., & Syed, Q. (2009). *Interpersonal violence and illicit drugs*. Retrieved from Liverpool: https://www.who.int/violenceprevention/interpersonal_violence_and_illicit_drug_use.pdf

Bardessono v. Michels, 3 Cal. 3d 780. (1970).

California Civil Code § 43.92. (2013).

Douglas, K., Hart, S., Webster, C., & Belfrage, H. (2013). Rating sheet for version 3 of the HCR-20. In *Mental health, law, and policy institute*. Simon Fraser University.

Fazel, S., Smith, N., Chang, Z., & Geddes, J. (2018). Risk factors for interpersonal violence: An umbrella review of meta-analyses. *The British Journal of Psychiatry, 213*(4), 609–614.

Friedman, S. H., Prakash, C., & Nagle-Yang, S. (2019). Postpartum psychosis: Protecting mother and infant. *Current Psychiatry, 4*(18), 13–21.

Gold, L., & Vanderpool, D. (2018). Legal regulation of restoration of firearms rights after mental health prohibition. *Journal of the American Academy of Psychiatry and the Law, 46*(3), 298–308.

Hartwig, T., Solis, L., & Lemmen, C. (2011). The duty to protect from third parties: Common law versus statute. *Journal of the American Academy of Psychiatry and the Law, 39*(4), 594–597.

Hospitalization of mentally ill definitions, O.R.C. 5122.01(A)(2004).

Johnson, R., Persad, G., & Sisti, D. (2014). The Tarasoff rule: The implications of interstate variation and gaps in professional training. *Journal of the American Academy of Psychiatry and the Law, 42*(4), 469–477.

Kontos, N., Taylor, J., & Beach, S. (2018). The therapeutic discharge II: An approach to documentation in the setting of feigned suicidal ideation. *General Hospital Psychiatry, 51*, 30–35.

Lipari v. Sears, Roebuck & Co., 497 F. Supp. 185 (D. Neb. 1980).

Merchants Nat. Bank & Trust Co. of Fargo v. United States, 272 F.Supp. 409 (D.N.D. 1967).

Michaelsen, K. (2017). Duties to third parties. In T. Wasser (Ed.), *Psychiatry and the law- basic principles* (pp. 35–51). Springer International Publishing.

Mumola, C., & Karberg, J. (2006). *Drug use and dependence, state and federal prisoners, 2004*. Retrieved from https://www.bjs.gov/content/pub/pdf/dudsfp04.pdf

Naidu v. Laird, 539 A.2d 1064 (Delaware 1988).

Patterson, T. (2012). Police chief: Suspect bought over 6,000 rounds of ammunition through Internet. *CNN*. Retrieved from www.cnn.com/2012/07/20/colorado-shooting-weapons/index.html

Peck v. Counseling Service of Addison County, 499 A.2d 422 (Vt. 1985).

Petersen v. Washington, 671 P.2d 230 (Wash. 1983).

PRMS (Producer). (2020). *Professional risk management services cause of loss- claims and lawsuits 1986-2019*. Retrieved from https://www.prms.com/media/2439/cause-of-loss-2019.pdf

Resnick, P., & Saxton, A. (2019). Malpractice liability due to patient violence. *Focus, 17*(4), 343–348. Retrieved from https://doi.org/10.1176/appi.focus.20190022

Saxton, A., Resnick, P., & Noffsinger, S. (2018). Chief complaint: Homicidal. Assessing violence risk. *Current Psychiatry, 17*(5), 27–35.

Scott, C., & Resnick, P. (2017). Clinical assessment of aggression and violence. In R. Rosner & C. Scott (Eds.), *Principles and practice of forensic psychiatry* (3rd ed., pp. 623–631).

Skeem, J., Kennealy, P., Monahan, J., et al. (2016). Psychosis uncommonly and inconsistently precedes violence among high-risk individuals. *Clinical Psychological Science, 4*(1), 40–49.

Soulier, M. F., Maislen, A., & Beck, J. C. (2010). Status of the psychiatric duty to protect, circa 2006. *Journal of the American Academy of Psychiatry and the Law, 38*(4), 457–473. Retrieved from https://www.ncbi.nlm.nih.gov/pubmed/21156904

Tarasoff v. The Regents of the University of California, 529 P.2d 553 (California Supreme Court 1974).

Tarasoff v. The Regents of the University of California, 17 Cal. 3d Cal. 3d 425 (California Supreme Court 1976).

Volk v. DeMeerleer, 386 P.3d 254 (Washington Supreme Court 2016).

Williams, T. (2019). What are "red flag' gun laws, and how do they work?. *New York Times*. Retrieved from https://www.nytimes.com/2019/08/06/us/red-flag-laws.html

Boundary Violations

14

Richard Martinez and Susan Hatters Friedman

While psychiatrists are much less likely to experience a malpractice claim than most colleagues in other medical specialties (Jena et al., 2011), claims involving boundary dilemmas and boundary violations warrant special consideration. Boundary violations historically were defined as inappropriate sexual relationships between psychiatrists (as well as other mental health therapists) and patients (Friedman & Martinez, 2019). Over the last 40 years, the concept of boundary violations has come to include inappropriate sexual relations, financial issues and dual relationships, as well as violations related to the internet and social media. Norris et al. (2003) described risk factors for clinician boundary problems. These include difficulty with limit setting, feelings of loneliness or shame, therapist fears of mortality and illness, and crises of life (whether in early life, midlife, or later life), as well as issues in one's own relationships and transition times such as employment changes and retirement. They further described that those at greatest risk of boundary violations are those who never conceptualize their own risk. A UK investigation of complaints against physicians for inappropriate relationships with patients found that 91% of the physicians investigated were men (Davies, 2015). Stress management, supervision when necessary with mentors, and avoidance of burnout may all help prevent these issues (Davies, 2015).

Boundaries and Boundary Violations

The concept of boundaries in psychiatry and other psychotherapeutic specialties begins with an appreciation of the special ethical requirements central to the patient-physician relationship. As far back as the Hippocratic Oath, the patient-physician relationship has been anchored in the principles of beneficence and nonmaleficence while stressing the importance of maintaining confidentiality and avoidance of exploitation of patients. "Into whatever homes I go, I will enter them for the benefit of the sick, avoiding any voluntary act of impropriety or corruption, including seduction of women and men, whether they are free men or slaves" (see Hippocratic Oath (2002), para. 9). Over time, the ethical requirements of the patient-physician relationship became codified in professional codes of ethics and extensively discussed in the medical and psychiatric literature.

The American Medical Association's (AMA's) *Code of Medical Ethics* has evolved from its initial 1847 version. In the current version of the AMA's Principles of Medical Ethics, the preamble makes clear that "a physician must recognize responsibility to patients first and foremost, as well as to society, to other health professionals, and to self" (American Medical Association, 2017, p. 1). Following the preamble, a list of principles provides guidance that stresses virtues such as honesty, compassion, and respect for all patients while reminding physicians of obligations to maintain patient confidences and privacy and to always place the patient's interests over self-interests. Other principles that round out the modern physician's ethical responsibilities include participation in community welfare activities and advocate for fair access to medical care. In addition to the preamble and principles, the *Code of Medical Ethics* includes chapters that contain opinions particularly relevant to the patient-physician relationship and boundary regulation. Sections that may be most useful include the Patient-Physician Relationship; Consent, Communication, and Decision-Making; Privacy, Confidentiality, and Medical Records; and Professional Self-Regulation (American Medical Association, 2017).

In addition to the Principles of Medical Ethics, the Opinions developed by the AMA Council on Ethical and Judicial Affairs (CEJA) are essential resources for clinicians wishing to better understand ethical obligations and profes-

R. Martinez
University of Colorado at Anschutz Medical Center, Denver, CO, USA
e-mail: Richard.martinez@cuanschutz.edu

S. H. Friedman (✉)
Division of Forensic Psychiatry, Case Western Reserve University, Cleveland, OH, USA
e-mail: Susan.hattersfriedman@case.edu

P. Ash et al. (eds.), *Malpractice and Liability in Psychiatry*, https://doi.org/10.1007/978-3-030-91975-7_14

sional boundaries. These opinions cover informed consent (Opinion 2.1.1); guidance in interacting with the media, electronic communication with patients, and professionalism in the use of social media (Opinions 3.1.5; 2.3.1; and 2.3.2); restrictions on romantic and sexual relationships with patients and family members (Opinions 9.1.1; 9.1.2); responsibilities to impaired colleagues (Opinion 9.3.2); and treating self or family (Opinion 1.2.1) (American Medical Association, 2017).

Of course, the practice of psychiatry (and other psychotherapeutic specialties) requires *awareness* of complex and unique dynamics particular to the patient-physician relationship. Therefore, in 1973, the American Psychiatric Association (APA) first published the *Principles of Medical Ethics: With Annotations Especially Applicable to Psychiatry*. In the 2013 edition, these annotations consider boundaries and provide guidance. Section 1.1 describes the psychiatrist's responsibility to deliver competent care with compassion and respect for human dignity and rights: "A psychiatrist shall not gratify his or her own needs by exploiting the patient. The psychiatrist shall be ever vigilant about the impact that his or her conduct has upon the boundaries of the doctor-patient relationship, and thus upon the well-being of the patient" (American Psychiatric Association, 2013, p. 3).

In Section 2, the *Annotations* provide further guidance on the concept of boundaries:

> The requirement that the physician conduct himself/herself with propriety in his profession and in all the actions of his or her life is especially important in the case of the psychiatrist… the necessary intensity of the treatment relationship may tend to activate sexual and other needs and fantasies on the part of both the patient and psychiatrist… the inherent inequality in the doctor-patient relationship may lead to exploitation of the patient. Sexual activity with a current or former patient is unethical. (American Psychiatric Association, 2013, p. 4)

Gutheil and Gabbard have contributed much to the psychiatric literature on boundary violations. Concerned about sexual misconduct malpractice claims in civil litigation and the growing number of complaints reported to medical licensing boards and district ethics committees, they proposed a theoretical risk management strategy that influenced a generation of practicing psychiatrists (Gutheil & Gabbard, 1993). With a risk-management approach, often described as the "slippery slope" model, Gutheil and Gabbard hoped to alert practitioners that harmful boundary violations could be avoided by mindful attention to aspects of the therapeutic relationship that might seem innocuous but could lead to harmful behaviors. As the authors wrote: "… fact finders—civil or criminal juries, judges, ethics committees or professional organizations, or state licensing boards—often believe that the presence of boundary violations (or even crossings) is presumptive evidence of, or corroborates allegations of sexual misconduct… smoke usually leads to fire; one can, however, find smoke where there is not fire, and yet fact finders may assume that where there's smoke, there's fire" (Gutheil & Gabbard, 1993, p. 189). Following this metaphor, the authors described a typology of boundary crossings that could reflect "smoke" and lead to "fire," and thus caution should be taken with each of these areas of the patient-physician relationship. Their typology of aspects of the relationship that required monitoring included consideration of role; time; place and space; money, gifts, and services; clothing; language; self-disclosure and related matters; and physical contact.

In earlier articles, Gabbard and Simon had described a series of minor boundary violations that were noted to precede eventual sexual exploitation of patients (Gabbard, 1989; Simon, 1989). This "slippery slope" understanding included a series of behaviors where the psychiatrist moved from last name to first name salutations, personal conversation and self-disclosure that intrude into the clinical work, seemingly innocuous physical contact such as pats on the shoulder progressing to hugs, meeting outside of the office, dinners with alcohol, and other social events, eventually culminating in sexual intimacy. In a later work, Gutheil and Brodsky (2008) provide an excellent summary of boundary dilemmas and provide recommendations that can guide clinicians in avoiding potential boundary problems and litigation.

The practice of psychiatry has changed dramatically in the last 30 years. Models based on the traditional psychotherapeutic patient-psychiatrist relationship when psychodynamic and psychoanalytic approaches were common in most psychiatric practices have receded. Today, psychiatrists work in a diversity of settings and contexts and draw on a myriad of theoretical approaches and techniques. In this changing practice of psychiatry, concepts of transference, countertransference, and the categorical approach of boundary violations may be less useful in managing boundary dynamics. In addition, patients are more diverse and come from a variety of ethnic, racial, and cultural backgrounds (Savin & Martinez, 2006), requiring sensitivity to dynamics rarely considered a generation ago. A model of boundary crossings and violations that was useful 30 years ago may have less practical value today. In addition, the concept of boundaries now extends beyond sexual exploitation, having importance in understanding dual relationships, prescribing for family and friends, and communicating with patients through email and social media.

To further appreciate the significance of boundary crossings and violations in professional misconduct, it is useful to review boundary violations and professional misconduct in health professionals who are referred for ethics remediation by licensing and other oversight entities. Caldicott and d'Oronzio (2015) published findings from the Professional/Problem-Based Ethics (ProBE) program, a national ethics education and professional remediation program offered in over six US and Canadian cities. They reviewed more than 1200 referrals of healthcare professionals from many health professional specialties including physicians, dentists, chiropractic practitioners, physical therapists, and others, over a 20-year period (1993–2013). Physicians constituted about 60% of their referrals over 20 years. Six medical specialties accounted for the physician participants with psychiatry representing 11% of the total number of physicians. In their typology of reasons for referral to ProBE, the authors coded a total of 38% of all referrals involved boundary crossings, 15% involved dual relationships, 11% for sexual relations with patients, and 8% of referrals involved inappropriate writing of prescriptions for friends, family, and others. The remainder of infractions that resulted in referral included an assortment of professional misconduct, including various forms of financial improprieties involved in the business operations of practice, misrepresentation in applications and license renewal, patient abandonment, and impairment while practicing. Boundary crossings clearly represented the largest group of referred practitioners, including physicians and other health professionals.

In a Canadian study, researchers constructed a database of all Canadian physicians disciplined by the provincial colleges of physicians and surgeons from 2000 to 2009 (Alam et al., 2012). The authors intended to determine whether psychiatrists were more likely than non-psychiatrists to commit professional misconduct including sexual boundary violations. There were 606 physicians disciplined in Canada during this 10-year period, including 82 psychiatrists. While psychiatrists make up 7% of all physicians in Canada, the number of psychiatrists in the database reflected 14% of all disciplined physicians, double the national proportion of psychiatrists. In addition, psychiatrists accounted for 20.3% of the total sexual misconduct offenses, again a disproportionate number when compared to non-psychiatric physicians. The authors concluded that psychiatrists had a greater risk of having disciplinary penalties not only in sexual misconduct but also in other unprofessional conduct and fraudulent behavior.

In the 1990s, some authors began to recognize the limitations of a model that was helpful in assessing potential risky behaviors that lead to boundary violations but discouraged variety and nuance in the patient-psychotherapist relationship that could offer potential benefits (Lazarus, 1994). In addition, as types of boundary dilemmas have expanded, involving the workplace as well as unique issues that have arisen with developments in social media and email, the "slippery slope" approach has been less useful in resolving and adjudicating the diversity of boundary dilemmas. A model that explored the differences between boundary crossings that might offer benefits to patients and boundary violations that are harmful was offered by Martinez (2000). Martinez's "graded risk" approach offered an alternative to the "slippery slope" approach that had come to dominate boundary analysis. Six factors are considered important to all boundary dilemmas, and, rather than offering proscriptions against certain boundary situations, each boundary dilemma is considered individually using a case-by-case analysis. The six factors used in this analysis include (1) the potential harm to the patient and the patient-physician relationship; (2) the potential benefit to the patient and the patient-physician relationship; (3) the presence or absence of coercive and exploitative elements in the boundary crossing; (4) the professional's motives and intentions; (5) the professional's aspiration to professional ideals of care; and (6) the context of the boundary crossing including cultural, ethnic, and racial considerations.

Martinez suggested that by considering the totality of these factors, a boundary crossing could be analyzed, and recommendations could be made to encourage, permit, discourage, or prohibit a particular boundary crossing. In addition, this analysis could occur prospectively and guide decisions about behaviors yet to occur, or be used retrospectively, providing guidance about behaviors that already occurred. Martinez's approach recognizes variety, diversity, and nuance in all boundary encounters. While some boundary violations are obvious, the negotiation of boundaries in the patient-psychiatrist relationship is central to treatment and providing care. To assume that one set of rules will solve these important areas of the therapeutic relationship is naïve. A psychiatrist must be mindful of the various ethical issues that may be in tension in any boundary encounter.

Boundary Violations and the Law

Historically, the concept of boundary violations came to be synonymous with sexual violations in the patient-physician relationship. As discussed earlier, beginning with the Hippocratic Oath, sexual relationships with patients were considered unethical and undermining of the moral foundation of physician professionalism. With a growing number of civil lawsuits, the APA evolved its position over a 40-year period, resulting in the present position that intimate relationships with current and former patients are always unethical. A review of some of the early sexual misconduct cases helps illustrate key concepts that continue to inform judgments and outcomes.

In *Roy v. Hartogs* (1976), Ms. Julie Roy was a psychiatric patient of Dr. Renatus Hartogs. Dr. Hartogs allegedly engaged in sexual relations with Ms. Roy over 13 months, claiming that this was part of her therapy. Ms. Roy sued Dr. Hartogs for emotional and mental injuries, having been psychiatrically hospitalized twice. Dr. Hartogs was found liable, and Ms. Roy was awarded damages.

Professional guidelines include the prohibition against sexual relationships with former patients (Appel, 2004). As well, sexual relationships with relatives of patients may be prohibited. In *Gladieux v. Ohio State Medical Board* (1999), Dr. Gladieux was a pediatrician who was alleged to have had sexual relationships with multiple mothers of his pediatric patients. This included the mother of a pediatric patient who had died of cancer. The medical board imposed a 2-year suspension of Dr. Gladieux's license, noting that his behavior was reprehensible.

Conversely, in *Long v. Ostroff* (2004), in which Dr. Ostroff was a family physician who had an affair with his patient's wife while caring for the patient, the Superior Court of Pennsylvania found that there were no grounds for malpractice. Dr. Ostroff entered into an intimate relationship with Mrs. Roseanne Long in September 1998 and continued this relationship for a 6-year period. In the initial motion to dismiss in Philadelphia County Court (*Long v. Ostroff*, 2003), the court noted that while the relationship began when Mr. and Mrs. Long were married, they divorced shortly afterwards. Dr. Ostroff did not reveal to Mr. Long that he was having a relationship with his now former wife over a 6-year period when he continued to be Mr. Long's primary care physician. The court concluded that Dr. Ostroff did not have a duty to his patient to inform him of the affair. On appeal to the Superior Court, the higher court agreed and found that there was no duty of care that prohibited an extramarital affair with a patient's spouse. The court stated that while such behavior may be "unethical," the behavior did not provide a cause of action for negligence against a family physician. To address these situations, the AMA has now provided opinions on the subject of intimate relationships with "key third parties," including spouses, parents, and important others and opined on the subject of sexual harassment (see AMA Opinions 9.1.2; 9.1.3). In Opinion 9.1.2, on the subject of romantic relationships with third parties, while there is no absolute rule, physicians are cautioned about their primary duty to the patient and that exploiting the vulnerability of a third party and behavior that detracts from the primary obligation to the patient can be considered unethical.

Malpractice insurance is unlikely to cover sexual misconduct with patients since this is not considered part of a professional service and rather is an intentional inappropriate action. While insurance carriers will provide initial support during the investigation of claims, many insurance policies exclude coverage for damages. In addition, psychiatrist-patient sexual relations are also illegal in many locations. MacIntyre and Appel (2020) provide an excellent summary of the current status of criminalization of sexual exploitation in the psychotherapist-patient relationship across 50 states. According to their study, over half the states now have specific laws banning intimate relationships between mental health providers, including psychiatrists, and their patients. State laws are variously worded in the criminalization of sexual acts between psychiatrists and their patients. In some states, whether a patient consents or assents to sexual acts is not exculpatory (Friedman & Martinez, 2019). However, in some jurisdictions the sexual act may only be illegal if it occurs in the consultation room or is alleged to be part of the treatment.

Whether or not states have criminalized intimate relationships between providers and patients, all such behavior is subject to civil action. While state medical boards have a clear position that sexual relationships with patients are unethical and subject to penalties, and have expanded the view that sexual misconduct includes an assortment of improprietous behaviors, issues of duties to report and penalties for failing to report continue to evolve (see Federation of State Medical Boards, 2020). Gulrajani (2020) has conceptualized the duty to report as a duty to protect, drawing on the AMA and APA ethics duties for physicians to report incompetent and unethical behaviors. He highlights recent high-profile cases, including sports doctor Larry Nassar, a former physician for the USA Gymnastics national team who was accused of assaulting 265 young women, as an example of the medical profession's failure to self-regulate in this area.

Of course, very few boundary dilemmas that may be ethically questionable have clear legal resolution or guidance. To illustrate, in AMA Opinion 1.2.1 (American Medical Association, 2017), it is recommended that "in general" physicians should not treat themselves or members of their family. However, the Opinion spells out circumstances where it may be permissible. Such situations would include emergency circumstances and for short-term minor problems. The Opinion stresses the importance of documentation and following up with the family member's primary physician. Avoiding sensitive and intimate care is stressed, and attention to the comfort level of the family member is important. If a physician treats a family member, it should be within the professional's scope of practice and expertise. Like many areas of physician practice, this is a moving target at present. With developments in the opioid abuse crisis, some states have considered laws that prohibit prescribing certain classes of medications for oneself or a member of one's family. The Federation of State Medical Boards (2021) recently issued a position statement to provide further guidance in this. In general, limiting self-treatment and treatment of family members is prudent. Physicians should become familiar with prohibitions and standards established within one's jurisdiction.

Digital Medicine and Boundaries: Emails and Social Media

With developments in the digital age, the practice of medicine, including psychiatry, has been radically transformed. The introduction of telepsychiatry platforms stands as one example of practice transformation that few imagined a generation ago. With the many positive developments introduced by digital technologies, new ethical problems involving patient email communication and professionals' engagement with social media have been identified. We see these ethical problems as appropriately conceptualized under the heading of boundary dilemmas.

Risks involved with emails with patients include misunderstandings, because of the inherent lack of body language and nonverbal cues or tone of voice in this type of communication. An additional concern is confidentiality (Farnan et al., 2013; Gutheil & Simon, 2005). The American College of Physicians-Federation of State Medical Boards (ACP-FSMB) position paper (Farnan et al., 2013) recommended guidelines that are established by physicians with patients regarding what may be communicated via email, and it is recommended only to use emails with patients who are attending their follow-up appointments. Electronic communications should be placed in the medical record as well. Within emails, problems may occur with confidentiality, inappropriate language, self-disclosure, countertransference issues, and lack of boundary with the end of a previous session (Friedman & Martinez, 2019; Gutheil & Simon, 2005). Further, emails which include inappropriate photos, which reveal sexual familiarity, or which are erotic may be what the outcome of malpractice cases hinge on (Gutheil & Simon, 2005). Thus, an inappropriate sexual liaison may have started before the inappropriate email, and the email is merely recording it.

The AMA Code of Ethics Opinion 2.3.1 acknowledges that electronic communication can be useful and can improve communication within the patient-physician relationship. However, special attention to privacy and confidentiality are required. Communication should be appropriate to clinical need and avoidance of blurring boundaries. Several useful recommendations from the opinion include protecting patient privacy and upholding standards of confidentiality; providing information to patients on the limitations and proper use of email correspondence; obtaining consent to use electronic communications; and making sure that one understands local laws on the issue of what constitutes a patient-physician relationship and duties of care.

The subject of receiving unsolicited emails from non-patients raises additional concerns. If a psychiatrist receives unsolicited emails, there are multiple additional issues of which one must be aware (Friedman et al., 2016). Unsolicited emails from unknown people may not be objective sources of information. They may not even be sent by the person who appears to have sent them. If the psychiatrist replies to an unsolicited email, there is a risk of creating a duty of care, despite not having the patient available for evaluation. Further, if one responds to an unsolicited email and creates a duty of care in a state where one is not licensed, one may be practicing medicine without a license, and the practitioner would not be covered by malpractice insurance. Although the physician may naturally desire to help someone who has sent an unsolicited email, these are important issues to consider. Potential solutions include not opening unsolicited emails or sending a standardized autoreply, for example, stating that the practitioner does not use email to conduct treatment or render advice.

If sending a personal reply to an unsolicited email, the physician should use much caution. Recupero (2005) has recommended a reply with a generic statement which reminds the sender of the lack of the patient-physician relationship. Unfortunately, replying and giving specific advice may appear to be establishing a physician-patient relationship even if the physician is only trying to be helpful. For example, the person receiving the email may believe that they have received important medical information and may not seek actual medical treatment in person (Friedman et al., 2016). It is prudent to encourage the person to seek help locally if a psychiatrist decides to reply, and to state that this response does not constitute the establishment of a patient-physician relationship.

Social media and email may both be vehicles of boundary violations. Separate from the problems created with emails, but an equally important area of professionalism in the electronic age, involves the use of social media. The American Medical Association (AMA), American College of Physicians (ACP), and Federation of State Medical Boards (FSMB) have published recommendations or position papers regarding online medical professionalism (see Farnan et al., 2013; Council of Ethical and Judicial Affairs, 2010).

The AMA's Council on Ethical and Judicial Affairs (CEJA) recommendations and guidelines for online professionalism have noted "the internet fosters disinhibition and feelings of anonymity and invisibility, which can promote either bad behavior or behavior that an individual would not engage in offline" (Council of Ethical and Judicial Affairs, 2010). The prudent psychiatrist should remember that behaviors online should be the same as the behavior in the clinic. As well, CEJA noted that those who are aware of unprofessional online contact by their colleagues should address it. Physicians have a duty to continue to promote trust in our profession. As CEJA noted, patient confidentiality and privacy should be maintained across all settings. Psychiatrists should use privacy settings to safeguard their personal details and monitor their internet footprint. The

ACP and the FSMB noted that "standards for professional interactions should be consistent across all forms of communication between the patient and physician, whether in person or online" (Farnan et al., 2013, p. 622).

Boundaries may be blurred when physicians and patients meet online on social media. These interactions can affect the public's perception of psychiatry. The ACP and FSMB discourage interactions with patients on social media outlets and recommend strict privacy settings. It is recommended that physicians have distinct personal media presence separated from professional social media accounts. Psychiatrists should monitor their social media persona, checking on what sort of information is available to the public with sensitivity not only to their individual reputations but also to the reputation of the profession as a whole. Using social media or dating Web sites exposes psychiatrists and other physicians to coming into contact with patients and resulting in undue familiarity.

If a psychiatrist is considering Googling a patient or searching for them on social media, the rationale behind this must be considered (Friedman & Martinez, 2019). The psychiatrist must consider whether there is benefit to the relationship and/or whether this is related to voyeuristic interest (Farnan et al., 2013). Greyson and colleagues (2012) surveyed violations of online professionalism and board actions. They found that the most common violation was inappropriate internet communication with patients (i.e., sexual communications). Additional reporting violations were internet prescribing without a relationship, physician credentials being misrepresented online, violating confidentiality online, not revealing conflicts of interest online, making derogatory remarks about patients online, intoxicated photos of physicians, and discriminatory remarks online. Disciplinary proceedings commonly followed and ended with informal warnings. Thus, problematic or risky behaviors online may include non-professional and inappropriate sexual interactions, misrepresenting credentials, mocking patients or others in healthcare, presenting oneself inappropriately online, "friending" patients on social media, voyeurism about patients online, dispensing medical advice without a relationship, and failure to maintain privacy and confidentiality (Friedman & Martinez, 2019).

Finally, in the time of the coronavirus pandemic, Zilber (2020) has offered reflections on how boundaries are moving in unexpected directions. She correctly observes that if a psychiatrist continues to see patients in the office, social distancing, masks, and welcoming behaviors require new sensitivity to boundaries. The shift to telepsychiatry for many psychiatrists involves rethinking workspace and self-disclosure in the encounter. Patients may be able to see the psychiatrist in his or her home. Virtual backgrounds or arrangements of one's virtual office have implications and open opportunities for discussion. The reality that both psychiatrist and patient are in a shared national and international crisis, with shared struggles and fears, may create "surreal boundary shifts" (Zilber, 2020).

Conclusion

While the concept of boundaries in the patient-physician relationship has historical precedent in the Hippocratic tradition, expansion of the concept of boundary dilemmas now includes patient-physician dynamics related to dual relationships, inappropriate prescribing for family and friends, relationships with patient relatives and family, and communication problems that develop in the context of social media and email. While this chapter has not covered all potential areas of malpractice liability related to the concept of boundary dilemmas, attention to boundaries will aid psychiatrists and other physicians in reducing risks and avoiding litigation. All physicians should be familiar with various professional codes published by the AMA and APA related to the patient-physician relationship and boundaries and follow developments in the AMA Opinions produced by CEJA. Ethical standards evolve over time and react to developments in science and culture, resulting in new standards with which all practitioners must be aware. Ignorance does not usually provide exculpation in the civil judicial system. For a profession to remain self-regulating, all practitioners must stay current and uphold the higher ethical standards that are required in professional practice.

Key Points

- Boundary issues include not only sexual relationships with patients but also relationships with patients' family members, dual relationships, inappropriate prescribing for family and friends, and communication issues with both social media and email.
- The "slippery slope" boundary issues paradigm describes a series of behaviors beginning with seemingly minor boundary violations but leading to sexual exploitation of patients.
- The "graded risk" approach to boundary analysis considers each dilemma on a case-by-case basis prospectively.
- Risk factors for boundary problems include stress from relationships, loneliness, employment stress and transition, and issues with limit setting—stresses that a psychiatrist may experience at any age.
- The AMA Code of Ethics opinions make recommendations about electronic communication with patients.
- Social media presence requires careful consideration of professionalism.

Acknowledgments Some of the conceptualizations in this chapter were previously presented in Friedman and Martinez (2019).

References

Alam, A., Kurdyak, P., Klemensberg, J., Griesman, J., & Bell, C. M. (2012). The characteristics of psychiatrists disciplined by professional colleges in Canada. *PLoS One, 7*(11), e50558. https://journals.plos.org/plosone/article?id=10.1371/journal.pone.0050558. Accessed March 30, 2021.

American Medical Association. (2017). *Code of medical ethics of the American Medical Association*. American Medical Association. Content also available at https://www.ama-assn.org/about/publications-newsletters/ama-principles-medical-ethics

American Psychiatric Association. (2013). *The principles of medical ethics: With annotations especially applicable to psychiatry* (2013 ed.). American Psychiatric Association. Content also available at https://www.psychiatry.org/psychiatrists/practice/ethics

Appel, J. M. (2004). May physicians date their patients' relatives? Rethinking sexual misconduct and disclosure after *Long v. Ostroff. Medicine and Health Rhode Island, 87*(5), 159–161.

Caldicott, C. V., & d'Oronzio, J. C. (2015). Ethics remediation, rehabilitation, and recommitment to medical professionalism: A programmatic approach. *Ethics and Behavior, 25*(4), 279–296. https://www.tandfonline.com/doi/full/10.1080/10508422.2014.930687?scroll=topandneedAccess=true. Accessed January 31, 2021.

Council of Ethical and Judicial Affairs. (2010). *CEJA Report 8-I-10*. https://www.ama-assn.org/sites/ama-assn.org/files/corp/media-browser/public/about-ama/councils/Council%20Reports/council-on-ethics-and-judicial-affairs/i10-ceja-professionalism-use-social-media.pdf. Accessed February 10, 2021.

Davies, M. (2015). Crossing boundaries: Dealing with amorous advances by doctors and patients. *British Medical Journal Careers, 351*, h5368. https://doi.org/10.1136/bmj.h5368. Accessed February 10, 2021.

Farnan, J. M., Sulmasy, L. S., Worster, B. K., Chaudhry, H. J., Rhyne, J. A., & Arora, V. M. (2013). Online medical professionalism: Patient and public relationships: Policy statement from the American College of Physicians and the Federation of State Medical Boards. *Annals of Internal Medicine, 158*(8), 620–627.

Federation of State Medical Boards. (2020). *Physician sexual misconduct: Report and recommendations of the FSMB workgroup on physician sexual misconduct*. https://www.fsmb.org/siteassets/advocacy/policies/report-of-workgroup-on-sexual-misconduct-adopted-version.pdf. Accessed February 10, 2021.

Federation of State Medical Boards. (2021). *Position statement: Treatment of self, family members and close relations*. https://www.fsmb.org/siteassets/advocacy/policies/position-statement-treatment-of-self-and-family-members-and-close-relations.pdf. Accessed May 31, 2021.

Friedman, S. H., Appel, J. M., Ash, P., Frierson, R. L., Giorgi-Guarnieri, D., Martinez, R., … Simpson, A. I. F. (2016). Unsolicited e-mails to forensic psychiatrists. *Journal of the American Academy of Psychiatry and the Law, 44*(4), 470–478.

Friedman, S. H., & Martinez, R. P. (2019). Boundaries, professionalism, and malpractice in psychiatry. *Focus, 17*(4), 365–371.

Gabbard, G. O. (Ed.). (1989). *Sexual exploitation in professional relationships*. APA Press.

Gladieux v. Ohio State Medical Board, Court of Appeals of Ohio, Tenth District, Franklin County. Decided: September 30, 1999.

Greysen, S. R., Chretien, K. C., Kind, T., Young, A., & Gross, C. P. (2012). Physician violations of online professionalism and disciplinary actions: A national survey of state medical boards. *JAMA, 307*(11), 1141–1142.

Gulrajani, C. (2020). A duty to protect our patients from physician sexual misconduct. *Journal of the American Academy of Psychiatry and the Law, 48*(2), 176–180.

Gutheil, T. G., & Brodsky, A. (2008). *Preventing boundary violations in clinical practice*. Guilford Press.

Gutheil, T. G., & Gabbard, G. O. (1993). The concept of boundaries in clinical practice: Theoretical and risk-management dimensions. *American Journal of Psychiatry, 150*(2), 188–196.

Gutheil, T. G., & Simon, R. I. (2005). E-mails, extra-therapeutic contact, and early boundary problems: The internet as a "slippery slope". *Psychiatric Annals, 35*(12), 952–960.

Hippocratic Oath. (2002).Translated by Michael North. National Library of Medicine. https://www.nlm.nih.gov/hmd/greek/greek_oath.html. Accessed February 10, 2021.

Jena, A. B., Seabury, S., Lakdawalla, D., & Chandra, A. (2011). Malpractice risk according to physician specialty. *New England Journal of Medicine, 365*(7), 629–636.

Lazarus, A. A. (1994). How certain boundaries and ethics diminish therapeutic effectiveness. *Ethics and Behavior, 4*(3), 255–261.

Long v. Ostroff, Philadelphia County Court of Common Pleas, 63 Pa. D and C.4th 444. Decided August 14, 2003.

Long v. Ostroff, Superior Court of Pennsylvania. Walter LONG, Appellant, v. Jonathan E. OSTROFF, D.O., Appellee. Decided: June 23, 2004.

MacIntyre, M. R., & Appel, J. M. (2020). Legal and ethics considerations in reporting sexual exploitation by previous providers. *Journal of the American Academy of Psychiatry and the Law, 48*(2), 166–175.

Martinez, R. (2000). A model for boundary dilemmas: Ethical decision-making in the patient-professional relationship. *Ethical Human Sciences and Services, 2*(1), 43–61.

Norris, D. M., Gutheil, T. G., & Strasburger, L. H. (2003). This couldn't happen to me: Boundary problems and sexual misconduct in the psychotherapy relationship. *Psychiatric Services, 54*(4), 517–522.

Recupero, P. R. (2005). E-mail and the psychiatrist-patient relationship. *Journal of the American Academy of Psychiatry and the Law, 33*(4), 465–475.

Roy v. Hartogs, 85 Misc.2d 891 (1976).

Savin, D., & Martinez, R. (2006). Cross-cultural boundary dilemmas: A graded-risk assessment approach. *Transcultural Psychiatry, 43*(2), 243–258.

Simon, R. I. (1989). Sexual exploitation of patients: How it begins before it happens. *Psychiatric Annals, 19*(2), 104–122.

Zilber, C. (2020). Surreal boundary shifts during the pandemic. *Psychiatric News*. APA Publishing Online April 9, 2020. https://psychnews.psychiatryonline.org/doi/10.1176/appi.pn.2020.4b25. Accessed May 30, 2021.

Breach of Confidentiality

15

Jacob M. Appel

Introduction

The physician's duty to hold a patient's private information in confidence dates back to the Hippocratic Oath and is now widely accepted as a "norm" in allopathic medicine (Higgins, 1989). Without such guarantees, patients might prove unwilling to reveal necessary information to their medical providers, especially the sort of personal divulgences often required for effective psychiatric care. In addition, disclosures by the physician that are "contrary to the individual's interest" are also "potentially detrimental to the public interest" as they will discourage other patients from confiding in their providers in the future (Çipi, 2012). Yet these duties must be balanced against competing obligations "to serve the commonweal and protect the health of others" that first arose in the late nineteenth century regarding the reporting of communicable diseases (Appel, 2019). Both common law and many state statutes recognize a duty of confidentiality. Breaches may expose a psychiatrist to tort liability for negligence if the standard of care is not upheld, but plaintiffs might also recover for breach of contract, invasion of privacy, and, if partial disclosure leads others to draw false conclusions, even defamation (Dickens & Cook, 2000). In contrast, the Health Insurance Portability and Accountability Act of 1996, a federal statute that imposes stiff penalties for breaches, does not allow for a private cause of action (Collins, 2019).

Private litigation over breaches of confidentiality remains relatively uncommon. While 15% of all "administrative actions, claims, and lawsuits" filed against psychiatrists between 1986 and 2018 were for such acts, a 2019 *Medscape* survey did not find unlawful disclosure to be among the top ten causes for lawsuits (Frierson & Joshi, 2019; Brooks, 2020). Several factors may discourage such suits, including the difficulty in establishing damages, which are often purely psychological or emotional, and a reluctance to endure further public exposure (Grabois, 1997–98). Potential litigants may fear a variation of the so-called Streisand Effect (Jansen & Martin, 2015), in which a trial over breach of confidentiality leads to broader and more detailed disclosure of private information. Suits may also be less frequent because psychiatrists value confidentiality highly and strive to preserve it (Grabois, 1997–98).

J. M. Appel (✉)
Department of Psychiatry, Icahn School of Medicine at Mount Sinai, New York, NY, USA

Legal Framework

History and Sources of Law

Confidentiality refers to the ethical and/or legal obligation of healthcare professionals to refrain from divulging private information regarding or obtained from patients. While confidentiality has long been considered an ethical norm in medicine, its legal status has evolved rapidly over the past two centuries. Physician-patient privilege—the right of patients to withhold the testimonial evidence of their providers from legal proceedings—was not historically recognized in the common law of the United States, for example, and the first state statute recognizing the right to prevent such testimony dates only to 1829 (*Dillenbeck v. Hess*, 1989). The American Medical Association adopted an "obligation of secrecy" in 1847—largely based on the earlier code of English physician Thomas Percival—but the parameters of this duty were uncertain (AMA, 1850). The best known confidentiality suit of the nineteenth century, the English case of *Kitson v. Playfair* (1896), addressed the accuracy of the disclosure, rather than the fact of the breach, and was resolved on defamation grounds (Marshall, 1966). The earliest American cases "involved physicians making extrajudicial disclosures of confidential information to third parties, in violation of state licensing statutes" (Grabois, 1997–98). These suits for confidentiality breaches largely failed on public policy grounds. For instance, in *Simonsen v. Swenson* (1920), the Nebraska Supreme Court upheld the disclosure of a false syphilis result to owners of a family-operated hotel where the

P. Ash et al. (eds.), *Malpractice and Liability in Psychiatry*, https://doi.org/10.1007/978-3-030-91975-7_15

patient was staying (Lawson, 1989). Even where the courts recognized such a duty, the exceptions proved broad. In the well-known case of *Berry v. Moench* (1958), often cited as favoring a confidentiality obligation, the Supreme Court of Utah addressed whether a psychiatrist might reveal a patient's private psychiatric history to the parents of his patient's romantic partner in order to protect the partner's interests (Grabois, 1997–98). The lenient standard the court imposed was that the psychiatrist was "obliged to consider the likelihood and the extent of benefit to the recipient, if the matter is true, as compared with the likelihood of injury and the extent thereof to the subject, if it prove false, or improper to reveal" (*Berry v. Moench*, 1958). Rather than a guarantee of protections, this approach afforded patients only a highly subjective cost-benefit analysis. The "watershed" case of *Humphers v. First Interstate Bank* (1985) proved the first major decision upholding tortious breach of a broad-based right to confidentiality (Appel, 2019). In that ruling, the Supreme Court of Oregon found against a physician who provided a woman subject to a closed adoption with information allowing her to identify her mother (*Humphers v. First Interstate Bank*, 1985).

Until the passage of the Health Insurance Portability and Accountability Act of 1996 (HIPAA), most regulation of private medical information occurred at the state level. One notable exception was Part 2 of 42 Code of Federal Regulations (42 C.F.R.), initially promulgated in 1975, which protects substance abuse records. Although 42 C.F.R. only applies to entities receiving federal assistance, the protections cover all providers offering maintenance or withdrawal therapies under a DEA license. However, courts have consistently held that these regulations do not give rise to private causes of action (*Chapa v. Adams*, 1999). The reality is that prior to HIPAA, states had enacted "some statutes restricting the use and disclosure of medical information," but few had embraced "a comprehensive approach" (Pritts, 2002). Many jurisdictions had adopted rules governing the disclosure of HIV status, and sometimes other sexually transmitted infections, but the result was a patchwork that often proved internally inconsistent and varied from state to state (Appel, 2019). Oklahoma offered one notable example: that state's rules on HIV confidentiality applied only to dentists and chiropractors, but not to physicians (Pritts, 2002).

Privilege—the right of a patient to withhold a physician's testimony from a legal proceeding—has also been governed historically by the states. At common law, the courts recognized just two such privileges: those between attorneys and clients and one between spouses. As late as the 1960s, only half of American states had adopted a physician-patient privilege by statute (Marshall, 1966). The Federal Rules of Evidence did not do so, and although all states have now embraced at least a limited physician-patient privilege, no such general protection currently exists in the federal courts.

A narrower psychotherapist-patient privilege was initially proposed by the Group for the Advancement of Psychiatry (GAP) in a 24-page report in 1960 (Slovenko, 2009). The need for such a privilege drew further attention when psychiatrist Joseph Lifschutz was briefly jailed for refusing to turn over records on the grounds that his other patients would no longer be able to trust their confidence with him (Martinez & Fox, 2018). In *Jaffee v. Redmond*, the US Supreme Court imposed such a privilege nationwide. Writing for a 7–2 majority, Justice John Paul Stevens observed that "effective psychotherapy…depends upon an atmosphere of confidence and trust in which the patient is willing to make a frank and complete disclosure of facts, emotions, memories, and fears" (*Jaffee v. Redmond*, 1996). It must be emphasized that the privilege is said to be "held" *by the patient*. Efforts to withhold testimony or medical records over the patient's objections are unlikely to succeed and can open the provider up to charges of contempt. In many jurisdictions, failure to maintain an adequate medical record is itself grounds for both professional discipline and negligence claims—and providers cannot shield themselves from this duty by asserting an alleged privilege of their own.

Grounds for Disclosure

HIPAA and state laws provide a range of exceptions to the general duty of confidentiality that vary considerably from jurisdiction to jurisdiction. Some of these exemptions dovetail with mandatory reporting laws. All states require providers to report child abuse discovered in professional situations under standards imposed by the Federal Child Abuse Prevention and Treatment Act (CAPTA) (42 U.S.C.A. § 5106g). Many states also impose a duty to report other threats to third parties or to the public including elder abuse, intimate partner violence, communicable and sexually transmitted diseases, wounds of specific origin (such as via gun, knife, and icepick), injuries resulting from "assaultive or abusive conduct," and impaired driving (Sachs et al., 1998). Of particular concern to psychiatrists is whether they must report the disclosure of a romantic relationship between a patient and her former provider (MacIntyre & Appel, 2020). The reporting of patients who are potentially unfit to own firearms, such as under New York State's SAFE Act, has also recently become an issue (Jacobs & Fuhr, 2016). One school of thought favors mandatory disclosure in these cases to protect the public, while another fears that requiring disclosure will over time reduce the willingness of patients to share confidences—thus damaging the therapeutic relationship without any long-term public benefit (Appel, 2009). In that sense, the mental health provider is said to have "dual loyalty"—both a fiduciary obligation to an individual patient and a duty to the commonweal as a public servant. The current trend favors disclosure. Psychiatrists should be familiar with the specific requirements in their jurisdiction regarding mandatory and discretionary reporting, as well as matters that may not be legally disclosed. When reporting, providers should inform patients that they are doing so unless the patient's interest in knowing is outweighed by a significant competing concern such as safety.

HIPAA permits the disclosure of PHI without the patient's consent "for treatment activities of a healthcare provider" including to non-covered entities (45 CFR 164). However, state laws vary considerably in this regard, and a number of states place further restrictions upon the unauthorized exchange of general information between healthcare providers; others prohibit this disclosure specifically with regard to psychiatric care and/or substance use (Jost, 2006). Several states including Florida, Michigan, and Washington prohibit such disclosures in non-emergent situations, while others "only [permit] sharing within a single facility or among state treatment programs" (Jost, 2006). In the absence of written authorization, a psychiatrist should not rely upon the broad exemption of HIPAA—which does not preempt state law in this area—but should be familiar with her own jurisdiction's specific rules governing information exchange between providers.

Disclosure may also be permitted—or required—to protect third parties. These duties were first outlined in the seminal California case of *Tarasoff v. Regents* (1976), discussed elsewhere in this volume, and generally require warning or protecting an identified third party. At least two states, Washington and Wisconsin, have extended this duty—and hence the right to breach confidentiality—to non-identified foreseeable victims (*Schuster v. Altenberg*, 1988; *Volk v. DeMeerleer*, 2016). The broad duty imposed in Washington State under *Volk v. DeMeerleer* (2016) has caused considerable controversy as it conflicts with the American Medical Association's Code of Ethics (Piel & Opara, 2018). Some jurisdictions have expanded the duty to breach confidentiality to protect third parties to include future risk of genetic diseases, but others have not (*Safer v. Estate of Pack*, 1996; *Pate v. Threlkel*, 1985). HIPAA also permits some degree of disclosure necessary to obtain payment for services, and even for fundraising purposes by hospital development offices (Prokopetz & Lehmann, 2014). However, the previously widespread practice of sharing medical information with patient's immediate relatives without first obtaining permission is now clearly actionable (Higgins, 1989).

HIPAA: Preemption and Expansion

HIPAA was intended to provide a "federal floor of safeguards to protect the confidentiality of medical information" (Olinde & McCard, 2005). State laws that are more restrictive still apply. Unfortunately, when "HIPAA and state laws conflict, and it is not clear which is more restrictive, the preemption provisions place healthcare providers in a quandary," especially as there is no mechanism for providers to request an advisory opinion from the Department of Health and Human Services (Slovenko, 2009). The Ohio courts, for example, have grappled with the question of whether a disclosure "authorized" under HIPAA can nonetheless breach state confidentiality standards (Tendam, 2018). HIPAA has also served indirectly as the basis for new causes of state action. For instance, in *Byrne v. Avery* (2018), the Connecticut Supreme Court addressed the case of an obstetrician who, when served with a subpoena in a paternity suit, did not "file a motion to quash the subpoena, appear in court, or even notify the plaintiff" but simply "mailed a copy of the plaintiff's medical file to the court" (Ray & Weiner, 2018). The court found that while HIPAA did not afford a private claim of action, the customary practice that resulted from HIPAA could inform the state's standard of care (*Byrne v. Avery*, 2018). Employers, such as hospitals and pharmacies, may also be held liable in some jurisdictions for negligent breaches by their employees (*Walgreen v. Hinchy*, 2015).

Types of Allegations

Claims for breach of confidentiality generally occur in state courts and claim that the psychiatrist negligently shared private information without permission from the patient or other legal justification and that the patient was injured as a result. The range of cases varies considerably. Many breaches occur inadvertently during the course of care—such as speaking to a patient's family member by telephone without first securing permission or accidentally leaving a patient's chart visible in a public place. These situations, as discussed below under risk reduction strategies, can often be avoided with general prudence. However, there are several specific areas that raise distinctive pitfalls including (1) evidentiary requests, (2) emergency care, (3) intentional disclosures, and (4) postmortem disclosures.

Evidentiary Requests

Psychiatrists may be asked to divulge confidences in matters before the court system. When such a request occurs without the color of legal authority, the provider should not comply absent authorization from the patient. In contrast, subpoenas cannot be ignored. A *subpoena duces tecum* may demand that the psychiatrist bring his or her records or notes. However, it is important to remember that subpoenas are not necessarily orders of a judge; they may be signed by an attorney or a court clerk. Under those circumstances, the psychiatrist should inform the patient so that he or she can object to the disclosure and seek a "qualified protective order" from the court. The words of psychiatrist Maurice Grossman may prove helpful here: "The frightening language of the document intimidates most recipients of subpoenas….If the recipient knew how easy it was to have a subpoena issued; if he knew how readily the subpoena could demand information when there actually was no legal right to command the disclosure of information; if he knew how often an individual releases information that legally he had no right to release because of intimidation, he would view the threat of the subpoena with less fear and greater skepticism" (Grossman, 1973, p. 245). When complying with a subpoena, a psychiatrist must be careful not to disclose information beyond the scope of the request (Ray & Weiner, 2018). If the subpoena is allegedly presented by an attorney working for a provider's own patient and does not contain a signed authorization for release of records, the psychiatrist should confirm its authenticity directly with the client. In contrast to attorney- and clerk-issued subpoenas, the psychiatrist should comply with all court orders—those directly issued by a judge—or attempt to have these court orders revoked or reversed through judicial process. Psychiatrists should consult their own attorneys (in hospital legal departments or at malpractice insurers) when possible to ascertain that the subpoena or court order is legitimate and compulsory. For example, an out-of-state subpoena or non-American court order may not be binding, and complying with such a request may open the provider up to liability for breach of confidentiality.

Emergency Care

One particular challenge for emergency department psychiatrists is how much confidential information to divulge during the course of a crisis. Both providers and patients often incorrectly believe that HIPAA prevents the disclosure of all medical information by default. In fact, unless the patient states otherwise, ER providers may inform "anyone who asks for the patient by name" that the patient is present in the hospital and, once the patient has been given an opportunity to refuse inclusion, other basic information available in the patient directory. But HIPAA allows further disclosure when "due to emergency treatment circumstances or incapacity, the patient has not been provided an opportunity to express his or her preference…if doing so is in the individual's best interest as determined in the professional judgment of the provider, and would not be inconsistent with any known preference previously expressed by the individual" (Health Information Privacy, 2013). State statutes and state court rulings generally follow similar principles. In an emergency, providers may contact a patient's family members and friends to learn relevant information about the patient's medical and psychiatric histories and recent conduct. However, disclosure should be limited to that necessary for care. Revealing unrelated history from the chart—especially on sensitive subjects—must be avoided. As a general rule, collateral information may be obtained in the emergency setting over a patient's objection if there is concern that the patient poses an acute risk to themself or others. It is less clear whether obtaining such information over the objections of the patient, in circumstances where the patient is willing to accept admission to alleviate the acute danger, might serve as the basis for a future cause of action.

Intentional Disclosures

Psychiatrists may wish to divulge patient information intentionally under various circumstances that are not required to protect the public. For example, the distinctive aspects of a patient's history, diagnosis, and treatment may prove educational when included in a publication or presented in a journal article, or a physician-author may hope to discuss a patient when writing about her own career or experiences. However, confidentiality laws and medical ethics do not afford providers with the right to reveal private patient information for broader education, intellectual, or literary purposes. In a famous case, poet-pediatrician William Carlos Williams published a story he had heard during medical rounds in *New Masses* in 1926 that resulted in a $5000 legal settlement (Slovenko, 1988). Under some circumstances, it may prove possible to obtain permission from a patient to write about him or her, but care should be used in order to avoid claims of duress. Often, tracking down the patient is no longer possible or the patient is deceased. Without permission, de-identification is required at a minimum so that third parties cannot recognize the patient. In situations where the patient might suffer harm from recognizing himself, including the reasonable but false belief that he might be identified by others, physician-authors may have a duty to disguise their depictions so that even the subjects cannot recognize themselves.

Intentional disclosure also arises when providers seek to conduct retrospective research. In addition to approval by an Institutional Review Board (IRB), human subject research generally requires the consent of the subjects if potentially identifiable data is used. When highly sensitive information such as mental health records are at issue, obtaining a government-issued certificate of confidentiality (CoC) from the appropriate governmental agency may be prudent. CoCs are designed to encourage participation in research and generally protects investigators from having to reveal confidential information about subjects during legal proceedings.

Historically, CoCs sometimes proved challenging for investigators to obtain. However, since the passage of the 21st Century Cures Act of 2016, federally funded medical research "in which identifiable, sensitive information is collected….including research on mental health" must be granted a CoC (Pub.L. 114–255 114–255). Research funded by other sources is also eligible for a CoC, although investigators are not required to obtain one. In addition, with advancing technologies in both informatics and genetics, researchers should be certain that de-identified data cannot be reattached to subjects or should warn subjects of this possibility.

Confidentiality After Death

The death of a patient raises distinctive concerns related to confidentiality and the law. These issues generated considerable public debate in 1991 surrounding Diane Wood Middlebrook's publication of a biography of poet Anne Sexton that drew upon 300 audio tapes of sessions with her psychiatrist, Dr. Martin T. Orne (Werth et al., 2002). Orne, who argued that Sexton "would have wanted the tapes released," faced extensive professional criticism for sharing them (Fox, 2007). The HIPAA Privacy Rule prevents disclosure of protected health information for 50 years but with exceptions. Most notable is that access is permitted "to a family member or other person who was involved in the individual's healthcare or payment for care prior to the individual's death, unless doing so is inconsistent with any prior expressed preference of the deceased individual that is known to the covered entity" (45 CFR 160.103). The American Medical Association (AMA) Code of Ethics permits disclosure narrowly, with the caveat that the provider must weigh breaching confidentiality against the "impact disclosure may have on the reputation of the deceased patient" (AMA, 2011). A patient's healthcare executor, usually the next of kin, generally has access to the deceased patient's records, and it is challenging to either prevent such access or to preclude the executor from disseminating this information once it is in his or her possession. A decedent's estate has standing to sue for breaches of confidentiality, and the next of kin may as well, but they will have to establish damages. It is not clear whether reputational damages for such breach of confidentiality can extend beyond the grave and under what circumstances. Whether a third party can win a claim against a provider who in good faith shares confidential information with the deceased's family, arguing poor judgment or violation of the decedent's wishes also remains unresolved. While lawsuits over breaches of postmortem confidentiality are likely to be rare, providers should not forget that their legal obligations in this area transcend death.

Psychotherapy Notes

Psychotherapy notes are afforded additional legal protections under HIPAA. The statute provides a precise definition: "notes recorded (in any medium) by a health care provider who is a mental health professional documenting or analyzing the contents of conversation during a private counseling session or a group, joint, or family counseling session and that are separated from the rest of the individual's medical record" (45 CFR 164). The term explicitly excludes information related to the modalities and frequencies of treatment, medication management, diagnosis, functional status, and clinical progress (45 CFR 164). Unlike routine progress notes and other medical records, which may be shared for a range of therapeutic, payment, and administrative reasons, disclosure of psychotherapy notes generally requires specific authorization from the patient. Even the patient may be denied access to his or her own psychotherapy notes (45 CFR 164). Narrow exceptions do exist for use in trainee education, to comply with mandatory reporting laws (such as those governing child abuse and neglect), in the context of *Tarasoff*-style warnings and prevent other imminent harms, and to defend against malpractice claims (Maio, 2003). An exception does *not* exist for sharing psychotherapy notes with other providers within the institution or on the treatment team. This limitation matters in practice because in states that accept HIPAA as guiding the standard of care, a provider who shares psychotherapy notes with another treating physician in the absence of authorization may open himself up to liability if that second provider shares the contents of those notes.

Reducing Risk

Communication

The fundamental rule for avoiding confidentiality breaches is for providers to know to whom they are divulging information and under what authority they are doing so. In the case of an adult patient with relevant decisional capacity, barring a court order, direct permission from the patient is generally required. In cases of incapacitation, providers may turn to the appropriate third-party decision-maker such as a proxy or surrogate. Information should generally not be divulged unless the identity of the recipient can be confirmed—since employers, parties involved in litigation with patients, and even journalists have been known to phone hospitals under false identities to secure protected health information (Harding, 2017). In a notorious prank, an Australian radio host tricked a nurse at London's King Edward VII's Hospital into believing the radio host was Queen Elizabeth II while inquiring about the pregnant Duchess of Cambridge (Crossly, 2014). These concerns will likely grow more pressing as "deepfake" technologies become increasingly realistic and widespread. Similar cautionary principles apply to the disclosure of written information and records. For instance, a jury awarded $1.25 million to an HIV+ patient whose diagnosis was inadvertently included in a file provided to a collections attorney (*M.O. v. Internal Medical Associates, Inc.*, 2013).

One particular and all-too-frequent source of concern is accidental disclosure that occurs during the course of direct care. In order to avoid these breaches, providers should ask family members and friends to step out of the room upon initial assessment or consultation to ascertain in private what information the patient does or does not want disclosed. In emergency and consult-liaison settings, efforts should be made to conduct evaluations in private so that other patients cannot overhear confidences. Office structures should also be designed to prevent breaches; telephones and fax machines should be appropriately located for necessary privacy, and computer monitors should be screened or shielded (Scott et al., 2007). Technology should be secured against breaches with encryption and sequestration. Finally, care should be taken when searching for patient information online: The very act of "plugging a patient's name into an Internet search engine…allows third parties with access to both search terms and URLs" to connect patients to specific diagnoses and healthcare facilities, potentially creating grounds for a claim of negligence (Appel, 2019).

Another concern is that of individuals under the employ of a psychiatrist intentionally accesses medical records without authorization and disclosing those records more broadly. While this is more often a concern for hospitals and healthcare institutions—examples include a high-profile internal breach involving the medical records of actress Farrah Fawcett at UCLA in 2006 and a similar attempt to access former President Bill Clinton's records at Columbia Presbyterian Hospital in 2004—an individual provider could be held liable for negligent hiring or supervision if his or her own office staff engages in misconduct (Ornstein, 2008; Bill Goes Home, 2004).

When breaches do occur, the patient should be informed immediately; a cover-up, if eventually discovered, may increase both the risk of litigation and its consequences. Data regarding the efficacy of apologizing for errors in reducing litigation is mixed (Boothman & Hoyler, 2013; McMichael et al., 2019). Many states have "apology laws" that exclude from evidence expressions of sympathy or admission of fault for unintended outcomes, but not all protect against admissions to breaches of confidentiality (Mastroianni et al., 2010). Providers may wish to consult their hospital legal departments or insurance carriers for specific guidance in this area.

Documentation

Any release of patient information to a third party should be documented in the medical record. HIPAA specifically requires written authorization for the release of protected health information except under specific circumstances. Verbal consent is acceptable in matters related to treatment and healthcare operations. The provider should document that the patient has sanctioned the disclosure and to whom. Ideally, if sensitive subjects (such as HIV status, mental health, reproductive decision-making, or substance use) are to be discussed, the chart should reflect specific permission to communicate about these matters. If the patient lacks capacity to grant consent, an alternative rationale for disclosure (e.g., consent by a proxy or surrogate, necessity for emergency medical care, etc.) should be documented. When appropriate, the method used to confirm the identity of the recipient should be documented as well (e.g., provider phoned telephone number of spouse that was previously documented in chart and spouse identified herself by name.) If medical care is discussed for the first time with third parties present, the provider should document that she obtained permission from the patient in private to proceed with these third parties present.

When breaching confidentiality without consent, such as to protect an identified 30 party or to comply with a state reporting statute, the justification for such a breach should be explained in detail. For example, it is generally insufficient to write that a child protective services agency was called because the provider had a reasonable suspicion of child abuse. Instead, the provider should document the factual basis upon which such abuse was suspected. Of note, in cases where reporting is discretionary (e.g., impaired driving or intimate partner violence in some jurisdictions) and a provider chooses *not* to report, the provider should document having considered reporting and the rationale for not doing so. This approach can provide protection in cases of lawsuits by third parties over the patient's subsequent conduct. In addition, if reporting later becomes necessary and leads to litigation, this historical record will help establish the physician's choice as one that stemmed from reflection and judiciousness.

Conclusion

Breaches of confidentiality lawsuits are distinct among malpractice claims in that they are largely avoidable. Unlike many other common causes for litigation (e.g., suicide and attempt, violence to third parties, incorrect management), decisions related to confidentiality rarely involve subjective decisions that implicate foreseeability, and outcomes do not depend upon the subtleties and debatable choices of diagnosis and treatment. Rather, most confidentiality claims can be prevented by simply recognizing the potential for breach in advance. Knowing when and with whom patient information may be shared is the critical element in avoiding suits for breach.

Key Points

- Confidentiality is essential to the psychiatrist-patient relationship and enables the open exchange of information necessary for care.
- Patients may assert privilege to withhold physicians' evidence from court, but physicians may not assert a privilege of their own accord.
- Confidentiality may be breached to protect the public or specific third parties in narrowly circumscribed areas, but these rules vary significantly from state to state.
- HIPAA and federal regulations governing the confidentiality of alcohol and drug abuse patient records do not create privacy causes of action but may influence state malpractice law through their impact on the industry custom and the standard of care.
- Providers should be certain under whose authorization they are acting when disclosing information.
- A diligent effort must be made to confirm the identity of the recipient prior to releasing information.
- Documentation related to disclosure should identify both the source of authority for the divulgence and the party to whom the information was divulged.

Acknowledgments Some of the conceptualizations in this chapter were previously presented in Appel (2019).

References

42 C.F.R.
42 U.S.C.A. § 5106g.
45 CFR 160.103.
45 CFR 164.
American Medical Association. (1850). *Code of ethics of the American Medical Association, adopted May 1847*. American Medical Association.
American Medical Association Code of Medical Ethics. (2011). Opinion 5.051: Confidentiality of medical information postmortem. *Virtual Mentor, 13*(7), 475–477.
Appel, J. M. (2009). Must physicians report impaired driving? Rethinking a duty on a collision course with itself. *The Journal of Clinical Ethics, 20*(2), 136–140.
Appel, J. M. (2019). Trends in confidentiality and disclosure. *Focus (American Psychiatric Publishing), 17*(4), 360–364.
Berry v. Moench, 8 Utah 2d 191 (1958).
Bill Goes Home. (2004, September 11). *New York Daily News*, p. 6.
Boothman, R., & Hoyler, M. M. (2013). The University of Michigan's early disclosure and offer program. *Bulletin of the American College of Surgeons, 98*(3), 21–25.
Brooks, M. (2020, January 28). Large percentage of psychiatrists sued for malpractice at least once. *Medscape*.
Byrne v. Avery Center for Obstetrics and Gynecology, P.C., 327 Conn. 540 (2018).
Chapa v. Adams, 168 F.3d 1036, 1038 (7th Cir. 1999).
Çipi, B. (2012). Ethical, juridical and historical aspects of medical confidentiality. *JAHR, 3*(1), 139–146.
Collins, J. D. W. (2019). Toothless HIPAA: Searching for a private right of action to remedy privacy rule violations. *Vanderbilt Law Review, 60*, 199.
Crossly, L. (2014, September 4). You should have stayed in Australia: Radio DJ who made hoax call to royal baby hospital is told she CAN'T give evidence to inquest of hanged nurse. *Daily Mail*.
Dickens, B. M., & Cook, R. J. (2000). Law and ethics in conflict over confidentiality? *International Journal of Gynecology & Obstetrics, 70*(3), 385–391.
Dillenbeck v. Hess, 73 N.Y.2d 278 (1989).
Fox, M. (2007, December 17). Diane Wood Middlebrook, Biographer, Dies at 68. *New York Times*.
Frierson, R. L., & Joshi, K. G. (2019). Malpractice law and psychiatry: An overview. *Focus (American Psychiatric Publishing), 17*(4), 332–336.
Grabois, E. W. (1997–98). The liability of psychotherapists for breach of confidentiality. *Journal of Law and Health, 12*, 39.
Grossman, M. (1973). The psychiatrist and the subpoena. *Journal of the American Academy of Psychiatry and the Law Online, 1*(4), 245–253.
Harding, D. (2017, June 16). Sun journalist "pretended to be related to Grenfell Tower victim" to get into hospital. *Yahoo News*.
Health Information Privacy. (2013). Department of Health and Human Services: https://www.hhs.gov/hipaa/for-professionals/faq/483/does-hipaa-permit-hospitals-to-inform-visitors-about-a-patients-location/index.html
Higgins, G. L. (1989). The history of confidentiality in medicine: The physician-patient relationship. *Canadian Family Physician Medecin de Famille Canadien, 35*, 921–926.
Humphers v. First Interstate Bank, 696 P.2d 527 (1985).
Jacobs, J. B., & Fuhr, Z. (2016). Preventing dangerous mentally ill individuals from obtaining and retaining guns: New York's SAFE Act. *Georgetown Journal of Law & Public Policy, 14*, 77.
Jaffee v. Redmond, 518 U.S. 1 (1996).
Jansen, S., & Martin, B. (2015). The Streisand effect and censorship backfire. *International Journal of Communication, 9*, 656–671.
Jost, T. S. (2006). Appendix B, Constraints on sharing mental health and substance-use treatment information imposed by federal and state medical records privacy laws. In Institute of Medicine (US) Committee on Crossing the Quality Chasm: Adaptation to Mental Health and Addictive Disorders. *Improving the quality of health care for mental and substance-use conditions: Quality Chasm Series*. National Academies Press.
Kitson v. Playfair and Wife (1896).
Lawson, C. M. (1989). Tort claims against health care providers for breach of confidentiality. *The Nebraska Medical Journal, 74*(6), 150–157.
M.O. v. Internal Medicine Associates, Inc. Monroe County Circuit Court – Indiana (2013).
MacIntyre, M. R., & Appel, J. M. (2020). Legal and ethics considerations in reporting sexual exploitation by previous providers. *The Journal of the American Academy of Psychiatry and the Law, 48*(2), 166–175.
Maio, J. E. (2003). HIPAA and the special status of psychotherapy notes. *Lippincott's Case Management, 8*(1), 24–29.
Marshall, T. K. (1966). Privileged occasions and professional secrecy. *Medicine, Science and the Law, 6*(2), 68–75.
Martinez, R., & Fox, P. (2018). Confidentiality in psychiatric practice. In L. H. Gold & R. L. Frierson (Eds.), *APA publishing textbook of forensic psychiatry*. American Psychiatric Association Publishing.

Mastroianni, A. C., Mello, M. M., et al. (2010). The flaws in state "apology" and "disclosure" laws dilute their intended impact on malpractice suits. *Health Affairs (Millwood), 29*(9), 1611–1619.
McMichael, B. J., Van Horn, R. L., & Viscusi, W. K. (2019). "Sorry" is never enough: How state apology laws fail to reduce medical malpractice liability risk. *Stanford Law Review, 71*(2), 341–409.
Olinde, J. F., & McCard, H. (2005). Understanding the boundaries of the HIPAA preemption analysis. *Defense Counsel Journal, 72*, 158.
Ornstein, C. (2008, April 3). Fawcett's cancer file breached. *Los Angeles Times*.
Pate v. Threlkel, 661 So. 2d 278 (1985).
Piel, J. L., & Opara, R. (2018). Does Volk v DeMeerleer conflict with the AMA code of medical ethics on breaching patient confidentiality to protect third parties? *AMA Journal of Ethics, 20*(1), 10–18.
Pritts, J. L. (2002). Altered states: State health privacy laws and the impact of the Federal Health Privacy Rule. *Yale Journal of Health Policy, Law, and Ethics, 2*, 327–364.
Prokopetz, J. J. Z., & Lehmann, L. S. (2014). Physicians as fundraisers: Medical philanthropy and the doctor-patient relationship. *PLoS Medicine, 11*(2), e1001600.
Pub.L. 114–255 114–255.
Ray, C. D., & Weiner, M. A. (2018). *Byrne v. Avery Center for Obstetrics and Gynecology, P.C., 327 Conn. 540 (2018): Yes, you can sue your health care provider if it discloses your medical records to your ex*. Connecticut Lawyer.
Sachs, C. J., Peek, C., Baraff, L. J., et al. (1998). Failure of the mandatory domestic violence reporting law to increase medical facility referral to police. *Annals of Emergency Medicine, 31*(4), 488–449.
Safer v. Estate of Pack, 677 A. 2d 1188 (1996).
Schuster v. Altenberg, 144 Wis.2d 223 (1988).
Scott, K., Dyas, J. V., Middlemass, J. B., et al. (2007). Confidentiality in the waiting room: An observational study in general practice. *The British Journal of General Practice: The Journal of the Royal College of General Practitioners, 57*(539), 490–493.
Simonsen v. Swenson, 104 Neb. 224 (1920).
Slovenko, R. (1988). *Psychiatry in law/law in psychiatry*. Routledge.
Slovenko, R. (2009). *Psychiatry in law/law in psychiatry*. Routledge.
Tarasoff v. Regents of University of California, 17 Cal.3d 425 (1976).
Tendam, M. L. (2018). The HIPAA-Pota-Mess: How HIPAA's weak enforcement standards have led states to create confusing medical privacy remedies. *Ohio State Law Journal, 79*(2), 411–450.
Volk v. DeMeerleer, 187 Wn2d 241 (2016).
Walgreen Co. v. Hinchy, 25 NE 3d 748 (2015).
Werth, J. L., Burke, C., & Bardash, R. J. (2002). Confidentiality in end-of-life and after-death situations. *Ethics & Behavior, 12*(3), 205–222.

Negligent Psychopharmacology

16

Brian K. Cooke

Adverse drug reactions are estimated to be the fourth leading cause of death in hospitalized patients (Federal Drug Administration [FDA], 2018). As research advances medical knowledge and contributes to the burgeoning development of medications, the profession of medicine has been more attentive to patient safety. One notable initiative, the Institute of Medicine's report from 1999, *To Err is Human: Building a Safer Health System* (Institute of Medicine, 2000), was a major step for the patient safety movement. Medical schools and residency training programs have joined the movement by integrating patient safety activities into their curricula. Healthcare professionals use root cause analysis (RCA) or morbidity and mortality (M&M) conferences to provide a safe venue to examine how patients have been harmed with the aim of improving the delivery of healthcare.

When considering the adverse events that may be the result of prescribing medications, psychiatrists must attend to a bevy of potential side effects. Black box warnings issued by the US Food and Drug Administration (FDA) represent the strictest disclosures of adverse effects. Medications commonly prescribed by psychiatrists are no different than other medications in this regard and, depending on the medication, have black box warnings for problems such as hepatotoxicity, fetal risk, pancreatitis, risks with concomitant opioid use, abuse and dependence, dementia-related psychosis, and serious rash. In 2004, a public health advisory was issued by the FDA, leading to a black box warning that antidepressants may cause increased suicidality risk in children, adolescents, and young adults with major depression or other psychiatric disorders (FDA, 2004). The events leading to this warning have been described elsewhere (Cohan, 2004) and are discussed further in Chap. 21. While controversial, this warning had a direct impact on psychiatrists and their patients, including declines in antidepressant use and depression diagnoses (Friedman, 2014).

While this chapter focuses on the risks of negligence, psychiatrists may also be sanctioned in criminal actions, state medical boards (see Chap. 33), and the US Drug Enforcement Administration. If a physician's gross negligence is the cause of a patient's death, then the physician can be charged with manslaughter, although these cases are rare (Ferner, 2000).

Legal Framework

Negligence has been defined as "conduct which falls below the standard established by law for the protection of others against unreasonable risk of harm" (American Law Institute, 1965). Cases of medical negligence arise following an adverse outcome, and physicians are held liable to compensate patients for injuries. Rothschild et al. (2002) noted, "Adverse drug events associated with malpractice claims were often severe, costly, and preventable."

In cases involving negligent psychopharmacology, the patient package inserts (PPI) for medications are commonly used to establish any dereliction and direct causation (Preskorn, 2014). The PPI is the label approved by the FDA describing the drug product's indication; who should take it; adverse events; instructions for uses in pregnancy, children, and other populations; and safety information (Federal Drug Administration, 2020). Although not intended to define the standard of care, the PPI includes relevant information that may be used to support or refute claims about the actions of the defendant physician.

Informed Consent

The practice of prescribing medications is not a passive experience but should usually follow a dynamic conversation. The physician and patient are engaged in a therapeutic relationship, often viewed as a partnership, in which the physician explains various recommendations, intended benefits, and potential risks; the patient as an autonomous agent may

B. K. Cooke (✉)
Department of Psychiatry and Behavioral Sciences, Emory University, Atlanta, GA, USA
e-mail: brian.cooke@emory.edu

P. Ash et al. (eds.), *Malpractice and Liability in Psychiatry*, https://doi.org/10.1007/978-3-030-91975-7_16

ask questions and decide which of the physician's proposed options is most favorable. This process, of course, represents informed consent. If absent or inadequate, and if the patient has suffered some harm, then informed consent becomes a focal point in alleged negligent psychopharmacology. Several notable landmark legal cases have helped define these parameters of informed consent.

In *Natanson v. Kline* (1960), Irma Natanson filed a malpractice suit against her physician, Dr. Kline, claiming she was not adequately informed of the risks of sustaining chest wall burns from cobalt radiation therapy as part of her treatment for breast cancer. The trial court found that the doctor was not negligent. Upon appeal, the Kansas Supreme Court held the trial court erred in their jury instructions regarding the amount of disclosure needed for a physician to obtain informed consent. The appellate court directed that the physician was obligated to disclose the elements of informed consent in "language as simple as necessary the nature of the ailment, the nature of the proposed treatment, the probability of success or of alternative, and perhaps the risks of unfortunate results and unforeseen conditions within the body" (p. 410). The Kansas Supreme Court stated, "The duty of the physician to disclose, however, is limited to disclosures that which a reasonable medical practitioner would make under the same or similar circumstances." This case established what is commonly referred to as "the reasonable practitioner standard" in regard to the amount of information disclosure required in the informed consent process.

In *Canterbury v. Spence* (1972), the District Court of Appeals held that a physician can be liable for malpractice for the failure to disclose severe, although rare, risks inherent in a medical procedure. In this case, Jerry Canterbury became paraplegic and incontinent after falling from his hospital bed following a laminectomy performed by Dr. Spence. Based on the principle of patient autonomy, the court disagreed with the professional medical standard described in *Natanson v. Kline* and redefined the standard for disclosure to be what a "reasonable person" would need to know regarding potential risks. This is referred to as the "reasonable person standard" regarding the amount of information disclosure required.

In *Clites v. Iowa* (1982), the Iowa Court of Appeals held that the failure to obtain informed consent for antipsychotic medications can be grounds for malpractice. Timothy Clites developed tardive dyskinesia after 5 years of treatment with antipsychotic medications for aggressive behavior while admitted to a state-operated residential facility. The court stated that "a competent patient has a fundamental right to decide to be left alone, absent an emergency situation." The court opined there is a "recognized standard that requires some form of informed consent prior to the administration of major tranquilizers," which includes an obligation to disclose the nature and probable consequences of the treatment.

Psychiatrists and Pharmaceutical Companies

In some medical malpractice lawsuits, the injured plaintiff may sue both the defendant physician and the drug manufacturer company. If the intended target is the pharmaceutical company, the physician will be dismissed from the suit. If the case proceeds against both, the drug manufacturer company may rely on the "learned intermediary doctrine" in an attempt to shift the focus, and ultimate responsibility, for any failure to warn about potential risks of the medication from the manufacturer to the prescribing physician (O'Reilly & Dalal, 2003). This stems from tort liability doctrine, which provides that "a manufacturer is not liable for failing to warn consumers of a product's potential risk so long as it provides a proper warning to the specialized class of people who are authorized to sell, install, or provide the product" (*Watts v. Medicis Pharm Corp*., 2015, p. 853). If the manufacturer provides an adequate warning to the physician, then the physician inherits the duty to provide the warning to the patient, which will be obtained with the patient's informed consent (Lin, 2020, pp. 215–216).

The phrase "learned intermediary" was first used in *Sterling Drug v. Cornish* in 1966. This 8th Circuit Court of Appeals case involved a woman who suffered extensive and permanent impairment of her vision resulting from the drug chloroquine phosphate, manufactured and sold by Sterling Drug under the trade name Aralen® and prescribed for arthritis. The appellee contended that the appellant "knew or should have known that some people would be so affected, and was negligent in its failure to warn doctors, including appellees' doctors, to be on the lookout for symptoms of the condition" (p. 84). The Court noted, "Moreover, in this case we are dealing with a prescription drug rather than a normal consumer item. In such a case the purchaser's doctor is a learned intermediary between the purchaser and the manufacturer. If the doctor is properly warned of the possibility of a side effect in some patients, and is advised of the symptoms normally accompanying the side effect, there is an excellent chance that injury to the patient can be avoided" (p. 85).

The rationale for the learned intermediary doctrine is that the physician, and not the drug manufacturer, is in the best position to communicate with the patient. The physician knows the patient's medical history. The drug manufacturer passes the information to the physician and thus avoids interfering in the physician-patient relationship. Equipped with the information from the drug manufacturer, physicians are better situated to explain to their patients the necessary medical terminology relevant to the drug's risks and benefits.

When psychiatrists supervise other healthcare professionals during a patient's treatment, they may assume vicarious liability in prescribing medications even if the alleged negligence was the result of the person they supervise. This concept of *respondeat superior* ("let the superior make answer") is another typical tort claim in medicine practice. The psychiatrist's duty to the patient may extend through any physician extender, nurse practitioner, or medical trainee under supervision (see Chap. 3).

Types of Allegations

Negligence in Prescribing, Administering, and Monitoring Medications

1. Prescribing

Negligent prescribing may stem from a physician's inadequate assessment and evaluation. Recommendations for what constitutes a thorough psychiatric evaluation have been described elsewhere, such as in textbooks and professional association guidelines. Allegations may focus on the physician's negligent medical decision-making with prescribing if it can be shown that a reasonable and prudent practitioner would have arrived at a different conclusion in similar circumstances. Negligence may be alleged if an inadequate assessment led to an incorrect diagnosis, or even if the physician conducted a thorough assessment but arrived at the wrong diagnosis. The wrong diagnosis will likely lead to the physician prescribing a medication that is not indicated for the patient's actual condition or may cause harm to the patient. Likewise, there may be alleged negligence if a physician made an accurate diagnosis but prescribed a medication that is not indicated for the patient's condition.

Prescribing too much of a quantity of a medication or too little is a common pitfall (Roth, 2007). Prescribing too much supplies the patient with an opportunity to misuse medications that have abuse potential or may increase the risk of overdose in a suicidal patient. Prescribing too little of a medication may place a patient at risk for inadequate treatment, withdrawal, or rebound symptoms if the patient's supply of mediation is abruptly interrupted. Lawsuits and other sanctions are more common when psychiatrists inappropriately administer, prescribe, dispense, or maintain records for controlled medications such as amphetamines, benzodiazepines, or opioids, but litigation has been brought in allegations involving all classes of psychiatric medications (Wettstein, 2017).

2. Administering

Negligent administering refers to delivering the medication by the wrong route, e.g., giving the drug intravenously instead of intramuscularly, and is not commonly seen in negligent psychopharmacology cases. If the physician has properly prescribed the medication, then problems of administering often involve nursing or other hospital staff rather than the physician. Administration of medication to patients without their knowledge, referred to as covert/concealed/or surreptitious administration, arguably runs afoul of informed consent and the right to refuse medication (Huang et al., 2012); although this practice is not uncommon in patients who lack competence (e.g., children) and may be underreported in psychiatric emergency settings.

3. Monitoring

Allegations of negligence may involve inadequate monitoring of medications. DiGiacomo and Sadoff (2015, p. 83) noted, "An early problem for psychiatrists using psychotropic medications was the unfamiliarity with unusual effects and the acceptance that bizarre symptoms were often related more to the psychiatric illness than to the medication used to treat the illness." Physicians should be familiar with and follow available standards and guidelines for medication monitoring. The ongoing monitoring of the patient's medical status may include checking drug levels or other biomarkers of possible side effects (e.g., clozapine, lithium, and antipsychotics). Failure to adequately monitor the patient's response and side effects to mediation will be characterized in the courtroom as patient abandonment.

Failure to Obtain Informed Consent or Adequate Informed Consent

Informed consent is just as much an art as a science. Providing a litany of warnings for every medication and alternative medication might dissuade patients from consenting to even the safest of medications. Instead, the psychiatrist should consider including the common side effects, the most serious potential side effects, and any others relevant for the patient's specific clinical scenario. Black box warnings should be included during the informed consent discussion; often, they communicate the potential for rare but dangerous side effects, such as injury or death.

Psychiatrists often treat patients who are competent to consent to medications but whose symptoms of mental illness may challenge the informed consent process. In this case, the psychiatrist should first determine if the patient truly is competent to make medical decisions or if a health-care proxy or guardian is needed. As competence may fluctuate, the psychiatrist may need to reexamine the patient's capacity to provide informed consent throughout the course of treatment. Confirming the patient's competence and absent an emergency exception, the psychiatrist then must be cautious to avoid overly simplifying or skipping the informed consent process (e.g., when initiating an antipsychotic medication in a paranoid patient with schizophrenia who is competent to consent to treatment).

Specific Areas of Risk

1. *Prescribing medications that have potential for abuse or addiction*

While all medications have the potential for adverse effects, some categories of medications have the potential for abuse or addiction. For the benzodiazepines, there is a black box warning that "concomitant benzodiazepine use with opioids may result in profound sedation, respiratory depression, coma, and death." Stimulants, commonly prescribed for attention-deficit/hyperactivity disorder, are noted in the patient package insert (PPI) to have "high abuse potential; avoid prolonged treatment, may lead to drug dependence…." Selection of benzodiazepines or stimulants relies on a clinical evaluation to assess for past or ongoing substance use disorders, patterns of prescription misuse, and other psychosocial risk factors that might precipitate abuse or dependence. When prescribed, psychiatrists should remain cognizant of the continued risk during the treatment course and utilize clinical judgment and laboratory monitoring (e.g., urine drug screens) where necessary to determine the appropriateness of continuing the prescriptions.

Psychiatrists should be aware if they are in a state that requires physicians to check the prescription drug monitoring program (PDMP) before prescribing a Schedule II or other controlled drug. They may verify this requirement by searching for the individual state PDMP or the state psychiatric society, as comprehensive national lists may be outdated. The PDMP is a useful tool that allows physicians to view which controlled substances patients have received and from which pharmacies. It can be used to verify that the patient has in fact received the prescription in question. More importantly, it will alert physicians if patients are prescribed potentially dangerous combinations of mediations (e.g., concomitant benzodiazepines and opioids) or duplicative prescriptions from other physicians, which may be unintentional or be evidence of "doctor shopping." As indicated by one example state's PDMP, a requestor (e.g., most commonly physicians and pharmacists but may include any healthcare professional) uses the application "to determine if a patient should be given or dispenses a prescription based on their prescription history. Requestors are the strongest line of defense to prevent prescription drug abuse" (Georgia PMP Aware user guide, 1).

The PDMP can be used as a therapeutic tool with the aim of increasing patient safety. Any discrepancies noted from the PDMP should be discussed with the patient. Errors may be found in the PDMP, as sometimes prescriptions do not appear in the list or may be erroneously included. Psychiatrists should be aware that searching the PDMP will display results limited to only the states which have been selected for the query. Introducing patients to the requirement of checking the PDMP before prescribing controlled substances can be included in a discussion of other relevant policies for prescribing controlled substances. Explaining the rationale for checking the PDMP will help patients appreciate the seriousness of these medications during an informed consent discussion.

Legislative changes mandating physicians to check the PDMP were commonly met with opposition. Physicians objected to difficulties with obtaining logins, accessing the database, additional time in patient workflow, and incomplete data from search results; prescriber utilization of PDMPs has also been noted to be low (Haffajee et al., 2014). Psychiatrists should understand that the process has been simplified with technological updates, integrating the PDMP into electronic health records, and the option to delegate other members of the healthcare team to assume the responsibility of checking patients.

Penalties for failure to check the PDMP vary among jurisdictions but may include disciplinary sanctions by the state's licensing board, professional misconduct charges that can result in permanent revocation of license, fines, and imprisonment (Haffajee et al., 2014). Additionally, there is increased civil liability risk for failure to check the PDMP. For example, negligence may be alleged if a patient overdoses, harming himself or another person, if it is argued that a reasonable and prudent physician would have checked the PDMP and modified the treatment plan based on identified safety concerns. As the potential penalties for failure to check a website may be perceived as harsh, some states have encouraged stipulations to make prescribers immune from liability for checking or failing to check the PDMP; it is unclear whether this provides any meaningful protection (Haffajee et al., 2014)

2. *Anticipating and managing adverse effects*

Negligence may be alleged if the psychiatrist does not adequately anticipate and manage adverse side effects. Fault may be found if the psychiatrist does not warn the patient of potential side effects listed in the PPI and then the patient has an injury as a direct result. For example, negligence may be argued if a psychiatrist did not warn the patient of the risk of sedation, dizziness, or orthostatic hypotension listed by the drug manufacturer, and then the patient fell and was injured.

Perhaps one of the most important adverse effects that may give rise to allegations of negligence is that of overdose, whether intentional or accidental, and death. The defendant psychiatrist may have deviated from the standard of care if he or she neglected to warn the patient of any inherent medical risks (e.g., cardiac arrhythmias); of the need to avoid ingesting other medications, substances, or foods (e.g., hypertensive crisis risk for the monoamine oxidase inhibitors – included as a Black Box warning); prescribed too high of a dose of medication; or dispensed too much medication to a patient at risk for overdose.

Childbearing age any potential fetal risks in Chap. 24, the psychiatrist should discuss with female patients of childbearing age the potential fetal risks, which might be listed as a black box warning (e.g., valproic acid) or included in pregnancy/lactation information listed for all medications. This discussion should be included in the informed consent process. Risk can be mitigated by careful consideration of medications prescribed in women of childbearing age regardless of her reporting about plans to conceive, monitoring the patient's use of contraception, desire to conceive, and pregnancy status.

Some medication side effects have been included in the *Diagnostic and Statistical Manual of Mental Disorders, 5th Edition* (DSM-5) (American Psychiatric Association, 2013), seemingly reflecting their frequency and highlighting the role psychiatrists have in preventing and managing them. The diagnostic criteria for these side effects can be found in the DSM-5 in the chapters of "Medication-Induced Movement Disorders and Other Adverse Effects of Medication." The listed movement disorders include neuroleptic-induced Parkinsonism, other medication-induced Parkinsonism, neuroleptic malignant syndrome, medication-induced acute dystonia, medication-induced acute akathisia, tardive dyskinesia, tardive dystonia, tardive akathisia, medication-induced postural tremor, other medication-induced movement disorder, antidepressant discontinuation syndrome, and other adverse effect of medication. Notably, the DSM-5 instructs the reader that these are not to be considered as mental disorders. While the inclusion of these diagnoses in the DSM-5 may be discussed by the forensic expert in cases of negligent psychopharmacology, it should be noted, "Although these movement disorders are labeled 'medication induced,' it is often difficult to establish the causal relationship between medication exposure and the development of the movement disorder, especially because some of these movement disorders also occur in the absence of medication exposure" (DSM-5, p. 709). Additionally, the "Cautionary Statement for Forensic Use of DSM-5" reminds the reader that while DSM-5 diagnostic criteria may be used as a reference for the courts and attorneys, that it was "developed to meet the needs of clinicians, public health professionals, and research investigators rather than all of the technical needs of the courts and legal professionals… the use of DSM-5 could be informed by an awareness of the risks and limitations of its use in forensic settings" (DSM-5, p. 25).

Allegations of negligent psychopharmacology may also focus on side effects reported by anecdotal evidence but not listed by the drug manufacturer. The medication's PPI will be examined to determine if the side effect was an expected result of the prescribed medication or could not have been anticipated. The strength of any prevailing research will support a contention that psychiatrists are responsible to remain informed of current medical knowledge.

Negligence may be alleged if it can be argued that the psychiatrist should have taken action to treat or prevent side effects from withdrawal. This could be seen in a variety of examples. Patients who seek care while in states of acute intoxication from substances or who are admitted to the hospital where they will no longer be able to continue receiving a substance may suffer injury if inadequately monitored and treated for withdrawal symptoms. While many substances do not have associated withdrawal states with heightened mortality or morbidity (e.g., opioids), psychiatrists must remember that withdrawal from the sedative, hypnotic, and anxiolytics may result in seizures, delirium tremens, or death. The substances that have the potential for potentially dangerous withdrawal states include certain prescribed psychiatric medications (e.g., benzodiazepines). Litigation may focus on the psychiatrist' efforts to monitor the patient's supply of medication, to prescribe a taper to mitigate withdrawal symptoms, or to refer the patient to a higher level of care (e.g., inpatient detoxification).

Although patients should be warned of the potential to experience discontinuation symptoms from the cessation of antidepressants, negligence would be difficult to prove as the commonly experienced symptoms (e.g., dizziness, tinnitus, paresthesia or "electric shock" sensations, poor sleep, or increased anxiety) are unlikely to cause damages; further, the symptoms of antidepressant discontinuation are "vague and variable" (DSM-5).

Off-Label Use

The FDA-approved indications of a medication typically align with the patient's diagnosis. It is well established, however, that physicians are permitted to prescribe medications for indications that are not specifically approved by the FDA. Otherwise known as off-label prescribing, this practice is both legal and common (Syed et al., 2021). The medical decision-making to prescribe off-label, however, should be supported and documented. Furthermore, psychiatrists may consider including this information in the informed consent discussion with the patient, e.g., explicitly stating that the proposed medication is not FDA approved for the patient's presumed diagnosis and the reason(s) why the physician is recommending the medication.

Disclosure of Errors

The psychiatrist may learn of errors related to their own prescribing of medications. Perhaps the wrong medication, dosage, or formulation was prescribed. Disclosure and apologizing to the patient may preserve the therapeutic relationship without increasing the potential for future litigation. Many states have apology laws to prevent the admissibility of a physician's apology as an admission of fault. While apology programs may lead to a rapid resolution of malpractice claims, it has been suggested that these programs may not decrease the number of claims (Konda & Torres, 2018). McMichael et al. (2019) offer an analysis of the consequences of apology laws on malpractice claims and physician liability.

3. *Supervision of physician extenders*

As described earlier, psychiatrists may be liable for damages incurred by the patient as a direct result of the actions of any paraprofessionals, physician extenders, or medical trainees who treated the patient under the psychiatrist's supervision. In one study (Myers et al., 2020) examining medical malpractice claims in which physician trainees were directly involved, inadequate supervision was a contributing factor in 24% of cases; the majority (74%) of these claims were procedure-related (e.g., puncture or laceration during surgery). In psychiatry, claims involving trainee negligence that result in legal action toward the supervisor more commonly involve sexual contact between the trainee and patient (see Chap. 14) and suicide by the patient (see Chap. 12) (Greene, 2019). Notably, a sub-analysis of the Malpractice Insurers Medical Error Prevention Study, a review of 1452 malpractice claims, found only one case involving a psychiatry trainee (Singh et al., 2007). Physicians maintain an obligation to monitor the competence of those whom they supervise, verify the quality of the work, modify the prescribed medications and treatment plan if indicated, and provide clinically relevant interventions no different than if the psychiatrist were solely responsible for the patient without the assistance of the extender (see Chap. 3).

Prescribing Risks in Specific Populations

Other areas of special risk with negligent psychopharmacology are described further elsewhere in this textbook, including prescribing to children and adolescents (Chap. 21), geriatric patients (Chap. 26), inmates in correctional facilities (Chap. 27), pregnant patients (Chap. 24), and patients located in a different state than the psychiatrist (Chap. 30).

Reducing Risk

Take a Thorough History Prior to Treatment

Taking a thorough history increases the likelihood of arriving at an accurate diagnosis and thus choosing a prudent treatment plan. Screening for underlying medical conditions may reveal comorbid diagnoses that could increase the adverse effects from medications. The psychiatrist should assess the patient's medication history to better understand the patient's response to prior trials of medications. One suggested mnemonic is that a good medication history will AVOIDM mistakes – asking about allergies, vitamins and herbs, old drugs and over-the-counter medications, interactions, dependence, and any medication problems in the family (FDA Drug Interactions, 2018).

Documentation

The psychiatrist should thoroughly document the clinical information relied upon to guide the treatment plan. Failure to maintain medical records may result in disciplinary action as a violation of state regulations. Furthermore, medical decision-making should be clear. The psychiatrist should note the rationale for treatment decisions including the need to start, increase, decrease, or discontinue any medications. Informed consent should also be documented in the medical record. The psychiatrist should record if the PDMP was checked, when clinically appropriate or required. If medications are adjusted between in-person encounters (e.g., during a telephone conversation with the patient between scheduled appointments), then the psychiatrist should remember to document the relevant clinical information and adjustments to prescriptions. The patient's report of side effects should be included, as well as the psychiatrist's interpretation of this report and any plans to monitor the medical symptoms and/or adjust medications. For female patients of childbearing age, psychiatrists should ask patients about their use of contraception. Any intentions of conceiving can be documented. Finally, psychiatrists should be mindful that if using an electronic health record and copying and pasting information, then the accuracy of the clinical information should be verified and updated accordingly (e.g., prescription dosages).

Ordering and Monitoring Labs, Weight, and Vital Signs

In addition to the clinical interview, psychiatrists may monitor the patient's response to medications by ordering and monitoring labs and vital signs when indicated. Some medications have recommended monitoring parameters (e.g., Clozapine REMS). For example, many antipsychotics carry a recommendation for checking the patient's fasting glucose at baseline if the patient has risk factors for diabetes. When prescribing stimulants, it is often recommended that psychiatrists should check the patient's blood pressure and heart rate at baseline and with dose increases and periodically and monitor the height and weight in pediatric patients. Drug levels should be monitored for some medications that have therapeutic ranges or may cause toxicity. As electronic health records are increasingly utilized, psychiatrists can take advantage of many available tools and reminders to assist in efforts to adequately monitor their patient's health status.

Maintain Up-to-Date Knowledge About Medications and Safety Information

Advances in scientific research rapidly develop our understanding of medicine. New safety warnings and recommendations for monitoring, however, may emerge for medications. Research trials may elucidate risks not previously captured by drug manufactures. Psychiatrists can take advantage of relevant FDA drug alerts, focus efforts on reading psychopharmacology updates, and choose maintenance of certification activities (e.g., continued medical education) that target deficits in outdated knowledge of medications.

Communicate with Patient, Family, and Other Involved Healthcare Professionals

Psychiatrists should regularly communicate with the patient and others who can provide helpful clinical information. If the patient is competent and there is no emergency exception, then a psychiatrist will need to obtain consent to communicate with outside sources. The patient's family may provide relevant information at the initial assessment and then later describe observations of the patient's response to medication. The psychiatrist may communicate with other healthcare professionals both during the initial assessment (e.g., a physical examination conducted by an internist) and as treatment progresses (e.g., referral to a specialist if concerned that the patient has developed side effects). If the patient is concurrently in treatment with a psychotherapist, then the psychiatrist should be cognizant of the risks of split treatment (Meyer & Simon, 1999), mitigating risk by communicating when there are safety concerns (see Chap. 3).

Key Points

- The process of informed consent has been influenced by landmark court cases directing psychiatrists to the amount of information that should be disclosed to the patient.
- In cases of alleged negligent psychopharmacology, a forensic expert retained by the plaintiff will likely offer an opinion that during the course of treatment, the defendant psychiatrist deviated from the standard of care which directly caused harm to the patient, often relating to the adverse effects from medication or other consequences of inadequate prescribing.
- Negligent psychopharmacology claims may stem from an inadequate assessment of the patient, leading the psychiatrist to miss important clinical data or arrive at an inaccurate diagnosis.
- Allegations of negligence may focus on a psychiatrist's failure to follow accepted recommendations for prescribing and monitoring the effects of medications.
- Psychiatrists should be especially careful in prescribing medications that have the potential for abuse or overdose, checking a prescription drug monitoring program if required or permitted in their jurisdiction.
- Psychiatrists should be aware of the safety information disclosed by drug manufacturers in the patient prescription insert and remain current with their medical knowledge pertaining to medication safety.
- Documentation in the patient's medical record should clearly show the clinical information gathered during the assessment, the psychiatrist's medical decision-making and rationale for the treatment plan, and the results of the informed consent process when prescribing medications.

References

American Law Institute, Restatement (Second) of Torts §282, 1965.

American Psychiatric Association. (2013). *Diagnostic and statistical manual of mental disorders: Diagnostic and statistical manual of mental disorders* (5th ed.). American Psychiatric Association.

Canterbury v. Spence, 464 F. 2d 772 (DC Cir. 1972).

Clites v. Iowa, 322 N.W.2d 917 (Iowa Ct. App. 1982).

Clozapine REMS. https://www.clozapinerems.com/CpmgClozapineUI/home.u. Accessed June 10, 2021.

Cohan, J. (2004). Psychiatric ethics and emerging issues of psychopharmacology in the treatment of depression. *Journal of Contemporary Health Law and Policy, 20*, 115–172. Available at https://scholarship.law.edu/jchlp/vol20/iss1/7

DiGiacomo, J. N., & Sadoff, R. L. (2015). Managing malpractice risks during psychopharmacologic treatment. In R. L. Sadoff (Ed.), *The evolution of forensic psychiatry: History, current developments, future directions*. Oxford University Press.

Federal Drug Administration (FDA). (2004). *Suicidality in children and adolescents being treated with antidepressant medications*. https://www.fda.gov/drugs/postmarket-drug-safety-information-patients-and-providers/suicidality-children-and-adolescents-being-treated-antidepressant-medications. Accessed July 7, 2021.

Federal Drug Administration (FDA). (2018). *Preventable adverse drug reactions: A focus on drug interactions*. https://www.fda.gov/drugs/drug-interactions-labeling/preventable-adverse-drug-reactions-focus-drug-interactions#:~:text=If%20these%20estimates%20are%20correct,%2C%20accidents%2C%20and%20automobile%20deaths. Accessed January 18, 2021.

FDA: How do I use prescription drug labeling. (2020). https://www.fda.gov/about-fda/project-renewal/how-do-i-useprescription-drug-labeling. Accessed December 17, 2021.

Ferner, R. E. (2000). Medication errors that have led to manslaughter charges. *BMJ, 321*(7270), 1212–1216. https://doi.org/10.1136/bmj.321.7270.1212

Friedman, R. (2014). Antidepressants' black-box warning--10 years later. *New England Journal of Medicine, 371*(18), 1666–1668.

Georgia PMP Aware user guide. https://georgia.pmpaware.net/login. Accessed July 1, 2021.

Greene, J. (2019). Ethical and legal considerations in supervision. In D. G. SG & K. M. Corcoran (Eds.), *Supervision in psychiatric practice: Practical approaches across venues and providers*. American Psychiatric Association.

Haffajee, R., Jena, A., & Weiner, S. (2014). Mandatory use of prescription drug monitoring programs. *Journal of the American Medical Association, 313*(9), 891–892. https://doi.org/10.1001/jama.2014.18514

Huang, E. K., McNiel, D. E., & Binder, R. L. (2012). Covert medication in psychiatric emergencies: Is it ever ethically permissible? *Journal of the American Academy of Psychiatry and the Law, 40*(2), 239–245.

Kohn, L., Corrigan, J., Donaldson, M. (Institute of Medicine). (2000). *To err is human: Building a safer health system*. National Academy Press.

Konda, S., & Torres, A. (2018). Practicing safe dermatology—Screening out liability. *Journal of the American Medical Association Dermatology, 154*(2), 142–143. https://doi.org/10.1001/jamadermatol.2017.4838

Lin, B. (2020). Federal right to try act: Heightened informed consent and price regulation measures will improve quality, autonomy, and exploitation issues. *Hastings Business Law Journal, 16*, 207–229. Also available at https://repository.uchastings.edu/hastings_business_law_journal/vol16/iss2/6

McMichael, B. J., Van Horn, R. L., & Viscusi, W. K. (2019). "Sorry" is never enough: How state apology laws fail to reduce medical malpractice liability risk. *Stanford Law Review, 71*(2), 341–409.

Meyer, D. J., & Simon, R. I. (1999). Split treatment: Clarity between psychiatrists and psychotherapists. *Psychiatric Annals, 29*(6), 327–332.

Myers, L. C., Gartland, R. M., Skillings, J., Heard, L., Bittner, E. A., Einbinder, J., Metlay, J. P., & Mort, E. (2020). An examination of medical malpractice claims involving physician trainees. *Academic Medicine, 95*(8), 1215–1222. https://doi.org/10.1097/ACM.0000000000003117

Natanson v. Kline, 187 Kan. 186, 354 P.2d 670 (Kan. 1960).

O'Reilly, J., & Dalal, A. (2003). Off-label or out of bounds? Prescriber and marketer liability for unapproved uses of FDA-approved drugs. *Annals of Health Law, 12*(2), 295–324.

Preskorn, S. H. (2014). Clinical psychopharmacology and medical malpractice: The four Ds. *Journal of Psychiatric Practice, 20*(5), 363–368.

Roth, L. (2007). Recognizing and avoiding common pitfalls in clinical psychopharmacology. *Psychiatric Times, 24*(8), 34–44. Retrieved from https://www.psychiatrictimes.com/view/recognizing-and-avoiding-common-pitfalls-clinical-psychopharmacology

Rothschild, J. M., Federico, F. A., Gandhi, T. K., Kaushal, R., Williams, D. H., & Bates, D. W. (2002). Analysis of medication-related malpractice claims: Causes, preventability, and costs. *Archives of Internal Medicine, 162*(21), 2414–2420. https://doi.org/10.1001/archinte.162.21.2414

Singh, H., Thomas, E. J., Petersen, L. A., et al. (2007). Medical errors involving trainees: A study of closed malpractice claims from 5 insurers. *Archives of Internal Medicine, 167*(19), 2030–2036. https://doi.org/10.1001/archinte.167.19.2030

Sterling Drug, Inc. v. Cornish, 370 F. 2d 82 (8th Cir. 1966).

Syed, S. A., et al. (2021). The law and practice of off-label prescribing and physician promotion. *Journal of the American Academy of Psychiatry and the Law, 49*(1), 53–59.

Watts v. Medicis Pharm Corp., 342 P.3d 847 (Ariz Ct Appeals 2015).

Wettstein, R. M. (2017). Specific issues in psychiatric malpractice. In R. Rosner & C. L. Scott (Eds.), *Principles and practice of forensic psychiatry* (3rd ed., pp. 297–305). CRC Press.

Abandonment and Unnecessary Commitment

17

Joy Stankowski and Renée Sorrentino

Psychiatrists, like most medical professionals, are not obliged to treat a patient unless they chose to do so. Once a psychiatrist has agreed to treat a patient, they have entered into a patient-physician relationship. A patient-physician relationship is established when a physician affirmatively acts by examining, diagnosing, or agreeing to treat a patient (Testa & West, 2010). The creation of a patient-physician relationship is important because it constitutes a contract in which the physician is legally and ethically obliged to treat the patient or to properly terminate the relationship. Termination refers to the cessation of treatment. Termination may occur by one party, coined "unilateral" termination, or by both parties, referred to as "termination by mutual agreement" (American Psychiatric Association, 2014).

Psychiatrists may choose to terminate with a patient when the treatment is no longer therapeutic. Noncompliance with treatment, frequent missed appointments, unpaid bills, or abusive behaviors are common reasons treatment may be no longer therapeutic (Mossman et al., 2010). Additionally, the retirement of a psychiatrist typically necessitates termination. *Abandonment* refers to the termination of a treatment relationship by a physician without allowing the patient to arrange suitable substitute treatment (Van Susteren, 2001). When patients terminate a treatment relationship, there is no issue of abandonment. Psychiatrists may be sued for medical malpractice under an abandonment claim. The first section of this chapter will review the legal framework for such claims and propose strategies to reduce liability in the setting of termination.

Further, physicians have several duties in caring for patients with mental illness. These include beneficence, or the duty to help, and non-maleficence, or duty to do no harm (Bush, 2010). These duties can create conflict for providers when a patient requires inpatient treatment but lacks the insight or capacity to agree to voluntary hospitalization. This scenario is not unusual in persons with mental illness, so the justification and process for involuntary confinement have a long history in psychiatry. Since involuntary confinement can have negative consequences, physicians who decide to initiate the process should ensure their decision-making process is well documented. The second section of this chapter will focus on unnecessary confinement and malpractice risk.

Legal Framework for Abandonment

Patients may feel abandoned, but this is not a sufficient basis for a legal claim of abandonment (Psychiatry [Edgemont], 2010). The legal basis for a claim of abandonment arises from the duties inherent in the patient-physician relationship. This relationship is considered different from other fiduciary relationships because of the susceptibility of the patient to injury if treatment is suddenly terminated and the power disparities that exist between a patient and a physician. The legal definition of a patient-physician relationship varies by jurisdiction. Physicians should consult their local medical board to learn the definition in their jurisdiction. The failure to treat a patient or to establish a substitute treatment provider is below the standard of care required by physicians and, as such, may be grounds for a malpractice claim. The legal argument in abandonment cases is that the patient claims the physician failed to maintain their duty to treat the patient or to establish a suitable substitute provider. Physicians are not required to find the suitable provider but are required to allow appropriate time for the patient to do so. Physicians may assist in the process by providing names of local clinics or referring the patient to the local medical society for referrals.

In *Williamson v. Liptzin* (1998), a landmark case involving patient abandonment, Dr. Liptzin was found negligent in the termination of psychiatric care for his patient, Mr.

J. Stankowski (✉)
Northcoast Behavioral Healthcare, Northfield, OH, USA

Case Western Reserve University, Cleveland, OH, USA

R. Sorrentino
Harvard Medical School, Boston, MA, USA
e-mail: rsorrentino@mgh.harvard.edu

P. Ash et al. (eds.), *Malpractice and Liability in Psychiatry*, https://doi.org/10.1007/978-3-030-91975-7_17

Williamson. Dr. Liptzin was a psychiatrist retiring from Student Psychological Services at the University of North Carolina at the end of the spring semester. He referred Mr. Williamson to another psychiatrist at the same clinic where he treated Mr. Williamson when Mr. Williamson returned for the fall semester. Mr. Williamson did not follow up with care, stopped taking his prescribed medications, and killed two University of North Carolina students 8 months later (the following January). The North Carolina court found Dr. Liptzin negligent for failing to communicate to the patient the importance of continued care, as well as for not ensuring care was established. Although the case was overturned on appeal 2 years later, it highlights the importance and expectation of the termination process (*Williamson v. Liptzin*, 1998).

Types of Allegations About Abandonment

The elements of an abandonment malpractice claim include termination of the patient-physician relationship that is done (1) unilaterally by the physician, (2) without notice or substitute treatment, and (3) at time when the patient is psychiatrically unstable (Professional Risk Management Services, n.d.). Abandonment allegations are unfounded in the absence of a patient-physician relationship. Non-patients may believe that a patient-physician relationship exists if the physician is acting in a medical capacity by offering medical advice or prescribing medications outside an established treatment relationship. The determination of whether such a relationship exists in ambiguous cases is answered by the court and/or a medical licensing board. If a relationship has been determined to exist, any of these claims may lead to a successful malpractice suit if damages arise from the deviation in care. Damages may directly flow from the physician's failure to appropriately terminate or indirectly from the physician's negligence (Van Susteren, 2001). Examples of damages include emotional suffering from untreated conditions or from fears related to the inability to access timely care.

Reducing Risk Regarding Abandonment

The first step in minimizing liability for abandonment claims is to be clear in the identification of whom one is treating. Non-patients may assume they are under a physician's care if they have met with them even once (independent of the clinical setting). The American Psychiatric Association (APA) advises psychiatrists on how to avoid creating an inadvertent patient-physician relationship (APA, 2014). More specifically, the guidelines outline the importance of defining a patient-physician relationship, including making it clear to friends or colleagues who ask for advice that one is not acting in the role of a treating physician. In addition, when answering questions from an audience about psychiatric care, the psychiatrist should clearly frame responses as general information that are not intended to establish a patient-physician relationship (APA, 2014). "Curbside" consultations (or consultations in which a patient is not formally evaluated but is reviewed with a colleague) may or may not constitute a patient-physician relationship depending on the jurisdictional definition of a physician-patient relationship.

Next, communicating with the patient about the end of care in a clear and consistent manner both with verbal discussion and written summary is essential. Terminations should be formal, documented, events. Patients may not understand that they are no longer patients if this information is not clearly communicated. The psychiatrist should educate the patient about treatment recommendations, indicating if care should continue, and, if so, the nature of the recommended care. For best practice, this discussion should be summarized in a follow-up letter to the patient which includes language such as termination, referral resources, and an end date for care. The reason for termination is not required in the letter but may be helpful in enhancing communication in some situations (Lippman & Davenport, 2011).

Although no specific time frame is referenced for appropriate termination of care, 30 days is generally considered appropriate time for a patient to secure a new treatment provider (APA, 2014). This time frame may be longer if the patient is located in an area where there is a relative shortage of psychiatrists. Terminating psychiatrists can minimize their risk of liability by providing resources for treatment, such as local mental health agencies or other physician referral services. However, it is not necessary for the psychiatrist to provide an exhaustive list of referrals.

Termination is not appropriate in a setting in which the patient is acutely ill or unstable, unless the patient has agreed and alternative care has been secured. Otherwise, patients who are acutely ill should be managed by the responsible psychiatrist until they are safely able to participate in the transfer of care (Mossman et al., 2010). This does not bar psychiatrists from terminating care when patients are psychiatrically hospitalized. It is acceptable to terminate care in such settings if the patient's care can be transferred to another psychiatrist in a timely way to ensure appropriate outpatient treatment.

In settings in which healthcare insurance or organizations refuse to pay for psychiatric care, the treating physician is responsible for the patient's care until other arrangements can be made (Mossman et al., 2010). In these situations, psychiatrists must provide care until the patient can be referred to alternative care. It is important to review the managed care company's policies regarding the transfer of psychiatric care in order to reduce liability related to termination of healthcare benefits. Psychiatrists contracting with various healthcare organizations should understand the contractual agreement and conditions regarding termination. Many insurance policies have their own policies and procedures for termination, including stricter policies for government insurances (Willis & Zerr, 2005). The nature of how to handle psychiatric terminations varies by organization and state. Consultation with local healthcare attorneys is important in avoiding liability in managed care settings. In the absence of specific guidelines, the psychiatrist should continue to treat the patient as they would any other patient until an alternative provider is available. The termination process may be delayed in situations in which the patient is no longer insured. Nonetheless, the treating psychiatrists must still apply their clinical judgment in providing care.

Patients may unilaterally terminate care by failing to attend appointments and return phone calls. Psychiatrists should make efforts to contact the patient by phone or by mail. If a patient remains unreachable, then a termination letter should be sent with specific instructions about how to access care and emergency coverage. Assisting patients in identifying an alternative provider may reduce liability since it establishes a clear effort to maintain continuity of care. This may include referral sources and the option to provide copies of medical records to a subsequent physician. It is important to consult with the local medical board as some state medical boards enumerate specific requirements about termination letters (Psychiatry [Edgemont], 2010).

Specific Risk Areas

Internal Abandonment

Patients may claim abandonment in the course of a treatment relationship, referred to as "internal abandonment," when the physician does not initiate treatment that is warranted or refuses to assist in accessing appropriate support (Medlaw, 2020). Examples include a psychiatrist who has not obtained an ECT consult for a severely depressed patient who has requested ECT, or a psychiatrist who refuses to complete necessary paperwork for disability transportation.

Pharmacology

Termination in the setting of pharmacologic management requires additional diligence on behalf of the treating psychiatrist to educate the patient on whether medications should be continued and, if so, how to obtain refills. Prescriptions should not be refilled beyond the identified termination date. The refilling of prescriptions suggests that the prescriber is still in a treatment relationship with the patient. If a patient has been advised to discontinue medications as part of the termination, the patient should be educated about potential side effects as well as how to access care if they encounter adverse side effects.

Expertise

The termination process includes providing resources for the patient to continue care. When a patient requires subspecialized treatment, such as treatment of refractory depression or treatment of a paraphilic disorder, finding such a specialist may be difficult. Depending on the geographic location, such specialists may be unavailable. Practicing in a rural area requires physicians to be mindful of the challenges of finding alternate providers. In these settings, it is imperative that the physician give adequate notice to the patient and support the transition to a new provider. The physician does not have a responsibility to find a subspecialist but does have a responsibility to refer the patient to another competent physician.

Noncompliant Patient

A psychiatrist may decide to terminate with a patient who is noncompliant with treatment. This noncompliance may take the form of missed appointments, failure to pay, or refusal to comply with the psychiatrist's treatment recommendations. Deciding to "fire" a patient should be based on the dissolution of a therapeutic relationship. Obtaining and documenting anonymous consultation with a colleague may be beneficial in decreasing liability by creating a record of diligence in termination (Mossman et al., 2010). The treating psychiatrist should make every effort to communicate the termination by contacting and writing the patient. If the patient is unreachable, this should be clearly documented.

Fired by a Patient

When a patient fires a psychiatrist, the patient-physician relationship is terminated, and the psychiatrist does not have any duty to provide treatment or treatment referrals. However, if the patient has fired the psychiatrist in the setting of acute psychiatric symptoms, the psychiatrist may have responsibilities to follow up with the patient to ensure the patient has expressed a consistent desire to terminate the treatment (Van Susteren, 2001). A patient who fires a psychiatrist in the setting of psychosis, for example, may not be competent in making this decision. In these situations, the reasoning behind the decision to fire the psychiatrist warrants further inquiry.

Psychiatrists on Leave

Psychiatrists who are unavailable by extended time off without emergency coverage or who do not respond to patient's questions posed in emails or phone calls may inadvertently abandon the patient (Jung & McDowell, 2020). Psychiatrists have a duty to provide emergency coverage when they are unavailable. The risk of inadvertent abandonment can be minimized by providing coverage when unavailable.

Documentation

Documentation and clear communication are the most effective ways of minimizing liability when terminating treatment. Documentation regarding termination should include a detailed note identifying the reason for termination, discussion with the patient, and referral plan, including coverage of medications and emergency care. One key component to an appropriate termination is to send the patient a letter identifying the termination of care and outlining the referral process as well as the anticipated time frame. The letter should clearly state the physician's opinion regarding the need for continued care and the rationale. To ensure the delivery of the letter, the physician may send the letter certified or ask the patient to sign and return the letter, indicating receipt.

Documentation should be timely and completed at the time of termination. Medical record entries that occur after a negative outcome are less credible than contemporaneous notes and should be avoided (see Chap. 5). Termination of the patient-physician relationship with appropriate notice, referral to a substitute provider, and continued care during the identified termination period minimizes liability in an abandonment claim.

Legal Framework for Unnecessary Confinement

Historically, involuntary confinement to an asylum or similar institution was seen as necessary both for the person with mental illness and for society. This confinement was justified by the legal principle of *parens patriae* (n.d.) ("parent of the country") (https://legaldictionary.thefreedictionary.com/parens+patriae), which enables the state to act respectively as guardian of a presumably incompetent individual, and police power (https://www.law.cornell.edu/constitution-conan/amendment-14/section-1/property-and-police-power) (Cornell Law School, n.d.), which enables the state to protect society against a person assumed to be mentally ill and dangerous. Although confinement under these principles was meant to be protective, in practice persons could find themselves committed indefinitely and stripped of certain rights with minimal due process. For example, commitment might be initiated by a relative, approved by a court, and extended by a hospital superintendent, all without a patient's input. Certification of mental illness was considered equivalent to a determination of legal incompetence, so committed patients were often deprived of rights such as the ability to refuse treatment. Even after hospitalization, some patients were considered incompetent for tasks such as parenting. Voluntary hospitalization, which might have afforded insightful patients some control over treatment, was prohibited in many states (Testa & West, 2010).

Systemic abuse led to calls for states to reform their civil commitment laws. In 1952 the Draft Act Governing Hospitalization of the Mentally Ill was published as a recommended model for states to adopt when revising mental health regulations (Applebaum, 2000). This Act encouraged voluntary hospitalization for mental illness, with involuntary commitment occurring only in cases of dangerousness due to mental illness. Patients facing commitment gained some legal rights, such as the ability to request a court hearing with full representation. Committed patients also gained rights; they were no longer considered globally incompetent and instead secured privileges such as visitation and freedom from non-medical restraint. Many states adopted all or part of the Act, but despite the improvements, abuses such as indefinite commitment continued.

In the following decades, several factors changed the management of mental illness. In the 1950s, chlorpromazine was discovered to have efficacy in the treatment of psychosis, and long-term hospitalizations were no longer necessary or appropriate in many cases. In the 1960s, the civil rights movement focused attention on individualism and autonomy and the ability of people with a mental illness to have a voice in their treatment settings and choices. Society began to consider that it was not only possible but desirable for patients to receive treatment in the less restrictive setting of the community. In *Lake v. Cameron* (1966), the D.C. Court of Appeals ruled that mentally ill persons must be held in the least restrictive treatment setting, so a patient cannot be detained in a hospital if appropriate community treatment is available. In *O'Connor v. Donaldson* (1975), the Court concluded that the state cannot confine a person with mental illness if they are neither dangerous nor in need of treatment. Mere "custodial care" is not sufficient justification for involuntarily detainment in a psychiatric hospital. In *Addington v. Texas* (1979), the Court raised the minimum standard of proof for involuntary hospitalization from a preponderance of the evidence (more likely than not) to the more substantial clear and convincing standard (significantly more likely than not). In raising the level of proof, the Court recognized that taking away an individual's liberty is of such import that due process demands more protection to the individual from being wrongly detained. In *Vitek v. Jones* (1980), the Court further supported due process under the 14th Amendment by holding that a prisoner could not be transferred to a mental hospital without proper procedures, such as adequate notice and right to a hearing with legal representation.

These US Supreme Court decisions established minimum constitutional standards for involuntary commitment. Although state statutes differ and in some cases are more protective of individual rights than federal guidelines, core criteria are dangerousness to self or others, or having a grave disability that makes one unable to care for oneself (Stone, 2016). Evidence of dangerousness must be established in a formal commitment hearing, but prior to this, physicians in most states may initiate a temporary emergency hold for purposes of assessment and observation (Hedman et al., 2016). In most jurisdictions, this hold is 3 business days which, in some cases, is sufficient time for assessment, stabilization, and discharge, all prior to a court-ordered commitment (Morris, 2020). In other cases, the emergency hold leads to a longer involuntary commitment. A physician's ability to independently initiate an emergency hold is therefore both a powerful tool and a source of liability, especially if the standard of care is not followed.

Types of Allegations Regarding Unnecessary Confinement

Physicians who do not obtain or document sufficient evidence of need for an involuntary hold can face allegations of malpractice or even false imprisonment (confining a person without consent, which may not be covered under standard malpractice insurance policies) (Thomas & Moore, 2013). Since the risk of not detaining a mentally ill and dangerous person is likely higher than the risk of holding a mentally person who turns out not to be dangerous, physicians often err on the side of caution and detain (Marett & Mossman, 2017). An involuntary hold, however, is not without potential negative consequences. Patients and society perceive involuntary psychiatric hospitalization as stigmatizing, coercive, and even akin to torture (Steinert, 2017). Patients experiencing self-stigma related to their detention may have a lower quality of life after hospitalization due to persistent feelings of shame and lowered self-esteem (Rusch et al., 2013). Physicians must therefore be careful to ensure that a decision to involuntarily detain someone is based on a solid foundation of data that includes the patient interview, record review, and collateral information. Although information may be limited in crisis situations, a prudent physician must make every effort to include these components in both decision-making and documentation.

Since the core criterion for involuntary commitment is dangerousness to self or others due to mental illness, all decision-making must include these determinations. Moreover it is the criterion required by the vast majority of states (Hedman et al., 2016). A physician filing paperwork for a temporary emergency hold should present evidence required by the state in which they practice and should do so in "good faith," with honest intent and conduct. Extending an emergency hold into an involuntary commitment, which could last weeks or months, requires a higher level of substantiation. The most important piece of data in this case is a personal examination of the patient. In the vast majority of states, patients have the right to see a healthcare professional for an involuntary commitment assessment (Hedman et al., 2016), and failure to provide such an assessment can be considered gross negligence in some jurisdictions (*Lanier v. Sallas*, 1986). Failure to conduct a personal assessment could also constitute a deficiency of federal (e.g., Centers for Medicare and Medicaid Services), hospital, and practice guidelines.

Another serious omission is confining a patient for inappropriate reasons or in an inappropriate setting – for example, committing a medically delirious patient to a psychiatric unit. Although a patient with delirium or substance intoxication could be dangerous, if the hold is not based on dangerousness due to mental illness, and/or the detainment is not in an appropriate setting, the hold may be invalid and even considered false imprisonment (Heldt et al., 2018). The purpose of psychiatric hospitalization is to provide assessment and treatment of a mental illness. If dangerousness is due to a medical cause, a hold on a psychiatric unit could delay appropriate medical care. Moreover, involuntary psychiatric commitment via a probate court impacts the patient's rights (e.g., the ability in the future to legally possess firearms) and reduces quality of life (Rusch et al., 2013). In sum, involuntary psychiatric holds should not be used for convenience or for conditions which will not benefit from assessment and treatment on a psychiatric unit.

Due diligence for pursuing an involuntary hold includes collecting relevant available collateral information. In the case of an acutely ill or uncooperative patient, third-party information can be critical. It cannot, however, form the sole basis for commitment. First, relying on the account of others potentially violates the ethical principle of respect for patient autonomy; patients have the right to make decisions about their own care (Entwistle et al., 2010). Second, family members and others providing information may knowingly provide false or misleading accounts (Witkin, 2019). The prudent physician will use collateral information as an adjunct to the clinical interview and other data.

Most states provide some immunity from malpractice and other claims in emergency situations so long as the physician initiating an involuntary hold acted in "good faith" (Marett & Mossman, 2017). Alternately, a provider who willfully or knowingly initiates an involuntary hold without reasonable cause may be held criminally liable. Physicians should remain mindful that commitment forms are often legally binding documents developed from state and federal requirements (Reeves et al., 1998) and as such should be completed thoroughly, honestly, and appropriately. Finally, even seemingly minor errors in paperwork, such as not dating or signing a form, can invalidate an involuntary hold and expose a physician to a malpractice case.

Reducing Risk

There are several steps physicians can take to reduce liability for claims of malpractice or false imprisonment. Before initiating an emergency hold, physicians should confirm and document that a patient is mentally ill and dangerous due to mental illness. It is also helpful (and in some states required) to assess and document the anticipated benefit of psychiatric hospitalization and that there is no less restrictive means of treatment. When extending a hold into a commitment, assessment requires a personal clinical interview, as well as a reasonable effort to make the evaluation as comprehensive as possible through collateral information.

Next, physicians should be aware of and understand the specific requirements for emergency holds and involuntary civil commitment in the state in which they practice. As mentioned above, in some jurisdictions, the simple failure of a physician to date a form renders the application invalid (Reeves et al., 1998). It is always the responsibility of the practitioner to be aware of relevant laws and requirements.

Documentation of all components of decision-making is essential. A prudent psychiatrist should be careful to note details of a personal interview with the patient. The note should include evidence of the presence of mental illness and further evidence that the patient poses a danger to self or others due to that mental illness. Co-occurring conditions such as substance intoxication should be included, but the primary reason for patient dangerousness must be mental illness. Finally, the physician should document that inpatient hospitalization is likely to be beneficial and is the least restrictive treatment setting.

All legal forms or affidavits should be completed carefully and fully, including physician printed name, signature, and date. A legible name and signature certifies that the physician performed a personal examination, and the date helps establish timing for the emergency or temporary hold.

In many cases, physicians are reluctant to communicate their decision to initiate an involuntary hold to the patient or family, fearing a negative reaction. Although each situation must be approached individually, honest and transparent communication can help educate the patient and the family and allay fears. Staff ultimately caring for the patient during the hold will also be appreciative of efforts to not make them responsible for delivering the news, and this continuity of care can help preserve a therapeutic alliance.

In sum, confinement in psychiatry is often required when a patient is dangerous due to mental illness. Ensuring that the confinement occurs under the right circumstances, and with the right documentation, can confirm its necessity and help avoid malpractice claims.

Key Points

- The establishment of a patient-physician relationship confers legal and ethical duties.
- Termination of a treatment relationship requires reasonable notice, treatment recommendations and referrals, and follow-up notice.
- Patients should be provided coverage during the termination period.
- A termination letter or follow-up notice should provide the termination date, coverage, and referral agencies.
- It may be helpful to consult with attorneys to understand specific guidelines regarding termination.
- Termination is not appropriate when patients are acutely ill and no appropriate, alternative timely care can be established.
- An involuntary hold removes a person's liberty and potentially creates stress and stigma.
- Initiating an involuntary hold therefore requires careful assessment, including an in-person interview and review of collateral information. It also requires knowledge of local state/regional requirements, including paperwork.
- The purpose of an involuntary hold is to treat mental illness in order to reduce dangerousness. Involuntary holds are not appropriate for non-psychiatric conditions.
- As always, decision-making should be carefully documented and communicated.

References

Addington v. Texas, 441 U.S. 418 (1979).

American Psychiatric Association. (2014). *APA quick practice guide: Ending the physician/patient relationship*. https://www.psychiatry.org/File%20Library/Psychiatrists/Practice/Practice-Management/Practice-Management-Guides/GeneralIssues-terminating-patient-relationships.pdf. Accessed June 6, 2021.

Applebaum, P. (2000). The draft act governing hospitalization of the mentally ill: Its genesis and its legacy. *Psychiatric Services, 2*(51), 190–194.

Bush, S. (2010). Formation of the physician-patient relationship: The Oregon Court of Appeals clarifies, but questions remain. *Physician Organizations, 13*(2), 11–13.

Cornell Law School. (n.d.). *Property and police power*. Retrieved from https://www.law.cornell.edu/constitution-conan/amendment-14/section-1

Entwistle, V. A., Carter, S. M., & McCaffery, K. (2010). Supporting patient autonomy: The importance of clinician-patient relationships. *Journal of General Internal Medicine, 25*(7), 741–745. https://doi.org/10.1007/s11606-010-1292-2

Hedman, L., Petrila, J., Fisher, W. H., Swanson, J. W., Dingman, D. A., & Burris, S. (2016). State laws on emergency holds for mental health stabilization. *Psychiatric Services, 67*(5), 529–535.

Heldt, J. P., Zito, M. F., Seroussi, A., Wilson, S. P., Schneider, P. L., Strouse, T. B., & Cheung, E. H. (2018). A medical incapacity hold policy reduces inappropriate use of involuntary psychiatric holds while protecting patients from harm. *Psychosomatics, 60*(1), 37–46.

Jung, S., & McDowell, R. H. (2020). Abandonment. In *StatPearls [Internet]*. StatPearls Publishing. Available from: https://www.ncbi.nlm.nih.gov/books/NBK563285/

Lake v. Cameron, 364 F.2d 657 (D.C. Cir. 1966).

Lanier v. Sallas, 777 F.2d 321 (5th Cir. 1986).

Lippman, H., & Davenport, J. (2011). Patient dismissal: The right way to do it. *The Journal of Family Practice, 60*(3), 135–140.

Marett, C., & Mossman, D. (2017). What is your liability for involuntary commitment based on faulty information? *Current Psychiatry, 16*(30), 21–33.

MedLaw. (2020). Dr. MedLaw Q&A: Patient abandonment. *Physicians Weekly*. Retrieved from https://www.physiciansweekly.com/dr-medlaw-qa-patient-abandonment-3/. Accessed June 6, 2021.

Morris, N. (2020). Reasonable or random: 72-hour limits to psychiatric holds. *Psychiatric Services in Advance, 72*(2), 210–212. https://doi.org/10.1176/appi.ps.202000284

Mossman, D., Ferrell, H., & Gilday, E. (2010). "Firing" a patient: May a psychiatrist unilaterally terminate care? *Current Psychiatry, 9*(12), 18–29.

O'Connor v. Donaldson, 422 U.S. 563 (1975).

Parens patriae. (n.d.). https://legaldictionary.thefreedictionary.com/parens+patriae. Accessed June 6, 2021.

Professional Risk Management Service. (n.d.). *Abandoenment? But there was no treatment relationship! PRMS*. Retrieved from https://www.prms.com/services/risk-management/abandonment. Accessed June 6, 2021.

Psychiatry (Edgemont). (2010). Terminating the treatment relationship. *Psychiatry (Edgemont), 7*(1), 40–42.

Reeves, R. R., Pinkofsky, H. B., & Stevens, L. (1998). Medicolegal errors in the ED related to the involuntary confinement of psychiatric patients. *American Journal of Emergency Medicine, 16*(7), 631–633.

Rusch, N., Muller, M., Lay, B., Corrigan, P. W., Zahn, R., Schonenberger, T., … Rossler, W. (2013). Emotional reactions to involuntary psychiatric hospitalization and stigma-related stress among people with mental illness. *European Archives of Psychiatry and Clinical Neuroscience, 264*, 35–43.

Steinert, T. (2017). Ethics of coercive treatment and misuse of psychiatry. *Psychiatric Services, 68*(3), 291–294.

Stone, D. (2016). There are cracks in the civil commitment process: A practitioner's recommendations to patch the system. *Fordham Urban Law Journal, 43*, 790. Retrieved from http://scholarworks.law.ubalt.edu/all_fac/1063

Testa, M., & West, S. (2010). Civil commitment in the United States. *Psychiatry (Edgemont), 7*(10), 30–40.

Thomas, J., & Moore, G. (2013). Medical-legal issues in the agitated patient: Cases and caveats. *The Western Journal of Emergency Medicine, 14*(5), 559–565. https://doi.org/10.5811/westjem.2013.4.16132

Van Susteren, L. (2001). Psychiatric abandonment: Pitfalls and prevention. *Psychiatric Times, 18*(8), https://www.psychiatrictimes.com/view/psychiatric-abandonment-pitfalls-and-prevention

Vitek v. Jones, 445 U.S. 480 (1980).

Williamson v. Liptzin appeal, 539 S.E.(2d) 313 (1998).

Willis, D., & Zerr, A. (2005). Terminating a patient: Is it time to part ways? *Family Practice Management, 12*(8), 34–38.

Witkin, M. (2019). The effect of collateral information on involuntary psychiatric commitment. *Current Psychiatry, 18*(2), e1–e2.

18 Negligent Psychotherapy

Karen B. Rosenbaum and Trent C. Holmberg

Joe Nocera, an investigative journalist for the New York Times, had a home in the Hamptons in a neighborhood called the Bayside, a beach town escape from New York City. When he first moved there in the early 2000s, he believed his neighbor to be a New York University affiliated psychiatrist to the stars, Dr. Isaac "Ike" Herschkopf. In the podcast, *The Shrink Next Door (TSND)*, Mr. Nocera details how he was invited to a party at what he thought was the doctor's home by a person dressed as a maintenance man. Inside the lavishly decorated property next door, which included a koi pond, pool, and miniature golf course, he saw pictures of the doctor posed with numerous famous people. A few days later the same "employee" dressed as a maintenance man invited Mr. Nocera and his wife to the home for dinner after which Dr. Herschkopf asked for a picture of the New York Times journalist, presumably for his wall of fame.

After this dinner the Noceras kept their distance but 2 years later learned from a neighbor that the "maintenance man" was Marty Markowitz, a patient of Dr. Herschkopf since 1981 and the actual owner of the lavish home next door. In the podcast, Mr. Nocera, through interviews of Marty Markowitz, family members, neighbors, and other patients, illustrates the ways in which Dr. Herschkopf allegedly took over every aspect of the life of Mr. Markowitz, including his family and friends, home, and business and financial affairs.

Through this story (which is now a 2021 television series on Apple TV starring Will Ferrell as Marty and Paul Rudd as Dr. Herschkopf), *TSND* illustrates the ways in which a therapist could potentially exploit a patient, specifically by abusing the transference relationship with a patient and exerting undue influence, crossing boundaries, giving ineffective and/or harmful treatment, and violating patient confidentiality. To illustrate these and other concepts pertaining to negligent psychotherapy, *TSND* narrative will be used throughout this chapter.

In 2019, Joe Nocera wrote that "The New York Department of Health lays out details of alleged misconduct from two of Isaac Herschkopf's former patients ahead of a September hearing." A notice of hearing document (2019) included allegations that Dr. Herschkopf became part owner of his patient's Swiss bank account and inhabited his patient's Southampton's home rent free. It also included that he made his patient perform "hundreds of hours of secretarial services." The notice also indicated that Dr. Herschkopf inappropriately touched another patient. The Department of Health ultimately revoked Dr. Herschkopf's medical license.

A majority of the allegations regarding psychotherapy can be divided into two major categories: errors of omission and errors of commission. Most actions against psychotherapists are brought as civil suits based on tort law (Hampton, 1984; Conte & Karasu, 1990). For malpractice in psychotherapy to be established, the patient/plaintiff must show there was a legal duty in the psychotherapist-patient relationship, that the psychotherapist breached this duty either due to an action (commission) or a failure to act (omission), that the patient suffered injury (emotional or otherwise) due to this breach of duty, and that the breach of duty directly and proximately caused the injury (see Chap. 1). Establishing malpractice in psychotherapy most often requires that an expert review the records and provide testimony at deposition or trial (see Chap. 9).

Violation of either ethical codes (a standard of conduct governing professionals) or laws (a body of rules governing a community) can also open a psychotherapist up to possible sanctions either by licensing boards (see Chap. 33), or through a civil suit, or both. For psychiatrists who are members of the American Psychiatric Association (APA), ethical guidelines provided by the APA will be summarized in this chapter.

K. B. Rosenbaum (✉)
Forensic Psychiatry Department, New York University Langone Medical Center, New York, NY, USA

T. C. Holmberg
Department of Psychiatry, University of Utah School of Medicine, Salt Lake City, UT, USA

P. Ash et al. (eds.), *Malpractice and Liability in Psychiatry*, https://doi.org/10.1007/978-3-030-91975-7_18

Types of Allegations

Ineffective Treatment

Ineffective treatment can be explained as an error of omission. In the landmark case, *Osheroff v. Chestnut Lodge* (1984), Dr. Rafael Osheroff, a depressed physician-patient, voluntarily admitted himself to Chestnut Lodge, a private psychiatric facility, and was treated for narcissistic personality disorder with long-term psychotherapy for 7 months, without being given the option to add antidepressant medication into his treatment plan, despite his requests for medication. His condition at Chestnut Lodge deteriorated. He was eventually transferred to another facility where he was treated with pharmacotherapy. His depression relented, and he was discharged within several weeks. He brought suit in 1982 against Chestnut Lodge. The court of appeals in the Maryland decision agreed with Dr. Osheroff's claim that accused Chestnut Lodge psychiatrists of "negligently failing to diagnose Osheroff's true condition, negligently treating him, and of providing inappropriate treatment for the illness he suffered." This case has been extensively written about as an example of negligent psychotherapy.

Before this case, there was a "respectable minority" doctrine, meaning if a respectable minority of clinicians agree with the treatment rendered, this could buffer against a malpractice claim. Klerman (1990) effectively argued that this doctrine "no longer holds if there is a body of evidence supporting the efficacy of a particular treatment and if there is agreement within the profession that this is the proper treatment of a given condition." In addition, the "respectable minority" has the obligation to explain all of the alternative treatments to the patient. Therefore, *Osheroff v. Chestnut Lodge* is also a case about informed consent.

Packman et al. (1994) commented that clinicians are at high risk for malpractice when they rely solely on psychotherapeutic approaches for all patients and when they do not refer patients appropriately for medication management if they are not able to administer medications or do not feel comfortable with the biological model.

Informed Consent and Medication Management (See Also Chap. 16)

Psychiatrists and any provider who prescribes psychotropic medications can be held liable for negligent prescribing. These errors are often errors of omission. Medication management is discussed in Chap. 16 and will not be covered in detail here. In regard to informed consent before initiating a course of psychotherapy, a patient has a right to know the nature and extent of his/her psychiatric issues, the risks and benefits of the proposed psychotherapeutic intervention, and what alternative courses of treatment there are, including no treatment.

Harmful Treatment, Adverse Reactions, and Negligent Diagnosis

The APA's *The Principles of Medical Ethics with Annotations Especially Applicable to Psychiatry* (2013) are more encompassing than the case law on malpractice in psychotherapy. If a psychiatrist/therapist follows all of the APA ethical guidelines, they will greatly reduce the risk of being involved in a malpractice suit. Some of these principles are especially relevant for the psychiatrist or other mental health provider practicing psychotherapy. The main points of these principles are the following:

- **Section 1.1**: "A psychiatrist shall not gratify his or her own needs by exploiting the patient" and "should be ever vigilant about the impact that his or her conduct has upon the doctor-patient relationship and thus upon the well-being of the patient."
- **Section 2.1**: "Sexual activity with a current or former patient is unethical."
- **Section 2.2**: The psychiatrist should guard against unduly influencing the patient by not using "the unique position of power afforded him/her by the psychotherapeutic situation to influence the patient in any way not directly relevant to treatment goals."
- **Section 4.1**: "Confidentiality is essential to psychiatric treatment." Exceptions are outlined in this section.
- **Section 8.2**: "When the psychiatrist's outside relationships conflict with the clinical needs of the patient, the psychiatrist must always consider the impact of such relationships and strive to resolve conflicts in a manner that the psychiatrist believes is likely beneficial to the patient."

In *TSND*, Dr. Herschkopf's patients gave examples of the therapist allegedly exerting undue influence over them, receiving expensive gifts, violating boundaries, and other clear ethical violations and violations of the physician maxim, "First Do No Harm."

Linden (2012) explained the difficulty in recognizing side effects (SEs) in psychotherapy. SEs of psychotherapy, unlike SEs of medications, can arise from a therapist's actions. Therefore, SEs in psychotherapy can develop into a potential legal issue as well as a clinical problem. Due to the lack of standardization of psychotherapeutic practice, it can be difficult to assess whether SEs were a result of a mistake by the clinician. Linden further characterized SEs as "unwanted events," defined as "events that occur parallel or in wake of the treatment" (Linden, 2012, p. 287). Linden suggests that unwanted events should be regularly discussed in supervision and training so that practitioners are aware of possible adverse events from psychotherapy.

An example of potentially harmful treatment is "reparative" or "conversion" therapy. The APA decided to declassify homosexuality as a mental disorder in 1973 (Drescher, 2015). Nevertheless, therapy aimed at eliminating or suppressing homosexuality continued as the practice was steadfastly supported by various political and religious organizations (Schroeder & Shidlo, 2001). In response, between 1998 and 2007, all of the major mental health professional organizations released statements opposing conversion therapy. By 2019, laws banning conversion therapy (mostly for minors) had been enacted in 18 states, the District of Columbia, and a number of localities (Mallory et al., 2019). These laws have been challenged from a constitutional (1st Amendment) standpoint, successfully at the Court of Appeals level in one recent case (*Otto v. City of Boca Raton*, 2020).

The first successful lawsuit regarding conversion therapy occurred in New Jersey in 2015 (*Ferguson* et al. *v. JONAH* et al. 2015). In the case, the jury unanimously determined that conversion therapy constituted consumer fraud, the fraud being the selling of services which the defendants claimed could change a person's sexual orientation from gay to straight. Subsequent similar lawsuits have established the proposition that therapists practicing conversion therapy are placing themselves in a position of liability.

An extreme example of an unwanted event caused by an incorrect treatment is the 1935 failure of his psychoanalyst to refer the celebrated composer George Gershwin to a neurologist in the face of obvious neurological symptoms which led to his death from a brain tumor in 1937 at just 38 years of age (Leffert, 2011). The failure to recognize his neurological symptoms (such as severe headaches, memory lapses, and olfactory hallucinations) as being neurological led to a negligent diagnosis and a failure on the part of his analyst to refer Mr. Gershwin in a timely manner, which could have possibly saved or at least prolonged his life.

Impaired Therapist (Psychiatric Illness, Physical Illness, and Substance Abuse – See Also Chap. 36)

The impaired therapist is susceptible to making both errors of commission and errors of omission. Quadrio (1992) in a review of "the problem of impaired therapists" explained that there are stressors on the practitioner at three levels: "A. Systemic/Structural; B. Systemic/Attitudinal; C. Individual/Intrapsychic." At the Systemic/Structural level, there are increasing regulations and decreasing autonomy, increasing financial costs, geographic mobility, increased competition from non-medical therapists, and a density of practitioners in urban areas. She describes Systemic/Attitudinal factors as including the culture in medicine of workaholism and competitive drive. Family support systems are often not prioritized. Due to gender inequality in medicine, women may settle for a lesser career track than their male counterparts. In terms of Individual or Intrapsychic factors, there is a self-selection and personality traits among doctors including a "difficulty with and tending to deny dependency needs." This may lead to self-medicating fatigue with drugs or alcohol. "Rigid ideologies" may also be a characteristic of some medical professionals.

The concept of burnout among physicians as well as other clinicians has been discussed more recently and can contribute to impaired judgment of the therapist/practitioner. Shanafelt (2009) prescribed finding enhanced meaning in work as a prescription for burnout syndrome, characterized in part by losing meaning and enthusiasm for patient care in the case of the psychotherapist. It is very important for the clinician to practice self-care to prevent the consequences of burnout.

Suicide (See Also Chap. 12)

Suicide (including suicide attempts) is one of the most common primary allegations in claims, lawsuits, and complaints made against psychiatrists. Claims in this area generally are errors of omission. Therapists who do not perform a suicide risk assessment, do not document the suicide risk assessment, or do not take appropriate action based on the patient's suicide risk open themselves up for liability.

When providing psychotherapy, it is advisable that the therapist perform and document a suicide risk assessment, identify and evaluate suicide risk factors, and weigh those against protective factors. In patient deaths from suicide, highly defensible cases where the psychiatrist or therapist delivered seemingly flawless treatment have been lost because of poor documentation.

In addition to performing (and updating) a suicide risk assessment, therapists would do well to develop and implement a reasonable treatment plan informed by the therapist's conclusion regarding the risk stratification of the patient. The treatment plan needs to be comprehensive, match the suicide risk, and be implemented appropriately. Therapists should also communicate with other providers involved in the patient's care and communicate with family or significant others when appropriate. They also need to provide adequate follow-up care after hospitalization.

Therapists should never alter a treatment record or add self-serving late entries after an adverse event, such as suicide (see Chap. 5). Finally, therapists should make efforts to keep abreast of new developments in the area of suicide risk assessment.

Failure to Document Appropriately

Failure to document treatment interactions can be seen as an error of omission. There is a long history of poor record keeping or failure to keep records contributing to successful malpractice cases. For example, Pope et al. (1978) explained that the failure to document and/or inadequate records can be used to demonstrate a lack of care on the part of the therapist and therefore liability. In the case of *Whitree v. State* (1968), a man was held in a state hospital for 12 years with virtually no written record of his care. Regarding suicide, Simon and Shuman (2009) explain that documentation of a risk assessment that is substandard can be worse than no documentation at all. It is important to document decision-making processes and document the "why," not just the "what." Failure to document care was also one of the allegations against "Ike" in *TSND.*

Patient Abandonment (See Also Chap. 17)

Patient abandonment could be seen as both an error of omission and an error of commission. Abandonment involves a failure to appropriately end a therapist-patient relationship. When a psychotherapist wishes to end the treatment relationship, adequate notice must be given to the patient. Pope et al. (1978) view "adequate notice" as a statement that gives the reason for termination, recommendations for follow-up care, and (when needed) appropriate aid in securing the new treatment.

The landmark case *Mazza v. Medical Mut. Ins. Co. of North Carolina* (1984) involved both errors of commission and omission. The plaintiff filed a civil action against his psychiatrist, alleging that his psychiatrist caused him injury and damage by engaging in sexual intercourse with the plaintiff's estranged wife and by abandoning the patient without reasonable notice. He was awarded compensatory and punitive damages. The Supreme Court of North Carolina reviewed the decision and affirmed the trial court's decision holding that it did not matter whether or not the defendant "intentionally" inflicted the negligence.

Performing Therapy Without Credentials or with False Credentials

Performing therapy without proper credentials, or misrepresentation of one's credentials, is not new. George Gershwin's psychoanalyst Gregory Zilboorg, a "fashionable analyst to see in New York" (Leffert, 2011), claimed to have credentials and degrees that he did not actually obtain. During the investigation into Zilboorg after Gershwin's untimely death, it became clear that Dr. Zilboorg did not receive a medical degree from the Psycho-Neurological Institute in St. Petersburg as he had claimed, because that institute did not have "degree-granting authority." In addition, he opened a private practice in psychoanalysis after receiving a medical degree from Columbia College of Physicians and Surgeons but with no internship or residency in psychiatry. He represented that he was in psychoanalytic training at the Berlin Psychoanalytic Institute for 2 years, but the program took at least 3 or 4 years to complete. In addition, although he was in private practice for about 20 years, there is no record of him ever holding a New York State medical license.

More recent examples of this phenomenon occur among some celebrity doctors. The Dr. Laura radio show (NNDB, 2019) was at its peak popularity in the 1990s and is still on the air. "Dr. Laura" speaks on "human interpersonal relations" and sometimes refers to herself as a "shrink." However, her PhD is in physiology, not psychology. She was granted a California Marriage, Family, and Child Therapist license in 1980. On her show, she often uses her Doctor platform to denounce sex outside of marriage, working mothers, abortion, premarital sex, and homosexuality and to emphasize the family unit. The television personality, Dr. Phil, has also come under scrutiny for misrepresenting his credentials (Belluz, 2016).

According to Van Tol (1990), it was estimated that at the time of the publication there were between 150 and 500 diploma mills in the United States, each of which may have granted up to 3000 illegitimate degrees. The most common diploma mills were in the fields of business, counseling and therapy, medicine and health, nutrition, education, and religion. "The demand for brokered credentials [paying for a degree] is heaviest in medicine and other health care fields" (Van Tol, 1990).

Confidentiality (See Also Chap. 15)

Between 2010 and 2019, confidentiality breaches accounted for 5% of lawsuits against psychiatrists covered by one major liability carrier (Professional Risk Management Services, 2020). In *TSND*, Marty Markowitz discussed a variety of confidentiality violations on Dr. Herschkopf's part. Marty stated that Dr. Herschkopf spoke to patients of his about other patients. He invited patients to the pool parties he threw at Marty's vacation home in the Hamptons. On one occasion, Marty recounted that Dr. Herschkopf had a celebrity patient send a fax intended for Dr. Herschkopf's eyes only to Marty's fax machine. Excerpts from unpublished novels Dr. Herschkopf had written allegedly incorporated some painful real-life events of one of his patients into one of his stories.

Duty to Warn/Protect (See Also Chap. 13)

Failure to warn or protect third parties from potential violence is an error of omission. Case law has established this duty in a majority of jurisdictions, dating back to the *Tarasoff* case in the 1970s. Generally speaking, a therapist will have discharged the duty to protect if the therapist hospitalizes the potentially dangerous patient and/or apprises a law enforcement agency of the threat and/or warns the intended victim. Since 1976, states have taken various approaches to the duty to protect, with some expanding the duty to protect (e.g., Washington State in *Volk v. DeMeerleer* [2016]) and others limiting the situations in which the therapist is required to warn or protect others (Soulier et al., 2010).

Finally, in every state, if a therapist has reason to believe that a patient is abusing a child, an elder, or another vulnerable person, a duty to report the abuse rests with the therapist. Failure to discharge this duty appropriately will place the therapist in a position of liability. This is an error of omission.

"Recovered" Memory Cases

Recovered memory cases (allegations of a therapist implanting false memories in a patient) are errors of commission. They fall under two categories previously discussed – harmful treatment and third-party liability. The most well-known case is *Ramona v. Ramona* (1994). In 1989, Holly Ramona, then in her late teens, sought treatment for bulimia and depression from a certified marriage and family therapist. The therapist allegedly suggested to Holly that her bulimia must have been caused by sexual abuse. Within several months of starting therapy, Holly came to believe that she had recovered repressed memories that her father, Gary Ramona, a Napa Valley wine company executive, had repeatedly raped her while she was a child over a period of 11 years. In 1990, Holly was hospitalized on a psychiatric unit. While there, a sodium amytal interview was performed under the supervision of a psychiatrist, ostensibly to clarify the accuracy of her recollections. Allegedly, the treatment team represented to Holly that the sodium amytal interview had confirmed her recovered memory of the repeated sexual abuse (Appelbaum & Zoltek-Jick, 1996). Holly confronted her father with the allegation in a hospital-coordinated family meeting. He denied the allegation. Mr. Ramona eventually lost his job and his wife filed for divorce. Additionally, Holly brought a civil suit against him for damages. A year later, Mr. Ramona sued the therapist, the psychiatrist, and the psychiatric hospital for negligent and intentional infliction of emotional distress (Appelbaum & Zoltek-Jick, 1996).

Mr. Ramona eventually won a jury verdict against all three defendants. Expert testimony supported Mr. Ramona's contention that the hospital, the psychiatrist, and the therapist were negligent. Without precedent, the jury reached a special verdict, based on their finding that each of the defendants had played a role in facilitating Holly's confrontation of her father, and therefore Mr. Ramona was a "direct victim" of their negligence. The "Direct Victim Test," termed by this case, proposes that when a therapist's behavior moves outside of the therapist-patient dyad and directly involves a non-patient, the therapist thereby assumes a duty to that person as well (Appelbaum & Zoltek-Jick, 1996). Mr. Ramona commented, "Holly's supposed memories are the result of defendants' drugs and quackery, not anything I did" (La Ganga, 1994).

This decision created a stir among the legal and mental health community as it seemed to represent an almost unprecedented expansion of the liability associated with practicing psychotherapy. Although it did not result in the flood of lawsuits that many predicted, it did establish a new area of liability for psychotherapists.

Sexual Misconduct and Sexual Boundary Violations (See Also Chap. 14)

Sexual misconduct claims typically involve errors of commission. In the landmark case *Roy v. Hartogs* (1976), a patient, Julie Roy, brought an action for damages against her psychiatrist. (This case is covered in more detail in Chap. 14.) Dr. Hartogs' malpractice insurance company refused to pay the $25,000 judgment in punitive damages that was levied against him for sexual activity that occurred in lieu of psychotherapy. He later unsuccessfully sued the company in an effort to get them to pay the judgment. Because insurers often consider sexual activity between therapist and patient to be intentional exploitation rather than mismanagement of therapy dynamics, they often set up policy language noting that any harm arising from sexual misconduct will not be covered. Their policy is that sexual activity with a patient does not constitute "professional services" (no matter how skillfully it is performed) so the clinician should be personally liable for this behavior. In order to exclude coverage for a claim or lawsuit, the insurer must advise the insured of the exclusion from coverage, usually by a "Reservation of Rights" letter. Alternatively, coverage for sexual misconduct is capped as a policy sub-limit for a mixed maximum amount such as $25,000.

Non-sexual Boundary Violations (See Also Chap. 14)

In *TSND*, Marty Markowitz describes a large number of non-sexual boundary crossings and violations in describing his decades-long therapy relationship with Dr. Herschkopf. Marty details how Dr. Herschkopf convinced Marty to let Dr. Herschkopf use Marty's home to throw lavish parties during which Dr. Herschkopf would present himself as the owner of the house. According to Marty, Dr. Herschkopf and his family stayed in the home. Dr. Herschkopf and his wife stayed in the master bedroom while Marty was relegated to a guest bedroom. Under a pseudonym, Dr. Herschkopf became intimately involved in managing and overseeing Marty's family business. Dr. Herschkopf convinced Marty to form a non-profit charitable foundation and to name Dr. Herschkopf (along with Marty and Dr. Herschkopf's wife) as the foundation's officers. In that role, Dr. Herschkopf had full control over where to direct the funds. Eventually, Marty was convinced to change his will to make the foundation the sole beneficiary. Dr. Herschkopf also used Marty to type Dr. Herschkopf's letters (including those involving patient care) and to transcribe Dr. Herschkopf's novels. Allegedly, Marty's time used to complete his doctor's administrative work was billed to Marty as therapy time.

Marty added that Dr. Herschkopf influenced Marty and other patients to write Dr. Herschkopf and/or his family members into their wills after isolating them from their families (see above). One patient, who had an estate valued at tens of millions of dollars, allegedly made Dr. Herschkopf's children the sole beneficiary in her will, making the will changes while she was in treatment with Dr. Herschkopf. Dr. Herschkopf also allegedly accepted expensive gifts from patients, including a $10,000 watch from one of them and expensive meals from others at restaurants where time spent dining was also charged as therapy session fees.

While boundary violations are not a frequent cause of action against psychiatrists, when non-psychiatrist therapists are sued (which itself is a rare event), boundary violations of some kind are the most frequent concern, surpassing child custody disputes, breaches of confidentiality, and suicide/suicide attempt in terms of frequency (Novotney 2016).

Strategies to Reduce Risk

- Psychiatrists should always document psychotherapy sessions.
- In difficult cases, therapists should obtain adequate supervision when necessary.
- It is important for clinicians to understand local Tarasoff/duty to third-party laws.
- Psychiatrists should abide by boundaries – a patient is always a patient.
- Psychiatry residency training programs should instruct trainees on potential areas of liability in psychotherapy.
- Abiding by ethical guidelines instituted by organizations that the therapist belongs to, such as the American Psychiatric Association, may help to prevent liability.

What Not to Do

In addition to not exploiting patients, other advice for things not to do include not allowing the discharge decision to be driven by insurance coverage determinations; never altering a treatment record after an adverse event; not entering into a dual role or multiple relationship with a patient if it can be avoided; not self-disclosing excessively; not using psychotherapeutic techniques that are experimental or unproven; and not using psychotherapeutic techniques without proper training. Where possible, do not have out of "office" (whether a physical or virtual office) contact with patients. The Office of Professional Medical Conduct, New York Department of Health determined that Dr. Herschkopf was guilty by a preponderance of evidence of seventeen charges pertaining to three patients. The charges included Negligence, Gross Negligence, Incompetence, Gross Incompetence, Exercising Undue Influence, Intent to Deceive, Moral Unfitness (which included exploiting the therapist-patient relationship for secondary gain), and failure to "maintain a record that accurately reflects the evaluation and treatment." The findings included that Dr. Herschkopf "showed little insight or remorse" throughout the proceedings and denied all of the charges. The penalty was the revocation of his license to practice medicine. (Determination and Order in the Matter of Isaac Steven Hercshkopf, 2021).

Key Points

- Psychotherapists should always document sessions, perform an adequate examination, and make an adequate diagnosis.
- Psychotherapists should develop and implement a reasonable treatment plan.
- Suicide risk should be reassessed on an ongoing basis, especially when changing level of care.
- Consultants and/or peer supervision should be used when needed, including case conferences if available.
- A patients' privacy should be protected.
- Psychiatrists should set and respect boundaries; sexual contact with a current or former patient is considered unethical and may be illegal

- Psychiatrists should obtain informed consent from patients before beginning treatment and continue to practice obtaining informed consent throughout the treatment. It is an ongoing dialogue, not a one-time event. This includes informing the patient of alternative treatments.

References

American Psychiatric Association. (2013). *The principles of medical ethics with annotations especially applicable to psychiatry 2013 edition*. APA.

Appelbaum, P. S., & Zoltek-Jick, R. (1996). Psychotherapists' duties to third parties: *Ramona* and beyond. *American Journal of Psychiatry, 153*(4), 457–465. https://doi.org/10.1176/ajp.153.4.457

Belluz, J. (2016). Dr. Phil is not a medical doctor. But he is now a paid spokesperson for a diabetes drug. *Vox*. Available at: https://www.vox.com/2016/2/26/11119788/dr-phil-diabetes. Accessed 3 Sept 2020.

Conte, H. R., & Karaku, T. B. (1990). Malpractice in psychotherapy: An overview. *American Journal of Psychotherapy, XLIV*(1), 232–246.

Drescher, J. (2015). Out of DSM: Depathologizing homosexuality. *Behavioral Sciences, 5*(4), 565–575. https://doi.org/10.3390/bs5040565

Ferguson et al. v. JONAH et al., No. L-5473-12, N.J. Super. Ct. Law Div. (2015).

Hampton, L. P. (1984). Malpractice in psychotherapy: Is there a relevant standard of care? *Case Western Reserve Law Review, 35*(252), 251–281.

Klerman, G. L. (1990). The psychiatric patient's right to effective treatment: Implications of Osheroff v. Chestnut Lodge. *American Journal of Psychiatry, 147*(4), 409–418.

La Ganga, M. L. (1994). Father Wins Suit in 'False Memory' Case. *The Los Angeles Times*.

Leffert, M. (2011). The psychoanalysis and death of George Gershwin: An American tragedy. *Journal of the American Academy of Psychoanalysis and Dynamic Psychiatry, 39*(3), 421–452.

Linden, M. (2012). How to define, find, and classify side effects in psychotherapy: From unwanted events to adverse treatment reactions. *Clinical Psychology and Psychotherapy, 20*(4), 286–296.

Mallory, C., Brown, T., & Conron, K. (2019). *Conversion Therapy and LGBT Youth Update*. Retrieved from the UCLA School of Law's Williams Institute website: https://williamsinstitute.law.ucla.edu/wp-content/uploads/Conversion-Therapy-Update-Jun-2019.pdf

Mazza v. Medial Mut. Ins. Co. of North Carolina, 311 N.C. 621, 319 S. E.2d 217. (1984).

New York State Department of Health State Board for Professional Medical Conduct, *In the Matter of Isaac Steven Herschkopf, MD Determination and Order*. April, 2021 New York, NY

NNDB. Profile of Laura Schlessinger. (2019). *Soylent Communications*. Available at: https://www.nndb.com/people/427/000022361/. Accessed 20 Aug 2020.

Nocera, J., & Wondery. (2019). 'The Shrink Next Door' Podcast. Available at: https://wondery.com/shows/shrink-next-door/. Accessed on 6 Dec 2020.

Nocera, J. (2019, Aug 6). New York Levels Allegations against *Shrink Next Door* Doctor. Bloomberg.com Available at: https://www.bloomberg.com/news/articles/2019-08-06/new-york-levels-allegations-against-shrink-next-door-doctor. Accessed on 7 Dec 2020.

Novotney, A. (2016). *5 Ways to avoid malpractice*. Monitor on psychology March 2016, Vol 47, No. 3. Retrieved from the American Psychological Association website: https://www.apa.org/monitor/2016/03/malpractice

Osheroff v. Chestnut Lodge, Court of Special Appeals of Maryland, No. 1016 September Term, 1984, 62 Md. App 519 490 A. 2d 720. (1985).

Otto v. City of Boca Raton, No. 19–10604, 11th Cir. (2020).

Packman, P. L., Cabot, M. G., & Bongar, B. (1994). Malpractice arising from negligent psychotherapy: Ethical, legal, and clinical implications of *Osheroff v.* Chestnut Lodge. *Ethics and Behavior, 4*(3), 175–197.

Pope, K. S., Simpson, N. H., & Weiner, M. F. (1978). Malpractice in outpatient psychotherapy. *American Journal of Psychotherapy, 32*(4), 493–602.

Professional Risk Management Services. (2020). Cause of Loss - Claims and Lawsuits 1986–2019. Retrieved from https://www.prms.com/media/2439/cause-of-loss-2019.pdf

Quadrio, C. (1992). Sex and gender and the impaired therapist. *Australian and New Zealand Journal of Psychiatry, 26*(3), 346–363.

Ramona v. Ramona (judgment on jury verdict) No 61898, Napa Cty Super Ct. (1994).

Roy v. Hartogs, 85 Misc.2d 891, 381 N.Y.S2d 587. (1976).

Schroeder, M., & Shidlo, A. (2001). Ethical issues in sexual orientation conversion therapies: An empirical study of consumers. *Journal of Gay & Lesbian Psychotherapy, 5*(3–4), 131–166. https://doi.org/10.1300/J236v05n03_09

Shanafelt, T. D. (2009). A prescription for preventing physician burnout and promoting patient-centered care. *Journal of American Medical Association, 302*(12), 1338–1340.

Simon, R. I., & Shuman, D. W. (2009). Therapeutic risk management of clinical-legal Dilemmas: Should it be a core competency? *Journal of the American Academy of Psychiatry and the Law, 37*(2), 155–161.

Soulier, M. F., Maislen, A., & Beck, J. C. (2010). Status of the psychiatric duty to protect, circa 2006. *Journal of the American Academy of Psychiatry and the Law, 38*(4), 457–473.

Tarasoff v. (1976). The Regents of the University of California, Supreme Court of California, 17 Cal. 3d 425, 551 P. 2d 334, 131 Cal Rptr. 14.

Van Tol, J. E. (1990). *Detecting, deterring and punishing the use of fraudulent academic credentials: A play in two acts*. 30 Santa Clara L. Rev. 791.

Volk v. DeMeerleer, 187 Wash. 2d 241. (2016).

Whitree v. State, 290 N.Y.S. 2nd 486, Ct. Cal. (1968).

Part IV

Practice Areas

Inpatient General Psychiatry

19

Charles W. Luther, Sara G. West, and Alan W. Newman

Inpatient hospitalization is considered the highest and most restrictive level of psychiatric care due to the inherent deprivation of liberty. As such, it is reserved for the most acutely ill and at-risk psychiatric patients. Several potential harms exist for psychiatric inpatients: suicide, violence, improper imprisonment, boundary violations, medication errors, elopement, and others. Suicide and attempted suicide represent 27% of all psychiatric malpractice claims, while incorrect treatment, breach of confidentiality, and medication issues represent another 23, 15, and 10 percent, respectively (Frierson & Joshi, 2019). There is no readily available data on the incidence of malpractice claims specifically involving inpatient psychiatric practice. Due to its association with a heightened risk of dangerousness, and because the act of discharge fits with a causal chain argument, inpatient practice is ripe for malpractice claims.

This chapter will describe clinical guidelines and actions designed to mitigate these risks. The authors will not define a minimum standard of care but rather aim to describe care that exceeds most plausible definitions of a minimum standard.

C. W. Luther (✉)
Department of Psychiatry, Case Western Reserve University School of Medicine, Southwest General Health Center, Cleveland, OH, USA
e-mail: Charles.Luther@case.edu

S. G. West
Department of Psychiatry, Case Western Reserve University School of Medicine, Cleveland, OH, USA

A. W. Newman
Department of Psychiatry, California Pacific Medical Center | Sutter Health, San Francisco, CA, USA
e-mail: alannewman@parkdietzassociates.com

Suicide

The failure to protect a patient from suicide or attempted suicide is the most common source of malpractice liability. The Joint Commission has long noted that the suicide of hospitalized patients is one of the most common sentinel events, comprising over 16% of the total sentinel events between 1995 and 2003 (Lieberman et al., 2004). Inpatient self-harm, including completed suicides, is the most common outcome leading to malpractice suits in behavioral health settings (Sher, 2015; Bongar et al., 1993; Ahn et al., 2020). In cases of inpatient suicide, certain failures are commonly associated with liability.

Inadequate Risk Assessment

Many patients admitted to an inpatient unit will have already been identified as being at high risk, leading some to question the value of risk categorization in preventing suicides once patients are in the inpatient environment (Large et al., 2011). Since most patients will be at "high" risk, the decision to place a patient on a specific type of precautions may depend on relying on the patient's self-report of active suicidality. Inpatient care teams should rely on a systematic suicide risk assessment rather than over-rely on the patient's own self-report. Busch et al. (2003) noted that 77% of patients who committed suicide denied suicidal ideation in their last documented communication. Patients may conceal plans to harm themselves in order to prevent interference with a planned suicide attempt, viewing the clinician as an obstacle to their planning (Resnick, 2002). For this reason, the safest strategy may be to make efforts for the unit to be as safe as possible for every patient on the unit (Large et al., 2011).

Though once common, so-called no-harm contracts provide little clinical utility. In a study of 76 suicides that occurred in a hospital or immediately after discharge, 28% had such a "contract" in place (Busch et al., 2003). These

P. Ash et al. (eds.), *Malpractice and Liability in Psychiatry*, https://doi.org/10.1007/978-3-030-91975-7_19

documents do not reduce the risk of self-harm, nor do they protect clinicians from liability (Drew, 2001; Simon, 1999); rather they may convey a false sense of security.

Physical Environment

Considerable efforts have been made in recent years to eliminate physical hazards present in hospital environments. The failure of hospitals to identify and mitigate these hazards is a major cause of malpractice liability (Ballard et al., 2008). Environment of care hazards include ligatures and anchor points, sharp objects, contraband items, cleaning chemicals, multistory buildings with poorly secured windows, and poorly monitored medications. Consistent with findings in other countries, the Joint Commission noted in a 1998 Sentinel Event Alert that 75% of inpatient suicides involved hanging and 20% involved jumping (Dong et al., 2005; Hunt et al., 2007; Lieberman et al., 2004). Mills et al. (2013) reviewed 243 suicide attempts or completions at inpatient VA hospital settings between 1999 and 2011: 44% of the incidents involved hanging, 16% involved strangulation, and 8% involved overdoses. Watts et al. (2012) attributed a decrease of suicides in the VA system from 2.64 to 0.87 per 100,000 admissions in part to their implementation of a checklist to identify and abate hazards on inpatient units. The Joint Commission has provided several resources on how to best eliminate physical hazards in hospital environments (The Joint Commission, 2020).

Inadequate Diagnosis and Treatment

Short hospital lengths of stay limit opportunities to address the underlying causes of a suicidal crisis. As multiple psychiatric diagnoses are associated with an elevated risk of suicidal behavior, an individualized and evidence-based approach to the patient's diagnosis and treatment is critical. Short-term dynamic risk factors have relevance in treating inpatients (Cassells et al., 2005). While depression is a well-established risk factor for suicidal behavior, a full response to oral medications for depression takes longer than the typical length of stay (van Calker et al., 2009). Additionally, although antidepressants show epidemiologic value in reducing the overall risk of suicide in a population, questions linger about potential worsening of suicidal thinking in some patients following the initiation of antidepressant medications (Courtet & Lopez-Castroman, 2017). For these reasons, providers should not consider the initiation of oral antidepressants solely sufficient to manage suicide risk. Though not routinely available, ECT and ketamine may provide a rapid decrease in suicidal thinking, and providers should consider the benefits of those treatments in very high-risk depressed patients (Alves et al., 2016; Dadiomov & Lee, 2019). Despite the limitations of oral antidepressants, there are short-term risk factors in many depressed patients that can be rapidly addressed, such as panic attacks and severe insomnia, which can be quickly and effectively treated with benzodiazepines or hypnotics (Fawcett, 1990). Command hallucinations, associated with elevated suicide risk in some patients, may respond rapidly to antipsychotic medications (Agid et al., 2006; Wong et al., 2013; Harkavy-Friedman et al., 2003). Both clozapine and lithium are well established in certain patient populations in reducing suicide risk (Meltzer, 2003; Griffiths et al., 2014).

Inpatient units using a "medication-only" approach have been criticized as lacking evidence (Jobes & Chalker, 2019). Hospital treatment teams have many opportunities to decrease suicide risk factors using various therapeutic approaches, including cognitive behavioral therapy, dialectical behavior therapy, and other models (Haddock et al., 2016; Jobes, 2017; Awenat et al., 2019). Malpractice liability management for inpatient suicide may include a careful assessment of the use of psychotherapeutic approaches with high-risk inpatients.

Failure to Monitor Patients at Elevated Risk

Upon admission, psychiatric inpatients are routinely monitored by staff. Solely relying upon every 15-min patient checks, though common, is problematic (Jayaram et al., 2007). Busch et al.'s (2003) study of 76 inpatient suicides noted that 42% of these patients were on every 15-min checks, and an additional 20% were on every 30-min checks. Hanging, often with ligature points below head height, has been with the most common method used in inpatient suicides, accounting for more than 70% of all cases in most studies (Mills et al., 2013; Achté et al., 1966; Proulx et al., 1997). Fifteen-minute intervals are sufficient time to cause significant harm, especially if the patient becomes aware of predictable patterns of observation times (Salim et al., 2006; Sakinofsky, 2014; Aneja et al., 2017). In contrast, one-on-one monitoring in person or by video is complicated by increased staffing needs, staff monitoring failures, or concerns about patient privacy (Jayaram et al., 2007; Cardell & Pitula, 1999; Appenzeller et al., 2020). The standard of care may require yet-to-be widespread electronic devices that could monitor pulse oximetry, heart rate, or other physiologic activity (Hayes, 2013; Masters & Wandless, 2005). Until such tools are developed, hospitals and providers should understand the benefits and limitations of monitoring strategies and be prepared to enact monitoring matched to the patient's level of risk.

Communication Failures

Communication failures are another source of potential malpractice liability, particularly when hospital policies on documentation and communication are not followed (Silverman et al., 1994). Since some patients may develop stronger therapeutic alliances with non-physician staff members, psychiatrists should rely on multidisciplinary treatment team meetings and a careful review of nursing and therapist notes rather than focus exclusively on their own assessments (Grant & Lusk, 2015).

Elopement

Elopement describes the "unauthorized absence of a patient from a mental health facility without permission" (Brumbles & Meister, 2013). Failure to prevent a patient from eloping is a source of significant malpractice liability (Feldkamp, 2018; Gerardi, 2007). Many studies have associated elopement with subsequent suicides and homicides (Bowers et al., 1998; Bowers et al., 2000; Crichton, 2011; Hunt et al., 2010).

Elopement risk can be mitigated by utilizing locked wards and reducing physical plant risk (Muir-Cochrane & Mosel, 2008). Even locked units may have design issues that allow windows to be opened, doors to be unlocked, and fences scalable. Bars on windows, secure doors, and un-scalable walls or fences can work against a welcoming therapeutic environment. Human errors can also contribute to elopement risk.

Hospitals can minimize the risks of elopement by better understanding the characteristics of patients who elope (Wilkie et al., 2014). While some patients elope due to command hallucinations or other symptoms, others may elope due to dissatisfaction with care, conflicts with staff, or concerns about personal or financial obligations (Davis et al., 1999). All staff should be aware of existing tools and interventions to minimize elopement risk (Bowers et al., 2005; MacAlister, 2013). When a patient is identified as being at elevated risk for elopement, it is helpful to communicate this risk to the entire team (Simon, 2008a).

Hospitals can minimize their risks of liability regarding elopement by having policies that address both prevention and protocols that assertively respond to elopements (Pages et al., 1998; Smith, 2012). Responses to elopement should be based on the patient's individual risk factors. Notifying hospital security, local law enforcement, treatment providers, family members, or housemates is a reasonable strategy to deliver diligent care and reduce risk.

Reducing Risk

- Hospitals should be aware of the physical plant risks that increase the risk of suicide attempts on a unit and elopement risk.
- Clinicians should assess risk and tailor monitoring and treatment plans in accordance.
- Hospitals should have policies and procedures to minimize elopements and respond to them.

Violence

Violence poses a risk during the hospital stay and in the post-discharge period. Case law has held that there is a duty to control a patient's violent behavior regardless of the absence of foreseeable victims, and any malpractice claim will rest upon whether the clinician was negligent in their assessment (Simon, 2008b).

In a study of 1136 men and women discharged from acute psychiatric units, Steadman et al. (2006) found 1-year rates of violence to be 28%, though the authors noted the limitations with generalizing these rates. Though studies vary, approximately 17% of psychiatric inpatients commit violence; male sex, involuntary admission status, schizophrenia, and alcohol use disorder are associated with higher risk (Iozzino et al., 2015).

Reducing Risk

Clinicians cannot predict or prevent all violence, though it is the standard of care to assess the risk for violence and to take clinically appropriate actions (Leong et al., 2003; Resnick & Saxton, 2019). Actuarial and structured clinical assessments are more accurate than clinical assessment alone (Mossman, 1994), though unstructured clinical judgment is most widely used in practice. Failure to use an actuarial or structured tool is not negligence, but their use is becoming more common in some high-risk forensic settings (Mossman, 2008; Resnick & Saxton, 2019). Solely relying on the patient's disavowal of violent thinking or planning is insufficient.

Utilizing a combination of empirically validated risk factors and clinical judgment, the Historical Clinical Risk Management-20 Scale assesses ten static, five dynamic, and five future risk factors (Howe et al., 2015). To assist with assessing near-term violence risk on an inpatient unit, the BRØSET is a six-item assessment with good psychometric properties (Almvik et al., 2000). Both represent enhanced assessments that when considered can appropriately discredit a claim of negligence.

Fisher (2016) outlined interventions to mitigate the risk of inpatient violence: adequate staffing, minimizing overcrowding and noise, structured therapeutic activities, enhanced monitoring during transition periods, de-escalation training, provision of medications targeting psychiatric etiology, and restraint and seclusion as least restrictive means as appropriate.

According to Price et al. (2018), effective de-escalation techniques emphasize:

- Maintaining respect and unconditional positive regard
- Adequate time and space, social cohesion
- Reducing hierarchical and physical barriers
- Rule flexibility and patient-centered locus of decision-making
- Staff authenticity, e.g., balancing authority vs. friendliness

Lavelle et al.'s (2016) study of 522 psychiatric inpatients showed a de-escalation success rate of 60%. Inpatient units should regularly train and implement these techniques.

Prior to discharge, the clinician should consider further actions commensurate with the level of risk simply because reducing the risk to zero is impracticable. For certain high-risk individuals with severe mental illness, an assisted outpatient commitment may be indicated, though it is far beyond the standard of care due to limited funding and availability (Cripps & Swartz, 2018). Simon (2008b) and Resnick and Saxton (2019) outlined other actions:

1. Developing collateral information from family, friends, and criminal justice sources
2. Conducting a family meeting for education and support
3. Conducting serial assessments as a process
4. Designing aftercare planning for rapid access and enhanced adherence
5. Assessing access to weapons
6. Pursuant to state law, enacting a duty to third parties (e.g., warning, involving law enforcement)
7. Incorporating a second opinion

Security, Officers, and Restraints

While most health professionals view the presence of hospital security as a critical element in addressing potential aggression by patients, hospital security can also create safety and liability risks in a hospital setting (Muir-Cochrane et al., 2020). There is limited empirical research regarding the use of security in hospital settings, and several articles in the media have raised concerns about the use of security officers creating risks to patients due to inadequate training or inappropriate use of lethal force (Lawrence et al., 2018; Rosenthal, 2016).

Hospital policies should delineate under which circumstances security can be utilized for aggressive behavior and how they should engage with clinical staff (Lawrence et al., 2018). One area of ongoing controversy regards the use of firearms by hospital security, particularly considering increasing awareness of the shootings of mentally ill patients by police outside of hospital settings (Blando et al., 2019; "How 3 Health System Executives,", 2016; Saleh et al., 2018).

Hospitals should also ensure that their security officers have adequate training in managing aggressive patients, especially with respect to verbal de-escalation techniques and other strategies to minimize the use of physical methods of restraint. The use of physical restraints with aggressive patients, whether by clinical staff only or with security officers' assistance, creates the risk of bodily injury to both staff and patients and liability risk due to these injuries (Recupero et al., 2011). Minimizing the need for physical restraints is the best way to avoid these injuries (American Psychiatric Association et al., 2003). When physical restraint is the only acceptable option, hospitals must ensure that security and clinical staff have adequate training to minimize patient and staff injuries and reduce liability risks from adverse outcomes (Recupero et al., 2011). Positional asphyxia is one adverse outcome that can potentially result from physical restraints, and hospital staff should be aware of individual patient risk factors that would make them more susceptible to an unfavorable outcome from physical restraints (Morrison et al., 2002; O'Halloran & Frank, 2000).

Civil Commitment

Admission to a psychiatric unit involves at least some deprivation of liberty, and this is unique in the practice of medicine. While psychiatric inpatients are often acutely mentally ill, if they are being admitted voluntarily, they retain the right to consent to their admission. This involves a clear understanding of the risks and benefits of the process without the interference of psychiatric symptoms (such as delusional beliefs). This concept was reinforced in 1990 by the US Supreme Court's decision in *Zinermon v. Burch* (1990). Voluntary admission has many benefits, including an increased therapeutic alliance as well as the avoidance of stigmatization and legal consequences that may result from a judicial hearing (such as inability to legally obtain a weapon). Consent for voluntary admission may also include the idea that, should the doctor and patient disagree about the need for continued hospitalization, almost any admission may shift from voluntary to involuntary (Garanki et al., 2014).

The philosophical justifications for involuntary hospitalization include access to treatment, the protection of patients from themselves at a time when they are too ill to make appropriate choices (*parens patriae*), and the protection of the community from potentially violent, mentally ill individuals (police powers). This, however, must be weighed against an individual's basic right to freedom. As suggested by the 1976 Wisconsin case *Lessard v. Schmidt*, some jurisdictions grant extra protections to the respondent during these civil commitment proceedings given the potential loss of liberty. At these formal hearings, the treating psychiatrist is often called upon to testify regarding just how ill the patient is while in the presence of the patient, which understandably can damage the therapeutic alliance and cause patients to lose trust in their treatment providers.

Reducing Risk

- Utilize the least restrictive means accounting for patient's decisional capacity.
- Document the clinical reasoning for choosing the legal status of admission (e.g., voluntary or involuntary).
- Adjust commitment status based on clinical picture and patient's wishes.

Treatment Modalities

One justification for deprivation of liberty associated with the process of civil commitment is the provision of treatment. Ideally, treatment decisions are made in conjunction with the patient and tailored to their specific goals. However, it occasionally falls upon the inpatient psychiatrist to administer medications to patients over their objection. In emergency situations, this can be done without court intervention. There are multiple mechanisms for non-emergent forced medications, and they vary among jurisdictions. The patient's rights-driven model exemplified in *Rogers v. Commissioner* (1983) again places the decision in the hands of the courts, which brings up many of the same issues as described in relation to civil commitment hearings. This situation is further often compounded by the administration of an unwanted intramuscular injection that may require the physical restraint of the patient. Acting in good faith with least restrictive means, supportive communication, and education to help the patient decreases liability.

There are several treatment modalities that are more readily available when an individual has been admitted to a psychiatric unit. The first is pro re nata (PRN) medications, which are administered by nurses as needed to patients based on their symptoms. When physicians provide clear indications and exceptions for administrating these medications and avoid writing for multiple medications to be given PRN for the same indication, they decrease the variability in how these treatment modalities is used.

Reducing Risk

- Tailor therapies based on patients' wishes, goals, symptoms, and diagnoses.
- Utilize least restrictive means for administering therapies.
- Document clinical justification for more intrusive modalities.

Boundaries

Sex on the hospital unit is the next topic that warrants consideration in terms of inpatient psychiatric malpractice. A risk averse policy would dictate the presence of a blanket ban on sexual activity in the hospital. That, however, fails to consider patients' fundamental human rights in an environment where so many other rights are limited (Maylea, 2019). Despite hospitals' prohibitions, two studies demonstrated that approximately one third of people on inpatient psychiatric units engage in some form of sexual activity (Warner et al., 2004; Welch & Clements, 1996). There are some events that are clearly criminal, namely, forced sexual contact, which may result in charges such as rape or gross sexual imposition. Other acts are definitively unethical, such as sexual contact between staff and patients. Consensual sex involving individuals with a guardian are more of a gray area. While it is possible to retain individual competencies with a court-appointed decision-maker in place, the presence of a guardian strongly suggests that the ward is vulnerable and may not be able to carefully weigh all the complex information necessary to make a competent decision to engage in sexual activity. Finally, the challenge occurs when two competent individuals consent to sex. While it may be uncomfortable, Dr. Maylea offers, "In policing the lawful bodily interactions of their patient and pushing sexual activity out of sight, clinicians may be breaching their duty of care to provide sexual health support and risk creating an environment in which the therapeutic relationship will be sacrificed to the enforcement of institutional policy" (Maylea, 2019, p. 1070).

As noted above, vulnerable populations (e.g., those with a guardian) may warrant an extra degree of protection on an inpatient unit, and this applies to those with intellectual limitations as well. Those diagnosed with intellectual disability have "deficits in adaptive functioning that result in failure to meet developmental and sociocultural standards for personal independence and social responsibility" (American Psychiatric Association, 2013, p. 33). Ideally, one would want to house such individuals in a specialized unit where the staff has had specific training to address issues unique to this population. As this design is not always logistically possible, staff may need to increase the frequency and intensity of their observation of these patients to ensure that they are not being exploited. Behavior plans also offer concrete rewards and consequences for the individual's actions in an environment that is unfamiliar and potentially frightening for the patient with intellectual deficits.

Reducing Risk

- Orient patients to safe boundaries while hospitalized.
- Enact policies regarding staff-patient boundaries.
- Devise boundary safety monitoring plans for vulnerable patients.

Discharge from Hospital

The post-discharge period is a time of increased risk of suicide and disruptions in access to care, and it is a unique and defined moment in psychiatric practice (Chung et al., 2017; Sowers & Rohland, 2004). Merely 30% of an adult Medicaid population received care within a week of discharge, and only 49% did so within a month (Stein et al., 2007). As such, clinicians would do well to anticipate discharge hurdles and communicate during care transitions with providers and community supports.

Reducing Risk

Discharge to a less restrictive setting has become routine care once acute psychiatric symptoms have been stabilized. Symptoms and risk often remain, and for this, diligent care planning and communication is key. Smith et al. (2017) described three actions to enhance the likelihood of successful transitions: liaising with providers, scheduling an aftercare appointment near the discharge date, and forwarding a summary of hospitalization. Further actions to reduce risk include:

- Supporting and educating families regarding discharge plans and expectations
- Stepping down to a less restrictive acute care setting, e.g., a crisis unit
- Addressing housing problems issues in the community
- Implementing case management
- Referral to substance use disorder treatment and medication-assisted treatment

Conclusion

The aforementioned malpractice risks can be a source of anxiety and uncertainty for clinicians. Understanding strategies to assess and mitigate the risk, while acknowledging that it often does not reduce to zero, will help to plan the clinical vector and to document the care provided. Such work will reduce the risk of malpractice claims in the inpatient setting.

Key Points

- Suicide and self-harm are the leading sentinel events most commonly associated with malpractice claims in an inpatient setting.
- Environment of care monitoring is key in reducing suicide risk; ligatures and anchor points are the most common source of risk.
- Clinical risk assessments that include both dynamic and static risk factors along with collateral information (rather than solely patient report) should be used routinely.
- Tailor patient monitoring frequency to clinical needs and avoid overreliance on every 15-min checks.
- Clinicians cannot predict violence accurately, though they ought to assess the risk. Although actuarial and structured clinical assessments afford more accuracy than unstructured clinical assessments, they are not yet the standard of care.
- De-escalation techniques to mitigate the risk of violence include unconditional positive regard, adequate time and space, rule flexibility, and patient-centered care.
- Hospital police and security officers should be trained to interact with psychiatric patients and clinical staff, and hospital policies should delineate circumstances and techniques for officer engagement (e.g., officers' use of guns).
- Physical restraints should be used as a last resort, and staff should regularly train in safe utilization and indications, particularly regarding positional asphyxia and individual patient risk factors.
- Civil commitment and forced medications require carefully weighing the patient's civil liberties against a need for both the individual's and the community's safety while adhering to local laws governing such procedures.
- There is clear precedent regarding the unethical nature of staff and patient intimate relationships; however, sex between patients is less clear. Educating both staff and patients about appropriate boundaries can serve to reinforce expectations and decrease liability.

References

Achté, K. A., Stenbäck, A., & Teräväinen, H. (1966). On suicides committed during treatment in psychiatric hospitals. *Acta Psychiatrica Scandinavica, 42*(3), 272–284. https://doi.org/10.1111/j.1600-0447.1966.tb01932.x

Agid, O., Seeman, P., & Kapur, S. (2006). The "delayed onset" of antipsychotic action—An idea whose time has come and gone. *Journal of Psychiatry and Neuroscience, 31*(2), 93–100.

Ahn, S. I., Lee, W., & Song, D. H. (2020). A descriptive study on the civil lawsuits of medical malpractice occurred during psychiatric ward treatment. *Psychiatry Investigation, 17*(9), 865. https://doi.org/10.30773/pi.2019.0350

Almvik, R., Woods, P., & Rasmussen, K. (2000). The BrØset violence checklist: Sensitivity, specificity, and interrater reliability. *Journal of Interpersonal Violence, 15*(12), 1284–1296.

Alves, L. P. C., Freire, T. F. V., Fleck, M. P. A., & Rocha, N. S. (2016). A naturalistic study of high-dose unilateral ECT among severely depressed inpatients: How does it work in the clinical practice? *BMC Psychiatry, 16*(1), 1–8. https://doi.org/10.1186/s12888-016-1095-z

American Psychiatric Association (Ed.). (2013). *Diagnostic and statistical manual of mental disorders* (5th ed., p. 33). American Psychiatric Association.

American Psychiatric Association, American Psychiatric Nurses Association, and the National Association for Psychiatric Health Systems. (2003). *Learning from each other: Success stories and ideas for reducing restraint/seclusion in behavioral health.* American Psychiatric Association, American Psychiatric Nurses Association, and the National Association for Psychiatric Health Systems. https://www.nabh.org/wp-content/uploads/2018/06/LearningfromEachOtherFINAL.pdf

Aneja, J., Jangli, S., Kulhara, P., & Bathla, M. (2017). Neuropsychiatric sequelae of attempted hanging and diagnostic dilemmas. *Industrial Psychiatry Journal, 26*(2), 239–242. https://doi.org/10.4103/ipj.ipj_46_15

Appenzeller, Y. E., Appelbaum, P. S., & Trachsel, M. (2020). Ethical and practical issues in video surveillance of psychiatric units. *Psychiatric Services (Washington, D.C.), 71*(5), 480–486. https://doi.org/10.1176/appi.ps.201900397

Awenat, Y. F., Peters, S., Gooding, P. A., Pratt, D., Huggett, C., Harris, K., Armitage, C. J., & Haddock, G. (2019). Qualitative analysis of ward staff experiences during research of a novel suicide-prevention psychological therapy for psychiatric inpatients: Understanding the barriers and facilitators. *PLoS One, 14*(9), e0222482. https://doi.org/10.1371/journal.pone.0222482

Ballard, E. D., Pao, M., Horowitz, L., Lee, L. M., Henderson, D. K., & Rosenstein, D. L. (2008). Aftermath of suicide in the hospital: institutional response. *Psychosomatics, 49*(6), 461–469. https://doi.org/10.1176/appi.psy.49.6.461

Blando, J. D., Cramer, R. J., & Szklo-Coxe, M. (2019). Hospital security programs and policies related to guns and other weapons. *Journal of Healthcare Management/American College of Healthcare Executives, 64*(3), 157–166. https://doi.org/10.1097/JHM-D-18-00046

Bongar, B., Maris, R. W., Berman, A. L., Litman, R. E., & Silverman, M. M. (1993). Inpatient standards of care and the suicidal patient. Part I: General clinical formulations and legal considerations. *Suicide and Life-threatening Behavior, 23*(3), 245–256.

Bowers, L., Jarrett, M., & Clark, N. (1998). Absconding: A literature review. *Journal of Psychiatric and Mental Health Nursing, 5*, 343–353.

Bowers, L., Jarrett, M., Clark, N., Kiyimba, F., & McFarlane, L. (2000). Determinants of absconding by patients on acute psychiatric wards. *Journal of Advanced Nursing, 32*(3), 644–649. https://doi.org/10.1046/j.1365-2648.2000.01523.x

Bowers, L., Simpson, A., & Alexander, J. (2005). Real world application of an intervention to reduce absconding. *Journal of Psychiatric and Mental Health Nursing, 12*(5), 598–602. https://doi.org/10.1111/j.1365-2850.2005.00879.x

Brumbles, D., & Meister, A. (2013). Psychiatric elopement: Using evidence to examine causative factors and preventative measures. *Archives of Psychiatric Nursing, 27*(1), 3–9. https://doi.org/10.1016/j.apnu.2012.07.002

Busch, K. A., Fawcett, J., & Jacobs, D. G. (2003). Clinical correlates of inpatient suicide. *The Journal of Clinical Psychiatry, 64*(1), 14–19. https://doi.org/10.4088/JCP.v64n0105

Cardell, R., & Pitula, C. R. (1999). Suicidal inpatients' perceptions of therapeutic and nontherapeutic aspects of constant observation. *Psychiatric Services, 50*(8), 1066–1070. https://doi.org/10.1176/ps.50.8.1066

Cassells, C., Paterson, B., Dowding, D., & Morrison, R. (2005). Long- and short-term risk factors in the prediction of inpatient suicide: Review of the literature. *Crisis, 26*(2), 53–63. https://doi.org/10.1027/0227-5910.26.2.53

Chung, D. T., Ryan, C. J., Hadzi-Pavlovic, D., Singh, S. P., Stanton, C., & Large, M. M. (2017). Suicide rates after discharge from psychiatric facilities, a systematic review and meta-analysis. *JAMA Psychiatry, 74*(7), 694–702.

Courtet, P., & Lopez-Castroman, J. (2017). Antidepressants and suicide risk in depression. *World Psychiatry, 16*(3), 317–318. https://doi.org/10.1002/wps.20460

Crichton, J. H. M. (2011). A review of published independent inquiries in England into psychiatric patient homicide, 1995–2010. *The Journal of Forensic Psychiatry and Psychology, 22*(6), 761–789. https://doi.org/10.1080/14789949.2011.617832

Cripps, S. N., & Swartz, M. S. (2018). Update on assisted outpatient treatment. *Current Psychiatry Reports, 20*, 112.

Dadiomov, D., & Lee, K. (2019). The effects of ketamine on suicidality across various formulations and study settings. *The Mental Health Clinician, 9*(1), 48–60. https://doi.org/10.9740/mhc.2019.01.048

Davis, B., Bowers, L., Jarrett, M., Clark, N., Kiyimba, F., & Mcfarlane, L. (1999). 1. Absconding: Why patients leave. *Journal of Psychiatric and Mental Health Nursing, 6*(3), 199–205. https://doi.org/10.1046/j.1365-2850.1999.630199.x

Dong, J. Y. S., Ho, T. P., & Kan, C. K. (2005). A case-control study of 92 cases of in-patient suicides. *Journal of Affective Disorders, 87*(1), 91–99. https://doi.org/10.1016/j.jad.2005.03.015

Drew, B. L. (2001). Self-harm behavior and no-suicide contracting in psychiatric inpatient settings. *Archives of Psychiatric Nursing, 15*(3), 99–106. https://doi.org/10.1053/apnu.2001.23748

Fawcett, J. (1990). Time-related predictors of suicide in major affective disorder. *American Journal of Psychiatry, 147*(9), 1189–1194. https://doi.org/10.1176/ajp.147.9.1189

Feldkamp, J. K. (2018). Regulatory and litigation risks of elopement. *Caring for the Ages, 19*(9), 8. https://doi.org/10.1016/j.carage.2018.08.006

Fisher, K. (2016). Inpatient violence. *Psychiatric Clinics of North America, 39*, 567–577.

Frierson, R. L., & Joshi, K. G. (2019). Malpractice law and psychiatry: An overview. *Focus: Journal of Life Long Learning in Psychiatry, 17*(4), 332–336.

Garanki, A., Shalenberg, E., Burstin, S. C., Brendel, R. W., & Appel, J. M. (2014). Voluntary psychiatric hospitalization and patient-driven requests for discharge: A statutory review and analysis of implication for the capacity to consent to voluntary hospitalizations. *Harvard Review of Psychiatry, 22*(4), 241–249.

Gerardi, D. (2007). *Elopement*. Retrieved November 5, 2020, from: http://www.psnet.ahrq.gov/web-mm/elopement

Grant, C. L., & Lusk, J. L. (2015). A multidisciplinary approach to therapeutic risk management of the suicidal patient. *Journal of*

Multidisciplinary Healthcare, 8, 291–298. https://doi.org/10.2147/JMDH.S50529
Griffiths, J. J., Zarate, C. A., & Rasimas, J. J. (2014). Existing and novel biological therapeutics in suicide prevention. *American Journal of Preventive Medicine, 47*(3 0 2), S195–S203. https://doi.org/10.1016/j.amepre.2014.06.012
Haddock, G., Davies, L., Evans, E., Emsley, R., Gooding, P., Heaney, L., Jones, S., Kelly, J., Munro, A., Peters, S., Pratt, D., Tarrier, N., Windfuhr, K., & Awenat, Y. (2016). Investigating the feasibility and acceptability of a cognitive behavioural suicide prevention therapy for people in acute psychiatric wards (the 'INSITE' trial): Study protocol for a randomised controlled trial. *Trials, 17*(1), 1–8. https://doi.org/10.1186/s13063-016-1192-9
Harkavy-Friedman, J. M., Kimhy, D., Nelson, E. A., Venarde, D. F., & Mann, J. J. (2003). Suicide attempts in schizophrenia: The role of command auditory hallucinations for suicide. *The Journal of Clinical Psychiatry, 64*(8), 871–874.
Hayes, L. M. (2013). Suicide prevention in correctional facilities: Reflections and next steps. *International Journal of Law and Psychiatry, 36*(3–4), 188–194. https://doi.org/10.1016/j.ijlp.2013.04.010
How 3 health system executives weighed decisions about armed security. (2016, September 14). *Becker's hospital review*. https://www.beckershospitalreview.com/hospital-management-administration/how-3-hospital-executives-weighed-decisions-about-armed-security.html
Howe, J., Rosenfeld, B., Foellmi, M., Stern, S., & Rotter, M. (2015). Application of the HCR-20 version 3 in civil psychiatric patients. *Criminal Justice and Behavior, 43*(3), 398–412.
Hunt, I. M., Kapur, N., Webb, R., Robinson, J., Burns, J., Turnbull, P., Shaw, J., & Appleby, L. (2007). Suicide in current psychiatric in-patients: A case-control study The National Confidential Inquiry into Suicide and Homicide. *Psychological Medicine, 37*(6), 831–837. https://doi.org/10.1017/S0033291707000104
Hunt, I. M., Windfuhr, K., Swinson, N., Shaw, J., Appleby, L., Kapur, N., & National Confidential Inquiry into Suicide and Homicide by People with Mental Illness. (2010). Suicide amongst psychiatric in-patients who abscond from the ward: A national clinical survey. *BMC Psychiatry, 10*, 14. https://doi.org/10.1186/1471-244X-10-14
Iozzino, L., Ferrari, C., Large, M., Nielssen, O., & de Girolamo, G. (2015). Prevalence and risk factors of violence by psychiatric acute inpatients: A systematic review and meta-analysis. *PLoS One, 10*(6), e0128536. https://doi.org/10.1371/journal.pone.0128536
Jayaram, G., Sporney, H., & Perticone, P. (2007). *The utility and effectiveness of 15-min checks in inpatient settings*. 4.
Jobes, D. A. (2017). Clinical assessment and treatment of suicidal risk: A critique of contemporary care and CAMS as a possible remedy. *Practice Innovations, 2*(4), 207–220. https://doi.org/10.1037/pri0000054
Jobes, D. A., & Chalker, S. A. (2019). One size does not fit all: A comprehensive clinical approach to reducing suicidal ideation, attempts, and deaths. *International Journal of Environmental Research and Public Health, 16*(19), 3606. https://doi.org/10.3390/ijerph16193606
Large, M., Ryan, C., & Nielssen, O. (2011). The validity and utility of risk assessment for inpatient suicide. *Australasian Psychiatry, 19*(6), 507–512. https://doi.org/10.3109/10398562.2011.610505
Lavelle, M., Stewart, D., James, K., Richardson, M., Renwick, L., Brennan, G., & Bowers, L. (2016). Predictors of effective de-escalation in acute inpatient psychiatric settings. *Journal of Clinical Nursing, 25*, 2180–2188.
Lawrence, R. E., Perez-Coste, M. M., Arkow, S. D., Appelbaum, P. S., & Dixon, L. B. (2018). Use of security officers on inpatient psychiatry units. *Psychiatric Services, 69*(7), 777–783. https://doi.org/10.1176/appi.ps.201700546
Leong, G. B., Silva, J. A., & Weinstock, R. (2003). Dangerousness. In R. Rosner (Ed.), *Principles and practice of forensic psychiatry* (2nd ed., pp. 565–571).
Lessard v. Schmidt, 413 F. Supp. 1318 (E.D. Wis. 1976).
Lieberman, D. Z., Resnik, H. L. P., & Holder-Perkins, V. (2004). Environmental risk factors in hospital suicide. *Suicide and Life-threatening Behavior, 34*(4), 448–453. https://doi.org/10.1521/suli.34.4.448.53740
MacAlister, D. (2013). A physical security evaluation tool for elopement prevention in a behavioural/mental health setting. *Journal of Healthcare Protection Management: Publication of the International Association for Hospital Security, 29*(1), 54–64.
Masters, K., & Wandless, D. (2005). Use of pulse oximetry during restraint episodes. *Psychiatric Services (Washington, D.C.), 56*, 1313–1314. https://doi.org/10.1176/appi.ps.56.10.1313
Maylea, C. (2019). The capacity of consent to sex in mental health inpatient units. *Australian and New Zealand Journal of Psychiatry, 53*(11), 1070–1079.
Meltzer, H. Y. (2003). Clozapine treatment for suicidality in schizophrenia international suicide prevention trial (InterSePT). *Archives of General Psychiatry, 60*(1), 82. https://doi.org/10.1001/archpsyc.60.1.82
Mills, P. D., King, L. A., Watts, B. V., & Hemphill, R. R. (2013). Inpatient suicide on mental health units in Veterans Affairs (VA) hospitals: Avoiding environmental hazards. *General Hospital Psychiatry, 35*(5), 528–536. https://doi.org/10.1016/j.genhosppsych.2013.03.021
Morrison, L., Duryea, P. B., Moore, C., & Nathanson-Shinn, A. (2002). *The lethal hazard of prone restraint: Positional asphyxiation (7018.01; p. 46)*. Protection and Advocacy.
Mossman, D. (1994). Assessing predictions of violence: Being accurate about accuracy. *Journal of Consulting and Clinical Psychology, 62*(4), 783–792.
Mossman, D. (2008). Violence risk: Is clinical judgment enough? *Current Psychiatry, 7*(6), 70–72.
Muir-Cochrane, E., & Mosel, K. A. (2008). Absconding: A review of the literature 1996–2008. *International Journal of Mental Health Nursing, 17*(5), 370–378. https://doi.org/10.1111/j.1447-0349.2008.00562.x
Muir-Cochrane, E., Muller, A., Fu, Y., & Oster, C. (2020). Role of security guards in Code Black events in medical and surgical settings: A retrospective chart audit. *Nursing and Health Sciences, 22*(3), 758–768. https://doi.org/10.1111/nhs.12725
O'Halloran, R. L., & Frank, J. G. (2000). Asphyxial death during prone restraint revisited: A report of 21 cases. *The American Journal of Forensic Medicine and Pathology, 21*, 39–52.
Pages, K. P., Russo, J. E., Wingerson, D. K., Ries, R. K., Roy-Byrne, P. P., & Cowley, D. S. (1998). Predictors and outcome of discharge against medical advice from the psychiatric units of a general hospital. *Psychiatric Services, 49*(9), 1187–1192. https://doi.org/10.1176/ps.49.9.1187
Price, O., Baker, J., Bee, P., Grundy, A., Scott, A., Butler, D., Cree, L., & Lovell, K. (2018). Patient perspectives on barriers and enablers to the use and effectiveness of de-escalation techniques for the management of violence and aggression in mental health settings. *Journal of Advanced Nursing, 74*, 614–625.
Proulx, F., Lesage, A. D., & Grunberg, F. (1997). One hundred inpatient suicides. *British Journal of Psychiatry, 171*(3), 247–250. https://doi.org/10.1192/bjp.171.3.247
Recupero, P. R., Price, M., Garvey, K. A., Daly, B., & Xavier, S. L. (2011). Restraint and seclusion in psychiatric treatment settings: Regulation, case law, and risk management. *The Journal of the American Academy of Psychiatry and the Law, 39*(4), 465–476.
Resnick, P., & Saxton, A. (2019). Malpractice liability due to patient violence. *Focus: The Journal of Lifelong Learning in Psychiatry, 17*(4), 343–348.

Resnick, P. J. (2002). Recognizing that the suicidal patient views you as an adversary. *Current Psychiatry, 1*(1), 8.
Rogers v. Commissioner, 390 Mass 489 (1983).
Rosenthal, E. (2016, February 12). Rosenthal: When the hospital fires the bullet—Google Scholar. *The New York Times*. https://scholar.google.com/scholar_lookup?hl=enandpublication_year=2016andjournal=New+York+Timesandauthor=E+Rosenthalandtitle=When+the+hospital+fires+the+bullet
Sakinofsky, I. (2014). Preventing suicide among inpatients. *The Canadian Journal of Psychiatry, 59*(3), 131–140. https://doi.org/10.1177/070674371405900304
Saleh, A. Z., Appelbaum, P. S., Liu, X., Scott Stroup, T., & Wall, M. (2018). Deaths of people with mental illness during interactions with law enforcement. *International Journal of Law and Psychiatry, 58*, 110–116. https://doi.org/10.1016/j.ijlp.2018.03.003
Salim, A., Martin, M., Sangthong, B., Brown, C., Rhee, P., & Demetriades, D. (2006). Near-hanging injuries: A 10-year experience. *Injury, 37*(5), 435–439. https://doi.org/10.1016/j.injury.2005.12.013
Sher, L. (2015). Suicide medical malpractice: An educational overview. *International Journal of Adolescent Medicine and Health, 27*(2), 203–206. https://doi.org/10.1515/ijamh-2015-5012
Silverman, M. M., Berman, A. L., Bongar, B., Litman, R. E., & Maris, R. W. (1994). Inpatient standards of care and the suicidal patient part II: An integration with clinical risk management. *Suicide and Life-threatening Behavior, 24*(2), 152–169. https://doi.org/10.1111/j.1943-278X.1994.tb00799.x
Simon, R. I. (1999). The suicide prevention contract: Clinical, legal, and risk management issues. *Journal of the American Academy of Psychiatry and the Law, 27*(3), 6.
Simon, R. I. (2008a). *Assessing and managing suicide risk: Guidelines for clinically based risk management* (p. 158). American Psychiatric Publishing.
Simon, R. I. (2008b). Clinically-based risk management of potentially violent patients. In R. I. Simon & K. Tardiff (Eds.), *Violence assessment and management* (1st ed., pp. 555–564). American Psychiatric Publishing.
Smith, T. A. (2012). Hospital security and patient elopement: Protecting patients and your healthcare facility. *Journal of Healthcare Protection Management: Publication of the International Association for Hospital Security, 28*(1), 7–20.
Smith, T. E., Abraham, M., Bolotnikova, N. V., Donahue, S. A., Essock, S. M., … Radigan, M. (2017). Psychiatric inpatient discharge planning practices and attendance at aftercare appointments. *Psychiatric Services, 68*(1), 92–95.
Sowers, W. E., & Rohland, B. (2004). American Association of Community Psychiatrists' principles for managing transitions in behavioral health services. *Psychiatric Services, 55*(11), 1271–1275.
Steadman, H. J., Mulvey, E. P., Monahan, J., Robbins, P. C., Appelbaum, P. S., Grisso, T., Roth, L. H., & Silver, E. (2006). Violence by people discharged from acute psychiatric inpatient facilities and by others in the same neighborhoods. *Archives of General Psychiatry, 55*, 393–401.
Stein, B. D., Kogan, J. N., Sorbero, M. J., Thompson, W., & Hutchinson, S. L. (2007). Predictors of timely follow-up care among Medicaid-enrolled adults after psychiatric hospitalization. *Psychiatric Services, 58*(12), 1563–1569.
The Joint Commission. (2020). *Suicide prevention resources*. https://www.jointcommission.org/-/media/tjc/documents/resources/patient-safety-topics/suicide-prevention/pages-from-suicide_prevention_compendium_5_11_20_updated-july2020_ep1.pdf
van Calker, D., Zobel, I., Dykierek, P., Deimel, C. M., Kech, S., Lieb, K., Berger, M., & Schramm, E. (2009). Time course of response to antidepressants: Predictive value of early improvement and effect of additional psychotherapy. *Journal of Affective Disorders, 114*(1–3), 243–253. https://doi.org/10.1016/j.jad.2008.07.023
Warner, J., Pitts, N., Crawford, M. J., Serfaty, M., Prabhakaran, P., & Amin, R. (2004). Sexual activity among patients in a psychiatric hospital wards. *Journal of the Royal Society of Medicine, 97*, 477–479.
Watts, B. V., Young-Xu, Y., & Mills, P. D. (2012). Examination of the effectiveness of the mental health environment of care checklist in reducing suicide on inpatient mental health units. *Archives of General Psychiatry, 69*(6), 588–592.
Welch, S. J., & Clements, G. W. (1996). Development of a policy on sexuality for hospitalized chronic psychiatric patients. *Canadian Journal of Psychiatry, 41*, 273–279.
Wilkie, T., Penney, S. R., Fernane, S., & Simpson, A. I. F. (2014). Characteristics and motivations of absconders from forensic mental health services: A case-control study. *BMC Psychiatry, 14*, 91. https://doi.org/10.1186/1471-244X-14-91
Wong, Z., Öngür, D., Cohen, B., Ravichandran, C., Noam, G., & Murphy, B. (2013). Command hallucinations and clinical characteristics of suicidality in patients with psychotic spectrum disorders. *Comprehensive Psychiatry, 54*(6), 611–617. https://doi.org/10.1016/j.comppsych.2012.12.022
Zinermon v. Burch, 494 U.S. 113 (1990).

Outpatient General Psychiatry

20

Stephen G. Noffsinger and Selena R. Magalotti

There are more than 42,000 psychiatrists practicing in the United States (Satiani et al., 2018). The majority of those psychiatrists deliver treatment in outpatient settings, such as private practices, clinics, community mental health centers, and intensive outpatient programs (Beck et al., 2018). Approximately 30 million outpatient psychiatric treatment encounters occur every year (Cherry et al., 2018). With every outpatient treatment encounter, the potential for malpractice litigation exists.

The psychiatrist practicing in the outpatient setting faces the special risk of malpractice litigation, due to several factors inherent to the outpatient setting:

- The initial outpatient psychiatric evaluation may be relatively incomplete, due to insufficient time allotted for the initial evaluation (typically 45–50 minutes), lack of collateral information at the initial evaluation (no past medical or psychiatric records and no information from family), and the possibility of incomplete and/or inaccurate self-disclosure of clinical information from the patient. The initial psychiatric evaluation relies almost exclusively on the patient's subjective report of his or her symptoms and past history, coupled with the psychiatrist's point-in-time clinical observations and mental status examination at the limited initial evaluation. Despite the psychiatrist's good faith efforts, an incomplete initial evaluation may result in an inaccurate diagnosis and resulting inaccurate treatment plan.
- As the length of stay for hospitalized patients continues to decline (Lee et al., 2012), outpatient psychiatrists may find themselves evaluating more acutely ill patients presenting for their initial outpatient evaluation after hospital discharge.
- Patients may be reticent to involve their partner and/or family member in the clinical discussion with the psychiatrist, for various possible reasons, which may result in the psychiatrist being unaware of important clinical information.
- The advent of telepsychiatry has been a mixed blessing. While allowing for the remote evaluation and treatment of patients, the accuracy and reliability of telepsychiatry evaluations have yet to be established. The legal regulation of telepsychiatry is in its infancy, and legal standards for telepsychiatry are unclear (Sorrentino et al., 2020).
- Psychological test measures and rating scales, which may assist in clarifying the diagnosis, are not typically readily available in the outpatient psychiatric setting.
- As the trend of closing inpatient psychiatry services continues (Shah et al., 2020), outpatient psychiatrists may find it increasingly difficult to hospitalize acutely ill patients.
- Follow-up outpatient encounters tend to be spaced weeks to months apart and may consist only of a brief interview and cursory mental status examination update. The lack of opportunity to fully update the clinical history and examination may result in perpetuating an inaccurate diagnosis and treatment plan.
- Psychiatrists are increasingly utilized for medication management only (Weissman, 2011) leaving little time in follow-up visits for exploration of relevant clinical issues and psychotherapy (which may, if they were to occur, result in relevant disclosures by the patient that result in an amended and more accurate diagnosis and treatment plan).

S. G. Noffsinger (✉)
University Hospitals Cleveland Medical Center, Cleveland, OH, USA

Case Western Reserve University School of Medicine, Cleveland, OH, USA

Case Western Reserve University School of Law, Cleveland, OH, USA

University of Akron School of Law, Cleveland, OH, USA
e-mail: Stephen.Noffsinger@UHhospitals.org

S. R. Magalotti
Case Western Reserve University School of Medicine, Cleveland, OH, USA

Northcoast Behavioral Healthcare, Northfield, OH, USA

P. Ash et al. (eds.), *Malpractice and Liability in Psychiatry*, https://doi.org/10.1007/978-3-030-91975-7_20

- Outpatient psychiatrists may see up to 25 to 30 patients daily. The risk of a malpractice claim increases proportionally in relation to the volume of patients seen daily.
- Due to the relative isolation of outpatient practice, the outpatient psychiatrist may find it difficult to obtain informal consultation with colleagues to discuss difficult or complex cases and may find it difficult to refer treatment-refractory patients to colleagues for a second opinion.
- Many psychiatrists in rural settings practice in clinical areas for which they have not received formal training. For example, a rural adult psychiatrist may find themselves evaluating children, due to the lack of accessible child and adolescent psychiatry services in their locale.
- The outpatient general psychiatrist may be not fully conversant with the issues and legal concepts that may result in a malpractice claim. The general psychiatrist may lack specific expertise in violence risk assessment, suicide risk assessment, the duty to protect third parties, standards for civil commitment, confidentiality/privilege, boundary issues, and informed consent, which most often form the basis of malpractice claims.

The Physician-Patient Relationship in the Outpatient Psychiatry Setting

As described in Chap. 1, a plaintiff in malpractice litigation bears the burden of proving, by a preponderance of the evidence, the four elements of malpractice: (1) duty, (2) dereliction of duty, (3) damages, and (4) a direct relationship between the dereliction of duty and damages.

The physician-patient relationship is a legally recognized "special relationship" which, once established, confers upon the psychiatrist several specific duties, including the duty to maintain confidentiality and to evaluate and treat the patient within the standard of care. The establishment of the physician-patient relationship (and corresponding duties) is clear in most instances, when the patient has overtly sought treatment and the physician affirmatively acts on a patient's behalf by examining, diagnosing, treating, or agreeing to do so. Once established, the physician is obligated to continue to treat the patient or to properly terminate the relationship (Blake, 2012; Frierson & Joshi, 2019).

However, instances do arise in outpatient practice when it is unclear whether a physician-patient relationship has been established and, therefore, whether a duty exists. Various courts have found:

- A physician-patient relationship has not been established when a physician is requested, but declines, to evaluate and treat a patient (*Hurley v. Eddingfield*, 1901; *Childs v. Weis*, 1969).
- Depending on jurisdiction, a physician-patient relationship may not always be considered to have been established when an informal "curbside" consultation takes place, as a professional courtesy to a colleague (*Mead v. Adler*, 2009). However, great care should be utilized when performing these types of consultations (see Chaps. 1 and 22).
- A traditional physician-patient relationship is not established when the examination is conducted at the behest of a third party, such as an examination for an employer, insurance company, or court. The intent of the independent medical examination is to inform the third party not to treat or diagnose the patient (State v. Herendeen et al., 2005; Simon & Shuman, 2007; Blake, 2012). However, limited duties do flow from the limited physician-patient relationship in an independent medical examination, including the duties to do no harm, to inform the examinee of any life-threatening conditions, and to address emergent clinical needs (Gold & Davidson, 2007).
- With respect to attending physicians supervising residents, a physician-patient relationship can be established between a physician who contracts, agrees, undertakes, or otherwise assumes the obligation to provide resident supervision at a teaching hospital and a hospital patient with whom the physician had no direct or indirect contact (*Lownsbury v. VanBuren*, 2002).
- A physician-patient relationship may be established when a psychiatrist offers clinical advice on a medical condition in a non-medical setting, e.g., comments to an acquaintance at a social gathering (Chesanow, 2017).

Specific Areas of Risk in the Outpatient Psychiatry Setting

Suicide/Attempted Suicide

Suicide is a major risk inherent to many of the common mental disorders seen in outpatient psychiatric practice. Depressive disorders, bipolar and related disorders, substance use disorders, psychotic disorders, and anxiety disorders all carry an increased lifetime risk for suicide and/or suicide attempts. Unfortunately, the death of a patient by suicide is not an uncommon experience for psychiatrists (Puttagunta et al., 2014; Ruskin et al., 2004; Simon, 2002).

Suicide is a common cause of malpractice litigation. It was the primary allegation in 13% of the 2010–2019 Psychiatric Risk Management Services claims (PRMS, 2020). Psychiatrists cannot reliably and accurately predict suicide. Suicide may occur even when the psychiatric standard of care was met or exceeded. The standard of care requires that (1) psychiatrists screen for elevated suicide risk during the initial evaluation by inquiring about current suicidal ideation and past suicide attempts, (2) conduct a reasonable suicide risk assessment when there are indicators of increased suicide risk (such as suicidal ideation, intent, plan, or a recent suicide attempt), and (3) develop a documented treatment plan, in response to the suicide risk assessment, to address dynamic suicide risk factors that may be reduced through treatment interventions. Damages that may flow from the outpatient psychiatrist's failure to comply with the standard of care in this area include wrongful death, psychological and physical pain/suffering, exacerbation of the underlying mental disorder, and loss of consortium.

The outpatient general psychiatrist may face suicide malpractice litigation due to:

- *Failure to screen for suicidal thoughts*: It is generally accepted that the psychiatrist should inquire about suicidal thinking at the initial evaluation, and during subsequent follow-up encounters if indicated, based on clinical judgment. Failure to do so may deviate from the standard of care. A comprehensive suicide risk assessment (see below) is not required at every treatment encounter, unless clinically indicated. If a suicide screening is negative, no further inquiry is required, unless there is contradictory information. However, a patient who endorses suicidal thinking, or who has other indicators of increased suicide risk, should undergo a reasonably comprehensive suicide risk assessment.
- *Failure to conduct a comprehensive suicide risk assessment when indicated*: When the psychiatrist has knowledge that the patient is at increased suicide risk, a reasonably comprehensive suicide risk assessment should be completed. Factors that should trigger a suicide risk assessment include a patient or knowledgeable person who informs the psychiatrist of the patient's suicidal ideation, suicidal intent, suicidal threats, recent suicide attempt, significant depression, or behaviors indicating increased suicide risk (see Chap. 12 for details on conducting a comprehensive suicide risk assessment). Failure to conduct a reasonably comprehensive suicide risk assessment, when warranted, is a frequent claim in psychiatric malpractice litigation. Psychiatrists are generally not liable if, using good faith professional judgment, a comprehensive suicide risk assessment was conducted but the psychiatrist makes an erroneous judgment about the severity of suicide risk. However, the outright failure to conduct a reasonably comprehensive suicide risk assessment, when warranted, is a failure to use professional judgment and therefore less defensible.
- *Inaccurate or incomplete suicide risk assessment*: Conducting a faulty suicide risk assessment may lead the psychiatrist to underappreciate suicide risk and may lead to a poor clinical outcome and subsequent malpractice claim. Reasonably comprehensive suicide risk assessments should contain the consideration of relevant static and dynamic suicide risk factors, protective factors, and an overall rating of suicide risk. If important suicide risk factors are ignored or not taken into consideration, the suicide risk assessment may be unreliable and/or inaccurate.
- *Failure to address dynamic suicide risk factors in the treatment plan*: Once identified as a dynamic risk factor in a suicide risk assessment, to the extent possible, each dynamic risk factor should have one or more corresponding treatment interventions implemented to reduce that risk. For example, a current severe depressive disorder or active substance use disorder is a dynamic suicide risk factor. Failing to recommend a treatment intervention(s) for these dynamic suicide risk factors may be below the standard of care and potentially lead to a poor clinical outcome and malpractice litigation (Jabbarpor & Jayaram, 2011).
- *Relying only on the patient's denial of suicide risk factors*: Patients who truly wish to complete suicide may not openly disclose their suicidal thinking, suicidal intent, and/or suicide plan. They may intentionally and falsely deny these important risk factors with the goal of avoiding hospitalization and/or preserving their ability to die from suicide. For that reason, if there is suspicion that the patient is not being truthful, the outpatient psychiatrist may benefit from seeking and considering collateral data that may confirm (or fail to confirm) the patient's denial of suicidal thinking/intent/plan. Collateral data may consist of observational data that may help to gauge the severity of current psychological symptoms (sleep, appetite, activity level, concentration, anxiety) and/or interviews of collateral informants (significant other or knowledgeable family members).
- *Failure to develop a safety plan*: Suicidal thinking and suicidal intent occur on an intermittent basis in many patients with elevated suicide risk, and the transition to a suicide attempt is often linked to impulsivity (Nock et al., 2008). For that reason, the standard of care requires that outpatients who are known to have elevated suicide risk have a safety plan in place to be used should their suicidal thinking/intent return and/or intensify. Components of a safety plan may include, when an emergency presents, instructions to return to the hospital or emergency department; calling a suicide hotline or 911; or calling the treating psychiatrist's office to arrange for an urgent intervention. Failure to construct a safety plan and to instruct the patient on the safety plan may be the basis of a malpractice claim.
- *Failure to involve family in safety plan*: A malpractice claim may allege that the outpatient psychiatrist should have involved the patient's family in the patient's

treatment, by informing the family of the patient's elevated suicide risk and/or safety plan. If the patient consents to the disclosure of clinical information to the family, or the patient is incompetent, the family may be a valuable tool in assisting to monitor for and reduce suicide risk. However, the outpatient psychiatrist is bound by the duty of confidentiality and may not disclose the patient's clinical information to family members without consent. Family involvement in the safety plan, therefore, requires the patient's consent.

Failure to Hospitalize

The outpatient psychiatrist who negligently or intentionally fails to hospitalize a patient who, in fact, requires psychiatric hospitalization may face malpractice litigation. Typically, at issue is whether a reasonable psychiatrist would perceive that the least restrictive setting to treat the patient's mental disorder is psychiatric hospitalization or, conversely, continued outpatient treatment. Elevated suicide or violence risk and the inability to care for self are common issues that justify the need for psychiatric hospitalization. Damages that may flow from the outpatient psychiatrist's failure to hospitalize the patient may include wrongful death, harm to third parties, delay in treatment, and/or exacerbation of the patient's illness.

Malpractice claims may assert that because the symptoms and behavior flowing from a patient's mental disorder met legal criteria for involuntary hospitalization, the outpatient psychiatrist was obligated to psychiatrically hospitalize the patient. However, this is an incorrect application of the principles of civil commitment. Legal standards for commitment only *permit*, but do not *require*, the outpatient psychiatrist to involuntarily hospitalize the patient. The critical issue to evaluate is determining the least restrictive treatment setting to address the patient's clinical needs (hospitalization or continued outpatient treatment).

Improper Commitment

When an outpatient psychiatrist pursues civil commitment (involuntary hospitalization) for a patient that the psychiatrist knows (or should know) does not meet the legal standards for commitment, a malpractice claim on the basis of false imprisonment may occur. Civil commitment is a major infringement on a patient's liberty interests, is highly stigmatizing (*Addington v. Texas*, 1979), and should only occur when the legal criteria for commitment are present. Most states' civil commitment statutes include a good faith immunity clause, protecting the psychiatrist who erroneously commits a patient in good faith. However, a psychiatrist who knowingly commits a non-committable patient could face malpractice liability (see Chap. 17).

Medication Issues

Medication errors are commonly alleged in malpractice litigation and include:

- *Prescribing an improper class of medication*: Prescribing only an antidepressant for a patient with a psychotic disorder, prescribing an antidepressant without a mood stabilizer for a patient with bipolar I disorder, or prescribing an antipsychotic to treat a primary anxiety disorder may lead to legal liability on the basis of prescribing an improper class or type of psychotropic medication. The damages that may flow from an improper class of medication error may include failure to treat the underlying illness, causing an exacerbation of the mental illness, and/or side effects from the erroneously prescribed medication.
- *Medication dosage errors*: Prescribing too small of a medication dose, leading to little or no therapeutic benefit – e.g., prescribing haloperidol 0.25 mg daily to treat a patient in an acute exacerbation of schizophrenia or prescribing lithium 100 mg daily to treat acute mania. Prescribing an excessive medication dose, leading to drug toxicity – e.g., prescribing ziprasidone 160 mg twice daily to maintain symptom remission in bipolar I disorder.
- *Prescribing contraindicated medications*: e.g., prescribing meperidine and a monoamine oxidase inhibitor, causing a hypertensive crisis and stroke.
- *Prescribing medications contraindicated in a specific medical condition*: e.g., prescribing large doses of benzodiazepines to a patient with impaired respiratory function, causing respiratory distress.
- *Medication side effects*: Patients experience medication side effects, to a lesser or greater extent, on a frequent basis. Medication side effects, even severe, do not equate with malpractice liability. The key issues are whether the prescribing physician informed the patient of the material risks of experiencing medication side effects in the course of obtaining informed consent (see below), whether the medication was indicated, whether the medication dosage was appropriate, and whether the physician appropriately monitored the patient for side effects.
- *Failure to monitor for medication side effects*: e.g., failing to monitor for lithium-induced renal failure or hypothyroidism, lithium toxicity, clozapine-induced agranulocytosis, and/or tardive dyskinesia. Tardive dyskinesia may also lead to claims of failure to obtain informed consent for treatment with antipsychotic medication.

- *Failure to order medication blood levels (when available and appropriate)*: for example, failure to order lithium or valproate blood levels.
- *Polypharmacy*: e.g., prescribing multiple medications from the same class of medications (e.g., multiple antipsychotic medications without clinical justification) or prescribing multiple classes of medications that result in toxicity.
- *Failure to inquire about medication allergies.*
- *Prescribing lethal volumes of medications to a suicidal patient*: for example, prescribing a 90-day supply of tricyclic antidepressants to a patient at high risk for suicide, therefore providing the means to complete suicide.
- *Creating drug dependence*: e.g., prescribing benzodiazepines on a long-term basis, leading to physiologic dependence, without informing the patient of the risk of dependence.
- *Prescribing off-label without informed consent*: Psychiatrists frequently prescribe psychotropic medications for non-FDA-approved indications, which is reasonable and acceptable. When prescribing off-label, the psychiatrist should inform the patient that the medication is being prescribed for an other-than-FDA-approved condition, so that the patient can truly give informed consent. There must be clinical justification and support in the scientific literature for prescribing for other-than-FDA-approved indications.
- *Failure to prescribe medications when indicated*: Psychiatrists cannot offer only the treatment options that they happen to personally favor or specialize in. Instead, the psychiatrist must develop and offer reasonable and ordinary treatment plans that contain mainstream treatment interventions. In a noteworthy case (*Osheroff v. Chestnut Lodge*, 1985), a malpractice jury found legal liability when the treating psychiatrist offered only psychodynamic psychotherapy for a patient with a severe major depressive disorder, and not antidepressant medications.

Misdiagnosis

Reasonable, effective treatment in the outpatient setting is possible when, after an appropriate evaluation, a reasonable diagnosis has been formulated based on the available data. An inaccurate diagnosis based either on a faulty database (e.g., failure to interview the patient, conduct a mental status examination, and/or review critical medical records) or misapplication of DSM-5 diagnostic criteria can lead to malpractice litigation. For example, if a psychiatrist misdiagnoses a psychotic patient as having only a depressive disorder, and adopts a treatment plan to treat only the misdiagnosed depressive disorder, the psychiatrist may face malpractice liability. An incorrect diagnosis was the primary allegation in 4% of the PRMS claims from 2010 to 2019 (PRMS, 2020).

Long-Term Treatment Issues

Malpractice litigation may arise over the course of extended outpatient treatment, due to allegations of:

- An improper or incomplete treatment plan
- Failure to adjust the diagnosis and treatment plan over the course of treatment, as additional clinical information becomes available through recurrent clinical encounters
- Insufficient or too infrequent outpatient treatment encounters
- Engaging in the wrong type of outpatient treatment
- Failure to refer to psychotherapist or internist/specialist for necessary consultation

Coordination of Care

Psychiatric patients in the outpatient setting may simultaneously receive mental health services from multiple providers. Patients frequently receive medication management from a psychiatrist and psychotherapy from an allied mental health professional. Malpractice litigation may allege that the outpatient psychiatrist failed to share clinical information and coordinate clinical care with the other treating mental health providers (see Chap. 3).

Breach of Confidentiality

The outpatient psychiatrist has a duty to keep the patient's personal and clinical information safeguarded. This duty of confidentiality is created by the physician-patient relationship and is described by HIPAA and state privacy laws. Narrow exceptions to confidentiality exist (e.g., child/elder abuse, public health issues, duty to protect, emergency coordination of care). If an outpatient psychiatrist breaches their patient's confidentiality needlessly, malpractice litigation may arise (see Chap. 15). This was the primary allegation in 5% of the 2010–2019 PRMS claims (PRMS, 2020).

Boundary Violations

The outpatient psychiatrist may face malpractice litigation for not observing professional boundaries (Friedman & Martinez, 2019). A boundary violation involves the patient being exploited or used for the mental health professional's own benefit or gratification. Boundary violations, in the most extreme form, involve sexual contact between a psychiatrist and patient (or former patient), which is never appropriate. A sexual boundary violation is never the patient's responsibility, as there is an inherent power imbalance in the physician-patient relationship making the patient incapable of providing informed consent for such activity (see Chap. 14).

Boundary violations are a less frequent malpractice allegation. A boundary violation was the primary allegation in only 2% of cases (PRMS, 2020) from 2010 to 2019. Most importantly, many psychiatric malpractice insurance policies treat sexual activity as an intentional tort and exclude liability coverage, leaving damages to be paid by the psychiatrist.

Harm to Third Parties

Outpatients with severe mental disorders may present elevated violence risk. Paranoid delusions and command hallucinations (Saxton et al., 2018) are especially concerning for violence among outpatients. Psychiatrists may evaluate violence risk using their clinical judgment and/or one of the many available violence risk assessment instruments. Despite research efforts, there is no generally accepted method or assessment instrument used to predict future violence reliably and accurately (Fazel et al., 2012). However, the standard of care requires the outpatient psychiatrist, when indicated, to conduct a good faith, reasonable violence risk assessment using their professional judgment, and to develop a treatment plan to address dynamic violence risk factors. Failure to do so may result in malpractice claims or wrongful death or physical injury damages.

When an outpatient harms a third party (such as a family member, acquaintance, or random person), malpractice litigation may result. *Tarasoff v. Regents* (1976) is a landmark California case that first outlined an outpatient mental health professional's duty to protect third parties. After *Tarasoff*, many states adopted duty to protect standards via statute and/or case law, describing specific circumstances when the duty to protect may attach and how the mental health professional may discharge their duty. The outpatient mental health professional's legal duty to protect obligations varies by state. Every outpatient practitioner should be aware of their state's relevant statutes and case law. State's legal standards vary, both with respect to civil immunity provisions and permissibility of breaching confidentiality (see Chap. 13 for more information) (National Conference of State Legislatures, 2018).

In the majority of jurisdictions, the duty to protect attaches only if the mental health professional has knowledge that the patient has made an explicit threat of causing serious physical harm or death to a readily identifiable person and the mental health professional believes that the patient has the ability and intent to carry out the threat (see, e.g., Ohio Revised Code 2305.51). Duty to protect statutes often describe the manner in which the mental health professional can discharge their duty, e.g., by psychiatrically hospitalizing the patient, breaching confidentiality and notifying law enforcement and/or the potential victim of the risk and/or conducting a good faith, reasonable violence risk assessment and tailoring the patient's treatment plan accordingly (*Littleton v. Good Samaritan*, 1988). Duty to warn or protect claims was the primary allegation in 1% of PRMS claims from 2010 to 2019 (PRMS, 2020).

Recently, the Supreme Court of Washington, in contrast with other jurisdictions, expanded the outpatient duty to protect in the State of Washington by requiring psychiatrists to exercise "reasonable care to act consistent with the standards of the mental health profession, in order to protect the foreseeable victims of his or her patient" even in the absence of an explicit threat toward an identifiable victim (*Volk v. DeMeerleer*, 2016; Resnick & Saxton, 2019).

Mismanagement of Medical Conditions

The outpatient psychiatrist may face legal liability for the failure to detect, diagnose, or manage a medical condition, independently or through consultation with other medical professionals:

- *Failure to detect evolving medical conditions and/or mistaking medical conditions for mental disorders*: e.g., an outpatient psychiatrist misperceives that their geriatric patient's evolving cognitive deficits are caused by a depressive disorder (not their recent head trauma) and fails to detect a subdural hematoma, causing morbidity for the patient and legal liability for the psychiatrist.
- *Failure to manage a medical condition*: e.g., a psychiatrist manages their patient's hypertension and lithium-induced hypothyroidism and elects not to refer the patient to an internist or endocrinologist. In the event of a bad outcome, malpractice may be alleged.
- *Failure to order relevant laboratory testing (to detect or manage a medical condition)*: e.g., failure to order brain imaging when indicated, failure to order thyroid function or renal function tests in patients prescribed lithium, and failure to monitor blood glucose, lipids, and cholesterol in a patient prescribed a second-generation antipsychotic medication.

Lack of Informed Consent

Informed consent consists of three requisite elements: information, competency, and voluntariness. Each element of informed consent may be the subject of malpractice litigation for the outpatient psychiatrist:

- *Information*: The psychiatrist, before prescribing and beginning a course of treatment, should disclose to a patient information about the proposed treatment that a reasonable patient would believe is material (*White v. Leimbach*, 2011; Noffsinger, 2012). Typically, this information includes the benefits and material risks of the proposed treatment and common side effects of the treatment. Psychiatric malpractice cases that allege lack of informed consent commonly assert that the treating psychiatrist failed to disclose important side effects of a proposed treatment. Examples include the failure to inform a patient that antipsychotic medications may cause tardive dyskinesia and/or metabolic syndrome or that clozapine may cause agranulocytosis, seizure, or severe constipation. The black box warning required by the Food and Drug Administration for certain antidepressant medications regarding the risk of suicidal behaviors in children and young adults may give rise to a lack of informed consent claim. Less commonly, informed consent claims may allege that the psychiatrist failed to warn the patient of the risks of discontinuing treatment (*Williamson v. Liptzin*, 2000).
- *Competency*: To competently consent to a proposed treatment, the patient must be able to understand the nature of their illness, the risks and benefits of the proposed treatment, the risks and benefits of alternative treatments, and the prognosis with and without the proposed treatment and be able to make a rational decision about accepting the proposed treatment. Outpatient psychiatrists should implement treatment plans only after reasonably confirming that their patient competently agrees to the treatment plan; otherwise, a lack of informed consent claim may result, even if the willing but incompetent patient agrees to the treatment.
- *Voluntariness*: Claims for coerced (involuntary) treatment occur mainly on inpatient psychiatric units and rarely occur in the outpatient setting.

Abandonment

The outpatient general psychiatrist should not abruptly terminate a patient's treatment without sufficient notice or a referral to another mental health practitioner. The outpatient psychiatrist is not obligated to evaluate and treat every patient that seeks treatment, nor is the outpatient psychiatrist obligated to continue to treat patients who are threatening, who are disruptive, or who fail to pay for services. However, the psychiatrist should give the patient ample notice of the termination and seek to refer the patient to another qualified mental health professional (see Chap. 17).

Practicing Outside of Expertise

Outpatient general psychiatrists should confine their practice to areas within their training and expertise. Evaluating and treating medical conditions outside the realm of psychiatry (or a psychiatrist's training in general medicine) may lead to a poor clinical outcome and malpractice claim. The outpatient general psychiatrist may be able to manage their patient's common medical conditions (diabetes, hypertension, heart disease, etc.) but should refrain from interpreting radiographic studies, polysomnograms, and EEGs, or practice in other areas, unless specifically trained in these areas.

Reducing Risk in the Outpatient Psychiatry Setting

Psychiatrists should take the following steps to reduce their risk of malpractice liability:

- Be thoroughly familiar with suicide and violence risk factors.
- Screen for suicidal thinking on a regular basis, especially with symptom exacerbation.
- Conduct a reasonably comprehensive suicide risk assessment when there are indicators of increased acute suicide risk.
- Implement and document specific interventions to treat elevated dynamic suicide risk factors.
- Do not rely exclusively on denial of suicidal thinking or suicidal intent from patients with increased acute suicide risk.
- Develop and implement a safety plan for patients at increased suicide risk.
- Conduct a reasonably comprehensive violence risk assessment when there are indicators of increased acute violence risk.
- Implement and document specific interventions to treat elevated dynamic violence risk factors.
- Be familiar with and implement their state's duty to protect laws.
- Know their state's involuntary hospitalization criteria.
- Carefully analyze the need for psychiatric hospitalization during periods of symptom exacerbation, balancing the patient's clinical needs with treatment in the least restrictive setting.
- Use (and document) DSM-5 criteria to justify clinical diagnoses.
- Obtain and review past psychiatric records, which may contain important clinical information.
- Make diagnoses using accepted methodology and a sufficient database.

- Prescribe psychotropic medications for FDA-approved conditions.
- When prescribing medications for non-FDA-approved conditions ("off-label"), clearly document the clinical rationale for the medication, and document that the patient was informed of and consented to the off-label use of the medication.
- Prescribe the appropriate class and dosage of psychotropic medications.
- Be aware of the relative and absolute contraindications for psychotropic medications.
- Inform the patient of the material risks and benefits of proposed treatments (including medication side effects) prior to obtaining informed consent.
- Reasonably ensure that the patient is competent to consent to treatments that you recommended.
- For incompetent patients, obtain consent for treatment from a substitute decision-maker (guardian, court, etc.).
- Be aware of FDA black box warnings and inform patients about them during the informed consent process.
- Monitor for medication side effects.
- Order medication blood levels when indicated.
- Avoid polypharmacy.
- Inquire about medication allergies.
- Do not prescribe lethal volumes of medications to patients at elevated suicide risk.
- Advise the patient of the risk of physiologic dependence when prescribing benzodiazepines.
- When warranted, revise the diagnosis and adjust the treatment plan as additional relevant clinical information is obtained.
- Schedule follow-up evaluations with sufficient frequency to adequately monitor the patient's clinical condition and response to treatment.
- Refer the patient to other health professionals (internist, neurologist, psychotherapist, etc.) when clinically indicated.
- Seek to coordinate clinical care with the patient's other treating mental health professionals.
- Maintain confidentiality of the patient's privileged clinical information.
- Breach confidentiality only with the patient's authorization, or in legally mandated exceptions to confidentiality.
- Avoid boundary violations.
- Be alert to the possibility of evolving or new medical conditions.
- Practice within his or her area of expertise.
- Refrain from abruptly terminating treatment.
- Seek consultation on difficult or complex cases, or when patients fail to respond to standard treatments.
- Be aware that documentation is critical, both in preventing and defending malpractice litigation. Progress notes should be legible (preferably typed) and descriptive and should document the rationale underlying the diagnosis, treatment plan, risk assessment, and decision-making process in areas that most often lead to malpractice claims.
- Psychiatrists should avoid offering clinical advice to non-patients or in non-clinical settings.
- Outpatient psychiatrists should stay abreast of evolving standards of treatment by reviewing practice guidelines, new advances, and new research that guides appropriate treatment. This is best accomplished through participation in an active continuing medical education program (Frierson & Joshi, 2019).

Key Points

- General outpatient psychiatrists bear malpractice risk. Common malpractice allegations include suicide, medication errors, misdiagnosis, harm to third parties, failure to hospitalize, lack of informed consent, breach of confidentiality, and mismanagement of co-morbid medical conditions. Documentation is critical, both in preventing and defending malpractice litigation.
- Assess and mitigate suicide risk. Screen for suicidal thinking on a regular basis. Conduct a suicide risk assessment when indicated. Address dynamic risk factors for suicide. Develop a safety plan. Do not prescribe lethal quantities of medication in patients at increased risk of suicide. Do not rely exclusively on denial of suicidal thinking or intent in patients with increased acute suicide risk.
- Assess and mitigate violence risk. Conduct a violence risk assessment when indicated. Address dynamic risk factors for violence. Know and follow your state's duty to protect laws.
- Consider the need for psychiatric hospitalization during periods of symptom exacerbation. Balance the patient's clinical needs with treatment in the least restrictive setting. Be familiar with your state's involuntary hospitalization criteria.
- Be mindful when prescribing. Prescribe psychotropic medications for FDA-approved conditions. Explain and document the use of off-label medication. Inform the patient or substitute decision-maker of the material risks and benefits of proposed treatments prior to obtaining informed consent.
- Diagnose thoughtfully. Use DSM-5 criteria to justify clinical diagnoses based on the patient interview and relevant collateral information. When warranted, revise the diagnosis and adjust the treatment plan as additional relevant clinical information is obtained.
- Follow up appropriately. Schedule follow-up evaluations with sufficient frequency to adequately monitor the patient's clinical condition and response to treatment.
- Seek consultation when clinically indicated. Be alert to the possibility of evolving or new medical conditions.

Coordinate care with the patient's other mental health professionals.

- Maintain confidentiality. Breach confidentiality only with the patient's authorization, or in legally mandated exceptions to confidentiality.

References

Addington v. Texas, 441 U.S. 418 (1979).

Beck, A.J., Page, C., Buche, J., Rittman, D., & Gaiser, M. (2018). University of Michigan Behavioral Health Workforce Research Center. Estimating the Distribution of the U.S. Psychiatric Subspecialist Workforce. UMSPH.

Blake, V. (2012). When is a patient-physician relationship established? *American Medical Association Journal of Ethics, 14*(5), 403–406.

Cherry, D., Albert, M., & McCaig, L. F. (2018). Mental health-related physician office visits by adults aged 18 and over: United States, 2012–2014. *NCHS Data Brief, no 311*. National Center for Health Statistics.

Chesanow, N. (2017). *When friends and family ambush you for free medical advice*. Retrieved from: https://www.medscape.com/viewarticle/882826_3

Childs v. Weis, 440 SW2d 104 (Ct Civ App Tx 1969).

Fazel, S., Singh, J. P., Doll, H., & Grann, M. (2012). Use of risk assessment instruments to predict violence and antisocial behaviour in 73 samples involving 24827 people: Systematic review and meta-analysis. *British Medical Journal, 345*, e4692. https://doi.org/10.1136/bmj.e4692

Frierson, R. L., & Joshi, K. G. (2019). Malpractice law and psychiatry: An overview. *Focus, 17*(4), 332–336.

Friedman, S. H., & Martinez, R. P. (2019). Boundaries, professionalism and malpractice in psychiatry. *Focus, 17*(4), 365–371.

Gold, L., & Davidson, J. E. (2007). Do you understand your risk? Liability and third-party evaluations in civil litigation. *Journal of the American Academy of Psychiatry and the Law, 35*(2), 200–210.

Hurley v. Eddingfield, 156 Ind 416, 59 NE 1058 (Ind 1901).

Jabbarpour, Y. M., & Jayaram, G. (2011). Suicide risk: Navigating the failure modes. *Focus, 9*(2), 186–193.

Lee, S., Rothbard, A. B., & Noll, E. L. (2012). Length of inpatient stay of persons with serious mental illness: Effects of hospital and regional characteristics. *Psychiatric Services, 63*(9), 889–895.

Littleton v. Good Samaritan Hospital Health Ctr., 39 Ohio St. 3d 86, 529 N.E.2d 449 (Ohio 1988).

Lownsbury v. Van Buren, 762 NE2d 354 (Ohio 2002).

Mead v. Adler, 231 Or App 451, 220 P3d 119 (Or 2009).

National Conference of State Legislators. (2018, Oct 12). *Mental Health Professionals' Duty to Warn*. Retrieved from: https://www.ncsl.org/research/health/mental-health-professionals-duty-to-warn.aspx

Nock, M., Borges, G., Bromet, E., Alonso, J., Angermeyer, M., Beautrais, A., & Williams, D. (2008). Cross-national prevalence and risk factors for suicidal ideation, plans and attempts. *British Journal of Psychiatry, 192*(2), 98–105. https://doi.org/10.1192/bjp.bp.107.040113

Noffsinger, S. G. (2012). *White v. Leimbech*: Informed consent updated. *Ohio Psychiatric Physician Association Insight Matters*. Spring 2012:19.

Ohio Revised Code section 2305.51.

Osheroff v. Chestnut Lodge, Inc., 62 Md. App. 519, 490 A.2d 720, cert. denied, 304 Md. 163, 497 A.2d 1163 (1985).

Professional Risk Management Services (PRMS). (2020). Cause of Loss – Claims and Lawsuits, 2010–2019.

Puttagunta, R., Lomax, M. E., McGuinness, J. E., & Coverdale, J. (2014). What is the prevalence of the experience of death of a patient by suicide among medical students and residents? A systematic review. *Academic Psychiatry, 38*(5), 538–541.

Resnick, P., & Saxton, A. (2019). Malpractice liability due to patient violence. *Focus, 17*(4), 343–348.

Ruskin, R., Sakinofsky, I., Bagby, R. M., Dickens, S., & Sousa, G. (2004). Impact of patient suicide on psychiatrists and psychiatric trainees. *Academic Psychiatry, 28*(2), 104–110.

Satiani, A., Niedermier, J., Satiani, B., & Svendsen, D. P. (2018). Projected workforce of psychiatrists in the United States: A population analysis. *Psychiatric Services, 69*(6), 710–713.

Saxton, A., Resnick, P., & Noffsinger, S. (2018). Chief complaint: Homicidal. Assessing violence risk. *Current Psychiatry, 17*(5), 27–35.

Shah, B., Leontieva, L., & Megna, J. L. (2020). Shifting trends in admission patterns of an acute inpatient psychiatric unit in the state of New York. *Cureus, 12*(7), e9285. https://doi.org/10.7759/cureus.9285

Simon, R. I. (2002). Suicide risk assessment: What is the standard of care? *Journal of the American Academy of Psychiatry and the Law, 30*(3), 340–344.

Simon, R. I., & Shuman, D. W. (2007). The doctor-patient relationship. *Focus, 5*(4), 423–431.

Sorrentino, R. M., DiCola, L. A., & Friedman, S. H. (2020). COVID-19, civil commitment and ethics. *Journal of the American Academy of Psychiatry and the Law, 48*(4), 436–441.

State v. Herendeen et al., 279 Ga 323, 613 SE 2d 647 (Ga 2005).

Tarasoff v. Regents of the University of California, 17 Cal. 3d 425 (Cal. 1976).

Volk v. DeMeerler, 386 P.3d, 254, 262 (Wash 2016).

Weissman, S. (2011). Are we training psychiatrists to provide only medication management? *Psychiatric Times, 28*(6).

White v. Leimbach, 131 Ohio St.3d 21, 2011-Ohio-6238.

Williamson v. Liptzin, 141 N.C. App. 1, 539 S.E.2d 313 (N.C. Ct. App. 2000).

21 Child and Adolescent Psychiatry

Peter Ash

While liability issues in the treatment of children and adolescents are similar in many ways to those involved in the assessment and treatment of adults, developmental differences, the involvement of parents in making treatment decisions, and the legal status of minors give rise to some significant differences. This chapter highlights these differences in the most common areas in which work with child and adolescent patients gives rise to malpractice actions and complaints to medical licensing boards.

Areas of Risk

Training and Credentialing

While a general psychiatrist who has not completed a fellowship in child and adolescent (C&A) psychiatry can legally treat children and adolescents, in the event of a malpractice suit, the psychiatrist's training in C&A psychiatry will be scrutinized, and the plaintiff may try to prove or imply to the jury that a non-fellowship trained psychiatrist should not be treating children at all. Therefore, a general psychiatrist who treats youth will want to be able to clearly demonstrate training and skill in treating the age range that included the child plaintiff. In jurisdictions that utilize a national standard of care (as opposed to a local standard), the psychiatrist will typically be held to the standard of a fully trained C&A psychiatrist. This can pose a dilemma to a general psychiatrist who wants to help children and adolescents in need, but who is practicing in a location where there is a grave shortage of C&A psychiatrists (e.g., much of the country, especially rural areas) (American Academy of Child & Adolescent Psychiatry, 2021).

P. Ash (✉)
Psychiatry and Law Service, Department of Psychiatry and Behavioral Sciences, Emory University, Atlanta, GA, USA
e-mail: peter.ash@emory.edu

Suicide Risk Assessment

From 1999 to 2007, the rate of suicide in 13–17-year-olds dropped about 25% to 3.58/100,00, and then over the next 12 years, it doubled to 7.12/100,000 in 2019; suicide became the second leading cause of death in that age group, accounting for about a quarter of all deaths (Centers for Disease Control and Prevention, 2021). Suicide is much less common in preadolescents than in adolescents or older age groups (0.57 per 100,000 for 6- to 12-year-olds) (Centers for Disease Control and Prevention, 2021).

Patient suicide is the second most common malpractice claim against psychiatrists who treat children and adolescents, after the fairly non-specific claim of "incorrect treatment" (Professional Risk Management Services, Personal communication, 2019). The general principles of assessing an adolescent's suicide risk are similar to assessing such risk in adults (see Chap. 12), but there are a number of significant differences, summarized in Table 21.1.

Suicidal ideation and attempts are surprisingly common in adolescents. The 2019 Youth Risk Behavior survey of high school students found that in the previous year, over 18% of high school students had seriously considered suicide, over 15% had made a plan, over 8% had made an attempt, and 2.5% had made an attempt that resulted in an injury sufficiently severe that it had to be treated by a doctor or nurse (Ivey-Stephenson et al., 2020). Girls had higher rates in all four categories than boys, although adolescent boys die from suicide at three times the rate of girls (15.88 per 100,000 for boys 15–18 years old in 2018 and 5.07 per 100,000 for girls) (Centers for Disease Control and Prevention, 2021). Given that the actual rate of suicides for 15- to 18-year-olds in 2018 was 10.59 per 100,000 (0.0106%), the ratio of seriously considering suicide and having a plan, generally considered to be a high-risk situation, to death from suicide is well over 1000:1. In this population, the specificity for accurately predicting suicide based simply on the risk factors of having suicidal ideation and a plan is quite low.

P. Ash et al. (eds.), *Malpractice and Liability in Psychiatry*, https://doi.org/10.1007/978-3-030-91975-7_21

Table 21.1 Key differences between suicidal adults and suicidal adolescents

Category	Compared to adults, for adolescents:
Risk factors	Suicide accounts for a higher proportion of all deaths
	Suicidal ideation is more common
	Suicide attempts are more common
	Disruptive behavior disorders (e.g., conduct disorder, oppositional defiant disorder) increase risk
	Contagion effects are more powerful
Diagnostic differences	Psychotic disorders are much less common
Symptoms	Although suicidal ideation is more common, suicidal ideation is more likely to be denied when asked about
	Lethality of means is more commonly misjudged
Treatment	SSRIs require more monitoring
	Family involvement in treatment is more important
Legal status	Legal consent for treatment usually needs to be provided by someone other than patient
	Hospitalization over the patient's objection, via parental consent, can often be accomplished without resorting to civil commitment
	Patient's responsibility for treatment compliance is reduced
Aftermath of completed suicide	Full discussion with parents less constrained by confidentiality limitations because parents control record release

Adapted from Ash (2012)

While a prior suicide attempt is often considered the most significant single risk factor, it is present in only a quarter of suicide deaths, as approximately three-quarters of youth suicide deaths occurred at the first attempt (McKean et al., 2018). Further complicating the issue of foreseeability of adolescent suicide, studies suggest that over half of the adolescents who died by suicide had a precipitating stressor that occurred within the 2 weeks preceding the suicide, many of which occurred within the 24 hours preceding the suicide, which allows for only a short time window for assessment and intervention (Annor et al., 2018; Marttunen et al., 1993; Harvard Injury Control Research Center, 2021).

These findings imply that historical risk factors alone have very limited predictive power in an individual case. Kingsbury (1993) identified four factors that are useful to consider in assessing suicidal intent in youth following a recent attempt (see Table 21.2). Malpractice actions involving adolescent suicide generally focus on the adequacy of the risk assessment and the steps taken to ameliorate risk. It is important in a risk assessment to consider the details specific to the case and document the reasoning used in weighing the identified risk factors in determining an intervention plan. Failure to identify or consider identified risk factors can lead to a plaintiff verdict. If the clinician identified and considered the risk factors, then the issue is one of clinical judgment.

Table 21.2 Assessing lethal intent of a recent suicide attempt

Clinical component	Example issues
Belief about intent	Purpose of the attempt Expectation of dying Lethality of means
Preparation	Saving up pills for overdose Saying good-bye Planning
Concealment	Planning attempt to avoid discovery: Timing so no one will rescue Choosing an isolated place
Communication	Telling others, directly or indirectly, about suicidal thinking Suicide note

Based on findings of Kingsbury (1993)

The most common issue in malpractice cases involving suicide of a child or adolescent outpatient is whether the patient should have been hospitalized. A safety plan that involves parents providing sufficient support, structure, and surveillance may allow a patient to be reasonably treated as an outpatient. Parental involvement and cooperation with the safety plan needs to be carefully assessed. Means restriction is also important: Brent et al. (2000) made the surprising finding that less than a third of parents of depressed adolescents were compliant with a recommendation to remove guns from the home.

When a suicidal adult declines a recommendation for hospitalization, the question becomes whether the patient meets civil commitment criteria. In most jurisdictions, since only a parent's consent is required for voluntary admission of a minor child, hospitalization can usually be achieved without needing to meet more stringent civil commitment criteria.

Documentation of a comprehensive assessment of suicidal risk is the best protection against a malpractice case, as a prospective plaintiff attorney will be scrutinizing the record carefully before taking the case (see Chap. 7). In difficult cases, such as where there are some risk factors but the clinician thinks, on balance, hospitalization is not necessary, remember Jonas Rappeport's (1984) suggestion: "When in doubt, Shout!" Ask another clinician to assess the patient and family, and document his or her judgment. The question in a malpractice case is whether the clinician acted reasonably. The opinion of a second reasonable clinician that was formulated at the time of decision can go a long way in undercutting the later opinion of a plaintiff expert who wasn't there and who had the advantage of knowing what ultimately occurred.

Medication

After "incorrect treatment" and suicide, medication issues are the most common issue in malpractice cases involving minor plaintiffs (Professional Risk Management Services, 2015).

Consent Issues

When a case involves an adverse reaction to medication, the issue of the adequacy of informed consent will be scrutinized. Most commonly, parents provide consent for the psychiatric treatment of minors, although depending on the jurisdiction, adolescents of a certain age may be able to provide legal consent in certain situations. While the assent of a minor is clinically useful, a legal consent is needed for prescribing (except in certain emergencies), so it is important for clinicians to be familiar with the laws in their own state. About half the states allow some adolescents to make some treatment decisions related to mental health or substance abuse care, most commonly either by specifying a specific age below 18 for consent or by allowing "mature minors" (generally not clearly defined) to consent (Kerwin et al., 2015). In those jurisdictions where a minor can consent, that consent authority is typically in addition to the ability of parents or guardians to consent. The clinician should keep in mind that a natural parent may not always be the appropriate decision-maker, such as when only one parent following divorce is awarded legal decision-making authority, when parental rights are terminated, or when the parent is a step-parent who has not legally adopted the child.

Off-Label Prescribing

Off-label prescribing is considerably more common with children than with adults, reflecting the fact that pharmaceutical companies frequently do not conduct the additional research studies necessary to obtain Food and Drug Agency (FDA) approval for use in children. Clinicians need not restrict prescribing to drugs that have received FDA approval for use with children – in fact, off-label prescribing occurs in about half of prescriptions written by C&A psychiatrists (Kearns & Hawley, 2014) – and the FDA and the courts have long recognized that such use is allowed (Beck & Azari, 1998). Good risk management nevertheless dictates that the prescribing clinician should be careful to obtain informed consent and document that such consent was obtained.

Black Box Warnings

A black box warning is the FDA's strictest warning highlighted in prescribing information. In 2004 the FDA began requiring a black box warning in product labeling of selective serotonin reuptake inhibitors (SSRIs) based on a pooled analysis which found that reports of suicidal thinking in children and adolescents increased from 2% on placebo to 4% on active drug (Hammad et al., 2006). In 2007, the FDA modified the warning to say that for those under age 25, youth on SSRIs should be "monitored appropriately" for adverse side effects, but did not define what constitutes appropriate monitoring (U.S. Food and Drug Administration, 2007). As a result, in a malpractice case involving an adverse event involving self-harm when a child or adolescent was on an SSRI, documentation of the informed consent process and the clinician's monitoring will be closely scrutinized. The FDA has issued other black box warnings for use in children and adolescents: the list of psychotropic medications with such warnings includes most first-generation antidepressants (amitriptyline, imipramine, and derivatives), aripiprazole (concern for suicidal thoughts in youth), valproic acid (birth defects if given to pregnant girls), opioids, and benzodiazepines when prescribed concomitantly with opioids.

Because black box warnings carry the official imprimatur of the FDA, good risk management dictates that the psychiatrist address those risks explicitly with the person consenting to the medication, and it is good practice to document that those possible side effects were discussed.

Ongoing Monitoring

The informed consent process begins when a medication is first prescribed, but is actually an ongoing process that takes into account how the patient is progressing and the development of side effects. Some side effects, such as weight gain or tardive dyskinesia, typically occur only after an initial treatment period or when prescribing medications long-term.

Documentation

A useful perspective in deciding how much to document is to assume that an adverse reaction to the medication occurred and the patient's attorney is scrutinizing the record. What information would the clinician want in the record? While the note need not be a verbatim transcript of the discussion, it should address that the risks and benefits were discussed, and particularly note that black box issues were talked about (for more details, see Chap. 16).

Danger to Others

Violence is surprisingly common in adolescence: self-report studies document that by age 17, 30–40% of boys and 16–32% of girls have committed a serious violent offense, defined as an aggravated assault, robbery, gang fight, or rape (U.S. Dept. Health and Human Services, 2001), although most of these offenses do not result in arrest. The onset of serious violence towards others is an adolescent phenomenon: the peak age for the onset of violent offending is in mid-adolescence, and it is uncommon for a person to first become violent after age 21 (Bernat et al., 2012; Elliott, 1994). Fortunately, for the majority of adolescents who engage in violence, violent offending is an adolescent phenomenon: most adolescents who engage in violence do not continue on to adult criminal careers (U.S. Dept. Health and Human Services, 2001).

Many of the principles in assessing violence risk in adults (see Chap. 13) also apply to work with adolescents, but because of developmental and legal differences, there are some significant differences, summarized in Table 21.3.

Aggression towards others in preadolescents is often a focus of clinical attention, but because of the lower lethality associated with violent preadolescents, aggression does not often lead to serious harm of the sort that gives rise to malpractice cases. With adolescent patients, the risk for violence tends to fall into two categories that require significantly different approaches. The first group includes those whose violence appears caused by mental illness or a severe developmental disorder. Examples include the psychotic and paranoid youth, the adolescent with an impulse control disorder, and patients with a developmental disorder that includes serious deficits in social judgment. For this group, the potential victim is most often a family member or someone the adolescent knows. Proper assessment and treatment of the underlying mental disorder is the main focus in achieving risk reduction. The second group includes those adolescents whose behavior involves criminal activity towards relative strangers and who are often involved with or referred by the juvenile justice system. These youth typically have a history of conduct disorder, multiple prior diverse offenses, repeated violent behavior, and association with delinquent peers. While this delinquent group also has a high rate of diagnosable mental disorder – studies suggest incarcerated youth have about triple the rate of normal populations (Teplin et al., 2002) – their violence risk is not easily explained by their mental disorder (Elkington et al., 2015). For this group, successful interventions to reduce violence risk focus on strategies that address criminogenic factors, such as involvement with a delinquent peer group. Because their delinquent behavior is driven by factors other than mental illness, treatment of the underlying mental conditions, while useful in alleviating suffering, has less effect on reducing violence risk.

Table 21.3 Key differences between violent adults and violent adolescents

Category	Compared to adults, for adolescents:
Risk factors	Impulsive violence towards others is more common
	Homicide accounts for a higher proportion of all deaths
	Violent careers are shorter
	Gang membership is a leading risk factor
	Psychosis and substance abuse are weaker risk factors
	School shooters are more likely to communicate threats to other students prior to shooting
Diagnostic differences	Psychotic disorder is less common
Behavior patterns	Violent behavior occurs more often by groups
Treatment	Peer group considerations are key
	Family involvement in treatment is more important
Legal	Someone other than the patient typically provides legal consent
	May be incompetent to waive rights against self-incrimination
	Hospitalization over the patient's objection can often be accomplished without resorting to civil commitment
	Patient's responsibility for treatment compliance is reduced
	Much criminal behavior is adjudicated in juvenile court

Adapted from Ash (2008)

As with adults, malpractice cases involving violence occur when a youth has seriously injured someone, and the question is whether the violence was reasonably foreseeable. If so, did the psychiatrist intervene appropriately, such as by hospitalizing the patient. As with adults at risk for suicide, asking about guns is important. Despite the fact that federal law makes it illegal for minors to own a handgun (Youth Handgun Safety Act, 1996), particularly in the delinquent group, access or ownership of handguns is very high. For example, in 2019, 6.7% of boys and 2% of girls reported carrying a gun other than for sport or hunting (Centers for Disease Control and Prevention (CDC), 2021). Usage is much higher among incarcerated delinquents, where studies have found rates of gun ownership of over 70% (Ash et al., 1996; Webster et al., 2002). With patients whose risk for violence is assessed as stemming from mental illness, risk assessment tends to focus on dynamic factors, such as particular stressors or triggers and details of parent-child interactions. For the more delinquent group, a number of risk assessment measures have been developed and may be utilized, including the Structured Assessment of Violence Risk for Youth (SAVRY); the Psychopathy Checklist, Youth Version (PCL-YV); and the Level of Service/Case Management Inventory (YLS/CMI). The drawback to these measures is that their correlations with future violence are fairly low (r = 0.25 to 0.30) (Olver et al., 2009), which implies that they are not very useful in predicting short-term violence in an individual case. Therefore, without significant evidence of intent to harm, treating psychiatrists are unlikely to be held liable for failing to prevent violence.

School Shooting Threats

The assessment of mass school shooting threats by K-12 students is different from other risk assessments for adolescent violence. School shootings are planned, not impulsive like most adolescent violence, and the risk in relying solely on an individual interview is that the possible shooter can easily lie about his or her intent. The most striking commonality found in K-12 shooters after the spate of school shootings in the 1990s is that almost all had communicated their intent to peers, but their threats had not been taken seriously (Vossekuil et al., 2002). This finding led school authorities to heighten surveillance of such communications by encouraging reporting of possible threats by peers and teachers. Even statements made in jest or to be provocative often trigger an immediate suspension and referral for evaluation. Because threats are so often made to others, collateral information, including talking to the youth's friends, is important, as well as the more usual sources of collateral information from parents and school personnel. For serious threats, involving a multidisciplinary team that includes school personnel and law enforcement is useful in obtaining information that may not be readily available to a clinician, such as examining the youth's computer for evidence of visiting Internet sites that focus on school shooting. Having such a team involved also reduces the clinician's liability in case of an adverse outcome.

A second significant difference in the assessment of a potential school shooter is that the risk factors that guide violence assessment in other contexts are frequently not useful. For example, a history of prior violence, a potent risk factor in most dangerousness assessments, is seldom present in the history of K-12 students who have committed mass violence (Vossekuil et al., 2002).

Details of techniques for assessing a potential school shooter are available in the literature (see, e.g., Fein et al., 2002; Cornell & Sheras, 2006; Ash, 2016; Kelly & McBride, 2019). From a liability perspective, the psychiatrist should recognize that these are specialized evaluations, that an interview of the individual suspect is rarely sufficient for gathering information, and that for serious threats, involvement of a team of evaluators including school personnel and law enforcement may be indicated.

Child Abuse and Neglect

Psychiatrists in all states have a mandatory duty to report suspected child abuse and neglect to the appropriate child protective services agency, and failure to recognize and report reasonable suspicion of abuse is malpractice (*Landeros v. Flood*, 1976). Psychiatrists may feel reluctant to report out of concerns that their patient (if an adult) or child's parents (if the patient is a child) will be angry at them. There is also risk that a parent may complain to the medical board about the report (PRMS, 2019). Finally, the psychiatrist may harbor concerns that the investigation will prove more disruptive and troublesome than the abuse or neglect itself. Nevertheless, such reports are required, and psychiatrists risk losing malpractice suits against them if they fail to report. In cases in which the psychiatrist is unclear as to whether there is an obligation to report, it is appropriate for the psychiatrist to call child protective services (CPS), lay out the nature of the concern without giving identifying information, and ask the protective services worker if those concerns require a formal report. If the answer is no, then the psychiatrist can document the conversation, including the name of the CPS worker, as this will provide strong protection in the event that the reasonableness of not reporting is later challenged. In making a report, the psychiatrist should keep in mind that in most jurisdictions, reporting waives confidentiality with regard to the findings that form the basis of the report; it does not waive confidentiality with regard to all information the psychiatrist knows about the patient.

The more complicated cases arise when the clinician does not suspect child abuse and later, when abuse is discovered, is sued for having failed to obtain the relevant information during treatment. Asking about abuse and neglect and documenting the responses should be a routine part of any child's initial evaluation. Some children will deny abuse when initially asked, and so a treating clinician should be sensitive to discovering symptoms that raise suspicion, but there is no clear syndrome of an abused child. It is also important that the psychiatrist not use leading questions which might encourage a false allegation. Once a psychiatrist has a reasonable suspicion, the question is whether to continue to investigate the possibility or simply file a report, a decision that will turn in large part on the psychiatrist's competence and experience in conducting abuse and neglect interviews. Psychiatrists do not have an obligation to investigate further once they have a reasonable suspicion – that's the job of child protective services – but they are not precluded from doing so if they think there is a good chance that gathering further information can be done rapidly and has a fair chance of disconfirming the suspicion.

On a child or adolescent inpatient unit, sexual molestation or abuse of one patient by another patient can give rise to a malpractice action. The issue will be whether the offending minor was known to be a risk. If the victim and perpetrator had different psychiatrists, the victim's treating psychiatrist will often be a defendant and may argue that since the perpetrator was not his patient, he or she had no way of knowing the perpetrator was a risk. The duty of the perpetrator's psychiatrist to alert others to the risk is often unclear and varies by jurisdiction. The hospital is also often also involved as a co-defendant, on the grounds that supervision by nurses and other staff was lax. One dilemma co-defendants often face is the temptation to defend themselves by arguing a co-defendant was at fault, not them. From the plaintiff's perspective, one defendant blaming another is a very positive situation – it helps establish liability, and plaintiffs seldom care just which defendant has to pay. The best protection against these cases is for an inpatient unit to have policies and practices that encourage reporting of potential abusers to the treatment team so that a treatment plan can be established which manages the risk.

Consent, Confidentiality, and Disclosure

Most commonly, even in jurisdictions in which some minors can consent to mental health treatment in certain situations, a parent or guardian provides consent for treatment. Clinicians should be familiar with the applicable laws in their jurisdiction so that they are obtaining valid consent. If the child's parents have divorced, it is advisable for the clinician to review the custody order or divorce decree specifying who can consent to medical treatment (PRMS, 2019).

Even in those jurisdictions where a minor can consent to treatment, parents or guardians typically have access to treatment records of a minor until the minor turns 18, which allows clinicians to use their discretion as to what treatment information to discuss with the responsible adult. The ability to release information to parents and involve them in treatment is helpful in communicating risks and potential adverse outcomes to parents, which can lower their incentive to file suit in case of an adverse result (see Chap. 7). The recent implementation of the ONC Cures Act Final Rule (2020) gives parents the right to read most of their children's healthcare records electronically without making a formal request or signing a release. This access should be taken into account when child and adolescent therapists discuss with their patients what confidentiality can be maintained. It may also present a dilemma to the psychiatrist when writing progress notes: a minor patient may disclose information that he or she does not want a parent to know, but if it is important to include the information in order to document the treater met the standard of care, the clinician is best advised to write it in the note. One option is for the psychiatrist to also keep "psychotherapy notes" as defined by HIPAA, which are a separate category of record that are considered part of the general medical record but are stored separately from it (Privacy Rule Definitions, 2001) and have more restricted access.

Child Custody Disputes

When a child patient's parents divorce and contest custody or visitation, one or both parents may try to bring the treating clinician into the conflict as either an evaluator of the custody question or as a fact witness to disclose aspects of the treatment the parent thinks will be helpful to his or her case. As a general matter, a treating clinician should stay out of the role of forensic evaluator because the two roles conflict (Kraus et al., 2011; Strasburger et al., 1997). Responding to a request, demand, or subpoena to provide information gained in the therapy, for example, to disclose a child patient's views about his parents or preference for which parent to live with, is more complex, as the parent, acting for the child, can often waive privilege. Nevertheless, releasing confidential information in court runs the risk of undermining the treatment because the youth may feel betrayed that his communications, told to the therapist to help him or her navigate all the loyalty conflicts and complexities of having one's parents divorce, may cause distress to one parent. From a liability standpoint, while testimony either as a treater or as a forensic evaluator is generally immunized from suit, it is not rare for a disgruntled parent in a custody dispute to make a complaint to the state medical board (PRMS, 2019). If expert opinion is being sought in a custody case, it is generally appropriate for a treating clinician to suggest to the parents and their attorneys that they agree to an independent custody evaluation where the evaluator would act in a forensic, rather than therapeutic, role. If testimony of the treater is still asked for, it may be appropriate for the therapist to point out the therapist's concern that such disclosure will likely undermine the treatment, that the test in custody cases is the best interest of the child, and that in the therapist's opinion, insisting on disclosure is likely not in the child's best interest.

Reducing Risk

As with risk areas in general psychiatry, the best protection is to provide appropriate assessment and treatment and document carefully. When dealing with issues that present increased risk of an adverse event, such as those discussed above, careful documentation is especially important. One approach is to imagine that the adverse effect unfortunately occurred and make sure to document those issues you think a plaintiff attorney would be looking for (see Chap. 7).

Malpractice Litigation

The statute of limitations (the amount of time a plaintiff has to file suit after the injury or discovery of the injury), typically between 2 and 7 years for adults, is longer for minors and varies by jurisdiction, with the most common rule being that it does not begin to run until the child patient turns 18. When the plaintiff child is still a minor, suits in most jurisdictions are filed by the parent on behalf of the child, rather than by the minor directly.

Because minors are limited legally in making decisions for themselves, parents have more involvement in treatment, and involvement of the parents in treatment will be examined as well as direct interactions with the minor patient. The clinician's advice to parents will be scrutinized. Children and adolescents are typically seen as less responsible for their actions than are adults, and although there is no clear research on the subject, this likely leads juries to shift more responsibility to the psychiatrist in cases that involve suicide or noncompliance with treatment. Finally, injured children are often seen sympathetically by juries who may then be more inclined to grant them compensation than they might with an adult plaintiff.

Key Points

- Psychiatrists who treat minors but have not completed a fellowship in child and adolescent psychiatry should be able to identify and document special training they have had in treating those age groups.
- In elevated risk situations, it is important to maintain a good alliance with and communication of risk to the youth's parents.
- Compared to assessing adults, the high prevalence of suicidal ideation and planning in adolescents complicates management.
- Off-label prescribing is common in treating youth but should involve increased attention to the informed consent process, especially the communication of black box warnings.
- Assessment of school shooting threats should not rely solely on an interview of the student making the threat, but should also involve obtaining collateral information from the student's friends, parents, and school personnel.
- Parents who are angry at their child's therapist for reporting suspected abuse or giving opinions in child custody and visitation disputes are more likely to make a complaint to a state medical board than to file a malpractice claim.
- Since parents can generally read their child's psychiatric records, care should be taken when writing in the chart about confidential information the patient does not want their parents to know about.
- In malpractice litigation, compared to adults, children and adolescents have less responsibility for complying with treatment and are likely to be seen as more sympathetic victims by juries.

Acknowledgments Some of the conceptualizations in this chapter were previously presented in Ash, P. (2019), Children are different: Liability issues in working with suicidal and dangerous youth. Focus, 17(4), 355-359; and in Ash, P. (2018), Medicolegal issues in prescribing medications to children and adolescents. In S. Vinson & E. Vinson (Eds.), Pediatric Psychiatry for Primary Care: A Clinician's Guide (pp. 96-106). New York, NY: Springer.

References

American Academy of Child & Adolescent Psychiatry. (2021). *Practicing child and adolescent psychiatrists*. www.aacap.org/aacap/Advocacy/Federal_and_State_Initiatives/Workforce_Maps/Home.aspx. Accessed January 20, 2021.

Annor, F. B., Zwald, M. L., Wilkinson, A., Friedrichs, M., Fondario, A., Dunn, A., et al. (2018). Characteristics of and precipitating circumstances surrounding suicide among persons aged 10–17 years – Utah, 2011–2015. *MMWR – Morbidity & Mortality Weekly Report, 67*(11), 329–332. https://doi.org/10.15585/mmwr.mm6711a4

Ash, P. (2008). Violence in children and adolescents. In R. I. Simon & K. Tardiff (Eds.), *The American Psychiatric Publishing textbook of violence assessment and management* (pp. 359–380). American Psychiatric Publishing.

Ash, P. (2012). Suicidal children, adolescents, and college students. In R. I. Simon & R. E. Hales (Eds.), *The American Psychiatric Publishing textbook of suicide assessment and management* (2nd ed., pp. 349–366). American Psychiatric Publishing.

Ash, P. (2016). School shootings and mental illness. In L. H. Gold & R. I. Simon (Eds.), *Gun violence and mental illness* (1st ed., pp. 105–126). American Psychiatric Association Publishing.

Ash, P., Kellermann, A. L., Fuqua-Whitley, D., & Johnson, A. (1996). Gun acquisition and use by juvenile offenders. *JAMA, 275*(22), 1754–1758.

Beck, J. M., & Azari, E. D. (1998). FDA, off-label use, and informed consent: Debunking myths and misconceptions. *Food and Drug Law Journal, 53*(1), 71–104.

Bernat, D. H., Oakes, J. M., Pettingell, S. L., & Resnick, M. (2012). Risk and direct protective factors for youth violence: Results from the National Longitudinal Study of Adolescent Health. *American Journal of Preventive Medicine, 43*(2 Suppl 1), S57–S66. https://doi.org/10.1016/j.amepre.2012.04.023

Brent, D. A., Baugher, M., Birmaher, B., Kolko, D. J., & Bridge, J. (2000). Compliance with recommendations to remove firearms in families participating in a clinical trial for adolescent depression. *Journal of the American Academy of Child & Adolescent Psychiatry, 39*(10), 1220–1226.

Centers for Disease Control and Prevention. (2021). *WISQARS fatal injury and violence data*. https://www.cdc.gov/injury/wisqars/fatal.html. Accessed January 21, 2021.

Centers for Disease Control and Prevention (CDC). (2021). *1991–2019 high school youth risk behavior survey data*. http://yrbs-explorer.services.cdc.gov/. Accessed April 11, 2021.

Cornell, D. G., & Sheras, P. (2006). *Guidelines for responding to student threats of violence*. Sopris West.

Elkington, K. S., Teplin, L. A., Abram, K. M., Jakubowski, J. A., Dulcan, M. K., & Welty, L. J. (2015). Psychiatric disorders and violence: A study of delinquent youth after detention. *Journal of the American Academy of Child & Adolescent Psychiatry, 54*(4), 302–312. https://doi.org/10.1016/j.jaac.2015.01.002

Elliott, D. S. (1994). Serious violent offenders: Onset, developmental course, and termination-The American Society of Criminology 1993 Presidential Address. *Criminology, 32*(1), 1–21.

Fein, R., Vossekuil, B., Pollack, W. S., Borum, R., Modzeleski, W., & Reddy, M. (2002). *Threat assessment in schools: A guide to managing threatening situations and to creating safe school climates*. U.S. Secret Service and U.S. Department of Education.

Hammad, T. A., Laughren, T., & Racoosin, J. (2006). Suicidality in pediatric patients treated with antidepressant drugs. *Archives of General Psychiatry, 63*(3), 332–339.

Harvard Injury Control Research Center. (2021). *Duration of suicidal crises*. https://www.hsph.harvard.edu/means-matter/means-matter/duration/. Accessed April 4, 2021.

Ivey-Stephenson, A. Z., Demissie, Z., Crosby, A. E., Stone, D. M., Gaylor, E., Wilkins, N., et al. (2020). Suicidal ideation and behaviors among high school students — Youth risk behavior survey, United States, 2019. *MMWR, 69*, 47–55. https://doi.org/10.15585/mmwr.su6901a6external

Kearns, M. A., & Hawley, K. M. (2014). Predictors of polypharmacy and off-label prescribing of psychotropic medications: A national survey of child and adolescent psychiatrists. *Journal of Psychiatric Practice, 20*(6), 438–447. https://doi.org/10.1097/01.pra.0000456592.20622.45

Kelly, M., & McBride, A. B. (Eds.). (2019). *Safe passage: A guide for addressing school violence*. American Psychiatric Association Publishing.

Kerwin, M. E., Kirby, K. C., Speziali, D., Duggan, M., Mellitz, C., Versek, B., et al. (2015). What can parents do? A review of state laws regarding decision making for adolescent drug abuse and mental health treatment. *Journal of Child & Adolescent Substance Abuse, 24*(3), 166–176. https://doi.org/10.1080/1067828X.2013.777380

Kingsbury, S. J. (1993). Clinical components of suicidal intent in adolescent overdose. *Journal of the American Academy of Child & Adolescent Psychiatry, 32*(3), 518–520.

Kraus, L. J., Thomas, C. R., Bukstein, O. G., Walter, H. J., Benson, R. S., Chrisman, A., et al. (2011). Practice parameter for child and adolescent forensic evaluations. *Journal of the American Academy of Child & Adolescent Psychiatry, 50*(12), 1299–1312. https://doi.org/10.1016/j.jaac.2011.09.020

Landeros v. Flood, 131 Cal Rptr 69, 555 P.2d 389 (Cal. 1976).

Marttunen, M. J., Aro, H. M., & Lonnqvist, J. K. (1993). Precipitant stressors in adolescent suicide. *Journal of the American Academy of Child & Adolescent Psychiatry, 32*(6), 1178–1183.

McKean, A. J. S., Pabbati, C. P., Geske, J. R., & Bostwick, J. M. (2018). Rethinking lethality in youth suicide attempts: First suicide attempt outcomes in youth ages 10 to 24. *Journal of the American Academy of Child & Adolescent Psychiatry, 57*(10), 786–791. https://doi.org/10.1016/j.jaac.2018.04.021

Olver, M. E., Stockdale, K. C., & Wormith, J. S. (2009). Risk assessment with young offenders: A meta-analysis of three assessment measures. *Criminal Justice and Behavior, 36*(4), 329–353. https://doi.org/10.1177/0093854809331457

ONC Cures Act Final Rule, 85 FR 25642 (2020).

Privacy Rule Definitions, 45 CFR 164.501 (2001).

PRMS. (2019). 10 things about...children and adolescents. *Rx for Risk, 27*(2), 3–4.

Professional Risk Management Services. (2015). The Psychiatrists' program cause of loss (2005–2014). *Rx for Risk, 23*(3), 7.

Professional Risk Management Services. (Personal communication, 2019). *The psychiatrists' program cause of loss (2009–2018)*.

Rappeport, J. R. (1984). Malpractice prevention. *Spring grove state hospital center*.

Strasburger, L. H., Gutheil, T. G., & Brodsky, A. (1997). On wearing two hats: Role conflict in serving as both psychotherapist and expert witness. *American Journal of Psychiatry, 154*(4), 448–456.

Teplin, L. A., Abram, K. M., McClelland, G. M., Dulcan, M. K., & Mericle, A. A. (2002). Psychiatric disorders in youth in juvenile detention. *Archives of General Psychiatry, 59*(12), 1133–1143.

U.S. Dept. Health and Human Services. (2001). *Youth violence: A report of the surgeon general*. Author.

U.S. Food and Drug Administration. (2007). *Revisions to product labeling*. http://www.fda.gov/downloads/Drugs/DrugSafety/InformationbyDrugClass/UCM173233.pdf. Accessed November 30, 2020.

Vossekuil, B., Fein, R., Reddy, M., Borum, R., & Modzeleski, W. (2002). *The final report and findings of the Safe School Initiative: Implications for the prevention of school attacks in the United States*. U.S. Department of Education, Office of Elementary and Secondary Education, Safe and Drug-Free Schools Program and U.S. Secret Service, National Threat Assessment Center.

Webster, D. W., Freed, L. H., Frattaroli, S., & Wilson, M. H. (2002). How delinquent youths acquire guns: initial versus most recent gun acquisitions. *Journal of Urban Health, 79*(1), 60–69.

Youth Handgun Safety Act. (1996). Youth Handgun Safety Act. *18 U.S.C. 922(x)* (Vol. 18 U.S.C. 922(x)).

Consultation-Liaison Psychiatry

22

Abhishek Jain

Consultation-liaison (C-L) psychiatry, or psychosomatic medicine, is a psychiatric subspecialty that studies and treats patients with comorbid psychiatric and general medical illnesses, somatoform disorders, and psychiatric symptoms resulting from primary medical conditions (Levenson, 2019). In practice, C-L psychiatrists usually provide hospital-based services in general medical settings or where mental health services are integrated with primary care (Levenson, 2019; Jain et al., 2015). While the mind-body interaction in medicine has been described for centuries, the American Board of Medical Specialties formally approved Psychosomatic Medicine as a subspecialty in 2003 (Levenson, 2019), and its standards continue to evolve.

C-L psychiatrists' unique role in providing consultation, rather than providing direct patient care, presents special responsibilities and liability considerations compared to those of treating physicians (Brendel & Schouten, 2007). In malpractice claims, one of the four commonly required elements involves establishing that the physician had a professional duty to a patient (see Chap. 1). While the goal of consultation is ultimately patient care, and C-L psychiatrists must meet acceptable standards of care when providing services, the consultant's duty may be thought of as to the practitioner who requested the consultation (Brendel & Schouten, 2007). However, the distinction between duty to the primary team (i.e., consultee) and duty to the patient may not always be absolute, particularly depending on the treatment setting, clinical circumstances, and institutional practices and expectations.

For example, a consultation may be requested for a specific question (e.g., "Does the patient have capacity to refuse surgery?") without an expectation of ongoing care and management. In other instances, which may also depend on the hospital and C-L service's established practices and policies, the requesting team may expect the C-L service to provide ongoing follow-up to the patient throughout the hospital admission and perhaps even actively manage and order medications and tests. In this latter circumstance, the C-L psychiatrist naturally has more direct responsibility (e.g., checking for potential drug-drug interactions before prescribing medications or following up on ordered labs) and in turn potentially greater liability. Moreover, these expectations and differences in practice might even change during the course of the same hospital admission. For instance, if a patient is in an intensive care unit, the intensivist may request consultations from multiple medical specialties with the understanding that the intensivist will ultimately be responsible for integrating the recommendations and making a final decision regarding the patient's care. On the other hand, the C-L psychiatrist may be expected, and better positioned, to make medication changes and order labs for a patient who has already been medically cleared for discharge and is awaiting transfer to an inpatient psychiatric hospital.

Medical consultations can also range from an informal "curbside" consult to a formally ordered consultation. While consultation is overall considered a relatively low-risk activity from a liability standpoint, the level of risk may vary (PRMS, 2014). For example, providing a "curbside" consultation to a colleague in the same subspecialty on a general topic (e.g., potential medication augmenting strategies for treatment-refractory depression) would typically be a low-risk activity (PRMS, 2014). Similarly, courts have rejected liability when informal treatment suggestions are offered, such as in staff meetings or an educational case conference (Olick & Bergus, 2003). However, in situations when the consultant's recommendations will foreseeably be relied upon and followed (e.g., emergency room resident informally asking the hospital's psychiatrist if an involuntary emergency admission can be cancelled for a patient who recently attempted suicide), the consultant may incur greater liability. Nonetheless, in order to prevail, the plaintiff would generally still need to prove, as in any other medical malpractice claims, that the consultation was negligent and that this negligence was a proximate cause in harming the patient (Olick & Bergus, 2003).

A. Jain (✉)
Department of Psychiatry, Columbia University Vagelos College of Physicians & Surgeons, New York, NY, USA

P. Ash et al. (eds.), *Malpractice and Liability in Psychiatry*, https://doi.org/10.1007/978-3-030-91975-7_22

Historically (Garrick & Weinstock, 1994), and based on a search using the term "consulting psychiatrist" through casetext.com at the time of writing this chapter, no published appellate level malpractice cases have been found of consulting psychiatrists being held liable. While this is reassuring, consulting psychiatrists have been named as defendants in malpractice cases (discussed in further detail below), unpublished malpractice claims against psychiatrists have been settled out of court, and medical consultants in other subspecialties have been held liable (Garrick & Weinstock, 1994). Thus, the following sections in this chapter will further detail how courts have interpreted liability of medical consultation generally and psychiatric consultation more specifically, unique challenges of providing psychiatric consultation in non-psychiatric medical settings, common legal issues that arise for C-L psychiatrists, and considerations to further reduce the likelihood of medical liability.

Liability Considerations in Medical Consultation

Seeking consultation from colleagues is routine practice in medicine. With a growing body of scientific information, increasing sub-specialization, and complex systems of care, seeking appropriate consultation is not only good practice but—along with documentation—has also been described as one of the "twin pillars" to prevent malpractice and enhance patient care (Gutheil & Appelbaum, 2000). Courts have even reasoned that holding informal "curbside" consultants accountable "would be detrimental in the long run to those seeking competent medical attention" and "would unacceptably inhibit the exchange of information and expertise among physicians" (Olick & Bergus, 2003; *Hill v. Kokosky*, 1990).

Nevertheless, consultants are not immune to malpractice claims (Suri, 2020), and courts may weigh various factors on case-by-case basis when assessing liability. Courts may consider the duty the consulting physician has to the primary treating physician versus the patient, which can include specific hospital policies and any contractual obligations (Suri, 2020). Cases can also hinge on the foreseeability of harm to the patient by the consulting physician's care, the extent the treating physician remained in control of care, and if it is reasonable and foreseeable that the patient or primary team would rely on the consultation recommendations (Olick & Bergus, 2003; Suri, 2020). Details such as the frequency, duration, and what the consultation entailed (e.g., examination, review of records, diagnosis, treatment, charge for services) might also play a role (Olick & Bergus, 2003; Suri, 2020). Further, some states may explicitly define physician-patient relationship by statute; for example, in Idaho medical malpractice cases, a physician-patient relationship is not formed when a physician provides consultation to another physician without seeing or examining the patient and without the expectation of payment (Idaho Code § 54-1821, 2020). Public policy implications (e.g., prevention of future harm, economic burden upon the physician, impact on the community) of liability decisions may also be taken into account by the courts (*Millard v. Corrado*, 2000). Additionally, the outcome of a case may depend on technical legal factors, such as whether the claim is brought under ordinary negligence—in which expert testimony is not required for a jury to determine whether the physician's conduct was reasonable—rather than as medical malpractice (Suri, 2020).

For example, in a 1995 New York case, the court found that a senior neurologist, who was supervising a postdoctoral chiropractic neurology resident, had a physician-patient relationship with a patient who had suffered a stroke. Although the senior neurologist had not physically examined the patient, reviewed the patient's medical history, or billed for his services, the court found that he had provided actual direction, rather than merely consultative advice, including a diagnosis and treatment instructions that had a direct bearing on the patient and therefore created a physician-patient relationship (Suri, 2020; *Gilinsky v. Indelicato,* 1995). Along similar lines, in a 1998 Illinois case, an appellate court reversed and remanded a trial court's summary judgment originally in favor of cardiac interventionists who were consulted by a treating cardiologist. According to the appellate court, a trier of fact might conclude that the cardiac interventionists "knew or should have known" their medical opinions were crucial in determining whether the patient could have an angioplasty; the treating cardiologist was not trained to read angiograms; and their medical opinions would be passed on to the patient (*Bovara v. St. Francis Hospital,* 1998).

Furthermore, in a 2000 Arizona case, a female patient died from a heart attack after being released from the emergency department. Her husband filed a malpractice action against the emergency room physician and the cardiologist who was "informally" consulted. Initially, the trial court granted summary judgment to the cardiologist based on reasoning that without an expressed or implied physician-patient relationship, the cardiologist owed no duty. However, the Arizona Court of Appeals reversed the decision. The court concluded that since the cardiologist reviewed the chart and provided a diagnosis which he knew the emergency room physician would rely upon, a sufficient relationship between the cardiologist and patient existed (*Diggs v. Arizona Cardiologists, Ltd.*, 2000).

On the other hand, in a 1990 Michigan case, the court found no relationship between consulting physicians and a patient when they spoke with the treating physician over the phone regarding birthing alternatives. In this case, the court reasoned that consulting physicians did not know, examine, or speak to the patient; the patient was not referred to them for treatment or consultation; and their opinions were to the treating physician as a recommendation that could be accepted or rejected (Olick & Bergus, 2003; *Hill v. Kokosky*, 1990). Similarly, in a 2001 Kansas case, the court found that a physician, who provided a neurological consult to a pediatric intensivist regarding a shuntogram that later resulted in permanent brain damage to the patient, did not have a physician-patient relationship with the patient. The court reasoned that the physician had only discussed the case in general terms and agreed to see the patient the next day, but he did not examine the patient, review the hospital chart, speak with the parents, or enter orders (*Irvin v. Smith*, 2001).

Likewise, in a 2012 Oregon case, an on-call neurosurgeon received a call from a resident and offered his opinion to admit the patient, but did not examine or treat the patient. The court discussed that a physician-patient relationship does not necessarily exist when offering advice to a colleague. The court described that "the question whether a physician's expression of an opinion constitutes a diagnosis [and a physician-patient relationship] will vary depending on, among other things, the customary practice within the relevant medical community, the degree and the level of formality with which one physician has assumed (or the other physician has ceded) responsibility for the diagnosis or treatment, the relative expertise of the two physicians, and the reasonable expectations, if any, of the patient under the circumstances" (*Mead v. Legacy Hospital System,* 2012).

Liability Considerations Specifically in Psychiatric Consultation

As noted, no published cases of consulting psychiatrists being held liable were found at the time of writing this chapter, and a casetext.com search revealed a limited number of appellate level malpractice cases with a consulting psychiatrist named as a defendant. Nonetheless, three recent case examples below provide some insight into how courts have thought about matters, such as scope of the psychiatric consultation, delineating recommendations from directives, and documentation.

In a 2009 New York case, a patient was brought to an emergency room complaining of "feeling overwhelmed by stress." An emergency room physician concluded that the symptoms were consistent with depression and consulted a psychiatrist to confirm that the patient was not suicidal or a risk to others and would not require involuntary admission. The psychiatrist completed the assessment and determined the patient would not require hospitalization and offered the patient a referral for outpatient psychiatric treatment. The patient left without being formally discharged, but returned 45 minutes later and was diagnosed with an ischemic stroke. Among the various complaints in the malpractice action, the patient alleged that the consulting psychiatrist failed "to perform a neurological examination and rule out a neurological etiology for his symptoms, develop a list of differential diagnoses, and refer the plaintiff for further diagnostic studies to work up neurological problems" (*Chin v. Long Island Coll. Hosp.*, 2014, p. 545). The lower court denied the consulting psychiatrist's motion to dismiss the complaint, but the appellate court decided that the court should have granted the motion. The appellate court stated, "Under these circumstances, where the plaintiff has been actively treated by an emergency room physician for any medical causes of his symptoms, and exhibited no clear signs of neurological problems at the time, the appellant [consulting psychiatrist] had no duty beyond properly performing an evaluation to determine whether the plaintiff was a danger to himself or others and would require involuntary admission for depression" (*Chin v. Long Island Coll. Hosp.*, 2014, p. xx).

In a 2013 Maine case, while more broadly regarding whether a day treatment program was defined as a healthcare provider, the court's decision considered that a psychiatrist's role of providing consultation was distinct from that of actually prescribing medical services. In this case, two strangers had sexually assaulted an intellectually disabled patient after she had been permitted to leave the property of the day treatment program. About a year prior to the assault, the consulting psychiatrist evaluated the patient to help develop an individual service plan (ISP). While the consultation provided important information to help develop the ISP, the evaluation did not tell the treatment staff "what to do," but only provided "recommendations," and medical services were not prescribed by the consulting psychiatrist or performed under his general direction. The court ultimately determined that the day treatment program was not a healthcare provider and the action against them cannot constitute an "action for professional negligence" (*D.S. v. Spurwink Services, Inc.*, 2013).

In a 2015 Louisiana case, an appellate court affirmed the trial court's dismissal of a patient's claims that a consulting psychiatrist's actions constituted defamation of character, intentional infliction of emotional distress, and violation of her privacy rights. The plaintiff-patient had been referred to the psychiatrist after the neurology department concluded that her multiple complaints were likely due to "conversion disorder" or "malingering." The psychiatrist interviewed her, reviewed her records, and issued a report. Allegations included that he "had treated her in a cruel and inappropriate manner, was verbally abusive to her, and had used inappropriate language toward her publicly, as memorialized in his consultation report" (*Conner v. Taylor,* 2015, p. *2). The appellate court found no error with the trial court dismissing the patient's defamation allegation on the basis that the psychiatrist's consultation report was rendered in his capacity as a consulting psychiatrist, was appropriately placed in the patient's medical records, and was not disseminated or discussed with others not involved in her medical treatment. Furthermore, regarding the claim of inflection of intentional emotional distress, the appellate court noted that while some of the statements in the report "are arguably (and perhaps unnecessarily) harsh and insulting … [the psychiatrist] had a duty as a consulting psychiatrist to evaluate her mental health and to generate a report for the medical team accurately reflecting his observations and conclusions" (*Conner v. Taylor,* 2015, p. *11).

Challenges and Opportunities in C-L Practice Settings

Building on the legal context and case examples, further appreciation of the unique challenges and opportunities of providing consultation in non-psychiatric settings can be important when considering liability issues. For instance, C-L practice settings vary from inpatient general medical hospitals to outpatient primary care offices, and different cultures and expectations (e.g., academic, community, specialized care) can frame how the consulting psychiatrist approaches cases. Not all tests or interventions (e.g., electroconvulsive therapy) may be readily available in a particular setting; therefore, recommending them may not be useful and unnecessarily bind the treatment team to an untenable course of action. Similarly, the C-L psychiatrist may need to consider the availability and level of staff training (e.g., monitoring of suicidal behavior), which can have implications for being able to manage safety concerns appropriately (Jain & Ackerman, 2015).

Other challenges in non-psychiatric settings, compared to the psychiatric setting, may include unique documentation and electronic medical records (EMR) systems. Generally, medical records serve multiple purposes, including critical information about the patient's history, communicating consultant's findings and recommendations to the primary treatment team, capturing necessary billing requirements for third-party payers, and, possibly, for reference in future litigation or legal purposes (Jain & Ackerman, 2015). Furthermore, patients or their families may also seek their medical records, including psychiatric consultation notes, and have greater access to information in their electronic medical record under the 21st Century Cures Act of 2016 (DesRoches et al., 2020). Thus the language (e.g., avoiding jargon and confusing abbreviations) and content (e.g., avoiding unnecessarily inflammatory details) are important to consider, which was highlighted in the above case example (*Conner v. Taylor,* 2015). Additionally, if the consulting psychiatrist is expected to enter orders, especially orders that might be unique to psychiatric care (e.g., transfer orders to an inpatient psychiatric unit) and unfamiliar to nursing and primary team, it can be helpful to verbally communicate and clarify this information to avoid confusion.

Additional considerations in C-L psychiatry may include limited privacy when interviewing the patient, especially if the patient is sharing a hospital room with another patient, has visitors, or has frequent medical care needs. Interruptions from other care providers are also expected in a busy hospital setting. Moreover, the patient may be unavailable due to being off the floor for testing or other procedures, transferred to another unit, or possibly even discharged prior to having a chance for follow-up. Similarly, as noted above, the primary medical setting may have limited psychiatric resources (e.g., limited psychiatric medical formulary or limited behavioral support staff). Thus, being mindful of these limitations can help C-L psychiatrists lessen the risk of a poor patient outcome. At the same time, by virtue of their unique expertise and training, C-L psychiatrists may also be able to work with primary teams, hospital administration, security, and legal counsel to address these challenges.

Common Medico-legal Issues in C-L Psychiatry

C-L psychiatrists are often consulted for and face unique medico-legal issues that arise in primary medical settings (Resnick & Sorrentino, 2005). Awareness of relevant legal issues can help C-L psychiatrists protect patient rights, be better informed when seeking risk management or legal consultation, and potentially reduce the risk of liability. Some key topics are highlighted here.

Capacity and Informed Consent

Assessment of patient's medical decision-making capacity, or simply capacity, has been described as the most common legal issue that arises in C-L psychiatry (Resnick & Sorrentino, 2006). One study cited that about 10% of consultation requests were for capacity (Kornfeld et al., 2009), though many more consultations frequently evolve into assessments of capacity (Jain & Ackerman, 2015). Broadly, capacity involves a patient's ability to communicate, understand, appreciate, and rationally manipulate information (Appelbaum, 2007). Relatedly, in order to provide valid informed consent (or informed refusal), a patient must have sufficient capacity, be provided adequate information, and make their decision voluntarily. While any physician can make a determination about capacity, psychiatric expertise can help flesh out whether the patient's decision-making is influenced by psychiatric or cognitive impairment. Thus, many complex medical decisions, and even potentially harmful choices by a patient (e.g., refusing hospitalization or treatment), often hinge on whether or not the patient has sufficient capacity. While a negative patient outcome is naturally undesirable, an appropriate assessment and clear documentation can help protect a patient's autonomy and provide protection in potential litigation.

Useful principles for C-L psychiatrists to keep in mind include that capacity is generally presumed in adults (even those with psychiatric illness), time-specific, and decision-specific (i.e., incapacity for one decision does not necessarily mean the patient lacks capacity for all decisions) (Ganzini et al., 2004). Clarifying the specific capacity question (e.g., "does the patient have capacity to consent to surgery"); gathering relevant clinical background regarding the medical urgency of the decision and the underlying condition that led to the concern for capacity; and approaches to help facilitate the patient's understanding (e.g., clarifying medical information) and restore their capacity (e.g., treating underlying delirium) can be helpful when providing consultation in these cases (Jain & Ackerman, 2015).

Treatment Refusal and Discharges Against Medical Advice

Patients of "sound mind" and with sufficient capacity generally have a right to refuse treatment and even leave the hospital against medical advice (AMA). C-L psychiatrists may provide consultation in these cases or perhaps assist with developing hospital procedures and policies (e.g., guidance to hospital security on preventing an incapacitated patient from physically leaving the hospital AMA). While a patient's capacity to make these decisions becomes central, C-L psychiatrists may also help facilitate communication between the primary team and the patient, resolve any conflicts, or help reduce the patient's fears about the medical course or treatment recommendations. Further, the C-L psychiatrist may help address underlying conditions (e.g., substance use withdrawal) or consider if an involuntary psychiatric admission is indicated. If no indication to hold the patient against his or her will is present, hospital and physician liability may not necessarily be absolved, and further discussing and carefully documenting a safety and follow-up plan with the patient can be useful (Brendel et al., 2019; Resnick & Sorrentino, 2006).

Substituted Decision-Making, Living Wills, and Advance Directives

If a patient lacks capacity, a consult psychiatrist may help the primary team navigate next steps. Typically, a surrogate decision-maker, who may have been previously assigned by the patient, statutorily defined (e.g., next of kin), or court-appointed (e.g., guardian), must be identified. Additionally, a patient may have an advance directive, which generally includes a living will (identifying desires about medical treatment) and durable power of attorney (who can make decision on behalf of the patient) if the patient becomes incapacitated (Resnick & Sorrentino, 2006). Despite passage of the federal Patient Self-Determination Act of 1990 that legally required hospitals to provide patients information about advance directives (PSDA, 1990), in one study of American adults only 26% had these provisions in place (Rao et al., 2014). Thus, addressing next steps when a patient lacks capacity can become complex. C-L psychiatrists can play a central role in these matters, and enlisting the hospital's legal counsel and ethics teams may also become necessary.

Confidentiality

With the wide availability and accessibility of electronic health records, being mindful of who may have access to consultation records is important (Jain et al., 2015). Under the Health Information Portability and Accountability Act (HIPAA, 1996), psychiatric records entered in the medical chart are part of the patient's general medical record (Brendel & Schouten, 2007). Medical records may be released for several purposes, such as treatment, payment, and healthcare operations, without requiring specific consent, and patients have broad rights to access their records; thus, care should be taken to limit documentation of information relevant to the consultation (Brendel et al., 2019). Additionally, exceptions to confidentiality and requirements for mandated reporters, such as situations involving duty to warn or protect, child abuse, elder abuse, infectious disease, or other safety considerations, are jurisdiction-specific and should be reviewed (Brendel et al., 2019). While physicians may face liability for failure to report in some situations, disclosures should be considered exceptions to the rule of protecting patient confidentiality, alternatives to releasing information should be explored, and if even if disclosure is necessary, efforts should be taken to share the minimum amount necessary (Brendel et al., 2019; Mermelstein & Wallack, 2008; Brendel & Schouten, 2007).

Restraints

Psychiatrists may be consulted to evaluate patients who are agitated or in need of restraints for the purposes of preventing falls or medical issues (e.g., lines, catheters, nasogastric tubes) (Resnick & Sorrentino, 2006). The Joint Commission and hospital policies generally have restrictive guidance regarding their use, and they are typically used as a last measure (Brendel et al., 2019). However, either overuse or failure to use when necessary may incur liability risk, and failure to follow policies may result in loss of medical facility accreditation (Resnick & Sorrentino, 2006).

Diagnoses

Misdiagnoses are common complaints in malpractice suits. Care and thought should be taken before concluding that a patient is exaggerating or intentionally producing symptoms (e.g., malingering or factitious disorder). These are frequent considerations in C-L psychiatry, and even if the conclusion is accurate, these can be prejudicial to patients and a potential source of lawsuits (Eisendrath & McNiel, 2004; Janofsky, 1994). Similarly, while rates of misdiagnosing an organic medical disease as a somatic symptom disorder (e.g., conversion disorder) have decreased from the 1960s to the 1990s (Stone et al., 2005; Espay et al., 2018), over- or underdiagnosing functional disorders (e.g., conversion disorder) can be harmful (Walzl et al., 2019), and careful review and documentation is important when considering these conditions.

Key Points

- Clarify the C-L psychiatrist's role. This includes whether the psychiatrist will be responsible for ordering medications and tests or only providing recommendations, along with the frequency and duration of follow-up. This may also depend on the institutional culture and policies.
- Clarify the consultation question. While the focus of consultation may evolve as the patient is being evaluated, clarifying the primary team's request can help avoid confusion and ensure that the key issues are addressed.
- Be mindful of documentation. The psychiatric consultation may be read by a wide audience, including potentially the patient or his or her family, so including only relevant information, avoiding prejudicial language, and providing clear reasoning behind diagnoses and recommendations are useful practices.
- Be clear with recommendations. C-L psychiatrists may use jargon or terminology that may be unfamiliar in nonpsychiatric settings. Further, at times the C-L psychiatrist may provide general suggestions (e.g., consider MRI) or stronger directives (e.g., please order lithium level); in the latter circumstance, instead of or prior to doing so, it may be more reasonable to call the primary team directly to avoid potential disagreement or "chart wars."
- Do not make unrealistic recommendations. Certain tests, procedures, or medications may be unavailable. In these circumstances, clarifying the availability of these options is important.
- Be cautious of informal "curbside" consultation. While these are common in daily practice, C-L psychiatrists may suggest a formal consultation when complex circumstances require direct examination of the patient, a specific diagnosis is offered, the consultation is being billed, the consultation is being documented, or the consultee is deferring to the consultant's recommendations rather than their own judgment (PRMS, 2014).
- Be familiar with key legal issues (e.g., capacity, informed consent, confidentiality) that frequently arise in C-L psychiatry.
- Consider ethics, legal, and peer consultation. As described, one of the pillars to avoid malpractice is appropriately seeking consultation, which holds true for consulting psychiatrists themselves.

References

Appelbaum, P. S. (2007). Clinical practice. Assessment of patients' competence to consent to treatment. *The New England Journal of Medicine, 357*(18), 1834–1840.

Bovara v. Francis Hospital, 298 Ill. App. 3d 1025 (Ill. App. Ct. 1998).

Brendel, R. W., & Schouten, R. (2007). Legal concerns in psychosomatic medicine. *The Psychiatric Clinics of North America, 30*(4), 663–676.

Brendel, R. W., Schouten, R., Nesbit, A., & Levenson, J. L. (2019). Legal and ethical issues. In J. L. Levenson (Ed.), *Psychosomatic medicine and consultation-liaison psychiatry* (3rd ed.). American Psychiatric Association Publishing.

Chin v. Long Island Coll. Hosp., 990 N.Y.S.2d 543 (N.Y. App. Div. 2014).

Conner v. Taylor, No. 2015 CA 0177 (La. Ct. App. Sep. 18, 2015).

D.S. v. Spurwink Servs., Inc., 65 A.3d 1196 (Me. 2013).

DesRoches, C. M., Leveille, S., Bell, S. K., Dong, Z. J., Elmore, J. G., Fernandez, L., Harcourt, K., Fitzgerald, P., Payne, T. H., Stametz, R., Delbanco, T., & Walker, J. (2020). The views and experiences of clinicians sharing medical record notes with patients. *JAMA Network Open, 3*(3), e201753.

Diggs v. Arizona Cardiologists, Ltd., 198 Ariz. 198 (Ariz. Ct. App. 2000).

Eisendrath, S. J., & McNiel, D. E. (2004). Factitious physical disorders, litigation, and mortality. *Psychosomatics, 45*(4), 350–353.

Espay, A. J., Aybek, S., Carson, A., Edwards, M. J., Goldstein, L. H., Hallett, M., LaFaver, K., LaFrance, W. C., Jr., Lang, A. E., Nicholson, T., Nielsen, G., Reuber, M., Voon, V., Stone, J., & Morgante, F. (2018). Current concepts in diagnosis and treatment of functional neurological disorders. *JAMA Neurology, 75*(9), 1132–1141.

Ganzini, L., Volicer, L., Nelson, W. A., Fox, E., & Derse, A. R. (2004). Ten myths about decision-making capacity. *Journal of the American Medical Directors Association, 5*(4), 263–267.

Garrick, T. R., & Weinstock, R. (1994). Liability of psychiatric consultants. *Psychosomatics, 35*(5), 474–484.

Gilinsky v. Joseph Rosario Indelicato, D.C., 894 F. Supp. 86 (E.D.N.Y. 1995).

Gutheil, T. G., & Appelbaum, P. S. (2000). *Clinical handbook of psychiatry and the law* (3rd ed.). Lippincott Williams & Wilkins Publishers.

Health Insurance Portability and Accountability Act of 1996, Publ L No 104–191. (1996).

Hill v. Kokosky, 186 Mich. App. 300 (Mich. Ct. App. 1990).

Idaho Code § 54-1821 (2020).
Irvin v. Smith, 272 Kan. 112 (Kan. 2001).
Jain, A., & Ackerman, K. D. (2015). Assessment of decision-making capacity. In D. Ackerman & A. F. DiMartini (Eds.), *Psychosomatic medicine*. Oxford University Press.
Jain, A., DiBarry, A. L., Gopalan, P., Azzam, P. N., & Whyte, E. M. (2015). Psychiatric consultation in the inpatient general medical setting. In D. Ackerman & A. F. DiMartini (Eds.), *Psychosomatic medicine*. Oxford University Press.
Janofsky, J. S. (1994). The Munchausen syndrome in civil forensic psychiatry. *The Bulletin of the American Academy of Psychiatry and the Law, 22*(4), 489–497.
Kornfeld, D. S., Muskin, P. R., & Tahil, F. A. (2009). Psychiatric evaluation of mental capacity in the general hospital: A significant teaching opportunity. *Psychosomatics, 50*(5), 468–473.
Levenson, J. L. (2019). Preface. In J. L. Levenson (Ed.), *Psychosomatic medicine and consultation-liaison psychiatry* (3rd ed.). American Psychiatric Association Publishing.
Mead v. Legacy Health Sys., 283 P.3d 904 (Or. 2012).
Mermelstein, H. T., & Wallack, J. J. (2008). Confidentiality in the age of HIPAA: A challenge for psychosomatic medicine. *Psychosomatics, 49*(2), 97–103.
Millard v. Corrado, 14 S.W.3d 42 (Mo. Ct. App. 2000).
Olick, R. S., & Bergus, G. R. (2003). Malpractice liability for informal consultations. *Family Medicine, 35*(7), 476–481.
Patient Self-Determination Act of 1990. 42, 1395 cc(a). 1990. U.S.C.
Professional Risk Management Services (PRMS). (2014). The "Curbside" Consult and what it means for you. RM-0199.
Rao, J. K., Anderson, L. A., Lin, F. C., & Laux, J. P. (2014). Completion of advance directives among U.S. consumers. *American Journal of Preventive Medicine, 46*(1), 65–70.
Resnick, P. J., & Sorrentino, R. M. (2005). Forensic issues in consultation-liaison psychiatry. *Psychiatric Times, 23*(14).
Resnick, P. J., & Sorrentino, R. M. (2006). Forensic considerations. In M. Blumenfield & J. S. Strain (Eds.), *Psychosomatic medicine*. Lippincott Williams & Wilkins Publishers.
Stone, J., Smyth, R., Carson, A., Lewis, S., Prescott, R., Warlow, C., & Sharpe, M. (2005). Systematic review of misdiagnosis of conversion symptoms and "hysteria". *BMJ (Clin Res Ed), 331*(7523), 989.
Suri, S. (2020). Action, affiliation, and a duty of care: physicians' liability in nontraditional settings. *Fordham L Rev, 89*, 301–342.
Walzl, D., Carson, A. J., & Stone, J. (2019). The misdiagnosis of functional disorders as other neurological conditions. *Journal of Neurology, 266*(8), 2018–2026.

Emergency Room Psychiatry

23

Jacob M. Appel

Introduction

The fast-paced, high-volume nature of care in many psychiatric emergency rooms raises distinctive challenges not encountered in other clinical settings. At the same time, emergency psychiatry as a separate field is relatively new (Moukaddam & Tucci, 2017). As a result, the standard of care for evaluation and treatment in psychiatric emergency rooms has not yet been clearly defined (Simpson & Monroe, 2018). Attempts have been made to generate consensus guidelines for practice (Allen et al., 2005; Wilson et al., 2012). However, the impact of these efforts has been blunted both by a shortage of empirically validated data and a broader skepticism among providers "regarding evidence-based guidelines and standardized measuring scales" (Damsa et al., 2007). The sheer range of conditions confronted by emergency room psychiatrists (e.g., psychotic disorders, mood disorders, substance use disorders, medical comorbidities, acute agitation, malingering, and a wide range of social stressors such as homelessness and food insecurity) require both a broad scope of clinical knowledge and an understanding of related "ethical and legal concepts" (Ostermeyer et al., 2017). Familiarity with relevant "federal and state laws pertaining to these significant medical-legal issues" is also crucial (Ostermeyer et al., 2017). Providing first-rate medical care can often, albeit not always, prove an effective method for avoiding both litigation and malpractice payouts.

Several aspects of the structure of emergency psychiatry in the United States are specifically conducive to malpractice claims (Slovenko, 2002). First, interactions between providers and patients tend to be short and discrete. The time-limited nature of these contacts may not allow for the goodwill and mutual trust that develops in long-term care relationships or even during the daily encounters of inpatient management. Second, regular shift changes—usually at either eight- or twelve-hour intervals—impede continuity of care. In private practice, the patient encounters the same provider at each session. In the inpatient and consult-liaison settings, the same team of full-time providers usually returns day after day. In contrast, many psychiatric emergency rooms are staffed by a rotating pool of clinicians, some of whom only work several non-consecutive days each month. The process of frequently transitioning care opens the door to misunderstandings and errors. Third, state laws limiting the length of stay in emergency rooms and financial pressures to render decisions quickly may impact the clinical choices of providers. Finally, the sheer volume of cases managed has been correlated with malpractice claims in the emergency setting (Carlson et al., 2018).

The nature of the care required in emergency settings also raises malpractice risk. Emergency room psychiatrists are called upon to make high stakes decisions with limited historical or corroborative information about their patients. These decisions involve assessment of risk and include weighing the dangers of suicide or violence against imposing severe restrictions upon individual autonomy. In extreme circumstances, they may require either physical or chemical restraints to prevent acutely dangerous behavior in the emergency setting. Often this must be done without knowing a patient's relevant medical background. Patients may present to a hospital's emergency department (ED) for the first time and, as a result of illness, prove poor historians. They may be unwilling or unable to reveal the names of outside mental health providers or collateral sources of information such as family members. This differs substantially from most outpatient settings, where an intake process secures detailed information on a patient's previous diagnoses, medication trials, risky behaviors, and other contacts with the mental health system. It also differs from many inpatient and consult-liaison encounters, when it is usually possible to obtain corroborative information from patients' families or friends

The part-time nature of emergency psychiatry work may also increase risk. Emergency room psychiatrists often lack the experience and expertise characteristic of specialists working in other psychiatric settings. Emergency psychiatry

J. M. Appel (✉)
Department of Psychiatry, Icahn School of Medicine at Mount Sinai, New York, NY, USA

P. Ash et al. (eds.), *Malpractice and Liability in Psychiatry*, https://doi.org/10.1007/978-3-030-91975-7_23

is not a recognized subspecialty by the American Board of Medical Specialties (ABMS), and only a small number of fellowship programs exist, all of which are not accredited by the Accreditation Council of Graduate Medical Education (ACGME). Most psychiatrists working in the emergency setting are not members of the American Association for Emergency Psychiatry (AAEP). Many psychiatrists practice part-time in the emergency department in order to support nascent private practices or as a bridge to other career opportunities. Short-term tenures combined with a lack of specialized training generate a distinct and potentially elevated risk of malpractice litigation.

Elements of Malpractice Specific to the Psych ED Setting

The four elements of malpractice required at common law and under most state statutes are (1) that the physician owed a professional duty to a patient; (2) that the physician breached that duty; (3) that the breach caused harm to the patient; and (4) that the harm led the patient to suffer physical or psychological damages (Bal, 2009; *Helling v. Carey,* 1974).

Duty and Dereliction

In the emergency setting, the physician-patient relationship with its concomitant duties generally commences when the patient presents for evaluation. The start of this obligation differs substantially from the outpatient setting, where providers may evaluate patients "in consultation" before entering into a formal treatment relationship. As a result of the Emergency Medical Treatment and Active Labor Act (EMTALA) of 1986, hospitals must "stabilize" any individual who presents suffering from "an emergency medical condition" (42 U.S. Code § 1395dd). In the ensuing decades, emergency rooms have become the "de facto safety net for many patients with mental illness," especially those with limited resources (Schmalz & Sawyer, 2020). Amendments to EMTALA in 1989 required "hospitals with the specialists needed to stabilize emergency medical conditions" to "accept patients from hospitals without the required specialists" (Schmalz & Sawyer, 2020). The liability for breaching this duty falls upon hospitals, rather than upon individual physicians, but an emergency psychiatrist inappropriately refusing transfers may create EMTALA liability for his employer (*Pham v. Black*, 2018).

General consensus has emerged regarding fundamental requirements of a standard-of-care encounter in the psychiatric emergency setting. These include "discerning the etiology of symptoms, assessing suicide and violence risk, and determining the need for psychiatric hospitalization" (Allen et al., 2005). Increased levels of control in the inpatient and ED settings, especially "over a patient's dangerous behavior," may elevate the risks of a malpractice suit (Tsao & Layde, 2007). Incidents that occur within the emergency room itself—such as a suicide in the ER—are highly likely to result in liability, whereas less control of a patient's behavior post-discharge may lessen liability, especially as the chronological distance between the date of discharge and the subsequent dangerous event increases.

Even in psychiatric emergency departments where residents or fellows provide the front-line care, direct evaluation of the patient by the attending physician should be expected (Sacchetti et al., 1992). A professional translator or translation service should be used with non-English-speaking patients unless the provider is fluent in the patient's preferred language (Kuhn, 1990). Urgent medical comorbidities should either be addressed directly or, when safe and necessary, patients should be referred to appropriate care (Zun, 2005). When possible, sexual assault survivors and victims of other crimes should be afforded access to the specific medical, psychological, and legal resources they require (Linden, 2011). Although many social issues faced by emergency room patients such as homelessness are often beyond the scope of individual providers to resolve in a systemic manner, all discharged patients must be ensured a safe disposition with meaningful access to food, shelter, medications, and essential ongoing medical treatment.

Causation

All jurisdictions require that the medical conduct cause the resulting injury for a patient or estate to recover damages. Historically, the level of causation required has been a so-called proximate cause; more recently, to avoid confusion by jurors, some states have switched to a standard that requires the provider's conduct to be a "substantial factor" in the patient's injury (Tsao & Layde, 2007). Under common law, defendants could offer a defense of "contributory negligence," in an attempt to avoid liability if the plaintiff contributed in any way to his own injury. This approach greatly favors physicians: A misdiagnosis or poor treatment decision leading to a suicide would not lead to a payout if the doctor could prove any intervening choice by the patient—such as missing a dose of medication—might have played a role in the negative outcome. Since the 1960s, states have adopted comparative responsibility systems in which a provider is only responsible to the degree that she contributed to the injury, and many states impose a requirement of more than 50% responsibility ("limited comparative negligence") for recovery. These limitations are particularly relevant in the emergency setting: Discharges of patients at chronic elevated risk of harm to themselves or others may raise questions as to whether a premature release or the underlying condition played a primary role in the negative events that followed. However, patients are still expected to minimize damages by pursuing appropriate care and may receive lower payouts in circumstances where they fail to do so (Adar, 2013).

Providers are usually responsible for injuries that arise inside the ED, much as they would be for those that occur in any other inpatient setting. However, as the chronological distance between evaluation and admission or discharge increases, the argument for causation between disposition and injury weakens. No hard-and-fast timetable absolves a provider from liability, but a panel of jurors will be more likely to hold a physician responsible for a suicide that occurs hours subsequent to release rather than weeks later. However, it is common practice for plaintiffs' attorneys to subpoena and depose all clinicians in the medical record if a patient suffers a negative outcome after inpatient discharge, so it is possible for an emergency department psychiatrist to be sued for "wrongful discharge" for a patient who was admitted to the hospital and not encountered again by the emergency department psychiatrist during the patient's inpatient stay.

Damages

Findings of negligence generally lead to the awarding of compensatory damages, which may cover payment for future treatment of the specific injury, resulting economic loss, and pain and suffering. In the emergency room setting, punitive damages may arise for wrongful admissions that result in unlawful detention (*Barker v. Netcare Corporation*, 2001).

Specific Areas of Risk

Wrongful Admission

Most emergency psychiatric liability arises as a result of negligence. One rare exception is the wrongful admission of patients to hospitals on an involuntary basis, which can also lead to claims of false imprisonment, an intentional tort, or even criminal charges. Historically, standards for admission were low and safeguards few. Yet a series of cases starting with *Lessard v Schmidt* (1972) have imposed significant limits on physicians' authority in this area. Many states now follow language similar to California's Lanterman-Petris-Short Act (1969) and require that an individual pose "a danger to others, or to himself or herself, or [be] gravely disabled as a result of the mental disorder" (California Welf. & Inst. Code §5000-5556 (1969)). At present, all states require that a patient pose some danger to the public or a threat to his own well-being to be hospitalized against his will—although the threshold and imminence of that danger or threat varies by jurisdiction. Federal law arguably imposes such a standard as well. In *O'Connor v. Donaldson* (1975), the US Supreme Court wrote that there is "no constitutional basis for confining such persons involuntarily if they are dangerous to no one and can live safely in freedom." Wrongful admission claims are now infrequent and rarely successful. Payouts are likely to result from overt breaches of law or ethical canons, such as acting out of malice, certifying a patient without a determination that the patient meets the standards for involuntary admission, or detaining a patient without personally examining him or her at all (*Plumadore v. New York*, 1980; *Riffe v. Armstrong*, 1996). Some courts have found that qualified immunity may exist for good faith determinations (*Glass v. Mayas*, 1992). Psychiatrists often benefit from considerable leeway in assessments of dangerousness. Yet providers are not shielded from "plainly incompetent" decisions that deprive patients of their liberties (*Rodriguez v. City of New York*, 1995). Since false imprisonment is an intentional tort, victims may be eligible for punitive as well as compensatory damages. Some liability policies may exclude or limit their coverage against such punitive claims or refuse to cover appeals from findings of intentional misconduct. Upon admitting a patient, providers should complete and sign the required legal paperwork and, except where permitted by law, no patient should be admitted to a psychiatric unit until the appropriate authorization forms—whether voluntary or involuntary—are completed.

Confidentiality/Reporting

The Health Insurance Portability and Accountability Act (HIPAA) of 1996, state laws and regulations, and customary practice all impose liability standards upon providers for breaches of confidentiality. One widespread misconception is that confidentiality laws, especially HIPAA, prevent providers from confirming the presence of patients in emergency departments. This is not the case. According to US Department of Health & Human Services guidance, HIPAA's "Privacy Rule permits a covered hospital or other covered health care provider to maintain in a directory certain information about patients – patient name, location in the facility, health condition expressed in general terms that does not communicate specific medical information about the individual" and to share this information with "anyone who asks for the patient by name" with the caveat that the patient must have the opportunity to restrict the information or to whom it is disclosed, or opt out of being included in the directory"

(Health Information Privacy, 2013). Most relevant in the psychiatric emergency setting, "Even when, due to emergency treatment circumstances or incapacity, the patient has not been provided an opportunity to express his or her preference about how, or if, the information may be disclosed, directory information about the patient may still be made available if doing so is in the individual's best interest as determined in the professional judgment of the provider, and would not be inconsistent with any known preference previously expressed by the individual" (Health Information Privacy, 2013). Critically, under HIPAA, providers can also exchange information with other providers essential for treatment of the patient such as providing collateral information between psychiatric emergency departments (45 CFR §§ 164.502(a)(1)(ii), 164.506(c)). Although violating HIPAA can impose severe civil and criminal consequences on covered entities, there is no cause for private action under the statute. Private causes of action generally occur in state courts under state malpractice laws.

Emergency room psychiatrists are often mandatory reporters. Every state imposes a duty to report child abuse under standards imposed by the Federal Child Abuse Prevention and Treatment Act (CAPTA) (42 U.S.C.A. § 5106g). Many states require the reporting of elder abuse, intimate partner violence, sexual relationships with previous providers, impaired driving, communicable diseases, and threats to public health (MacIntyre & Appel, 2020). Providers may be held liable for failing to warn third parties of a range of dangers from interpersonal violence to risk of infection. At the same time, providers can also be held liable for breaching duties of confidentiality. Knowledge of specific state law in this area, or consultation with a hospital or insurer legal expert, is essential in these matters.

Malingering

The feigning of psychiatric illness for secondary gain is a common phenomenon in the emergency setting with estimates of malingering reported as high as 1 in 5 presenting patients (Rumschik & Appel, 2019). However, "a patient's dishonesty about his presenting complaint does not necessarily mean that the patient does not have a legitimate need" (Hamilton & Feldman, 2007). It may be useful to divide malingerers into categories: "soft malingerers" presenting as a result of social service failures like homelessness and "hard malingerers" who may be avoiding judicial (e.g., arrest) or extrajudicial (e.g., from a loan shark) consequences for conduct (Appel, 2019). Multiple validated tests for detecting malingering exist, but many are time-consuming to conduct and not well-suited for the emergency setting. The Structured Interview of Reported Symptoms (SIRS), for example, has a specificity of 97.5%, but requires 30–40 minutes to administer (Zubera et al., 2015). The Miller Forensic Assessment of Symptom Test (M-FAST) is the most promising of tests for the emergency room, as it can be administered in 5–10 minutes (Zubera et al., 2015). However, its sensitivity and specificity run lower than that of the SIRS, so it should only be used in cases where the pre-test probability of malingering runs high (Zubera et al., 2015). All of these tests require some level of engagement by the patient, which may not be forthcoming. Another, often more practical approach involves a comparison of the patient's observed behavior and symptoms with those of known psychiatric illnesses (Zubera et al., 2015).

A diagnosis of malingering can open up the provider to liability in multiple ways. First, malingering is a derogatory and stigmatizing label that, once documented, may affect a patient's future care. As a result, it can lead to claims of defamation (Weiss & Dell, 2017). Second, many patients engaged in malingering are also prone to high-risk behavior. Therefore, even a patient claiming suicidal thoughts but who was accurately diagnosed with malingering in the ER and discharged, and who subsequently dies of an overdose, poses a challenge to the provider: In hindsight, a case of malingering may be mistaken for one of improper care. To avoid these scenarios, providers should document in detail the patient's statements and behaviors that lead to the diagnosis. A likely motivation should also be included, since one should be reluctant to label a patient as malingering without a clear indication that the patient is pursuing specific secondary gain.

Negligent Discharge

One of the most common causes of action against ER psychiatrists is negligent discharge. The frequency of these cases should not be surprising, as one of the most fundamental responsibilities of the emergency room provider is patient triage. It should be emphasized that the discharge itself is not actionable, but rather the damages that result from such a discharge. These damages may stem from misdiagnosis, leading to medical or psychiatric decompensation. Alternatively, they may result from failure to adequately assess the risk that a patient poses a danger to himself or to others. Providers must avoid discharging patients as a result of positive countertransference, especially in the absence of collateral information (Sulkowicz, 1999). Pressures for premature discharge from family members must also be resisted. Both patients and relatives will sometimes offer to sign waivers absolving providers of responsibility for future self-harm or dangerousness, but these are unlikely to carry any significant weight during litigation.

Reducing Risk: Communication and Documentation

Communication

Communication is the "cornerstone of the physician-patient relationship," and multiple studies have revealed a correlation between a "breakdown" in communication and subsequent litigation (Huntington & Kuhn, 2003). Up to 55% percent of all claims may stem from communication failures between physicians and patients (CRICO Strategies, 2016). The advantages of good communication are particularly apparent in the emergency setting, ensuring that patients understand what to anticipate in times of crisis. Even when the emergency department is busy, physicians should introduce themselves to patients briefly in a timely manner, provide a rough sense of how long a delay they can expect before formal evaluation, and ask if they have any pressing needs in the interim (Granger, 2013). When medical errors do occur, some data suggests that direct apologies by physicians reduce litigation costs (Walling & Ackerman, 2006). A number of states have adopted laws that exclude apologies by physicians from being used against them in court, although their efficacy remains controversial (McMichael et al., 2019). Psychiatrists should be familiar with their own institution's policies in this regard. On a much more routine level, apologizing for inconveniences that are not errors—a long wait time, a noisy environment—can reassure the patient at no risk and establish rapport, which in turn may reduce the likelihood of subsequent litigation.

Documentation

Clear documentation in the emergency setting is essential to prevent liability (Ferguson et al., 2018). In fact, "good care combined with good documentation is the surest way to avoid being a defendant in a malpractice action" (Simpson & Stacy, 2004). The purpose of this documentation, from a liability-deterring standpoint, is to explain the clinical choices made, as well as those alternatives considered but rejected, and the rationale for doing so. In litigation, a detailed description of the decision-making process can prove highly protective. The quality of documentation may also influence whether a malpractice defense attorney will accept a case on a physician's behalf (Simpson & Stacy, 2004).

At a minimum, in the emergency department, every patient should have a note written by the attending of record on every shift (Sacchetti et al., 1992). The attending physician should also document any significant changes in the patient's condition including the uses or removal of physical restraints. Under no circumstances should a patient be discharged or transferred from a psychiatric emergency department without an attending note which includes a safety assessment and a justification for release. The standard of care is less clear in circumstances where the psychiatric team functions as a consultation service for patients who are officially under the care of a medical attending in an emergency department. The optimal approach—and one employed by the majority of medical centers—remains for the attending to staff the consult in real time, evaluating the patient and documenting pertinent findings. However, a sizeable number of hospitals allow for residents or fellows to evaluate these consultation cases and then discuss the cases via phone with an attending off-site, which likely meets the threshold of the respectable minority doctrine for avoiding liability (Appel et al., 2013–2014). No clear case law exists on this consultation model of emergency psychiatric treatment. (It is important to note that attendings should be careful not to bill for direct evaluation of patients they have not personally evaluated to avoid liability, disciplinary measures, and possible criminal sanction for fraud.) The rise of telepsychiatry and video evaluation may render this issue moot, as attending psychiatrists may increasingly be able to conduct direct emergency evaluations from off-site.

Situations often arise when a patient would benefit from admission but wishes to leave and does not pose an acute danger; in such cases, common practice is to document the patient's choice and that no legal grounds exist to hold the patient further under the circumstances. Similarly, if the patient refuses medical treatment and is allowed to do so, the chart should include both a statement that treatment was offered and a brief capacity assessment demonstrating that the patient possessed the capacity to refuse.

A fast-paced environment with multiple providers requires clear documentation of the chain of interaction between providers. When starting a shift, the physician should record in the chart of each patient the name of the provider from whom she obtained "sign out"; when transferring a patient out of the psychiatric emergency department—such as to a medical ED or floor—the name of the accepting attending should be recorded as well. Anyone reviewing the chart should be able to discern which provider was responsible for a particular patient at any moment. The chart should also clarify the reasons for ordering PRN medications. When such medications are administered involuntarily, such as in response to agitation or violence, the specific purpose and legal justification for the order should be documented in the chart.

Discharge from the emergency department requires specific safeguards: a careful screen for potential suicide or violence, a safety plan reviewed with the patient, and, when available, collateral information obtained from a patient's outpatient providers and family. All of these should be specifically documented. Many psychiatric patients pose some chronic risk of harm to themselves or others, and hospitalization may be contraindicated. In these cases, providers should document why the risk is not currently acute or elevated and that the patient is at his baseline. Occasionally, individuals who do not suffer from mental illness will present to emergency rooms posing a threat to others. When legally permissible and appropriate, these cases should be reported to law enforcement and the report documented prior to discharge.

Conclusion

Emergency psychiatry differs from other areas of psychiatry in that providers have no say in choosing or screening their patients and can rarely build lasting rapport. They must often make rapid decisions based upon limited information. In addition, they confront numerous legal and ethical obligations that are governed by laws that vary considerably between states. Emergency psychiatrists should familiarize themselves with the basic legal principles and their duties and should know the particular applications within their jurisdictions. They should be equally comfortable drawing upon expert help. Hospitals generally have both legal and risk management teams that can offer important, complementary—but not interchangeable—guidance when complex cases arise. On nights and weekends, a senior administrator may be on call to address high stakes concerns. By drawing upon the expertise of others, providers can frequently offset the structural causes of increased liability on the emergency setting.

Key Points

- While emergency room psychiatrists encounter a wide range of clinical conditions and ethical challenges, providing first-rate medical care can often prove an effective method for avoiding both litigation and malpractice payouts.
- Structural factors leading to increased risk of malpractice claims against emergency psychiatrists include the short, discrete nature of patient-provider interactions, frequent shift changes that disrupt continuity of care, limits upon durations of stay, and the sheer volume of patient encounters.
- Emergency psychiatrists should be familiar with federal and states laws pertaining to their area of practice.
- The physician-patient relationship with its concomitant duties generally commences when the patient presents to the emergency room for evaluation.
- As a result of the Emergency Medical Treatment and Active Labor Act of 1986, hospitals must stabilize any individual who presents suffering from an emergent medical condition.
- The standard of care in the psychiatric emergency setting includes identifying the likely cause of symptoms, assessing the risk for suicide and violence, and determining the need for acute psychiatric hospitalization.
- Wrongful admission may lead to claims of false imprisonment, an intentional tort, rendering victim eligible for punitive as well as compensatory damages.
- While malingering is common in the emergency setting, psychiatrists open themselves up to liability if they diagnose malingering without clear evidence of intended secondary gain.
- Breakdowns in communication are a leading cause of litigation for psychiatrists, and diligent efforts should be made to keep patients informed regarding their care.
- Effective documentation explains in detail the clinical choices made, as well as those alternatives considered but rejected, and the rationale for doing so.

References

42 U.S. Code § 1395dd.

45 CFR §§ 164.502(a)(1)(ii), 164.506(c).

Adar, Y. (2013). Comparative negligence and mitigation of damages: Two sister doctrines in search of reunion. *Quinnipiac Law Journals, 31*(783), 9.

Allen, M., Currier, G., et al. (2005). The expert consensus guideline series. Treatment of behavioral emergencies 2005. *Journal of Psychiatric Practice, 11*(Suppl 1), 5–108.

Appel, J. M., Kapley, D., et al. (2013–2014). Mental health innovation vs. psychiatric malpractice: Creating space for reasonable innovation. *Faulkner Law Review, 5*(1), 131–163.

Appel, J. M. (2019). At psychiatric emergency rooms, fake patients take a heavy toll. *Undark*. https://undark.org/2019/03/07/the-malingering-pandemic/

Bal, B. S. (2009). An introduction to medical malpractice in the United States. *Clinical Orthopaedics and Related Research, 467*(2), 339–347. https://doi.org/10.1007/s11999-008-0636-2

Barker v. Netcare Corporation. (2001). Franklin County Court of Common Pleas Ohio 98 CV-09-7239.

California Welf. & Inst. Code §5000-5556 (1969)

Carlson, J. N., Foster, K. M., Pines, J. M., et al. (2018). Provider and practice factors associated with emergency physicians' being named in a malpractice claim. *Annals of Emergency Medicine, 71*(2), 157–164.e4.

CRICO Strategies. (2016). *Malpractice risks in communication failures: 2015 annual benchmarking report*. Cambridge, MA.

Damsa, C., Andreoli, A., et al. (2007). Quality of care in emergency psychiatry: Developing an international network. *European Psychiatry: The Journal of the Association of European Psychiatrists, 22*, 411–412.

Federal Child Abuse Prevention and Treatment Act (CAPTA) (42 U.S.C.A. § 5106g).

Ferguson, B., Geralds, J., Petrey, J., & Huecker, M. (2018). Malpractice in emergency medicine-a review of risk and mitigation practices for the emergency medicine provider. *The Journal of Emergency Medicine, 55*(5), 659–665.

Glass v. Mayas, 794 F.Supp. 470 (E.D.N.Y. 1992).

Granger, K. (2013). Healthcare staff must properly introduce themselves to patients. *BMJ, 347*, f5833.

Hamilton, J. C., & Feldman, M. D. (2007). Functional analysis of malingering in the emergency department. *Psychiatric Times*.

Health Information Privacy. (2013). Department of Health and Human Services: https://www.hhs.gov/hipaa/for-professionals/faq/483/does-hipaa-permit-hospitals-to-inform-visitors-about-a-patients-location/index.html

Helling v. Carey, 83 Wash. 2d 514, 519 P.2d 981 (1974).

Huntington, B., & Kuhn, N. (2003). Communication gaffes: A root cause of malpractice claims. *Proceedings (Baylor University, Medical Center), 16*(2), 157–161.

Kuhn, W. (1990). Malpractice and emergency medicine. *Emergency Medicine Reports, 11*(2).

Linden, J. A. (2011). Clinical practice. Care of the adult patient after sexual assault. *New England Journal of Medicine, 365*(9), 834–841.

Lessard v. Schmidt, 349 F. Supp. 1078 (E.D. Wis. 1972).

MacIntyre, M. R., & Appel, J. M. (2020). Legal and ethics considerations in reporting sexual exploitation by previous providers. *The Journal of the American Academy of Psychiatry and the Law, 48*(2), 166–175.

McMichael, B. J., Van Horn, L., & Viscusi, K. (2019). "Sorry" is never enough: How state apology Laws fail to reduce medical malpractice liability risk. *Stanford Law Review, 71*(2), 341–409.

Moukaddam, N., & Tucci, V. T. (2017). Emergency psychiatry: Ten years later. *Psychiatric Clinics of North America, 40*, xiii–xiv.

Ostermeyer, B., Shoaib, A. N., & Deshpande, S. (2017). Legal and ethical challenges, part 1: General population. *The Psychiatric Clinics of North America, 40*(3), 541–553.

O'Connor v. Donaldson 422 US 563 (1975).

Pham v. Black, 347 Ga. App. 585 (Ga. Ct. App. 2018).

Plumadore v. New York 427 N.Y.S.2d (N.Y.App.Div. 1980).

Riffe v. Armstrong, 477 S.E.2d 535 (1996).

Rodriguez v. City of New York, 72 F.3d 1051 (2d Cir. 1995).

Rumschik, S. M., & Appel, J. M. (2019). Malingering in the psychiatric emergency department: Prevalence, predictors, and outcomes. *Psychiatric Services, 70*(2), 115–122.

Sacchetti, A., Carraccio, C., & Harris, R. H. (1992). Resident management of emergency department patients: Is closer attending supervision needed? *Annals of Emergency Medicine, 21*(6), 749–752.

Schmalz, A., & Sawyer, N. T. (2020). The EMTALA loophole in psychiatric care. *The Western Journal of Emergency Medicine, 21*(2), 244–246. https://doi.org/10.5811/westjem.2019.10.45332

Simpson, S., & Stacy, M. (2004). Avoiding the malpractice snare: Documenting suicide risk assessment. *Journal of Psychiatric Practice, 10*(3), 185–189.

Simpson, S. A., & Monroe, C. (2018). Implementing and evaluating a standard of care for clinical evaluations in emergency psychiatry. *Journal of Emergency Medicine, 55*, 522–529.e2.

Slovenko, R. (2002). *Psychiatry in law/law in psychiatry*. Routledge.

Sulkowicz, K. J. (1999, December). Psychodynamic issues in the emergency department. *Psychiatric Clinics of North America, 22*(4), 911–922.

Tsao, C. I., & Layde, J. B. (2007). A basic review of psychiatric medical malpractice law in the United States. *Comprehensive Psychiatry, 48*(4), 309–312.

Walling, R. J., & Ackerman, S. S. (2006). Having to say you're sorry: A more efficient medical malpractice insurance model. *Contingencies, 18*, 46–49.

Weiss, K., & Dell, L. (2017). Liability for diagnosing malingering. *Journal of the American Academy of Psychiatry and the Law, 45*, 339–347.

Wilson, M., Pepper, D., et al. (2012). The psychopharmacology of agitation: Consensus statement of the American Association for Emergency Psychiatry Project BETA Psychopharmacology Workgroup. The western. *Journal of Emergency Medicine, 13*, 26–34.

Zubera, A., Raza, M., Holaday, E., et al. (2015). Screening for malingering in the emergency department. *Academic Psychiatry, 39*, 233–234.

Zun, L. S. (2005). Evidence-based evaluation of psychiatric patients. *The Journal of Emergency Medicine, 28*(1), 35–39.

24 Reproductive Psychiatry

Susan Hatters Friedman, Aimee Kaempf, and Nina Ross

Introduction

Reproductive psychiatry focuses on the treatment of mental health disorders related to reproduction. Providing psychiatric treatment during pregnancy and postpartum requires a specialized knowledge of the relationship between the reproductive cycle and mental health. Psychiatric issues during the reproductive life cycle include premenstrual mood disorders; mental health issues related to infertility, loss, and birth trauma; psychiatric illnesses during pregnancy and the postpartum; and the treatment of mental illness in menopause. This chapter will primarily focus on malpractice related to pregnancy, the postpartum, and parenting. Issues related to malpractice within reproductive psychiatry include informed consent for reproductive decisions such as abortion and permanent contraception; psychiatric hospitalization during the perinatal period, including the use of seclusion and restraints; prescribing psychiatric medications to women during pregnancy and postpartum; abandonment or failure to treat women in pregnancy or postpartum which may lead to wrongful death by suicide or infanticide; and dual agency in parenting or custody evaluations.

S. H. Friedman (✉)
Departments of Psychiatry, Pediatrics, Reproductive Biology, and Law, Case Western Reserve University, Cleveland, OH, USA
e-mail: SJH8@Case.edu

A. Kaempf
Department of Psychiatry, University of Arizona, Tucson, AZ, USA

N. Ross
Department of Psychiatry, University Hospitals/Case Western Reserve University, Cleveland, OH, USA
e-mail: Nina.ross@uhhospitals.org

Specific Areas of Risk

Informed Consent

Informed consent is especially important in the context of reproductive healthcare decisions. Such decisions are often time-sensitive and irreversible, involve multiple stakeholders, can be mired in socio-political controversy, and may evoke strong emotions among patients and caregivers (American College of Obstetricians and Gynecologists [ACOG], 2021). When women with psychiatric disorders are faced with reproductive decisions, medical decision-making capacity may be called into question. Medical decision-making capacity consists of four key abilities: (1) the ability to communicate choices, (2) the ability to understand relevant information, (3) the ability to appreciate the situation and its consequences, and (4) the ability to rationally manipulate information (Appelbaum & Grisso, 1988).

The presence of a mental disorder does not automatically equate to incapacity. Women with psychiatric illnesses may exhibit symptoms with varying degrees of severity, meaning whether one has the capacity to make medical decisions may fluctuate over time (Appelbaum & Grisso, 1988; McCullough et al., 2002). Additionally, capacity to make medical decisions is task-specific, with criteria for competency becoming more stringent as the consequences of a woman's choice become more significant (American Medical Association [AMA], 2016). A woman may lack capacity for one treatment decision while maintaining capacity for another. The ethical principle of autonomy mandates that clinicians involve patients in all treatment decisions to the greatest extent feasible in accordance with the patient's medical decision-making capacity. Whenever possible, treatment to restore decisional capacity should be pursued in order to avoid depriving a woman of her right to make healthcare decisions. However, when a woman lacks medical decision-making capacity, generally the clinician must identify an appropriate surrogate decision-maker.

P. Ash et al. (eds.), *Malpractice and Liability in Psychiatry*, https://doi.org/10.1007/978-3-030-91975-7_24

Women with mental illness or disability have been denied reproductive freedoms throughout history (ACOG, 2017). Compared to women with no mental health history, women with psychiatric illness have higher rates of contraception non-adherence, risky sexual behaviors, and unintended pregnancies; thus, family planning is an important consideration in this population (Miller, 1997). Abortion and non-reversible contraception are two procedures with permanent consequences that require knowledgeable participation on the part of the patient (or surrogate), free of manipulation or coercion (ACOG, 2021; AMA, 2016). Such decisions are ethically complex and become even more challenging in the context of mental illness (ACOG, 2017).

Failure to obtain informed consent for any procedure, including abortion and permanent contraception, may be grounds for a malpractice claim, or even a criminal charge of battery. Psychiatrists may be called upon to assess medical decision-making capacity or offer other input when women with mental illness face reproductive decisions. For psychiatrists involved in such cases, the risk of legal ramifications can be minimized by obtaining consultation when warranted and ensuring thorough documentation of the informed consent dialogue, the assessment of medical decision-making capacity, and the patient's (or surrogate's) treatment decision (AMA, 2016).

Informed Consent: Abortion

Between 2011 and 2017, 18–21% of all pregnancies in the United States ended in abortion (Jones et al., 2019). Nationally, approximately half of all pregnancies are unintended, and one out of four women in the United States will have an abortion in her lifetime (Jones & Jerman, 2017). The decision to terminate a pregnancy is profound, irreversible, and time-dependent, necessitating knowledgeable and voluntary participation. Pre-abortion counselling includes a thorough review of all pregnancy termination options including risks, benefits, and anticipated outcomes of each procedure. Discussion of alternatives such as continuing pregnancy and adoption should be non-directive and free of any attempt to persuade or manipulate a woman's decision (ACOG, 2021). The values and beliefs of clinicians, partners, or other stakeholders should not interfere with voluntary decision-making (ACOG, 2021).

The effect of elective abortion on mental health has been debated in the literature. Overall, research has shown that having an abortion does not increase a woman's risk for mental illness and that the relative risk of psychiatric illness after an abortion is of no greater risk to mental health than carrying a pregnancy to term (American Psychological Association, 2008). In some jurisdictions, the informed consent process surrounding abortion is complicated by policies aimed at restricting abortion access. Some statutes may require women seeking abortions be provided with government-scripted materials regarding certain aspects of abortion and fetal development, some of which may contain biased or medically inaccurate information. Such statutes place clinicians in the ethically problematic situation of being legally mandated to provide inaccurate and potentially misleading information to patients (Vandewalker, 2012). Psychiatrists involved in abortion-related decisions should be familiar with relevant legal regulations in their area and how such policies may impact the informed consent process. Psychiatrists may be called upon to assess capacity to provide informed consent for adolescents seeking a judicial bypass of parental consent or for patients experiencing mental illness. While the requirement of informed consent has been clearly established in the legal and medical systems, it is unclear how a court in a malpractice suit will reconcile these statutes and their impact on informed consent.

Informed Consent: Permanent Contraception

Female permanent contraception is one of the most common methods of birth control used in the United States (Kavanaugh & Jerman, 2018). Permanent contraception for women with psychiatric disorders has a dubious history, with eugenics movements of the early twentieth century prompting many states to adopt statutes permitting compulsory "sterilization of mental defectives," regardless of the woman's reproductive preferences (Kundnani, 2013; *Buck v. Bell*, 1927). Compared to women with no disabilities or with exclusively physical disabilities, women with cognitive disabilities are more likely to have undergone tubal ligation or hysterectomy and at younger ages (Li et al., 2018).

Decisions regarding permanent contraception among women with psychiatric illness raise several ethical concerns. Respect for a woman's reproductive autonomy should guide considerations of permanent contraception (ACOG, 2017). Pre-sterilization counselling should include a focus on the woman's reproductive preferences and should underscore the permanence of the procedure. Reversible birth control methods, particularly long-acting reversible contraception, should be offered as alternatives. Coercive, or non-voluntary sterilization is unethical and should never be performed. Clinicians should be aware of any biases (explicit or implicit) that may impact reproductive health recommendations and care (ACOG, 2017).

Most women with mental illness retain capacity to make reproductive health decisions and should be permitted to consent to or to decline permanent contraception (Diekema, 2003). In cases where capacity fluctuates over time, clinicians should strive to assess patients when psychiatric treatment and mental health functioning are maximized (Appelbaum & Grisso, 1988). If a woman is legally incompetent to make reproductive healthcare decisions, courts may approve permanent contraception. However, such authorizations are becoming increasingly controversial and should be limited to situations in which sterilization is overwhelmingly considered the best and lone option for the woman unable to give consent (Kundnani, 2013; Rowlands & Amy, 2019). In sum, providing ethical female permanent contraception involves ensuring access to sterilization for women who desire it while simultaneously protecting against coercive or abusive practices, especially among individuals with mental disorders and other populations whose reproductive rights have historically been discounted (ACOG, 2017).

Psychiatric Hospitalization

Pregnancy Screening During Psychiatric Hospitalization

In 2016, approximately 400,000 women of childbearing age were admitted to psychiatric hospitals across the United States (Health Services Advisory Group [HSAG], 2018). Yet patients' reports of sexual, contraceptive, and menstrual histories are often unreliable (Goyal et al., 2015). Knowledge of pregnancy status upon psychiatric admission is essential to incorporating relevant risk/benefit analyses into treatment decisions and to minimize adverse pregnancy outcomes related to teratogenic medication use and other interventions (American Psychiatric Association [APA], 2010). Despite being a key element of medical evaluation, pregnancy testing is not uniform across inpatient psychiatric facilities, with testing rates ranging from 59% to 94% (HSAG, 2018). Failure to determine the pregnancy status of psychiatrically hospitalized women prevents informed treatment decisions by clinicians and patients and has the potential to cause severe, preventable harm to both the fetus and mother—leading to malpractice liability. Even when testing is negative, pregnancy screening during psychiatric hospitalization provides an opportunity to discuss contraception and family planning options in a population that is potentially exposed to teratogenic medications and that is at high risk for unintended pregnancies (HSAG, 2018; du Toit et al., 2018).

Psychiatric Admission for Pregnant Women

Mental illnesses (e.g., mood, anxiety, and psychotic disorders) are common during the perinatal period and can lead to negative outcomes for the infant and mother if not treated. In most instances, psychiatric illness in pregnant and postpartum women can be successfully treated with outpatient interventions such as social support, lifestyle modifications, therapy, and medication management (Mental Health America, 2018). Less commonly, severe mental disorders occur in the perinatal period, either as a new-onset illness or as a continuation of a chronic psychiatric condition (Jones et al., 2014). Severe mood or psychotic episodes can give rise to psychiatric exigencies including suicidality, aggression, psychotic denial of pregnancy, delusions involving the baby, poor infant care, and thoughts of infanticide. Women with such symptoms often require psychiatric hospitalization for safety and stabilization. Assessing the need for psychiatric admission involves consideration of the severity of symptoms, degree of impairment, presence of psychosis, level of social support, psychiatric history, dangerousness to self, and risk of harm to the infant or others (Jones et al., 2014). Failure to appropriately hospitalize a pregnant or lactating woman could result in a malpractice suit for a variety of reasons, including wrongful death (suicide or homicide).

Pregnant women with severe mental illness face logistical barriers to psychiatric hospitalization. Some psychiatric facilities automatically exclude pregnant women from admission. Others exclude women at greater than 32 weeks' gestational age and/or women with high-risk pregnancies. Thus, in an already strained mental healthcare system (Torrey et al., 2019), pregnant women with severe mental illness have even fewer options. Furthermore, inconsistent requirements for medical clearance and admission can make the process of psychiatrically hospitalizing a pregnant woman confusing and burdensome, leading to prolonged emergency department waits and delays in care (Lee et al., 2016). If psychiatric admission is denied due to pregnancy, women may be admitted to medical or obstetrical units to receive psychiatric treatment through a consultation service. This arrangement is problematic because most medical/obstetric units lack the secure, therapeutic environment and specially trained staff provided in mental health facilities and are therefore ill-equipped to offer around-the-clock, comprehensive care for severely mentally ill patients (Lee et al., 2016). Failure to hospitalize due to lack of bed availability or unit policy is not a defense to a malpractice claim.

Psychiatric Admission for Postpartum Women

In the United States, postpartum admission rates to mental healthcare facilities are estimated to be 1–2 per 1000 births, most commonly for postpartum psychosis (Jones et al., 2014). In general, specialized perinatal mental health resources are scarce. Joint mother-baby inpatient psychiatry units, available in Europe and other parts of the world, have not been adopted in the United States (Jones et al., 2014; Kosman et al., 2020). Hence, the decision to hospitalize a woman soon after childbirth is particularly challenging because psychiatric admission entails separation of the mother from her infant, interruptions in breastfeeding, added caregiving demands on other family members, stigma contributing to feelings of shame and guilt, and difficulties with post-discharge readjustment to caring for a newborn (Wisner et al., 1996; Kosman et al., 2020). Not all psychiatric facilities have the staff or resources to accommodate women with basic postpartum needs, such as supervised visits with the baby, lactation consultation, obstetrics follow-up, and access to breast pumps and storage equipment. Such limitations may deter new mothers from agreeing to inpatient care despite being in crisis. The risks and benefits of psychiatric admission, either on a voluntary or involuntary basis, must be carefully weighed while adhering to ethical principles of beneficence, non-maleficence, autonomy, and justice. Decision-making is complicated by the need to factor in the impact of hospitalization on the mother-infant relationship. Despite the many possible dilemmas, hospitalization remains a necessary intervention whenever the safety of the mother, newborn, or others is at stake, and no less restrictive suitable alternatives are available (Jones et al., 2014; Kosman et al., 2020). Psychiatrists confronted with the difficult task of determining whether or not to psychiatrically hospitalize a woman in the postpartum period may minimize malpractice risk through detailed documentation of the decision-making process as well as through consultation with colleagues.

Seclusion and Restraint

The use of seclusion and restraint (S & R) in psychiatric treatment is controversial and highly regulated. It should be reserved for situations in which there is an imminent risk of harm to the pregnant woman, her fetus/newborn, or others, and other reasonable means such as verbal de-escalation or increased staffing are unsuccessful or unavailable (Recupero et al., 2011). Unnecessary use of S & R (i.e., to punish or control a patient who does not pose an imminent risk of harm) may be grounds for a lawsuit alleging constitutional rights violations or excessive use of force (Recupero et al., 2011). Perinatal agitation is considered a psychiatric-obstetrical emergency and is associated with negative outcomes including premature delivery, low birth weight, placental abnormalities, spontaneous abortion, and postnatal death (Aftab & Shah, 2017). Interventions should proceed from least restrictive to more restrictive and may include verbal de-escalation, environmental changes, oral or intramuscular medications, placement in a seclusion room, and, as a last resort, physical restraint (Wilson et al., 2015).

Pregnancy places women at increased risk of injury during S & R. Potential adverse health effects associated with the use of S & R during pregnancy include discomfort, impaired mobility, increased fall risk, delays in assessment and care during obstetrical emergencies, and increased risk of blood clots (ACOG, 2016). Later in pregnancy, physical restraints may place pressure on the uterus and contribute to inferior vena cava compression syndrome resulting in decreased placental blood flow. Thus, pregnant women after 20 weeks' gestation require left lateral decubitus positioning with elevation of the right hip (Wilson et al., 2015). During childbirth and postpartum, restraints interfere with normal labor and delivery, breastfeeding, and mother-infant bonding (ACOG, 2016). Close observation is essential during any S & R episode and should include frequent monitoring of vital signs as well as fetal heart tones and movement (Recupero et al., 2011; Wilson et al., 2015). Detailed documentation of events surrounding S & R, including a patient's preceding behaviors and attempts at de-escalation, helps protect mental health clinicians and facilities against claims that S & R was needlessly or inappropriately implemented (Recupero et al., 2011).

Malpractice Liability from Psychiatric Treatment (or Lack Thereof) During Pregnancy and the Postpartum

Psychiatrists who treat reproductive age women must be aware of the impact of psychiatric illness and treatment on potential pregnancies. As previously noted, almost half of pregnancies in the United States are unplanned (Finer & Zolna, 2016). Compared to women without psychiatric illness, women with psychiatric illness are more likely to have unplanned or unwanted pregnancies (Møller-Olsen et al., 2018; Miller, 1997). Between weeks 3 and 8 of pregnancy is the most significant period of organogenesis (Niebyl & Simpson, 2012) which can occur before many women realize they are pregnant. A woman may therefore be taking a potentially teratogenic psychiatric medication during this crucial organogenesis window. Psychiatrists who treat women of reproductive age must keep in mind that a patient could become pregnant, either intentionally or unintentionally. Thus, it is critical that medication choices in this population take into account the potential for pregnancy. Whenever possible, psychiatrists should opt for agents that are safer in pregnancy. Psychiatrists should discuss the safety of medication in pregnancy prior to the woman becoming pregnant. Patients should be educated that in the event of pregnancy, they should contact their psychiatrist rather than suddenly stopping medications on their own (Friedman et al., 2021).

There is a common misconception that pregnancy is protective against psychiatric illness (Cohen, 2001), when, in fact, pregnancy and the postpartum period are times of significant vulnerability to psychiatric illness (Davé et al., 2010). Discontinuation of psychiatric medication during pregnancy significantly increases the risk of illness relapse (Cohen, 2001; Viguera et al., 2012). Furthermore, psychiatrists who stop a woman's medication upon learning that she is pregnant place the woman and fetus at risk for sequela of abrupt medication discontinuation – and themselves at risk of an abandonment lawsuit.

However, the psychiatric treatment of pregnant patients often prompts malpractice concerns. In particular, psychiatrists worry that psychiatric medications may adversely affect the fetus. Physicians are typically more concerned about errors of commission compared to errors of omission (Friedman et al., 2018; Friedman, 2015; Miller, 2009). In reproductive psychiatry, this bias causes physicians to excessively worry about harm from prescribing a medication and to not adequately consider the harms from inadequately treated psychiatric illness.

Inadequately treated psychiatric illness can lead to adverse maternal and fetal outcomes, which in turn can lead to malpractice suits. In the most severe cases, inadequately treated psychiatric illness can result in suicide and homicide, including neonaticide and infanticide. Each of the many risk factors common among mothers with serious mental illness can adversely impact fetal and infant health.

Treatment of psychiatric illness during pregnancy requires weighing the risks of medications against the risks of inadequately treated psychiatric illness. There is no risk-free option. However, steps can be taken to make thoughtful, evidence-based decisions that minimize adverse maternal and fetal outcomes as well as mitigate the risk of a malpractice suit. Ideally, physicians should incorporate preventative ethics by discussing the possibility of future pregnancies with women of reproductive age (Friedman et al., 2018; Friedman, 2015; Miller, 2009). This process can proactively identify and prevent future dilemmas, such as the dilemma that occurs when a woman who has achieved psychiatric stability on a potentially teratogenic medication must decide whether or not to stop the medication when she is pregnant. As in any patient encounter, physicians should assess the risks of the treatments and act as "learned intermediaries," conveying risks of a treatment to their patients (Friedman & Hall, 2013).

Psychiatrists are familiar with assessing the risks of a treatment to an adult patient, but they are typically less familiar with assessing the risks of a psychiatric treatment to a fetus. Psychiatrists should also be able to critically assess existing data and new reports about a medication's risks during pregnancy. Traditionally, the US Food and Drug Administration (FDA) classified medications' safety during pregnancy using five risk categories: A, B, C, D, and X (Department of Health and Human Services, 2014). This classification system was widely criticized for its misleading simplicity that resulted in an emphasis on a drug's risks, without any providing meaningful description of these risks or providing any information about the risks of undertreated maternal psychiatric illness (Cohen, 2001; Department, 2014). In response to this criticism, the FDA developed the Pregnancy and Lactation Labeling Rule in 2015 (Department, 2014). This rule removed the categories and mandated the inclusion of more descriptive information on packaging, including a description of its potential risks during pregnancy and lactation and the data from which these risks were derived (Department, 2014).

Risks of treatment need to be weighed with risks of psychiatric illness, described in Table 24.1. Typically, five reproductive domains are considered when evaluating the effect of a psychiatric medication on fetal outcomes: intrauterine demise, prematurity, congenital malformations, neonatal syndromes, and neurobehavioral problems (Miller, 1997; Friedman & Hall, 2013; Wisner et al., 2000). Ethical and legal concerns have traditionally prohibited the enrollment of pregnant women in randomized controlled trials (Institute of Medicine, 1994; Kaye, 2019; Lyerly et al., 2008). As such, most information about the impact of psychiatric medication during pregnancy is from observational studies, such as retrospective analyses and exposure registries. Observational studies have many limitations, including confounding effects, selection bias, and classification bias (Friedman & Hall, 2013; Gueyffier & Cucherat., 2019). Physicians must carefully interpret these studies while being mindful of their limitations. Treating psychiatrists should be aware of conflicting studies about medications in pregnancy as well as the risk of untreated illness. An algorithm for treating women of childbearing age may be useful (Fig. 24.1). Consulting potential references online, such as womensmentalhealth.org, as well as colleagues, is helpful.

Table 24.1 Risk of treatment versus risk of psychiatric illness formulation in pregnancy

	Risk of medication	Risk of psychiatric illness
Woman	Medication side effects Adverse pregnancy events	Suicide Homicide Medical comorbidities Substance use Adverse pregnancy events Impaired maternal-infant bonding
Fetus	Adverse pregnancy events Intrauterine death Abnormal growth Congenital malformations Neonatal syndromes Neurobehavioral outcomes	Adverse pregnancy events Intrauterine death Abnormal growth Congenital malformations Neonatal syndromes Neurobehavioral outcomes Impaired maternal-infant bonding

If a medication potentially poses a risk of an adverse fetal outcome, physicians should accurately describe this risk to their patients. Care should be taken to distinguish the absolute risk of an adverse outcome from the relative risk of an adverse outcome (Friedman et al., 2018; Friedman, 2015). Absolute risk of an adverse outcome should be accompanied by information about the severity of this outcome should it occur. For example, lithium is well-known to cause Ebstein's anomaly, a heart defect in which the tricuspid valve is not properly formed. However, the incidence and severity of this defect are much more limited than previously thought. Ebstein's anomaly initially was found to have an incidence of 3% in women exposed to lithium, a figure generated from a database on women prescribed lithium who self-reported adverse events, compared to a 1 in 20,000 incidence in the general

Fig. 24.1 Algorithm – psychiatric treatment of women of childbearing age

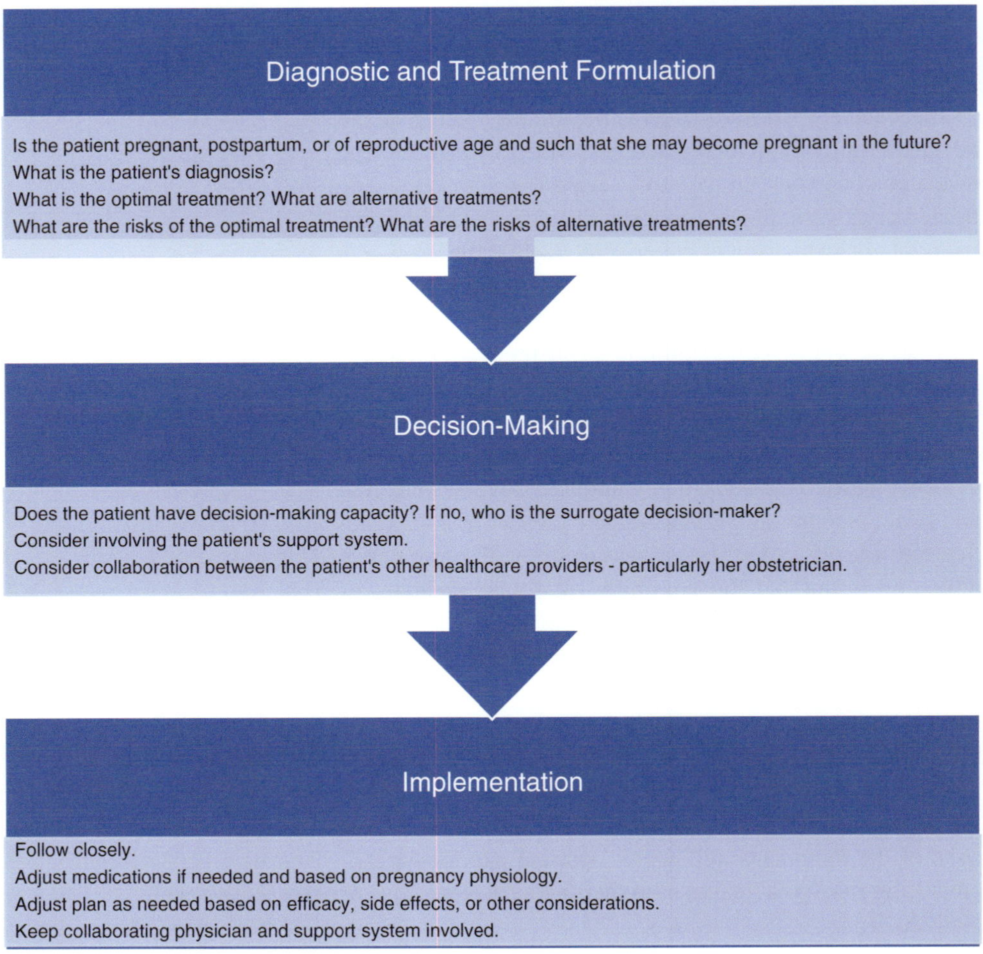

population (Niebyl 2012; Weinstein & Goldfield, 1975). Observational studies have since shown that actual incidence of Ebstein's anomaly is much smaller, present in about 0.6% of lithium-exposed infants compared to 0.18% in unexposed infants (Patorno et al., 2017). Furthermore, though more severe cases require surgery, others require only close monitoring (Kron & Roeser, 2017; Knott-Craig et al., 2012). Psychiatrists who treat pregnant patients must convey the risks of a medication, including the likelihood and severity of adverse outcomes. A woman who had responded to lithium previously may very well decide to take lithium after receiving evidence-based, accurate information about its risks to her and her fetus.

Pregnancy trimester can affect a medication's teratogenic potential as well as medication efficacy. For example, first trimester exposure to valproic acid has a well-established risk of neural tube defects as well as other congenital malformations (Koren et al., 2006). However, prescribing valproic acid to a woman who is 20-week pregnant, after the neural tube has largely formed, minimizes the risk of congenital malformations due to valproic acid, although seizures may be a risk due to sudden withdrawal at delivery. Dosage requirements may change in pregnancy and postpartum and can be anticipated.

Other considerations can limit the risk of adverse outcome to woman and fetus. Pregnant patients, in particular, should be prescribed the minimum effective dose and the minimum number of effective medications (Friedman, 2015; Friedman & Hall, 2013). Prescribing a lower than effective dose confers the risks both of the medication and undertreated psychiatric illness (Friedman & Hall, 2013). Polypharmacy can synergistically increase the likelihood of malformations (Sadowski et al., 2013). Psychiatrists should also ask women if they plan to breastfeed and, if so, inform patients about the bioavailability of the medication when ingested through breastmilk and potential risks.

After ascertaining that the patient is capable of providing informed consent, involving the patient's support system in these discussions can be helpful in providing emotional support for the patient and identifying additional concerns (Wisner et al., 2000). Should capacity become impaired in the future, this discussion also allows the patient to communicate her preferences so that a surrogate decision-maker can make decisions in accordance with her preferences. Malpractice suits typically arise from adverse health outcomes coupled with patients and their families having negative feelings such as guilt, shame, and anger (Gutheil, 2004;

Hickson et al., 1992). These feelings can be evoked by problems with a physician's communication skills, including the perception that a physician is judgmental, insensitive, unavailable, or withholding important information (Witman et al., 1996; Gutheil, 2004; Hickson et al., 1992). Physicians who take the time to have clear, honest, thoughtful conversations with their female patients of childbearing age and their support systems may meaningfully reduce their risk of lawsuits, even if an adverse outcome occurs.

Treatment decisions may change throughout the course of pregnancy, as circumstances and psychiatric illnesses change. The physician should be prepared to work collaboratively with the patient and her support persons and alter the treatment plan if indicated. Collaboration with the patient's obstetrician can be extremely helpful, both in treatment formulations and in adjusting the treatment plan as indicated.

Treatment decisions may also include involuntary medications, long-acting medications, and electroconvulsive therapy. For example, a physician who believes a pregnant patient requires involuntary medication should consider the risks of this medication administration to the woman and fetus, which in this case includes the inherent risks of the medication and the risks of its administration including possible use of restraints (Friedman et al., 2018). A patient for whom involuntary medications are being considered is likely more psychiatrically ill, and the risks of her psychiatric illness to her health and her fetus' health are more severe than someone with mild psychiatric illness. A psychiatrist who believes a pregnant patient might benefit from a long-acting psychiatric medication should consider the risks of this medication and the fact that less information is known about its dissemination across the placenta (Friedman et al., 2018). A patient for whom a long-acting psychiatric medication is indicated may have a history of poor medication compliance and psychotic illness. Similarly, if electroconvulsive therapy is indicated, the physician should identify the risks of ECT and the risks of alternative treatments, based on critical appraisal of up-to-date literature, and discuss this information with the patient who can make an informed choice (Coshal et al., 2019).

Novel treatments of psychiatric illness may prompt questions about whether or not implementation of this treatment is the standard of care and how to best convey the risks associated with these treatments. One such relatively new treatment is brexanolone, an intravenous γ-aminobutyric acid modulator for treatment of moderate to severe postpartum depression (Meltzer-Brody et al., 2018; U.S. Food and Drug Administration, 2019). Considering novel treatments for a patient should again follow a similar decision-making framework. Novel treatments inherently have less data and more uncertainty about their risks to both mother and infant, and this uncertainty should be conveyed.

The health of woman and her fetus is inextricably linked (Walker et al., 2015). It is also imperative to consider woman and fetus as a dyad, rather than as adversaries (Miller, 2009; Friedman et al., 2018). Psychiatrists who appropriately treat pregnant women with psychiatric illness not only reduce their own risks of malpractice, but actively promote the health of both woman and fetus.

Wrongful Death: Infanticide

The risk of infanticide should be considered in the postpartum, especially among women who are contemplating suicide. Jennings et al. (1999) found that among mothers with depression, 41% had thoughts of harming their young child, compared to 7% of controls. Infant factors may also increase risk; among mothers of infants with colic, one quarter had infanticidal thoughts during colic episodes (Levitzky & Cooper, 2000). Many more mothers will experience such thoughts than will act on them.

Despite the frequency, psychiatrists still often do not ask about mothers having thoughts of harming their child (Friedman et al., 2008). Mothers who were suicidal may attempt or commit an "extended suicide," believing that the loving mother would take her child with her in death. Alternatively, a psychotic mother may kill her child or infant because of delusional reasons. Various motives for child murder include altruistic, acutely psychotic, unwanted child, spouse revenge, and, most commonly, fatal child maltreatment (often from chronic abuse or neglect), each suggesting their own preventive strategies (Friedman & Resnick, 2007).

Friedman and Resnick (2007) noted that a psychiatrist treating a mother should evaluate whether she has hallucinations or delusions about the children, which may elevate her risk toward the child. Psychiatrists should assess for risk of infanticide systematically similarly to how they do for suicide (Friedman & Resnick, 2007). A tick—box general risk assessment for homicide may not include specific risk items for risk to children and thus would not be useful in this regard. Of note, postpartum exacerbation or onset of obsessive-compulsive disorder (OCD) is common (Booth et al., 2014). Psychiatrists should be careful to distinguish ego-dystonic violent obsessions from true violent ideation or psychosis and note their markedly different risk implications (Booth et al., 2014).

Wrongful Death by Suicide in Pregnancy or the Postpartum

Lawsuits about wrongful death may occur during the pregnancy or postpartum period related to suicide or infanticide, which was alleged to occur because of lack of appropriate treatment. Suicide has been noted to be responsible for up to one-fifth of deaths in the postpartum period (Lindahl et al., 2005), and risk factors for suicide should be considered in pregnancy and postpartum (Sidhu & Friedman, 2020).

Marriage may be less of a protective factor against suicide for women than it is for men (Vijayakumar, 2015). Relationship problems, prior psychiatric hospitalization, substance abuse, mental health symptoms, younger age, and a limited supports system may elevate the risk (Lindahl et al., 2005; Gold et al., 2012; Comtois et al., 2008). It should also be noted that thoughts of suicide are not rare in the peripartum. Specifically, Lindahl et al. (2005) noted that at 18 weeks' gestation, about 10% of women endorsed thoughts of self-harm and 7% did so at 32 weeks pregnant. Similarly, by 6 months postpartum, 7–15% reported some thoughts of self-harm. Further, women may self-report suicidal thoughts when they are actually experiencing infanticidal thoughts, in order to get help (Barr & Beck, 2008).

Dual Agency

Occasionally, a reproductive psychiatrist or general psychiatrist may be asked by a parent to provide a forensic opinion about that patient's capacity to parent or for child custody. However, the reproductive or general psychiatrist should be aware that such an assessment is a forensic assessment. This is different than a clinical assessment; there is a lack of normal doctor-patient confidentiality. Further, the report and testimony may be perceived to harm the patient despite the clinician's good intentions. Ethical and legal dilemmas exist when a psychiatrist attempts to serve as both the forensic evaluator and the treating clinician. Friedman et al. (2021) noted "clinicians not trained in forensic assessment should be wary of performing parenting capacity assessments for legal purposes." Budd (2005) noted common mistakes include failure to disclose the evaluation's purpose, failure to disclose the lack of confidentiality, over-relying on a single source of information (compared to forensic evaluations where collateral information is critical), as well as making overstated recommendations and conclusions.

Conclusions

Various potential types of malpractice are possible within reproductive psychiatry. Psychiatrists should therefore consider the reproductive potential of any woman of childbearing age and should use caution to provide appropriate evaluation and treatment.

Key Points

- Autonomy mandates that women be involved in reproductive health decisions to the greatest extent possible, in accordance with medical decision-making capacity.
- Psychiatrists who treat a woman of reproductive age must recognize that she could become pregnant during treatment; therefore, pregnancy status should be assessed regularly, and psychiatrists should have a working knowledge of relatively safe medications in pregnancy.
- Failure to provide adequate psychiatric treatment to a pregnant patient could increase the risk of facing abandonment and wrongful death malpractice lawsuits.
- When treating a pregnant patient, psychiatrists should discuss the risks and benefits of treatments and alternatives with the woman, her support system where possible, and her other healthcare providers.
- Psychiatrists should accurately appraise a treatment plan's potential risks, as well as the risks of undertreated psychiatric illness.
- Despite systemic barriers to psychiatric admission during the perinatal period, hospitalization remains a necessary intervention whenever the safety of the mother, the newborn, or others is at stake, and no less restrictive alternatives are available.
- Psychiatrists should complete both a suicide risk assessment and a homicide/infanticide risk assessment when seeing a pregnant or postpartum woman.
- Acting as both the treating psychiatrist and the expert witness/report writer should be avoided in parenting capacity or custody cases related to dual agency issues.

References

American College of Obstetricians and Gynecologists (ACOG) Committee on Ethics. (2017). Sterilization of women: Ethical issues and considerations. *Obstetrics and Gynecology, 129*(4), e109–e116. https://doi.org/10.1097/AOG.0000000000002023

ACOG Committee on Ethics. (2021). Informed consent and shared decision making in obstetrics and gynecology. *Obstetrics & Gynecology, 137*(2), e34–e41.

ACOG Committee on Health Care for Underserved Women. (2011, reaffirmed 2016). Health care for pregnant and postpartum incarcerated women and adolescent females. *Obstetrics & Gynecology, 118*(5), 1198–1202.

Aftab, A., & Shah, A. (2017). Behavioral emergencies: Special considerations in the pregnant patient. *The Psychiatric Clinics of North America, 40*(3), 435–448. https://doi.org/10.1016/j.psc.2017.05.017

American Medical Association (AMA). (2016). *Opinions on consent, communication & decision making*. Retrieved from the AMA website. https://www.ama-assn.org/sites/default/files/media-browser/code-of-medical-ethics-chapter-2.pdf

American Psychiatric Association. (2010). *Practice guideline for the treatment of patients with major depressive disorder* (3rd ed.). Available at https://psychiatryonline.org/pb/assets/raw/sitewide/practice_guidelines/guidelines/mdd.pdf. Accessed 15 Sep 2020.

American Psychological Association, Task Force on Mental Health and Abortion. (2008). *Report of the APA task force on mental health and abortion*. Retrieved from the American Psychological Association website. http://www.apa.org/pi/wpo/mental-health-abortion-report.pdf

Appelbaum, P., & Grisso, T. (1988). Assessing patients' capacities to consent to treatment. *The New England Journal of Medicine, 319*(25), 1635–1638.

Barr, J., & Beck, C. (2008). Infanticide secrets: Qualitative study on postpartum depression. *Canadian Family Physician, 54*(12), 1716–1717.

Booth, B., Friedman, S., Curry, S., Ward, H., & Stewart., S. (2014). Obsessions of child murder: Underrecognized manifestations of obsessive-compulsive disorder. *Journal of the American Academy and the Law, 42*(1), 66–74.

Buck v. Bell 274 U.S. 200 (1927).

Budd, K. (2005). Assessing parenting capacity in a child welfare context. *Children and Youth Services Review, 27*(4), 429–444.

Cohen, L. (2001). Limitations of pregnancy risk categories. Retrieved from the MGH Center for Women's Mental Health website. https://womensmentalhealth.org/obgyn/limitations-of-pregnancy-risk-categories/

Comtois, K., Schiff, M., & Grossman, D. (2008). Psychiatric risk factors associated with postpartum suicide attempt in Washington State, 1992–2001. *American Journal of Obstetrics and Gynecology, 199*(2), 120–1e1.

Coshal, S., Jones, K., Coverdale, J., & Livingston, R. (2019). An overview of reviews on the safety of electroconvulsive therapy administered during pregnancy. *Journal of Psychiatric Practice, 25*(1), 2–6. https://doi.org/10.1097/PRA.0000000000000359

Davé, S., Petersen, I., Sherr, L., & Nazareth, I. (2010). Incidence of maternal and paternal depression in primary care: A cohort study using a primary care database. *Archives of Pediatrics and Adolescent Medicine, 164*(11), 1038–1044. https://doi.org/10.1001/archpediatrics.2010.184

Department of Health and Human Services Food and Drug Administration. (2014). 21 CFR Part 201: Content and format of labeling for human prescription drug and biological products: Requirements for pregnancy and lactation labeling. *Federal Register, 79*(233), 72064–72103.

Diekema, D. (2003). Involuntary sterilization of persons with mental retardation: An ethical analysis. *Mental Retardation and Developmental Disabilities Research, 9*, 21–26. https://doi.org/10.1002/mrdd.10053

du Toit, E., Jordaan, E., Niehaus, D., Koen, L., & Leppanen, J. (2018). Risk factors for unplanned pregnancy in women with mental illness living in a developing country. *Archives of Women's Mental Health, 21*(3), 323–331. https://doi.org/10.1007/s00737-017-0797-7

Finer, L., & Zolna, M. (2016). Declines in unintended pregnancy in the United States, 2008–2011. *New England Journal of Medicine, 374*(9), 843–852. https://doi.org/10.1056/NEJMsa1506575

Friedman, S. H. (2015). The ethics of treating depression in pregnancy. *Journal of Primary Care and Community Health, 7*(1), 81–83.

Friedman, S. H., & Hall, R. (2013). Antidepressant use during pregnancy: How to avoid clinical and legal pitfalls. *Current Psychiatry, 12*(2), 10–17.

Friedman, S. H., Hall, R., & Sorrentino, R. (2018). Involuntary treatment of psychosis in pregnancy. *Journal of the American Academy of Psychiatry and the Law, 46*(2), 217–223. https://doi.org/10.29158/JAAPL.003759-18

Friedman, S.H., Kaempf, A., Landess, J, & Kauffman, S. (2021, in press). Forensic issues in reproductive psychiatry. In L. A. Hutner, L. Catapano, S. Nagle-Yang, K. Williams, & L. Osborne (Eds.), *APA textbook of women's reproductive mental health*. American Psychiatric Association Publishing.

Friedman, S. H., & Resnick, P. J. (2007). Child murder by mothers: Patterns and prevention. *World Psychiatry, 6*(3), 137–141.

Friedman, S. H., Sorrentino, R. M., Stankowski, J. E., Holden, C. E., & Resnick, P. J. (2008). Psychiatrists' knowledge about maternal filicidal thoughts. *Comprehensive Psychiatry, 49*(1), 106–110.

Gold, K., Singh, V., Marcus, S., & Palladino, C. (2012). Mental health, substance use and intimate partner problems among pregnant and postpartum suicide victims in the National Violent Death Reporting System. *General Hospital Psychiatry, 34*(2), 139–145.

Goyal, M., Hersh, A., Badolato, G., Luan, X., Trent, M., Zaoutis, T., & Chamberlain, J. M. (2015). Underuse of pregnancy testing for women prescribed teratogenic medications in the emergency department. *Academic Emergency Medicine, 22*(2), 192–196. https://doi.org/10.1111/acem.12578

Gueyffier, F., & Cucherat., M. (2019). The limitations of observation studies for decision making regarding drugs efficacy and safety. *Thérapie, 74*(2), 181–185. https://doi.org/10.1016/j.therap.2018.11.001

Gutheil, T. (2004). Suicide, suicide litigation, and borderline personality disorder. *Journal of Personality Disorders, 18*(3), 248–256. https://doi.org/10.1521/pedi.18.3.248.35448

Health Services Advisory Group, prepared for the Centers for Medicare & Medicaid Services (2018). Inpatient psychiatric facility outcome and process measure development and maintenance project methodology report: Screening for Pregnancy Measure. Retrieved from CMS.gov. https://www.cms.gov/Medicare/Quality-Initiatives-Patient-Assessment-Instruments/MMS/Downloads/IPF-Methodology-Report-Screening-for-Pregnancy.pdf

Hickson, G., Clayton, E., Githens, P., & Sloan, F. (1992). Factors that prompted families to file medical malpractice claims following perinatal injuries. *Journal of the American Medical Association, 267*(10), 1359–1363. https://doi.org/10.1001/jama.1992.03480100065032

Institute of Medicine (US) Committee on Ethical and Legal Issues Relating to the Inclusion of Women in Clinical Studies. (1994). In A. Mastroianni, R. Faden, & D. Federman (Eds.), *Women and health research: Ethical and legal issues of including women in clinical studies*. National Academies Press (US).

Jennings, K., Ross, S., Popper, S., & Elmore, M. (1999). Thoughts of harming infants in depressed and nondepressed mothers. *Journal of Affective Disorders, 54*(1–2), 21–28.

Jones, I., Chandra, P., Dazzan, P., & Howard, L. (2014). Bipolar disorder, affective psychosis, and schizophrenia in pregnancy and the post-partum period. *The Lancet, 384*(9956), 1789–1799.

Jones, R., & Jerman, J. (2017). Population group abortion rates and lifetime incidence of abortion: United States, 2008–2014. *American Journal of Public Health, 107*(12), 1904–1909. https://www.guttmacher.org/article/2017/10/population-group-abortion-rates-and-lifetime-incidence-abortion-united-states-2008

Jones, R., Witwer, E., & Jerman, J. (2019) *Abortion incidence and service availability in the United States, 2017*. Retrieved from the Guttmacher Institute website. https://www.guttmacher.org/report/abortion-incidence-service-availability-us-2017.

Kavanaugh, M., & Jerman, J. (2018). Contraceptive method use in the United States: Trends and characteristics between 2008, 2012 and 2014. *Contraception, 97*(1), 14–21. https://doi.org/10.1016/j.contraception.2017.10.003

Kaye, D. (2019). The moral imperative to approve pregnant women's participation in randomized clinical trials for pregnancy and newborn complications. *Philosophy, Ethics, and Humanities in Medicine, 14*(1):11. Published 2019 Sep 6. https://doi.org/10.1186/s13010-019-0081-8

Knott-Craig, C., Goldberg, S., Ballweg, J., & Boston, U. (2012). Surgical decision making in neonatal Ebstein's anomaly: An algorithmic approach based on 48 consecutive neonates. *World Journal of Pediatrics Congenital Heart Surgery, 3*(1), 16–20. https://doi.org/10.1177/2150135111425933

Kosman, K., Almeida, M., Salama, K., Salzman, C., & Teslyar, P. (2020). Inpatient hospitalization for postpartum depression: Implications for mother and infant. *Harvard Review of Psychiatry, 28*(4), 279–286. https://doi.org/10.1097/HRP.0000000000000253

Koren, G., Nava-Ocampo, A., Moretti, M., Sussman, R., & Nulman, I. (2006). Major malformations with valproic acid. *Canadian Family Physician, 52*(4), 441–447.

Kron, I., & Roeser, M. (2017). Management of Ebstein's anomaly. *Annals of Cardiothoracic Surgery, 6*(3), 266–269. https://doi.org/10.21037/acs.2017.05.03

Kundnani, R. (2013). Protecting the right to procreate for mentally ill women. *Southern California Review of Law and Social Justice, 23*(1), 59–89.

Lee, S., Tucci, V., Moukaddam, N., Worley, A., & Shah, A. (2016). Pregnant and virtually abandoned: The multiple hurdles of medically clearing and admitting a pregnant patient to an inpatient psychiatric unit. *Journal of Psychiatry and Mental Health, 1*(1). https://doi.org/10.16966/2474-7769.105

Levitzky, S., & Cooper, R. (2000). Infant colic syndrome—Maternal fantasies of aggression and infanticide. *Clinical Pediatrics, 39*(7), 395–400.

Li, H., Mitra, M., Wu, J. P., Parish, S. L., Valentine, A., & Dembo, R. S. (2018). Female sterilization and cognitive disability in the United States, 2011–2015. *Obstetrics and Gynecology, 132*(3), 559–564. https://doi.org/10.1097/AOG.0000000000002778

Lindahl, V., Pearson, J., & Colpe, L. (2005). Prevalence of suicidality during pregnancy and the postpartum. *Archives of Women's Mental Health, 8*(2), 77–87.

Lyerly, A., Little, M., & Faden, R. (2008). The second wave: Toward responsible inclusion of pregnant women in research. *International Journal of Feminist Approaches to Bioethics, 1*(2), 5–22. https://doi.org/10.1353/ijf.0.0047

McCullough, L., Coverdale, J., & Chervenak, F. (2002). Ethical challenges of decision making with pregnant patients who have schizophrenia. *American Journal of Obstetrics and Gynecology, 187*(3), 696–702. https://doi.org/10.1067/mob.2002.125767

Meltzer-Brody, S, Colquhoun, H, Riesenberg, R., Epperson, C., Deligiannidis, K., Rubinow, D. Li, H., Sankoh, A., Clemson, C., Schacterle, A., Jonas, J., & Kanes S. (2018, September 29). Brexanolone injection in post-partum depression: two multicentre, double-blind, randomised, placebo-controlled, phase 3 trials [published correction appears in Lancet;392(10153):1116]. *Lancet*, 392(10152):1058–1070. doi:https://doi.org/10.1016/S0140-6736(18)31551-4.

Mental Health America. (2018). Perinatal mental health. Available from: https://www.mhanational.org/issues/position-statement-49-perinatal-mental-health

Miller, L. (1997). Sexuality, reproduction, and family planning in women with schizophrenia. *Schizophrenia Bulletin, 23*(4), 623–635. https://doi.org/10.1093/schbul/23.4.623

Miller, L. (2009). Ethical issues in perinatal mental health. *Psychiatric Clinics of North America, 32*(2), 259–270. https://doi.org/10.1016/j.psc.2009.02.002

Møller-Olsen, C., Friedman, S., Prakash, C., & North, A. (2018). Clinical characteristics of maternal mental health service users treated with mood stabilizing or antipsychotic medication. *Asia-Pacific Psychiatry, 10*, e12304. https://doi.org/10.1111/appy.12304

Niebyl, J., & Simpson, J. (2012). Drugs and environmental agents in pregnancy and lactation: Embryology, teratology, epidemiology. In S. G. Gabbe, J. R. Niebyl, J. L. Simpson, M. B. Landon, H. L. Galan, E. R. M. Jauniaux, & D. A. Driscoll (Eds.), *Obstetrics: Normal and problem pregnancies* (6th ed.). Elsevier.

Patorno, E., Huybrechts, K., Bateman, B., Cohen, J., Desai, R., Mogun, H., Cohen, L., & Hernandez-Diaz, S. (2017). Lithium use in pregnancy and the risk of cardiac malformations. *New England Journal of Medicine, 376*(23), 2245–2254. https://doi.org/10.1056/NEJMoa1612222. PMID: 28591541; PMCID: PMC5667676.

Recupero, P., Price, M., Garvey, K., Daly, B., & Xavier, S. (2011). Restraint and seclusion in psychiatric treatment settings: Regulation, case law, and risk management. *The Journal of the American Academy of Psychiatry and the Law, 39*(4), 465–476.

Rowlands, S., & Amy, J. (2019). Sterilization of those with intellectual disability: Evolution from non-consensual interventions to strict safeguards. *Journal of Intellectual Disabilities: JOID, 23*(2), 233–249. https://doi.org/10.1177/1744629517747162

Sadowski, A., Todorow, M., Yazdani, B., Koren, G., & Nulman, I. (2013). Pregnancy outcomes following maternal exposure to second-generation antipsychotics given with other psychotropic drugs: A cohort study. *British Medical Journal Open, 3*(7), e003062. https://doi.org/10.1136/bmjopen-2013-003062

Sidhu, N., & Friedman, S. (2020). Suicide and gender. In L. Gold & R. Frierson (Eds.), *The American Psychiatric Association publishing textbook of suicide risk assessment and management* (pp. 293–304). American Psychiatric Association Publishing.

Torrey, E., Jaffe, D., Entsminger, K., Geller, J., & Stanley, J. (2019). The shortage of public hospital beds for mentally ill persons: A report of the treatment advocacy center. Retrieved from the Treatment Advocacy Website. https://mentalillnesspolicy.org/imd/shortage-hospital-beds.html

United States Food and Drug Administration. (2019). FDA approves first treatment for post-partum depression. Retrieved from FDA website. https://www.fda.gov/news-events/press-announcements/fda-approves-first-treatment-post-partum-depression

Vandewalker, I. (2012). Abortion and informed consent: How biased counseling laws mandate violations of medical ethics. *Michigan Journal of Gender & Law, 19*(1), 1–70.

Viguera, A., Nonacs, R., Cohen, L., Tondo, L., Murray, A., & Baldessarini, R. (2012). Risk of recurrence of bipolar disorder in pregnant and nonpregnant women after discontinuing lithium maintenance. *American Journal of Psychiatry, 157*(2), 179–184. https://doi.org/10.1176/appi.ajp.157.2.179

Vijayakumar, L. (2015). Suicide in women. *Indian Journal of Psychiatry, 57*(Suppl 2), S233.

Walker, E., McGee, R., & Druss, B. (2015). Mortality in mental disorders and global disease burden implications: A systematic review and meta-analysis. *JAMA Psychiatry, 72*(4), 334–341. https://doi.org/10.1001/jamapsychiatry.2014.2502

Weinstein, M., & Goldfield, M. (1975). Cardiovascular malformations with lithium use during pregnancy. *American Journal of Psychiatry., 132*(5), 529–531. https://doi.org/10.1176/ajp.132.5.529

Wilson, M., Nordstrom, K., Shah, A., & Vilke, G. (2015). Psychiatric emergencies in pregnant women. *Emergency Medicine Clinics of North America, 33*(4), 841–851. https://doi.org/10.1016/j.emc.2015.07.010

Wisner, K., Jennings, K., & Conley, B. (1996). Clinical dilemmas due to the lack of inpatient mother-baby units. *International Journal of Psychiatry in Medicine, 26*(4), 479–493. https://doi.org/10.2190/NFJK-A4V7-CXUU-AM89

Wisner, K., Zarin, D., Holmboe, E., Appelbaum, P., Gelenberg, A., & Leonard, H. (2000). Risk-benefit decision making for treatment of depression during pregnancy. *American Journal of Psychiatry, 157*(12), 1933–1940. https://doi.org/10.1176/appi.ajp.157.12.1933

Witman, A., Park, D., & Hardin, S. (1996). How do patients want physicians to handle mistakes? A survey of internal medicine patients in an academic setting. *Archives of Internal Medicine, 156*(22), 2565–2569.

Addiction Psychiatry

25

Ryan C. Wagoner

Addiction psychiatry is both an officially recognized subspecialty of psychiatry and a prominent component of the work that many general psychiatrists do every day. In all areas of medicine where addictive substances are prescribed, physicians run the risk of patients overusing their medications, at times with catastrophic results. This risk is even more pronounced in psychiatry, where the patient population already struggles with finding ways to cope with stressors and may turn to abusing substances to alleviate their suffering. When compounded with a psychiatrist's role of often treating substance use disorders, addiction psychiatry is deeply ingrained into the practice of the larger specialty.

In the area of addictions, malpractice risk arises in multiple areas for a psychiatrist. Some of these risks are specific to the treatment of substance use disorders, but others are encountered in general clinical practice. This leads to addiction psychiatry malpractice risk being a concern for all psychiatrists who engage in clinical practice. Exploring these risks and how best to reduce them in clinical practice is the focus of this chapter.

Risk During General Clinical Practice

Benzodiazepines are often used in the treatment of anxiety disorders and are clinically warranted in many psychiatric patients (Balon & Starcevic, 2020). Because most psychiatrists do not prescribe opiates or treat physical pain, benzodiazepines represent one of the few examples of a controlled substance that a psychiatrist may routinely prescribe. However, the use of benzodiazepines is not without risk. Overdose risk for benzodiazepines has been an increasing issue in the United States, particularly when other controlled substances are prescribed (Bachhuber et al., 2016; Agarwal & Landon, 2019). Risk associated with the use of these medications also differs based upon age, as more and more evidence suggests that elderly individuals may be more susceptible to increased side effects from benzodiazepines (Markota et al., 2016; Zhong et al., 2015). In a clinical setting, benzodiazepines provide a challenge in both their risk for dependence and withdrawal. As this class of medications is widely used in primary care and psychiatry, these risks are a persistent consideration for psychiatrists on a regular basis in an outpatient setting. Psychiatrists should be cognizant of these competing risks and how to address them with the best available evidence.

The other class of controlled substances that psychiatrists may employ are stimulant medications. Stimulants are a mainstay of treatment for attention-deficit/hyperactivity disorder (ADHD) (Arnsten, 2006), as well as other conditions for which they are less commonly used, such as narcolepsy (Bassetti et al., 2019). While the withdrawal from these medications may not be as profound or as medically dangerous as that of benzodiazepines, in most circumstances, dependence on these medications can be problematic. Stimulant misuse and diversion can occur with these medications, due to their similar effects to illicit stimulants (Wilens et al., 2008).

Overprescribing and Dependence

With the advent of the Diagnostic and Statistical Manual of Mental Disorders, 5th edition (DSM-5), a shift occurred in the diagnosis of substance-related disorders. Gone are the competing interests of abuse versus dependence; instead, a more unified diagnosis of a substance use disorder is used to describe an individual with problematic patterns of substance use leading to clinically significant impairment or distress (American Psychiatric Association, 2013). The potential for liability, though, does not begin and end with the diagnosis of a substance use disorder; instead, the misuse of a controlled substance in a patient who has shown signs of

R. C. Wagoner (✉)
Department of Psychiatry and Behavioral Neurosciences, University of South Florida, Tampa, FL, USA
e-mail: ryanwagoner@usf.edu

P. Ash et al. (eds.), *Malpractice and Liability in Psychiatry*, https://doi.org/10.1007/978-3-030-91975-7_25

dependence on the medication can be sufficient to raise liability concerns for a psychiatrist.

Like it or not, physicians are often the gatekeepers to limit medications which may have the potential for misuse amongst patients. Some of these medications, such as benzodiazepines and stimulants, are classified as controlled substances and have specific regulations regarding their use. For example, according to US Federal Regulation 1306.12, refilling a prescription for a Schedule II controlled substance (such as stimulant medications) is prohibited. However, up to a 90-day supply may be authorized under specific conditions (Drug Enforcement Administration, 2020). This presents the first potential area for liability with addictive substances: prescribing outside of what is legally authorized.

Prescribing outside of the legal and regulatory bounds laid down by federal and state governments is fraught with peril. Failure to follow the law in this regard opens the psychiatrist up to regulatory oversight, civil liability, and even criminal liability. Particularly in the malpractice arena, if a bad outcome occurs in a case and the law regulating prescriptions was not followed, then it is quite difficult to mount a defense that the illegal prescriptions are within the prevailing standard of care. This bright line in prescribing regulations necessitates the need for psychiatrists to know the regulations surrounding controlled substances and follow those regulations when writing for medications such as benzodiazepines and stimulants.

While prescribing regulations around controlled substances can provide clear guidance around their use, clinical judgment about the appropriate prescription of these substances can be less clear, but no less important. For example, stimulant medications are primarily used by psychiatrists in the treatment of ADHD. The clinician must determine if a patient meets the appropriate criteria for diagnosis of this condition and discuss the risks and benefits of using stimulant medications. If a psychiatrist deviates from typical prescribing, such as using a stimulant for attention problems in an individual who does not meet full criteria for ADHD, the psychiatrist should consider whether they can justify this choice from a clinical perspective and if it meets the prevailing standard of care.

The second area for liability when prescribing potentially addictive substances arrives in failing to recognize dependence and misuse in patients. Individuals who are "addicted" to a prescribed substance may seek to obtain increasing amounts of the medication (or similar prescriptions from other providers – i.e., doctor shopping), due to a compulsive desire to take the substance, despite harmful consequences (National Institute on Drug Abuse, 2018). The gatekeeper role of the practitioner can be placed in conflict with the patient's wishes at those times. This type of situation becomes most prominent when a patient obtains a large amount of medication from a provider due to his or her dependence and has a bad outcome, such as an intentional or accidental overdose.

Not every situation of medication dependence or misuse will be detectible, and absolute certainty about how patients utilize their medications is not expected. Rather, reasonable care should be taken to explore clear situations where dependence or misuse behavior is potentially occurring. For example, if a patient is constantly requesting early refills of a controlled substance and increasing doses, with other evidence of dependence, then a reasonable psychiatrist should address this behavior in some way. Many states require investigation into prescription filling practices by patients through electronic databases that must be checked prior to writing for a controlled substance (Lin et al., 2017). These state-specific regulations again offer guidance on standards that must be met when prescribing these substances to avoid both malpractice situations and criminal penalties.

The third area where liability can occur when prescribing addictive substances to patients is diversion. Drug diversion is characterized by individuals obtaining or illegally using prescription medicines (Centers for Disease Control, 2020). This behavior can occur in both the outpatient setting and within medical facilities. It can also arise in any area of the medical supply chain, from the prescribing physician through to the patient to whom the prescription is given (Berge et al., 2012). The problems posed by diversion of controlled substances to third parties are similar to those previously mentioned in this chapter, but with an added layer of a patient willfully committing what is often a criminal act. A psychiatrist who is aware of controlled substances being diverted has a responsibility to take action related to this behavior, preferably in an expedient fashion. Although a psychiatrist is not a police officer tasked with bringing wrongdoers to justice, continuing to prescribe a controlled substance without an intervention in this situation raises major liability concerns.

Under-Prescribing and Withdrawal

Overprescribing is not the only peril involved in the utilization of controlled substances by psychiatrists. Due to the risks of withdrawal, abrupt cessation of a medication can also be a major concern in terms of risk and liability. For some medications, such as stimulants, withdrawal symptoms can be distressing, but show much less physical effects than other controlled substances (Pasic, 2017). However, benzodiazepines carry significant risks in withdrawal, such as seizures, which threaten serious injury or death in the wrong circumstances (Balon & Starcevic, 2020).

The potential for malpractice related to withdrawal from controlled substances begins with the prescription itself. High doses of medications like benzodiazepines increase the risk for withdrawal (Balon & Starcevic, 2020) and may require tapering if the patient ever requires cessation of this medication. Careful consideration of the appropriate circumstances in which high-dose benzodiazepines and stimulants are warranted should be assessed by the provider regularly, as this type of prescribing leads to a higher risk of withdrawal and correspondingly more complex management.

Controlled substances may need to be discontinued for a number of reasons, including missed appointments, side effects from the medications, choice to stop this particular therapy, or misuse of the substance. A psychiatrist should consider the potential risks of discontinuation of a medication in each of these circumstances and what options are available to mitigate the effect. This does not automatically entitle a patient to a continued supply of a controlled substance at whatever dose he or she demands, even if he or she is abusing it. Rather, psychiatrists may consider how best to balance appropriate prescribing with minimizing the risk of harm to their patients. For example, if a patient was overusing a high-dose benzodiazepine he or she was prescribed, the psychiatrist can consider multiple options to address taking the patient off this medication, including but not limited to a truncated tapering prescription, referral to an inpatient detoxification unit, or facilitating the patient having access to community resources which could mitigate his or her withdrawal. Often, the choice of which option to use will be guided both by the unique aspects of the case and the policies of the psychiatrist's place of employment. Recommendations for tapers of various medications vary widely and attempt to balance both expediency and comfort of the patient (Lader & Kyriacou, 2016). Due to the lack of an agreed upon schema for management of benzodiazepine withdrawal, psychiatrists should be aware of various tapering strategies and use their clinical judgment to assess which they will use.

Like many aspects of decision-making by physicians, a major limitation of appropriately managing potential withdrawal is knowing that a problem exists. While a psychiatrist should attempt to make sure that a patient has sufficient medication to last until his or her next appointment, a myriad of reasons can lead to the patient running out of a controlled substance, including changes to appointment times, changes in as-needed medication utilization, or overuse by the patient. In a situation where a patient runs out of these medications, appropriate policies should be in place at the psychiatrist's place of business to deal with these requests for refills. A more problematic issue occurs when the patient requests a refill and the on-call psychiatrist does not know the patient; in those situations, referral to specialized "walk-in" services or an emergency department may be warranted, to allow for examination and more in-depth discussion about why the prescribed medication has run out.

Risk when Treating Addictions

While almost all psychiatrists will engage in the practice of prescribing controlled substances at some point in their career, many also specifically treat issues related to addictions. In this specific arena, the principles previously discussed in this chapter, such as monitoring for overuse and mitigating the risk of withdrawal, become even more relevant on a regular basis. In addition to these risks, psychiatrists who treat addictions often engage in medication-assisted treatments (MATs) to treat addictions for specific substances. MATs can significantly increase the rates of successful abstinence in treatment for multiple substances, primarily in opioid use disorders (Connery, 2015). The medications used in MAT can present unique challenges and liability risks. In this chapter, we discuss three potential MATs that psychiatrists may use and the liability considerations they entail.

Methadone

Methadone is a long-acting full opioid agonist which is used to treat opioid use disorder (Substance Abuse and Mental Health Services Administration [SAMHSA], 2020b). This medication is often referred to as the gold standard in the treatment of opioid use disorders with MATs (Connery, 2015). Methadone is a unique medication when prescribed, as it can be used for two different purposes, with different regulations. When methadone is prescribed as a medication to treat pain, it is handled similar to many other Schedule II medications. However, when methadone is prescribed specifically to treat the symptoms of an opioid use disorder, a different set of regulations and requirements is imposed (SAMHSA, 2015).

This difference in regulatory requirements necessitates that psychiatrists should be clear as to the reason that they are utilizing methadone. When psychiatrists decide to use methadone in their practice, they should be aware both of the appropriate clinical prescribing of the medication and of the regulations surrounding the prescription. Regulatory requirements for the prescribing of methadone to treat an opioid use disorder can be quite stringent. Federal regulations require that in most circumstances, methadone may only be dispensed through an accredited opioid treatment program (OTP). One exception to this is often referred to as the "three-day rule," in which a practitioner may administer methadone for up to 72 hours (in 1 day increments) under an emergency withdrawal situation (DEA, 2020). However, even this exception has strict criteria on the timeframe of when this medication can be administered and emphasizes that methadone cannot simply be "prescribed," but must be "administered" (DEA, 2020), which solidifies the idea that this is not often a "take-home" medication. Another exception is found later in the same section of the DEA regulations, in which a physician can administer methadone to maintain or detoxify a patient who is being treated at a hospital for a medical or surgical condition other than addiction (DEA, 2020).

Guidelines produced by the Substance Abuse and Mental Health Services Administration (SAMHSA) lay out many aspects of proper use of methadone in opioid treatment programs, including appropriate drug testing, what systems of care are appropriate, dosage recommendations, and when "take-home" medications are appropriate (SAMHSA, 2015). Psychiatrists involved in prescribing methadone should be familiar with these guidelines, as practicing outside of them would be quite difficult to justify as an acceptable standard of care. In addition, many states also have further regulations on the use of methadone for treatment of an opioid use disorder above those mandated by the federal government. In the context of potential liability, a psychiatrist not only should be aware of all these regulations but should be vigilant to stay up to date with revisions and changes, as these can directly affect his or her clinical practice with this medication.

Dosing requirements for methadone can be complex, and multiple conversion charts are available, including from the Centers for Disease Control (2020). A particular concern in the use of methadone is that as higher doses of methadone are used, the conversion factor into morphine equivalents increases. Thus, the risk for overdose can increase exponentially as more methadone is prescribed. In addition, the use of other types of medications at the same time, including opioids and benzodiazepines, further increases the risk of overdose (Caplehorn & Drummer, 2002). In terms of liability, a careful consideration of overdose risk is a prominent feature of prescribing methadone.

Overuse of methadone is less of a concern in the treatment of opioid use disorder if the practitioner is following the guidelines for proper administration and the patient is receiving limited take-home doses of methadone. However, if a psychiatrist is using methadone to treat a patient's pain, then a serious risk of overuse and overdose can occur. In those circumstances, the psychiatrist should first consider if he or she is in the proper treatment role to manage the patient's pain. If they determine that they are the appropriate physician to manage this issue, they should develop clear reasoning for why this is and consider the problems with both overuse and withdrawal from this controlled substance, which were discussed previously in this chapter.

Buprenorphine

Buprenorphine is a partial opioid agonist that is also used to treat opioid use disorders (SAMHSA, 2020a). Unlike methadone, buprenorphine has less stringent regulations and can be prescribed outside of an accredited opioid treatment program if the physician has completed federally mandated training and received a special DEA waiver to prescribe buprenorphine for opioid replacement therapy (SAMHSA, 2020a). Limits on the number of patients a prescriber can currently manage on buprenorphine are mandated, so providers should be aware of the most recent numbers allowed. Although buprenorphine induction is typically initiated in an office or facility, buprenorphine is often prescribed as a "take-home" medication that is not administered from the facility directly, which is a major difference from most methadone treatment.

Similar to methadone, guidelines for prescribing buprenorphine are produced by SAMHSA (Centers for Substance Abuse Treatment, 2004). However, a major difference is that many of the guidelines are recommendations rather than hard and fast regulations. Although these are recommendations and are not required by law, psychiatrists should be familiar with the treatments proposed, as documents like this one are often considered when establishing a standard of care in malpractice cases. When practitioners deviate from these recommendations, they should have a clear and documented rationale as to why they have chosen to do so, in the event a malpractice case arises after a bad outcome.

Often, buprenorphine formulations are given along with naloxone, which decreases the likelihood of diversion and misuse. However, even if naloxone is not included in the formulation, important side effects of buprenorphine, such as respiratory depression, are often less than those of full opioid agonists (SAMHSA, 2020a). Despite this decrease in risk for overdose (Bell et al., 2009), buprenorphine can still be overused, either through obtaining a formulation without naloxone or by using enough to overcome naloxone's effect (Lavonas et al., 2014). Although the "high" associated with buprenorphine would be expected to be much less compared to many other opioids that are abused (due to the partial agonist effect), this does not prevent individuals from trying. Particularly when used in combination with other sedating drugs, such as benzodiazepines, this can present a risk for overdose. Diversion is also a concern, both for intoxicating effects and for individuals to mitigate their withdrawal symptoms outside of seeing a medical professional (Lavonas et al., 2014). As described earlier in this chapter, careful consideration should be made about the risks of overuse and withdrawal with this medication, and appropriate steps should be taken by the practitioner if these factors are identified.

Naltrexone

Naltrexone works in a much different way than other MATs, as it does not replace the addictive substance of interest.

Rather, it reduces the euphoric and sedative effects of opioids and alcohol through blockade of target receptors (SAMHSA, 2020c). Naltrexone is also different than the other MATs discussed in this chapter because it does not have its own risk for misuse or withdrawal. However, the interaction between naltrexone and opioid medications should be considered, as naltrexone could precipitate withdrawal from opiates if taken too closely in time. Naltrexone can also interact with substances of abuse by decreasing tolerance (Ritter, 2002). Patients who decide to stop using naltrexone and return to opioid use may find that their tolerance is greatly reduced; this leads to a danger of accidental overdose if an individual immediately returns to his or her previous pattern of use. Discussions about this potential outcome with patients can reduce the potential for overdose and the associated potential liability.

Naltrexone itself can cause side effects and appropriate discussion of the risks and benefits of the medication, like all prescriptions, should take place. In particular, psychiatrists should consider monitoring of liver function in individuals taking naltrexone, as serious complications are possible between this medication and hepatic functioning (LiverTox, 2020). Finally, like MATs, naltrexone is often less successful when used in a vacuum. Rather, integrating this medication as part of a more comprehensive addiction treatment plan is often recommended (Connery, 2015), and psychiatrists should consider if other resources are warranted during treatment.

Reducing Risk in Addiction Treatment

The use of medications with addictive potential, as well as the treatment of addictions themselves, holds unique risks for potential psychiatric malpractice, as detailed earlier in this chapter. While many of these risks can be reduced with typical advice found throughout this text, special strategies can also be quite useful. The first is knowing the laws and guidelines surrounding the prescribing of both controlled substances and medication-assisted treatments (MATs). While practitioners may chafe at the idea of having their clinical practice tightly scrutinized, these statutes and regulations provide a bright line in many cases of what kind of clinical practice is allowed or not, ranging from the amount of medication that can be prescribed to what other services should also be provided. Careful following of these laws will decrease both criminal and civil liability.

The second area of risk reduction in this arena is in clinical documentation. Virtually every discussion addressing liability in medicine centers around documentation. However, when focusing on addictive substances, which treatment is selected is not the primary concern; rather, acknowledging the presence of an issue and taking action supports the minimum standard of care. For example, if a patient has unusual filling habits of their controlled substance, this does not immediately require the practitioner to discontinue the medication and document that they have chastised the patient. Instead, a wide variety of clinical decisions could arise from this situation, based on the unique aspects of why this unusual filling habit occurred. Different practitioners could disagree on how best to address the situation in their clinical judgment. However, the action most likely to lead to increased risk for malpractice is to do nothing and to fail to document consideration towards the issue at all. Thus, providing a recognition of the problem and at least a minimum amount of rationale behind why a particular action was taken (or not taken) can substantially decrease risk in these situations.

Documentation becomes keenly important in areas where clear guidance is not available, such as tapering of controlled substances. When reviewing the literature for a taper schedule for benzodiazepines, for example, a myriad of choices pops up with often conflicting recommendations (Lader & Kyriacou, 2016). The decision of which piece of literature to give the most credence is often left to the psychiatrist. In such a situation, clinical documentation can be helpful in providing a rationale for why a particular taper is chosen. Citations of relevant literature in a clinical note are not required; rather, even a simple sentence about a planned strategy to mitigate withdrawal or the reason behind this can show a psychiatrist's firm standing within the standard of care in many situations.

The third area of risk reduction related to addictions is proper prescribing based on the clinical situation. Psychiatrists can fall into the trap of prescribing ever-increasing amounts of controlled substances, due to subjective concerns of patients. Psychiatrists can also become frustrated by the addictive behaviors of patients and wish to quickly remove the offending substance, despite the potential for risky withdrawal. In both circumstances, psychiatrists should base their clinical practice on the most appropriate prescribing practices available to them. Patients should have a say in their care, but should not dictate prescriptions that are beyond the comfort level of the psychiatrist. By the same token, anger with a patient should not lead to removing substances that can precipitate withdrawal, without a clear plan and consideration of the risks inherent in this action. The earlier that proper prescribing is initiated, based on evidence and manufacturer guidelines, the less the risk for later complications stemming from high doses of controlled substances and MATs. Many institutions and psychiatrists institute policies about limiting the use of controlled substances in practice, with some going so far as to ban the prescription of any stimulants or benzodiazepines in their clinics. This likely stems from multiple areas of concern, including potential liability when prescribing these substances, frustration with patients who take these medications, or logistics problems in ensuring appropriate prescribing practices. However, as noted previously in this chapter, many of the potential liability risks when prescribing benzodiazepines and stimulants can be mitigated by knowing the legal regulations, documenting appropriately, and using sufficient clinical judgment.

Key Points

- Addiction psychiatry and the corresponding risks for liability occur in both a sub-specialized setting and typical clinical practice.
- Misuse and dependence can introduce increased risks for malpractice when controlled substances are prescribed.
- Withdrawal and the potential for serious side effects should be mitigated, both with appropriate prescriptions of controlled substances and a consideration for tapering.
- Medication-assisted treatments (MATs) can increase the potential for successful treatment of substance use disorders but also introduce unique considerations for mitigating liability, including following specific regulations around their use.
- Risk can be reduced in this area through knowledge of medication-specific regulations, appropriate clinical documentation, and proper prescribing of controlled substances based on the clinical situation.

References

Agarwal, S. D., & Landon, B. E. (2019). Patterns in outpatient benzodiazepine prescribing in the United States. *JAMA Network Open, 2*(1), 1–11.

American Psychiatric Association. (2013). *Diagnostic and statistical manual of mental disorders, fifth edition (DSM-5)*. American Psychiatric Association.

Arnsten, A. F. T. (2006). Stimulants: Therapeutic actions in ADHD. *Neuropsychopharmacology, 31*, 2376–2383.

Bachhuber, M. A., Hennessy, S., Cunningham, C. O., Starrels, J., & L. (2016). Increasing benzodiazepine prescriptions and overdose mortality in the United States, 1996–2013. *American Journal of Public Health, 106*(4), 686–688.

Balon, R., & Starcevic, V. (2020). Role of benzodiazepines in anxiety disorders. In Y. K. Kim (Ed.), *Anxiety disorders. Rethinking and understanding recent discoveries* (pp. 367–388). Springer.

Bassetti, C. L. A., Adamantidis, A., Burdakov, D., Han, F., Gay, S., et al. (2019). Narcolepsy – Clinical spectrum, aetiopathophysiology, diagnosis and treatment. *Nature Reviews Neurology, 15*, 519–539.

Bell, J. R., Butler, B., Lawrance, A., Batey, R., & Salmelainen, P. (2009). Comparing overdose mortality associated with methadone and buprenorphine treatment. *Drug and Alcohol Dependence, 104*(1), 73–77.

Berge, K. H., Dillon, K. R., Sikkink, K. M., Taylor, T. K., & Lanier, W. L. (2012). Diversion of drugs within health care facilities, a multiple-victim crime: Patterns of diversion, scope, consequences, detection, and prevention. *Mayo Clinic Proceedings, 87*(7), 674–682.

Caplehorn, J. R. M., & Drummer, O. H. (2002). Fatal methadone toxicity: Signs and circumstances, and the role of benzodiazepines. *Australian and New Zealand Journal of Public Health, 26*(4), 358–362.

Centers for Disease Control (CDC). Calculating total daily dose of opioids for safer dosage. https://www.cdc.gov/drugoverdose/pdf/calculating_total_daily_dose-a.pdf. Accessed 12/21/2020.

Centers for Substance Abuse Treatment. (2004). *Clinical guidelines for the use of buprenorphine in the treatment of opioid addiction. Treatment improvement protocol (TIP) series 40*. Substance Abuse and Mental Health Services Administration.

Connery, H. S. (2015). Medication-assisted treatment of opioid use disorder: Review of the evidence and future directions. *Harvard Review of Psychiatry, 23*(2), 63–75.

Drug Enforcement Administration (DEA), U.S. Department of Justice. Title 21 Code of Federal Regulations, Part 1306 – Prescriptions. https://www.deadiversion.usdoj.gov/21cfr/cfr/2106cfrt.htm. Accessed 12/16/2020.

Lader, M., & Kyriacou, A. (2016). Withdrawing benzodiazepines in patients with anxiety disorders. *Current Psychiatry Reports, 18*(8), 1–8.

Lavonas, E. J., Severtson, S. G., Martinez, E. M., Bucher-Bartelson, B., Le Lair, M., et al. (2014). Abuse and diversion of buprenorphine sublingual tablets and film. *Journal of Substance Abuse Treatment, 47*(1), 27–34.

Lin, H. C., Wang, Z., Boyd, C., Simoni-Wastila, L., & Buu, A. (2017). Associations between statewide prescription drug program (PDMP) requirement and physician patterns of prescribing opioid analgesics for patients with non-cancer chronic pain. *Addictive Behaviors, 76*, 348–354.

LiverTox: Clinical and Research Information on Drug-Induced Liver Injury. (2020). *Naltrexone*. National Institute of Diabetes and Digestive and Kidney Diseases.

Markota, M., Rummans, T. A., Bostwick, J. M., & Lapid, M. I. (2016). Benzodiazepine use in older adults: Dangers, management, and alternative therapies. *Mayo Clinic Proceedings, 91*(11), 1632–1639.

National Institute on Drug Abuse. (2018). Understanding drug use and addiction drug facts. https://www.drugabuse.gov/publications/drugfacts/understanding-drug-use-addiction. Accessed 12/19/2020.

Pasic, J. (2017). Amphetamine withdrawal. In K. D. Nordstrom & M. P. Wilson (Eds.), *Quick guide to psychiatric emergencies* (pp. 217–220). Springer.

Ritter, A. J. (2002). Naltrexone in the treatment of heroin dependence: Relationship with depression and risk of overdose. *Australian and New Zealand Journal of Psychiatry, 36*(2), 224–228.

SAMHSA (Substance Abuse and Mental Health Services Administration). (2015). Federal guidelines for opioid treatment programs.

SAMHSA (Substance Abuse and Mental Health Services Administration). (2020a). Buprenorphine. https://www.samhsa.gov/medication-assisted-treatment/medications-counseling-related-conditions/buprenorphine. Accessed 12/21/2020.

SAMHSA (Substance Abuse and Mental Health Services Administration). (2020b). Methadone. https://www.samhsa.gov/medication-assisted-treatment/medications-counseling-related-conditions/methadone. Accessed 12/21/2020.

SAMHSA (Substance Abuse and Mental Health Services Administration). (2020c). Naltrexone. https://www.samhsa.gov/medication-assisted-treatment/medications-counseling-related-conditions/naltrexone. Accessed 12/21/2020.

Wilens, T. E., Adler, L. A., Adams, J., Sgambati, S., Rotrosen, J., et al. (2008). Misuse and diversion of stimulants prescribed for ADHD: A systematic review of the literature. *Journal of the American Academy of Child & Adolescent Psychiatry, 47*(1), 21–31.

Zhong, G., Wang, Y., Zhang, Y., & Zhao. (2015). Association between benzodiazepine use and dementia: A meta-analysis. *PLoS One, 10*(5), 1–16.

Geriatric Psychiatry

26

Marilyn Price

Throughout the world, demand for geriatric mental health services is expected to grow exponentially in the coming years. In the United States, the size of the population over 65 grew by over a third within the past decade alone (U.S. Census Bureau, 2020), and adults over 65 are expected to account for nearly a quarter of the national population by 2060 (Colby & Ortman, 2015). Medical advances have dramatically increased the human lifespan; patients who in previous centuries would have succumbed to heart disease, cancer, and infectious diseases are today living well into their octogenarian and nonagenarian years. With increasing age comes an increasing risk for neuropsychiatric disorders such as minor neurocognitive disorder (mNCD) and major neurocognitive disorder (MNCD). The treatment of severe mental illness (SMI) in older patients may require specialized training and experience, as symptoms and treatment response can vary throughout the lifespan. Unfortunately, demand for geriatric psychiatrists already vastly exceeds supply, and older patients are often treated by clinicians with less specialized expertise, such as primary care physicians (American Psychiatric Association, Council on Geriatric Psychiatry, 2019).

Despite the complexity and potential for adverse events that often accompany the care of older patients, malpractice lawsuits against psychiatrists caring for elderly patients occur less frequently. Data of claims (written demands for money outside of litigation) and lawsuits against psychiatrists insured by the malpractice carrier PRMS from 2010 to 2019 indicate that only about 10% involve a patient over the age of 60 (D. Vanderpool, personal communication, December 1, 2020). Several factors contribute to fewer claims being filed. First, proving causation in elderly patients can be quite difficult due to the increasing prevalence of comorbid medical conditions and polypharmacy with age (Faust, 2012). Deaths from intentional drug ingestion combined with volitional decrease in nutrition may be misclassified as death from natural causes. Second, damages are typically limited, as future earnings and lost wages for an older adult are considerably less than those for younger adults injured in the prime of their working years. Despite the low frequency of claims, however, geriatric psychiatrists—as subspecialists—may be held to a higher standard than that of general psychiatrists (Meyer, 2006).

In psychiatry, most medical malpractice lawsuits result from patient suicides (Tsao & Layde, 2007). Suicides in inpatient settings are more likely to result in malpractice claims than those occurring among outpatients (Tsao & Layde, 2007). Other frequent causes for lawsuits in psychiatry include medication-related errors or adverse events, ECT-related adverse outcomes, failure to obtain informed consent, negligent psychotherapy, sexual misconduct, injury to third parties, abandonment, false imprisonment, breach of confidentiality, and negligent supervision (Meyer, 2006; Tsao & Layde, 2007).

Suicide

Suicide is the 16th leading cause of death for persons over the age of 65 (Centers for Disease Control and Prevention, 2018). Suicide is also an oft-overlooked risk in the care of older adults:

> Older patients' medical records were less likely to have evidence of 1) screening for impulsivity and firearms access and 2) engagement in safety planning, referrals for mental health services, and consideration of psychiatric hospitalization. (Simons et al., 2019, p. 604)

These facts are troubling, considering that elderly patients are at elevated risk for suicide (Malin et al., 2018). White males over the age of 65 are at the highest risk for suicide. Data from the Centers for Disease Control (CDC) indicated that in 2019, suicide was the 15th most common cause of death in males 65 and older. Firearms were used in 75% of completed suicides, indicating that psychiatrist should

M. Price (✉)
Assistant Professor of Psychiatry (PT), Law and Psychiatry Service, Massachusetts General Hospital, Harvard Medical School, Boston, MA, USA
e-mail: MPRICE3@mgh.harvard.edu

P. Ash et al. (eds.), *Malpractice and Liability in Psychiatry*, https://doi.org/10.1007/978-3-030-91975-7_26

inquire about access to firearms as this is a significant risk factor. Suffocation was used in 11% and poisoning in 7% (CDC WISQARS, 2021). Suicide was not among the top 20 causes of death for females over the age of 65 in the United States (CDC WISQARS, 2021).

Risk factors include the presence of psychiatric disorders, physical illness, neurocognitive decline, diminished functional capacity, death of a spouse, and loss of social networks. Conducting suicide risk assessments can identify those at risk and allow for timely and effective intervention (Price & Howard, 2020; Hernandez et al., 2021). Some common warning signs for suicide that raise concern in younger patients, such as giving away one's belongings or writing a will, may not be viewed as warning signs among older adults, so suicide risk may be overlooked. Risk factors for suicide in older adults also include male gender (Hedna et al., 2020), negative feelings about one's health status (Lee et al., 2018), psychiatric disorders such as depression (Lapierre et al., 2011), onset or diagnosis of NCD (Malin et al., 2018), hopelessness (Hernandez et al., 2021), functional impairment (Malin et al., 2018), being prescribed opioids or benzodiazepines (Voaklander et al., 2008), and stressful life events such as the loss of a spouse (Lapierre et al., 2011; Price & Howard, 2020), to name only a few. Risk factors vary between subgroups of older adults (e.g., being unmarried increases risk in older men but not older women) (Hedna et al., 2020), so risk assessments should take the patient's gender, age, and other factors into account. The risk for suicide among men increases steadily with advancing age once a patient has reached the age of 65 (Malin et al., 2018). Unfortunately, few rigorous scientific studies have explored the efficacy of suicide prevention interventions for older adults (Chauliac et al., 2020). When an elderly patient dies by suicide, a poor alliance with the patient's family members increases the likelihood of a malpractice suit (Malin et al., 2018).

Diagnosis

Errors in diagnosis represent the most common cause of all medical malpractice claims in the United States (Schaffer et al., 2017), and allegations of misdiagnosis account for 34% of all payout amounts (Gower, 2020). Although the term "pseudodementia" has fallen out of favor, depression and other conditions are frequently mistaken for neurocognitive disorder (NCD) in older adults. Unlike cognitive impairment due to a neurodegenerative disease process, however, many other causes of a dementia-like presentation are amenable to treatment. Psychiatrists should approach differential diagnosis carefully when evaluating patients with suspected NCD. In fact, "[t]he prevalence of dementia in the United States *declined significantly* between 2000 and 2012" (Langa et al., 2017, p. 51).

Physicians should consider the possibility of underlying medical problems that may respond to treatment and which may cause irreversible damage if not diagnosed and treated in time, such as memory loss due to an operable tumor or normal pressure hydrocephaly (Howe, 2011). Particularly in elderly patients, the initial symptoms of physical illness are often psychological or behavioral in nature. A change in mental status due to the onset of delirium often signifies the presence of infection or other somatic conditions in older adults (Metzger et al., 2018). Underlying medical conditions, many of which are treatable, are frequently misdiagnosed as functional NCDs in older patients (van der Feltz-Cornelis et al., 2020).

Sensory impairments should be considered in the differential diagnosis for older adults. Age-related hearing loss is associated with depression and cognitive decline (Rutherford et al., 2018). Sensory impairments can also increase the risk for suicidal ideation in older adults (Park & Lee, 2020). In older patients, treatable impairments can result in symptom-driven behavior that could be misdiagnosed as NCD. For example, a patient who is uncommunicative could be suffering from hearing loss, not dementia-related apathy. Furthermore, untreated sensory impairments are known to increase the risk of adverse outcomes in the elderly (Holzer & Gluck, 2018).

Depression is prevalent among older adults and can account for a wide variety of physical and psychological symptoms, including aggression (Gilmore et al., 2020), cognitive decline (Gallagher et al., 2016), and an increased risk for falls (Grenier et al., 2014). Late-life depression is treatable in over 80% of cases, and several evidence-based practices have been studied for the treatment of depression in older adults (CDC and NACDD, 2009). Many patients are not informed that depression is associated with an increased risk for dementia (Survey, 2013), a fact which can be important in treatment planning.

Capacity, Informed Consent, and Advance Directives

McNary (2017) identifies informed consent and capacity to consent to treatment as important areas for risk management in the treatment of elderly patients, both of which can be affected by a variety of different variables, including illness, treatment response, medications, and psychodynamic factors. Capacity assessments should be tailored to the specific decision or activity being considered, and a patient may lack the capacity for some decisions while retaining capacity for others.

Because the prevalence of neurocognitive impairment increases with advancing age, psychiatrists who treat elderly patients should appreciate the importance of communicating with a patient's family members as well as the possibility that the patient's ability to make treatment decisions may be impaired (McNary, 2017). When a patient lacks the capacity to make a treatment decision, the decision falls to a substitute decision-maker or proxy. McNary (2017) suggests requesting copies of any legal documents that authorize a third party to make medical decisions on behalf of the patient. When such documents have not been executed, treatment decisions often fall to the patient's closest relatives, which can be an especially challenging process for loved ones (Gaster et al., 2017). Working carefully with authorized substitute decision-makers is an important step in legal risk management, particularly when treating older patients.

The Patient Self-Determination Act of 1990 requires hospitals and nursing homes to provide patients with information regarding the availability and use of medical advance directives as well as the right to refuse treatment (Frolik & Kaplan, 2010). For patients in the early stages of a neurodegenerative disease process, the psychiatrist may advise the patient to create advance directives for healthcare and to consult with an attorney to plan for the likelihood of future impairment. Gaster and colleagues provide helpful examples of specific advance directive language to help direct future treatment decisions in later and advancing stages of MNCD (Gaster et al., 2017). Psychiatric advance directives are also gaining in popularity, and the psychiatrist may wish to encourage patients with chronic or relapsing mental illness to complete one if they have not already (McNary, 2017).

There is growing recognition of a right to sue for wrongful life or wrongful survival when a patient's advance directive refusing treatment is not honored (Bartylla, 2020). Evidence suggests that patients' advance directives declining life-sustaining measures are "routinely ignored" by physicians (Peters Jr., 1998), in violation of the ethical principle of honoring patient autonomy. Because the right to refuse treatment is well established in US law (*Cruzan v. Director*, 1990), patients or their representatives can bring suit when violations of advance directives occur. Liability for failing to honor a patient's advance directive can be based on common law such as battery, lack of informed consent, negligence, intentional infliction of emotional distress, and breach of contract (Pope, 2017). Assessing a patient's code status and honoring any do-not-resuscitate (DNR) orders and other advance directives is therefore a critical step from both an ethical and risk management perspective.

Safety and Capacity for Independent Living

The care of older patients often necessitates assessments for safety and the capacity to live independently. Incapacity for self-care increases a patient's vulnerability to abuse and neglect, accumulating and worsening medical problems, eventual placement in long-term care, and mortality (Naik et al., 2008). In some patients, a new inability to manage one's financial affairs can be an early warning sign of mNCD and future cognitive decline.

Psychiatrists may need to advise older patients or their families about the current or likely future necessity of driving cessation, particularly for patients with age-related sensory impairments or NCD (American Psychiatric Association, 2016). Compared to drivers aged 30 to 59, accidents involving drivers over 80 carry over four times the rate of motor vehicle accident (MVA) fatalities (Cohn, 2009), and the risk of fatal MVAs increases with age (Ratnapradipa et al., 2021). Additionally, many jurisdictions require physicians to report impaired drivers (Collier, 2012). Failing to provide advice regarding the safety of driving has resulted in liability for treating physicians. In *Coombes v. Florio* (2007), a 75-year-old patient who had been told it was safe to resume driving was involved in an MVA resulting in the death of a 10-year-old child. The physician had prescribed medications with sedating properties that could be more pronounced in older patients, but the patient had not been warned about these and other risks associated with his treatment. The Massachusetts Supreme Court found that the victim had a cause of action against the physician.

Psychiatrists treating elderly patients should also consider the safety of the patient's home environment and living situation, particularly when medical frailty is present or decisional capacity is impaired. Falls represent a significant risk for elderly patients, and the consequences of a fall can be severe, frequently leading to hospitalization and hastened functional decline. Some home modifications that reduce the risk of falls, such as the removal of rugs, are easily accomplished and carry little to no cost to the patient or his or her family. Geriatric psychiatrists should avoid prescribing medications that increase the risk of falls unless their benefits outweigh their risks for a particular patient. Wandering behaviors may place frail or cognitively impaired patients at additional risk, although technological safeguards such as GPS monitoring may help to lessen risk while maximizing patient autonomy (Liu et al., 2017). In inpatient hospital settings and long-term care facilities, patient wandering leading to adverse events can result in litigation; it is estimated that roughly 10% of lawsuits filed against nursing homes involve resident elopement (Williams, 2002).

Elder Abuse and Neglect

In most states, physicians are mandatory reporters of elder abuse or neglect (Frolik & Kaplan, 2010; McNary, 2017). The definition of elder abuse varies from one state to the next (Frolik & Kaplan, 2010) and may include physical, psychological, sexual, or financial abuse and neglect (McNary, 2017; Storey, 2020). Financial abuse is prevalent, and a vulnerable patient's physician may be the first person to recognize its warning signs (Lachs & Pillemer, 2015). Unfortunately, elder abuse and neglect are common among both community-dwelling older adults and those in residential treatment settings, with an estimated 11% of community-residing older adults experiencing abuse within the past year (Williams et al., 2020).

Psychiatrists should be familiar with common risk factors for elder abuse among potential victims as well as in caregivers. Victim risk factors include physical health problems, mental health problems, substance abuse, dependency (of the elder or his or her caregiver), stress and poor coping skills, attitudes and negative beliefs, prior abuse victimization, and relationship problems (Storey, 2020). Clinicians should be attentive to signs of elder abuse, such as suspicious burns or bruises, reports of new sexually transmitted infections, unexplained and significant changes in weight or sleep, seclusion, unusual fear, a disparity between assets and lifestyle, sudden failures to meet financial obligations, failures to fill prescriptions, poor hygiene, dehydration, pressure ulcers, and lack of corrective measures—such as eyeglasses or hearing aids—for sensory impairments (McNary, 2017).

In residential care settings such as assisted living facilities, rehabilitation centers, and skilled nursing facilities, a patchwork of laws throughout the United States are intended to protect residents. When abuse or neglect takes place in an institutional setting, patients or their representatives may be able to bring action under state elder abuse laws, some of which allow for the assessment of damages for pain and suffering of the victim (Brashier, 2010). Malpractice litigation against nursing homes is also on the rise (Kapp, 2009). Dehydration and malnutrition among residents represent an increasing proportion of claims against long-term care facilities (Braun & Capezuti, 2000); other frequent causes for lawsuits in the nursing home setting are decubitus ulcers, falls, weight loss, infections, physical abuse, and wrongful death (Kapp, 2009). Complaints against nursing facilities for elder abuse and neglect, and the incidence of adverse events due to substandard care, appear to be increasing (Harrington et al., 2020).

Agitation, Violence, and Disinhibition

Behavioral and psychological symptoms of dementia, which are found in over 90% of patients with NCD (Aarsland, 2020), can pose significant treatment challenges in geriatric psychiatry. These symptoms, including agitation, can lead to physically aggressive behavior, potentially resulting in harm to the patient or others (Gilmore et al., 2020). Agitation can be understood as:

> (1) occurring in patients with a cognitive impairment or dementia syndrome; (2) exhibiting behavior consistent with emotional distress; (3) manifesting excessive motor activity, verbal aggression, or physical aggression; and (4) evidencing behaviors that cause excess disability and are not solely attributable to another disorder (psychiatric, medical, or substance-related). (Cummings et al., 2015, p. 7)

Several factors carry an increased risk for frequent agitation, including age, severity of NCD, delusions, anxiety, euphoria, and irritability (Veldwijk-Rouwenhorst et al., 2017). The ability to communicate one's needs can be significantly impaired in patients with MNCD, and a patient who is unable to express his or her needs verbally may engage in aggressive or otherwise agitated behavior in an effort to obtain help (Surti et al., 2018).

Aggression in older patients may be reactive (i.e., a response to modifiable factors in the environment) or proactive (i.e., premeditated), and effective treatment for the two types may be different (Volicer, 2021). Reactive aggression may respond to treatment improvements such as milieu changes and effective pain control, whereas proactive aggression may be more likely to require treatment with antipsychotic medication (Volicer, 2021). Aggression may also be a warning sign of an underlying medical problem, inadequately treated pain, and other unmet needs (Surti et al., 2018). Although preventing injury to the patient or others is of critical importance when aggressive behavior emerges, psychiatrists should remember that its presence may signify an underlying problem that requires treatment.

In long-term care settings, the use of restraint and seclusion to control problematic behavior is recognized as a warning sign of poor-quality care (Kapp, 2018). Restraints may be physical, as in the case of devices which restrict freedom of movement, or chemical, as in the use of medications to control a patient's behavior rather than to treat his or her medical condition. Although the use of restraints may be appropriate in some situations for which other interventions have failed, evidence suggests that restraints do not improve the safety of elderly patients; in fact, there is evidence that restraint use can *increase* the risk of falls and other adverse events (Braun & Capezuti, 2000).

Substance Abuse

Although substance abuse is less prevalent in seniors (Burgard & Kohn, 2018), substance use disorders are a growing and under-recognized problem among older adults in the United States (American Psychiatric Association [APA], 2015). As the APA notes, older adults—and especially older women—are more sensitive to the toxic effects of substances due to general medical aspects of the aging process (APA, 2015). Among older adults, alcohol use disorder is the most common substance use disorder (Jemberie et al., 2020), and marijuana addiction is growing more prevalent (Burgard & Kohn, 2018). Mirroring trends across age cohorts, opioid misuse is also increasing; from 2002 to 2014, the misuse of opioids doubled among adults 65 and older (Weiss et al., 2018). Elderly patients experiencing withdrawal from alcohol or other substances often experience heightened withdrawal severity, potentially raising risk: "[p]rofessional liability may increase due to the high rate of mortality from untreated delirium tremens, failure to diagnose, or inadequate treatment" (Burgard & Kohn, 2018, p. 259). Psychiatrists working with elderly patients should also be cognizant of the risk for drug diversion by patients themselves or by their caregivers. Elder abuse experts have characterized opioid-related elder abuse as an escalating problem in the US healthcare system (Roberto et al., 2021).

Prescribing and Psychopharmacology

Prescribing for older patients carries special risks due to the prevalence of underlying medical conditions, heightened sensitivity to medication side effects, and the potential for drug-drug interactions (Das et al., 2021). Such risks are further heightened among frail patients residing in long-term care facilities such as nursing homes, whose residents often suffer from medical multi-morbidity and take several medications concurrently, which can significantly complicate treatment planning (American Psychiatric Association, 2019). In all patients, but particularly the elderly, polypharmacy increases the risk for adverse events and iatrogenic harm (Fozdar & Holzer, 2018).

Although the presence of severe mental illness (SMI) is associated with increased mortality (Fuller-Thomson et al., 2020), more patients with SMI today are living into old age than in previous generations. Treatments well studied for younger patients with SMI often have less empirical support for their use in older adults (Young et al., 2017), and the risk for adverse effects may be greater (Das et al., 2021). Psychiatrists who typically treat younger patients may need to modify their practice patterns when prescribing for older adults.

Antipsychotics

The prescription of antipsychotic medications in elderly patients carries special risks and requires a nuanced risk-benefit analysis, especially when prescribing off-label use medications. In 2005 and 2010, the Food and Drug Administration (FDA) issued black box warnings that antipsychotics may confer an increased mortality risk in elderly patients with dementia (Szmulewicz et al., 2018). Adverse events associated with antipsychotic medications in older patients include extrapyramidal symptoms, excess sedation, falls, hastened cognitive decline, and increased risk for stroke, myocardial infarction, pneumonia, hip fractures, and mortality (Nørgaard et al., 2020; Zuidema et al., 2015). However, there is evidence supporting the effectiveness of antipsychotics for the treatment of aggression and psychosis in elderly patients with MNCD (Zuidema et al., 2015). The American Psychiatric Association (APA) recently approved a position statement that:

> Aggression, agitation, and psychosis are highly prevalent in patients with MNCD and cause great suffering. Their presence is associated with a worse prognosis. While non-pharmacological approaches are generally recommended as first-line treatments, they are often ineffective in the treatment of aggression, agitation and psychosis, and the judicious use of antipsychotic medications may be appropriate. (American Psychiatric Association, Council on Geriatric Psychiatry, 2020, p. 1)

Compliance with the APA's Practice Guideline on the Use of Antipsychotics to Treat Agitation or Psychosis in Patients with Dementia (Reus et al., 2016) can help to lessen the risk of adverse outcomes and ensure that the psychiatrist's practices are consistent with the current standard of care.

Antidepressants

There is mixed evidence regarding the efficacy and tolerability of antidepressants among older adults with major depressive disorder and other conditions (Tham et al., 2016). Side effects associated with some antidepressant medications that may be minor in younger patients, such as dry mouth and changes in bowel habits, can be more problematic among the elderly due to factors more prevalent in old age, including dysphagia, fall risk, and susceptibility to malnutrition and dehydration (Tham et al., 2016).

Benzodiazepines

Older adults are among the most frequent recipients of benzodiazepine prescriptions, and the rate of such prescriptions—often in conjunction with other prescription medications—has been rising in recent years (Altmann et al.,

2020). Benzodiazepines have been reported to increase the risk for falls (McNary, 2017) and as a method of suicide (Voaklander et al., 2008) in elderly patients. There is also some evidence, albeit controversial, suggesting a possible link between benzodiazepines and MNCD (Burgard & Kohn, 2018).

Prescribing: General Recommendations

Because elderly patients may not accurately report all medications they are currently taking, requesting that patients bring all current medications to the office can help to lessen risk (McNary, 2017). Providing written information about prescribed medications, their appropriate use, and associated risks (such as the risk for impaired driving or an increased risk for falls) may also help to decrease the risk of adverse events and subsequent liability (McNary, 2017). Patients should be informed about off-label use of a medication, and this should be appropriately documented. Special caution is warranted regarding polypharmacy in older adults. In one large nationwide study of patients with NCD who were treated with antipsychotic medication, mortality risk was significantly increased when benzodiazepines were added but decreased when adding antidepressants (Nørgaard et al., 2020). Aggressive and violent behavior poses special problems when it is nonresponsive to behavioral interventions. As discussed above, antipsychotics may be effective, but there is some—albeit limited—evidence of benefit from β-blockers, valproate, carbamazepine, and lithium in patients with NCD-related aggression (Newman, 2012). Physicians who prescribe for elderly patients should be familiar with the American Geriatrics Society's Beers Criteria ® for potentially inappropriate medications in the elderly (2019 American Geriatrics Society Beers Criteria ® Update Expert Panel, 2019), which were recently updated.

Non-pharmacological Treatment

There is some limited evidence supporting the use of non-pharmacological treatment options for agitation in NCD (Gilmore et al., 2020; Meyer & O'Keefe, 2020). Psychotherapy may be helpful for psychiatric conditions in old age (Meyer & O'Keefe, 2020). One option that psychiatrists may consider in treating anxiety is an initial period of psychopharmacology combined with evidence-based psychotherapy, followed by ongoing psychotherapy (Wetherell et al., 2013). Music therapy and reminiscence also show promise (Gilmore et al., 2020; Meyer & O'Keefe, 2020).

Electroconvulsive therapy (ECT) and other neuromodulatory treatments have been shown to be helpful in geriatric psychiatry. Generally, ECT is well tolerated in older adults and may carry lower risk than many psychopharmacological treatment options (Gad et al., 2018; Spaans et al., 2018). Among older adults with depression, ECT is associated with gains in life expectancy, clinical improvement, and time to response (Gad et al., 2018). The superiority of ECT over pharmacotherapy in depression for older adults is independent of numerous risk factors including hypercholesterolemia, hypertension, and other chronic conditions (Spaans et al., 2018).

COVID-19

The COVID-19 pandemic has dramatically impacted geriatric medicine. In addition to SARS-CoV-2's well-documented adverse impact on mortality for the elderly, some have speculated that the pandemic may also contribute to increased suicide rates among older adults (Wand et al., 2020). In both community-dwelling seniors and those living in long-term care facilities, COVID-19-related factors can increase risks for elder abuse and neglect (Makaroun et al., 2020). Among COVID-19 patients of all age groups, there is a higher risk for drug-drug interactions (Preskorn & Quadri, 2020), a factor which carries added danger for older patients. Early recognition and diagnosis of COVID-19 in elderly patients may be challenging, as delirium may be the only symptom initially (Kennedy et al., 2020). Furthermore, even without social isolation and loneliness, pandemic-related factors appear to be giving rise to an increasing burden of psychiatric conditions among the elderly (Uvais, 2020). Behavioral and psychological symptoms of dementia can pose significant ethical and logistical challenges during COVID-19 containment measures, and decisions regarding isolation, enforcement of mask requirements, movement restrictions, and related issues can be fraught with difficulties (Fahed et al., 2020; Nkodo et al., 2020).

Concerned about the potential for a wave of lawsuits in the wake of the COVID-19 pandemic, some states issued temporary executive orders intending to shield medical providers and others from liability for COVID-related adverse outcomes (Cioffi & Rinaldi, 2020; Terry, 2020). While immunity from liability may seem attractive to some, Sklar and Terry (2020) suggest that shielding long-term care facilities from lawsuits may worsen existing problems with poor safety measures and low-quality care. In attempts to combat the pandemic's spread, many long-term care facilities and inpatient treatment settings have implemented visitor bans, a practice which raises concerns about vulnerable patients' psychosocial needs, civil rights, and the availability and involvement of substitute decision-makers (Bronsther, 2020). Other measures intended to reduce risk, such as transferring vulnerable patients to other facilities, have had unforeseen tragic consequences (Temple-Raston, 2020).

Concluding Recommendations

The APA has published several position statements which may be helpful to geriatric psychiatrists in reducing the risk for malpractice and liability, including opinions on substance use disorders (American Psychiatric Association, 2015), assessing the ability to operate a motor vehicle (American Psychiatric Association, Council on Geriatric Psychiatry, 2016), the role of psychiatrists in nursing homes (American Psychiatric Association, Council on Geriatric Psychiatry, 2019), and, as previously mentioned, the use of antipsychotic medications in patients with NCD (American Psychiatric Association, Council on Geriatric Psychiatry, 2020). Treatment guidelines are also available from organizations such as the American Geriatrics Society (AGS) (2019 American Geriatrics Society Beers Criteria ® Update Expert Panel, 2019). McNary underscores the importance of proactive communication with the patient's family members and other caregivers, including providing written information about the patient's condition, ensuring that caregivers understand treatments and their potential side effects, and including the patient in treatment decision-making (McNary, 2017).

Key Points

- Adults over 65 are expected to account for nearly a quarter of the national population in the United States by 2060, resulting in an increase in neuropsychiatric disorders such as minor neurocognitive disorder (mNCD) and major neurocognitive disorder (MNCD).
- Only 10% of claims (written demands for money outside of litigation) and lawsuits against psychiatrists involve a patient over the age of 60.
- Fewer claims are filed regarding elderly patients because proving causation can be quite difficult due to the increasing prevalence of comorbid medical conditions and polypharmacy with age. Deaths from suicide by overdose or volitional decrease in nutrition may be misclassified as death from natural causes.
- The rates of death from suicide increase with age; white males 65 and older are demographically at highest risk of death from suicide.
- Risk factors for suicide in the elderly include mental illness, physical illness, family stressors including loss of spouse/partner, social isolation, financial stressors, and social factors.
- Firearms are the most commonly used method in suicide in the elderly population.
- Common areas of liability related to treating older adults include prescribing medications off-label and prescribing medications with black box warnings.
- There has been an increase in lawsuits for wrongful life or wrongful survival when a patient's advance directive refusing treatment is not honored.

References

Aarsland, D. (2020). Epidemiology and pathophysiology of dementia-related psychosis. *Journal of Clinical Psychiatry, 81*(5), AD19038BR1C. https://doi.org/10.4088/JCP.AD19038BR1C

Altmann, H., Stahl, S. T., Gebara, M. A., et al. (2020). Coprescribed benzodiazepines in older adults receiving antidepressants for anxiety and depressive disorders: Association with treatment outcomes. *Journal of Clinical Psychiatry, 81*(6), 20m13283. https://doi.org/10.4088/JCP.20m13283

American Geriatrics Society Beers Criteria ® Update Expert Panel. (2019). American Geriatrics Society 2019 Updated AGS Beers Criteria® for potentially inappropriate medication use in older adults. *Journal of the American Geriatrics Society, 67*(4), 674–694.

American Psychiatric Association. (2015). *Position statement on substance use disorders in older adults*. American Psychiatric Association. https://www.psychiatry.org/File%20Library/About-APA/Organization-Documents-Policies/Policies/Position-Substance-Use-Disorders-in-Older-Adults.pdf. Accessed December 1, 2020.

American Psychiatric Association, Council on Geriatric Psychiatry. (2016). *Position statement on the role of psychiatrists in assessing driving ability*. American Psychiatric Association. https://www.psychiatry.org/File%20Library/About-APA/Organization-Documents-Policies/Policies/Position-2016-Assessing-Driving-Ability.pdf. Accessed December 1, 2020.

American Psychiatric Association, Council on Geriatric Psychiatry. (2019). *Position statement on the role of the psychiatrist in nursing facilities*. American Psychiatric Association. https://www.psychiatry.org/File%20Library/About-APA/Organization-Documents-Policies/Policies/Position-Psychiatrists-in-Nursing-Facilities.pdf. Accessed February 13, 2021.

American Psychiatric Association, Council on Geriatric Psychiatry. (2020). *Position statement on the use of antipsychotic medication in patients with major neurocognitive disorder*. American Psychiatric Association. https://www.psychiatry.org/File%20Library/About-APA/Organization-Documents-Policies/Policies/Position-Antipsychotic-Medication-Major-Neurocognitive-Disorder.pdf. Accessed December 19, 2020.

Bartylla, B. (2020). The next chapter of "wrongful life": Concepts for "wrongful survival" in comparative analysis. *Cambridge Law Review, 5*(1), 104–134.

Brashier, R. C. (2010). *Mastering elder law*. Carolina Academic Press.

Braun, J. A., & Capezuti, E. A. (2000). A medico-legal evaluation of dehydration and malnutrition among nursing home residents. *Elder Law Journal, 8*, 239–296.

Bronsther, R. (2020). Visitor restrictions during COVID-19 pandemic may impact surrogate medical decision-making. *Journal of Patient Experience, 7*(4), 428–429.

Burgard, M., & Kohn, R. (2018). Substance use disorders in the elderly. In J. C. Holzer, R. Kohn, J. M. Ellison, & P. R. Recupero (Eds.), *Geriatric forensic psychiatry: Principles and practice* (pp. 253–263). Oxford University Press.

Centers for Disease Control and Prevention. (2018, June). Suicide risking across the US. *Vital Signs*. Available at https://www.cdc.gov/vitalsigns/suicide/modules/June-Vital-Signs-Transcript-6.4.18.pdf. Accessed October 13, 2019.

Centers for Disease Control and Prevention. *Web-based Inquiry Statistics Query and Reporting System (WISQARS): Leading cause of death reports. Leading causes of death by age group United States 2019*. Available at https://www.cdc.gov/injury/wisqars/fatal.html. Accessed March 1, 2021.

Centers for Disease Control and Prevention (CDC) and National Association of Chronic Disease Directors (NACDD). (2009). *The state of mental health and aging in America, issue brief #2: Addressing depression in older adults: Selected evidence-based programs*. NACDD.

Chauliac, N., Leaune, E., Gardette, V., Poulet, E., & Duclos, A. (2020). Suicide prevention interventions for older people in nursing homes and long-term care facilities: A systematic review. *Journal of Geriatric Psychiatry & Neurology, 33*(6), 307–315.

Cioffi, A., & Rinaldi, R. (2020). COVID-19 and medical liability: A delicate balance. *Medico-Legal Journal, 88*(4), 187–188.

Cohn, J. (2009). Increased driving regulations for the elderly: A case study in New York calling for the expansion of current regulations. *Albany Government Law Review, 2*, 304–327.

Colby, S. L., & Ortman, J. M. (2015, March). *Projections of the size and composition of the U.S. population: 2014 to 2060*. Current Population Reports, P25-1143. United States Census Bureau. https://www.census.gov/content/dam/Census/library/publications/2015/demo/p25-1143.pdf. Accessed December 1, 2020.

Collier, R. (2012). Physicians open to ideas on how to assess and discuss fitness to drive. *Canadian Medical Association Journal, 184*(4), E207–E208.

Coombes v. Florio, 877 N.E.2d 567 (Mass. 2007).

Cruzan v. Director, Missouri Department of Health, 497 U.S. 261 (1990).

Cummings, J., Mintzer, J., Brodaty, H., et al. (2015). Agitation in cognitive disorders: International Psychogeriatric Association provisional consensus clinical and research definition. *International Psychogeriatrics, 27*(1), 7–17.

Das, A., Minner, R., Krain, L., & Spollen, J. (2021). Delirium on clozapine: A tale of friend turned foe—A case report. *International Journal of Psychiatry in Medicine, 56*(6), 446–458. https://doi.org/10.1177/0091217420972827

Fahed, M., Barron, G. C., & Steffens, D. C. (2020). Ethical and logistical considerations of caring for older adults on inpatient psychiatry during the COVID-19 pandemic. *American Journal of Geriatric Psychiatry, 28*(8), 829–834.

Faust, D. (2012). Criteria for appraising scientific status I. In D. Faust (Ed.), *Coping with psychiatric and psychological testimony* (6th ed., pp. 42–87). Oxford University Press.

Fozdar, M. A., & Holzer, J. C. (2018). Psychopharmacological agents, side effects, and black box warnings. In J. C. Holzer, R. Kohn, J. M. Ellison, & P. R. Recupero (Eds.), *Geriatric forensic psychiatry: Principles and practice* (pp. 121–127). Oxford University Press.

Frolik, L. A., & Kaplan, R. L. (2010). *Elder law in a nutshell* (5th ed.). West.

Fuller-Thomson, E., Lung, Y., West, K. J., Keyes, C. L. M., & Baiden, P. (2020). Suboptimal baseline mental health associated with 4-month premature all-cause mortality: Findings from 18 years of follow-up of the Canadian National Population Health Survey. *Journal of Psychosomatic Research, 136*, 110176. https://doi.org/10.1016/j.jpsychores.2020.110176

Gad, H., Bateman, D., & Holtzheimer, P. E. (2018). Neurostimulation therapies, side effects, risks, and benefits. In J. C. Holzer, R. Kohn, J. M. Ellison, & P. R. Recupero (Eds.), *Geriatric forensic psychiatry: Principles and practice* (pp. 129–140). Oxford University Press.

Gallagher, D., Kiss, A., Lanctot, K., & Herrmann, N. (2016). Depressive symptoms and cognitive decline: A longitudinal analysis of potentially modifiable risk factors in community dwelling older adults. *Journal of Affective Disorders, 190*, 235–240.

Gaster, B., Larson, E. B., & Curtis, J. R. (2017). Advance directives for dementia: Meeting a unique challenge. *Journal of the American Medical Association, 318*(22), 2175–2176.

Gilmore, M. C., Stebbins, L., Argüelles-Borge, S., Trinidad, B., & Golden, C. J. (2020). Development and treatment of aggression in individuals with dementia. *Aggression and Violent Behavior, 54*, 101415. https://doi.org/10.1016/j.avb.2020.101415

Gower, J. (2020). *2020 medical malpractice payout analysis*. Diederich Healthcare. https://www.diederichhealthcare.com/the-standard/2020-medical-malpractice-payout-analysis/. Accessed December 1, 2020.

Grenier, S., Payette, M. C., Langlois, F., Vu, T. T. M., & Bherer, L. (2014). Depressive symptoms are independently associated with recurrent falls in community-dwelling older adults. *International Psychogeriatrics, 26*(9), 1511–1519.

Harrington, C., Mollot, R., Edelman, T. S., Wells, J., & Valanejad, D. (2020). U.S. nursing home violations of international and domestic human rights standards. *International Journal of Health Services, 50*(1), 62–72.

Hedna, K., Hensing, G., Skoog, I., Fastbom, J., & Waern, M. (2020). Sociodemographic and gender determinants of late-life suicide in users and non-users of antidepressants. *European Journal of Public Health, 30*(5), 958–964.

Hernandez, S. C., Overholser, J. C., Philips, K. L., Lavacot, J., & Stockmeier, C. A. (2021). Suicide among older adults: Interactions among key risk factors. *International Journal of Psychiatry in Medicine, 56*(6), 408–421. https://doi.org/10.1177/0091217420982387

Holzer, J. C., & Gluck, P. (2018). Patient safety and risk reduction in geriatric psychiatry patients. In J. C. Holzer, R. Kohn, J. M. Ellison, & P. R. Recupero (Eds.), *Geriatric forensic psychiatry: Principles and practice* (pp. 141–145). Oxford University Press.

Howe, E. G. (2011). Ethical challenges when patients have dementia. *Journal of Clinical Ethics, 22*(3), 203–211.

Jemberie, W. B., Padyab, M., Snellman, F., & Lundgren, L. (2020). A multidimensional latent class analysis of harmful alcohol use among older adults: Subtypes within the Swedish Addiction Severity Index registry. *Journal of Addiction Medicine, 14*(4), e89–e99.

Kapp, M. B. (2009). The liability environment for physicians providing nursing home medical care: Does it make a difference for residents? *Elder Law Journal, 16*, 249–293.

Kapp, M. B. (2018). Forensic issues in long-term care psychiatry. In J. C. Holzer, R. Kohn, J. M. Ellison, & P. R. Recupero (Eds.), *Geriatric forensic psychiatry: Principles and practice* (pp. 147–154). Oxford University Press.

Kennedy, M., Helfand, B. K. I., Gou, R. Y., et al. (2020). Delirium in older patients with COVID-19 presenting to the emergency department. *JAMA Network Open, 3*(11), e2029540. https://doi.org/10.1001/jamanetworkopen.2020.29540

Lachs, M. S., & Pillemer, K. A. (2015). Elder abuse. *New England Journal of Medicine, 373*(20), 1947–1956.

Langa, K. M., Larson, E. B., Crimmins, E. M., et al. (2017). A comparison of the prevalence of dementia in the United States in 2000 and 2012. *JAMA Internal Medicine, 177*(1), 51–58.

Lapierre, S., Erlangsen, A., Waern, M., et al. (2011). A systematic review of elderly suicide prevention programs. *Crisis, 32*(2), 88–98.

Lee, H., Seol, K. H., & Kim, J. W. (2018). Age and sex-related differences in risk factors for elderly suicide: Differentiating between suicide ideation and attempts. *International Journal of Geriatric Psychiatry, 33*(2), e300–e306.

Liu, L., Cruz, M., Ruptash, T., Barnard, S., & Juzwishin, D. (2017). Acceptance of global positioning system (GPS) technology among dementia clients and family caregivers. *Journal of Technology in Human Services, 35*(2), 99–119.

Makaroun, L. K., Bachrach, R. L., & Rosland, A. M. (2020). Elder abuse in the time of COVID-19—Increased risks for older adults and their caregivers. *American Journal of Geriatric Psychiatry, 28*(8), 876–880.

Malin, M. A., Jimenez-Madiedo, C., & Kohn, R. (2018). Suicidal behavior in the elderly and its forensic implications. In J. C. Holzer, R. Kohn, J. M. Ellison, & P. R. Recupero (Eds.), *Geriatric forensic psychiatry: Principles and practice* (pp. 283–292). Oxford University Press.

McNary, A. L. (2017). Managing your aging patient population. *Innovations in Clinical Neuroscience, 14*(3–4), 41–44.

Metzger, E. D., Holzer, J. C., & Brendel, R. W. (2018). Forensic issues in geriatric psychiatry consult liaison service and the right to accept and refuse treatment. In J. C. Holzer, R. Kohn, J. M. Ellison, & P. R. Recupero (Eds.), *Geriatric forensic psychiatry: Principles and practice* (pp. 113–119). Oxford University Press.

Meyer, C., & O'Keefe, F. (2020). Non-pharmacological interventions for people with dementia: A review of reviews. *Dementia, 19*(6), 1927–1954.

Meyer, D. J. (2006). Psychiatry malpractice and administrative inquiries of alleged physician misconduct. *Psychiatric Clinics of North America, 29*, 615–628.

Naik, A. D., Teal, C. R., Pavlik, V. N., Dyer, C. B., & McCullough, L. B. (2008). Conceptual challenges and practical approaches to screening capacity for self-care and protection in vulnerable older adults. *Journal of the American Geriatrics Society, 56*(S2), S66–S70.

Newman, W. J. (2012). Psychopharmacologic management of aggression. *Psychiatric Clinics of North America, 35*(4), 957–972.

Nkodo, J. A., Camus, V., & Fougère, B. (2020). Ethical issues in the management of patients with behavioral and psychological symptoms of dementia during COVID-19 containment: Examples from institutions in France. *American Journal of Geriatric Psychiatry, 28*(12), 1332–1333.

Nørgaard, A., Jensen-Dahm, C., Gasse, C., Wimberley, T., Hansen, E. S., & Waldemar, G. (2020). Association of benzodiazepines and antidepressants with 180-day mortality among patients with dementia receiving antipsychotic pharmacotherapy: A nationwide registry-based study. *Journal of Clinical Psychiatry, 81*(4), 19m12828. https://doi.org/10.4088/JCP.19m12828

Park, J., & Lee, O. E. (2020). Association between vision impairment and suicidal ideation among older adults: Results from National Survey on Drug Use and Health. *Disability & Health Journal, 13*(4), 100939. https://doi.org/10.1016/j.dhjo.2020.100939

Peters, P. G., Jr. (1998). The illusion of autonomy at the end of life: Unconsented life support and the wrongful life analogy. *University of California at Los Angeles Law Review, 45*(3), 673–732.

Pope, T. M. (2017). Legal briefing: New penalties for disregarding advance directives and do-not-resuscitate orders. *Journal of Clinical Ethics, 28*(1), 74–81.

Preskorn, S. H., & Quadri, S. (2020, October 20). Why are patients with COVID-19 at risk for drug-drug interactions? *Psychiatric Times*. https://www.psychiatrictimes.com/view/why-patients-with-covid19-risk-drug-drug-interactions. Accessed November 7, 2020.

Price, M., & Howard, P. (2020). Suicide in elderly population. In L. H. Gold & R. L. Frierson (Eds.), *Suicide risk assessment and management* (3rd ed., pp. 251–263). American Psychiatric Association.

Ratnapradipa, K. L., Pope, C. N., Nwosu, A., & Zhu, M. (2021). Older driver crash involvement and fatalities, by age and sex, 2000–2017. *Journal of Applied Gerontology, 40*(10), 1314–1319. https://doi.org/10.1177/10.1177/0733464820956507

Reus, V. I., Fochtmann, L. J., Eyler, A. E., et al. (2016). *The American Psychiatric Association practice guideline on the use of antipsychotics to treat agitation or psychosis in patients with dementia*. American Psychiatric Association.

Roberto, K. A., Teaster, P. B., Lindberg, B. W., & Blancato, R. (2021). A first (and disturbing) look at the relationship between the opioid epidemic and elder abuse: Insights of human service professionals. *Journal of Applied Gerontology, 40*(10), 1231–1235. https://doi.org/10.1177/0733464820947279

Rutherford, B. R., Brewster, K., Golub, J. S., Kim, A. H., & Roose, S. P. (2018). Sensation and psychiatry: Linking age-related hearing loss to late-life depression and cognitive decline. *American Journal of Psychiatry, 175*(3), 215–224.

Schaffer, A. C., Jena, A. B., Seabury, S. A., Singh, H., Chalasani, V., & Kachalia, A. (2017). Rates and characteristics of paid malpractice claims among US physicians by specialty, 1992–2014. *JAMA Internal Medicine, 177*(5), 710–718.

Simons, K., Van Orden, K., Conner, K. R., & Bagge, C. (2019). Age differences in suicide risk screening and management prior to suicide attempts. *American Journal of Geriatric Psychiatry, 27*(6), 604–608.

Sklar, T., & Terry, N. P. (2020). States are making it harder to sue nursing homes over COVID-19: Why immunity from lawsuits is a problem. *The Conversation*. https://theconversation.com/states-are-making-it-harder-to-sue-nursinghomes-over-covid-19-why-immunity-from-lawsuits-is-a-problem-139820. Accessed July 3, 2020.

Spaans, H. P., Kok, R. M., Bouckaert, F., et al. (2018). Vascular risk factors in older patients with depression: Outcome of electroconvulsive therapy versus medication. *International Journal of Geriatric Psychiatry, 33*(2), 371–378.

Storey, J. E. (2020). Risk factors for elder abuse and neglect: A review of the literature. *Aggression and Violent Behavior, 50*, 101339. https://doi.org/10.1016/j.avb.2019.101339

Surti, G. M., Stanton, L., & Kohn, R. (2018). Violence and aggression in the elderly: Nondirected aggression and clinical causation. In J. C. Holzer, R. Kohn, J. M. Ellison, & P. R. Recupero (Eds.), *Geriatric forensic psychiatry: Principles and practice* (pp. 199–212). Oxford University Press.

Survey. (2013). Survey finds shortfalls in the quality of mental health care for older Americans. *Psychiatric Services, 64*(2), 203.

Szmulewicz, A. G., Ferraris, A., Rodriguez, A., et al. (2018). All-cause mortality in older adults with affective disorders and dementia under treatment with antipsychotic drugs: A matched-cohort study. *Psychiatry Research, 265*, 82–86.

Temple-Raston, D. (2020, December 24). *The tragedy of "St. Joe's"*. NPR.org. https://www.npr.org/2020/12/24/947120581/the-tragedy-of-st-joes. Accessed December 29, 2020.

Terry, N. P. (2020). Liability and liability shields. In S. Burris, S. de Guia, L. Gable, D. E. Levin, W. E. Parmet, & N. P. Terry (Eds.), *Addressing legal responses to COVID-19* (pp. 199–204). Public Health Law Watch.

Tham, A., Jonsson, U., Andersson, G., Söderlund, A., Allard, P., & Bertilsson, G. (2016). Efficacy and tolerability of antidepressants in people aged 65 years or older with major depressive disorder—A systematic review and a meta-analysis. *Journal of Affective Disorders, 205*, 1–12.

Tsao, C. I., & Layde, J. B. (2007). A basic review of psychiatric medical malpractice law in the United States. *Comprehensive Psychiatry, 48*, 309–312.

United States Census Bureau. (2020, June 25). *65 and older population grows rapidly as baby boomers age*. U.S. Census Bureau Press. https://www.census.gov/newsroom/press-releases/2020/65-older-population-grows.html. Accessed August 16, 2020.

Uvais, N. A. (2020). Psychological impact of the COVID-19 pandemic among the elderly: A case series from India. *Primary Care Companion to CNS Disorders, 22*(4), 20com02675. https://doi.org/10.4088/PCC.20com02675

van der Feltz-Cornelis, C. M., Allen, S. F., & van Eck van der Sluijs, J. F. (2020). Misdiagnosis of an underlying medical condition as Conversion Disorder/Functional Neurological Disorder (CD/FND) still occurs. *General Hospital Psychiatry, 65*, 43–46.

Veldwijk-Rouwenhorst, A. E., Smalbrugge, M., Wetzels, R., et al. (2017). Nursing home residents with dementia and very frequent agitation: A particular group. *American Journal of Geriatric Psychiatry, 25*(12), 1339–1348.

Voaklander, D. C., Rowe, B. H., Dryden, D. M., et al. (2008). Medical illness, medication use and suicide in seniors: A population-based case-control study. *Journal of Epidemiology & Community Health, 62*(2), 138–146.

Volicer, L. (2021). Importance of distinguishing reactive and proactive aggression in dementia care. *Journal of Geriatric Psychiatry & Neurology, 34*(3), 243–247. https://doi.org/10.1177/0891988720924706

Wand, A. P. F., Zhong, B. L., Chiu, H. F. K., Draper, B., & De Leo, D. (2020). COVID-19: The implications for suicide in older adults. *International Psychogeriatrics, 32*(10), 1225–1230.

Weiss, A. J., Heslin, K. C., Barrett, M. L., Izar, R., & Bierman, A. S. (2018). *Opioid-related inpatient stays and emergency department visits among patients aged 65 years and older, 2010 and 2015. HCUP Statistical Brief #244*. Agency for Healthcare Research and Quality. https://www.hcup-us.ahrq.gov/reports/statbriefs/sb244-Opioid-Inpatient-Stays-ED-Visits-Older-Adults.pdf. Accessed September 18, 2020.

Wetherell, J. L., Petkus, A. J., White, K. S., et al. (2013). Antidepressant medication augmented with cognitive-behavioral therapy for generalized anxiety disorder in older adults. *American Journal of Psychiatry, 170*(7), 782–789.

Williams, J. L., Racette, E. H., Hernandez-Tejada, M. A., & Acierno, R. (2020). Prevalence of elder polyvictimization in the United States: Data from the National Elder Mistreatment study. *Journal of Interpersonal Violence, 35*(21–22), 4517–4532.

Williams, L. (2002). Resident elopement: Case study and lessons learned. *Nursing homes: Long-term care management*, pp. 42–45.

Young, R. C., Mulsant, B. H., Sajatovic, M., et al. (2017). GERI-BD: A randomized double-blind controlled trial of lithium and divalproex in the treatment of mania in older patients with bipolar disorder. *American Journal of Psychiatry, 174*(11), 1086–1093.

Zuidema, S. U., Johansson, A., Selbaek, G., et al. (2015). A consensus guideline for antipsychotic drug use for dementia in care homes. Bridging the gap between scientific evidence and clinical practice. *International Psychogeriatrics, 27*(11), 1849–1859.

Correctional Psychiatry

27

Anthony Tamburello and Chinye Azuh-Showole

Introduction

Jails and prisons are widely regarded as higher-risk settings for healthcare-related lawsuits (Trestman et al., 2015). While there is little research directly comparing liability by treatment setting for psychiatrists, insurers share this view (Dyer, 2020). In correctional settings, psychiatrists may be sued less often than non-psychiatric medical providers (Chapman, 2020). Regardless, psychiatrists may find it difficult to get malpractice coverage if they work with inmates (Knuppel, 2011). Cognizant of the risk of being sued, psychiatrists may be reticent to work in these facilities because of how this may affect their future insurability (Schlanger, 2003). Prison doctors who are sued by inmates are also nearly four times as likely to have a board action taken against their license compared with providers in the community (Dabney & Vaughn, 2016; McCoin, 2018).

In this chapter, we will discuss liability for providers of psychiatric care in correctional settings. Readers interested in mental health-related suits against correctional officers or administrators are referred to Ross's text on Liability in Criminal Justice Settings (2018); those interested in systems-based correctional litigation and monitoring thereof are referred to Metzner's articles on these subjects (Metzner, 2002; Metzner, 2009).

A. Tamburello (✉)
University Correctional Health Care, Piscataway, NJ, USA

Department of Psychiatry, Rutgers University-Robert Wood Johnson Medical School, Piscataway, NJ, USA
e-mail: Anthony.tamburello@rutgers.edu

C. Azuh-Showole
Department of Psychiatry, Rutgers University-Robert Wood Johnson Medical School, Piscataway, NJ, USA
e-mail: c.ashowole@rutgers.edu

Theories of Liability

Inmates may sue psychiatrists under several different legal theories. In state courts, they may bring a legal action for ordinary medical malpractice (See Chap. 1). However, inmates may also sue state government entities in federal court for a violation of civil rights under 42 U.S.C.A. §1983. In *Estelle v. Gamble* (1976), the US Supreme Court held that "deliberate indifference by prison personnel to a prisoner's serious illness or injury constitutes cruel and unusual punishment contravening the Eighth Amendment" (p. 97). *Bowring v. Godwin* (1977) expanded the Gamble decision to apply to prison mental health services. *Bell v. Wolfish* (1979) extended these healthcare rights to pretrial detainees (i.e., those in jails and detention centers) under the 14th amendment; the same deliberate indifference standard applies to these individuals (*Butler v. Fletcher,* 2006). While healthcare services in jails and prisons may be provided by outside agencies or companies, being employed by a contracted vendor does not protect one against a §1983 suit (Daniel, 2009).

Though §1983 (which specifically refers to actions "under color" of state law) does not apply in federal settings, inmates in federal correctional facilities may sue a prison official under a *Bivens* action (*Bivens v. Six Unknown Named Agents of Federal Bureau of Narcotics,* 1971) for a constitutional claim or may file a malpractice suit under the Federal Tort Claims Act. Such federal tort claims are difficult to pursue, as federal inmates must first exhaust administrative remedies such as filing a complaint with the Board of Prisons (Center for Justice Democracy, 2015; Schwartz, 2014). If housed in a privately-run federal prison, *Bivens* does not apply, and the inmate must seek redress under whatever state tort law is available (*Minneci v. Pollard,* 2012).

Theoretically, psychiatrists could also be sued should their actions interfere with an inmate's access to services or programs in violation of the Americans with Disabilities Act (ADA), though these cases are typically directed towards deficiencies in healthcare systems. Mental health services for incarcerated persons are considered "services, programs, or

P. Ash et al. (eds.), *Malpractice and Liability in Psychiatry*, https://doi.org/10.1007/978-3-030-91975-7_27

activities of a public entity" under the ADA. For example, investigators from the Department of Justice criticized policies such as subjecting inmates with serious mental illness to solitary confinement or disciplinary charges for self-injurious behavior as violations of the ADA (Dlugacz et al., 2019).

Deliberate Indifference

While courts have sometimes inconsistently applied this legal concept (Ross, 2010), deliberate indifference is more difficult for a plaintiff to prove than the negligence that may be seen in ordinary medical malpractice (Daniel, 2009). In *Farmer v. Brennan* (1994), the US Supreme Court held that a *subjective* standard applied to cases of deliberate indifference. In other words, the state actor must have actual knowledge of the serious medical need and then failed to act. It is insufficient for the plaintiff to show that the correctional healthcare provider "should have known." While work in correctional settings remains high-risk for litigation, *Farmer* shifted the balance in favor of defendants. In a large study of inmate civil rights lawsuits, findings in favor of correctional personnel substantially increased (71% to 83%) after *Farmer* and were typically delivered by summary judgment (Ross, 2010).

Healthcare staff in jails and prisons are given substantial deference by the courts if they provide reasonable care consistent with medical standards and ethics (Vaughn, 1997). A bad outcome by itself is not deliberate indifference (*Sylvester v. City of Newark,* 2005). Minor errors or delays in treatment are unlikely to meet this standard, and inmate claims viewed by the courts as frivolous are likely to be dismissed (Vaughn, 1995; *Johnson v. Hamilton,* 2006). A medication error that is not life-threatening is unlikely to be serious enough to rise to the level of a civil rights violation. Inmates consistently do not prevail in suits where the issue at hand is a disagreement about the type, dosage, or quantity of medication prescribed (Vaughn, 1997). If a prisoner contributed to a bad outcome through non-adherence with treatment or intentional self-injury, this may be considered a defense against an allegation of deliberate indifference. Most examples of this though are in refusals of medical care (Farber, 2007).

It is not necessary however that a medical problem be life-threatening to be considered a serious medical need. Any diagnosis from a physician that requires treatment, or a condition that would be obvious to a layperson as requiring medical attention, is likely to be considered sufficiently serious (Friedman, 1992). While a single negligent medical act is unlikely to result in a ruling for an inmate plaintiff, courts have found deliberate indifference for failure to correct a known error (*Spann v. Roper*, 2006) or for repeated negligent acts (Friedman, 1992). When denied medication for a serious illness, an inmate plaintiff is likely to prevail (Vaughn, 1995). The longer the delay in providing treatment and the more suffering resulting from such delay, the greater the risk of liability (Vaughn, 1995; Vaughn, 1997). Providing cursory care or continuing a treatment that has been established as ineffective could make providers subject to liability (Friedman, 1992; Cohen, 2020). While courts have not found a right for inmates to have outside consultation to resolve disputes between inmates and the facility's medical staff (Vaughn, 1997), ignoring the advice of outside consultants could be a cause of action for deliberate indifference (Cohen, 2020).

Failure of a constitutionally based claim does not preclude an inmate from also suing for medical negligence in state court (Daniel, 2009), though this pathway carries its own difficulties. The Prison Litigation Reform Act of 1996 (PLRA) sets procedural rules, such as exhausting administrative remedies, that have greatly limited this strategy. Factors such as non-adherence with a treatment regimen or misuse of medication may be considered contributory negligence (Daniel, 2009).

Standard of Care

In the third edition of Psychiatric Services in Correctional Facilities (2016), the American Psychiatric Association asserts, "The fundamental policy goal for correctional mental healthcare is to provide the same quality of mental health services to each patient in the criminal justice system that *should be available* in the community" (p. 5).

Ruiz v. Estelle (1980), a federal district court case, largely set the bar for the components required for a minimally adequate healthcare system in prison (see Table 27.1).

In brief, failure to adequately evaluate inmate patients for mental illness and suicidality, to provide clinically appropriate treatment and monitoring, or to document such treatment

Table 27.1 Components of a minimally adequate correctional healthcare system (Ruiz v. Estelle, 1980)

A systematic program for screening and evaluating inmates in order to identify those who require mental health treatment
Treatment entails more than segregation and close supervision of inmate patients
Treatment requiring the participation of trained mental health professionals, employed in sufficient numbers to identify and treat in an individualized manner those treatable inmates suffering from serious mental disorders
Accurate, complete, and confidential records of the mental health treatment process
Prescription and administration of behavior-altering medications in dangerous amounts, by dangerous methods, or without appropriate supervision and periodic evaluation is an unacceptable method of treatment
A basic program for the identification, treatment, and supervision of inmates with suicidal tendencies is a necessary component of any mental health treatment program

could all expose the psychiatrist to liability. These services must all be provided regardless of their cost to the correctional system. Inadequate funding has been roundly rejected by federal courts as a defense to a civil rights violation (Vaughn, 1997).

The National Commission on Correctional Health Care (NCCHC) and the American Correctional Association (ACA) publish standards for healthcare within jails and prisons. While the organizations themselves have suggested that these represent the standard of care (Griffith, 2020), and trial courts may sometimes refer to them as such, the Supreme Court has declined the "wholesale adoption of professional standards" when determining if a constitutional violation has occurred (Metzner, 2002).

Special Liability Risks in Correctional Settings

Suicide

In *Taylor v. Barkes* (2015), the US Supreme Court held that it has never established "a right to the proper implementation of adequate suicide prevention protocols," (p. 3) adding, "No decision of this Court even discusses suicide screening or prevention protocols" (p. 4). While this may provide some cover for correctional systems with inadequate policies for suicide risk management, an inmate patient's completed suicide is by far the healthcare outcome at highest risk for legal entanglement (Ross, 2010). Most of these cases result in settlements (Olivero & Roberts, 1990).

Generally, for the plaintiff to prevail in a suit related to a correctional suicide, the defendant must be shown to have acted intentionally or with "reckless disregard" for an inmate's risk for suicide (Olivero & Roberts, 1990). Causes of action in suicide cases against psychiatrists include inadequate psychiatric examination, failure to consider conspicuous risk factors in assessing suicide risk, failure to implement suicide precautions when aware of risk factors, failure to communicate with other providers or custody staff, abrupt discontinuation of psychiatric medication in an inmate otherwise at risk for suicide, and repeated examples of delayed or denied medical treatment (Daniel, 2009). No-harm contracts, which were found in 13% of suicide deaths in jails and lockups, do not protect psychiatrists from liability (Hayes, 2010).

In *Drake v. Koss* (2006), the Eight Circuit Court of Appeals ruled that the correctional staff were not deliberately indifferent in failing to prevent a serious suicide attempt because they were influenced by the views of a state hospital psychiatrist that the inmate's prior self-injurious behaviors were manipulative. The suit against the hospital psychiatrist was settled. Deliberate self-harm is a marker for increased suicide risk in the community (Olfson et al., 2012). Considering the high rates of malingering in jails and prisons, providers in these settings are wise to avoid being dismissive of suicidality (Cummings & Thompson, 2009). Medication decisions related to a suicide can also be a source of liability. In *Williams v. Mehra* (1999), the Sixth Circuit Court of Appeals found that a psychiatrist's prescription of a pill form of a tricyclic antidepressant to an inmate with a history of overdose (when a liquid form was available) could have been found to have been deliberately indifferent.

Solitary Confinement

Also referred to as isolated confinement, restricted housing, administrative segregation, disciplinary segregation, or similar terms, solitary confinement is the housing of an inmate for disciplinary, protective, medical, investigative, administrative, or other reasons in a manner that substantially restricts access to social interaction, recreation, property, and other institutional programming and services. The practice of solitary confinement has often subjected correctional systems to class action litigation (Metzner, 2002) and may be a factor as well in suits targeting healthcare providers. In *Palakovic v. Wetzel* (2017), the plaintiff had brief visits with a psychologist in solitary confinement and a prescription for an antidepressant but was denied access to a psychiatrist. The Third Circuit Court of Appeals opined that the defendants, inclusive of the mental health staff, were deliberately indifferent by "substituting solitary confinement for treatment."

Informed Consent

While some argue that the inherently coercive nature of a correctional environment makes true consent impossible (Veneziano, 1986), psychiatrists ordinarily have a duty to obtain informed consent from inmates for non-emergency psychotropic medications. Federal courts have supported this as an inmate right (Tamburello et al., 2018), though the Third Circuit Court of Appeals in *White v. Napoleon* (1990) qualified that "prisoners may not bring treatment to a halt, insisting on answers to questions that are unreasonable, time-wasting or intended to turn the doctor-patient relationship into a battle for control over treatment" (p. 113). Emergency treatment is a clear exception in situations when the inmate is a present danger to self or others (*Chambers v. Ingram,* 1988). Besides emergency treatment, exceptions for informed consent can be found in non-emergency forced medications for seriously mentally ill prisoners following an administrative hearing (*Washington v. Harper,* 1990).

In *Johnson v. Tinwalla* (2017), a psychiatrist prescribed antipsychotic medication to a patient who had immediately revoked written consent for it. This particular patient was in a sexual violent predator program and was not considered eligible for a *Harper* hearing because he was not technically an inmate. Although the defendant psychiatrist claimed that the patient never refused the medication, it was administered to him in a cup along with an assortment of other medications. The court considered the actions of the psychiatrist not only deliberately indifferent but also a battery.

Adverse Drug Reactions

In *Chambers v. Ingram* (1988), a psychiatrist prescribed haloperidol to a jail inmate who later admitted to feigning illness, but unfortunately suffered seizures after taking the medication. He had refused this medication specifically because of the risk of seizure, though alleged that he continued to take it on threat of being forced. The Seventh Circuit Court of Appeals opined that the actions of the doctor may have been negligent but were not deliberately indifferent. This suggests that if the inmate has knowledge of potential risks, physicians are unlikely to be successfully sued under §1983 for an adverse drug reaction.

In contrast, the Ninth Circuit Court of Appeals in *Ortiz v. City of Imperial* (1989) considered a jail doctor deliberately indifferent for prescribing sedatives without an examination to an inmate patient in alcohol withdrawal who had recently suffered a head injury and who later died from complications thereof. The court indicated that deliberate indifference does not require a complete failure to treat and that liability can be incurred if prescribers ignore a known danger of the medication.

In *Arroyo v Li* (2014), a federal district court judge ruled that tardive dyskinesia was a serious medical need and failing to diagnose or treat it in an inmate could be deliberate indifference. In this case, the plaintiff psychiatrist had been notified by psychiatrists from previous state prisons, but had disagreed with their diagnosis. Later a diagnosis of tardive dyskinesia was confirmed by other physicians, including outside neurologists.

Supervision of Providers of Psychiatric Services

Correctional systems increasingly rely on physician extenders to provide psychiatric services at lower cost. A psychiatrist acting as a collaborating physician for an advanced practice nurse (APN) or physician assistant (PA) may worry about their vicarious liability (see Chap. 1). Such concern may be generally unwarranted. Based on a 2017 insurance dataset, less than 1% of paid malpractice claims for APNs were for those practicing in a prison setting (Nurses Service Organization, 2017). Far more claims were reported by APNs working in community physician offices and skilled nursing facilities compared to those working in correctional settings. Claims related to psychiatric work were less common than claims for non-psychiatric prison healthcare services, comprising only 6.5% of the total, with suicide and improper prescribing of controlled medication being the most common causes of action (Nurses Service Organization, 2012).

In §1983 litigation, state actors are held responsible for their own conduct, not necessarily that of their subordinates (*Monell v. Department of Soc. Svcs,* 1978; *Barkes v. First Correctional Medical, Inc,* 2014). While courts have come to different conclusions on these matters, the action of hiring an unqualified professional, or a failure to train, supervise, or control them, could be a source of liability (Olivero & Roberts, 1990; Vaughn, 1995).

Supervisors of psychiatric professionals at any level could be held liable for deliberate indifference by offering financial incentives for avoiding the provision of care to inmates as a cost-saving measure. An egregious example of this can be found in the case of a jail physician who was paid a bonus for every 911 call that was avoided, though other cost-cutting measures that limit access to care may also incur liability (Robbins, 1999). Conversely, Rutgers University Correctional Health Care noticed a decrease in cases and payouts to inmates related to a cost-based agreement with the New Jersey Department of Corrections that removed financial incentives to restrict care (Trestman et al., 2015).

Hunger Strikes

Hunger strikes are a common problem in correctional settings, and psychiatrists may be asked to intervene to try to address relevant mental health factors. An inmate is likely to see forced feeding as an assault and may try to sue the involved healthcare staff. Generally, case law, legislation, and regulations in the United States have supported forced feeding of inmates engaging in a hunger strike, despite widespread opposition by professional organizations (Reeves et al., 2017).

While it is unlikely that a psychiatrist will be asked to directly participate in forced feeding, cases may allege improper intervention by a physician during a hunger strike (Dabney & Vaughn, 2016). In one example, an inmate alleged that forced feeding was improperly justified by a diagnosis of borderline personality disorder (*Department of Public Welfare v. Kallinger,* 1990). A bad outcome with a hunger strike as a backdrop may be a source of §1983 litigation. In 2019, the Kentucky Department of Corrections settled a lawsuit from the family of an inmate who died after refusing nearly all his meals for several weeks but was not considered to be on a hunger strike because he occasionally accepted tea. Allegations within the suit included inadequate access to psychiatric care (Clarke, 2020).

Discharge Planning

Most inmates complete a sentence and return to the community, where the structure and accessibility of treatment resources are different. In the weeks following release, former inmates with mental health or substance use disorders are at particularly high risk for recidivism (SAMHSA, 2017). In terms of aftercare, critical psychiatric services include providing a written summary of the inmate's needs, making referrals for appropriate continuity of care in the community, and providing a clinically appropriate temporary supply of medication (Metzner, 2002). In *Wakefield v. Thompson* (1999), the Ninth Circuit Court of Appeals held that the state has a duty to provide to the inmate a "supply sufficient to ensure that he has that medication available during the period of time reasonably necessary to permit him to consult a doctor and obtain a new supply" (p. 4). In *Charles v. Orange County* (2019), the Second Circuit Court of Appeals held that appropriate discharge planning, including the provision of a supply of medication for mentally ill inmates, was considered a part of "in-custody medical care," and failure in this regard could be a violation of inmates' civil rights.

Reducing Risk

Quality Clinical Care

The best defense against a malpractice suit is for it to be unnecessary in the first place. Providing the best possible care in jails and prisons may feel like an aspirational goal considering operational factors like staffing, access to inmate patients, medication formulary controls, availability of counseling and ancillary services, and various stressors indigenous to these settings. Nevertheless, a thorough psychiatric evaluation and a treatment plan that carefully considers inmate preferences and environmental limitations will prevent most undesired clinical outcomes. Care for a serious mental health problem should never be ignored, denied, or unnecessarily delayed (Ross, 2010). Quality control measures, including a peer review process, can greatly improve clinical care and reduce liability (Danto, 1997).

Collateral Information

Acquiring and documenting information from collateral sources can be helpful in difficult or complicated cases. Medical records and family contacts may shed light on past and recent signs of serious mental illness, treatment response, and suicidal behavior. Once the provider has access to additional information though, it can be a double-edged sword from a liability perspective. It is essential that documentation support that this information was considered in management decisions, whether or not it changed diagnosis or treatment.

Continuity of Care

Psychiatrists should use caution before changing a treatment plan that they inherited from another professional. Several legal actions have occurred in the context of abrupt discontinuation of medication on transfer into a correctional system (Vaughn, 1995; Daniel, 2009). While a fresh assessment could be an opportunity to reduce the risks of polypharmacy or unindicated medications, it is wise to defer changes until the responsible psychiatrist appreciates the rationale for the treatment in question.

Documentation

Keeping accurate, complete, and confidential records is a basic component of adequate prison mental healthcare (*Ruiz v. Estelle,* 1980). Documentation may protect the psychiatrist from successful lawsuits by demonstrating timely responses to inmates' serious medical needs, as well as adequate assessment and reasonable treatment planning. In *Estelle v. Gamble* (1976), the US Supreme Court was persuaded that prison doctors were not deliberately indifferent by records indicating that Gamble had been seen 17 times over the course of 3 months and had been prescribed medications for his physical injury. While heroic levels of medical attention have not been demanded by the courts, it is critically important that a defendant psychiatrist can prove via contemporaneous documentation that the inmate plaintiff had access to clinically appropriate care for any identified serious mental health needs.

Informed Consent and Non-adherence

Psychiatrists should obtain informed consent for psychotropic medication consistent with institutional policies and procedures. There are many reasons why an inmate may not take medication as prescribed, such as not wanting to appear weak to other inmates or to save medication with the intent to divert it (Tamburello et al., 2018). In a structured correctional setting, a psychiatrist may be made aware of non-adherence from nursing or custody staff. When medication is prescribed for a serious mental illness, knowledge of non-adherence is ignored at the prescriber's peril. Psychiatrists should promptly identify and manage non-adherence, including pursuing a *Harper* hearing if appropriate and available at the institution. Increased observation and management of non-adherence in inmate patients who are seriously mentally ill, actively disturbed, or otherwise at risk for violence will reduce liability (Danto, 1997). Should the institution lack a policy on non-emergency forced medications, consideration should be given to transfer the inmate to a facility capable of managing the situation.

Suicide Risk Management

Following the recommendations above will go a long way in reducing suicide risk. When conducting a suicide risk assessment, the professional should go beyond simply eliciting a "no" to the question of suicidal ideation by synthesizing all the available information and forming a treatment plan to address the identified risk factors. Consider risks specific to prison including (but not limited to) single-cell housing, environmental stressors (such as conflicts with staff or peers), disciplinary problems, and adverse legal, social, financial, or occupational developments (Knoll, 2010). Psychiatrists should be well versed in the institution's policies and procedures regarding suicide risk management. They should advocate as needed for adequate processes for the screening of inmates for suicide risk factors, as well as periodic training about suicide risk identification and management for all staff who have contact with inmates (Daniel, 2009).

Extra care should be taken in higher-risk situations including any intake or return to the facility (e.g., from the community, court, and outside trips), substance withdrawal (Danto, 1997), mental anguish (Olivero & Roberts, 1990), and incidents of increased confinement (e.g., disciplinary, protective, or medical housing), especially when not housed with a cellmate (Reeves & Tamburello, 2014). Orders for increased observation should be appropriate to the level of risk and should exclude access to items which the inmate may use to self-injure (Knoll, 2010). A close working relationship with custody, administration, and other healthcare staff will facilitate communication and prompt management of at-risk inmates (Ross, 2010).

Suicide rating scales, which are typically normed for community samples, by themselves are not sufficient to prevent a suicide and related liability. A low score on a suicide rating scale may be falsely reassuring and may result in an inadequate response to a suicidal threat. Mental health staff should be mindful that the conditions of suicide watch in jails and prisons are invariably unpleasant, with the usual restrictions of property and clothing that could be used for self-injury. Thus, denial of suicidal ideation in this setting may not be reliable and should not be the sole reason for reducing the level of observation (Hayes, 1998).

The psychiatrist should consider appropriate alternatives for psychotropic medications with particular lethality such as tricyclic antidepressants (Daniel, 2009). When available and appropriate, creative prescribing strategies for inmates at risk for overdose, such as using a liquid or crushed form that is difficult to hoard, should be considered. By avoiding the prescription of unindicated medications, the psychiatrist protects not only the patient but potentially others in the facility who may unwittingly (or wittingly) be subjected to a risky medication intended for someone else.

Accreditation

While not universally regarded as authoritative in terms of the standards of care in correctional medicine (Robbins, 1999; Metzner, 2002), accreditation by a professional organization such as the NCCHC or the ACA may offer some medicolegal protection (Griffith, 2020). Psychiatrists are wise to support such credentialing as it represents a meaningful commitment of resources by the facility to implement policies and procedures that prioritize the provision of adequate healthcare services to inmates.

Professional Liability Coverage

Before accepting work at a correctional facility, psychiatrists should learn if their employer will indemnify their work, as well as that of the work of those under their supervision. For state employees, indemnification is the norm. Contractors may need to find private professional liability coverage if not offered by their employer. Providers should be aware of "hold harmless" clauses in their employment contract that may limit or exclude them from coverage by requiring them (rather than the facility) to accept responsibility for a poor psychiatric outcome (Knoll, 2010).

Key Points

- While healthcare lawsuits frequently occur in a correctional setting, courts generally grant deference to defendants if the care provided was reasonable.
- Psychiatrists in jails and prisons may be sued either in state court for medical negligence or in federal court for a civil rights violation for deliberate indifference to an inmate's serious mental health needs.
- Suicide is the outcome most likely to result in litigation against a psychiatrist in these settings, though liability concerns are emerging for care related to adverse drug reactions, solitary confinement, hunger strikes, and discharge planning.

- Quality clinical care, documentation, informed consent, continuation or careful discontinuation of medications on transfer from other settings, addressing non-adherence, and suicide risk management are key strategies to reduce liability.

References

American Psychiatric Association Work Group to Revise the APA Guidelines on Psychiatric Services in Correctional Facilities, and American Psychiatric Association Task Force to Revise the APA Guidelines on Psychiatric Services in Jails and Prisons. (2016). *Psychiatric services in correctional facilities* (3rd ed.). American Psychiatric Association.

Arroyo v. Li, No. 3: CV-13-1506, 2014 WL 4215524, M.D. Pa (2014).

Barkes v. First Correctional Medical, Inc., 766 F.3d 307, 310-311, C.A.3 (2014).

Bell v. Wolfish, 441 US 520 (1979).

Bivens v. Six Unknown Named Agents of Federal Bureau of Narcotics, 403 U.S. 388 (1971).

Bowring v. Godwin, 551 F.2d 44, 47, 4th Cir (1977).

Butler v. Fletcher, No. 05-3480, 465 F.3d 340, 8th Cir (2006).

Center for Justice Democracy at New York Law School. (2015). *FAQ – civil justice and prison health care: All locked up and behind bars*. https://centerjd.org/system/files/PrisonHealthCareFAQF_0.pdf. Accessed October 29, 2020.

Chambers v. Ingram, 858 F.2d 351, 7th Cir (1988).

Chapman, R. (2020). *Personal communication, Chapman Law Group*, 10/14/2020.

Charles v. Orange County, No. 17-3506, 2d Cir (2019).

Clarke, M. (2020). *$400,000 settlement in lawsuit over Kentucky prisoner's starvation death*. https://www.prisonlegalnews.org/news/2020/oct/1/400000-settlement-lawsuit-over-kentucky-prisoners-starvation-death/. Accessed November 6, 2020.

Cohen, F. (2020). Three takes on deliberate indifference. *Correct Care, Summer, 6*.

Cummings, D., & Thompson, M. (2009). Suicidal or manipulative? The role of mental health counselors in overcoming a false dichotomy in identifying and treating self-harming inmates. *Journal of Mental Health Counseling, 31*(3), 201–212.

Dabney, D. A., & Vaughn, M. S. (2016). Incompetent jail and prison doctors. *The Prison Journal, 80*(2), 151–183.

Daniel, A. E. (2009). Suicide-related litigation in jails and prisons: Risk management strategies. *Journal of Correctional Health Care, 15*(1), 19–27.

Danto, B. L. (1997). Suicide litigation as an agent of change in jail and prison: An initial report. *Behavioral Sciences & the Law, 15*(4), 415–425.

Department of Public Welfare v. Kallinger, 134 Pa. Commonwealth Ct. 415, 580 A.2d 887 (1990).

Dlugacz, H. A., Droubi, L., & Gallagher, M. (2019). Custodial suicide and class action remedies: Current obstacles and future directions. *Behavioral Sciences & the Law, 37*(3), 281–303.

Drake v. Koss, 439 F.3d 441, 8th Cir (2006).

Dyer, W. (2020). *Personal communication, HCP National Insurance Services*, 10/15/2020.

Estelle v. Gamble, 429 U.S. 97 (1976).

Farber, B. J. (2007). *Civil liability for inadequate prisoner medical care – An introduction*. http://www.aele.org/law/2007JBSEP/2007-09MLJ301.pdf. Accessed November 3, 2020.

Farmer v. Brennan, 511 U.S. 825, 836 (1994).

Friedman, M. C. (1992). Cruel and unusual punishment in the provision of prison medical care: Challenging the deliberate indifference standard. *Vanderbilt Law Review, 45*(4), 921–949.

Griffith, D. (2020). The best defense is a good offense (and a good set of standards). *Correct Care, Summer*, 12–14.

Hayes, L. M. (1998). Controversial issues in suicide prevention. *American Jails*, 19–23.

Hayes, L. M. (2010). *National study of jail suicide: 20 years later*. http://www.ncianet.org/wp-content/uploads/2015/06/national-study-of-jail-suicide-20-years-later.pdf. Accessed October 12, 2020.

Johnson v. Hamilton, No. 0501453, U.S. App. Lexis 16767, 8th Cir (2006).

Johnson v. Tinwalla, 855 F.3d 747 (2017).

Knoll, J. L. (2010). Suicide in correctional settings: Assessment, prevention, and professional liability. *Journal of Correctional Health Care, 16*(3), 188–204.

Knuppel, J. (2011). *Physicians who treat inmates are at greater risk of litigation*. https://www.kevinmd.com/blog/2011/07/physicians-treat-inmates-greater-risk-litigation.html. Accessed October 13, 2020.

McCoin, M. (2018). *California jail doctor faces medical board discipline for negligent care*. https://www.prisonlegalnews.org/news/2018/jan/31/california-jail-doctor-faces-medical-board-discipline-negligent-care/. Accessed October 14, 2020.

Metzner, J. L. (2002). Class action litigation in correctional psychiatry. *Journal of the American Academy of Psychiatry and the Law, 30*(1), 19–29.

Metzner, J. L. (2009). Monitoring a correctional mental health care system: The role of the mental health expert. *Behavioral Sciences & the Law, 27*(5), 727–741.

Minneci v. Pollard, 132 S. Ct. 617 (2012).

Monell v. Department of Soc. Svcs, 436 U.S. 658 (1978).

Nurses Service Organization: Nurse Practitioner Claim Report: 4th Edition – A Guide to Identifying and Addressing Professional Liability Exposures. (2017). https://aonaffinity-blob-cdn.azureedge.net/affinitytemplate-dev/media/nso/images/documents/cna_cls_np_exec_101617_cf_prod_asize_online_sec.pdf. Accessed November 4, 2020.

Nurses Service Organization: Nurse Practitioners 2012 Liability Update. (2012). http://www.hpso.com/Documents/Individuals/Professional%20liability/NP_Claims_Study_2012.pdf. Accessed November 4, 2020.

Olfson, M., Marcus, S. C., & Bridge, J. A. (2012). Emergency treatment of deliberate self-harm. *Archives of General Psychiatry., 69*(1), 80–88.

Olivero, J. M., & Roberts, J. B. (1990). Jail suicide and legal redress. *Suicide and Life-threatening Behavior, 20*(2), 138–147.

Ortiz v. City of Imperial, 884 F.2d 1312, 9th Cir (1989).

Palakovic v. Wetzel, 854 F. 3d 209 – Court of Appeals, 3rd Cir (2017).

Prison Litigation Reform Act (PLRA), 42 U.S.C. § 1997e (1996).

Reeves, R., & Tamburello, A. C. (2014). Single cells, segregated housing, and suicide in the NJ DOC. *Journal of the American Academy of Psychiatry and the Law, 42*(4), 484–488.

Reeves, R., Tamburello, A. C., Platt, J., et al. (2017). Characteristics of inmates who initiate hunger strikes. *Journal of the American Academy of Psychiatry and the Law, 45*(3), 302–310.

Robbins, I. P. (1999). Managed health care in prisons as cruel and unusual punishment. *Journal of Criminal Law and Criminology, 90*(1), 195–237.

Ross, D. L. (2010). The liability trends of custodial suicides. *American Jails, 24*(1), 37–47.

Ross, D. L. (2018). *Civil liability in criminal justice* (7th ed.). Routledge.

Ruiz v. Estelle, 503 F. Supp. 1265, S.D. Texas (1980).

SAMHSA. (2017). *Guidelines for successful transition of people with mental or substance use disorders from jail and prison: Implementation guide*. https://store.samhsa.gov/sites/default/files/d7/priv/sma16-4998.pdf. Accessed November 3, 2020.

Schlanger, M. (2003). *Inmate litigation*. https://repository.law.umich.edu/articles/1296/. Accessed October 13, 2020.

Schwartz, M. A. (2014). *Section 1983 litigation*, 3rd ed. https://www.fjc.gov/sites/default/files/2014/Section-1983-Litigation-3D-FJC-Schwartz-2014.pdf. Accessed October 13, 2020.

Spann v. Roper, No. 05-2721, U.S. App. Lexis 17480, 8th Cir (2006).

Sylvester v. City of Newark, No. 03-2486, 147 Fed. Appx. 566, 6th Cir (2005).

Tamburello, A., Metzner, J., Ferguson, E., et al. (2018). AAPL practice resource for prescribing in corrections. *Journal of the American Academy of Psychiatry and the Law Online Supplement, 46*(2). http://www.jaapl.org/content/46/2_Supplement. Accessed November 4, 2020.

Taylor v. Barkes, 135 S. Ct. 2042 (2015).

Trestman, R. L., Ferguson, W., & Dickert, J. (2015). Behind bars: The compelling case for academic health centers partnering with correctional facilities. *Academic Medicine, 90*(1), 16–19.

Vaughn, M. S. (1995). Section 1983 civil liability of prison officials for denying and delaying medication and drugs to prison inmates. *Issues in Law & Medicine, 11*(1), 47–76.

Vaughn, M. S. (1997). Civil liability against prison officials for prescribing and dispensing medication and drugs to prison inmates. *Journal of Legal Medicine, 18*(3), 315–344.

Veneziano, C. A. (1986). Prison inmates and consent to treatment: Problems and issues. *Law and Psychology Review, 10*, 129–146.

Wakefield v. Thompson, 177 F.3d 1160, 1163, 9th Cir (1999).

Washington v. Harper, 494 U.S. 210 (1990).

White v. Napolean, 897 F.3d 103, 13, 3rd Cir (1990).

Williams v. Mehra, 186 F.3d 685, 6th Cir (1999).

Forensic Psychiatry

28

Renée Sorrentino and Ryan C. W. Hall

Individuals practicing the subspecialty of forensic psychiatry are often accustomed to testifying in malpractice cases, but they are rarely the defendant in such suits. However, forensic evaluators are not immune to medical malpractice claims. In 2002, Binder (2002) identified several factors which led to a shift in the accountability of experts, including an increase in the number of physicians acting as expert witnesses, an increase in attorney malpractice, and a perceived absence of protections for the injured party. In addition, classic legal safeguards such as prosecution for perjury, cross-examination, and rules related to admissibility of evidence were perceived as ineffective in stopping or deterring unprincipled evaluators (Binder, 2002). These factors have, in part, contributed to the shift of increased liability for serving as a forensic expert (Professional Risk Management Services [PRMS], 2017; Binder, 2002).

Besides malpractice concerns, forensic practitioners may have to consider other legal pitfalls including negligence claims, intentional torts, claims related to federal civil rights law, contract law violation, board complaints, and confidentiality concerns (Gold & Davidson, 2007; Blake, 2011; Bonnici et al., 2017). Just as it is hard to know the national standard of psychiatric care at times, the standard of care for forensic psychiatry may be even more nebulous given the multiple subspecialties and various issues that may arise in a single lawsuit (Knoll & Gerbasi, 2006; Cooke et al., 2017). Furthermore, the ultimate service that a forensic expert renders is an opinion, and it is often the case that reasonable and knowledgeable opposing experts can have a difference of opinion (Knoll & Gerbasi, 2006). It is also not uncommon for experts to focus on or believe that some information has more weight or significance than other pieces of information (e.g., facts of the case; specifics of the medical literature). This can result in the inclusion of certain pieces of information in a report or final opinion that another expert finds less relevant. This, again, is not necessarily inappropriate, unethical, or malpractice. A problem arises when the difference in opinion is due to extreme bias, extreme misapplication of the scientific literature, or outright dishonesty. Several professional organizations, such as the APA, have instituted a review mechanism to censure members who provide forensic opinions which the organization interprets as intentionally extremely one-sided or made without adequate empirical evidence or support (Friend, 2003; Knoll & Gerbasi, 2006; Gold & Davidson, 2007).

This chapter will review medical malpractice claims and medical board complaints in the forensic psychiatry setting. This chapter is not meant to set guidelines or standards, but to highlight potential issues for the forensic psychiatric practitioner. It should be noted that ethics and legality are not always the same. It is a general recommendation that if one adheres to forensic and general psychiatric ethics, the risk of malpractice lawsuits or other type of professional disciplinary action is minimized.

General Concepts for Reducing Forensic Risk

Efforts to reduce claims of medical malpractice and disciplinary actions include an understanding of the legal requirements for forensic work in the jurisdiction in which the work is completed. These include an awareness of the licensure guidelines for forensic work; knowledge of the exceptions to confidentiality, including mandatory report guidelines; and the case law which defines the duty and extent of the doctor-patient relationship for forensic evaluations. Specifics for varying areas will be addressed in subsections of this chapter.

In addition to knowledge of the legal mandates related to forensic work, forensic psychiatrists working as expert

R. Sorrentino (✉)
Harvard Medical School, Boston, MA, USA
e-mail: rsorrentino@mgh.harvard.edu

R. C. W. Hall
University of Central Florida, Orlando, FL, USA

University of South Florida, Tampa, FL, USA

Barry University Dwayne O. Andreas School of Law, Orlando, FL, USA

P. Ash et al. (eds.), *Malpractice and Liability in Psychiatry*, https://doi.org/10.1007/978-3-030-91975-7_28

witnesses may decrease their liability risk by following the tenets of professional organizations, continuing education in the field over the course of one's career, as well as adhering to forensic guidelines. Organizations such as the American Academy of Psychiatry and the Law (AAPL) provide resource documents for completing forensic examinations. Experts who generally adhere to professional and ethical guidelines from such professional organizations are demonstrating that their work is at the very least commensurate with, if not above, the standard of care in their field. Therefore, these individuals are less likely to be found liable of medical malpractice or professional misconduct.

Generally, keeping up-to-date with the forensic literature may also be helpful. For example, articles published by senior academic experts may highlight trends and advances in the field, as well as communicate particular common sense advice learned from experience. For example, Binder (2002) outlined practical risk reduction advice, such as "not overstating opinions," accepting cases within one's own area of expertise, and keeping the attorney informed of one's opinion and any changes that may relate to conclusions. The implementation of the ethical notions of honesty, striving for objectivity, and courtesy for all parties involved in the process may also mitigate the risk of liability (Anfang & Wall, 2006; Knoll & Gerbasi, 2006; Glancy et al., 2015; Anfang et al., 2018; Booth et al., 2019).

Immunity

Before discussing the specifics of malpractice concerns, it is important to identify that testifying experts may be granted varying forms of immunity, which are designed to allow them to express their opinions honestly without fear of legal reprisals. However, these immunities are not ironclad and may only apply to certain aspects of the forensic process (Gold & Davidson, 2007). For example, there is the notion of witness immunity or a "quasi-judicial immunity." This immunity exists when an individual is testifying, doing work for "the court," or potentially in circumstances where medicolegal matters are in question (Gold & Davidson, 2007; Coffey et al., 2017; Weiss & Van Dell, 2017). However, witness immunity applies only to testimonial aspects (e.g., opinions in report or stated in open court) and may not fully cover all aspects of the evaluation, such as the data gathering or in-person interactions (Gold & Davidson, 2007; Coffey et al., 2017; Weiss & Van Dell, 2017). Although rarely an issue in a psychiatric examination, witness immunity may not apply to physical harm caused during a forensic physical examination (e.g., forensic orthopedic examination) (Gold & Davidson, 2007). Although rare, it is possible for there to be a malpractice claim for emotional infliction of harm stemming from a forensic psychiatric interview. For this to occur, case law often requires that the behavior of the evaluator be outrageous and "so severe that no reasonable person could be expected to endure it" (Chen & LeBourgeois, 2006).

The immunities discussed above most clearly apply to evaluations for criminal or civil courts. However, forensic psychiatrists may practice in many different venues, and not all evaluations are conducted with the end result of providing testimony or a written report (e.g., treatment of incarcerated individuals) (Gold & Davidson, 2007). So other grounds for a lawsuit may arise, such as Federal 1983 actions for violations of an inmate's constitutional rights. The concept of sovereign immunity may apply in forensic maltreatment malpractice cases if the forensic psychiatrist is employed by the state or federal government (King & Pinals, 2017).

Duty in Forensic Cases

The first component in a malpractice claim is whether there was a professional duty owed to the patient. This duty arises from the creation of a doctor-patient relationship. The subspecialty of forensic psychiatry is generally considered the practice of medicine even though there is a limited doctor-patient relationship (Gold & Davidson, 2007; Glancy et al., 2015; Anfang et al., 2018). Multiple professional organizations, such as the American Medical Association (AMA), have taken such a position, hence the concern for negligent medical care or "medical malpractice" in forensic work (Friend, 2003; Gutheil & Bursztajn, 2003; Knoll & Gerbasi, 2006; Anfang et al., 2018; Gold & Davidson, 2007).

The definition of a doctor-patient relationship varies by jurisdiction, but may include forensic settings. Courts have defined whether a doctor-patient relationship existed in a forensic case based on specific facts in individual cases (Bonnici et al., 2017). Educating an evaluee about a diagnosis, the need for treatment, and treatment modalities may constitute a doctor-patient relationship and thereby confer a duty owed to the evaluee (Marrette & Mossman, 2017). Some courts have recognized a "limited" doctor-patient relationship in the setting of an independent medical examination (IME), including the following duties: not to injure the evaluee, to properly diagnose, to inform the evaluee about a potentially serious medical condition ("duty to disclose"), and to maintain confidentiality by disclosing only relevant information to third parties (PRMS, 2017). In cases in which the courts have not recognized a doctor-patient relationship, claimants may pursue claims of negligence. Negligence claims, unlike medical malpractice claims, have longer statutes of limitations, do not require expert witnesses, and may not be covered by malpractice insurance (Gold & Davidson, 2007). Although outside the scope of this chapter, forensic psychiatrists should be aware of liability claims independent of malpractice, including defamation, breach of confidentiality or contract, and other intentional torts (Gold & Davidson, 2007).

It is generally recommended that a treating clinician not serve as a forensic expert for his or her own patients. Literature highlights that this may affect the fiduciary relationship that already exists between a treater and his or her patient and that it may strain the relationship (Booth et al., 2019). In addition, if a patient is dissatisfied with the forensic opinion, it may result in a treatment malpractice suit. According to Gold and Davidson (2007), "The situation most fraught with the risk of malpractice liability arises when psychiatrists agree to perform a forensic evaluation or to provide court testimony for patients whom they have been treating clinically" (p. 206).

Specific Areas of Risk

Contractual Agreements

When the physician works as an expert for a retaining attorney, this is often seen as a contractual role (e.g., "at-will employee") (Friend, 2003). It is the attorney's obligation to assess and hire the expert. To limit potential legal implications from a "legal malpractice suit," it is best to appropriately identify one's areas of expertise and publications and not to exaggerate in a subspecialty area. Such misattributions are not likely to lead to a medical malpractice suit, but could lead to a contractual violation or fraud charge (Gold & Davidson, 2007). These types of lawsuits may not be covered by traditional medical malpractice but are relatively uncommon.

Licensure Considerations

The identification of forensic psychiatry as a subspecialty in medicine results in some unique considerations, such as if state licensure is needed to perform an evaluation in a neighboring state, as well as whether malpractice insurance actually covers forensic "medical malpractice" (Simon & Shuman, 1999; Gold & Davidson, 2007).

When practicing forensic psychiatry outside of one's home state, the question of medical licensure in the state in which the evaluation occurs should be addressed (Simon & Shuman, 1999). If one does not clarify this situation, it can lead to testimony being rejected, potential board actions taken, criminal charges (felony or misdemeanor charge for practicing without licensure), and lack of malpractice coverage (Simon & Shuman, 1999). There are multiple ways this can be approached. The simplest approach is for the expert to contact the Board of Medicine in the state where the evaluation is to take place to see if there are any special requirements for performing an IME (Simon & Shuman, 1999). Some experts have included in their contract that the hiring attorney, who knows the laws regarding experts in the jurisdiction where they practice, will evaluate and make sure all appropriate licensure requirements are known to the expert. Another option is that the expert will do the evaluation in conjunction with a licensed physician from that state (Simon & Shuman, 1999).This often circumvents licensure requirements with the out-of-state expert having a consulting relationship, which has been historically allowed by medical boards. When working with a licensed, consulting physician, there may be restrictions in terms of how a report is authored and if both physicians can testify or not, depending on the jurisdiction. Even when working in conjunction with another expert, it is important to review the state medical board's criteria for expert work to understand potential limitations or the need for additional certification. For example, the state of Florida has a relatively easy to obtain "expert witness certification" which allows for expert work such as conducting an evaluation and providing testimony (Fla. Stat. § 458.3175, 2020).

An additional caveat to the licensure issue is telehealth evaluations. This is an option that has become more accepted due to the COVID-19 pandemic and may be attractive for attorneys who are trying to limit costs. Again, if one is engaging in a telehealth evaluation, it is important to be aware of the state laws where the evaluee is located. In emergent situations, such as a natural disaster or pandemic, some of these state laws that restrict out-of-state practice are suspended by executive order (see Chap. 32). In addition to licensure, privacy concerns should also be taken into account, such as using HIPAA-compliant technology (Klein, 2011). It is also a good idea to consult with malpractice carriers prior to the forensic evaluation to see if there is additional coverage or concern that may arise from conducting a telehealth forensic evaluation since this is an evolving field.

Confidentiality and Mandated Reporting

In general, the law requires physicians to report cases of suspected child or elder abuse. This may raise an ethical dilemma for forensic psychiatrists considering that many forensic settings obligate the examiner to protect information under the attorney-client privilege. States vary in how they address forensic mandated reporting. For example, some states, like Maryland and Oregon, specifically create an exclusion to mandated reporting for criminal proceedings (Kapoor & Zonana, 2010). Strategies to minimize liability related to mandated reporting requirements include understanding the laws in the specific jurisdiction, informing the referring parties of limitations to confidentiality, and informing the referring party if there are plans to notify authorities (Kapoor & Zonana, 2010).

Tarasoff Warnings

If there is a legitimate safety concern, depending on the jurisdiction, a *Tarasoff*-type warning may need to be issued (Gold & Davidson, 2007). Since the doctor-patient relationship is limited, the *Tarasoff* duty may also be more circumscribed in a forensic evaluation. For example, since the forensic evaluator does not have the traditional doctor-patient treatment relationship, there is some question as to whether a forensic evaluator could involuntarily hospitalize an evaluee in some jurisdictions. In general, the forensic literature recommends the following: inform the evaluee that he or she requires hospitalization, inform the evaluee's treating physician that the evaluee needs to be hospitalized, or inform the evaluee's lawyer (Gold & Davidson, 2007; Anfang et al., 2018).

Failing a Daubert Challenge

To date, the authors are not aware of any expert having faced medical malpractice claims for failing a *Daubert* challenge. However, there have been case reports of lawyers refusing to pay an expert who did not "survive" a *Daubert* challenge (Gutheil & Bursztajn, 2005). This may lead to legal disputes related to contract issues or how services were presented, but not medical malpractice issues specifically (Gold & Davidson, 2007). It needs to be remembered that it is the judge who makes the determination of whether an expert "survives" a *Daubert* challenge and meets the criteria for admissibility (Gutheil et al., 2003; Gutheil & Bursztajn, 2005). The determination of whether an opinion is admissible in and of itself is not a ruling on negligence of the expert. Many factors go into the determination of admissibility, such as whether the expert is the appropriate expert to be commenting on the topic, whether the expert had the correct information to render an opinion, and whether the expert's credentials and basis for their opinion are appropriately communicated to the judge (Gutheil & Bursztajn, 2003). Therefore, the determination of admissibility in a *Daubert* challenge also depends on the behavior of the retaining attorney (e.g., selection of the expert, how the attorney intended to use the expert, and skill of lawyering when addressing the *Daubert* challenge) (Friend, 2003; Gutheil & Bursztajn, 2003).

Public Statements outside of the Courtroom

Although not a traditional malpractice claim, there are other potential intentional torts that could arise while doing a forensic interview, such as defamation (e.g., slander or libel), invasion of privacy, or violation of fiduciary duty of confidentiality (Gold & Davidson, 2007; Weiss & Van Dell, 2017). It should be noted that intentional torts are often not covered by malpractice insurance, and this type of action is often limited to specific situations where quasi-judicial immunity does not apply (Coffey et al., 2017; Gold & Davidson, 2007; Weiss & Van Dell, 2017). Slander and libel cases are rarely brought against forensic experts, in part because they are often hard to prove. Experts can further minimize this risk by striving for objectivity, reviewing collateral information, identifying sources, and formulating a well-reasoned opinion (Knoll & Gerbasi, 2006; Cooke et al., 2014; Weiss & Van Dell, 2017; Booth et al., 2019). Although factual errors may occur, it is the intentional inclusion of factual errors or misleading information that may raise the concern for defamation.

If one chooses to write about his or her forensic legal experiences more as an exposé or biography, claims such as invasion of privacy or breach of contract can occur, as well as malpractice claims (Blake, 2011). Many of the legal and ethical issues regarding writing on forensic cases are similar to writing about clinical patients. These concerns have been discussed in depth in other texts or legal rulings, such as the landmark case of *Doe v. Roe.* (Doe v. Roe, 1977; Blake, 2011). Forensic evaluations may retain some degree of confidentiality, even if testimony is given in the public venue of open court. As mentioned before, quasi-judicial immunity may cover statements made as part of the act of testifying, and some statements may become part of the public domain, but that does not mean that statements made outside of testimony are still covered. This is a complex area in the field of law (Cooke et al., 2014; Weiss & Van Dell, 2017). In order to be able to discuss one's forensic work in public, the individual may want to consult with a lawyer to see what the expert's First Amendment rights are compared to privacy issues of those being discussed, as well as what would be considered public domain, and how the public interest exemption may apply (Blake, 2011; Cooke et al., 2014). In addition, a written release from the evaluee would help to reduce future ethics concerns or legal challenges that could occur (Blake, 2011; Cooke et al., 2014).

Fitness for Duty Evaluations

There are often concerns about completing fitness-for-duty evaluations; however, many states and jurisdictions have acknowledged that risk assessment is more of an art than an empirical science (Anfang et al., 2005; Anfang & Wall, 2006; Friend, 2003; Gold & Davidson, 2007). It is generally important to be up-to-date on the standards of performing such evaluations to help ensure that the assessments are conducted appropriately (e.g., "reasonable care") and that conclusions are supported (Anfang et al., 2005; Anfang & Wall, 2006; Knoll & Gerbasi, 2006; Gold & Davidson, 2007; Anfang et al., 2018). In general, a forensic evaluator cannot be successfully sued for merely formulating an opinion, even an unfavorable one, unless the opinion is false or reckless (Anfang et al., 2005; Chen & LeBourgeois, 2006; Gold & Davidson, 2007; Weiss & Van Dell, 2017). In addition, the notion of "professional medical judgment" makes it hard to hold a physician liable for errors in professional judgment as long as his or her decisions were based on a proper medical foundation and technique (Gold & Davidson, 2007; Weiss & Van Dell, 2017). Many different groups and associations have recommendations or resource documents available to help examiners stay up-to-date on medical knowledge. For forensic psychiatrists, the American Academy of Psychiatry and the Law's (AAPL) *Practice Guideline for the Forensic Assessment* resource document, as well as the *AAPL Practice Resource for the Forensic Evaluation of Psychiatric Disability* are often helpful (Glancy et al., 2015; Anfang et al., 2018). In addition, the American Psychiatric Association (APA) has a resource document on violent patients, which was released in 2012 (Buchanan et al., 2012). Again, it is important to have collateral records and to have performed a structured evaluation when formulating one's opinion to reduce the risk of a liability claim (Anfang et al., 2005; Anfang & Wall, 2006; Anfang et al., 2018). The use of screening instruments may also help with formulating the opinion or demonstrating that a structured objective approach was used (Anfang et al., 2005; Anfang et al., 2018).

Medical Board Complaints

An additional area of risk for forensic psychiatrists is Board of Medicine complaints/actions (Anfang & Wall, 2006; Coffey et al., 2017; Gold & Davidson, 2007). It is often easier for somebody who feels he or she has been maligned by a forensic expert to file a complaint with the state medical licensure board than to bring a lawsuit (Coffey et al., 2017). Malpractice insurance may or may not cover board investigations, depending on the specifics of the insurance rider (Gold & Davidson, 2007). The rules related to statutory evidence levels are also different for board actions.

Individuals may also file complaints with professional organizations (Knoll & Gerbasi, 2006; Gold & Davidson, 2007). Courts have ruled that professional organizations are allowed to censure members based on provided testimony if they conclude that it is biased or not representative of the current knowledge base of the field (Friend, 2003; Knoll & Gerbasi, 2006; Gold & Davidson, 2007). Again, this is a case where following traditional medical ethics is protective, especially since it may be the society's or Board of Medicine's ethics positions that will be the basis for action or inaction against a forensic practitioner's status or license (Gold & Davidson, 2007).

Documentation

Clear documentation supporting medical decision-making is an essential component in risk management. Expert witnesses may decrease liability by outlining costs, retainers, deadlines and licensure requirements, policies regarding maintaining records, and ownership of videotaped interviews (if used in the evaluation), reports, and written/types notes in a contractual agreement. Documentation of records reviewed and collateral sources of information used to support opinions should be clearly identified. In general, obtaining an evaluee's written consent to participate in the evaluation, especially in a civil evaluation, and an acknowledgment of the limits of confidentiality and who will have access are also good practice.

Key Points

- Because a limited doctor-patient relationship exists in most forensic evaluations, forensic psychiatrists can be sued or reported to the state medical board or professional organizations.
- Treating psychiatrists should avoid performing forensic evaluations on their patients where possible.
- Providing opinions within the standard practices as advised by professional organizations will mitigate against malpractice or professional complaints.
- Awareness of the legal guidelines regarding licensure, confidentiality, and mandated reporting should include forensic practice.
- Forensic experts are afforded some immunity in legal settings, but this immunity is limited and does not cover all actions.

References

Anfang, S. A., Faulkner, L. R., Fromson, J. A., & Gendel, M. H. (2005). The American Psychiatric Association's resource document on guidelines for psychiatric fitness-for-duty evaluations of physicians. *Journal of the American Academy of Psychiatry & the Law, 33*(1), 85–88.

Anfang, S. A., & Wall, B. W. (2006). Psychiatric fitness-for-duty evaluations. *Psychiatric Clinics of North America, 29*(3), 675–693.

Anfang, S. A., Gold, L. H., & Meyer, D. J. (2018). AAPL practice resource for the forensic evaluation of psychiatric disability. *Journal of the American Academy of Psychiatry & the Law, 46*(1 Supplement), S2–S47.

Binder, R. L. (2002). Liability for the psychiatrist expert witness. *American Journal of Psychiatry, 159*, 1819–1825.

Blake, V. (2011). When doctors pick up the pen-patient-doctor confidentiality breaches in publishing. *Virtual Mentor, 13*(7), 485–489.

Bonnici, D., Bonnici, K. B., Weinstock, R., & Garrick, T. (2017). Liability of the forensic psychiatrist. In *Principles and practice of forensic psychiatry* (3rd ed., pp. 83–89). CRC Press.

Booth, B. D., Watts, J., & Dufour, M. (2019). Lessons from Canadian courts for all expert witnesses. *Journal of the American Academy of Psychiatry & the Law, 47*(3), 278–285.

Buchanan, H., Binder, R., Norko, M., & Swartz, M. (2012). Resource document on psychiatric violence risk assessment. *American Journal of Psychiatry, 169*(3), 1–10.

Chen, T., & LeBourgeois, H. W. (2006). Malpractice action stemming from court-ordered independent medical examination. *Journal of the American Academy of Psychiatry & the Law, 34*(4), 563–565.

Coffey, C. A., Brodsky, S. L., & Sams, D. M. (2017). I'll see you in court…again: Psychopathology and hyperlitigious litigants. *Journal of the American Academy of Psychiatry & the Law, 45*(1), 62–71.

Cooke, B. K., Goddard, E. R., Werner, T. L., Cooke, E. O., & Griffith, E. E. (2014). The risks and responsible roles for psychiatrists who interact with the media. *Journal of the American Academy of Psychiatry & the Law, 42*(4), 459–468.

Cooke, B. K., Worsham, E., & Reisfield, G. M. (2017). The elusive standard of care. *Journal of the American Academy of Psychiatry & the Law, 45*(3), 358–364.

Doe v. Roe, 400 N.Y.Supp. 2d 668 (1977).

Fla. Stat. § 458.3175 (2020). Expert Witness Certificate.

Friend, A. (2003). Keeping criticism at bay: Suggestions for forensic psychiatry experts. *Journal of the American Academy of Psychiatry & the Law, 31*(4), 406–412.

Glancy, G. D., Ash, P., Bath, E. P., Buchanan, A., Fedoroff, P., Frierson, R. L., Harris, V. L., Hatters Friedman, S. J., Hauser, M. J., Knoll, J., Norko, M., Pinals, D., Price, M., Recupero, P., Scott, C. L., & Zonana, H. V. (2015). AAPL practice guideline for the forensic assessment. *Journal of the American Academy of Psychiatry & the Law, 43*(2 Suppl), S3–S53.

Gold, L. H., & Davidson, J. E. (2007). Do you understand your risk? Liability and third-party evaluations in civil litigation. *Journal of the American Academy of Psychiatry & the Law, 35*(2), 200–210.

Gutheil, T. G., & Bursztajn, H. (2003). Avoiding ipse dixit mislabeling: Post-Daubert approaches to expert clinical opinions. *Journal of the American Academy of Psychiatry & the Law, 31*(2), 205–210.

Gutheil, T. G., & Bursztajn, H. J. (2005). Attorney abuses of Daubert hearings: Junk science, junk law, or just plain obstruction? *Journal of the American Academy of Psychiatry & the Law, 33*(2), 150–152.

Gutheil, T. G., Hauser, M., White, M. S., Spruiell, G., & Strasburger, L. H. (2003). "The whole truth" versus "the admissible truth": An ethics dilemma for expert witnesses. *Journal of the American Academy of Psychiatry & the Law, 31*(4), 422–427.

Kapoor, R., & Zonana, H. (2010). Forensic evaluations and mandated reporting of child abuse. *Journal of the American Academy of Psychiatry & the Law*, (38), 49–56.

King, I. G., & Pinals, D. A. (2017). Clinician immunity against claims of malpractice and constitutional violations. *Journal of the American Academy of Psychiatry & the Law, 45*(4), 495–497.

Klein, C. A. (2011). Cloudy confidentiality: Clinical and legal implications of cloud computing in health care. *Journal of the American Academy of Psychiatry & the Law, 39*(4), 571–578.

Knoll, J., & Gerbasi, J. (2006). Psychiatric malpractice case analysis: Striving for objectivity. *Journal of the American Academy of Psychiatry & the Law, 34*(2), 215–223.

Marrette, C. P., & Mossman, D. (2017). Considering work as an expert witness? Look before you leap! *Current Psychiatry, 16*(9), 44–48.

Professional Risk Management Services (PRMS). (2017). Rx for Risk: Addressing risk management. *PRMS., 25*(1).

Simon, R. I., & Shuman, D. W. (1999). Conducting forensic examinations on the road: Are you practicing your profession without a license? *Journal of the American Academy of Psychiatry & the Law, 27*(1), 75–82.

Weiss, K. J., & Van Dell, L. (2017). Liability for diagnosing malingering. *Journal of the American Academy of Psychiatry & the Law, 45*(3), 339–347.

Malpractice in Psychiatric Research

29

Robert L. Trestman, Anita S. Kablinger, and Allison O. McKell

At its heart, clinical research in psychiatry is exploration and innovation. It is the hypothesis-driven process by which psychiatrists learn more of the underlying pathophysiology of disease, new approaches to care, and a plethora of knowledge domains that allow mental health clinicians to prevent or treat mental illness. Just as with clinical practice, ethical and legal requirements have grown to support an increasingly complex and sophisticated process of psychiatric research. The text below seeks to provide information for practicing clinicians.

Background and Context of Psychiatric Research Malpractice and Liability

Practice Versus Research

Research vs. Clinical Roles: A critical concept to recognize is that the fundamental goals and activities undertaken in the performance of biomedical research are not always aligned with regular clinical practice (Morreim, 2004). It is generally accepted that the relationship between physician and patient is one of trust and that the physician accepts a responsibility to act in the best interests of the patient. In contrast, the investigator-subject relationship is less clear, especially if the clinical trial investigator is concurrently a practicing physician. Indeed, advancing science for society's benefit while maintaining the Hippocratic Oath tenet of "do no harm" can be a fragile balance.

To help address this conundrum, one of the seminal documents for modern human research subject protections, The Belmont Report, states that:

> the term "practice" refers to interventions that are designed solely to enhance the well-being of an individual patient or client and that have a reasonable expectation of success. The purpose of medical or behavioral practice is to provide assessment, diagnosis, treatment or preventive therapy to particular individuals. By contrast, the term "research" designates an activity designed to test an hypothesis, permit conclusions to be drawn, and thereby to develop or contribute to generalizable knowledge (expressed, for example, in theories, principles, and statements of relationships). Research is usually described in a formal protocol that sets forth an objective and set of procedures designed to reach that objective. (Belmont Report, 1979, pg 3)

The Belmont Report also acknowledges that the lines between research and practice can be murky, noting that "[r]esearch and practice may be carried on together when research is designed to evaluate the safety and efficacy of a therapy" (pg. 4). When these situations occur, however, they "need not cause any confusion regarding whether or not the activity requires review; the general rule is that if there is any element of research in an activity, that activity should undergo review for the protection of human subjects" (pg. 4). This guidance supports the idea that even when research and clinical activities comingle, research is occurring and thus the degree of duty towards the patient-subject in malpractice terms is arguable.

Research Ethics and Regulatory Oversight: The ethical aspects of clinical research were shaped over the last 100 years by events of scientific malfeasance. Some well-known examples of these transgressions are the atrocities committed in the name of research during the Holocaust, the Tuskegee syphilis study, studies exposed by the Beecher Paper, the development of HeLa cells, and the death of Jesse Gelsinger (Gross, 2016; Jones et al., 2016). As a result, important evolutionary documents guiding ethical experimentation involving human subjects were developed, which include The Nuremberg Code, The Declaration of Helsinki,

R. L. Trestman (✉) · A. S. Kablinger
Department of Psychiatry and Behavioral Medicine, Carilion Clinic and Virginia Tech Carilion School of Medicine, Roanoke, VA, USA
e-mail: rltrestman@carilionclinic.org; ASKablinger@carilionclinic.org

A. O. McKell
Office of Organizational Integrity and Compliance, Carilion Clinic, Roanoke, VA, USA
e-mail: aomckell@carilionclinic.org

P. Ash et al. (eds.), *Malpractice and Liability in Psychiatry*, https://doi.org/10.1007/978-3-030-91975-7_29

Table 29.1 Important documents in research ethics (adapted from Fischer IV, 2006, Schiz Bull)

Nuremberg Code (1947)
Declarations of Geneva (1949) and Helsinki (1964)
Common Rule (1974)
Belmont Report (1979)
Council for International Organizations of Medical Sciences Guidelines (CIOMS, 1982)
International Conference on Harmonization (ICH, 1996)
National Bioethics Advisory Commission Report (1998)
Revised Common Rule (2018)

The Belmont Report, and the US Federal Policy for the Protection of Human Subjects, known as "the Common Rule" (Table 29.1). Central to human research ethics in the United States, The Belmont Report was disseminated in 1979 by the National Commission for the Protection of Human Subjects of Biomedical and Behavioral Research and includes the primary principles of (1) *respect for persons* (through informed consent), (2) *beneficence* (via risk/benefit analysis), and (3) *justice* (through appropriate selection of subjects) (Adashi et al., 2018).

While physicians continuously encounter the regulatory landscape in performance of clinical duties, new challenges arise when those clinicians also engage in research. In the United States, an alphabet soup of federal agencies exists that are specific to research oversight or include research guidelines as part of their agency's funding mechanisms (Table 29.2). The Institutional Review Board (IRB) is perhaps the most recognized of the research oversight requirements and was established by the US federal government as part of Title II of the National Research Act of 1974. IRBs function to protect the rights and interests of human subjects participating in scientific research and, themselves, abide by specific rules and regulations of function (National Institute of Health, 2020; Federal Drug Administration, 2019). Clinical studies also benefit from the use of data safety monitoring boards (DSMBs) that provide scheduled, unblinded study monitoring with regard to patient safety that may lead to ending studies early (National Institute of Mental Health, 2015). A DSMB is an additional oversight body that is study-specific and independent of the IRB (Ellenberg et al., 2002). Not all studies will require a DMSB, and those that do typically contain some combination of the following elements: a large study population, multiple study sites, intervention(s) that can induce unacceptable risks, major endpoints (e.g., death, inferiority with safety implications), aim to provide definitive safety and efficacy information, or if it could be ethically important to stop the trial early (Ellenberg et al., 2002).

In addition to domestic regulations, international guidelines spanning industrialized countries' pharmaceutical development were rigorously outlined in the International

Table 29.2 A sampling of major US agencies that oversee regulations and policies relevant for biomedical research. Many more federal and state oversight bodies and regulations not listed here can also impact psychiatric research

US Federal Agency	Research oversight function	Relevant regulations
National Institutes of Health (NIH)	Oversight of federal grant application, awards, and associated research, including financial COIs	Responsibility of applicants for promoting objectivity in research for which PHS funding is sought (42 C.F.R. part 50, subpart F) Revised common rule
Food and Drug Administration (FDA)	Oversight and review/approval body for medical drug and device studies	Food drug and cosmetics act of 1938 and its amendments
Office of Human Research Protections (OHRP)	Oversight body for research studies with human subjects	Revised common rule Belmont report
Office of Research Integrity (ORI)	Oversight body for research integrity, the responsible conduct of research, and scientific misconduct for PHS-funded studies	Public health service policies on research misconduct, at 42 C.F.R. part 93.301
Office of Civil Rights (OCR)	HIPAA-related breaches in privacy and security for all studies that use PHI and electronic medical records	Health insurance portability and accountability act of 1996 and its amendments HITECH act of 2009
Centers for Medicare & Medicaid Services (CMS)	Oversees Medicare payments for clinical trial participation	National Coverage Determination for routine costs in clinical trials False claims act Physician payments sunshine act
Substance Abuse and Mental Health Services Administration	Oversees correct use and protection of patient medical records for those participating in "part 2" programs	Confidentiality of alcohol and drug abuse patient records, CFR 42, part 2

Conference on Harmonization of Technical Requirements for Registration of Pharmaceuticals for Human Use (ICH). ICH E6 or *The Guideline for Good Clinical Practice* (GCP) is the hallmark which each investigator must follow (ICH E6, 2016). Numerous administrative bodies, guidelines, regulatory offices, and specialized contracts exist. Specific to psychiatry, the National Bioethics Advisory Commission Report provided recommendations for *Research Involving Persons with Mental Disorders That May Affect Decision Making Capacity* (National Bioethics Advisory Commission Report, 1998). Research regulations are not only laws; they often also provide detailed descriptions of what is considered acceptable standard practices in research and can be considered synonymous to the concept of "standard of care" that is presented in malpractice suits.

Distinct Characteristics of Psychiatry Research: An inherent difficulty in research involving psychiatric illness is the absence of objective or biomarker measurements such as laboratory tests or neuroimaging that are common endpoints in other biomedical studies. Clinical trials that assess the utility of a novel antihypertensive, for example, define specific numerical endpoints to demonstrate efficacy. In psychiatry, scales are often utilized as primary outcome measurements for efficacy trials and focus on clusters of symptoms to produce quantitative data. However, measures vary widely (consider cognition, mood, psychosis) and are difficult to translate into clinically relevant changes in patient functioning (Carrier et al., 2017). Thus, in terms of potential malpractice, it can be particularly problematic to define "standard of care" or "standard research practices" for psychiatric research projects.

Clinical Malpractice Versus Research Malpractice

What constitutes malpractice within the world of clinical research can be difficult to define. When we reference malpractice in this context, do we intend traditional and formulaic definitions provided by the idea of medical negligence? Do we operate under that legal paradigm in which a defendant has a duty to a plaintiff, that the defendant breaches that duty, and that the breach in duty causes an injury resulting in some harm to the plaintiff? Or do we consider the term "malpractice" a colloquial catch-all term to mean any legal-related incident?

Civil Actions: A key component of malpractice tort is the role of the defendant in the care of the plaintiff. Separation of clinician from clinical researcher is not an a priori conclusion when it comes to human subject trials, and both ethical and legal issues have been a focus of discussion. One commonly held perspective insists that a fiduciary duty between physician and patient cannot exist due to the divergence between medical practice and research (Miller & Brody, 2003; Miller & Brody, 2002). Although research and clinical care do have different primary goals, many argue that the obligation of beneficence and non-maleficence remains and that medical negligence in research studies may occur (Morreim, 2004). Another common question in research-related lawsuits is whether the use of a placebo control arm in a study equates to medical negligence. Glass and Waring (2005) propose that placebo-controlled trials indeed represent a risk for physician researchers that may predispose them to civil liabilities. They argue that a placebo, as an inert substance, delays treatment in those who have psychiatric illness for which there are effective agents and that informed consent as to the nature of trial participation does not constitute an adequate defense. From a medical rather than legal viewpoint, Miller (2000) provides a thoughtful and robust reasoning on the use of placebo given a study's "scientific merit, risks are at an acceptable minimum and justified by the anticipated benefits…, patient volunteers give informed consent, [and that] investigators offer short-term treatment optimization at the conclusion of research participation." This is particularly relevant in psychiatric research, as the placebo response rate may at times be significant (Gopalakrishnan et al., 2020). While use of placebos in studies is only one potential liability, it is an important one to consider when conducting psychiatric research.

Criminal Proceedings: Physicians are some of the most recognized defendants in popular culture surrounding the US legal system; however, their profession still resides in a relatively privileged position. Criminal proceedings against medical doctors due to their professional actions are exceedingly rare, likely due in part to "idealization bias." Idealization bias in this case is the elevation of the medical profession and presumption that doctors always act in good faith, only thinking to benefit the patient. These assumptions can lead to lack of more serious repercussions, even in cases where beneficence is demonstrably not present (Richardson, 2009). Criminal prosecution of research physicians as a result of their research activities is also infrequent. Like the concept of idealization bias, "societal benefit bias" occurs since biomedical research is held to have significant benefits for society despite its inherent risks (Richardson, 2009). While these biases are powerful, researchers can still be subject to criminal prosecution in extreme cases, often associated with financial fraud (Department of Justice U.S. Attorney's Office Northern District of Ohio, 2020; Dyer, 2020).

Research Regulatory Enforcement: Noncompliance with research-related regulations may be viewed as a type of malpractice, a research malpractice. This is especially true in instances of alleged scientific misconduct. Scientific misconduct is defined as "[f]abrication, falsification, or plagiarism in proposing, performing, or reviewing research, or in reporting research results" and typically occurs when investigators depart from accepted best practices and ethical standards for conducting research. Investigating scientific misconduct is a legalized process whereby allegations must be proven by a preponderance of the evidence (i.e., more likely than not). There are strict statutory guidelines for how an investigation should take place as well as the timing for findings to be presented to the federal Office of Research Integrity (ORI) for research funded by the Public Health Service (Public Health Service Policies on Research Misconduct, 2005).

Other federal regulatory agencies also possess the ability to investigate concerns or reports of misdeeds (see Table 29.2). The consequences for researchers and their institutions can be substantial and may include loss of reputation, required retraction of publications, return of research funds, as well as other significant financial sanctions (Gross, 2016). Depending on the facts of the case, individual researchers can be held civilly and criminally liable. For civil malpractice or negligence suits, the US judicial system allows that statutes or regulations can provide a basis for standard of care (Jansson, 2003). In research cases, this is especially relevant for the practices surrounding the provision of informed consent. Regulatory compliance in biomedical research is critical, and failure to do so can increase the risk of legal repercussions. However, research physicians and their institutions should remember that meeting those requirements and following an IRB-approved protocol do not necessarily offer full protection. Previous case law suggests that at times the court finds research performed in line with an IRB-approved protocol to be a partial defense, and in other instances it may not (Jansson, 2003). In fact, IRBs themselves are at risk for being named as co-defendants (Shaul et al., 2005; Icenogle, 2003). At first glance, research regulations may seem to be benign "check boxes"; however, they can play a central role in clinical trial litigation.

Key Concepts and Associated Risks for Legal Repercussions

Informed Consent

Informed consent and the capacity to provide informed consent for participation in mental health research studies are at the core of psychiatric human subject trials and thus are often central to associated malpractice claims. Informed consent must be given voluntarily and includes comprehension by the subject of the research procedure, its purpose, risks and anticipated benefits, and alternative procedures and the opportunity to ask questions and/or prematurely leave the trial at any time after consent. Coercion or undue influence and the capacity of the individual to participate in studies are viewed as two of the most important principles governing human subject research (Fischer IV, 2006).

Case #1: Dan Markingson, a patient with first episode schizophrenia, consented to a trial comparing antipsychotic medications. He died from suicide 6 months later after family concerns voiced repeatedly to investigators during the study. The central concerns with this case include capacity and informed consent, coercion, investigator financial conflict of interest, and lack of patient oversight. This tragic case remained in the news with multiple updates and public reaction for over 10 years without satisfactory answers (Stone, 2014; Olsen, 2008).

The National Bioethics Advisory Committee (NBAC) was a presidentially commissioned group established in 1995 that deliberated and provided a report in 1998 entitled "Research Involving Persons with Mental Disorders That May Affect Decision-making Capacity." The NBAC made multiple recommendations that strengthened human research protection in the areas of informed consent, surrogate decision-making, the roles of assent and objection, and minimizing risk while maximizing potential benefit. One concern considered was the recommendation for a formal, independent assessment of capacity for potential subjects in mental health research, but this suggested that patients with mental illness are incapable of consent unless assessed to be capable first. Capacity concerns remain an important issue of every mental health research paradigm (Crigger, 2001).

It is important to note that the presence of psychiatric disorders does not render a person automatically unable to consent for research. Evidence exists for the retention of the ability to consent despite serious mental illness and that consent can be maximized through the use of teaching aids and assessment instruments (Dubois et al., 2011). However, some vulnerable populations (that may have overlap at times with mental illness) are explicitly described with whom extra care must be considered for human subject research. These populations include children and adolescents, elderly participants, pregnant women and neonates, and prisoners (Fischer IV, 2006).

In terms of potential torts, informed consent is again a focal point. In her article on litigation in clinical research, Morreim (2004) describes that for the first half of the twentieth century, lack of informed consent was a strict liability issue that could result in battery claims. However, she reveals the courts subsequently changed course, indicating that improper informed consent in medicine did not necessarily equate to battery and rather was more akin to medical negligence. This change was important because battery does not require the demonstration of harm, only proof that touching was unwanted, whereas negligence requires a burden of proof for causation and demonstrable harm. Additionally, battery is much more likely to result in criminal prosecution and is often not covered by malpractice insurance, requiring the defendant to pay financial penalties themselves (Morreim, 2004).

Privacy

Physicians navigate the realm of patient privacy daily, especially psychiatrists who often deal in the most sensitive of medical, psychological, and interpersonal information. Such practitioners are intimately familiar with federal regulations surrounding protected health information (PHI), such as the Health Insurance Portability and Accountability Act (HIPAA) and 42 CFR Part 2- Confidentiality Of Substance Use Disorder Patient Records, colloquially known as "Part 2."

Research seeks to disseminate knowledge and clinical trial findings, but physician researchers should remember that privacy concerns for subjects remain paramount. The best way to avoid improper disclosures is to obtain authorizations from research subjects whenever possible. When that is not possible, both HIPAA and Part 2 allow for some research exceptions to disclosure restrictions. However, similar to informed consent, it is not up to the researcher to determine when disclosure authorization is not necessary. Instead, an IRB reviews the proposed research and decides whether it is appropriate to grant full or partial waiver of HIPAA or Part 2 disclosure authorization. An example of a study that frequently receives these IRB-granted waivers would be a medical record review that only collects and analyzes deidentified data and that intends to aggregate results reporting in public venues.

Breaches in confidentiality carry stiff penalties—both civil and criminal (Alder, 2015). In relation to malpractice suits, there must be a breach of duty as well as defined harm. The duties of the research investigator to his or her subject rest strongly upon the informed consent process and its documentation. If the investigator uses or disseminates PHI in a manner inconsistent with that consented to by the subject, nor as a protocol modification approved by an IRB, then the investigator arguably defaults on his or her contractual obligations. If the research subject can demonstrate harm, such as a negative impact on his or her employment, then her or she may be successful in seeking legal recourse.

Conflicts of Interest

Complex relationships with the biomedical industry exist within both clinical practice and research. Many investigators and academic institutions work alongside industry partners to develop investigational products, design clinical trials, and provide feedback for continued research and development. Individual physicians also may consult for the pharmaceutical company with whom they participate in clinical trials. Ideally, these activities support the best interests of patients and research subjects; however, there are instances when that may not occur which can result in a conflict of interest (COI). However, studies have found that COIs are not always disclosed or disclosed fully by investigators (Confronting, 2018; Dunn et al., 2016). Moreover, research demonstrates that physicians may prescribe up to three times as many drugs from the company from which they receive remuneration (Carey & Harris, 2008). Bias of treatment choice based on this financial gain has repeatedly been reported leading to enactment of the Sunshine Act in 2013, providing transparency of monetary payments made to physicians (Confronting, 2018). It is easy to see why many instances of research malpractice and misconduct have been tied to an investigator and/or institutional COI.

Case #2: AstraZeneca was found guilty of marketing the antipsychotic drug Seroquel for non-FDA-approved illnesses in 2006, utilizing physicians to promote the product as safe for these illnesses. Physicians were also willingly placed as authors on ghostwritten articles expanding on beneficial trials of Seroquel that the physicians had not themselves performed. The US Department of Justice fined AstraZeneca $520 M for dishonest marketing (Pharmaceutical Integrity Coalition, 2010).

The existence of a COI is not itself malpractice, but it can certainly be a motivating factor behind poor decision-making that leads to harmful errors. To avoid COI-related issues, there are accepted methods to navigate research team members' COIs, such as disclosing these situations to their institution and to the public or by removing a conflicted study team member from certain research activities (Confronting Conflict of Interest, 2018; Dunn et al., 2016). If these best practices surrounding the management of COIs in research are not followed and harm arises to a research subject, a malpractice suit could follow.

Strategies to Avoid or Mitigate Risks

Education/Training/Certification

The conduct of clinical research requires technical, ethical, and legal expertise. Qualified, experienced researchers graduating from medical schools are not common, and their numbers are declining each year (Meador, 2015). Despite arduous requirements in medical school and graduate medical training, clinical research knowledge and first-hand experience in clinical trials are limited and vary across clinicians (Blanchard et al., 2018). A lack of such expertise can drastically increase research-related risks to a clinician or organization.

Research ethics are mandated teaching by the Accreditation Council for Graduate Medical Education (ACGME) in psychiatry residency education. However, programs are often challenged to successfully present this important topic, given that few psychiatrists engage in clinical research, the existence of multiple demands in attaining skills for different settings (ED, inpatient, outpatient, C/L), and the lack of specific guidelines or content to utilize in residency programs for this purpose. Academic organizations within psychiatry have developed and shared curricula to address this need (Beresin et al., 2003). Physician-scientist training programs also exist that can act as a bridge between mentored postdoctoral research and graduate medical training (Blanchard et al., 2018).

Post-residency opportunities can also strengthen investigator participation in clinical research. The Association of Clinical Research Professionals (ACRP) has published Principal Investigator (PI) competencies and offers certification (Certified Principal Investigator and Maintenance of Certification). A consensus of the Clinical and Translational Science Awards (CTSA) Consortium Enhancing Clinical Research Professionals' Training and Qualification provides this competency-based approach (Calvin-Naylor et al., 2017); Vulcano (2012) demonstrated that outcome data of CPI certification as a predictor of investigator regulatory compliance.

Logistics/Operations

Following a robust research education program, logistics and operations may be the next most important tool to avoid an environment where malpractice and misconduct flourish. A collection of technically trained and specialized personnel are recommended to support the performance of biomedical research from clinical research coordinators and research assistants to administrators and compliance specialists. Navigating the complex tasks of grants, clinical trial agreements, subject screening and enrollment, regulatory document maintenance, and more can be overwhelming even for programs conducting small numbers of clinical trials. In the authors' experience, situations of inadequate research oversight are unfortunately not uncommon and can lead to significant risks and consequences as highlighted in the case study below:

Case #3: A recent case in the news (Carey, 2016) describes an NYU researcher engaging in a clinical trial in patients with PTSD, with a compound that had marijuana-like effects. Psychedelic drugs such as LSD, psilocybin, and ketamine have been a renewed focus of research, particularly in those with PTSD. In this case, reports indicated that there was lax institutional oversight on subject safety and the FDA found falsified records and failure to keep accurate histories (Carey, 2016). In this case, the PI was suspended from study participation and later resigned. NYU also shut down the study. No other consequences have been reported as of December 2020.

In order to appropriately support study teams, several key elements are needed: engaged principal investigators (PIs), extensive research infrastructure, and protected research time for study team members. Institutions need to ensure that clinical research is given adequate time and resources to protect the science, the researchers, and, most importantly, the research subjects. Principal investigators have the ultimate responsibility for the studies that they conduct. Though delegation of specific duties is often acceptable, the PI retains that primary responsibility if they are not fulfilled accurately.

Malpractice Insurance and Insurance Riders

Malpractice insurance is necessary for any practicing physician in today's litigious environment. Physician researchers do well to understand what their malpractice policies (or those of their employer) cover and do not cover. Research studies are often not included, which can expose the provider and/or his or her institution up to much higher levels of financial penalty. Physicians who engage in research should first check with their malpractice insurance provider to determine whether their coverage includes the planned research activities. It is critical that this occurs *before* research activities begin. For those physicians performing research at larger universities or academic medical centers, their institution may provide coverage as is the case with the authors' institution, the University of Washington, and others. Small practice partnerships or solo practitioners should be extra diligent in verifying their protection. If a physician's inquiry uncovers that such research activities are not covered or are only covered in a limited capacity, they should seek additional coverage. Some malpractice insurers may offer insurance riders for clinical research that can be added to existing policies for an increased fee. In other cases, it may be necessary to seek out a stand-alone research malpractice policy.

Indemnification Clauses

Another important strategy that can help physician researchers and their institutions avoid or limit legal exposure is through assignment of indemnification. Clinical trial agreements (CTAs) are complex documents fraught with numerous potential pitfalls for researchers and their institutions. One of the most critical elements to review when negotiating a CTA is the indemnification clause. These paragraphs set up the framework for who is liable, under what circumstances they are liable, and what remedy are they required to provide (and to whom). One should not assume "boiler plate language" is adequate protection. Seemingly inconsequential word choices can have catastrophic repercussions in the event of a lawsuit by a research participant. Thus, it is important for whomever reviews and signs off on the CTA to have a clear understanding of the legal responsibilities and liabilities assigned to the sponsor and those assigned to whomever is conducting the study.

No-Fault Research Injury Compensation

The United States remains one of the only industrialized nations that conducts research trials without a compensation mechanism for research subjects who are injured as a result of participation in a clinical trial (Chapman et al., 2019; Henry et al., 2015). Morality and access barriers aside, civil litigation may be an appropriate option in cases of negligence or where fault can be determined. However, research injuries often do not fall under those umbrellas (Chapman et al., 2019). When those criteria are less clear or unmet, the lack of a standard mechanism for injured research subjects to seek remedy can lead to additional lawsuits and associated expenses. Creation of a no-fault compensation system is supported by evidence in other countries and could lead to an overall decrease in legal costs (Chapman et al., 2019; Henry et al., 2015). Creation and adoption of such a system will require cooperation and advocacy by community members, sponsors, institutions, policy makers, and clinical researchers.

Summary/Concluding Remarks

The search for new knowledge to improve the human condition is essential, challenging, and painstaking work. It can place our patients at risk and, if we are not careful, may also jeopardize an investigator's career as well. It is important that, before initiating psychiatric research, all involved are clear about the goals of the study and the processes needed for its safe conduct. Institutional awareness and support are critical components, as the regulatory oversight is substantial. The potential exposure to litigation of the principal investigator, the research team members, and the institution during the process of psychiatric research requires ongoing learning and careful communication among all stakeholders.

Key Points

- The fundamental goals and activities undertaken in the performance of biomedical research are not always aligned with those of regular clinical practice.
- The 1979 Belmont Report includes the primary principles of (1) respect for persons (through informed consent), (2) beneficence (via risk/benefit analysis), and (3) justice (through appropriate selection of subjects).
- In terms of potential malpractice exposure, it can be particularly problematic to define "standard of care" or "standard research practices" for psychiatric research projects.
- While use of placebos in studies is only one potential liability, it is an important one to consider when conducting psychiatric research.
- Regulatory compliance in biomedical research is critical, and failure to do so can increase the risk of legal repercussions. However, research physicians and their institutions should remember that meeting those requirements and following an IRB-approved protocol is necessary but may not be sufficient to provide full protection.
- The existence of a conflict of interest (COI) is not itself malpractice, but it can certainly be a motivating factor behind poor decision-making that leads to harmful errors.
- The conduct of clinical research requires technical, ethical, and legal expertise. Despite arduous requirements in medical school and graduate medical training, clinical research knowledge and first-hand experience in clinical trials are still limited.
- Successfully navigating the complex tasks of grants, clinical trial agreements, subject screening and enrollment, regulatory document maintenance, and more requires a coherent and supportive institutional infrastructure.
- Physicians who engage in research should first check with their malpractice insurance provider to determine whether their coverage includes the planned research activities.

References

Adashi, E. Y., Walters, L. B., & Menikoff, J. A. (2018). The Belmont report at 40: Reckoning with time. *American Journal of Public Health, 108*(10), 1345–1348.

Alder, S. (2015). What are the penalties for HIPAA violations? *HIPAA Journal*. https://www.hipaajournal.com/what-are-the-penalties-for-hipaa-violations-7096/. Accessed 17 Dec 2020.

Beresin, E. V., Baldessarini, R. J., Alpert, J., & Rosenbaum, J. (2003). Teaching ethics of psychopharmacology research in psychiatric residency training programs. *Psychopharmacology, 171*(1), 105–111.

Blanchard, M., Burton, M. C., Geraci, M. W., Madaio, M. P., Marsh, J. D., Proweller, A., Rockey, D. C., Salata, R. A., Tan, W., Williams, C. S., Zaidi, M., & Todd, R. F. (2018). Best practices for physician-scientist training programs: Recommendations from the alliance for academic internal medicine. *American Journal of Medicine, 131*(5), 578–584.

Calvin-Naylor, N. A., Jones, C. T., Wartak, M. M., Blackwell, K., Davis, J. M., Divecha, R., Ellerbeck, E. F., Kieburtz, K., Koziel, M. J., Luzuriaga, K., Maddox, J., Needler, N. A., Murphy, S., Pemberton, K., Radovich, C., Rubenstein, E. P., Selker, H. P., Tenaerts, P., Unsworth, K., … Shanley, T. P. (2017). Education and training of clinical and translational study investigators and research coordinators: A competency-based approach. *Journal of Clinical and Translational Science, 1*(1), 1–10.

Carey, B. (2016). *An N.Y.U. study gone wrong, and a top researcher dismissed*. https://www.nytimes.com/2016/06/28/health/nyu-cannabis-ptsd-psychiatry.html?_r=2. Accessed 15 Oct 2020.

Carey, B., & Harris, G. (2008). *Psychiatric group faces scrutiny over drug industry ties*. https://www.nytimes.com/2008/07/12/washington/12psych.html. Accessed 15 Oct 2020.

Carrier, F., Banayan, D., Boley, R., & Karnik, N. (2017). Ethical challenges in developing drugs for psychiatric disorders. *Progress in Neurobiology, 152*, 58–69.

Chapman, C. R., Sukumaran, S., Tsegaye, G. T., Shevchenko, Y., & Caplan, A. L. (2019). The quest for compensation for research-related injury in the United States: A new proposal. *The Journal of Law, Medicine & Ethics, 47*(4), 732–747.

Confronting conflict of interest. (2018). *Nature Medicine, 24*, 1629. https://doi.org/10.1038/s41591-018-0256-7.

Crigger, B. J. (2001). National Bioethics Advisory Commission. National Bioethics Advisory Commission Report: Ethical and policy issues in international research. *IRB, 23*(4), 9–12.

Department of Justice U.S. Attorney's Office Northern District of Ohio. (2020, July 31). *Eight Charged in Scheme to Defraud FDA and Falsify Records Used in Clinical Research Trials* [Press Release]. Retrieved from https://www.fda.gov/inspections-compliance-enforcement-and-criminal-investigations/press-releases/eight-charged-scheme-defraud-fda-and-falsify-records-used-clinical-research-trials

Dubois, J., Bante, H., & Hadley, W. B. (2011). Ethics in psychiatric research: A review of 25 years of NIH-funded empirical research projects. *American Journal of Bioethics Primary Research, 2*(4), 5–17.

Dunn, A. G., Coiera, E., Mandl, K. D., & Bourgeois, F. T. (2016). Conflict of interest disclosure in biomedical research: A review of current practices, biases, and the role of public registries in improving transparency. *Research Integrity and Peer Review, 1*, 1. https://doi.org/10.1186/s41073-016-0006-7

Dyer, O. (2020). US ex-doctor who ran fraudulent clinical trial sites is sentenced to 28 years in prison. *British Medical Journal, 371*, m3946.

Ellenberg, S. S., Fleming, T. R., & DeMets, D. L. (2002). Introduction. In S. Senn & V. Barnett (Eds.), *Data monitoring committees in clinical trials* (pp. 1–18). Wiley.

FDA. (2019). Institutional Review Boards (IRBs) and Protection of Human Subjects in Clinical Trials | FDA. Accessed 1 Dec 2020.

Fischer, B. A., IV. (2006). A summary of important documents in the field of research ethics. *Schizophrenia Bulletin, 32*(1), 69–80.

Glass, K., & Waring, D. (2005). The physician/investigator's obligation to patients participating in research: The case of placebo-controlled trials. *Journal of Law, Medicine and Ethics, 33*(3), 575–585.

Gopalakrishnan, M., Zhu, H., Farchione, T. R., Mathis, M., Mehta, M., Uppoor, R., & Younis, I. (2020). The trend of increasing placebo response and decreasing treatment effect in schizophrenia trials continues: An update from the US Food and Drug Administration. *Journal of Clinical Psychiatry, 81*(2), 19r12960.

Gross, C. (2016). Scientific misconduct. *Annual Review of Psychology, 67*, 693–711.

Henry, L. M., Larkin, M. E., & Pike, E. R. (2015). Just compensation: A no-fault proposal for research-related injuries. *Journal of Law and the Biosciences, 2*(3), 645–668.

Icenogle, D. L. (2003). IRBs, conflict and liability: Will we see IRBs in court? Or is it when? *Clinical Medicine & Research, 1*(1), 63–68.

ICH. (2016). *Guideline for good clinical practice*. https://database.ich.org/sites/default/files/E6_R2_Addendum.pdf. Accessed 1 Dec 2020.

Jansson, R. L. (2003). Notes and comments, researcher liability for negligence in human subject research: Informed consent and researcher malpractice actions. *Washington Law Review, 78*(1), 229–263.

Jones, D. S., Grady, C., & Lederer, S. E. (2016). "Ethics and clinical research"—The 50th anniversary of Beecher's bombshell. *New England Journal of Medicine, 374*(24), 2393–2398.

Meador, K. (2015). Decline of clinical research in academic medical centers. *Neurology, 131*(5), 578–584.

Miller, F. G. (2000). Placebo-controlled trials in psychiatric research: An ethical perspective. *Biological Psychiatry, 47*(8), 707–716.

Miller, F. G., & Brody, H. (2003). The clinician-investigator: Unavoidable but manageable tension. *Kennedy Institute Ethics Journal, 13*(4), 329–346.

Miller, F. G., & Brody, H. (2002). What makes placebo-controlled trials unethical? *American Journal of Bioethics, 2*(2), 3–9.

Morreim, E. H. (2004). Litigation in clinical research: Malpractice doctrines vs. research realities. *The Journal of Law, Medicine & Ethics, 32*(3), 474–484.

National Bioethics Advisory Commission. (1998). *Research involving persons with mental disorders that may affect decision-making capacity*. 1998. https://www.georgetown.edu/research/nrcbl/nbac/capacity/TOC.htm. Accessed 1 Nov 2020.

National Commission for the Protection of Human Subjects of Biomedical and Behavioral Research. (1979). *The Belmont report: Ethical principles and guidelines for the protection of human subjects of research*. U.S. Department of Health and Human Services. https://www.hhs.gov/ohrp/regulations-and-policy/belmont-report/read-the-belmont-report/index.html

National Institutes of Health. (2020). https://grants.nih.gov/policy/humansubjects/single-irb-policy-multi-site-research.htm. Accessed 10 Dec 2020.

National Institute of Mental Health. (2015). *Policy governing independent safety monitors and independent data and safety monitoring boards*. https://www.nimh.nih.gov/funding/clinical-research/policy-governing-independent-safety-monitors-and-independent-data-and-safety-monitoring-boards.shtml. Accessed 12 Dec 2020.

Olsen, J. (2008). https://www.twincities.com/2008/05/17/dan-markingson-had-delusions-his-mother-feared-that-the-worst-would-happen-then-it-did/. Accessed 15 Oct 2020.

Pharmaceutical Integrity Coalition, (2010). https://www.pharmaceuticalintegritycoalition.org/recent/astrazeneca/. Accessed 15 Oct 2020.

Public Health Service Policies on Research Misconduct; Final Rule. Department of Health and Human Services, 70 Fed. Reg. *28370* (May 17, 2005) (to be codified at 42 CFR Parts 50 and 93).

Richardson, L. S. (2009). When human experimentation is criminal. *Journal of Criminal Law and Criminology, 99*(1), 89–134.

Shaul, R. Z., Birenbaum, S., & Evans, M. (2005). Legal liabilities in research: Early lessons from North America. *BMC Medical Ethics, 6*(4). https://doi.org/10.1186/1472-6939-6-4

Stone, J. (2014). https://blogs.scientificamerican.com/molecules-to-medicine/umn-how-many-deaths-have-occurred-during-your-clinical-trials/. Accessed 15 Oct 2020.

Vulcano, D. M. (2012). CPI™ certification as predictor of clinical investigators' regulatory compliance. *Drug Information Journal, 46*(1), 84–87.

Part V

Special Topics

Telepsychiatry

30

Shabana Khan and Abhishek Jain

Telehealth is the use of communication technologies to provide health-related services. The Health Resources and Services Administration (HRSA) more specifically defines it as "the use of electronic information and telecommunication technologies to support long-distance clinical health care, patient and professional health-related education, public health, and health administration" (HRSA, 2020). While the COVID-19 pandemic propelled the use of telehealth nationally – with one large academic medical center reporting a 683% increase in urgent and 4345% increase in non-urgent virtual visits over a 6-week period from March to April 2020 (Mann et al., 2020) – this modality has existed for more than half a century. The first use of video communications to deliver medical care occurred in 1959 at the University of Nebraska when two-way, closed-circuit, interactive television was used, largely in psychiatry, for medical education and treatment (Wittson & Benschoter, 1972). The term "telepsychiatry" was first used in 1969 to describe consultations conducted from Massachusetts General Hospital to a clinic at Logan International Airport (Dwyer, 1973). Today, video-based telepsychiatry involves the use of live videoconferencing for the provision of a variety of services including psychiatric evaluations, behavioral therapies, medication management, patient education, and clinician-to-clinician consultations (American Psychiatric Association [APA], 2020b). Additional telehealth technologies include asynchronous (not live) or store-and-forward modalities (e.g., emails, texts), remote patient monitoring, and mobile health (mHealth).

Prior to the COVID-19 pandemic, legal, regulatory, and reimbursement hurdles (e.g., prescribing restrictions, licensure requirements, lack of payment parity) often limited the practice of telepsychiatry. During the pandemic, flexibilities at the state and federal level – such as by the Centers for Medicare & Medicaid Services (CMS) and Drug Enforcement Administration (DEA) – allowed significant expansion of telepsychiatry and enabled many Americans to access mental healthcare (Hoffman, 2020). Furthermore, states such as New York have provided temporary malpractice immunity, except for gross negligence (Executive Order No. 202.10, New York, 2020). While these flexibilities allowed psychiatrists to rapidly shift to almost exclusively virtual practices during this critical time, many had little or no prior telepsychiatry knowledge or experience and had to quickly consider important administrative, clinical best practice, and technical aspects of this modality (APA, 2020a; Shore et al., 2018). As with in-person care, telepsychiatry services can carry liability risks and, although they have so far been limited, malpractice claims may increase as telehealth becomes more prevalent (Becevic et al., 2020). At the same time, evidence also suggests that availability of certain telemedicine services, such as in critical care settings, may help reduce risk of liability (Becker et al., 2019b). Thus, understanding and appreciating key telepsychiatry legal and regulatory issues can help reduce malpractice and licensure violation risks (Becker et al., 2019a; Becker et al., 2019b; Fields, 2020). This chapter will review these considerations for psychiatrists who provide telepsychiatry services.

Medical Malpractice and Licensure Violation Risks in Telemedicine

In a study of about 94,000 medical liability claims from 2004 to 2013, only 196 involved telemedicine – with diagnostic error and failure to respond as commonly cited allegations – and only 56 of those claims resulted in payment (Becker et al., 2019b). In a more recent 2019 study, a sample of 551 medical malpractice cases from a 1-month period (October to November 2018) was reviewed. None of these cases involved claims regarding direct-to-consumer (DTC) telemedicine (via phone, smartphone, or computer) healthcare

S. Khan (✉)
NYU Grossman School of Medicine, New York, NY, USA
e-mail: Shabana.Khan@nyulangone.org

A. Jain
Department of Psychiatry, Columbia University Vagelos College of Physicians & Surgeons, New York, NY, USA
e-mail: aj2798@cumc.columbia.edu

P. Ash et al. (eds.), *Malpractice and Liability in Psychiatry*, https://doi.org/10.1007/978-3-030-91975-7_30

services. While this is a relatively small sample from a brief duration and does not account for claims that were unreported, unresolved, settled, or confidentially decided, the findings suggest the relatively low liability risk of providing DTC services. The authors discussed that, as a potential explanation for the absence of these malpractice cases, telemedicine at that time was primarily used by lower-risk specialties for lower-risk conditions (e.g., sinus problems, allergies). Moreover, many practices may not offer controlled substance prescriptions or other higher-risk treatments through telemedicine (Fogel & Kvedar, 2019). However, these reviews occurred prior to the COVID-19 pandemic, after which the use of telemedicine became more prevalent across a wider range of subspecialties and levels of risk.

While the reported number of telemedicine malpractice cases thus far has been low, the regulation and practice of telemedicine may be impacted by legal considerations beyond civil litigation. One such noteworthy case, Hageseth v. Superior (2007), resulted in a criminal conviction of practicing medicine without an appropriate license and underscores potential risks surrounding online prescribing (Fields, 2020). In 2005, John McKay, a 19-year-old Stanford University student in California, requested fluoxetine via the India-based online company usanetrx.com. Mr. McKay completed a questionnaire that was forwarded to JRB Health Solutions headquartered in Florida, and a request was subsequently relayed to "physician subcontractor" Dr. Christian Hageseth. Dr. Hageseth was located and licensed to practice medicine in Colorado, but was not licensed to practice medicine in California. Without contacting or examining Mr. McKay, Dr. Hageseth submitted an online prescription that was filled by a pharmacy in Mississippi and mailed to Mr. McKay in California. Weeks later, Mr. McKay was intoxicated with alcohol, completed suicide by carbon monoxide poisoning, and had a detectable amount of fluoxetine in his blood. The San Mateo County District Attorney filed a criminal complaint charging Dr. Hageseth with a felony for willfully and unlawfully practicing medicine in California without a valid license. The defense sought relief on the grounds that the alleged conduct (prescribing fluoxetine) occurred outside California and therefore the court lacked jurisdiction. The California Court of Appeals rejected this appeal and reasoned that a criminal offense via the Internet is still subject to California laws and "it makes no difference that the charged conduct took place in cyberspace rather than real space" (Hageseth v. Superior Court, 2007; Egelko, 2008). Eventually, the physician was sentenced to 9 months in jail in 2009 after pleading No Contest to a felony count of practicing medicine without a license (Dremann, 2009).

On the one hand, cases such as this may send a warning and help regulate inappropriate prescribing of medication via the Internet. On the other hand, the potentially deleterious impact on telehealth from this case was raised by critics such as Dr. Hageseth's attorney who in 2009 stated, "Telemedicine is now dead . . . No doctor in his or her right mind would now pursue telemedicine unless licensed in all 50 states" (Egelko, 2009). On balance, for practitioners this case highlights that practicing in another state without a license may open up the potential for legal consequences, such as criminal charges and convictions, beyond civil malpractice claims (Fields, 2020). While in malpractice claims the plaintiff must prove that a physician's action (or inaction) was a proximate cause that led to a patient's injury or death; in this criminal case the physician's action itself (without necessarily linking it directly to the patient outcome) was sufficient for criminal conviction. Indeed, Mr. McKay's parents also filed a civil lawsuit against Dr. Hageseth; however, experts for both plaintiff and defense concluded that the fluoxetine was not a cause of Mr. McKay's death, and the suit was eventually dropped (Egelko, 2009).

Whereas the jurisdictional argument in a civil proceeding (e.g., medical malpractice) may have been considered differently, and enforcing civil penalties in another state may have been challenging (Egelko, 2009), California law "generally permits the punishment of a defendant . . . for any crime committed 'in whole or in part' in the state" (Hageseth v. Superior Court, 2007). Thus, with these factors taken into account, the decision to reach across state lines and prosecute Dr. Hageseth for criminal charges was perhaps a more accessible legal remedy to curtail inappropriate prescribing by an out-of-state physician to California residents. Also noteworthy from this case is that the court deemed it is unacceptable for practitioners to claim ignorance that prescribing medication over the Internet, without medical license in the state where the patient is located, is unlawful (Hageseth v. Superior Court, 2007). Practitioners must additionally consider that defending these types of criminal charges may not typically fall under the protection and liability coverage of malpractice insurance. Furthermore, in some situations a third party may even face liability for accepting prescriptions from an out-of-state physician, as was raised in a case involving a Louisiana-licensed physician who prescribed home-health services in Mississippi (Frazier v. Univ. of Miss. Med. Ctr., 2018).

Telepsychiatry Legal, Regulatory, and Practice Considerations

Licensure

As noted, the general rule is that a physician must be licensed in the jurisdiction where the patient is located (the originating site) at the time of the visit. While this can be a significant hurdle to the practice of telehealth across state lines, disregard or unawareness of this requirement may open the physician to legal consequences. While some states may have exceptions for consultation, follow-up care, or reciprocity agreements, each state has specific provisions. Licensure exceptions may also include care provided as an employee or contractor of the US Department of Veterans Affairs (Veterans E-Health and Telemedicine Support Act, 2017) or the military. A few states even offer a limited telemedicine license or registration.

As of the writing of this chapter, 29 states, the District of Columbia, and Guam are members of the Interstate Medical Licensure Compact (IMLC), an agreement among participating jurisdictions to streamline the licensure process for physicians (IMLC, 2021). A physician must hold a full, unrestricted license in a compact-member state (the state of principle licensure) before applying for full licensure in other compact states. While the IMLC may expedite the time to obtain licensure in these jurisdictions, a physician must still keep up to date with regulatory, continuing education, and other requirements in each respective state he or she intends to practice. Physicians should review these licensure requirements of the jurisdiction where the patient is located and should be aware that malpractice policies are likely to exclude coverage for unlicensed activities.

In the context of the COVID-19 pandemic, many states temporarily waived or modified licensure requirements for telehealth and some states expedited licensure for retired physicians (Federation of State Medical Boards, 2021). These flexibilities are time-limited and tied to state emergency declarations and/or executive orders. While this patchwork of variable state-by-state changes can be complex and a barrier to practicing telehealth across state lines, practitioners must remain abreast of rapidly changing requirements.

Internet Prescribing and Controlled Substances

Internet prescribing refers to a practitioner prescribing a medication to a patient based upon an interaction that has taken place online. These practices must be appropriately reviewed and commensurate with each jurisdiction's laws and regulations (Carlson & Thompson, 2005). Provisions in each state are typically outlined in a statute called a medical practice act. State medical boards interpret and enforce this act by authorizing physician licensure and investigating and disciplining violations. It can be helpful to keep in mind that, similar to practitioners, state medical boards have the challenge of adapting to evolving technology and practice standards, regulatory changes, and scientific developments.

In 2001, Ryan Haight died at age 18 after overdosing on hydrocodone/acetaminophen (Vicodin) purchased over the Internet. The Ryan Haight Online Pharmacy Consumer Protection Act of, 2008 was passed in response to this tragedy with the intent to target rogue Internet pharmacies. The Act requires practitioners to conduct at least one in-person medical evaluation of a patient before prescribing a controlled substance (Ryan Haight Act, 2008). While there are seven "practice of telemedicine" exceptions to the Ryan Haight Act requirement for an initial in-person medical evaluation, these exceptions are very narrow and generally do not apply to most current practices of telemedicine. One exception is the practice of telemedicine being conducted by a practitioner who has obtained a "special registration." Despite the Ryan Haight Act being passed 13 years ago, the special registration has yet to be defined or activated despite the Substance Use-Disorder Prevention that Promotes Opioid Recovery and Treatment (SUPPORT) for Patients and Communities Act setting a deadline of October 24, 2019, for the Drug Enforcement Administration (DEA) to promulgate final regulations for the special registration (SUPPORT Act, 2018). Thus, this requirement for an in-person medical evaluation has been a significant obstacle to the legitimate practice of telemedicine. This limitation has particularly impacted the use of telemedicine for medication-assisted treatment for opioid use disorder and stimulant medication to treat individuals with attention deficit hyperactivity disorder. Telemedicine practitioners and several professional organizations have been advocating for over a decade for the DEA to remove this requirement of an in-person examination if a practitioner is acting in the usual course of his or her practice and issuing the controlled substance for a legitimate medical purpose (Caudill, 2018). Nonetheless, this remains an important provision for practitioners of telemedicine.

Another Ryan Haight Act telemedicine exception is a declaration of a public health emergency by the Secretary of the US Department of Health and Human Services (HHS), which occurred in January 2020. In response to this declaration, the DEA adopted policies to allow DEA-registered practitioners to prescribe controlled substances without an in-person examination if the prescription is for a legitimate medical purpose, if the practitioner is acting in his or her usual course of professional practice, and if the communication is conducted via live, interactive audio-video (DEA, 2020). Moreover, on March 23, 2020, the DEA issued guidance that waived, for the duration of the public health emergency, the requirement for DEA-registered practitioners to obtain a separate DEA registration in each state in which he or she dispenses a controlled substance (DEA, 2020). Obtaining a separate DEA registration and having to list a unique physical address in each state has been a longstanding hurdle to providing telehealth care across state lines. On March 31, 2020, the DEA issued additional guidance, also for the duration of the public health emergency, allowing authorized practitioners to prescribe buprenorphine to new and existing patients with opioid use disorder via telephone without first conducting an examination in-person or via telemedicine. This may only be done if the practitioner determines that an adequate evaluation of the patient can be conducted via telephone. Though these changes made at the federal level have been helpful to provide care to patients during the COVID-19 crisis, practitioners must also comply with practice standards and other applicable federal and state laws and regulations, which do not always align.

Informed Consent

Prior to the COVID-19 pandemic, about 40 jurisdictions included some sort of telehealth informed consent requirement in their statutes, administrative code, Medicaid and other payer policies, and/or rules regulating healthcare professionals. Telehealth informed consent can include explanation of what telehealth is; potential risks (including those related to privacy and security), benefits, and alternatives; patient's right to refuse or stop treatment; and contingencies for technical issues. The requirement may apply to the Medicaid program, a specific specialty, or all telehealth encounters in the state depending on the policy and may be verbal, written, or both. The requirement for formal informed consent is typically reserved for higher-risk decisions, such as invasive procedures and experimental studies, and not usually required for a patient's choice regarding how he or she wishes to receive services. Some experts note requiring a written or verbal informed consent misrepresents telehealth as a different form of care. Furthermore, significant state-by-state variability exists with respect to informed consent requirements for telehealth (Center for Connected Health Policy [CCHP], 2020).

Establishing a Physician-Patient Relationship

Physicians should review state and payer rules, as well as guidance by their organization or practice on what constitutes establishing a physician-patient relationship. State laws and regulations differ with respect to defining establishment of a patient-physician relationship for purposes of treatment via telemedicine. All states allow a physician to establish a relationship with a new patient via telemedicine; however, there are state-specific nuances (American Medical Association, 2018). For telepsychiatry practice across state lines, the laws and regulations of the state where the patient is located are relevant. Payers may also have requirements that a physician-patient relationship must be established in order to be able to bill for telemedicine services. Understanding when and how a physician-patient duty attaches is important to consider in the context of medical malpractice.

Credentialing and Privileging

Hospital-based telepsychiatry services can increase access to specialty care for underserved populations and help address workforce maldistribution and shortages. Practitioners must be credentialed and privileged before providing in-person or telehealth patient care services at hospitals or other healthcare organizations. Credentialing is the process of assessing and verifying that a practitioner's license status and qualifications are in good standing to provide services. Privileging authorizes a practitioner's specific scope of patient care services based on factors including the practitioner's license, education, training, competence, judgment, and ability to perform privileges.

Practitioner credentialing is governed by the bylaws and policies of a hospital, and a telehealth practitioner providing care for multiple originating site hospitals within a large network may need to be credentialed at each of the hospitals, as well as at the site where the practitioner is located (distant site). This time- and resource-intensive process can be an administrative barrier to widespread telehealth implementation (Baker-Whitcomb & Harvey, 2018). In 2011, the Center for Medicare and Medicaid Services (CMS) approved regulations (CMS, 2011), and the Joint Commission (TJC) developed standards (TJC, 2012) allowing originating site hospitals receiving telehealth services to accept the credentialing and privileging decisions made by the hospital or entity providing the telehealth service (distant site). This streamlined process, known as credentialing by proxy, is voluntary and can help cut down on credentialing-related time, expense, and duplication of effort. In order for a hospital to use the credentialing-by-proxy process, there must be a written agreement between the two relevant parties, the distant site hospital must be a Medicare-participating hospital or telemedicine entity, and hospitals must ensure that their bylaws meet the requirements for this process (CCHP, 2021a).

Improper credentialing of physicians can expose hospitals to vicarious liability such as claims of negligent credentialing if this lack of diligence resulted in a patient injury. With respect to credentialing-by-proxy for physicians practicing telehealth, practices that may lead to claims of negligent credentialing include an originating site hospital relying on the credentialing and privileging information from a distant site, and the distant site's credentialing process or decision was flawed; or an originating site hospital relying on the distant site's credentialing process without a written agreement indicating that the distant site telehealth credentialing and privileging processes met the Medicare Conditions of Participation.

Malpractice Insurance

Practitioners should confirm that their malpractice carrier provides coverage for telepsychiatry services that they provide or intend to provide and should consider obtaining written assurances that the policy covers telehealth malpractice lawsuits. While some states, such as Hawaii, may require malpractice insurers to provide "coverage for telehealth that shall be equivalent to coverage for the same services provided via face-to-face contact between a health care provider and a patient," not all states require malpractice insurance carriers to cover telehealth (HI Revised Statutes §671–7(a) (2017); CCHP, 2021c). Additionally, if the practice of telepsychiatry occurs across state lines, the psychiatrist and patient may be in different states with different liability laws, damage caps, statutes of limitations, or standards of care. Psychiatrists should confirm that the policy extends coverage to all states in which they will be practicing and that the malpractice carrier itself is licensed in those states (CCHP, 2021b).

Privacy and Security

Telepsychiatry technical best practices include a secure point-to-point connection; private high-speed network; fully encrypted data transmission; compliance with relevant federal laws and regulations including the Health Insurance Portability and Accountability Act (HIPAA) and Health Information Technology for Economic and Clinical Health (HITECH) Act; compliance with relevant state laws and regulations; and contractual assurances such as business associate agreements to outline methods that will be used by third-party partners to ensure protection of the data.

Environmental considerations include ensuring that both clinician and patient are in private locations during a telehealth visit. Clinician and patient education and guidance on appropriate use of technology and environmental considerations can help mitigate privacy and security risks. With technologies such as remote patient monitoring, privacy risks around data collection, use, and sharing must be considered (Hall & McGraw, 2014).

On March 17, 2020, the US Department of Health and Human Services (HHS) Office for Civil Rights (OCR) announced it will exercise its enforcement discretion and will not impose penalties for noncompliance with the regulatory requirements under the HIPAA Rules against covered healthcare practitioners in connection with the good faith provision of telehealth specifically during the COVID-19 nationwide public health emergency (HHS, 2020). OCR indicated that under this notice, covered healthcare practitioners may use popular applications that allow for video chats, including Apple FaceTime, Facebook Messenger video chat, Google Hangouts video, Zoom, or Skype, to provide telehealth without risk that OCR might seek to impose a penalty for noncompliance with the HIPAA Rules related to the good faith provision of telehealth during the public health emergency. While this change was temporarily made at the federal level during the public health emergency, a psychiatrist must also consider organization protocols as well as state laws and regulations regarding health information and what is required to protect it.

Standard of Care and Scope of Practice

State laws and medical board regulations generally require that the standard of care for telemedicine be consistent with that of an in-person encounter to ensure that patients receive quality and safe care. Psychiatrists should also review state-specific scope of practice laws. Telehealth practitioners should practice within the scope of their profession and consult national medical professional organizations' standards. Of particular consideration are circumstances in which telepsychiatrists also supervise mid-level providers (e.g., nurse practitioners) through consultation via videoconferencing. Each jurisdiction has unique regulations, and malpractice carriers may need to be notified before psychiatrists engage in these activities.

Additional Clinical and Safety Considerations

One of the opportunities and challenges of telemedicine is being able to provide services remotely in rural settings. Practitioners may or may not be familiar with the local area of the patient; thus, learning about available local services – such as mobile crisis and psychiatric emergency departments – can be useful when there is a need to escalate care. Developing relationships with community healthcare professionals can also help with continuity of care and considerations for referrals. Gaining general awareness and understanding of the patient's community can be accomplished virtually and allow for the delivery of culturally appropriate healthcare. Over time, practitioners describe being able to identify local pharmacies and services and even giving detailed directions to patients and their families despite never having physically been in those areas themselves.

Other practical considerations include having the patient's contact information (phone number and physical location at the time of the visit) readily available if there is break in the videoconferencing connection, or if a safety issue arises and local emergency or crisis services need to be activated. Telepsychiatrists should also outline a back-up plan in the event of a technology glitch, such as transitioning to telephone to complete the visit. Basic legal considerations, such as civil commitment laws and procedures, mandated reporting, and duty to warn or protect requirements, are important especially if the practitioner is providing services in another state. As with in-person encounters, careful documentation is important. Practitioners should note that there may be specific documentation requirements for telehealth encounters in statutes, administrative codes, payer policies, and/or organization protocols. These requirements may include indicating whether informed consent was obtained, type of technology used, time spent providing services, and location of patient and/or practitioner at the time of the encounter.

Further considerations include obtaining vital sign measurements, performing a targeted virtual physical examination, or conducting an Abnormal Involuntary Movement Scale (AIMS) test when clinically indicated. These assessments can be conducted via video, for example, by having the patients measure their blood pressure, pulse, or pulse oxygen saturation if they have remote monitoring devices available at home or check their pulse manually. If the patient is physically present in a setting such as a hospital or clinic at the time of the visit, healthcare professionals who are at the site with the patient may be able to measure vital signs or assist with a physical examination with guidance from the offsite telepsychiatrist.

Conclusion

With the increased use of telepsychiatry, especially since the COVID-19 pandemic, this modality has become a prevalent feature in mainstream healthcare and is likely to continue at least in some form in the future. Organizations including the APA, American Academy of Child and Adolescent Psychiatry (AACAP), American Telemedicine Association (ATA), CCHP, and the National Consortium of Telehealth Resource Centers (NTRCs) offer resources to help psychiatrists navigate the legal and regulatory landscape (see Table 30.1). Knowledge of clinical, legal, and regulatory considerations relevant to the practice of telepsychiatry can help psychiatrists reduce the risk of licensure violations and medical malpractice.

Key Points

- Telehealth is the use of communication technologies to provide health-related services.
- While telehealth has existed for more than half a century, the COVID-19 pandemic rapidly expanded its use nationally.
- Previous state and federal legal, regulatory, and reimbursement restrictions were relaxed and enabled easier access to healthcare during the COVID-19 pandemic.
- While the reported number of telemedicine malpractice cases thus far has been low, the increased use of telemedicine across a wider range of situations and risk levels, and evolving practice standards, may raise unique liability and legal considerations.
- Psychiatrists should confirm that their malpractice carrier provides coverage for telepsychiatry services.
- Psychiatrists should be aware of relevant telemedicine legal and regulatory requirements and exceptions surrounding Internet prescribing, controlled substances, informed consent, establishing a physician-patient relationship, credentialing and privileging, privacy and security, standards of care, and scope of practice.

Table 30.1 Telepsychiatry legal and regulatory resources

AACAP Telepsychiatry Toolkit	Up-to-date topics in the practice of pediatric telepsychiatry Developed jointly by the Telepsychiatry Committees of AACAP and the American Psychiatric Association (APA) https://www.aacap.org/AACAP/Clinical_Practice_Center/Business_of_Practice/Telepsychiatry/toolkit_videos.aspx. Accessed December 29, 2020
AACAP Pediatric Telepsychiatry Curriculum	Pediatric Telepsychiatry for graduate medical education (GME) and continuing medical education (CME) https://www.aacap.org/App_Themes/AACAP/Docs/clinical_practice_center/business_of_practice/Telepsych/Pediatric_Telepsychiatry_Curriculum_Oct_2020-web.pdf. Accessed December 29, 2020
AACAP Clinical Update (2017)	Telepsychiatry with children and adolescents https://www.jaacap.org/article/S0890-8567(17)30333-7/pdf. Accessed December 29, 2020
APA Telepsychiatry Toolkit	Up-to-date topics in the practice of general telepsychiatry Developed by the APA Telepsychiatry Committee https://www.psychiatry.org/psychiatrists/practice/telepsychiatry/toolkit. Accessed December 29, 2020
APA and the American Telemedicine Association (ATA) Best Practices (2018)	Best practices in videoconferencing based telemental health https://www.liebertpub.com/doi/pdf/10.1089/tmj.2018.0237. Accessed December 29, 2020
Center for Connected Health Policy (CCHP)	Research and analyses of telehealth policy and federal/state legislation and regulations https://www.cchpca.org. Accessed December 29, 2020
National Consortium of Telehealth Resource Centers (NTRCs)	Assistance, education and information in telehealth Collaborative network of 12 regional and 2 national centers funded by HHS https://www.telehealthresourcecenter.org. Accessed December 29, 2020

- As a general rule, a physician should be licensed in the jurisdiction where the patient is located.
- Practical considerations, such as having a plan if there are technological or connection issues during a patient encounter, being able to contact emergency services in the patient's local area if needed, and knowledge of relevant jurisdiction-specific laws (e.g., civil commitment and mandated reported), can be useful.

References

American Medical Association. (2018). *50 State Survey: Establishment of a patient-physician relationship via telemedicine*. https://www.ama-assn.org/system/files/2018-10/ama-chart-telemedicine-patient-physician-relationship.pdf

American Psychiatric Association. (2020a). *Psychiatrists' use of telepsychiatry during COVID-19 public health emergency*. https://www.psychiatry.org/File%20Library/Psychiatrists/Practice/Telepsychiatry/APA-Telehealth-Survey-2020.pdf. Accessed 29 Dec 2020.

American Psychiatric Association. (2020b). *What is Telepsychiatry?* https://www.psychiatry.org/patients-families/what-is-telepsychiatry. Accessed 29 Dec 2020.

Baker-Whitcomb, A., & Harvey, J. (2018). Benefits and barriers to telehealth credentialing by proxy. *Telemedicine and e-Health, 24*(11), 922–926.

Becevic, M., Sheets, L. R., Wallach, E., McEowen, A., Bass, A., Mutrux, E. R., & Edison, K. E. (2020). Telehealth and telemedicine in Missouri. *Missouri Medicine, 117*(3), 228–234.

Becker, C. D., Dandy, K., Gaujean, M., Fusaro, M., & Scurlock, C. (2019a). Legal perspectives on telemedicine part 1: Legal and regulatory issues. *The Permanente Journal, 23*, 18.293.

Becker, C. D., Dandy, K., Gaujean, M., Fusaro, M., & Scurlock, C. (2019b). Legal perspectives on telemedicine part 2: Telemedicine in the intensive care unit and medicolegal risk. *The Permanente Journal, 23*, 18.294.

Carlson, D., & Thompson, J. (2005). The role of state medical boards. Virtual mentor: Ethics. *Journal of the American Medical Association, 7*(4), 311–314.

Caudill, R. (2018). *Update on developments with Ryan Haight and online prescribing*. American Psychiatric Association Telepsychiatry Blog. https://www.psychiatry.org/psychiatrists/practice/telepsychiatry/blog/update-on-developments-with-ryan-haight-and-online-prescribing. Accessed 29 Dec 2020.

Center for Connected Health Policy. (2020). *State Telehealth Laws and Reimbursement Policies Spring 2020 Report*. https://www.cchpca.org/sites/default/files/2020-05/CCHP_%2050_STATE_REPORT_SPRING_2020_FINAL.pdf. Accessed 29 Dec 2020.

Center for Connected Health Policy. (2021a). *Credentialing and Privileging*. https://www.cchpca.org/telehealth-policy/credentialing-and-privileging. Accessed 2 Jan 2021.

Center for Connected Health Policy (2021b). *Malpractice*. https://www.cchpca.org/telehealth-policy/malpractice. Accessed 2 Jan 2021.

Center for Connected Health Policy (2021c). Current State Laws & Reimbursement Policies. https://www.cchpca.org/telehealth-policy/current-state-laws-and-reimbursement-policies. Accessed January 2, 2021.

Centers for Medicare and Medicaid Services. (2011). *Condition of participation: Governing body*. 42 CFR. https://www.govinfo.gov/content/pkg/CFR-2011-title42-vol5/pdf/CFR-2011-title42-vol5.pdf. Accessed 29 Dec 2020.

Dremann, S. (updated 2009, March 10). *Doctor convicted in internet prescriptions case*. Palo Alto online. https://www.paloaltoonline.com/news/2009/03/10/doctor-convicted-in-internet-prescriptions-case. Accessed 30 Dec 2020.

Drug Enforcement Administration. (2020). *COVID-19 information page*. https://www.deadiversion.usdoj.gov/coronavirus.html. Accessed 29 Dec 2020.

Dwyer, T. F. (1973). Telepsychiatry: Psychiatric consultation by interactive television. *The American Journal of Psychiatry, 130*(8), 865–869.

Egelko, B. (2008, December 30; Updated 2012, February 9). *Father blames son's suicide on 'telemedicine.'* SFGATE. https://www.sfgate.com/news/article/Father-blames-son-s-suicide-on-telemedicine-3178535.php. Accessed 8 Dec 2020.

Egelko, B. (2009, April 18; updated 2012, February 8). 'Telemedicine' doctor gets 9 months in jail. SFGATE. https://www.sfgate.com/health/article/Telemedicine-doctor-gets-9-months-in-jail-3164016.php. Accessed 30 Dec 2020.

Executive Order No. 202.10, New York. (2020). *Continuing temporary suspension and modification of laws relating to the disaster Emergency*. https://www.governor.ny.gov/news/no-20210-continuing-temporary-suspension-and-modification-laws-relating-disaster-emergency. Accessed 29 Dec 2020.

Federation of State Medical Boards. (2021). *COVID-19 resource directory*. https://www.fsmb.org/advocacy/covid-19/. Accessed 2 Jan 2021.

Fields, B. G. (2020). Regulatory, legal, and ethical considerations of telemedicine. *Sleep Medicine Clinics, 15*(3), 409–416.

Fogel, A. L., & Kvedar, J. C. (2019). Reported cases of medical malpractice in direct-to-consumer telemedicine. *Journal of the American Medical Association, 321*(13), 1309–1310.

Frazier v. Univ. of Miss. Med. Ctr., CIVIL ACTION NO. 3:16-CV-976-DPJ-FKB (S.D. Miss. Oct. 24, 2018).

Hageseth v. Superior Court, 150 Cal. App. 4th 1399, 59 Cal. Rptr. 3d 385 (Cal. Ct. App. 2007).

Hall, J. L., & McGraw, D. (2014). For telehealth to succeed, privacy and security risks must be identified and addressed. *Health Affairs (Project Hope), 33*(2), 216–221.

Health Resources and Services Administration. (2020). *What is telehealth?* https://www.hhs.gov/hipaa/for-professionals/faq/3015/what-is-telehealth/index.html. Accessed 29 Dec 2020.

HI Revised Statutes §671–7(a) (2017). Accessed January 2, 2021.

Hoffman, D. A. (2020). Increasing access to care: Telehealth during COVID-19. *Journal of Law and the Biosciences, 7*(1).

Interstate Medical Licensure Compact. (2021). https://www.imlcc.org/a-faster-pathway-to-physician-licensure/. Accessed 2 Jan 2021.

Mann, D. M., Chen, J., Chunara, R., Testa, P. A., & Nov, O. (2020). COVID-19 transforms health care through telemedicine: Evidence from the field. *Journal of the American Medical Informatics Association, 27*(7), 1132–1135.

Ryan Haight Online Pharmacy Consumer Protection Act of 2008. https://www.govinfo.gov/content/pkg/BILLS-110hr6353enr/pdf/BILLS-110hr6353enr.pdf.

Shore, J. H., Yellowlees, P., Caudill, R., Johnston, B., Turvey, C., Mishkind, M., Krupinski, E., Myers, K., Shore, P., Kaftarian, E., & Hilty, D. (2018). Best practices in videoconferencing-based telemental health April 2018. *Telemedicine and e-Health, 24*(11), 827–832.

Substance Use-Disorder Prevention that Promotes Opioid Recovery and Treatment (SUPPORT) for Patients and Communities Act of

2018. https://www.congress.gov/bill/115th-congress/house-bill/6. Accessed 29 Dec 2020.

The Joint Commission. (2012). Final revisions to telemedicine standards. https://www.jointcommission.org/-/media/tjc/documents/standards/jc-requirements/revisions_telemedicine_standardspdf.pdf?db=web&hash=80DD5BCB3FE622C42BEE956C35611376

U.S. Department of Health & Human Services. (2020). *Notification of Enforcement Discretion for Telehealth Remote Communications During the COVID-19 Nationwide Public Health Emergency*. https://www.hhs.gov/hipaa/for-professionals/special-topics/emergency-preparedness/notification-enforcement-discretion-telehealth/index.html. Accessed 29 Dec 2020

Veterans E-Health and Telemedicine Support (VETS) Act of 2017. https://www.congress.gov/115/bills/s925/BILLS-115s925es.pdf. Accessed 20 Jan 2021.

Wittson, C. L., & Benschoter, R. (1972). Two-way television: Helping the Medical Center reach out. *The American Journal of Psychiatry, 129*(5), 624–627.

31 Malpractice and the Internet

Patricia R. Recupero

Many commentators have argued that information and communications technology (ICT) is fundamentally changing the doctor-patient relationship. The use of the Internet for psychiatrist-patient communication may impact the therapeutic alliance and the psychiatrist's risk for malpractice liability. The COVID-19 pandemic fueled the rapid adoption of Internet-based tools among nearly all mental health professionals, many of whom were unfamiliar with the malpractice risks that such technology entails. This chapter reviews several Internet-specific liability issues that psychiatrists may encounter and offers suggestions for risk management.

The Psychiatrist-Patient Relationship: Establishment of a Duty of Care

For a medical malpractice claim to succeed, the plaintiff must show that a physician-patient relationship—which confers a duty of care—exists between the patient and the defendant physician (see Chap. 1). For cases involving the Internet, the question of whether a physician-patient relationship exists is not always straightforward. However, courts have found that the relationship, with its corresponding duty of care, can be established in the absence of face-to-face interaction between the physician and the patient (Diwan, 2012; Recupero, 2005; Terry & Wiley, 2016).

In *White v. Harris* (2011), a state appellate court held that a physician-patient relationship and corresponding duty of care had been established between a psychiatrist and a patient whom he had evaluated through a one-time, 90-minute consultation conducted via videoconferencing technology for a telepsychiatry research study. Following this one-time session, the psychiatrist completed a consultation including the patient's history, the psychiatrist's diagnostic impressions, and recommendations for a course of treatment via follow-up care by another clinical provider. This consultation explicitly stated that no further treatment would be provided by the psychiatrist who had evaluated the patient for the research study. Nearly a year later, the patient died following an intentional overdose on medications, none of which had been prescribed by the psychiatrist from the research study. Nonetheless, the telepsychiatrist from the study was named as a defendant in a malpractice suit filed by the patient's parents, and the appellate court held that a duty of care had been established by the one-time, 90-minute telepsychiatry consultation (*White v. Harris*, 2011).

The existence of a physician-patient relationship can also be established by the physician's response to unsolicited requests for medical advice or information (Recupero, 2005). The communication between the psychiatrist and patient (or a third party acting on the patient's behalf) need not be as formal as telepsychiatry sessions for a duty of care to be established. The existence of such a duty will depend upon the extent and nature of interactions between the psychiatrist and a patient (or third party) (Recupero, 2005); the greater the degree of interaction, the greater the likelihood that a physician-patient relationship will be established (Recupero, 2006). The following examples illustrate a sliding scale of interactivity and corresponding malpractice liability risk:

1. No interaction (e.g., the patient visits the psychiatrist's website but does not establish contact with the psychiatrist's office; low risk of liability).
2. Low interaction (e.g., the psychiatrist's website contains a free electronic screening tool, which visitors to the website can complete; the user's responses prompt an automated response encouraging the website visitor to make an appointment with the psychiatrist).
3. Low-to-moderate interaction (e.g., the psychiatrist responds in general terms to an unsolicited email from a prospective patient; no diagnosis or personalized advice is offered or suggested, but the email contains links to information about mental health on the NIMH website, information about the psychiatrist's fees and insurance

P. R. Recupero (✉)
Warren Alpert Medical School of Brown University, Providence, RI, USA
e-mail: Patricia_Recupero@Brown.edu

P. Ash et al. (eds.), *Malpractice and Liability in Psychiatry*, https://doi.org/10.1007/978-3-030-91975-7_31

plans accepted, and a link to an electronic appointment-request form).

4. Moderate interaction (e.g., the psychiatrist performs a one-time evaluation of a patient and generates a final report and/or referral to another healthcare provider).
5. Moderate-to-high interaction (e.g., the psychiatrist issues prescriptions to someone with whom they have been connected via the Internet).
6. Ongoing, extensive interaction (e.g., the Internet is used to conduct an ongoing therapeutic relationship with a patient; higher risk of liability).

Incidents similar to the first level (no interaction) are unlikely to establish a duty of care, while cases similar to the sixth level (ongoing, extensive interaction) more clearly establish the professional relationship and its associated legal responsibilities. Liability in intermediate levels of interaction (e.g., responses to unsolicited emails, Friedman et al., 2016) may depend upon the facts in a particular case and upon the rules and jurisdiction(s) in question.

The decision to establish a psychiatrist-patient relationship carries some unique considerations for Internet-related cases. For example, the psychiatrist must determine which patients are appropriate for Internet-based treatment or even adjunctive incidental Internet communications. Interstate licensure issues may also be a major concern. Consider a psychiatrist who commutes into Manhattan from Connecticut and who holds a medical license in New York but not in Connecticut. The psychiatrist may treat patients who also travel to New York for appointments but who live near the state border in Connecticut or New Jersey. Even if the psychiatrist-patient relationship is well-established for face-to-face treatment in New York, medical licensure and jurisdiction issues could arise regarding any treatment conducted virtually, particularly if the physician does not have a medical license for the state in which a patient is located. Furthermore, the psychiatrist's medical malpractice insurance may limit coverage to treatment that takes place in New York.

Parameters of the Duty and the Standard of Care

The establishment of the psychiatrist-patient relationship and a corresponding duty of care is a separate question from the extent or parameters of that duty. The parameters of the duty depend upon the specific factors in a case; the responsibilities of a psychiatrist merely providing consultation through a review of medical records, for example, may be different from those of an attending physician on a psychiatric inpatient unit. Similarly, the extent of duties expected of a psychiatrist providing Internet-based services may differ from those of clinicians practicing in traditional, face-to-face settings. However, some courts may hold psychiatrists to the same standard of care regardless of whether treatment and professional activities are conducted in person or online. As acknowledged by the Court in *White v. Harris* (2011), expert testimony is typically required in order to define the standard of care.

Some commentators have argued that telepsychiatrists should be held to a *higher* standard of care than psychiatrists working in traditional modalities, due to differences between traditional and remote psychiatry (Serri, 2016). One shortcoming of Internet-based treatment is its limitations during emergencies. Should a patient become acutely suicidal or violent in the psychiatrist's office, the psychiatrist can accompany the patient to the emergency department or call ambulance services and wait with the patient until they arrive; in both cases, the psychiatrist is likely already familiar with the local emergency departments and other area resources, such as mobile crisis response teams, and may even have their phone numbers saved on speed dial. When a remote patient is in crisis, however, the psychiatrist must utilize resources local to the patient, which carries potentially unforeseen logistical complications, as when geographically isolated patients must wait a long time for Emergency Medical Services to arrive; furthermore, the patient may not even be at home.

Today, the standard of care for psychiatrists—including those who do not practice telemedicine—arguably includes a duty to understand and use Internet and communications technology (ICT) competently in the provision of patient care. The Institute of Medicine's core competencies for health professions include the use of information technology (Hilty et al., 2020). Furthermore, during the COVID-19 public health emergency, this duty required treating patients remotely so as to lessen infection transmission risks associated with face-to-face appointments. The physician's duty includes a responsibility to help patients make informed decisions about their care and to set reasonable expectations about care provision. When deciding whether to use particular forms of technology to conduct or augment psychiatric care, informed consent involves disclosing the purposes, risks, and benefits of a given treatment, as well as alternatives to its use and safeguards that may be employed to lessen any risks. For example, when using applications (apps) and other software, informed consent may require disclosure of risks to patient confidentiality (Edwards-Stewart et al., 2019).

In some cases, the psychiatrist-patient relationship may be adversely affected by the use of Internet-based therapy (Shore, 2020). The oft-perceived lack of formality inherent in computer-mediated communication may affect patients' behavior; in a survey of telehealth consumers, many reported multitasking during telemedicine appointments, including viewing other media, driving a vehicle, and drinking alcohol (DrFirst, 2020). If the decision to conduct the psychiatrist-patient relationship through the Internet results in decrements to the quality of the therapeutic alliance, the risk of adverse events may increase. The physician-patient relationship is an important factor in determining the likelihood of suicidal behavior, for example (Schultz et al., 2020). A poor physician-patient relationship may also increase the risk that patients or their representatives may pursue litigation if adverse events occur.

Dereliction of Duty

Once a duty of care has been established, the legal inquiry in psychiatric malpractice cases turns to whether the doctor's conduct breached that duty and failed to conform to the applicable standard of care. Recent growth in direct-to-consumer telemedicine marketing has raised concern about whether these services depart from an acceptable standard of care (Fogel & Kvedar, 2019). Although medical malpractice cases involving telemedicine have been rare, most to date have involved physicians prescribing over state lines without performing an in-person physical examination (Ackerman, 2019). In *Hageseth v. The Superior Court of San Mateo County* (2007), a Colorado-based physician, who wrote antidepressant prescriptions for a young man attending college in California, was convicted for practicing medicine without a license in California (a felony charge resulting in a 9-month jail sentence) following the patient's suicide. The defendant psychiatrist had never personally evaluated the patient—neither in person nor even via telepsychiatry. The patient's father also pursued malpractice litigation against the psychiatrist, and the physician was required to surrender his Colorado medical license (Egelko, 2008).

Failing to monitor patients for high-risk symptoms, or to adequately review and supervise subordinate clinicians or employees, represents another area rife with potential for dereliction of duty. In one case, a physician based in Saipan came to the attention of regulators when three high-risk patients for whom he had written prescriptions for Suboxone received medical treatment from other providers (*In the Matter of Gahlinger*, 2014a; *In the Matter of Gahlinger*, 2014b). The state medical board noted that the physician had never met with the three patients in person; instead, he had met with two of them briefly via videoconferencing with the help of an assistant located in Utah (*In the Matter of Gahlinger*, 2014a).

The failure to obtain a patient's informed consent to the use of particular forms of ICT may also breach the standard of care. Some jurisdictions have statutes or codes specifically requiring the physician to obtain written informed consent to treatment via telepsychiatry, for example (Shore, 2020). Failing to disclose risks associated with other forms of technology (such as short message service (SMS) text messaging, patient portals, and mobile health apps) before using them with patients may also constitute a departure from the standard of care (Shore, 2020). Inherent within the responsibility to obtain a patient's informed consent to the use of such technologies is the psychiatrist's duty to understand their use, risks, benefits, alternatives, and safeguards.

Disclaimers or other written statements declaring a physician-patient relationship nonexistent or terminated are unlikely to protect a psychiatrist who abandons a patient in need of further care. In the case of *White v. Harris* mentioned above, the appellate court found that "[t]he doctor had a duty of due care in his professional contact with decedent, which was not extinguished by the ministerial act of termination of their professional relationship" (*White v. Harris*, 2011, p. 205). Particularly when evaluating or treating patients at high risk for suicide, violence, substance abuse, high-risk medical conditions, or acute psychiatric decompensation, the standard of care may require the psychiatrist to arrange for follow-up services and, potentially, to initiate commitment proceedings if involuntary hospitalization is clinically appropriate.

Causation

Having established a duty of care, its parameters, and a breach of that duty, the question turns to causation, an especially challenging element in psychiatric negligence cases. Suicide is the most common reason for medical malpractice claims in psychiatry (Serri, 2016), but it is a complex phenomenon, typically with no single cause. This complexity can be problematic for plaintiffs attempting to show causation in a psychiatric malpractice action. Serri notes that courts in recent years have focused on the question of foreseeability—a different concept from predictability—in determining causation in suicide cases (Serri, 2016). Thus, if a patient's suicide attempt is reasonably foreseeable, the nexus between the psychiatrist's breach of duty and subsequent harm may be more easily demonstrated.

When a patient is injured as a result of a psychiatrist's reliance upon technology, liability may attach to the physician (Smith & Fotheringham, 2020), who is acting in the role of a learned intermediary in the application of that technology. For example, suppose that the psychiatrist relies upon artificial intelligence (AI) tools built into an Internet-based platform through which the patient communicates with the treatment team. These AI tools may purport to identify patients at risk for suicide or violent behavior by automatically monitoring content that patients share through a mobile health application or social media. If the psychiatrist fails to conduct thorough risk assessments and relies, instead, on the AI system's risk screening algorithm to identify patients in need of further evaluation, a defense of "but the patient wasn't flagged as high-risk by the system" is not likely to protect the physician from liability. Such shortcuts and tools may be attractive from an efficiency perspective, but they do not absolve the physician of their duty of care to the patient.

When harm befalls a patient or others due to the *patient's* reliance on technology, and not upon the treating psychiatrist's recommendations or care, the psychiatrist is not likely to be held liable, as the proximate or direct cause of harm would be something other than the psychiatrist's conduct.

Damages

The determination of damages when psychiatric treatment is provided through the Internet can be complex: "physicians and patients may be located in states with different liability laws, statutes of limitations, standards of care or damage caps" (Ackerman, 2019). Adverse consequences for the psychiatrist in Internet-related negligence may include civil awards as well as criminal sentences and administrative sanctions such as censure by a state medical board. Determinations of damages for Internet-related psychiatric malpractice will likely be similar to cases *not* involving the Internet.

Areas of Risk and Mitigation of Risk

To minimize the risk of malpractice and other forms of liability, psychiatrists can be cognizant of several additional areas of risk with respect to the use of ICT as discussed below.

Diagnosis

Misdiagnosis is the most common allegation in telemedical malpractice (The Doctors Company, 2020). A review of closed claims found that the most common missed diagnoses were cancer, stroke, and infection (The Doctors Company, 2020). Psychiatrists employing Internet technology to treat patients can remain vigilant toward the possibility of underlying medical conditions that could explain a patient's presentation. It is also important to note the shortcomings of ICT in diagnostic accuracy, including the loss of data such as vital signs, ambulation, olfactory stimuli, and nuanced visual cues, such as tremor or the development of a rash or other allergic reaction (Serri, 2016). Early recognition of side effects and extrapyramidal symptoms may also be more challenging over the Internet; for example, assessing for cogwheel rigidity may not be feasible in the absence of a face-to-face physical examination.

Prescribing and Health Information Exchange

Prescribing, particularly the prescription of controlled substances in the absence of a face-to-face relationship, is one of the practices most likely to give rise to liability (The Doctors Company, 2020). Collaborative care and coordination of care with the patient's other providers can help to mitigate such risks. States have established Prescription Drug Monitoring Programs (PDMPs) to track prescriptions for controlled substances, and physicians are typically expected to check the PDMP's database before prescribing controlled substances to a patient (Dike et al., 2019). Some commentators have expressed concern that heath information exchange (HIE) like PDMPs "may heighten clinicians' duties to search for patient information generated by other clinicians" (Mangalmurti et al., 2010, p. 2062). However, obtaining extensive medical records from previous treatment providers is not the current standard of care in outpatient psychiatry (Recupero & Harms, 2015). Rather, the Internet can help to facilitate care coordination between psychiatrists and patients' other clinicians, such as primary-care providers, ideally improving the quality of care that a patient receives and *lessening* the risk of adverse events that could lead to malpractice lawsuits. In psychiatry, special issues may be posed by patient access to clinical information within the electronic medical record. Although patients in the past could request access to their medical records, few patients did so in practice, whereas obtaining such access today can be accomplished with only a few clicks of a mouse or even via smartphone while the patient is awaiting an appointment.

Social Media

Social media platforms carry numerous legal and ethical risks for psychiatrists. Interacting with patients or their families through social networking sites or apps is rife with potential for boundary violations (see Chap. 14) (Gabbard et al., 2011), and using social media to discuss patient care involves significant risks to patient confidentiality, even when precautions are taken to enhance privacy. Sharing de-identified case information may lead to inadvertent breaches of confidentiality, for which doctors have been held liable (*In the matter of Thran*, 2011). One recent development in which psychiatrists should exercise caution is the growth in private professional interest groups on social media. Content shared to "private" groups on many SNS (social networking site) platforms remains within the control of the SNS developer or the company that owns the platform (Crotty & Mostaghimi, 2014).

Smartphone Apps and mHealth

Smartphone applications (apps) for mental health have proliferated in recent years (Terry & Wiley, 2016), and many patients already use such software. Physicians unfamiliar with their use, development, and diversity may view such apps as harmless and useful adjuncts to psychiatric care. However, most apps are developed with commercial interests at heart, not patient protection, and few employ evidence-based practices (Melcher & Torous, 2020; Torous & Roberts, 2017). Most of the top-ranking apps marketed for depression and smoking cessation, for example, share users' data with third parties such as Google and Facebook, but most fail to disclose this clearly in their privacy policies (Huckvale et al., 2019).

There are, however, some evidence-based mental health apps available, and psychiatrists can help to educate patients about their use, as well as the drawbacks to apps not grounded in empirical evidence. The American Psychiatric Association (APA) has developed an evaluation model for mHealth apps (https://www.psychiatry.org/psychiatrists/practice/mental-health-apps), and the APA's Ethics Committee has responded to member questions about ethical considerations in the use of mHealth apps (APA, 2020). Terry and Wiley (2016) note that a duty of care may be ascribed to healthcare professionals who participate in the development of mHealth apps or similar technology. If the psychiatrist is, in fact, involved in the development, marketing, or evaluation of an mHealth app, patients should be apprised of this fact during informed consent discussions (APA, 2020). Because mental health apps constitute new technology, "…there is no clear standard of care in these areas, and no specific case law has yet addressed this issue in the context of utilizing mobile apps as an adjunct to psychotherapy" (Edwards-Stewart et al., 2019, p. 283).

Patients' Internet Use

Even when treatment is not conducted via the Internet, a patient's Internet use can carry implications for the provider's risk of liability. At a minimum, some basic digital literacy can help to improve the psychiatrist's own privacy protection (Dixon et al., 2020). Conducting a therapeutic relationship over the Internet merits a higher level of digital literacy in both provider and patient. Especially helpful is some familiarity with common Internet abbreviations and conventions, such as the meanings of emoticons and emoji, which can be used to communicate suicidal or homicidal ideation.

Suicidal patients can easily find pro-suicide material and how-to suicide instructions on the Internet (Recupero, 2020; Recupero et al., 2008), and patients with substance use disorders can purchase drugs with abuse potential online (Klein & Kandel, 2011). Others, frustrated with the cost or side effects of prescribed medications, may purchase medications or supplements online to self-treat problematic symptoms (Coe et al., 2019; Mash & Leo, 2020). Medications ordinarily only available through a physician's prescription are also sold online, sometimes with minimal to no involvement or oversight by medical professionals (Klein, 2011). Many of these suppliers are located in foreign jurisdictions and may not be subject to the same regulatory requirements as domestic pharmacies (Klein, 2011). Failing to appreciate the severity of a patient's Internet gaming or other problematic Internet use (PIU) or the gravity of its implications for the patient's well-being can be another area of risk. Severe PIU shares similarities with other behavioral addictions and has been linked to suicidal and homicidal behavior (Recupero, 2008). Social media, in particular, may be risky for patients in acute mania or psychosis, as disinhibited or symptom-driven use of livestreaming or commenting can go viral quickly, potentially creating a damaging digital footprint.

Caution is warranted before using the Internet or social media to search for information about patients (Dike et al., 2019). Sometimes termed "patient-targeted Googling," such practices carry the potential for unforeseen ethical problems (APA, 2020; Dike et al., 2019). However, the use of patient-directed searches may be clinically appropriate in some cases, when it is performed for the patient's benefit and not the psychiatrist's curiosity (Ince et al., 2020).

Technological Failures, Errors, and Data Security

The potential for technological failures, such as the loss of a broadband Internet connection on either end, is a well-known drawback to the use of the Internet in psychiatry. The best way to mitigate this risk is advance planning for such contingencies. During initial intake, the psychiatrist can obtain phone numbers and other contact information for the patient and their local providers and caregivers in the event of lost Internet access, as well as information regarding rescue services in the patient's location, in case the patient becomes acutely suicidal or violent during Internet-based treatment.

Advanced technology, such as artificial intelligence (AI), carries special implications for malpractice (Price II et al., 2019). Some predictive analytics tools show promise for automated identification of patients at increased risk, potentially facilitating early intervention and averting adverse events. For example, machine learning and natural language processing (NLP) are currently being studied for the identification of psychosis, suicide, violence, and relapse risks (Edgcomb & Zima, 2019; Just et al., 2017; Koutsouleris et al., 2020 and Ni et al., 2020). However, the duty of care cannot be delegated to an algorithm, and psychiatrists retain responsibility for ensuring that patient care conforms to an acceptable standard of care. Speech-to-text transcription tools are limited, and transcription errors—on the physician's or the patient's end—as well as autocorrect-induced errors, may be common (Diwan, 2012). In one illustrative case, a physician accidentally prescribed Flomax to a female patient for whom he intended to prescribe Flonase (Troxel, n.d.).

Security problems and data breaches represent another area of technological failures and errors. The purveyors of the popular videoconferencing software, Zoom, were censured recently by the Federal Trade Commission for misleading consumers about the platform's security (In the matter of Zoom, 2020). Purchasing data-breach insurance may be one option to limit liability; some malpractice policies already include built-in data-breach coverage. Security tools such as two-factor authentication, encryption, advanced privacy settings, and secure patient portals help to reduce risk (Crotty & Mostaghimi, 2014; The Doctors Company, 2020). Physicians using the Internet in the course of patient care should maintain compliance with HIPAA regulations, such as by having software vendors sign business-associate agreements (Crotty & Mostaghimi, 2014). Elhai and Frueh (2016) provide an explanation of security risks associated with different forms of ICT (such as wireless networks), steps that can be taken to reduce risk, different types of encryption that may be available, instructions for accessing free and low-cost security-enhancing tools, and a review of the difficulty of installing and implementing specific security tools.

Informed Consent

Obtaining a patient's informed consent to the use of the Internet in psychiatric treatment confers some protection against liability (Edwards-Stewart et al., 2019). The standard by which the adequacy of informed consent is judged varies from state to state. At a minimum, patients should be warned about risks to confidentiality and shortcomings of Internet-based treatment. It bears noting that telepsychiatry, which enjoys a strong base of empirical support, is distinct from other Internet-based treatment modalities (e.g., e-therapy), which carry their own unique risks and benefits (Recupero & Rainey, 2005). ICT can enhance the informed consent process; for example, many videos for patient education are freely available online. Before using the Internet to communicate with patients, psychiatrists may wish to ask patients to sign a written agreement indicating their understanding and acceptance of relevant risks. However, agreements and disclaimers attempting to exculpate a psychiatrist from all liability may not be upheld by courts.

Conclusion

Helpful risk-management advice is typically available from medical malpractice insurance carriers (Recupero, 2018), who have a vested interest in reducing the likelihood of adverse outcomes and subsequent lawsuits. For example, one insurance provider recommends completing a Refusal-of-Care form when a patient is asked to come in for a face-to-face appointment but refuses to do so due to COVID-related fears or some other reason (The Doctors Company, 2020). Clinical practice guidelines (CPGs), resource documents, ethics opinions, and other resources from professional societies also contain valuable information about Internet-related risks and their mitigation. Such guidelines are available from the American College of Physicians (Farnan et al., 2013), the American Telemedicine Association (Shore et al., 2018), the Federation of State Medical Boards (Farnan et al., 2013), the APA (APA, 2020; Shore et al., 2018), and various subspecialty organizations, government agencies, and regulatory bodies like the Joint Commission, to name only a few.

Key Points

- The use of the Internet carries special implications for psychiatric malpractice.
- A psychiatrist-patient relationship and the corresponding duty of care can be established in the absence of in-person, face-to-face contact.
- Liability risk increases on a sliding scale with increasing levels of interaction between the psychiatrist and a prospective patient.
- There are risks as well as benefits associated with the use of the Internet in clinical psychiatry, and discussion of risks to patients should be included in informed-consent conversations.
- Several areas carry additional malpractice risk for psychiatrists who use the Internet in clinical practice, such as prescribing controlled substances, monitoring high-risk patients, and supervising subordinate workers.
- Legal issues, such as malpractice insurance coverage and assessment of damages, may be especially complex when the psychiatrist and patient are physically located in different jurisdictions.
- Psychiatrists should exercise care in the use of new technology, such as artificial intelligence (AI) tools, mobile health applications (apps), and social media; many popular apps have been created with minimal clinical oversight or scientific evidence, and many carry significant risks to privacy.
- Patients' Internet use may also carry implications for malpractice risk, and psychiatrists should endeavor to stay well-informed about the ways in which patients may be using the Internet, even when one is not providing any Internet-based services.

References

Ackerman, B. G. (2019, April 17). Is the doctor in? Medical malpractice issues in the age of telemedicine. *National Law Review, 9*, 107. https://www.natlawreview.com/article/doctor-medical-malpractice-issues-age-telemedicine. Accessed December 9, 2020.

American Psychiatric Association. (2020). Recent opinions of the APA Ethics Committee on *The Principles of Medical Ethics with Annotations Especially Applicable to Psychiatry* (2020). Washington, D.C.: American Psychiatric Association. https://www.psychiatry.org/File%20Library/Psychiatrists/Practice/Ethics/APA-Recent-Ethics-Opinions-2020.pdf. Accessed December 14, 2020.

Coe, M. A., Pillitteri, J. L., Sembower, M. A., Gerlach, K. K., & Henningfield, J. E. (2019). Kratom as a substitute for opioids: Results from an online survey. *Drug & Alcohol Dependence, 202*, 24–32.

Crotty, B. H., & Mostaghimi, A. (2014). Confidentiality in the digital age. *British Medical Journal, 347*, g2943. https://doi.org/10.1136/bmj.g2943

Dike, C. C., Candilis, P., Kocsis, B., Sidhu, N., & Recupero, P. R. (2019). Ethical considerations regarding internet searches for patient information. *Psychiatric Services, 70*(4), 324–328.

Diwan, R. M. (2012). Measuring malpractice in modern mobile medicine. *Virginia Journal of Social Policy & Law, 20*(2), 221–239.

Dixon, L. B., Adler, D. A., Berlant, J., et al. (2020). Managing our public selves. *Psychiatric Services, 71*(11), 1196–1198.

(The) Doctors Company. (2020). *Your patient is logging on now: The risks and benefits of telehealth in the future of healthcare*. Napa, CA: The Doctors Company. https://www.thedoctors.com/siteassets/pdfs/12482_telehealth_whitepaper_080420_f.pdf. Accessed December 14, 2020.

DrFirst. (2020, October 28). *DrFirst survey: 44% of Americans have used telehealth services during coronavirus pandemic but some admit not paying attention*. Rockville, MD: DrFirst. https://drfirst.com/press-releases/survey-44-americans-telehealth-coronavirus-pandemic/. Accessed December 21, 2020.

Edgcomb, J. B., & Zima, B. (2019). Machine learning, natural language processing, and the electronic health record: Innovations in mental health services research. *Psychiatric Services, 70*(4), 346–349.

Edwards-Stewart, A., Alexander, C., Armstrong, C. M., Hoyt, T., & O'Donohue, W. (2019). Mobile applications for client use: Ethical and legal considerations. *Psychological Services, 16*(2), 281–285.

Egelko, B. (2008, December 30). Father blames son's suicide on 'telemedicine.' *SF Gate*. https://www.sfgate.com/news/article/Father-blames-son-s-suicide-on-telemedicine-3178535.php. Accessed December 23, 2020.

Elhai, J. D., & Frueh, B. C. (2016). Security of electronic mental health communication and record-keeping in the digital age. *Journal of Clinical Psychiatry, 77*(2), 262–268.

Farnan, J. M., Sulmasy, L. S., Worster, B. K., et al. (2013). Online medical professionalism: Patient and public relationships: Policy statement from the American College of Physicians and the Federation of State Medical Boards. *Annals of Internal Medicine, 158*(8), 620–627.

Fogel, A. L., & Kvedar, J. C. (2019). Reported cases of medical malpractice in direct-to-consumer telemedicine. *JAMA, 321*(13), 1309.

Friedman, S. H., Appel, J. M., Ash, P., Frierson, R. L., Giorgi-Guarnieri, D., Martinez, R., et al. (2016). Unsolicited e-mails to forensic psychiatrists. *Journal of the American Academy of Psychiatry and the Law, 44*(4), 470–478.

Gabbard, G. O., Kassaw, K. A., & Perez-Garcia, G. (2011). Professional boundaries in the era of the internet. *Academic Psychiatry, 35*(3), 168–174.

Hageseth v. The Superior Court of San Mateo County, 150 Cal. App. 4th 1399, 59 Cal. Rptr.3d 385 (Cal. Ct. App. 2007).

Hilty, D., Chan, S., Torous, J., Luo, J., & Boland, R. (2020). A framework for competencies for the use of mobile technologies in psychiatry and medicine: Scoping review. *JMIR mHealth & uHealth, 8*(2), e2229. https://doi.org/10.2196/12229

Huckvale, K., Torous, J., & Larsen, M. E. (2019). Assessment of the data sharing and privacy practices of smartphone apps for depression and smoking cessation. *JAMA Network Open, 2*(4), e192542. https://doi.org/10.1001/jamanetworkopen.2019.2542

In the matter of Alexandra Thran, M.D., No. C10-156, Consent Order, April 13, 2011 (State of Rhode Island Department of Health, Board of Medical Licensure and Discipline).

In the matter of the licenses of Paul M. Gahlinger to practice as a physician/surgeon and to prescribe and administer controlled substance in the state of Utah, No. DOPL 2014-329, Stipulation and Order, July 21, 2014a. https://dopl.utah.gov/orders/2014-329_SO_2014-07-21.pdf. Accessed December 1, 2020.

In the matter of the licenses of Paul M. Gahlinger, MD, to practice as a physician/surgeon and to administer and prescribe controlled substances in the state of Utah, No. DOPL 2014-329, Emergency Order, July 8, 2014b. https://dopl.utah.gov/orders/2014-329_EO_2014-07-08.pdf. Accessed December 1, 2020.

In the matter of Zoom Video Communications, Inc., No. 192 3167. Agreement containing consent order. https://www.ftc.gov/system/files/documents/cases/1923167zoomacco2.pdf. Accessed December 21, 2020.

Ince, H. Y., Streeter, C. C., Maksimowski, M., & Garakani, A. (2020). Window to his world: Using a patient's YouTube channel to help diagnose chronic mania. *Journal of Psychiatric Practice, 26*(4), 324–328.

Just, M. A., Pan, L., Cherkassky, V. L., et al. (2017). Machine learning of neural representations of suicide and emotion concepts identifies suicidal youth. *Nature Human Behavior, 1*, 911–919.

Klein, C. A. (2011). Psychotropics without borders: Ethics and legal implications of internet-based access to psychiatric medications. *Journal of the American Academy of Psychiatry and the Law, 39*(1), 104–111.

Klein, C. A., & Kandel, S. (2011). www.mydrugdealer.com: Ethics and legal implications of internet-based access to substances of abuse. *Journal of the American Academy of Psychiatry and the Law, 39*(3), 407–411.

Koutsouleris, N., Dwyer, D. B., Degenhardt, F., et al. (2020). Multimodal machine learning workflows for prediction of psychosis in patients with clinical high-risk syndromes and recent-onset depression. *JAMA Psychiatry*, ePub online ahead of print, December 2, 2020; https://doi.org/10.1001/jamapsychiatry.2020.3604

Mangalmurti, S. S., Murtagh, L., & Mello, M. M. (2010). Medical malpractice liability in the age of electronic health records. *New England Journal of Medicine, 363*(21), 2060–2067.

Mash, J. E., & Leo, R. J. (2020). Phenibut: A novel nootropic with abuse potential. *Primary Care Companion to CNS Disorders, 22*(4), 19l02587. https://doi.org/10.4088/PCC.19l02587

Melcher, J., & Torous, J. (2020). Smartphone apps for college mental health: A concern for privacy and quality of current offerings. *Psychiatric Services, 71*(11), 1114–1119.

Ni, Y., Barzman, D., Bachtel, A., Griffey, M., Osborn, A., & Sorter, M. (2020). Finding warning markers: Leveraging natural language processing and machine learning technologies to detect risk of school violence. *International Journal of Medical Informatics, 139*, 104137. https://doi.org/10.1016/j.ijmedinf.2020.104137

Price, W. N., II, Gerke, S., & Cohen, I. G. (2019). Potential liability for physicians using artificial intelligence. *Journal of the American Medical Association, 322*(18), 765–1766.

Recupero, P. R. (2005). E-mail and the psychiatrist-patient relationship. *Journal of the American Academy of Psychiatry and the Law, 33*(4), 465–475.

Recupero, P. R. (2006). Legal concerns for psychiatrists who maintain web sites. *Psychiatric Services, 57*(4), 450–452.

Recupero, P. R. (2008). Forensic evaluation of problematic internet use. *Journal of the American Academy of Psychiatry and the Law, 36*(4), 505–514.

Recupero, P. R. (2018). The internet and telepsychiatry. In L. H. Gold, R. L. Frierson, & R. I. Simon (Eds.), *Textbook of forensic psychiatry* (3rd ed., pp. 347–360). American Psychiatric Publishing.

Recupero, P. R. (2020). Social media and the internet. In L. H. Gold & R. L. Frierson (Eds.), *Textbook of suicide assessment and management* (3rd ed., pp. 355–368). American Psychiatric Publishing.

Recupero, P. R., & Harms, S. E. (2015). Outpatient psychiatrists' practices for requesting prior treatment records. *Journal of the American Academy of Psychiatry and the Law, 43*(4), 444–450.

Recupero, P. R., Harms, S. E., & Noble, J. M. (2008). Googling suicide: Surfing for suicide information on the internet. *Journal of Clinical Psychiatry, 69*(6), 878–888.

Recupero, P. R., & Rainey, S. E. (2005). Informed consent to e-therapy. *American Journal of Psychotherapy, 59*(4), 319–331.

Schultz, K., Sandhu, S., & Kealy, D. (2020). Primary care and suicidality among psychiatric outpatients: The patient-doctor relationship matters. *International Journal of Psychiatry in Medicine*; ePub online ahead of print, November 29, 2020; https://doi.org/10.1177/0091217420977994

Serri, T. (2016). An examination of the impact of malpractice law on telepsychiatry clinicians & clients with suicidal ideations. *Akron Law Review, 50*(4), 933–964.

Shore, J. H. (2020). Managing virtual hybrid psychiatrist-patient relationships in a digital world. *JAMA Psychiatry, 77*(5), 541–542.

Shore, J. H., Yellowlees, P., Caudill, R., et al. (2018). Best practices in videoconferencing-based telemental health. *Telemedicine Journal & e-Health, 24*(11), 827–832.

Smith, H., & Fotheringham, K. (2020). Artificial intelligence in clinical decision-making: Rethinking liability. *Medical Law International, 20*(2), 131–154.

Terry, N. P., & Wiley, L. F. (2016). Liability for mobile health and wearable technologies. *Annals of Health Law, 25*, 62–97.

Torous, J., & Roberts, L. W. (2017). Needed innovation in digital health and smartphone applications for mental health: Transparency and trust. *JAMA Psychiatry, 74*(5), 437–438.

Troxel, D. B. (n.d.). *Electronic health record closed claims study: An expert analysis of medical malpractice allegations*. The Doctors Company.

White v. Harris, No.10-246, 36 A.3d 203 (Vt. 2011).

Practicing During Disasters and Public Health Emergencies

32

Kaustubh G. Joshi

Threats to human health can come from various disaster scenarios, including infectious diseases (e.g., COVID-19), environmental phenomena (e.g., hurricanes, floods, earthquakes, forest fires), or man-made disasters (e.g., industrial accidents, wars, terrorist attacks). These scenarios create the possibility that the demand for mental health resources will exceed capacity such that hospitals and clinics will be unable to meet the mental health needs of the affected communities. Disasters and the resulting demand for mental health services also create challenges in meeting legal obligations related to psychiatric practice (e.g., meeting standards of care, having the authority to prescribe medications, or maintaining patient confidentiality).

Psychiatrists practicing in these difficult times may be concerned about failing to meet these legal obligations and the resulting civil or criminal liability. Ideally, all psychiatrists (those who live and work in the disaster area as well as volunteers from other states) would be able to care for patients without fear of facing unreasonable liability risks. However, psychiatrists' concern or confusion about various legal protections, or lack of thereof, during disasters and public health emergencies may interfere with their responsiveness and willingness to offer their services; thus, the need for legal clarity is crucial to their provision of assistance during disasters and public health emergencies (Pope & Palazzo, 2010).

Liability Concerns

Liability risks exist with all psychiatric scenarios, especially when there is a suboptimal or an unanticipated outcome. Disasters and public health emergencies can result in limited choices for both patients and psychiatrists. Patient preferences for specific healthcare options may carry less weight, and providers may have fewer treatment options available to them (Altman et al., 2019).

There are three broad categories of potential liability claims during disasters and public health emergencies: suboptimal medical care (e.g., negligence, abandonment, lack of informed consent), a regulatory or administrative breach (e.g., practicing without proper state licenses, Emergency Medical Treatment and Active Labor Act (EMTALA) violation, Health Insurance Portability and Accountability Act (HIPAA) Privacy Rule violation), and wanton behavior (e.g., criminal acts) (Altman et al., 2019). Other types of potential claims include constitutional violations (e.g., equal protection claims) and lack of preparedness for emergencies (Altman et al., 2019). Denial of treatment in a routine healthcare environment may increase the chance of being sued; however, malpractice claims for denial of treatment after disasters are infrequent (Altman et al., 2019). Evidence suggests that during disasters, healthcare providers at greatest risk of being sued are those who live and work in the disaster-affected area and report to work instead of evacuating (Altman et al., 2019; Courtney & Hodge, 2011; Pou, 2013).

Negligence

Changes in the usual standard of practice in psychiatry may be necessary to save as many lives as possible during disasters and public health emergencies. When providing care, the legal standard of care is generally based on what a reasonable provider of the same specialty would do in similar circumstances (Lambert & Wertheimer, 2017). During a disaster or public health emergency, the psychiatrists' actions are judged by evaluating whether the psychiatrist acted consistently with how a reasonable psychiatrist in a similar situation would have acted (Lambert & Wertheimer, 2017). During major emergencies when resources are scarce, the focus of mental health services shifts from individualized

K. G. Joshi (✉)
Department of Neuropsychiatry and Behavioral Science, University of South Carolina School of Medicine, Columbia, SC, USA
e-mail: kaustubh.joshi@uscmed.sc.edu

P. Ash et al. (eds.), *Malpractice and Liability in Psychiatry*, https://doi.org/10.1007/978-3-030-91975-7_32

patient care to providing essential services to those most in need among vulnerable populations (Hodge et al., 2010). Due to a lack of time and/or available resources, psychiatrists may provide treatment that is different from that which the "reasonably prudent" psychiatrist would normally provide (Pope & Palazzo, 2010). Defining what a reasonable psychiatrist would do in an emergency is difficult when access to and the use of resources differ even within the same locality (Hodge & Courtney, 2010).

Psychiatrists may have to provide emergent medical care which may result in an adverse outcome (e.g., applying a tourniquet to a patient's badly injured limb without the patient's consent but then the patient later loses that limb, or prescribing an antibiotic to prevent sepsis but then the patient develops anaphylaxis). These scenarios for example could give rise to ordinary negligence claims of practicing outside the usual scope of practice, especially for clinicians and healthcare entities lacking immunity during disasters and public health emergencies. These clinicians and healthcare entities may be unsure how courts may judge their actions if patients are harmed as a result of shifts to the standards of care during such emergencies. Assessing legal standards of care is inherently patient-centered, subject to considerable discretion by adjudicators, and highly variable (Hodge & Courtney, 2010). Fortunately, medical malpractice claims have not typically multiplied in emergencies (Hodge & Courtney, 2010).

In such a malpractice case, providing evidence that a reasonable psychiatrist would have made similar decisions in a disaster environment becomes more difficult. Real-time documentation of medical decision-making, a primary defense for psychiatrists' actions, could be affected because, for example, a lack of electricity renders the electronic medical record (EMR) inoperable; however, psychiatrists could consider writing on paper and then transferring to the EMR once the EMR is back online. For similar reasons, prior medical records may not be available for review, and this may impact the care provided. Additionally, environmental conditions may rapidly change such that it is impossible to maintain the usual level of information sharing, communication, and collaboration with patients when healthcare decisions must be made (Altman et al., 2019). These factors can contribute to the perception of suboptimal care. In addition, determining what a "reasonable and prudent" practitioner would do under similar circumstances can be difficult to assess in crises as the standards of care may change frequently to address communal needs (Hodge et al., 2010). Deviation from the normal standard of care need not give rise to malpractice liability during disasters and public health emergencies; however, the standard of care in emergency situations is open to interpretation (Pope & Palazzo, 2010).

Practicing Without Proper State Licensure and Improper Prescribing

Liability for practicing without a properly recognized state medical license can occur when out-of-state providers show up at an unfamiliar facility that needs emergency manpower (Altman et al., 2019). As care is deemed to have been provided where the patient was physically present when services were provided, liability can also occur when providing services to patients who have been displaced to a different state where the psychiatrist does not have a medical license (e.g. a psychiatrist in South Carolina continues to have telehealth appointments with a college student who returns home to Georgia due to COVID-19 restrictions on campus, but that psychiatrist does not have a Georgia medical license). During COVID-19, many states modified licensing requirements to allow for emergency licensing of qualified medical personnel (Federation of State Medical Boards, 2020).

The federal Social Security Act allows for the modification of state licensing requirements; however, the modification of licensure requirements is primarily a matter for the individual states (Pope & Palazzo, 2010). Clinicians can usually avail themselves of each state's medical licensing requirements by reviewing that state's medical board website. Numerous legal provisions facilitate the emergency deployment of healthcare providers and allow them to temporarily practice and prescribe medications in the state experiencing the emergency. For example, once a state's governor declares an official state of emergency, certain licensure waiver or reciprocity laws become active (Rukow et al., 2011).

For example, the Emergency Management Assistance Compact (EMAC), which all states have joined, allows healthcare providers licensed in one state to provide care in the state affected by the emergency (Emergency Management Assistance Compact, 2020). This also includes the ability to write prescriptions, consistent with the terms of the psychiatrist's licensure (Rukow et al., 2011). However, the EMAC generally applies to state and local government agents, and not psychiatrists practicing in private facilities (Rukow et al., 2011). Many states have enacted laws to allow out-of-state psychiatrists to practice and, when appropriate, to prescribe medications during an emergency. For example, some states have enacted laws waiving licensure requirements for psychiatrists serving in the affected jurisdiction as long as they are properly licensed in their home state (Rukow et al., 2011). Other states have enacted laws allowing registered volunteer healthcare providers to offer their services during a declared disaster through a local host organization (Rukow et al., 2011). Federal healthcare providers licensed in any state are authorized to practice and prescribe in any federal facility (e.g., Veterans Affairs hospital) before, during, and after emergencies, thus allowing for quicker mobilization and facilitation of their abilities to reach those affected populations (Rukow et al., 2011).

During emergencies, psychiatrists must adhere to federal and state laws that regulate prescribing medications. The ultimate authority to prescribe medications is granted by the state where the provider is licensed. In emergencies, if providing care in a different state, prescribing laws remains in effect unless they are temporarily suspended or altered by federal/state emergency declaration. These laws contain limited emergency provisions, which may facilitate the prescription and dispensing of certain psychotropic medications to individuals who depend on these medications to treat a chronic mental health condition (Rukow et al., 2011). Despite systems in place that allow for prescribing during emergencies, psychiatrists may have to juggle complying with emergency laws once they are activated and simultaneously adhering to "nonemergency" laws that can remain in place during emergencies (Rukow et al., 2011). For example, some states have laws prohibiting healthcare providers from writing prescriptions for individuals they have not examined or with whom they have not established a doctor-patient relationship. During an emergency in these states, especially if the demand for mental health services is high and there is a shortage of mental health providers, these providers will have a limited time to take a history, reach a diagnosis, and determine whether they need to prescribe medications. Unless states waive this provision of the law, psychiatrists will have to determine, on a case-by-case basis, whether they have had sufficient opportunity to examine an individual and establish a doctor-patient relationship in accordance with the state's law before they can prescribe medications (Rukow et al., 2011).

Abandonment, Informed Consent, HIPAA Privacy Rule Breach, and the Duty to Warn and Protect

When a psychiatrist takes an affirmative step to provide care to an individual, it may create a physician-patient relationship and a duty on behalf of the psychiatrist within the applicable standard of care (Lambert & Wertheimer, 2017). In disasters, the usual expectations and parameters associated with physician-patient relationships can change. Psychiatrists may have to cease treating some patients so that they can focus their time or resources elsewhere; this could open up liability concerns regarding claims of abandonment (Altman et al., 2019). At times, psychiatrists may refuse to treat patients outright, creating conflicts with the Emergency Medical Treatment and Active Labor Act (EMTALA) and its state counterparts.

During emergencies, informed consent standards remain in place, but the requirement may be adjusted (Lambert & Wertheimer, 2017). Informed consent requirements may be reassessed to enable effective delivery of emergency mental health services and oral consent may supplant a written consent.

Patients' protected health information could be more easily compromised during crises. A lack of electricity or destroyed equipment may render normally protected modes of communication and documentation inoperable, increasing the chances of unintentional leaks or public exposure of protected health information (Altman et al., 2019). Rationing resources, arranging transportation, or making evacuation decisions, especially for patients with special needs, are moments vulnerable to potential privacy breaches (Altman et al., 2019).

Psychiatric patients sometimes make threats toward third parties that could potentially result in harm. In some state jurisdictions, psychiatrists have a duty to warn third parties of potential harm, while other state laws include a duty to protect. If there is a duty to warn, it may include the use of certain measures, such as notifying the intended victim or reporting a dangerous person to the police. In disaster conditions, psychiatrists may find it difficult to meet this duty due to difficulty assessing an individual's "dangerousness" for a variety of reasons: a lack of prior information/medical history, unavailability of law enforcement officials, and inability to locate the intended victim (Lambert & Wertheimer, 2017) if there has been evacuation or displacement of persons. Due to a lack of hospital beds and other resources during disasters, it may be difficult for psychiatrists to hospitalize patients and thereby meet their duty to protect third parties from harm by their patients.

Immunity from Liability

Psychiatrists should feel comfortable serving in expanded capacities on the frontlines of disasters and public health emergencies. As such, they need to be shielded from medical tort liability. There are no comprehensive national liability protections for all healthcare providers during disasters and public health emergencies (Altman et al., 2019). In addition to the Federal Torts Claim Act and state tort laws, limited immunity is often provided through a patchwork of additional federal and state laws and regulations. This immunity depends upon several factors such as applicable regulations, nature of the services provided, and whether healthcare professionals are volunteering their services (i.e., they are not being paid for providing their services) (Lambert & Wertheimer, 2017). These federal and state laws can be complex and are frequently modified. Despite these liability protections, there is usually no immunity due to willful or wanton acts, gross negligence, providing care while intoxicated, or criminal acts (Lambert & Wertheimer, 2017).

Federal Laws, Declarations, and Waivers

Most of the laws providing liability protections are triggered once a disaster or public health emergency is declared. Additional federal laws can be enacted that provide additional liability protections, especially to volunteers. The main federal law involving public health emergencies is the Public Health Service Act (PHSA) (Public Health Service Act of 1944). This Act authorizes the US Department of Health and Human Services (HHS) Secretary to declare a public health emergency, activating the Secretary's emergency powers to provide states with resources and personnel to respond to the emergency and to waive or modify certain legal requirements. A public health emergency declared under PHSA is separate and distinct from a presidential declaration of emergency under the National Emergencies Act (National Emergencies Act of 1976) or from a gubernatorial request to the President for a declaration of emergency under the Stafford Act (Stafford Disaster Relief and Emergency Assistance Act of 1988). PHSA does not contain immunity or liability protections; however, the determination of a public health emergency is a prerequisite for the activation of liability provisions in other laws, such as the Public Readiness and Emergency Preparedness (PREP) Act (Public Readiness and Emergency Preparedness Act of 2005). The PREP Act provides broad immunity to volunteer health professionals (VHPs) who administer or use countermeasures covered by declarations issued by the HHS Secretary, such as the declaration issued during the COVID-19 pandemic for certain medical products to be used against this illness (US Department of Health and Human Services, 2020). However, PREP Act immunity is not absolute.

When the President declares a major disaster or an emergency under the Stafford Act or an emergency under the National Emergencies Act and the HHS Secretary declares a public health emergency, the HHS Secretary can authorize waivers under Section 1135 of the Social Security Act (called "1135 waivers") to waive or modify certain EMTALA, Medicare, Medicaid, state licensure, and HIPAA requirements, as determined by the Centers for Medicare and Medicaid Services (CMS) (US Department of Health and Human Services, 2019). These waivers or modifications allow providers, who provide services in good faith during an emergency when they may be unable to comply with normal statutory requirements, to be reimbursed and exempted from sanctions (absent fraud or abuse) (Altman et al., 2019). Additionally, 1135 waivers are effective for only a set period of time; therefore, responders whose efforts precede or exceed the time of period of formal declaration may be left unprotected (Altman et al., 2019). CMS may grant "blanket" waivers to all similarly impacted providers in the disaster area depending on the scope, severity, and duration of the disaster (Altman et al., 2019). The 1135 waivers only apply to federal program requirements (e.g., Medicare and Medicaid). State law and gubernatorial authority determine state modifications to professional licensure requirements, credentialing or privileging at certain facilities, and authorization for emergency protections for certain healthcare providers (Altman et al., 2019).

Outside of disasters and public health emergencies, there are two standing volunteer liability reform laws to prevent medical tort liability from deterring volunteer health professionals (VHPs): Health Insurance Portability and Accountability Act (HIPAA) (Health Insurance Portability and Accountability Act of 1996) and Volunteer Protection Act (VPA) (Volunteer Protection Act of 1997). HIPAA, specifically Section 194, extends eligibility for Federal Tort Claims Act liability protections to VHPs at qualifying free clinics, provided the clinic sponsors the VHPs by submitting an application to the Health Resources and Services Administration (American Medical Association, 2020).

VPA provides liability protections to VHPs who are performing services for nonprofit organizations or government entities (American Medical Association, 2020). These protections apply to uncompensated volunteers for acts of ordinary negligence committed within the scope of their responsibilities. They are not liable for economic damages caused by providing medical care within the scope of their volunteer responsibilities although this exemption does not extend to noneconomic damages, e.g., losses for physical and emotional pain, suffering, and mental anguish (Volunteer Protection Act of 1997). VPA only protects VHPs practicing with a license as required by the law in the state where the harm occurred, unless state authorities allow for licensure exceptions. VPA preempts state laws that are inconsistent with VPA, unless those state laws provide greater liability protection for VHPs (American Medical Association, 2020). However, VPA protections are limited. For example, VPA protects only volunteers, not healthcare providers working in their regular nonemergency roles and capacities (Pope & Palazzo, 2010). A nonprofit or government agent can still bring civil claims against VHPs (Pope & Palazzo, 2010). VPA does not preempt certain state laws that put conditions on volunteers such as risk management requirements, vicarious liability, and a financially secure form of recovery for intended victims (Pope & Palazzo, 2010).

State Laws

States have a variety of liability protections that could apply to physicians providing care in an emergency, especially those serving as volunteers. All 50 states and the District of Columbia have enacted Good Samaritan laws. These laws, which do not need an official declaration of an emergency in order to be applicable, generally protect VHPs from liability when volunteering in good faith and without compensation at the scene of an emergency (Lambert & Wertheimer, 2017). Good Samaritan protections may also apply to care provided by VHPs in a hospital if VHPs are not on duty and do not charge a fee (Lambert & Wertheimer, 2017). However, the effect and scope of Good Samaritan laws vary dramatically from state to state. Some states include hospital settings as an emergency scene in their statutes, while others expressly exclude hospitals from their statutes (Pope & Palazzo, 2010). There are states that only include declared emergencies, while other states' statutes are drawn to broadly cover all emergency situations (Pope & Palazzo, 2010).

There are limitations to Good Samaritan laws. Many Good Samaritan statutes only apply to volunteers, and not all states have statutes that allow healthcare providers to be designated as such (Pope & Palazzo, 2010). Therefore, receiving compensation would take a provider outside the scope of the statute. Most states only shield action taken at the scene of an accident. Thus, immunity would not extend to a hospital emergency room, or in the aftermath of an emergency, as normal conditions slowly return (Pope & Palazzo, 2010). Therefore, Good Samaritan liability protection would apply to the more common scenario of assisting at the scene of a car crash, but not necessarily to treating individuals in the emergency department after a hurricane or during a pandemic (Pope & Palazzo, 2010). Furthermore, state laws vary considerably on what constitutes "good faith" and "without compensation," that is, whether protection applies for a provider who is otherwise salaried in a regular job (Altman et al., 2019).

Some states extend various liability protections to care provided by VHPs, often as part of an official response, in public health emergencies, states of emergencies, or other state-declared disaster proclamations issued by governors (American Medical Association, 2020). State laws also provide liability protections for VHPs providing care in a free clinic, nonprofit hospital, nonprofit organization, or as part of a government organization (American Medical Association, 2020). Volunteer protection statutes do not require an emergency declaration and may protect volunteers working on behalf of nonprofit and governmental entities from liability when responding to an emergency or disaster situation (Lambert & Wertheimer, 2017).

States have enacted Compact or Uniform laws, which include liability protections for volunteers responding to a declared emergency across state lines (American Medical Association, 2020). These protections are not automatic and are limited in their applicability. For example, the Emergency Management Assistance Compact (EMAC) only becomes effective once a state of emergency has been declared. The EMAC provides immunity to officers from the state that is rendering aid to the state requesting aid, in which officers are considered agents of the requesting state for tort liability and immunity purposes (American Medical Association, 2020). These individuals will not be liable for acts or omissions rendered in good faith; however, EMAC does not provide liability protection for actions constituting willful misconduct, gross negligence, or recklessness (Pope & Palazzo, 2010). For EMAC protections to apply, a state must make a request to another state(s) through EMAC, and such request must be formally accepted by the rendering state (American Medical Association, 2020). Of note, the EMAC does not require participating states to actually provide aid (Emergency Management Assistance Compact, 2020).

The Uniform Emergency Volunteer Health Practitioner Act (UEVHPA) allows state governments to give reciprocity to other states' licensees during a declared emergency so that covered individuals may provide emergency health services without meeting the disaster state's licensing requirements (Uniform Law Commission, 2020). Since 2007, the UEVHPA has been enacted in 17 states, the District of Columbia, and US Virgin Islands (Uniform Law Commission, 2020). This Act grants immunity from civil liability to out-of-state licensed health professionals for gratuitous care provided in a declared emergency (American Medical Association, 2020). There are limitations to whom UEVHPA applies, including out-of-state physicians who have registered in advance or during an emergency (American Medical Association, 2020).

Some states have crafted executive orders that are put into effect during a disaster or public health emergency. Most of these executive orders, which can include extending liability protections, are similar to what other states have done by adopting the model acts referenced above (Pope & Palazzo, 2010). These orders are not actual laws but only become effective when the governor signs them at the time of the disaster or public health emergency. They are also time-limited and must be reissued in subsequent disasters and public health emergencies.

Non-Volunteer Healthcare Providers

Non-volunteer (salaried or paid) healthcare providers are more likely to bear the brunt of providing care during a disaster or public health emergency, especially in the early stages before VHPs arrive. However, legislation does not address the associated disproportionate liability risk burden of non-volunteer healthcare providers (Altman et al., 2019; Hodge et al., 2009). In contrast to volunteers and government employees, non-volunteer providers performing their regular job duties during a disaster or public health emergency are generally not provided immunity from negligence by most legislation

(Altman et al., 2019; Pope & Palazzo, 2010). One exception is the PREP Act, which provides immunity for all providers from claims that may arise from dispensing a specific countermeasure during a declared public health emergency (Altman et al., 2019; Public Readiness and Emergency Preparedness Act of 2005). Some states have enacted the Model State Emergency Health Powers Act, which may offer immunity from negligence if the non-volunteer healthcare provider is rendering care under contract with or at the request of a state (Altman et al., 2019). However, non-volunteer healthcare providers who practice from their office or a local hospital will not receive protection through these laws (Altman et al., 2019). Good Samaritan laws may not apply unless care is provided at a scene of an emergency.

A small number of states have attempted to bridge this legislative gap by enacting laws that provide immunity more broadly for healthcare providers, regardless of volunteer or compensation status (Altman et al., 2019). Elements of these states' laws include acting in response to a declared emergency or disaster in which there is a recognized depletion of resources attributable to the disaster, at express or implied request of the state government, and consistent with emergency plans (Altman et al., 2019).

Conclusion

Disasters and public health emergencies create the high likelihood that the demand for mental health resources will exceed capacity such that the mental health needs of the affected communities may not be met. This surge also creates challenges in meeting legal obligations related to practicing psychiatry. There are increased potential liability risks when attempting to treat patients during disasters or public health emergencies; however, statutory protections that prevent liability may be enacted when a government official (e.g., state governor) declares an official state of emergency. Although there are federal and state laws that provide healthcare providers protections from liability during these situations, there is a discrepancy in the protections afforded non-volunteer healthcare providers compared to volunteer healthcare providers. The most important step to reducing liability risk for providers during a disaster or public health emergency, regardless of the type and location of practice, is to remain informed and stay prepared (Altman et al., 2019).

Key Points

- The resulting demand in mental health needs during disasters and public health emergencies can create challenges in meeting legal obligations related to practicing psychiatry.
- Suboptimal medical care, regulatory/administrative breaches, and wanton behavior are three board categories of potential liability claims.
- There are no national comprehensive national liability protections for all healthcare providers during disasters and public health emergencies.
- Limited immunity is often provided through a patchwork of federal and state laws and regulations.
- There is a discrepancy in the protections afforded non-volunteer healthcare providers compared to volunteer healthcare providers.

References

Altman, R. L., Santucci, K. A., Anderson, M. R., & McDonnell, W. M. (2019). American Academy of Pediatrics Committee on Medical Liability and Risk Management. Understanding liability risks and protections for pediatric providers during disasters. *Pediatrics, 143*(3), e20183893.

American Medical Association. (2020). Liability protections for health care professionals during COVID-19. Retrieved from https://www.ama-assn.org/practice-management/sustainability/liability-protections-health-care-professionals-during-covid-19

Courtney, B., & Hodge, J. G. (2011). For the Pediatric Emergency Mass Critical Care Task Force. Legal considerations during pediatric emergency mass critical care events. *Pediatric Critical Care Medicine, 12*(6 Supplement), S152–S156.

Emergency Management Assistance Compact (EMAC). (2020). Retrieved from https://www.emacweb.org/

Federation of State Medical Boards. (2020). U.S. States and Territories Modifying Licensure Requirements for Physicians in Response to COVID-19. Retrieved from https://www.fsmb.org/siteassets/advocacy/pdf/state-emergency-declarations-licensures-requirementscovid-19.pdf

Health Insurance Portability and Accountability Act. (1996). Pub. L. 104–191, 110 Stat. 1936.

Hodge, J. G., & Courtney, B. (2010). Assessing the legal standard of care in public health emergencies. *Journal of American Medical Association, 303*(4), 361–362.

Hodge, J. G., Garcia, A. M., Anderson, E. D., & Kaufman, T. (2009). Emergency legal preparedness for hospitals and health care personnel. *Disaster Medicine and Public Health Preparedness, 3*(2 Supplement), S37–S44.

Hodge, J. G., Rutkow, L., & Corcoran, A. J. (2010). Mental and behavioral health legal preparedness in major emergencies. *Public Health Reports, 125*(5), 759–762.

Lambert, K., & Wertheimer, M. (2017). American Professional Agency: Risk management in disaster response. Retrieved from https://www.aacap.org/App_Themes/AACAP/Docs/resource_centers/disaster/resource_group/resources/orgs/RMDisasterResp.pdf

National Emergencies Act of 1976. Pub. L. 94–412, 90 Stat. 1255.

Pope, T. M., & Palazzo, M. F. (2010). Legal briefing: Crisis standards of care and legal protections during disasters and emergencies. *The Journal of Clinical Ethics, 21*(4), 358–367.

Pou, A. M. (2013). Ethical and legal challenges in disaster medicine: Are you ready? *Southern Medical Journal, 106*(1), 27–30.

Public Health Service Act of 1944. Pub. L. 78–410, 58 Stat. 682.

Public Readiness and Emergency Preparedness Act of 2005. Pub. L. 109–148, 119 Stat. 2818.

Rukow, L., Vernick, J. S., Wissow, L. S., et al. (2011). Prescribing authority during emergencies: Challenges for mental healthcare providers. *Journal of Legal Medicine, 32*(3), 249–260.

Stafford Disaster Relief and Emergency Assistance Act of 1988. Pub. L. 100–707, 102 Stat. 4689.

Uniform Law Commission. (2020). Emergency Volunteer Health Practitioners Act. Retrieved at https://www.uniformlaws.org/committees/community-home?CommunityKey=565933ce-965f-4d3c-9c90-b00246f30f2d

US Department of Health and Human Services. (2019). 1135 Waivers. Retrieved from https://www.phe.gov/Preparedness/legal/Pages/1135-waivers.aspx

US Department of Health and Human Services. (2020). Declaration under the public readiness and emergency preparedness act for medical countermeasures against COVID-19. *Federal Register, 85*(52), 15198–15203.

Volunteer Protection Act of 1997. Pub. L. 105–19, 111 Stat. 221.

Part VI

Complaints

Medical Board Complaints

33

Jacqueline Landess and Brian Holoyda

Dr. David Israelstam was licensed to practice psychiatry for over 30 years when he encountered problems with the state medical board (SMB) (State of Wisconsin Medical Examining Board, 2011). Dr. Israelstam was seeing a woman for monthly medication management. She intentionally overdosed on medication and was hospitalized. Dr. Israelstam visited the patient while she was hospitalized, discussed her history of sexual abuse, and hugged her. In a later interview with the patient, he also discussed his relationship problems with women in his life and discussed the patient's sexuality. Due to these behaviors, the SMB reprimanded Dr. Israelstam and required him to complete a program addressing patient-provider boundaries.

Ten years later, he once again encountered the SMB after a complaint was filed alleging that he asked a female patient if she wanted to have a sexual relationship with another man who had Asperger's disorder. The female patient was under guardianship and had a history of post-traumatic stress disorder, intellectual disability, and other psychiatric problems. Dr. Israelstam ultimately stipulated to disciplinary actions in this matter, including a fine and training on professional boundaries (Wisconsin Medical Examining Board, 2011). Unfortunately, Dr. Israelstam's contacts with the SMB were not over. Several years following this incident, he was charged and then convicted of possession of child pornography (Cullen, 2013). He voluntarily surrendered his license at that time.

Dr. Israelstam's story highlights the typical disciplinary and regulatory functions of a SMB. He also fits a general profile of those most likely to be disciplined: male gender, involvement in direct patient care, and in practice for longer than 20 years (Morrison & Wickersham, 1998). However, one might argue that the SMB's investigation and actions were not harsh enough earlier, and perhaps Dr. Israelstam's child pornography problem could have been discovered sooner. On the other hand, this case also touches on the tension between the SMB's various missions of protecting the public from unprofessional conduct of physicians and maintaining an appropriate scope of authority and discipline while respecting physicians' legal rights.

History of SMBs

The first SMBs were established in the mid-1800s and legitimized by a Supreme Court decision in 1889 which upheld West Virginia's medical practice act as constitutional (*Dent v. West Virginia*, 1889). In subsequent decisions, the Court relied on state precedent to emphasize the importance of and constitutional basis for SMB authority, citing the state's police powers under the tenth Amendment to protect the public from "ignorant pretenders and charlatans" and "incapacity as well as deception and fraud" (*Hawker v. New York*, 1898, p. 195).

By 1910, nearly all states had SMBs (Johnson & Chaudhry, 2012). In 1912, the Federation of State Medical Boards (FSMB) was created. The FSMB is a nonprofit organization that has no formal authority over SMBs but is a prominent resource for SMBs. SMBs join on a voluntary basis and, as of 2020, there are 71 member boards, including both allopathic and osteopathic medical boards (FSMB, 2020). The FSMB provides support, advocacy, model legislation, and education to state members. It is also a cosponsor of the US Medical Licensing Exam (USMLE) along with the National Board of Medical Examiners (NBME), creator of the Physician Data Center, and coordinator of the Federation Credential Verification Service (FCVS) and other services intended to expedite or ease the administrative burdens of physician licensure.

Notably, in their early stages, SMBs' primary focus was to protect physicians' scope of practice and prevent unlicensed physicians from practicing (Johnson & Chaudhry, 2012). However, by the mid-twentieth century, due to pressure from the American Medical Association (AMA), the

J. Landess (✉)
Department of Psychiatry, Medical College of Wisconsin, Milwaukee, WI, USA

B. Holoyda
Martinez Detention Facility, Martinez, CA, USA

P. Ash et al. (eds.), *Malpractice and Liability in Psychiatry*, https://doi.org/10.1007/978-3-030-91975-7_33

public, and other entities, SMBs began to increasingly focus on detection, investigation, and discipline of unprofessional physicians (Johnson & Chaudhry, 2012). Today, these roles, along with licensure, are the primary functions of a SMB.

Medical Practice Acts and Structure of SMBs

Medical Practice Acts (MPAs) exist in every state, which establish the SMB and define its composition and scope of authority. The MPA usually gives the SMB or a designated agency the power to make rules which govern the practice of medicine in the state. The MPA establishes criteria for medical licensure and physician discipline, which typically includes continuing medical education requirements, licensure fees, requirements for medical education, and the terms of each license. They may also specify what disciplinary actions the SMB may take against a physician, define specific offenses and potential fines, and describe confidentiality requirements of investigative and disciplinary proceedings. Impaired physician reporting requirements are also often included in the MPA (see Chap. 36).

The structure and authority of SMBs vary by state. In many states, the SMB functions as an independent, semi-independent, or advisory agency. Most function independently (Federation of State Medical Boards [FSMB], 2018a). In addition to overseeing physicians, most SMBs oversee physician assistants, and some SMBs may also oversee professions such as acupuncturists, physical therapists, and massage therapists (Bovbjerg et al., 2006). A few states, such as Illinois and New York, have separate boards for licensing and discipline. Other states have separate boards for allopathic and osteopathic medicine. Most boards are comprised of both public and physician members; the FSMB has recommended that 25% of SMB membership should be members of the public (FSMB, 2018b). As of 1999, all but three SMBs had public members (Johnson & Chaudhry, 2012). SMBs may have additional requirements; for instance, the Florida SMB requires that at least one member of the Board be 60 years or older (Florida Board of Medicine, 2021). SMB members are usually appointed by the state's governor and are often nominated by state medical societies or other organized medicine groups. Terms may vary but range from 3 to 8 years (Bovbjerg et al., 2006). Funding for SMBs usually comes from physician licensing and fees (FSMB, 2018a).

Grounds for Discipline

The FSMB recommends that an MPA empower an SMB to initiate proceedings against "unprofessional, improper, incompetent, unlawful, fraudulent, deceptive, or unlicensed practice of medicine" (FSMB, 2018b). Unprofessional conduct tends to be vaguely defined, which leaves the SMB with broad discretion in deciding how to pursue investigations and disciplinary action. For instance, the Illinois Medical Practice Act mentions 48 instances which can be grounds for discipline, ranging from license revocation to reprimand. These include the following: felony conviction; gross negligence in practice; engaging in "dishonorable" conduct; habitual or excessive use of controlled substances with impairment; patient abandonment; repeated failure to collaborate with a physician assistant, advanced practice nurse, or licensed prescribing psychologist; confidentiality violations; fraud; sexual misconduct; mental illness resulting in inability to practice safely; or "a pattern of practice or other behavior which demonstrates incapacity or incompetence to practice" (Illinois Medical Practice Act, 1987). Thus, while certain occurrences objectively meet the potential threshold for discipline (such as a felony conviction or alleged sexual misconduct), others could conceivably encompass many behaviors (e.g., "dishonorable" conduct) that may be subjectively defined. As illustrated within the Illinois MPA, SMBs can deny licensure or discipline physicians who have been convicted of felonies. This practice was held to be constitutional by the US Supreme Court (*Hawker v NY*, 1898). Furthermore, physicians can be disciplined for crimes of "moral turpitude," including even misdemeanor offenses not directly related to the practice of medicine (Rakatansky, 2011). How *moral turpitude* is defined is less clear, though there should be statutory guidance. An Ohio court, relying on Black's Law Dictionary, defined it as: "[A]n act or behavior that gravely violates moral sentiment or accepted moral standards of [the] community and is a morally culpable quality held to be present in some criminal offenses" (Black's Law Dictionary, 1991, p. 698). Notably, state courts have upheld SMB decisions in which a physician has been disciplined following a conviction for tax fraud or evasion (*Rossiter v. State Med Board of Ohio*, 2004; *Haley v. Medical Disciplinary Board*, 1991). The reasoning generally is that the physician has raised doubt as to his or her character or honesty, traits regarded as essential in the treatment and care of patients.

With social media and an increased online presence, physicians should also be wary of posts and online behaviors which could constitute unprofessional conduct. For instance, SMBs were "likely" or "very likely" to pursue investigations in cases where physicians inappropriately contacted patients, used patient images without consent, or misrepresented credentials online (Greysen et al., 2013).

SMB Complaint Procedure and Investigations

One of the SMB's central functions is to receive and resolve complaints against its licensees. Complaints may come from a variety of sources besides patients, including members of the public, other physicians, malpractice claims notifications, police, medical staff, hospitals, managed care organizations, professional societies, and courts. Some states have anonymous reporting or allow for complaints to be filed online (Sy, 2016). Anonymous reporting is controversial due to the risk of bad faith reporting, including reports by competitors or disgruntled patients' intent on pursuing frivolous claims. On the other hand, some states, such as Wyoming, do not allow anonymous reporting and require a written complaint that is signed, with the patient and physician's name and a detailed narrative (Wyoming Board of Medicine, 2020). Data comparing and contrasting rates of discipline between states with anonymous and non-anonymous complaints is lacking. Unlike malpractice actions, SMB complaints typically have no statute of limitations.

The most common complaints are related to a deviation from the standard of care, including overprescribing medicine, failure to diagnose, failure to respond to a call from the hospital to help a patient in a traumatic situation, and failure to provide medical tests in a timely manner (FSMB, 2018a).

The FSMB outlines the nine steps that the SMB follows in the complaint process, summarized in Fig. 33.1 (FSMB, 2018a):

1. *Assess for jurisdiction*: The SMB first determines if it has the authority to investigate the complaint under the state's MPA. If not, the board may refer the complaint to an agency with jurisdiction. If no such jurisdiction is found, the board notifies the complainant that the board has no jurisdiction.
2. *Prioritize case and initiate investigation*: Based on the allegations made, the SMB determines if there is an imminent threat to the public. If there is an imminent threat, the board may suspend the physician's license and order him or her to stop seeing patients. If not, the SMB will prioritize the case and may initiate an investigation.

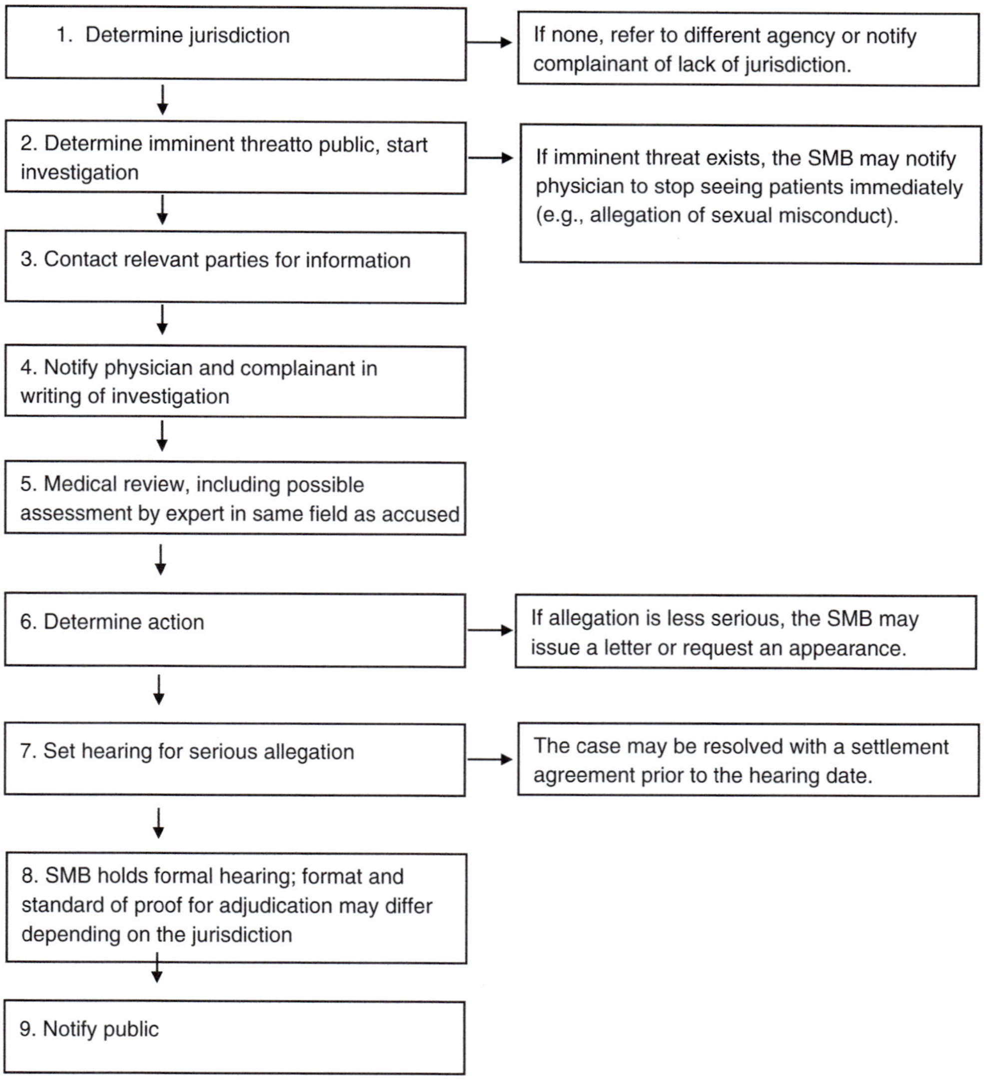

Fig. 33.1 Summary of the state medical board complaint process. (Adapted from FSMB, 2018a)

The SMB may also close a case before investigation if the conduct is deemed too minor to warrant an action, such as minor billing disputes, failure to provide sufficient patient parking, or refusal to accept certain insurances (Bovbjerg et al., 2006). In 2014, one-quarter of complaints to the Texas Medical Board were closed before an investigation was launched (Page, 2015).

3. *Proceed with investigation and contact all parties*: The SMB launches an investigation, which may vary in depth. For some complaints, the board may contact the physician directly and request records to determine grounds for further assessment. In cases requiring substantial work, the board may open a comprehensive investigation and contact all relevant individuals and facilities to request information regarding the alleged event. The Medical Board of California indicates that investigative steps may include the following: generating and serving investigational subpoenas; executing search warrants; interviewing the complainant, any witnesses, and the physician; inspecting the location of the alleged events; and conducting undercover operations (Medical Board of California, 2019). In cases related to treatment and care, the SMB may request medical records from a physician, which could potentially disclose the identity of the complainant (Medical Board of California, 2019). Complaint and investigation details remain confidential and do not enter the public record (Medical Board of California, 2019). In a case study of six states, three-quarters of reports close during the investigation, due to a lack of sufficient evidence, without moving forward (Bovbjerg et al., 2006).
4. *Issue formal notification to physician and complainant*: At some point following the initiation of the investigation, the SMB will contact the physician. The SMB sends a letter to the physician stating the allegation and may request relevant records. The SMB also notifies the complainant. The physician is legally entitled to a hearing with due process procedural rights.
5. *Medical review*: Board investigators conduct a review of the case to determine if a patient's medical care has been impacted or if the complaint involves other behavioral or ethical problems. As part of the investigation, the board may obtain an outside opinion from an expert who practices in the same medical specialty as the accused physician. SMBs must only show substandard or unethical conduct, which is different from the standard required in malpractice claims, where the plaintiff must establish negligence and damages (Frierson & Joshi, 2019).
6. *Decide on potential charges or action*: After reviewing the evidence from the investigation, the SMB will decide whether there is sufficient evidence to support potential disciplinary action. At this point, the SMB may propose any number of actions, including making a formal complaint against the physician, which could result in license suspension or revocation and/or imposition of fines. For less serious cases, the board may issue a letter of concern, request an appearance, or require a physical, medical, or psychiatric competency evaluation (Table 33.1).

Table 33.1 Disciplinary options for a state medical board (FSMB, 2018a)

Disciplinary action	Definition
Reprimand	Warning or letter of concern
Conditions imposed	Must fulfill conditions to avoid sanction
Administrative fine	Monetary penalty, may be up to $25,000 in some states
Probation	License monitored for a certain period of time
Administrative action	Non-punitive-no effect on license
License restriction	Limiting the scope of practice (i.e., cannot prescribe narcotics)
License suspension	Cannot practice for a specific period of time
License revocation	Can no longer practice medicine in that state
Voluntary surrender of license	
Denial of license	

7. *Set a hearing*: For serious or contested cases, the SMB may schedule a hearing to allow formal review of the case and an additional opportunity for the physician to respond. The complaint may be settled before the hearing date with a settlement offer made to the full board.
8. *Adjudicate*: The SMB holds a formal hearing, which may resemble a nonjury trial in civil court. Generally, states follow one of several approaches. The SMB may directly hear the arguments in the case. Alternatively, a hearing officer may conduct a preliminary hearing with a full hearing before the SMB to follow. An alternative approach is to have an administrative law judge hear the case. In many states, assistant attorneys general help the SMB prosecute the case. At the hearing, there may be witnesses and presentation of evidence. The board then decides if there has been a violation of the state's MPA. The standard of proof required to confirm a practice violation varies by jurisdiction (FSMB, 2018a). Some states require a preponderance of evidence standard (i.e., more likely than not), while others require evidence beyond a reasonable doubt (the same standard required in criminal cases). Still other states require different standards, depending on the allegations. For instance, in Arizona, the standard is clear and convincing evidence unless there is alleged sexual misconduct, in which case the standard is preponderance of the evidence (FSMB, 2018a). If the SMB finds a violation of the MPA, it will impose a disciplinary action on the physician (Table 33.1).
9. *Public notice*: If there is a violation of the state's Medical Practice Act and the board imposes disciplinary action,

the information becomes public record and is shared with other SMBs via the FSMB's Physician Data Center. It is also reported to the National Practitioner Data Bank (NPDB) (NPDB, 2020).

Trends and Research in SMB Actions

The Federation of State Medical Boards (FSMB) publishes data on the trends in physician disciplinary action carried out by SMBs. In its most recent report from 2018, the FSMB summarized state medical board actions taken in 2017 (FSMB, 2018a). The organization reported that state medical boards disciplined 4081 physicians that year, a number that has remained relatively constant over the last decade. Of those, 1866 were disciplined for the first time. An additional 1339 were subject to a reciprocal action for an action taken by another state medical board. This may occur when a physician is licensed in multiple states and one SMB is notified that the physician received an adverse action in another jurisdiction; in such cases, the SMB in each state where the physician is licensed may open its own investigation. In terms of actions taken, 711 physicians were put on probation, 656 had their licenses suspended, and 248 had their licenses revoked. The remaining physicians who were disciplined received less severe punishments (e.g., fines, public or private reprimand, etc.)

Over the decade from 2008 to 2017, the number of board actions involving reprimands, requirements for additional continuing medical education, license suspensions, and license surrenders has all increased, while the number involving administration, fines, conditions imposed, probation, license revocation, license denial, and others has decreased. The FSMB does not report data on the basis of physician specialty.

There is limited empirical literature on complaints made to SMBs. Enbom and colleagues reviewed sexual misconduct complaints brought to the Oregon Board of Medical Examiners between 1991 and 1995 (Enbom & Thomas, 1997), and 1998 to 2002 (Enbom et al., 2004). From 1991 to 1995, 100 complaints of alleged sexual misconduct were filed against 80 licensees, two of whom were women. Thirty-nine percent of allegations involved sexual impropriety (e.g., inappropriate comments, gestures, or violations of patient privacy), 31% involved sexual transgressions (e.g., sexualized or inappropriate touching short of sexual contact), and 30% involved sexual violations (i.e., a sexual relationship). Physicians in the specialties of family practice, obstetrics and gynecology, and psychiatry had a higher proportion of complaints. There were a total of 390 practicing psychiatrists in the state of Oregon during that time period, of whom nine had sexual misconduct complaints filed against them (2.3%). In addition, psychiatrists had the greatest proportion of medical board actions reported to the NPDB compared to other specialties. Such actions included voluntary limitation of one's license, retiring or surrendering one's license in lieu of disciplinary action, revocation, or suspension. In their follow-up study of the Oregon Board of Medical Examiners' sexual misconduct complaints received between 1998 and 2002, Enbom et al. (2004) found that only two complaints were made against 469 psychiatry licensees (0.4%), both of which were reportable. Other specialties with a greater proportion of sexual misconduct complaints during that period were, in descending order, plastic surgery, neurology, family medicine, obstetrics and gynecology, and internal medicine. These findings suggest that psychiatrists in the state of Oregon remain at higher risk than most specialties for sexual misconduct claims, which are often reportable to the NPDB. This finding is consistent with a previous study on all physicians disciplined for sex-related offenses between 1981 and 1996, which demonstrated that psychiatrists were the most likely specialty to be disciplined for sex-related offenses (Dehlendorf & Wolfe, 1998).

There is comparatively more known about the disciplinary actions taken by medical boards against physicians, including psychiatrists. In California between 1995 and 1997, 375 physicians were disciplined for 465 offenses (Morrison & Wickersham, 1998). The most frequent causes for discipline were negligence or incompetence (34%), abuse of alcohol or other drugs (14%), inappropriate prescribing practices (11%), inappropriate contact with patients (10%), and fraud (9%). These reasons are consistent with findings from other SMBs (Cardarelli et al., 2004; Clay & Conatser, 2003). Disciplinary actions included stayed suspension of license (45%), revocation of license (21%), reprimand (21%), and actual suspension of license (13%). Various studies have found that male gender, non-white ethnicity, lack of board certification, international medical school education, and greater length of time in practice are associated with an increased risk of disciplinary action (Cardarelli et al., 2004; Khaliq et al., 2005; Kohatsu et al., 2004).

In a study focused on psychiatrists in the state of California during a 30-month period, Morrison and Morrison (2001) found that 75 psychiatrists were disciplined by the state medical board, representing 13% of all physicians disciplined. Psychiatrists were significantly more likely than nonpsychiatrists to be disciplined for inappropriate conduct (27%, including sexual and nonsexual behaviors) and negligence or incompetence (17%). In this study, women psychiatrists were less likely to be disciplined. Claiming child psychiatry as a practice specialty significantly increased the risk of disciplinary action, whereas psychoanalysts were less likely than other psychiatrists to be disciplined. International medical graduate status and board certification did not affect the likelihood of psychiatrists being disciplined.

Not surprisingly, unprofessional conduct in training may be a harbinger for future similar behaviors. Papadakis et al.

(2005) conducted a retrospective study, which showed that physicians who were disciplined by SMBs were three times more likely to have behaved unprofessionally in medical school as compared to a control group. In particular, these students were more likely to have demonstrated "irresponsibility, diminished capacity for self-improvement, poor initiative, impaired relationships with students, residents and faculty, impaired relationships with nurses, and unprofessional behavior associated with being anxious, insecure or nervous" (p. 2676). Increased emphasis on education about and discussion of boundary issues during undergraduate and graduate medical training, as well as early detection of stress, burnout, depression, and substance problems, could potentially help reduce unprofessional conduct as a trainee and subsequently as a practicing physician.

Lastly, states vary in terms of how often they discipline physicians, though it is not clear how to interpret this data (Harris & Byhoff, 2017). Are states with fewer disciplinary actions negligent in their regulation or doing a better job in prevention? States also differ in terms of discipline severity, with some states consistently leveling harsher punishments than others. Public Citizen, a consumer advocacy organization, has released reports in which it critiques SMBs that have lower rates of or less severe disciplinary actions (Robeznieks, 2013). It has asserted that higher SMB rates of discipline correlate with a higher degree of public safety. While this may be an incorrect inference, Public Citizen and others have noted that SMBs tend to have less ability to enact effective discipline when they are inadequately funded and do not have broad authority (Bovbjerg et al., 2006; Robeznieks, 2013). However, Public Citizen's approach does not adequately consider that less severe SMB actions may be effective in addressing public safety risk while also providing the physician an opportunity to continue practice once rehabilitated or censured. In other words, the punishment may more aptly fit the crime.

Facing a Board Complaint

Physicians facing a medical board complaint may feel angry, resentful, anxious, or bewildered. Some may contemplate suicide or a change in career (Bourne et al., 2016). Even if physicians have done nothing wrong, they may fear humiliation and a loss of reputation and income. Others fear seeking needed mental health treatment due to the risk of SMB sanctions (Miles, 1998). A survey conducted by Hendin et al. (2007) noted that 37% of SMB executive directors believed that the presence of a mental health diagnosis was sufficient to impose sanctions on a physician and indicated that they treat physicians receiving psychiatric care differently than those receiving medical care. In addition, many states have questions on their licensure applications that ask about a history of mental health treatment and disorders. If these questions do not link impairment to the presence of a mental health disorder, they may violate the American with Disabilities Act (ADA) and be illegal, not to mention deter the physician from being truthful, seeking treatment, or applying for a license in that state (Polfliet, 2008).

As noted previously, many complaints do not reach the investigative stage (Page, 2015). If they do, the SMB will usually send the physician a notification and request for a response within a certain time frame. The physician should be prudent and timely in responding to the SMB (Landess, 2019). Physicians may make the mistake of minimizing the complaint, either not responding at all, responding late, or doing so hastily before consulting with an attorney. Physicians should be cautious and prudent as they proceed and take all SMB requests seriously (Sweeney, 2020). The consequences of a disciplinary action are far-reaching and could prevent the physician from earning a living, could lead to a report to the NPDB, or could lead to inability to obtain licensure in other states.

Physicians should first contact their malpractice carrier, as many insurers provide legal representation for SMB issues. If not, they should retain an attorney who is familiar with the SMB process and administrative law. The physician should work in conjunction with the attorney to draft a response to the SMB and refrain from discussing the details with colleagues or the complainant. The physician should not alter or destroy patient records which are requested. In addition, he or she should always consult with his or her attorney before agreeing and presenting to even informal hearings before the SMB, conversations with investigators, or the like (Landess, 2019). Statements made during SMB investigations can be discovered and used in future malpractice actions or board investigations.

If the investigation progresses to a final hearing and adjudication, which is usually public, the physician should be familiar with the general process of these proceedings and burden of proof. Physicians retain basic constitutional rights during these proceedings such as the right to procedural due process, which includes the right to notice, to confront witnesses and examine evidence, to a hearing, and to be represented by an attorney. If due process is not followed, this could be the basis for an appeal. When communicating with the SMB, the physician should be honest but not condescending or defensive. The physician should answer promptly and professionally to questions asked. He or she should remain humble while explaining his or her perspective and narrative of events and not blame or express anger toward the complainant (Finger, 2015).

If the SMB returns with an unfavorable decision to the physician, he or she may appeal, though there is often a very small window to do so. Since the SMB is an administrative agency, the appellate court's analysis is limited in scope. As an example, an appellate case in Arkansas stated: "When reviewing such decisions, we uphold them pursuant to the [MPA] if they are supported by substantial evidence and are not arbitrary, capricious, or characterized by an abuse of discretion" (*Ahmad v. Ark. State Med. Bd.*, 2018, pg. 228). Arbitrary and capricious is further defined as lacking a rational basis or relying on a finding of fact which is erroneous. The Arkansas court noted that if a decision is found to be supported by substantial evidence, it cannot be arbitrary or capricious. Furthermore, the decision could not be "unduly harsh" and if so would be considered capricious. To wit, the Arkansas Supreme Court stated: "To permanently bar an individual from the profession that he studied and prepared himself for, and has practiced for many years, apparently in a law-abiding manner, requires proof that makes it clearly evident that that individual had embarked on a calculated course of willfully violating the law" (*Ark. State Bd. of Pharmacy v. Patrick*, 1968, p. 269). Thus, given the narrow basis on which to assert an appeal, a physician may find it difficult to succeed.

Some physicians may turn to additional resources during or after undergoing a board investigation. The Center for Physician Rights (CPR) is a nonprofit organization created to help physicians who believe they have been "wrongfully subjected to an unfair medical board disciplinary process, physician health program fitness for duty evaluation, or peer review process, and have been deprived of due process or other protected legal rights" (Center for Physician Rights, 2021). CPR states its primary goal is to advocate for government accountability and oversight of SMBs, as well as increased transparency of the administrative process, and to provide support, guidance, and education of physicians affected by SMB actions.

Conclusion

SMBs serve a critical and important role in regulating medicine and protecting the public from incompetent, unethical, and unprofessional physician misconduct. However, SMBs have been simultaneously criticized for being overly lenient with physician discipline, too subjective with their decision-making, or having no mechanism to correlate disciplinary actions with improved healthcare quality in the state. An SMB's disciplinary function is primarily reactive rather than preventative, but many SMB members have expressed a desire to take a more proactive approach to promoting physician health, education, and accountability before escalation to a SMB complaint (Bovbjerg et al., 2006). The common causes for discipline include negligent or incompetent behavior, substance abuse, inappropriate prescribing, and inappropriate contact with patients. Research suggests that psychiatrists may be more likely to be accused of and disciplined for sexually inappropriate behavior with patients.

Ultimately, there is no doubt that facing an SMB complaint is one of the more stressful events in a physician's career. A physician in this situation should immediately seek legal counsel and consider any complaint to be serious, given the potential impact on the physician's career, reputation, and ability to make a living, if disciplined. All physicians should familiarize themselves with their state's MPA, which can provide insight regarding what might constitute unprofessional conduct and the scope of the SMB's authority. Physicians should also review information on their state's SMB website, which may outline expectations about continuing medical education (CME) and advertising, and describe other professional standards for physicians to maintain licensure and good standing in the state. Physicians should proactively seek out this information and incorporate these standards into their practice.

Key Points

- Medical practice acts (MPAs) exist in every state and describe the function, composition, and authority of state medical boards (SMBs).
- SMBs may initiate investigations and discipline physicians for unprofessional conduct, which is often vaguely defined but can include crimes of "moral turpitude"; these are crimes that may not be directly related to the practice of medicine, such as tax evasion.
- In 2018, SMBs disciplined approximately 4000 physicians nationwide, a number that has remained relatively constant over the last decade.
- Some studies have demonstrated that psychiatrists are more likely than nonpsychiatrists to have sexual misconduct complaints filed against them and to be disciplined for inappropriate sexual and nonsexual conduct.
- Although many complaints do not reach the investigative stage, a physician who receives notification of a board complaint should consult with his or her malpractice carrier and/or an attorney before sending a response.
- If a SMB investigation proceeds to adjudication, a final hearing will occur. The physician has certain due process rights at this stage. The standard of proof required at this hearing differs by state and/or offense and ranges from preponderance of evidence (i.e., more likely than not) to beyond a reasonable doubt. If the SMB finds that the physician has violated the MPA, it may invoke disciplinary actions, which includes reprimands, fines, license restrictions, revocations, suspensions, or similar actions.

Acknowledgments Some of the conceptualizations in this chapter were previously presented in Landess (2019).

References

Ahmad v. Ark. State Med. Bd., 542 SW3d 224, 228 (2018).

Ark. State Bd. of Pharmacy v. Patrick, 423 SW2d 265, 269 (1968).

Black, H. D. (1991). *Black's law dictionary* (6th ed., p. 698). West.

Bourne, T., Vanderhaegen, J., Vranken, R., et al. (2016). Doctors' experiences and their perception of the most stressful aspects of complaints processes in the UK: An analysis of qualitative survey data. *BMJ Open, 6*, e011711.

Bovbjerg R., Aliagathe, P., & Gittler, J. (2006). *State discipline of physicians; assessing state medical boards through case studies*. U.S. Department of Health and Human Services. https://aspe.hhs.gov/basic-report/state-discipline-physicians-assessing-state-medical-boards-thruogh-case-studies#process. Accessed December 24, 2020.

Cardarelli, R., Licciardone, J. C., & Ramirez, G. (2004). Predicting risk for disciplinary action by a state medical board. *Texas Medicine, 100*(1), 84–90.

Center for Physician Rights. (2021). https://www.physicianrights.net/?r_done=1. Accessed March 1, 2021.

Clay, S. W., & Conatser, R. R. (2003). Characteristics of physicians disciplined by the State Medical Board of Ohio. *Journal of the American Osteopathic Association, 103*(2), 81–88.

Cullen, S. (2013). Madison psychiatrist with history of inappropriate behavior charged with possessing child pornography. *Wisconsin State Journal*. https://madison.com/wsj/news/local/crime_and_courts/madison-psychiatrist-with-history-of-inappropriate-behavior-charged-with-possessing-child-pornography/article_49145d8a-8209-11e2-a1de-0019bb2963f4.html. Accessed December 25, 2020.

Dehlendorf, C. E., & Wolfe, S. M. (1998). Physicians disciplined for sex-related offenses. *JAMA, 279*(23), 1883–1888.

Dent v. West Virginia., 129 U.S. 114 (1889).

Enbom, J. A., Parshley, P., & Kollath, J. (2004). A follow-up evaluation of sexual misconduct complaints: The Oregon Board of Medical Examiners, 1998 through 2002. *American Journal of Obstetrics and Gynecology, 190*(6), 1642–1650.

Enbom, J. A., & Thomas, C. D. (1997). Evaluation of sexual misconduct complaints: The Oregon Board of Medical Examiners, 1991 to 1995. *American Journal of Obstetrics and Gynecology, 176*(6), 1340–1346.

Federation of State Medical Boards. (2018a). U.S. medical regulatory trends and actions 2018. https://www.fsmb.org/SysSiteAssets/advocacy/publications/us-medical-regulatory-trends-actions.pdf. Accessed December 26, 2020.

Federation of State Medical Boards (2018b). Guidelines for the structure and function of a state medical and osteopathic board. https://www.fsmb.org/siteassets/advocacy/policies/guidelines-for-the-structure-and-function-of-a-state-medical-and-osteopathic-board.pdf. Accessed December 26, 2020.

Federation of State Medical Boards (2020). About FSMB. https://www.fsmb.org/about-fsmb/. Accessed December 20, 2020.

Finger, A.L. (2015). Four things not to do at a medical board hearing. *Medscape Psychiatry*. https://www.medscape.com/viewarticle/821629_1. Accessed December 24, 2020.

Florida Board of Medicine (2021). The Board. https://flboardofmedicine.gov/the-board/. Accessed December 27, 2020.

Frierson, R. L., & Joshi, K. G. (2019). Malpractice law and psychiatry: An overview. *Focus, 17*(4), 332.

Greysen, S. R., Johnson, D., Kind, T., et al. (2013). Online professionalism investigations by state medical boards: First, do no harm. *Annals of Internal Medicine, 158*(2), 124–130.

Haley v. Medical Disciplinary Board., 818 P.2d 1062 (1991).

Harris, M. A., & Byhoff, E. (2017). Variations by state in physician disciplinary actions by U.S. medical licensure boards. *BMJ Quality and Safety, 26*, 200–208.

Hawker v. New York, 170 U.S. 189, 195 (1898).

Hendin, H., Reynolds, C., Fox, C., et al. (2007). Licensing and physician mental health: Problems and possibilities. *Journal of Medical Licensure and Discipline, 93*(2), 6–11.

Illinois Medical Practice Act of 1987. 225 Illinois Compiled Statutes 60. https://www.ilga.gov/legislation/ilcs/ilcs3.asp?ActID=1309. Accessed December 22, 2020.

Johnson, D., & Chaudhry, H. (2012). *Medical licensing and discipline in America*. Lexington Books.

Khaliq, A. A., Dimassi, H., Huang, C. Y., Narine, L., & Smego, R. A. (2005). Disciplinary action against physicians: Who is likely to get disciplined? *American Journal of Medicine, 118*(7), 773–777.

Kohatsu, N. D., Gould, D., Ross, L. K., & Fox, P. J. (2004). Characteristics of physicians disciplined by the State Medical Board of Ohio. *Archives of Internal Medicine, 164*(6), 653–658.

Landess, J. (2019). State medical boards, medical licensure, and discipline in the United States. *Focus, 17*(4), 337–342.

Medical Board of California. (2019). Questions and Answers About Investigations. https://www.mbc.ca.gov/Publications/Brochures/Investigations.aspx. Accessed December 10, 2020.

Morrison, J., & Morrison, T. (2001). Psychiatrists disciplined by a state medical board. *American Journal of Psychiatry, 158*(3), 474–478.

Morrison, J., & Wickersham, P. (1998). Physicians disciplined by a state medical board. *JAMA, 279*(23), 1889–1893.

Miles, S. H. (1998). *JAMA, 280*(10):865.

National Practitioner Data Bank. (2020) About us. https://www.npdb.hrsa.gov/topNavigation/aboutUs.jsp. Accessed December 12, 2020.

Page, L. (2015). The black cloud of a medical board investigation. *Medscape Psychiatry*. https://www.medscape.com/viewarticle/853911. Accessed December 10, 2020.

Papadakis, M. A., Teherani, A., Banach, M. A., Knettler, T. R., Rattner, S. L., … Hodgson, C. S. (2005). Disciplinary action by medical boards and prior behavior in medical school. *New England Journal of Medicine, 353*(25), 2673–2682.

Polfliet, S. J. (2008). A national analysis of medical licensure applications. *Journal of the American Academy of Psychiatry and Law, 36*(3), 369–374.

Rakatansky, H. (2011). Criminal convictions and medical licensure. *AMA Journal of Ethics*. https://journalofethics.ama-assn.org/article/criminal-convictions-and-medical-licensure/2011-10. Accessed December 15, 2020.

Robeznieks, A. (2013). Where's doc disciplinary data? Federation of state medical boards drops annual summary; public citizen vows it controversial ranking still in the works. *Modern Healthcare*. https://www.modernhealthcare.com/article/20130726/MAGAZINE/307279958/where-s-doc-disciplinary-data. Accessed December 25, 2020.

Rossiter v. State Medical Board of Ohio, 155 Ohio App. 3d 689 (2004).

State of Wisconsin Medical Examining Board (2011) In the matter of disciplinary proceedings against David M. Israelstam. https://online.drl.wi.gov/decisions/2011/ORDER0000903-00006118.pdf. Accessed December 26, 2020.

Sweeney J. (2020) Dangers of a medical board investigation: how to protect yourself. *Medscape Psychiatry*. https://www.medscape.com/viewarticle/940672#vp_2. Accessed December 16, 2020.

Sy, T. (2016). Facing a medical board investigation. MD Edge. https://www.mdedge.com/cardiology/article/115465/practice-management/facing-medical-board-investigation?sso=true. Accessed December 15, 2020.

Wyoming Board of Medicine. Complaint process. http://wyomedboard.wyo.gov/consumers/file-a-complaint. Accessed December 26, 2020.

34 Ethics Complaints

Charles C. Dike and Keri Ann Stevenson

The ethics tradition is deeply rooted in the field of medicine. At its inaugural meeting in 1847, the American Medical Association (AMA) adopted its *Code of Medical Ethics*, drawing heavily on the code of medical ethics published by English physician and philosopher Thomas Percival in 1803 (Riddick, 2003). The newly established AMA *Code of Medical Ethics* was prepared "for the government of the medical profession" (AMA, 1847, p. 92) and outlined the duties, obligations, and rights of physicians in caring for patients and serving the public (AMA, 1847). Since 1847, the code has been revised many times and renamed *The Principles of Medical Ethics (AMA Principles).* The document currently consists of nine statements that describe the standards physicians demand of themselves and the behaviors expected by society (AMA, 2001). As stated in the preamble, the principles "are not laws, but standards of conduct that define the essentials of honorable behavior for the physician" (AMA, 2001, p. 1). Although not laws, violation of these *AMA Principles* can result in professional sanctions through state medical licensing boards that may jeopardize a physician's medical career. Notably, the AMA does not investigate ethics complaints against physicians but directs those who wish to file complaints to do so with the applicable state medical licensing board (AMA Ethics Group, 2020).

In psychiatry, ethics problems can arise that are not fully explicated in the *AMA Principles.* The American Psychiatric Association (APA) addressed this problem by publishing *The Principles of Medical Ethics with Annotations Especially Applicable to Psychiatry* in 1973 (APA, 2013b) (*APA Annotations*), a document that has been revised several times over the years. It contains the nine ethics statements outlined in the *AMA Principles*, accompanied by varying numbers of corresponding sub-statements specifically related to the practice of psychiatry. For example, under Section 4 of the *AMA Principles*, "A physician shall respect the rights of patients, colleagues, and other health professionals, and shall safeguard patient confidences and privacy within the constraints of the law" (APA, 2013b, p. 6), the *APA Annotations* include 14 additional statements specifically relevant to psychiatry. These include, for example, "When, in the clinical judgment of the treating psychiatrist, the risk of danger is deemed to be significant, the psychiatrist may reveal confidential information disclosed by the patient" (APA, 2013b, p. 7). As such, this sub-statement specifically addresses risk management obligations of psychiatrists that are not as applicable to other physicians. Additionally, the APA has published the *APA Commentary on Ethics in Practice*, a tool that is intended to help psychiatrists understand and apply these psychiatric ethics principles in their practice (APA, 2015).

Several subspecialty organizations have adopted their own codes of ethics to address their special circumstances. These include the American Academy of Psychiatry and the Law (AAPL), the American Academy of Child and Adolescent Psychiatry (AACAP), and the American Society of Addiction Medicine (ASAM) (AACAP, 2014; AAPL, 2005; ASAM, 2019). However, psychiatric subspecialty organizations do not enforce their own ethics policies but instead refer complainants to the APA or to a state medical licensing board (Candilis et al., 2014). Although ethics guidelines of any organization usually apply to members of that organization, psychiatrists who practice in a subspecialty area in which they do not hold professional membership can sometimes be held to the ethics standards of that subspecialty association (*Sugarman*, 1996).

Physicians who engage in unethical conduct risk both causing harm to patients and tarnishing the reputation of the profession. Therefore, ethics violations are treated seriously and can result in significant consequences, including sanctions, which are reportable to the state medical licensing board and the National Practitioner Data Bank (Meyer &

C. C. Dike (✉)
Department of Psychiatry, Yale University, New Haven, CT, USA
e-mail: charles.dike@yale.edu

K. A. Stevenson
Department of Psychiatry and Neurobehavioral Sciences, University of Virginia, Charlottesville, VA, USA
e-mail: kas4ka@virginia.edu

P. Ash et al. (eds.), *Malpractice and Liability in Psychiatry*, https://doi.org/10.1007/978-3-030-91975-7_34

Price, 2012). Other consequences of ethics violation may include loss of malpractice insurance coverage and failure to qualify as managed care providers. As such, in renewing physician contracts and credentialing, hospitals and insurance carriers routinely ask, "Have you ever been disciplined by or had your privileges restricted by a professional organization, health care facility, or licensing board for any matter concerning your professional practice?" (Hilliard, 2003). Physicians should therefore not only be conversant with medical and psychiatric ethics but also strive to comply with them.

Ethics Complaints Versus Malpractice Claims

Violations of ethics guidelines may attract malpractice claims if they directly cause harm to a patient. However, despite the close relationship between them, ethics complaints differ from malpractice claims in many ways.

First, while malpractice claims specifically allege that a healthcare provider's failure to provide proper care directly resulted in patient harm, ethics complaints simply allege that a physician has engaged in unethical conduct, regardless of whether harm has occurred (Hilliard, 2003; Meyer & Price, 2012).

Second, while malpractice claims must be filed by the harmed patient, the patient's legal guardian, or the patient's surviving next of kin (in the case of a wrongful death lawsuit), ethics complaints can be filed by anyone with direct knowledge of the unethical conduct. This includes patients, family members or friends of patients, colleagues of the psychiatrist, or even concerned members of the public. Unlike in malpractice cases in which claimants must obtain and pay for legal representation, there is no cost involved in filing an ethics complaint (Meyer & Price, 2012).

Third, while the standard of care in malpractice cases is what the "average prudent physician" would do in similar circumstances, in the peer review adjudication process of ethics complaints, the pertinent standard is the ethics code of the organization by which a member physician has agreed to abide (Meyer & Price, 2012).

Fourth, unlike in malpractice cases in which the investigation is limited to the physician's conduct that harmed the patient, the peer review investigative process of an ethics committee can include material that was not part of the original complaint and involves "prospective judgments about the respondent physician's capacity and motivation to conform his practice of medicine to the applicable standard of care" (Meyer & Price, 2012, p. 195).

Fifth, although there can be collateral career consequences for physicians who have had multiple or egregious malpractice claims made against them, the main factor at stake in malpractice cases is money, that is, the amount that is required to make the patient "whole" again, which can be substantial. In contrast, no money is directly at stake in ethics complaints; complainants receive nothing more than a response regarding the outcome of the investigation. However, the legal cost of the defense against complaints to the ethics committee, or to state medical licensing boards, can be significantly burdensome to psychiatrists.

Unfortunately, physicians sometimes must defend against both an ethics complaint and a malpractice suit, as some complainants file ethics complaints against physicians with the hope that a peer review sanction will help bolster a subsequent malpractice claim to promote financial settlement in lieu of trial (Meyer & Price, 2012). Further, evidence gathered by investigating boards may be subject to discovery by a plaintiff's attorney in a subsequent malpractice case (Hilliard, 2003).

APA Procedures for Investigating Ethics Complaints

Unlike the AMA, which does not investigate ethics complaints, the APA has comprehensive procedures for handling complaints of unethical conduct by its members that can be found on the APA website (APA, 2013a). Complaints to the APA's ethics committee can only proceed if the psychiatrist is a member of the APA, and even then, only in the absence of ongoing medical licensing board investigation or litigation. APA ethics investigations do not occur concurrently with any other investigation. As ethics guidelines apply only to individual members of an organization, nonmembers cannot be held liable or accountable by the association. However, medical licensing boards have an obligation to investigate any (ethics) complaints brought to the board. While the consequences of an adverse finding by a medical licensing board could directly impact a practitioner's ability to practice, for an organization's ethics committee, only the status of membership in the organization is at risk (APA, 2013a).

The APA is comprised of a centralized, national body with district branches (DBs) located in states. Large states may have many district branches, for example, California has five while New York State has 14, but most have only one branch. The APA's ethics committee is organized in similar fashion; in addition to the national ethics committee (hereafter referred to as APA Ethics Committee), every district branch is expected to have an ethics committee (DB Ethics Committee). Most, but not all, DBs of the APA have an ethics committee. Ethics complaints are investigated by the DB Ethics Committee or, in the absence of one, by appropriate representatives of the district branch. In smaller states, the DB may refer all ethics complaints to the state medical board for investigation. Complaints that come directly to the APA Ethics Committee will be referred to the appropriate DB Ethics Committee for processing (APA, 2013a).

As noted earlier, any individual with direct knowledge of an unethical issue could lodge a complaint with the ethics committee. The ethics committee may also commence investigation when members become aware of extrinsic evidence of unethical conduct, either through the media, the medical licensing board, or legal decisions. For ethics investigation triggered by extrinsic evidence, the ethics committee is the complainant (APA, 2013a).

Investigation of a member of the profession for an ethics violation is a serious issue that should be handled with sensitivity, respect, and confidentiality. Specific procedures should be followed to protect both the complainant and the psychiatrist. The complainant must be willing to sign an agreement that information generated from the ethics investigation or hearing will remain confidential and will not be used for any other purpose. It does not, however, preclude an attorney or a regulatory body from asking the psychiatrist if they are aware of ever having been the subject of an ethics investigation or sanctioned by a professional organization for unethical conduct.

Informing a psychiatrist that he or she is being investigated for an ethics complaint has serious consequences for the psychiatrist. In addition to severe emotional distress, the psychiatrist is obligated to disclose the information on medical license renewal application forms, hospital privileging forms, and any employment-related application. This would be required even if the psychiatrist were completely exonerated following investigation. Therefore, the psychiatrist should not be informed until after the ethics committee has determined there is a high probability of an ethics violation.

As discussed earlier, the APA ethics guidelines operate on nine *Principles*. Complaints brought to the ethics committee must demonstrate violation of at least one of the principles. The job of the ethics committee is to determine which principle has been breached by an accused member in order for the complaint to have merit. In addition to a written and signed complaint, the DB Ethics Committee asks for and reviews additional documents submitted by the complainant. If it is determined that none of the *Principles* were violated, the committee will state so in writing to the complainant and to the APA Ethics Committee and stop the investigation. The complainant may appeal to the APA Ethics Committee within 30 days of receiving such notice (APA, 2013a).

However, if an ethics violation is strongly suspected after reviewing the complaint, the committee will inform the psychiatrist. The DB Ethics Committee may ask the psychiatrist to submit documents that may refute the allegations. The committee will also inform the psychiatrist of the potential for a formal hearing in front of the ethics committee and the rights of the psychiatrist at the hearing, including the rights to be defended by legal counsel, to present witnesses, and to examine or cross-examine the complainant or the complainant's witnesses. Depending on the severity of the alleged ethics violation, the accused psychiatrist could be offered an educational option, completion of which would resolve the complaint and avert a hearing. If the accused psychiatrist or the ethics committee elects to proceed with a hearing, the complainant is informed of the process involved and that the complainant reserves the right to attend with a witness or support person (APA, 2013a).

The review of ethics violations follows a defined process. Any decision reached by the DB Ethics Committee will be presented to the DB executive council and to the APA Ethics Committee. A psychiatrist found to have violated APA ethics has a period of up to 30 days from the date of the DB's decision to appeal the decision to the APA Ethics Committee. Even absent an appeal, the APA Ethics Committee reviews the complaints and all the documents the DB Ethics Committee reviewed to come to its decision. The APA Ethics Committee may uphold the decision or ask for further clarification and consideration by the DB Ethics Committee.

If it is determined after a hearing that no violation of ethics occurred, such will be communicated in writing to the complainant following approval of the DB executive council and the APA Ethics Committee. If, on the other hand, it is determined that unethical conduct occurred and the DB executive council and the APA Ethics Committee concur, there are several options available for sanctioning the accused member after expiration of the appeals process described earlier. These include reprimand, suspension, or expulsion from the association, depending on the severity of the ethics violation. The complainant is informed of the decision at this stage, including the chosen method of sanction (APA, 2013a).

While reprimand, the least severe sanction, is confidential, suspension, the next severe sanction, includes publication of the decision and the member's name in *Psychiatric News* and the DB Newsletter (or other forms of DB communication). Additionally, the member is reported to the state medical licensing board and the National Practitioner Data Bank. The same publication and reporting requirements are true for when a member is expelled from the association, the most severe sanction. Expulsion cannot proceed, however, until after the APA Board of Trustees has reviewed the case and affirmed the decision (APA, 2013a). Regardless of the sanction option chosen, additional requirements and conditions may be imposed on the accused member. If an APA member resigns from the APA after an ethics complaint is received but before its resolution, the member's name is published in *Psychiatric News* and the DB Newsletter or any other DB communication vehicle.

Common Ethics Violations and Consequences

Despite the possible sanctions described earlier, expulsions from the APA are rare, with, for example, only two reported in *Psychiatric News* between 2000 and 2006. During that period, four members resigned from the organization in the course of an ethics investigation (Sondheimer & Klykylo, 2008). Recent data regarding the types and outcomes of ethics complaints made against psychiatrists are surprisingly sparse. Preliminary data (currently in press) from the APA Ethics Committee's survey of DB Ethics Committees in 2019–2020 indicate that clinical practice issues are the commonest reasons for ethics complaints, followed by boundary violations. This does not appear to be significantly different from previous findings over the years.

In 1976, an APA DB reported that it received 44 ethics complaints over a 4-year span, broken into seven categories (in order of frequency): miscellaneous, undue influence, sexual contact, lack of cooperation with providing insurance or tax forms, improper advertising, excessive fees, and improper diagnosis resulting in loss of job. Although in many cases the committee believed the complaints were justified, they only voted for a finding of unethical conduct in two cases; the others reportedly lacked sufficient proof to find against the psychiatrist (Zitrin & Klein, 1976).

In 1992, a member of the APA Ethics Committee published an analysis of approximately 5 years of data on complaints against members, with a focus on complaints against female psychiatrists. Prevalence rates of ethics complaints were 1.1% against male members and 0.4% against female members. After investigation, a greater percentage of complaints against women than men (60% vs 39%) were dismissed. At that time, complaints of sexual involvement with patients constituted the largest category of complaints, comprising 33% of the complaints against male and 27% of the complaints against female psychiatrists (Mogul, 1992).

Sexual misconduct is an especially common form of ethics violation in medicine and psychiatry (see also Chap. 14). While the APA ethics guidelines prohibit romantic relationships between psychiatrists and current or past patients (APA, 2013a), the AMA Code of Medical Ethics prohibits such relationships with current patients only (AMA, 2016). Indeed, the APA Ethics Committee also warns against intimate relationships between psychiatrists and significant third parties (family or caretakers) of current or past patients due to the high risk of exploitation of the third party or breach of patient confidentiality (APA, 2020).

However, inappropriate sexual behavior is only one form of boundary violation that occurs in psychiatry. Unlike boundary crossings, which are less serious behaviors that carry a risk of harming the patient but may also enhance the therapeutic relationship (e.g., accepting an inexpensive hand-made gift), boundary violations (e.g., accepting expensive gifts, sexual relations with patients) are more likely to cause harm to patients. In committing boundary violations, psychiatrists take advantage of patients and undermine or threaten their treatment goals (Sidhu & Srinivasaraghavan, 2000). Unfortunately, many ethics complaints against psychiatrists involve some form of boundary violation, most of which are sexual.

The body of literature regarding nonsexual boundary violations in psychiatry is more limited, possibly because these violations could be more covert and difficult to recognize, especially in early stages (Musselman, 2019). However, two recent cases demonstrate the extremes of problematic nonsexual boundary violations. In *Pierce v. Oremland*, Dr. Oremland, a prominent California psychiatrist, was accused of inducing a patient both to give him at least 12 works of highly valued art and to invest in an investment firm with which Dr. Oremland had a relationship. He was also accused of using the patient as a private detective (including to investigate other patients) and a handyman. Additionally, Mr. Pierce alleged that Dr. Oremland used him as a "personal servant" (Rosenfield, 2016). The psychiatrist argued that the patient consented to their business dealings and that the art he received from the patient was given willingly as payment for psychiatric treatment (Rosenfield, 2016). According to court records, the case subsequently settled for an undisclosed amount in 2016 (Pierce, 2016).

In *The Shrink Next Door,* a popular Wondery podcast (discussed in more detail in Chap. 18), a psychiatrist is accused of exploiting his patient for personal gain over three decades. According to a New York state board complaint document, the alleged unethical behaviors of the psychiatrist included influencing the patient to allow the psychiatrist to move into his home as if it were his (while the patient moved to the guest chambers), to will his house to the psychiatrist's wife, to will his fortune to an organization the psychiatrist directed, to add the psychiatrist as a joint owner of his bank account, to appoint the psychiatrist as his power of attorney, to pay the psychiatrist millions of dollars in fees for treatment, and other egregious acts. The psychiatrist denied the claims, stating that the patient was acting of his own free will (Nocera, 2019; Weintraub, 2019). Of note, the psychiatrist resigned from the APA in 2016 during an ethics investigation, and the New York Department of Health revoked his license in April 2021, although an appeal may be pending (New York Department of Health, 2021).

Ethics violations like those common among APA members also occur with other mental health practitioners. The American Psychological Association, which has its own code of ethics, regularly reports findings of investigations of ethics complaints it conducts. Data from 2015 indicates that while 64 complaints were received, only eight cases were opened that year after the preliminary investigation. Half of the opened cases were for sexual misconduct and the rest for clinical practice issues related to confidentiality, inappropriate follow-up/termination, insurance/fee problems, and other inappropriate professional behavior. In reviewing and adjudicating five cases that year, the American Psychological Association Ethics Committee recommended expulsion in two cases, stipulated resignation in two cases, and probation until completion of directives by the licensing board in one case (American Psychological Association, 2016).

Conclusion

The principles of psychiatric ethics are organized around practices that are in the best interests of patients and do not cause them harm. A psychiatrist's conduct and treatment recommendations should uphold the organization's ethics standard, maintenance of which should engender trust and cooperation from patients. Violation of the organization's principles of ethics could have deleterious effect on patients and the profession and discourage patients from seeking much-needed care. While malpractice claims often involve infringement of professional ethics, not all ethics violations are malpractice. However, a malpractice claim may be raised against a psychiatrist with potential career-ending consequences when a breach of ethics principles directly causes serious harm to a patient. Even when a malpractice claim is not filed, ethics complaints could negatively affect a psychiatrist's emotional equilibrium and ability to practice without restrictions. The burden, therefore, is on psychiatrists to practice within the boundaries of the ethics guidelines of their psychiatric association and those of the subspecialty areas within which they practice.

Key Points

- Psychiatrists as physicians are expected to uphold the standards of conduct that are defined in the ethics guidelines of the American Medical Association, the American Psychiatric Association, and relevant subspecialty organizations.
- Unlike in malpractice claims, in ethics complaints it is not necessary to demonstrate that patient harm resulted from the psychiatrist's behavior.
- A finding of unethical conduct against a physician by the ethics committee does not result in financial compensation for the patient, but a malpractice finding does.
- While the APA enforces its ethics through its ethics committees, the AMA refers all ethics complaints against physicians to the local medical licensing board.
- The APA has detailed procedures for handling complaints of unethical conduct by its members, with only the psychiatrist's APA membership status being at risk in the adjudicative process.
- APA sanctions against a psychiatrist for breach of ethics may include reprimand, suspension, or expulsion.
- A psychiatrist who resigns from the APA in the middle of an ethics investigation will be reported in *Psychiatric News* and local District Branch communication outlets.
- Due to required reporting, additional consequences for ethics violations may include loss of malpractice insurance coverage, failure to qualify as a managed care provider or to be credentialed by a health system, and loss of a medical license.
- In cases of unethical behavior resulting in patient harm, physicians may need to defend against both an ethics complaint and a malpractice suit.
- Common ethics complaints made against psychiatrists include clinical practice issues and boundary violations, with most of the latter being sexual in nature.

References

American Academy of Child and Adolescent Psychiatry. Codes of Ethics (2014). https://www.aacap.org/App_Themes/AACAP/docs/about_us/transparency_portal/aacap_code_of_ethics_2012.pdf. Accessed December 5, 2020.

American Academy of Psychiatry and the Law. Ethics Guidelines for the Practice of Forensic Psychiatry (2005). https://www.aapl.org/ethics-guidelines. Accessed December 5, 2020.

AMA Ethics Group Frequently asked questions on ethics (Undated) (cited 2020, December 2). https://www.ama-assn.org/about/publications-newsletters/frequently-asked-questions-ethics. Accessed December 2, 2020.

American Medical Association. Code of Medical Ethics (1847). https://www.ama-assn.org/sites/ama-assn.org/files/corp/media-browser/public/ethics/1847code_0.pdf. Accessed December 2, 2020.

American Medical Association. Code of Medical Ethics Chapter 9: Opinions on professional self-regulation (2016). https://www.ama-assn.org/sites/ama-assn.org/files/corp/media-browser/code-of-medical-ethics-chapter-9.pdf. Accessed December 28, 2020.

American Medical Association. Principles of Medical Ethics (2001). https://www.ama-assn.org/sites/ama-assn.org/files/corp/media-browser/principles-of-medical-ethics.pdf. Accessed December 2, 2020.

American Psychiatric Association. APA Commentary on Ethics in Practice (2015). https://www.psychiatry.org/File%20Library/Psychiatrists/Practice/Ethics/APA-Commentary-on-Ethics-in-Practice.pdf. Accessed December 2, 2020.

American Psychiatric Association. Ethics (2013a). https://www.psychiatry.org/psychiatrists/practice/ethics. Accessed March 21, 2021.

American Psychiatric Association. Opinions of the ethics committee on the principles of medical ethics, Question A9 (2020). https://www.psychiatry.org/psychiatrists/practice/ethics. Accessed March 21, 2021.

American Psychiatric Association. The Principles of Medical Ethics with Annotations Specifically Applicable to Psychiatry (2013b). https://www.psychiatry.org/psychiatrists/practice/ethics. Accessed March 21, 2021.

American Psychological Association Ethics Committee. (2016). Report of the ethics committee, 2015. *American Psychologist, 71*(5), 427–436.

American Society of Addiction Medicine. Public Policy Statement on Medical Ethics with Annotations Applicable to Addiction Medicine

(2019). https://www.asam.org/docs/default-source/public-policy-statements/public-policy-statement-on-medical-ethicsa98c2894 72bc604ca5b7ff000030b21a.pdf?sfvrsn=2e3048c2_2. Accessed December 5, 2020.

Candilis, P. J., Dike, C. C., Meyer, D. J., Myers, W. C., & Weinstock, R. (2014). Should AAPL enforce its ethics? Challenges and solutions. *The Journal of the American Academy of Psychiatry and the Law, 42*(3), 322–330.

Hilliard, J. T. (2003). The threat worse than malpractice. *Medical Economics, 80*, 38.

Meyer, D. J., & Price, M. (2012). Peer review committees and state licensing boards: Responding to allegations of physician misconduct. *The Journal of the American Academy of Psychiatry and the Law, 40*(2), 193–201.

Mogul, K. M. (1992). Ethics complaints against female psychiatrists. *The American Journal of Psychiatry, 149*(5), 651–653.

Musselman, M. (2019). The Shrink Next Door: A tale of boundary violations. *AAPL Newsletter*, *44*(3), 7 and 25.

New York Department of Health (2021). Available at https://apps.health.ny.gov/pubdoh/professionals/doctors/conduct/factions/FileDownloadAction.action?finalActionId=12569andfileName=HRG+133525.pdfandfileSeqNum=2

Nocera, J. (2019). The Shrink Next Door. Wondery. https://wondery.com/shows/shrink-next-door/. Accessed December 10, 2020.

Pierce v. Oremland (2016). Order to show cause RE dismissal. Superior Court of California County of San Francisco. https://webapps.sftc.org/ci/CaseInfo.dll?CaseNum=CGC15545622andSessionID=9F4CE95847DCAF6F619A5E3B1768E6A2DFC22CE0. Accessed March 21, 2021.

Riddick, F. A. (2003). The code of medical ethics of the American Medical Association. *The Ochsner Journal, 5*(2), 6–10.

Rosenfield, S. (2016). Art and psychiatry on trial: the strange case of Pierce v. Oremland (Internet). KQED Inc. 2. https://www.kqed.org/arts/12146947/art-and-psychiatry-on-trial-the-strange-case-of-pierce-v-oremland. Accessed December 20, 2020.

Sidhu, N., & Srinivasaraghavan, J. (2000). Ethics and medical practice: Why psychiatry is unique. *Indian Journal of Psychiatry, 58*(6), 199–202.

Sondheimer, A. N., & Klykylo, W. M. (2008). The ethics committees of the American Academy of Child and Adolescent Psychiatry and the American Psychiatric Association: History, process, education, and advocacy. *Child and Adolescent Psychiatric Clinics of North America, 17*(1), 225–236.

Sugarman v. Board of Registration in Medicine (1996) 422 Mass. 338.

Weintraub, H. (2019). In the matter of Isaac Steven Herschkopf, M.D. New York State Department of Health State Board for Professional Misconduct. https://apps.health.ny.gov/pubdoh/professionals/doctors/conduct/factions/FileDownloadAction.action?finalActionId=12569andfileName=CHRG+133525.pdfandfileSeqNum=1. Accessed December 10, 2020.

Zitrin, A., & Klein, H. (1976). Can psychiatry police itself effectively? The experience of one district branch. *American Journal of Psychiatry, 133*(6), 653–656.

Negative Reviews on the Internet

35

Alan W. Newman

Introduction

For over two decades, online reviews have become increasingly common as a method for consumers to inform their medical decision-making. The percentage of patients using physician review sites has increased from 25% in 2008 to over 60% in 2020 (Marrero et al., 2020). Despite these sites' ubiquity and popularity with patients, most providers do not routinely check these sites to see what is posted about themselves (Samora et al., 2016). Yet, most providers who choose to check these sites will find at least one comment with false or inaccurate information (Samora et al., 2016).

The Business of Physician Ratings

More than 60 websites provide some kind of patient review of health services (Samora et al., 2016). The most commonly used sites included Vitals, Healthgrades, RevolutionHealth, RateMDs, and ZocDoc (Samora et al., 2016). In addition to specialized medical websites, the business review website Yelp is one of the most popular services for finding information about healthcare providers. While Yelp is most commonly associated with reviews of bars and restaurants, one of the site's developers has said that his motivation to start the site came from his difficulties in finding information about local doctors (Liu et al., 2019). The news website US News and World Report also has a large health website similar to specialized sites like Vitals and Healthgrades.

None of the major online review sites treat psychiatry differently than other medical specialties, despite the many unique aspects of psychiatric practice. Despite the fact that psychiatric practices would be expected to have a disproportionate number of patients seeking care for personality disorders or illnesses that impact mood or reality testing, none of the sites take into consideration elements that may adversely impact the reviews of psychiatrists compared with non-psychiatrists. Furthermore, the major sites do not take into consideration the practice setting of the evaluated psychiatrists: a psychiatrist working in a community mental health center specializing in chronic psychosis is treated no differently than a private practice psychiatrist working exclusively with cash-paying patients.

Though some may know about various health websites, perhaps most patients begin their searches using Internet search engines like Google, Bing, and Yahoo! These websites have long used automated algorithms to scan websites to determine how search results appear to the individual user. Most search algorithms recognize that a search that includes the letters "DR" or "MD" is likely searching for information about a healthcare provider (Luo, 2019). The developers of physician review websites utilize protocols that allow those searching for doctors to find their sites. Upon arriving at these sites, one will typically find patient comments and an overall rating between one and five stars. Review sites do not simply collect comments from patients. Some collect information on a provider's history of malpractice cases, medical board actions, and other publicly available information (Luo, 2019).

Some sites are called "closed-looped" sites, meaning that they verify that the person leaving the review is indeed the reviewed clinician's patient (Barreto & Whitehair, 2017). However, most review sites are "open-looped," meaning that anyone can log in and make a comment. Lacking authentication, fake negative reviews on these sites can be written by a competitor, a stalker, or a "troll" (i.e., someone deliberately trying to sow discord online). Even genuine patients can enlist dozens of friends to write additional negative reviews. Likewise, non-authenticated sites can have fake positive reviews written by the provider, friends, or paid online freelancers claiming to be happy patients. Despite these risks, patients increasingly rely on online sources for information about physicians and other healthcare issues (Azu et al., 2012).

A. W. Newman (✉)
Department of Psychiatry, California Pacific Medical Center | Sutter Health, San Francisco, CA, USA
e-mail: newmanaw@sutterhealth.org

P. Ash et al. (eds.), *Malpractice and Liability in Psychiatry*, https://doi.org/10.1007/978-3-030-91975-7_35

The genre of physician rating sites continues to evolve. Most sites allow consumers to rate physicians on a point scale, frequently rating them between 1 and 5 points, with many also allowing free-text comments to be added (Brody & Elhadad, 2010; Luo, 2019). The variation in methodologies and business models used by various online rating sites has made it challenging to perform research using information from these sites. Because they are created for commercial rather than academic or public policy purposes, attempts to scientifically analyze information posted on these sites is challenged by numerous limitations (Brody & Elhadad, 2010).

Healthcare review sites engage in a number of business practices of concern to physicians. Psychiatrists who type their name into many of these sites' search boxes will find not only reviews of their practice but also the ratings of many of their local competitors. Some review sites have a subscription model for physicians that will change what consumers will find on their search. For example, Healthgrades' lower-tier subscription will move negative reviews lower on the page as well as remove ads for competing providers, while the more expensive subscription option will, among other benefits, elevate subscribers' profiles on competitors' pages (Luo, 2019). Many psychiatrists might reasonably balk at paying a company to deemphasize comments that the platform itself solicited and published.

An increasing percentage of the US population reports that online reviews of physicians are important when choosing a physician. A recent study found that 59% of respondents considered rating sites important in choosing a physician (Hanauer et al., 2014). Unsurprisingly, several studies support that younger patients are more likely to use online rating sites (Burkle & Keegan, 2015; Murphy et al., 2019).

Despite the fear of negative reviews, numerous studies support that the majority of ratings and comments about physicians on online review sites are positive (Ornstein, 2016; Liu et al., 2019; Burkle & Keegan, 2015; Marrero et al., 2020). One study showed that while 9% of those leaving comments on physician review sites left *only* negative reviews, an additional 27% left a mix of positive and negative reviews (Burkle & Keegan, 2015). Younger patients may be more likely to leave negative reviews than older patients (Burkle & Keegan, 2015). The bulk of negative reviews appear to focus less on the doctor's knowledge or the quality of care and more on unhappiness with the clinician's interpersonal skills or actions by the clinic staff (Azu et al., 2012; Online Doctor Complaints Primarily About Customer Service, 2016).

Physicians may fear that negative online reviews will cost them business and harm their professional reputations. This fear is not unfounded: one study showed that 27% of patients strongly agreed that negative online reviews would cause them to avoid care from that physician (Burkle & Keegan, 2015). Another survey noted that 37% of respondents rejected a physician due to poor online ratings (Hanauer et al., 2014). Though losing a quarter of potential patients due to negative reviews is a valid concern, this statistic also suggests that the majority of patients would not use negative reviews alone to sway a decision. Furthermore, there has been increased attention over the past few years of the problem of obtaining truthful and reliable information online (Lazer et al., 2018). As awareness of how false information spreads on the Internet increases, consumers may approach negative comments with more skepticism than 15 years ago when many of these sites started.

Regardless of the industry, proactively leaving comments takes time and effort, and most customers do not write reviews. At the same time, those with highly negative experiences may be more likely to post comments out of anger, a desire for justice, or a perceived duty to inform others. Given that an extremely negative experience may be more likely to lead to a review than an unremarkable experience, posted reviews may be skewed away from the average person's experience. There is little question that online reviews only describe a fraction of total clinical encounters (Murphy et al., 2019).

Research on Online Physician Reviews

Few studies on rating sites focus on psychiatry as a distinct specialty, and most studies only review physicians as a group rather than by unique specialties. In addition to the lack of specific studies on psychiatric patient ratings, physician rating sites have many deficiencies as measures of clinical competence and quality. Emmert noted multiple problems in performing research on information obtained from doctor rating sites (Emmert et al., 2013). They noted that databases fail to list many doctors. Only a small percentage of doctors on websites are evaluated at all, with a smaller percentage evaluated by multiple patients. They also noted that the rating systems used on different sites are different enough to limit meta-analyses or other meaningful reviews on this data. Another deficiency of rating sites comes from the anonymity of the reviewer: information claiming to be from genuine patients can be entered by non-patients (including the rated doctor or that doctor's competitors). If the rated physician cannot identify the specific incident, they will have difficulty learning from the feedback, but if they can identify the incident, they are at risk of violating privacy rules by responding to the specific incident. Perhaps most importantly, there is little evidence that these websites improve either patient outcomes or physician performance.

Samora noted numerous ethical issues that impact research performed on data from these sites (Samora et al., 2016). Because these sites do not authenticate the raters, an unethical physician can manipulate the ratings in their own favor. Some companies offer rated physicians opportunities to pay for ways to improve their ratings, further impacting the quality of data generated from these sites.

Many researchers have attempted to extract useful information from online review sites. This research is challenging due to the fact that these companies are competing businesses using proprietary methods that they are generally unwilling to share outside of their own companies. Furthermore, without knowledge of how many reviews reflect the truthful experiences of actual patients, some conclusions drawn from this research may be invalid.

One approach used in several studies involves the linguistic analysis of words used in comments to identify useful patterns of information (King et al., 2014; Grabner-Kräuter & Waiguny, 2015; Schindler & Bickart, 2012). One study suggested that reviews that were more "factual" rather than "emotional" were perceived as having more credibility (Grabner-Kräuter & Waiguny, 2015). A study on commercial product online reviews suggests that reviews with poor spelling and grammar are considered less valuable, while those considered more entertaining to read are more valuable (Schindler & Bickart, 2012).

Positive Reviews

As discussed above, most physician reviews are positive. A review of 63 studies by Hong found a mean value of 3.89 on a 5-point scale, with a median of 4 out of 5 (Hong et al., 2019). In addition, doctors with a larger number of reviews may benefit from being perceived as a "sought-after practitioner" (Grabner-Kräuter & Waiguny, 2015). Just as negative reviews may harm a provider, several studies support that many consumers choose a physician based on a positive review on online rating sites (Hanauer et al., 2014). Some studies suggest that positive online reviews may better correlate with traditional measures of quality than negative reviews (Murphy et al., 2019; Leibovich, 2018), while another study showed that online reviews were not correlated with Press Ganey patient satisfaction surveys (Widmer et al., 2018).

The correlation between physician communication and patient satisfaction was known long before the Internet era (Woolley et al., 1978). One study found that bedside manner was the most common reason a provider received the highest review, while the lowest ratings were most commonly due to poor bedside manner, perceptions of dishonesty or undue pressure by the doctor, and staff rudeness (Shemirani & Castrillon, 2017). While these issues are clearly related to patient satisfaction, they do not directly address issues about the clinical competence of the physician.

Negative Reviews

The impact of negative reviews has been studied for a number of different medical specialties (Liu et al., 2019). While a surgical or dermatological practice may seem very different from a psychiatric one, most studies show that many reviews focus on issues common to all medical practices, such as the interpersonal skills of the doctor, attitudes of the office staff, and issues related to billing and appointments (Liu et al., 2019).

Fake Reviews

Many physicians are concerned about the accuracy and reliability of online review sites (Burkle & Keegan, 2015). While "closed-looped" sites like Healthgrades attempt to verify that the one leaving the review is a patient of the rated doctor, there is no evidence that any of the online rating sites vet the truthfulness of any review, and without proactive action by the physician or health employer, it is unlikely that a negative comment will be removed or flagged on a rating site (Burkle & Keegan, 2015). Because most physician review sites do not verify the rater, physicians face the same risks that most businesses face regarding both positive and negative fake reviews. Disreputable companies, sometimes using low-paid online workers from anywhere in the world, may pay for fake positive reviews about their own company or for negative ones about a rival (Segal, 2011). While Amazon, Yelp, and other companies report using algorithms to identify many fake reviews, physicians should probably not assume that these tools will remove the risk of fake reviews (Segal, 2011; Frojo, 2013; Schoolov, 2020).

Beyond the world of healthcare websites, fake negative reviews have been used as a weapon against businesses. Social media sites have made it easy for large numbers of people to be recruited to give negative reviews to those expressing support for ideas or views that the reviewers find objectionable, leading to a sudden flood of poor reviews (Carman, 2019). This practice, sometimes known as "review-bombing," can be spontaneous or coordinated (Wordsworth, 2019). While some of these behaviors may reflect genuine but misguided activism, others may simply be "internet trolls" engaged in provocative behavior for the purpose of getting attention and sowing discord. In an era of extremely polarized political discourse, pseudoscience, and conspiracy theories, physicians who post opinions on social media sites like Facebook or Twitter should be mindful that their practices could be attacked by those who disagree with their views.

Physician Responses to Negative Reviews

Taking Reviews Seriously

While physicians may feel defensive and angry about negative reviews, doctors may use online reviews as opportunities to address areas where improvements are needed (Luo, 2019; Murphy et al., 2019; Vanderpool, 2017). Clinicians should be open to the possibility that even a scathing negative review may identify previously unrecognized deficiencies in providing a positive patient experience. One negative review on a single health website is better than ten across multiple sites, and prompt attention to issues identified in a bad review can prevent an even larger problem in the longer term.

Removal Requests

Some negative reviews may reflect misunderstandings or describe problems that have been resolved. Regardless of whether a negative online review accurately reflects a patient's experience or current reality, most clinicians would prefer not to see negative reviews about them and may wish to see them removed.

What may seem like the most straightforward strategy – asking the Internet company to remove the review – is probably the least likely to succeed (O'Donnell & Alltucker, 2018). Unless the physician can prove the negative review is fraudulent or otherwise violates the site's rules, the company will not remove individual reviews. Facebook does not allow individual reviews of a business page to be removed, but they do have a setting that will enable the page owner to remove all reviews – positive and negative – from a page (Cvetkovic, 2020). Yelp allows a physician or other reviewed business to flag a comment, which is then reviewed by an automated process (Burkle & Keegan, 2015). This process can identify hate speech, suspicious activity, and some fake reviews, but rather than weighing in on factual disputes, the most the company will likely do is to categorize the review as "recommended" or "not currently recommended" (Segal, 2011; Frojo, 2013; O'Donnell & Alltucker, 2018). As discussed above, some of these companies will minimize the visibility of negative reviews if the physician subscribes to a paid premium account (Luo, 2019).

Some providers will reach out to the patient to attempt to address their concerns and possibly convince them to remove the negative comment (Azu et al., 2012). If the clinic is aware of the identity of the patient, reaching out directly and offline may be safer than responding to the online post itself. Unfortunately, an unhappy patient may be further angered by the outreach and continue to post new complaints, now complaining about the efforts to get them to remove the original comment.

A tempting but risky strategy is responding to the negative comment on the website itself. The doctor risks violating HIPAA if their response to the patient reveals personalized health information (Ornstein, 2016; Luo, 2019). Some doctors have foolishly posted details of the patient's care in their response to the negative comment, exposing themselves to significant liability and potential fines (Ornstein, 2016).

Some large healthcare employers have policies that prevent physicians from responding to online comments (Ornstein, 2016). A physician employed by a university or large health system should consult with his or her company policies before responding to a negative review.

Search Engine Algorithms and Profile Claiming

Patients may attempt to learn more about a doctor by "Googling" them (i.e., typing the doctor's name into the search engine at www.google.com). Psychiatrists are well-advised to enter their own name into the major search engines to see what is said about them online, both positive and negative, and on which sites. Most psychiatrists will find their name on the same sites that review any other physician, such as vitals.com, healthgrades.com, zocdoc.com, webmd.com, ratemds.com, and usnews.com/doctors. An additional benefit of online self-searching is discovering physicians with a very similar name. A negative review on one physician's page could easily have been intended for a similarly named colleague. Asking a commenter to remove a comment that was clearly intended for a different physician is not an unreasonable request.

Google uses a complex algorithm to determine how search results appear on a user's page, and search results will appear differently, depending on information Google has gathered about the person entering the search information (*Google's Search Algorithm and Ranking System – Google Search*, n.d.). While the results of a Google search may look different to different users, there are actions that a clinician can take to elevate positive information and lower negative information in a potential patient's search results (Azu et al., 2012). Most health review sites allow the clinician to "claim" their profile, which can enable them to correct inaccurate information and address some negative comments in a manner that can mitigate the impact of negative reviews (Luo, 2019). If not obvious when searching one's own pages, most health websites have a "frequently asked questions section" that will guide the physician on how to claim their page.

While some sites attempt to convince providers of the benefits of premium accounts, the simple act of claiming one's online presence across various "free" services may yield many benefits. Doximity, a physician networking site, creates automatic profiles for all US physicians, and "claiming" one's Doximity page was shown in one study to significantly lower where negative reviews appear in a Google search (Widmer et al., 2019).

While it may be difficult to eliminate most negative reviews from the Internet, pushing negative reviews further down the results may decrease the likelihood that they will be seen by prospective patients, particularly if the negative reviews are not on the first page of results. While a physician with negative reviews would doubtless prefer that those comments be removed rather than simply lowered in search results, there is empirical support that the order in which positive and negative reviews appear on sites indeed influences patient perceptions (Li et al., 2015).

Positive Reviews

Some providers will try to offset negative reviews by asking genuine patients to post their own reviews (Luo, 2019). While hospitals and large practices often seek testimonials from satisfied patients, psychiatrists especially should be mindful of boundary issues and other ethical concerns created by soliciting what is ultimately marketing work for the physician's practice. Rather than assertively seeking reviews from individual patients, some practices simply put up a sign or provide a paper card with a link to the review site (Luo, 2019).

Some physicians engage in the unethical strategy of writing their own fake positive reviews or asking friends or staff to do the same, hoping that these reviews will elevate the doctor's scores and push down negative reviews. Creating fake reviews violates the rules of health websites and may expose providers in some states to legal liability (Vanderpool, 2017). If multiple reviewers are logged from the same physical location, automated software may detect and flag these reviews. Having positive reviews flagged as "untrustworthy" may create additional reputation concerns.

Arbitration Agreements

Similar to arbitration agreements demanded by some healthcare providers to bypass litigation, some providers have required patients to sign a waiver explicitly requiring the patient to not post negative comments online as a condition of receiving care (Ornstein, 2016; Samora et al., 2016). In addition to the fact that patients under such agreements may simply post anonymous and anonymized negative reviews, arbitration contracts can be challenged or struck down for a variety of reasons (Bal & Brenner, 2010; Vanderpool, 2017; Allen, 2000).

Litigation

To date, lawsuits against the major internet sites for negative reviews have been dismissed (Vanderpool, 2017; McKinnell, 2019). Without that option, one strategy chosen by some physicians is to file a lawsuit against the patient making the negative comment (O'Donnell & Alltucker, 2018). Although defamation is the most common claim made in these suits, other legal arguments include allegations that the patient engaged in "tortious interference with business relations," "tortious interference with contracts," and "tortious interference of privacy" (Vanderpool, 2017; O'Donnell & Alltucker, 2018). While these lawsuits are usually unsuccessful, there are many cases where physicians have won large judgments against patients for behaviors, including negative online reviews (Vanderpool, 2017; O'Donnell & Alltucker, 2018). As these cases garner significant media attention and sometimes public sympathy for the patient, physicians should carefully consider whether a defamation lawsuit creates greater risks to their professional reputation than the negative online review itself (Ornstein, 2016; O'Donnell & Alltucker, 2018; Mather, 2019; Rozner, 2018; Luo, 2019). In one well-publicized case, a Botox-providing physician with multiple one-star rantings sued at least 12 reviewers (Goldberg, 2020).

Some companies, for a fee, will work to improve a doctor's Web presence. While a clinician may balk at paying money to improve their online reputation, these efforts are likely to be more successful and less costly than protracted litigation (Azu et al., 2012).

An alternative to suing patients or paying subscriptions to the review sites is working with companies that specialize in reputation management. Some of these companies proactively solicit physicians to provide these services (Samora et al., 2016). These companies identify available information about a provider across the Internet and use various strategies to elevate positive reviews and mitigate negative comments (Luo, 2019). Although some reputation management services are provided by large, specialized firms with names like WebiMax and Reputation Resolutions, the services they provide may be excessive for the typical clinician dealing with a handful of negative reviews but may be of value to doctors with a large number of negative reviews spanning multiple health sites. Less expensive reputation management services may be found on websites marketing the work of solo freelancers. Given the unregulated nature of many of these services, psychiatrists should carefully investigate the practices of anyone they hire for reputation management to ensure that they engage in lawful activity consistent with the provider's ethical business practices.

Conclusions

In conclusion, online reviews of physicians are likely here to stay. Physicians should take negative reviews seriously and seek insights from them to improve the experiences of future patients, especially as it relates to staff demeanor and patient communication. Some negative reviews may be inevitable, but physicians can minimize their disruptive impact by learning about the common health websites and "claiming" their profiles. Careful outreach to unhappy patients may lead to some reviews being modified or deleted. A physician can ethically create an environment to increase their total number of reviews and expect that most of these reviews will be positive and lessen the impact of unfavorable ones. For those with multiple negative reviews across many sites, a financial investment in reputation management specialists or subscriptions to premium health websites may improve the provider's online brand.

Key Points

- Online reviews are popular with patients and are often used to select providers.
- Review sites typically rate psychiatrists no differently than any other physician.
- Most negative reviews of physicians focus on the patient's interactions with the doctor and clinic staff rather than the quality of care provided.
- Physicians should use negative reviews as opportunities to improve on the quality of the patient experience.
- Physicians may improve their online reputation by being aware of what is said about them online, by claiming their online profile, and by engaging in ethical practices to encourage patient reviews.
- Physicians should be aware of the risks of responding directly to negative reviews, engaging in litigation against reviewers, or paying third parties for online reputation management.

References

Allen, J. (2000, April 24). With arbitration's pros, cons, what's a patient to do? *Los Angeles Times*. https://www.latimes.com/archives/la-xpm-2000-apr-24-he-22804-story.html. Accessed July 5, 2021.

Azu, M. C., Lilley, E. J., & Kolli, A. H. (2012). Social media, surgeons, and the internet: An era or an error? *The American Surgeon, 78*(5), 555–558. https://doi.org/10.1177/000313481207800537

Bal, S., & Brenner, L. (2010, March). Physician-patient arbitration agreements: Make sure they are understood by all. *Orthopedics Today*. https://www.healio.com/news/orthopedics/20120325/physician-patient-arbitration-agreements-make-sure-they-are-understood-by-all. Accessed July 5, 2021.

Barreto, J. E., & Whitehair, C. L. (2017). Social media and web presence for patients and professionals: Evolving trends and implications for practice. *PM&R: The Journal of Injury, Function, and Rehabilitation, 9*, S98–S105. https://doi.org/10.1016/j.pmrj.2017.02.012

Brody, S., & Elhadad, N. (2010). Detecting salient aspects in online reviews of health providers. *AMIA Annual Symposium Proceedings, 2010*, 202–206.

Burkle, C. M., & Keegan, M. T. (2015). Popularity of internet physician rating sites and their apparent influence on patients' choices of physicians. *BMC Health Services Research, 15*, 416. https://doi.org/10.1186/s12913-015-1099-2

Carman, A. (2019, August 28). Angry fans keep wrecking podcasts with one-star reviews. *The Verge*. https://www.theverge.com/2019/8/28/20835812/podcast-review-bomb-apple-castbox-one-star. Accessed July 5, 2021.

Cvetkovic, S. (2020, January 22). *How to turn off & delete Facebook reviews*. https://blog.reviews.io/how-to-delete-turn-off-facebook-reviews. Accessed July 1, 2021.

Emmert, M., Sander, U., & Pisch, F. (2013). Eight questions about physician-rating websites: A systematic review. *Journal of Medical Internet Research, 15*(2), e2360. https://doi.org/10.2196/jmir.2360

Frojo, R. (2013, September 24). Five ways Yelp is stamping out fake reviews. *San Francisco Business Times*. https://www.bizjournals.com/sanfrancisco/blog/2013/09/five-ways-yelp-stamps-out-fake-reviews.html. Accessed July 1, 2021.

Goldberg, N. (2020, June 19). "Scamming" Manhattan Botox doctor with litigious history sues yet another client over bad Yelp review. *New York Daily News*. https://www.nydailynews.com/new-york/ny-manhattan-botox-doctor-sues-patient-yelp-review-20200619-4xpg6lo2ofhbrksmm4zke2uzre-story.html. Accessed July 1, 2021.

Google's Search Algorithm and Ranking System – Google Search. (n.d.). Retrieved March 27, 2021, from https://www.google.com/search/howsearchworks/algorithms/. Accessed July 1, 2021.

Grabner-Kräuter, S., & Waiguny, M. K. (2015). Insights into the impact of online physician reviews on patients' decision making: Randomized experiment. *Journal of Medical Internet Research, 17*(4), e93. https://doi.org/10.2196/jmir.3991

Hanauer, D. A., Zheng, K., Singer, D. C., Gebremariam, A., & Davis, M. M. (2014). Public awareness, perception, and use of online physician rating sites. *JAMA, 311*(7), 734. https://doi.org/10.1001/jama.2013.283194

Hong, Y. A., Liang, C., Radcliff, T. A., Wigfall, L. T., & Street, R. L. (2019). What do patients say about doctors online? A systematic review of studies on patient online reviews. *Journal of Medical Internet Research, 21*(4), e12521. https://doi.org/10.2196/12521

King, R. A., Racherla, P., & Bush, V. D. (2014). What we know and don't know about online word-of-mouth: A review and synthesis of the literature. *Journal of Interactive Marketing, 28*(3), 167–183. https://doi.org/10.1016/j.intmar.2014.02.001

Lazer, D. M. J., Baum, M. A., Benkler, Y., Berinsky, A. J., Greenhill, K. M., Menczer, F., Metzger, M. J., Nyhan, B., Pennycook, G., Rothschild, D., Schudson, M., Sloman, S. A., Sunstein, C. R., Thorson, E. A., Watts, D. J., & Zittrain, J. L. (2018). The science of fake news. *Science, 359*(6380), 1094–1096. https://doi.org/10.1126/science.aao2998

Leibovich, B. C. (2018). Correlation of online physician reviews and overall patient satisfaction. *Mayo Clinic Proceedings, 93*(4), 404–405. https://doi.org/10.1016/j.mayocp.2018.02.021

Li, S., Feng, B., Chen, M., & Bell, R. A. (2015). Physician review websites: Effects of the proportion and position of negative reviews on readers' willingness to choose the doctor. *Journal of Health Communication, 20*(4), 453–461. https://doi.org/10.1080/10810730.2014.977467

Liu, C., Uffenheimer, M., Nasseri, Y., Cohen, J., & Ellenhorn, J. (2019). "But his yelp reviews are awful!": Analysis of general surgeons' yelp reviews. *Journal of Medical Internet Research, 21*(4), e11646. https://doi.org/10.2196/11646

Luo, J. (2019). A guide for the 21st century psychiatrist to managing your online reputation, your privacy, and professional use of social media. *Psychiatric Clinics of North America, 42*(4), 649–658. https://doi.org/10.1016/j.psc.2019.08.011

Marrero, K., King, E., & Fingeret, A. L. (2020). Impact of surgeon gender on online physician reviews. *Journal of Surgical Research, 245*, 510–515. https://doi.org/10.1016/j.jss.2019.07.047

Mather, K. (2019, December 12). *Doctor sues patient for $25,000 over negative Yelp review: "I can't believe it"*. https://www.yahoo.com/now/doctor-sues-patient-for-25000-over-negative-yelp-review-191902439.html. Accessed July 1, 2021.

McKinnell, J. (2019, September 16). *Doctor suing Google over negative reviews "invited criticism", tech giant claims*. https://www.abc.net.au/news/2019-09-16/google-defamation-case-sydney-doctor-sues/11516182. Accessed July 1, 2021.

Murphy, G. P., Radadia, K. D., & Breyer, B. N. (2019). Online physician reviews: Is there a place for them? *Risk Management and Healthcare Policy, 12*, 85–89. https://doi.org/10.2147/RMHP.S170381

O'Donnell, J., & Alltucker, K. (2018, July 18). Doctors, hospitals sue patients who post negative comments, reviews on social media. *USA TODAY*. https://www.usatoday.com/story/news/politics/2018/07/18/doctors-hospitals-sue-patients-posting-negative-online-comments/763981002/. Accessed July 1, 2021.

Online Doctor Complaints Primarily About Customer Service. (2016, April 26). *Vanguard Communications*. https://vanguardcommunications.net/patient-complaints/

Ornstein, C. (2016, May 27). Doctors fire back at bad Yelp reviews – And reveal patients' information online. *Washington Post*. https://www.washingtonpost.com/news/to-your-health/wp/2016/05/27/docs-fire-back-at-bad-yelp-reviews-and-reveal-patients-information-online/. Accessed July 1, 2021.

Rozner, L. (2018). Manhattan doctor sues patient for $1 million for posting negative reviews online. CBS News New York. https://www.cbsnews.com/newyork/news/million-dollar-online-review-lawsuit/. Accessed July 1, 2021.

Samora, J. B., Lifchez, S. D., & Blazar, P. E. (2016). Physician-rating web sites: Ethical implications. *The Journal of Hand Surgery, 41*(1), 104–110.e1. https://doi.org/10.1016/j.jhsa.2015.05.034

Schindler, R. M., & Bickart, B. (2012). Perceived helpfulness of online consumer reviews: The role of message content and style. *Journal of Consumer Behaviour, 11*(3), 234–243. https://doi.org/10.1002/cb.1372

Schoolov, K. (2020, September 6). *Amazon reviews: Thousands are fake, here's how to spot them*. https://www.cnbc.com/2020/09/06/amazon-reviews-thousands-are-fake-heres-how-to-spot-them.html. Accessed July 1, 2021.

Segal, D. (2011, May 21). A rave, a pan, or just a fake? *The New York Times*. https://www.nytimes.com/2011/05/22/your-money/22haggler.html. Accessed July 1, 2021.

Shemirani, N. L., & Castrillon, J. (2017). Negative and positive online patient reviews of physicians – 1 vs 5 stars. *JAMA Facial Plastic Surgery, 19*(5), 435–436. https://doi.org/10.1001/jamafacial.2016.2039

Vanderpool, D. (2017). What can I do about a negative online review? *Innovations in Clinical Neuroscience, 14*(5–6), 31–32.

Widmer, R. J., Maurer, M. J., Nayar, V. R., Aase, L. A., Wald, J. T., Kotsenas, A. L., Timimi, F. K., Harper, C. M., & Pruthi, S. (2018). Online physician reviews do not reflect patient satisfaction survey responses. *Mayo Clinic Proceedings, 93*(4), 453–457. https://doi.org/10.1016/j.mayocp.2018.01.021

Widmer, R. J., Shepard, M., Aase, L. A., Wald, J. T., Pruthi, S., & Timimi, F. K. (2019). The impact of social media on negative online physician reviews: An observational study in a large, academic, multispecialty practice. *Journal of General Internal Medicine, 34*(1), 98–101. https://doi.org/10.1007/s11606-018-4720-3

Woolley, F. R., Kane, R. L., Hughes, C. C., & Wright, D. D. (1978). The effects of doctor-patient communication on satisfaction and outcome of care. *Social Science & Medicine. Part A: Medical Psychology & Medical Sociology, 12*, 123–128. https://doi.org/10.1016/0271-7123(78)90039-1

Wordsworth, R. (2019, March 25). The secrets of "review-bombing": Why do people write zero-star reviews? *The Guardian*. http://www.theguardian.com/games/2019/mar/25/review-bombing-zero-star-reviews

36 Impaired Psychiatrists

Doris C. Gundersen

Simply weeding out detected offenders did not materially advance the safety of patients, was needlessly wasteful of valuable medical skills and, not least, was inhumane. (Dilts & Sargent, 2003)

Impairment

The nomenclature historically used in early regulatory law and public policy statements, as well as scientific literature, to describe ill, but not necessarily functionally impaired physicians, included the term "impaired physician" (Gendel & Cooper, 2017). It was not until 2013 that the Federation of State Medical Boards (FSMB) published new guidelines to address the return to work of physicians who had been out because of "illness," a less pejorative/stigmatizing description than "impairment," for those physicians who required treatment but never endangered their patients.

"Impairment" is often used interchangeably with "illness" or even "incompetence," although each term has a very specific meaning. An "ill physician" is one who is symptomatic of disease or who has sustained injury, whereas an "impaired physician" has lost functionality rendering him or her unable to deliver safe medical care (Gendel & Cooper, 2017). The formal definition of impairment is the inability to practice medicine with reasonable skill and safety due to illness or injury (Anfang et al., 2005). Physicians who are not functionally impaired but suffer from *a potentially impairing illness* should always be distinguished from a frankly impaired physician who cannot deliver safe patient care. Importantly, illness in a physician commonly predates the development of frank impairment by a lengthy period (Carr et al., 2017). Identifying and evaluating physician illness and impairment can be challenging because of variable manifestations of disease as well as the physician's tendency to suppress, deny, or minimize problems (Boisaubin & Levine, 2001).

D. C. Gundersen (✉)
Department of Psychiatry, University of Colorado, Denver, CO, USA
e-mail: doris.gundersen@ucdenver.edu

Incompetence, on the other hand, generally implies an insufficient knowledge base or skill level of a physician, which can also threaten patient safety. Of course, a physician can be ill but competent, ill and incompetent, impaired but competent, or impaired and incompetent. When impairment is suspected, a fitness-for-duty evaluation should be conducted by an independent evaluator to ensure that the physician in question can perform the specific functional tasks required for his or her specialty. Guidelines for conducting such an evaluation are published by the American Psychiatric Association and are addressed in scientific journals (American Psychiatric Association, 2004; Anfang et al., 2005). In the absence of illness or impairment, referral for a competency evaluation conducted by special centers with the requisite expertise to determine competency for a specific specialty or subspecialty in medicine should be pursued before a physician is returned to work (Saravia, 2017).

It is estimated that about 15% of physicians will experience impairment at some point in their medical careers (Boisaubin & Levine, 2001). The incidence of impairment among psychiatrists is not precisely known. This is because most studies on this subject apply to physicians in general and are dated. However, available evidence supports that psychiatrists have a higher prevalence of impairment related to psychiatric conditions, inclusive of substance abuse and personality disorders (Swearingen, 1990). While impairment has many potential etiologies, substance use disorders are the most studied cause (Candilis et al., 2019). Other causes of impairment include profound fatigue (as with burnout or sleep deprivation), age-related motor skill deficits, or cognitive decline (Candilis et al., 2019).

Although physicians may not be at higher risk for impairment relative to other professionals in safety-sensitive employment (i.e., attorneys, pilots), unique factors related to personality, life experiences, and medical training may pre-

P. Ash et al. (eds.), *Malpractice and Liability in Psychiatry*, https://doi.org/10.1007/978-3-030-91975-7_36

dispose them to mental illness, such as depression and substance use disorders (Boisaubin & Levine, 2001). Like many other professionals, physicians are unusually achievement-oriented and conscientious and tend to deny their own personal problems. These traits can contribute to professional success but, when taken to an extreme, can lead to poor health and/or impairment (Boisaubin & Levine, 2001).

An impaired physician may be observed to look ill, be delinquent in charting or dictations, show a decline in work performance (leading to medical errors), engage in unethical or illegal behavior, and ultimately receive patient complaints, thereby increasing the risk for medical board sanctions (Myers, 2019). State medical boards (SMB) as well as physician health programs (PHP) recognize how essential it is to identify illness and impairment among physicians to protect the public from injury and protect the physician from negative consequences, including license suspension or revocation, untreated illness, and even death (Boisaubin & Levine, 2001).

Risk Factors for Illness in Physicians

Physicians are less likely than the general population to seek medical or mental health attention when needed (Candilis et al., 2019). They are commonly reluctant to obtain a primary care physician and, instead, self-diagnose and self-treat (Pullen et al., 1995; Firth-Cozens, 2018). They also tend to work, even when they are ill (Giæver et al., 2016).

Fears related to confidentiality and privacy likely fuel this behavior as does stigma (especially for mental illnesses and addiction). Prioritizing their patients' needs over their own is another potential obstacle to seeking needed medical care (Candilis et al., 2019). Additionally, characteristics common among physicians include perfectionism, difficulty delegating authority, and critical self-judgment which may interfere with help-seeking behavior (Ziegler, 2016). Toxic or disruptive work environments, loss of agency or autonomy, excessive work demands and associated long clinical hours, and exhaustion increase the risk for illness (Myers, 2019). Finally, external factors such as challenging life events (e.g., death of a friend or family member, marital discord, financial stressors) can heighten a physician's stress and risk for illness (Carr et al., 2017).

The Health of Psychiatrists

In general, the physical health of physicians is good. For almost all physical conditions, physicians experience a lower mortality rate than the general population (Frank & Segura, 2009). When compared to other professional groups as well as the general population, male physicians have greater longevity and female physicians engage in more self-care (Frank et al., 2001; Firth-Cozens, 2018).

However, the culture of medicine has traditionally afforded low priority to mental health conditions, and the picture is less positive for physicians (Reidar, 2019; Firth-Cozens, 2018). Of importance, psychiatric conditions have the potential to induce impairment in practicing physicians absent early intervention and treatment.

Specific observations about the health of psychiatrists are important to note. Again, as a group, physicians tend to be physically healthier than the general population. However, among psychiatrists, significantly raised mortality rates are observed compared with other physicians. Additionally psychiatrists have higher rates of ischemic heart disease, injury, poisoning, and colon cancer (Carpenter et al., 2003; Firth-Cozens, 2018).

Frank et al. (2001) found that female psychiatrists tended to be older compared to female physicians at large (possibly because they had changed specialties), more likely to be current or ex-smokers, unmarried, and in poorer health.

Psychiatrists are at higher risk for developing mental illness during their professional careers compared to other specialists (Braquehais et al., 2015). Longitudinal studies in the United Kingdom show that psychiatrists as a group suffer from unusually high stress levels and have the highest levels of job dissatisfaction. Additionally, psychiatrists, like laboratory-based physicians, experience the highest levels of depression (Baldwin et al., 1997; Firth-Cozens, 1999, 2000, 2018).

Reasons for this elevated risk may include stress created by organizational policies and procedures, limited support, and lack of agency. Excessive work and related emotional exhaustion are common, in addition to individual stressors experienced by physicians at large. Factors that increase stress in the practice of psychiatry are varied and include contending with patient violence and suicides, limited resources (i.e., a shortage of beds for patients needing hospitalization), social isolation (particularly for the private practitioner), and systems issues, including conflicts that arise between a psychiatrist's perceived responsibility toward patients and limitations placed on treatment by formulary restrictions and insurance companies. Finally, psychiatrists may be drawn to the profession because of a family history of psychiatric illness (conferring genetic risk on the physician) or even personal experiences with mental health problems (Kerebih et al., 2019).

A 2015 survey of Canadian psychiatrists found that while 31.6% of the 487 psychiatrists who responded to a health questionnaire acknowledged having experienced mental illness, only 42% reported that they would disclose their illness to family or friends (Kumar, 2007). A variety of cross-sectional studies have demonstrated that psychiatrists suffer higher rates of depression and burnout (Kumar et al., 2005) compared to their physician peers in other specialties. In a survey conducted by Medscape, 35% of responding psychiatrists endorsed burnout (Kane, 2019). This is true for psychiatrists participating in physician health programs (PHPs), peer assistance services that provide a confidential avenue for physicians needing treatment, as well as those in the general physician population (Braquehais et al., 2015).

Of concern, suicide is more common among psychiatrists compared to hospital employed physicians (Hawton et al., 2001; Firth-Cozens, 2018). Higher suicide rates among psychiatrists have been observed over several decades in the United States and in the United Kingdom (Hawton et al., 2001). Reports of stress, depression, and substance misuse appear to be more elevated among psychiatrists (Firth-Cozens, 2018). One retrospective study of 1218 physicians in a Barcelona PHP found that psychiatrists were more likely to be referred to a PHP on a mandatory basis rather than being self-referred. The 72 psychiatrists admitted to this program were more likely to be of advanced age and require treatment in a hospital setting (Braquehais et al., 2015). Additionally, numerous studies have shown that psychiatrists appear to be subject to more disciplinary actions by medical boards than their physician peers in other specialty areas.

The highest rates of physicians misusing multiple drugs are found among psychiatrists and emergency medicine physicians (Firth-Cozens, 2018). In a study examining self-reported, past year substance abuse, psychiatrists used more benzodiazepines compared to other specialties (Hughes et al., 1999). Psychiatry residents have the highest lifetime use of cigarettes, cocaine, LSD, and marijuana compared to other specialties (Shore, 1982; Myers & Weiss, 1987; Braquehais et al., 2015). Both male and female psychiatrists were overrepresented in a study following physician members of Alcoholics Anonymous. It is thought that this is perhaps related to psychiatrists being more comfortable and/or willing to share information about their addiction in a group setting (Firth-Cozens, 2018). A Medscape Survey of physicians in all specialty groups demonstrated that psychiatrists were the most help-seeking specialty (45%), compared to internists (26%) and general surgeons (17%) (Kane, 2020).

While the aging process can increase cognitive difficulties in physicians at large (Turnbull et al., 2000), there is no evidence suggesting that aging psychiatrists experience any increased problems professionally (Firth-Cozens, 2018).

In terms of behavioral problems, psychiatrists, predominately men, are twice as likely to be disciplined by a state medical board due to sexual boundary violations compared to all other physician groups (Firth-Cozens, 2018). In a study of the California Medical Board comparing matched groups of disciplined and non-disciplined physicians, there were twice as many psychiatrists among the disciplined group, most likely for sexual relationships with patients (Morrison & Morrison, 2001). Apart from the legal and professional ramifications, these findings suggest greater difficulties for some psychiatrists, particularly with sexual boundaries. Given these findings and considering the immense harm caused to patients and the profession, it is important to identify underlying causes leading to poor judgment and sexual misconduct early and to plan treatment interventions (Firth-Cozens, 2018). Historically, medical boards have contended with sexual boundary violations with harsh discipline, including revocation of licensure (Carr et al., 2017). However, the vast majority of physicians engaging in professional sexual misconduct have underlying health conditions (i.e., a manic episode), psychosocial problems (divorce, midlife crisis), or personality disorders (narcissistic and dependent traits) and are amenable to treatment. With treatment and monitoring through a PHP, the recidivism rates have been demonstrated to be quite low (Brooks et al., 2012; Carr et al., 2017).

Duty to Report an Impaired Colleague

The AMA (2017) Ethics Opinion 9.32 outlines the ethical obligation that physicians must report impaired, incompetent, or unethical colleagues consistent with applicable law. In April 2016, the Federation of State Medical Boards (FSMB) adopted a "Position Statement on the Duty to Report" and noted that such a report fulfills one's duty of beneficence by intervening on situations, which potentially pose patient harm (FSMB, 2016). This duty to report is generally incorporated into each state's Medical Practice Act created through legislation and is similar across different jurisdictions. SMBs rely on such reports because it is through a complaint-based process that they strive to protect the public. There are exceptions to this reporting obligation. In most states, if a psychiatrist is treating another physician for behavioral, mental health, or substance abuse, no reporting requirement is involved, unless, in the opinion of the treating psychiatrist, the impaired practitioner/patient presents a danger to himself, herself, or others. This is true regardless of whether or not the practitioner is a participant in a PHP. However, this reporting obligation often fails. Physicians who identify a potentially impaired physician often experience conflicting emotions because of their relationship with the individual who may be a friend, colleague, mentor, or practice partner (Mossman & Farrell, 2011). Not trusting their own observations or falsely believing they do not have a responsibility may also contribute to a physician's failure to report (Candilis et al., 2019). Additionally, concerns about retribution, harming a colleague's career, and fears of legal risks may contribute to a physician's reluctance to report (FSMB, 2016).

In one survey of 3504 physicians, 96% of respondents agreed that physicians should report an impaired colleague.

However, only 45% who were aware of a colleague's impairment did so (FSMB, 2016). In another survey of 2938 physicians conducted in 2010, about a third were aware of an impaired or incompetent colleague and failed to report, violating the Medical Practice Act in their respective states (DesRoches et al., 2010). When anonymously surveyed, 7–10% of male and 3–4% of female physicians acknowledge past sexual contact with a patient. However, reports to the National Practitioner Data Bank do not reflect these numbers (Carr, 2003; Carr et al., 2017).

Physicians may wish to consult with their malpractice carrier before reporting a colleague. The common signs observed in an impaired practitioner include poor personal hygiene, a failure to return calls or pages (or frank absenteeism), changes in mood or emotions, appearing sleep deprived, slurring speech (possibly with the odor of alcohol), a pattern of patient complaints, and more medical errors (Mossman & Farrell, 2011).

To preserve the reputation and integrity of the medical profession, self-regulation must occur. For this to be successful, changes in regulatory bodies and physician behavior are necessary to make the duty to report less conflictual or anxiety-provoking. The AMA and other professional organizations have encouraged state medical boards to only inquire about current impairment and not to require disclosure of past illness. Additionally, state medical boards have been asked not to distinguish between physical illness and mental illness in their inquiries in order to reduce implicit bias related to the stigma mental illness carries (Candilis et al., 2019). Finally, the option of making good faith, anonymous complaints may improve the reporting process. Educating physicians about the fact that the majority of impaired physicians, once treated and recovered from illness, return to clinical practice in good standing may encourage reports to SMBs (Mossman & Farrell, 2011). Physician health programs with safe harbors (e.g., a report to the PHP of an impaired colleague rather than the SMB satisfies the duty) receive many more voluntary referrals than mandated referrals, and interventions more frequently occur before impairment develops, protecting the patient population as well as the ill physician.

Physician Health Programs

Clearly, the best way to protect patients from harm and preserve the integrity of the psychiatric profession is to continue with efforts to change the culture of medicine so that a healthy physician workforce is emphasized through education, promotion of self-care, and the availability of appropriate resources for ill physicians to obtain assistance before they become impaired. This need was recognized several decades ago and led to the development of the modern physician health program.

As far back as 1958, formal efforts were made to address issues pertaining to physician illness and impairment. Historically, the FSMB identified addiction among physicians as a disciplinary problem rather than a health problem, consistent with the belief that addiction was a moral failure, rather than the disease we know it is today. A physician could be disciplined for merely carrying a diagnosis, even if they were not impaired (Gundersen, 2015). This sanction-oriented approach to illness has limited effectiveness as it is likely to encourage physicians to avoid disclosure of their problems (Gendel & Cooper, 2017). With this approach alone, a physician who is ill but not impaired may be unfairly punished, and while the intent is to protect patients from harm, the exact opposite may occur if the physician is removed from practice in the context of an already strained healthcare system experiencing physician shortages. Legal measures alone (SMB discipline or peer review processes) cannot remedy unprofessional behavior caused by illness or impairment. Similarly problematic is the American Board of Medical Specialties' stance to disallow physicians to sit for board certification or recertification examinations if they are on a stipulated agreement with a medical board for an illness (American Board of Medical Specialties, 2021). This is viewed as a practice restriction even though the monitored physician is not restricted within their scope of expertise. Downstream consequences of delayed certification include difficulty credentialing with hospitals and insurance companies, which interferes with a physician's livelihood (Gendel & Cooper, 2017).

In February 1973, the AMA Council on Mental Health (1973) published a landmark policy paper: "The Sick Physician: Impairment by Psychiatric Disorders, Including Alcoholism and Drug Dependence." The Council emphasized the ethical responsibility for a physician to address a colleague's inability to practice medicine adequately due to physical or mental disorders (Gundersen, 2015).

Ultimately, the FSMB called for the development of a model program to assist physicians through rehabilitation and protect the public by placing recovering physicians on probation to monitor their health, which encouraged the development of physician health programs (formerly called impaired physician health programs). In the early 1970s, treatment programs specifically designed to treat addicted physicians emerged. Many of the thought leaders in this field were recovered physicians with a passion to help colleagues similarly afflicted. Finally, in 1974, model legislation was developed that offered a therapeutic alternative to discipline in regard to physician illness. A flurry of articles published in the late 1970s served to educate and raise awareness about physician addiction. By 1980, less than a decade after the

AMA's policy paper, all but three of 54 US states and territories had established PHPs (Gundersen, 2015).

From the 1990s through the 2010s, PHPs were established in most states and internationally (Kunyk et al., 2016) to provide a confidential resource for physicians suffering from potentially impairing conditions (Carr et al., 2017).

In 1990, the Federation of State Physician Health Programs (FSPHP) was born out of a need for individual state programs to work together in discussing and promoting best practices and especially to influence national public policy. The mission of the FSPHP is "to support physician health programs in improving the health of medical professionals, thereby contributing to quality patient care" (Federation of State Physician Health Programs, 2018). Annual meetings were convened to share program developments, create clinical guidelines and other policies (derived mostly from collective clinical experiences working with physicians given the paucity of physician health research at the time), and publish findings as experience working with physicians matured. In 2001, the Joint Commission created a new Medical Staff Standard (2.6) requiring hospitals to separate disciplinary matters from those pertaining to a physician's health status, an early effort to focus on assistance rather than punishment for ill or impaired physicians (Gundersen, 2015).

The most effective PHPs in the United States have within their authorizing legislation a safe harbor or confidential track, which allows for physician anonymity from SMBs, provided no patient harm has occurred and the physician in question has not been criminally charged. This provision is extremely important to draw physicians with "potentially impairing illness" into the PHP for evaluation prior to the onset of functional impairment (Carr et al., 2017). Fortunately, stakeholder agencies, including the FSMB, the FSPHP, the American Society of Addiction Medicine, the APA, and the AMA, support this model, as do most state medical societies. In this scenario, a report to the PHP obviates the need for a concerned colleague to make a report to the state's regulatory body. To remain anonymous to SMBs, PHP participants must remain fully cooperative with evaluation, treatment, and health monitoring (Carr et al., 2017). Such contingency contracting is highly successful in the rehabilitation of physicians who otherwise might develop impairment and pose harm to the public (Crowley, 1984). The leverage created by a potential report to a SMB improves treatment compliance and the likelihood of rehabilitation. Predictably, with this safe harbor provision, voluntary/self-referrals to PHPs have increased 300–900% (Carr et al., 2017).

The success of the PHP model has been demonstrated in recent research on outcomes. For example, Brooks et al. (2013) studied whether physicians affiliated with a PHP affected the number of "claims paid" by their malpractice carriers. The study showed that claims were paid less often for physicians who were involved in a PHP intervention, compared to a control group of physicians in the community with no history of problematic behavior or PHP involvement. While the PHP participants had a higher risk of malpractice claims at the initiation of their PHP involvement, their risk dropped substantially (20% lower than controls) following a PHP intervention.

Similarly, the success rate for PHP participants with substance use disorders exceeds comparable rates observed in the general population by a large margin (Carr et al., 2017). Because of the high recovery rates (sustained sobriety) from addiction via the PHP model, it has been proposed that a similar model be developed for addicted patients in the general population and other patients suffering from chronic or relapsing diseases such as depression, diabetes, and hypertension (DuPont & Humphreys, 2011; Carr et al., 2017).

While largely successful, PHPs have drawn criticism from some detractors who believe PHPs hold too much power over the physicians they serve and that due process for physicians who disagree with a PHP's recommendations is lacking. Contrary to these beliefs, PHPs have no subpoena power and cannot impose discipline or alter licensure status. Participation is strictly voluntary unless the physician is already involved with a SMB and mandated for evaluation. PHP participants can choose to work directly with their SMB in lieu of PHP involvement (Carr et al., 2017). With turnover at SMBs, which can be frequent, PHPs may encounter new or increased scrutiny. Finally, some patient safety organizations demand full transparency and are opposed to the confidential tracks afforded to ill physicians. For these reasons, PHPs must be expertly staffed, continue to improve upon evidence-based guidelines (in conjunction with the FSPHP and other stakeholder agencies), and vigorously promote the need for more research. These efforts are likely to balance the tensions between patient safety advocates and PHPs. With adequate funding and support, PHPs are well positioned to address a variety of problems physicians encounter during their careers. Primary prevention, including combating the epidemic of burnout, depression, and suicide, will require research and coordinated efforts between PHPs, SMBs, medical schools, residencies, and national organizations involved in the practice of medicine (Carr et al., 2017).

Conclusions

Identifying physicians suffering from potentially impairing illnesses can be challenging due to defense mechanisms employed by individual physicians, including denial or minimization of illness. External factors, including a sanction-based approach to illness, may inhibit physicians from reporting impaired colleagues despite their ethical and legal obligations to do so. Deep-rooted stigma, particularly concerning mental illness, and concerns about maintaining confidentiality may drive treatment underground so that ill physicians self-treat and fail to receive optimal medical and/or psychiatric care.

In the last decade, as burnout among physicians has increased exponentially, efforts have been made to raise awareness about the occupational hazards of practicing medicine with emphasis on self-care and illness prevention. However, physicians generally remain reluctant to seek care, especially in jurisdictions lacking preserved confidentiality. PHPs offering a safe harbor from SMB involvement have observed an increase in self-referred physicians, highlighting the importance confidentiality plays in help-seeking behavior for ill physicians. With confidentiality, PHPs can provide earlier intervention than SMBs, which operate on a complaint-driven model. Physicians are generally brought to the attention of regulatory bodies after patient harm occurs and when the ill physician has progressed to impairment.

Regarding psychiatrists, more research is needed understand why this medical specialty experiences more illness than other specialties and what remedies are needed to reduce overall morbidity and mortality. Finally, exploring the factors contributing to a higher rate of discipline among psychiatrists is equally important.

Key Points

1. Illness, impairment, and incompetence are sometimes used interchangeably but have distinct meaning when assessing a physician's fitness for duty.
2. Confidentiality appears to be a deciding factor in whether or not a physician seeks help on a voluntary basis.
3. Psychiatrists are less healthy than other medical specialists, and the etiologies for this are largely unknown.
4. The majority of physicians fail to report impaired colleagues to SMBs. Consideration should be given to allow physicians to report their impaired colleagues to PHPs, in lieu of a SMB report, which affords more confidentiality to the physician needing help and reduces the fear of disciplinary action, while concurrently protecting the public from harm.
5. Research to better understand the higher rates of discipline among psychiatrists is needed.

References

AMA Council on Mental Health. (1973). The sick physician. Impairment by psychiatric disorders, including alcoholism and drug dependence. *JAMA, 223*(6), 684–687.

American Board of Medical Specialties. (2021). *Board certification requirements*. https://www.abms.org/board-certification/board-certification-requirements/. Accessed June 13, 2021.

American Medical Association. (2017). *Code of medical ethics of the American Medical Association*. American Medical Association. Also available at https://www.ama-assn.org/about/publications-newsletters/ama-principles-medical-ethics

American Psychiatric Association. (2004). *Resource document guidelines for psychiatric "fitness for duty" evaluations of physicians*. Available at https://www.psychiatry.org/psychiatrists/search-directories-databases/library-and-archive/resource-documents. Accessed June 6, 2021.

Anfang, S. A., Faulkner, L. R., Fromson, J. A., & Gendel, M. H. (2005). The American Psychiatric Association's resource document on guidelines for psychiatric fitness-for-duty evaluations of physicians. *Journal of the American Academy of Psychiatry and the Law, 33*, 85–88.

Baldwin, P. J., Dodd, M., & Wrate, R. W. (1997). Young doctors' health—I. How do working conditions affect attitudes, health and performance? *Social Science & Medicine, 45*(1), 35–40.

Boisaubin, E. V., & Levine, R. E. (2001). Identifying and assisting the impaired physician. *American Journal of the Medical Sciences, 322*, 31–36.

Braquehais, M. D., Bel, M. J., Lusilla, P., Valero, S., Mozo, X., Casas, M., et al. (2015). Psychiatrists admitted to a physicians' health programme. *Occupational Medicine, 65*(6), 499–501.

Brooks, E., Gendel, M. H., Early, S. R., Gundersen, D. C., & Shore, J. H. (2012). Physician boundary violations in a physician's health program: A 19-year review. *Journal of the American Academy of Psychiatry and the Law, 40*(1), 59–66.

Brooks, E., Gendel, M. H., Gundersen, D. C., Early, S. R., Schirrmacher, R., & Shore, J. H. (2013). Physician health programmes and malpractice claims: Reducing risk through monitoring. *Occupational Medicine, 63*(4), 274–280.

Candilis, P. J., Kim, D. T., Sulmasy, L. S., & for the ACP Ethics Professionalism and Human Rights Committee. (2019). Physician impairment and rehabilitation: Reintegration into medical practice while ensuring patient safety: A position paper from the American College of Physicians. *Annals of Internal Medicine, 170*(12), 871–879. https://doi.org/10.7326/M18-3605

Carpenter, L. M., et al. (2003). Mortality of doctors in different specialties: Findings from a cohort of 20,000 NHS consultants. *Occupational and Environmental Medicine, 54*, 388–395.

Carr, G. (2003). Professional sexual misconduct--an overview. *Journal of the Mississippi State Medical Association, 44*(9), 283–300.

Carr, G. D., Hall, P. B., Finlayson, A. J., & DuPont, R. L. (2017). Physician health programs: the US model. In K. J. Brower & M. B. Riba (Eds.), *Physician mental health and well-being, integrating psychiatry and primary care* (pp. 265–294). Springer.

Crowley, T. J. (1984). *Contingency contracting treatment of drug-abusing physicians, nurses, and dentists (NIDA Research Monograph 46)* (pp. 68–83). U. S. Government Printing Office.

DesRoches, C., Rao, S., Fromson, J., Birnbaum, R., Lessoni, L., Vogeli, C., & Campbell, E. (2010). Physicians' perceptions, preparedness for reporting, and experiences related to impaired and incompetent colleagues. *JAMA, 304*(2), 187–193.

Dilts, S. L., & Sargent, D. A. (2003). The law and physician illness. In R. Rosner (Ed.), *Principles and practice of forensic psychiatry* (2nd ed., pp. 171–179). Arnold.

DuPont, R. L., & Humphreys, K. (2011). A new paradigm for long-term recovery. *Substance Abuse, 32*(1), 1–6.

Federation of State Physician Health Programs. (2018). https://www.fsphp.org. Accessed June 3, 2021.

Firth-Cozens, J. (1999). The psychological problems of doctors. In Firth-Cozens, J. & Payne, R.L. (eds). Stress in health professionals: Psychological and organizational causes and interventions. : Wiley.

Firth-Cozens, J. (2000). The person or the job? Longitudinal studies of UK doctors. In *Healthcare workers: Their health risks and how to minimise them (Berzelius Symposium 52)*. Royal Society of Medicine.

Firth-Cozens, J. (2018). *Improving the health of psychiatrists*. Published online by Cambridge University Press. https://www.cambridge.org/core/journals/advances-in-psychiatric-treatment/article/improving-the-health-of-psychiatrists. Accessed June 13, 2021.

Frank, E., Boswell, L., Dickstein, L. J., & Chapman, D. P. (2001). Characteristics of female psychiatrists. *American Journal of Psychiatry, 158*(2), 205–212.

Frank, E., & Segura, C. (2009). Health practices of Canadian physicians. *Canadian Family Physician, 55*(8), 810–811.

FSMB. (2016). *Position statement on duty to report*. https://www.fsmb.org/siteassets/advocacy/policies/position-statement-on-duty-to-report.pdf. Accessed June 2, 2021.

Gendel, M. H., & Cooper, P. D. (2017). The law and the physician – Ill physicians. In R. Rosner & C. L. Scott (Eds.), *Principles and practice of forensic psychiatry* (3rd ed., pp. 203–211). CRC Press.

Giæver, F., Lohmann-Lafrenz, S., & Løvseth, L. T. (2016). Why hospital physicians attend work while ill? The spiraling effect of positive and negative factors. *BMC Health Services Research, 16*, 548. https://doi.org/10.1186/s12913-016-1802-y

Gundersen, D. (2015, March 20). President's message. *FSPHP Newsletter*.

Hawton, K., Clements, A., Sakarovitch, C., Simkin, S., & Deeks, J. J. (2001). Suicide in doctors: A study of risk according to gender, seniority and specialty in medical practitioners in England and Wales, 1979–1995. *Journal of Epidemiology and Community Health, 55*(5), 296–301.

Hughes, P. H., Storr, C. L., Brandenburg, N. A., Baldwin, D. C., Anthony, J. C., & Sheehan, D. V. (1999). Physician substance use by medical specialty. *Journal of Addictive Diseases, 18*(2), 23–37. https://doi.org/10.1300/J069v18n02_03.

Kane, L. (2019). *Medscape national physician burnout, depression & suicide report*. https://www.medscape.com/slideshow/2019-lifestyle-burnout-depression-6011056. Accessed June 13, 2021.

Kane, L. (2020). *Medscape national physician burnout & suicide report 2020: the generational divide*. https://www.medscape.com/slideshow/2020-lifestyle-burnout-6012460#2. Accessed June 13, 2021.

Kerebih, H., Salelew, E., & Hailesilassie, H. (2019). Factors associated with medical students' choice of psychiatry as future specialty: A cross-sectional study. *Advances in Medical Education and Practice, 10*, 751–758.

Kumar, S. (2007). Burnout in psychiatrists. *World Psychiatry, 6*(3), 186–189.

Kumar, S., Hatcher, S., & Huggard, P. (2005). Burnout in psychiatrists: An etiological model. *International Journal of Psychiatry in Medicine, 35*(4), 405–416.

Kunyk, D., Inness, M., Reisdorfer, E., Morris, H., & Chambers, T. (2016). Help seeking by health professionals for addiction: A mixed studies review. *International Journal of Nursing Studies, 60*, 200–215.

Morrison, J., & Morrison, T. (2001). Psychiatrists disciplined by a state medical board. *American Journal of Psychiatry, 158*, 474–478.

Mossman, D., & Farrell, H. (2011). Physician impairment: When should you report? *Current Psychiatry, 10*(9), 67–71.

Myers, M. F. (2019). The mentally ill physician: Issues in assessment, treatment and advocacy. *Canadian Journal of Psychiatry, 64*(12), 823–837.

Myers, T., & Weiss, E. (1987). Substance use by interns and residents: An analysis of personal, social and professional differences. *British Journal of Addiction, 82*, 1091–1099.

Pullen, D., Cam, D. E., Doughty, M. V., Lonie, C. E., & Lyle, D. (1995). The medical care of doctors. *Medical Journal of Australia, 162*(9), 481–484.

Reidar, T. (2019). "Work and mental health in doctors": A short review of Norwegian studies. *Porto Biomedical Journal, 4*(5), 50.

Saravia, A. (2017). *Determining whether a physician is competent to practice medicine is complex*. https://www.hcplive.com/view/determining-whether-a-physician-is-competent-to-practice-medicine-is-complex-. Accessed June 2, 2021.

Shore, J. (1982). The impaired physician four years after probation. *JAMA, 248*, 3127–3130.

Swearingen, C. (1990). The impaired psychiatrist. *Psychiatric Clinics of North America, 13*(1), 1–11.

Turnbull, J., Carbotte, R., Hanna, E., Norman, G., Cunnington, J., & Kaigas, T. (2000). Cognitive difficulty in physicians. *Academic Medicine, 75*(2), 177–181.

Ziegler, P. Z. (2016). What you need to know when treating physicians: Issues, sensitivities and considerations. *Psychiatric Times, 33*(6), https://www.psychiatrictimes.com/view/what-you-need-know-when-treating-physicians-issues-sensitivities-and-considerations

Index

P. Ash et al. (eds.), *Malpractice and Liability in Psychiatry*, https://doi.org/10.1007/978-3-030-91975-7

MIX
Papier aus verantwortungsvollen Quellen
Paper from responsible sources
FSC® C105338

If you have any concerns about our products,
you can contact us on
ProductSafety@springernature.com

In case Publisher is established outside the EU,
the EU authorized representative is:
Springer Nature Customer Service Center GmbH
Europaplatz 3, 69115 Heidelberg, Germany

Printed by Libri Plureos GmbH
in Hamburg, Germany